For My One, True Love
XOXO

PICASSO SCULPTURE

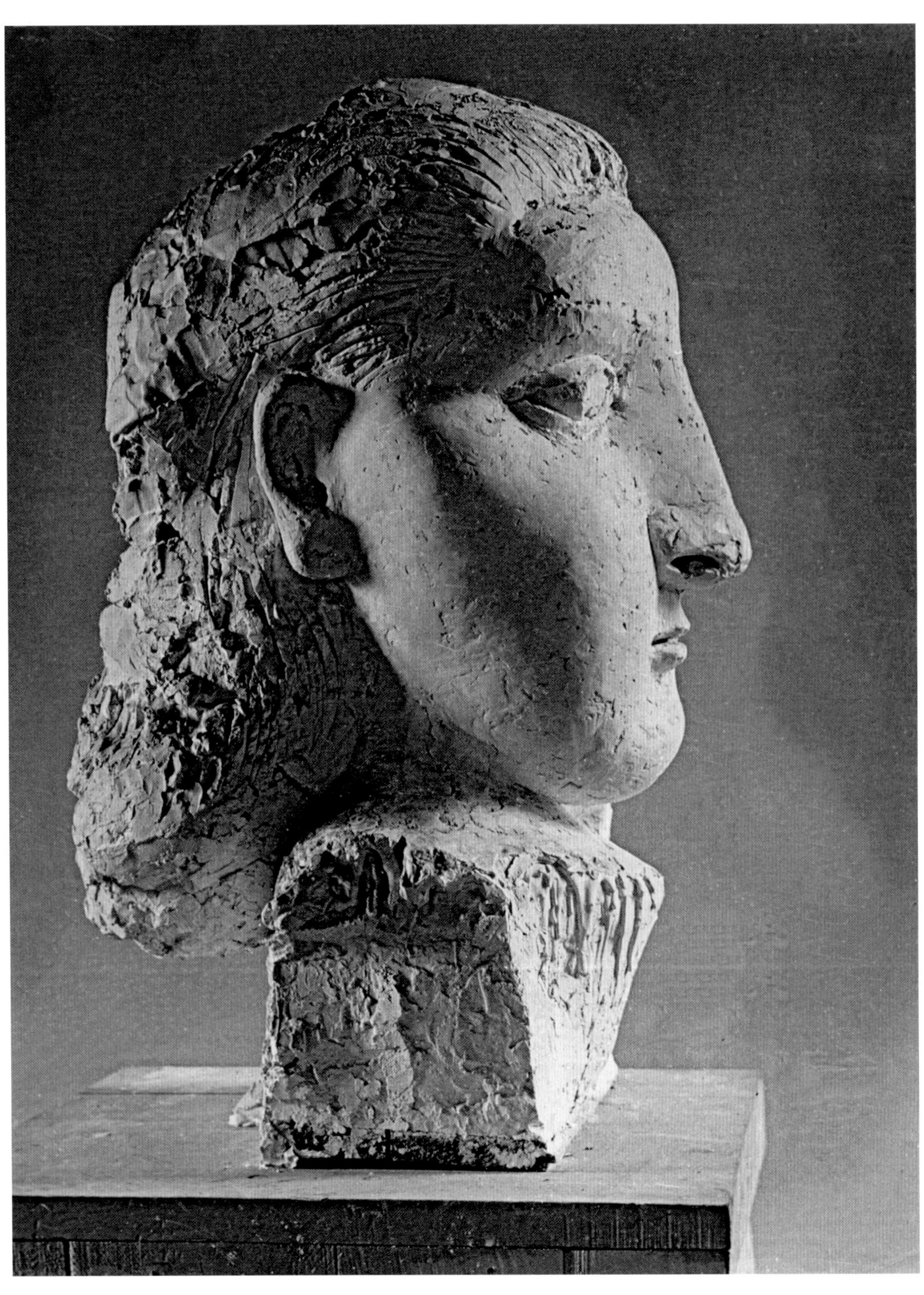

PICASSO
SCULPTURE

ANN TEMKIN | ANNE UMLAND

with

VIRGINIE PERDRISOT, MUSÉE NATIONAL PICASSO–PARIS

and

LUISE MAHLER and **NANCY LIM**

The Museum of Modern Art, New York

Published in conjunction with the exhibition *Picasso Sculpture* at The Museum of Modern Art, New York, September 14, 2015–February 7, 2016. Organized by The Museum of Modern Art in collaboration with the Musée national Picasso–Paris. Organized by Ann Temkin, The Marie-Josée and Henry Kravis Chief Curator of Painting and Sculpture, and Anne Umland, The Blanchette Hooker Rockefeller Curator of Painting and Sculpture, The Museum of Modern Art; with Virginie Perdrisot, Curator of Sculptures and Ceramics at the Musée national Picasso–Paris.

Hyundai Card

The exhibition at MoMA is made possible by Hyundai Card.

Major support is provided by Monique M. Schoen Warshaw, Marie-Josée and Henry Kravis, Robert Menschel and Janet Wallach, and Sue and Edgar Wachenheim III.

Generous funding is provided by Cornelia T. Bailey.

Additional support is provided by the MoMA Annual Exhibition Fund.

This exhibition is supported by an indemnity from the Federal Council on the Arts and the Humanities.

Support for the publication is provided by The International Council of The Museum of Modern Art; the Jo Carole Lauder Publications Fund of The International Council of The Museum of Modern Art; and The Museum of Modern Art's Research and Scholarly Publications endowment established through the generosity of The Andrew W. Mellon Foundation, the Edward John Noble Foundation, Mr. and Mrs. Perry R. Bass, and the National Endowment for the Humanities' Challenge Grant Program.

Produced by the Department of Publications, The Museum of Modern Art, New York
Christopher Hudson, Publisher
Chul R. Kim, Associate Publisher
David Frankel, Editorial Director
Marc Sapir, Production Director

Edited by Rebecca Roberts with Thomas Fredrickson, Nancy Grubb, Alexander Provan, Sarah Resnick, and Elizabeth Smith
Designed by McCall Associates, New York
Production by Matthew Pimm
Color separation, printing, and binding by Brizzolis SA, Madrid

Sharon Bowman translated portions of Chapters 4, 5, 6, and 8 from the French.

This book is typeset in HVD Brandon and Monotype Ysobel.
The paper is 150 gsm Creator Silk.

Published by The Museum of Modern Art
11 West 53 Street
New York, New York 10019-5497
www.moma.org

First edition. Second printing

Library of Congress Control Number: 2015947162
ISBN: 978-0-87070-974-6

Distributed in the United States and Canada by ARTBOOK | D.A.P.
155 Sixth Avenue, 2nd floor, New York, New York 10013
www.artbook.com

Distributed outside the United States and Canada by Thames & Hudson Ltd
181A High Holborn, London WC1V 7QX
www.thamesandhudson.com

Illustrations:

Front cover: *Head of a Woman* (detail). Boisgeloup, 1931–32. Plaster, produced as plaster proof in April 1937 by M. Renucci, 52 ½ × 25 ⅝ × 28 in. (133.4 × 65 × 71.1 cm). The Museum of Modern Art, New York. Gift of Jacqueline Picasso in honor of the Museum's continuous commitment to Pablo Picasso's art. See plate 56

Front fabric stamping: *Figure*. Paris, October 1928. Iron wire and sheet metal, 14 ¾ × 3 15/16 × 7 11/16 in. (37.5 × 10 × 19.6 cm). Musée national Picasso–Paris. Dation Pablo Picasso, 1979; on long-term loan to the Centre national d'art et de culture Georges Pompidou, Paris. Musée national d'art moderne/Centre de création industrielle. See plate 34

Back cover: The entrance hall at Picasso's villa La Californie, Cannes, 1956. Photograph by Edward Quinn

Page 2: *Head of a Woman* (1941), plaster. Paris, rue des Grands-Augustins, 1943. Gelatin silver print, printed 1943–[71], 11 ¾ × 8 ⅞ in. (29.8 × 22.5 cm). Photograph by Brassaï. Musée national Picasso–Paris. Purchase, 1996

Page 31: *Head of a Woman* (1931) and other plaster sculptures at the Château de Boisgeloup, December 1932 (detail). Gelatin silver print, printed c. 1960, 11 ⅝ × 9 in. (29.5 × 22.8 cm). Photograph by Brassaï. Musée national Picasso–Paris. Purchase, 1986

Printed and bound in Spain

CONTENTS

Hyundai Card

HYUNDAI CARD is proud to be the lead sponsor of the exhibition *Picasso Sculpture* at The Museum of Modern Art, bringing to viewers the most extensive survey of Pablo Picasso's work in three dimensions to be mounted in the United States in more than forty years.

For Picasso, sculpture was both uniquely personal and profoundly experimental. Never formally trained in the practice, he approached it with a sense of freedom and curiosity, creating radically innovative works that continually reimagined what sculpture could be. This landmark exhibition, bringing together nearly 150 of Picasso's extraordinarily inventive works in three dimensions, presents a focused overview of this less familiar aspect of the artist's oeuvre.

A long-term sponsor of The Museum of Modern Art, supporting over thirty exhibitions at the Museum since 2006, Hyundai Card is delighted to make *Picasso Sculpture* possible.

FOREWORD

THIS VOLUME is published on the occasion of the exhibition *Picasso Sculpture,* which continues a long-standing tradition at The Museum of Modern Art of major exhibitions dedicated to the groundbreaking art of Pablo Picasso (1881–1973). *Picasso Sculpture* is the first full-scale survey of the artist's profoundly innovative and influential work in three dimensions to be mounted in the United States in nearly half a century, the last such exhibition having taken place in 1967, also at this museum. We are delighted to revisit Picasso's remarkable achievement as a sculptor from a twenty-first-century perspective, at a moment when this body of work carries fresh relevance for contemporary artists.

Picasso Sculpture extends a historic partnership between The Museum of Modern Art and the Musée national Picasso—Paris. Because Picasso retained the majority of his sculptures during his lifetime, a large number of them entered the founding collection of the Musée Picasso following the settlement of his estate. Today the Musée houses the most extensive collection of Picasso's sculpture in the world; approximately one-third of the sculptures in the present exhibition come from this single source. We owe a tremendous debt of gratitude to Laurent Le Bon, president of the Musée Picasso, for his unstinting generosity and enthusiastic support of this project. His collaborative spirit has been fundamental to the realization of the exhibition. We also gratefully acknowledge the positive response that his predecessor, Anne Baldassari, gave to our initial proposal and her thoughtful encouragement during its early planning phases.

That we have been able to mount this exhibition is due not only to the sympathetic cooperation of the Musée Picasso, but also to the graciousness of Picasso's heirs: Maya Widmaier Picasso, Claude Ruiz-Picasso, Dr. and Mrs. Eric Thévenet, Catherine Hutin, Marina Ruiz-Picasso, and Mr. and Mrs. Bernard Ruiz-Picasso. We deeply appreciate their kind support as they extend the historic legacy of goodwill toward this museum established by the artist. We express our profound gratitude to all those who have lent work to the exhibition; their generosity has been vital to the realization of this ambitious undertaking.

I warmly salute the exhibition's organizers, Ann Temkin, The Marie-Josée and Henry Kravis Chief Curator of Painting and Sculpture, and Anne Umland, The Blanchette Hooker Rockefeller Curator of Painting and Sculpture, and their colleague Virginie Perdrisot, Curator of Sculptures and Ceramics at the Musée Picasso, as well as Luise Mahler, Assistant Curator, and Nancy Lim, Curatorial Assistant, Department of Painting and Sculpture, The Museum of Modern Art. An exhibition of this scope and ambition could have come about only as the result of great dedication and outstanding teamwork. Special thanks are due to the entire staff at The Museum of Modern Art, virtually all of whom have contributed directly or indirectly to *Picasso Sculpture.*

This exhibition is made possible by the generosity of Hyundai Card. Major support is provided by Monique M. Schoen Warshaw, Marie-Josée and Henry Kravis, Robert Menschel and Janet Wallach, and Sue and Edgar Wachenheim III. Additional support is provided by Cornelia T. Bailey and by the MoMA Annual Exhibition Fund. We are grateful for the support provided for this publication by The International Council of The Museum of Modern Art, the Jo Carole Lauder Publications Fund of The International Council of The Museum of Modern Art, and The Museum of Modern Art's Research and Scholarly Publications endowment established through the generosity of The Andrew W. Mellon Foundation, the Edward John Noble Foundation, Mr. and Mrs. Perry R. Bass, and the National Endowment for the Humanities' Challenge Grant Program. Finally, we extend our great appreciation to the Federal Council on the Arts and the Humanities, which provided an indemnity for the exhibition.

Glenn D. Lowry
Director, The Museum of Modern Art

LENDERS TO THE EXHIBITION

Albright-Knox Art Gallery, Buffalo
Art Gallery of Ontario, Toronto
The Art Institute of Chicago
Baltimore Museum of Art
Centre national d'art et de culture Georges Pompidou, Paris. Musée national d'art moderne/
Centre de création industrielle
Fine Arts Museums of San Francisco
Fondation Beyeler, Riehen/Basel, Beyeler Collection
Fundación Almine y Bernard Ruiz-Picasso para el Arte
Hirshhorn Museum and Sculpture Garden, Smithsonian Institution, Washington, D.C.
Kravis Collection
Leonard A. Lauder Cubist Trust
Musée d'art moderne de la Ville de Paris
Musée national Picasso–Paris
Musée Picasso, Antibes
Museo Nacional Centro de Arte Reina Sofía, Madrid
Museo Picasso Málaga
Museum Ludwig, Cologne
The Museum of Fine Arts, Houston
Nasher Sculpture Center, Dallas
Philadelphia Museum of Art
Private collections
Private collection. Courtesy Thomas Ammann Fine Art AG, Zurich
Staatliche Museen zu Berlin, Nationalgalerie, Museum Berggruen
Staatsgalerie Stuttgart
Tate

ACKNOWLEDGMENTS

THE HONOR of organizing this exhibition has brought with it a great debt of gratitude to countless people on whose knowledge, hard work, and generosity we have relied for every aspect of the project. First and foremost we echo the Museum's director, Glenn D. Lowry, in expressing our profound thanks to Laurent Le Bon, president of the Musée national Picasso–Paris, for making this occasion possible by allowing some fifty sculptures from the Musée's collection to come to New York City. Laurent's fairness, resourcefulness, and magnanimous spirit have guided the richly rewarding collaboration between our museums at every step. We also thank Anne Baldassari, former president of the Musée Picasso, for enthusiastically agreeing to partner with us on this ambitious undertaking and sharing her deep knowledge during the early stages of its planning.

This exhibition could be realized only because it met with the trust of those individuals charged with the guardianship of Picasso's extraordinary legacy. We deeply appreciate the exceptional generosity and gracious support granted us by the artist's heirs, Maya Widmaier Picasso, Claude Ruiz-Picasso, Dr. and Mrs. Eric Thévenet, Catherine Hutin, Marina Ruiz-Picasso, and Mr. and Mrs. Bernard Ruiz-Picasso. They understand the indispensable role they play in a project of this sort, and they made time for our needs amid endless demands on their schedules and good will.

Sculptures lent by institutions and private collectors across Europe and the United States join the works from the collection of the Musée Picasso and MoMA in our presentation of this remarkable aspect of Picasso's career. We prevailed upon friends old and new to make available works that are in many cases fixtures in gallery displays, unusually fragile, or both. We especially thank: Janne Sirén, Albright-Knox Art Gallery; Matthew Teitelbaum and Kenneth Brummel, Art Gallery of Ontario; Douglas Druick and Stephanie D'Alessandro, Art Institute of Chicago; Doreen Bolger and Oliver Shell, Baltimore Museum of Art; Bernard Blistène and Brigitte Léal, Centre national d'art et de culture Georges Pompidou, Paris, Musée national d'art moderne/Centre de création industrielle; Colin Bailey and Timothy Burgard, Fine Arts Museums of San Francisco; Sam Keller and Theodora Vischer, Fondation Beyeler; Melissa Chiu and Valerie Fletcher, Hirshhorn Museum and Sculpture Garden; Fabrice Hergott, Musée d'art moderne de la Ville de Paris; Jean-Louis Andral and Isabelle Le Druillennec, Musée Picasso, Antibes; Manuel Borja-Villel and Rosario Peiro Carrascoat, Museo Nacional Centro de Arte Reina Sofía; José Lebrero Stals, Museo Picasso Málaga; Yilmaz Dziewior, Katia Baudin, and Stephan Diederich, Museum Ludwig; Gary Tinterow, Museum of Fine Arts, Houston; Jeremy Strick and Jed Morse, Nasher Sculpture Center; Timothy Rub and Matthew Affron, Philadelphia Museum of Art; Oliver Berggruen, Udo Kittelmann, and Felicia Rappe, Staatliche Museen zu Berlin, Nationalgalerie, Museum Berggruen; Christiane Lange and Ina Conzen, Staatsgalerie Stuttgart; and Nicholas Serota, Tate. We also extend our sincere thanks to the collectors who have graciously parted with works that occupy major places in their homes: Marie-Josée and Henry Kravis, Leonard A. Lauder Cubist Trust, and several individuals who wish to remain anonymous.

We are delighted to acknowledge the fundamental contribution of Werner Spies, who pioneered scholarship on the subject of Picasso's sculpture, and to thank him for his gracious reception of this project. Yve-Alain Bois, Elizabeth Cowling, and Carmen Giménez formed the exhibition's spirited Advisory Committee. Their expertise, accrued over years of intensive work on Picasso and related subjects, immeasurably enriched our thinking and our working process. With characteristic generosity, Cowling also offered rigorous feedback on the catalogue manuscript. We thank Diana Widmaier Picasso for sharing with us archival research that represents years of intensive work toward a catalogue raisonné of the sculptures. We are pleased to recognize the gracious assistance of Judith Ferlicchi and Olivia Speer at DWP Editions. We also thank Diana for her thoughtful role in the matter of important loans. Our warm appreciation goes to John Richardson, who took generous interest in this project amidst the demands of completing volume four of his biography of the artist.

Over the course of the exhibition's development, many individuals kindly contributed key assistance related to loans, scholarly research, and the exhibition's presentation: William Acquavella, Doris Ammann, Stephanie Ansari, Oliver Barker, Agnès de la Beaumelle, François Bellet, Marie-Laure Bernadac, Emily Braun, Marie Brisson, Olivier Camu, Michael Cary, Sabine Cordesse, Evelyne Ferlay, Michael Findlay, Tatyana Franck, Larry Gagosian, Magali Gaugy, Arne Glimcher, Philippe Grimminger, Blair Hartzell, Yuhi Hasegaza, Delphine Huisinga, Pepe Karmel, Elizabeth Kujawski, Sandrine Ladrière, Carolyn Lanchner, Elizabeth Lebon, Marie-Josèphe Lesieur, Catherine Manchada, David Nash, Christine Piot, Lionel Pissarro, Rebecca Rabinow, Bernardo Laniado Romero, Christian Scheidemann, Oliver Shell, Lorna Surtees, Vérane Tasseau, and Sylvain Troilo. A number of conservators collaborated with us in pursuing important research questions. For this we would like to acknowledge Agnes Conin, Claire Guérin, Florence Half-Wrobel, Andrew Lins, Sally Malenka, Chantal Quirot, and Kendra Roth. The assembly of the large number of images contained in this catalogue has been a particularly challenging task, and for their assistance in this regard we extend particular thanks to Francesca Calmarini, Wolfgang Frei, Béatrice Hatala, Janet Hicks, Hanna Nelson, Michael Slade, and Kenjiro Yamakawa.

At the Musée Picasso we have many kind friends to thank. All accommodated the needs of this project despite the innumerable challenges and demands posed by the reopening of their museum during the course of this past year. We are deeply grateful for the contributions of Virginie Perdrisot, Curator of Sculptures and Ceramics, who has been a cheerful and insightful partner during our numerous research trips to Paris and who has unstintingly shared with us her knowledge of the institution's collection. Our many hours together in the storerooms of the Musée Picasso are among our most special memories from this project. We thank Cécile Godefroy for providing indispensable research support for this catalogue. Registrar Audrey Gonzalez expertly organized the myriad details involved in the loans from the Musée Picasso. Violette Andrès, Sophie Annoepel-Cabrignac, Emilie Bouvard, Laure Collignon, Laura Couvreur, Pierrot Eugene, Nathalie Leleu, Sonny Raharison, and Jeanne Sudour all generously helped us with a wide range of requests involving curatorial and archival matters. We also gratefully recognize the work of Antoine Amarger, Emilie Augier-Bernard, Franck Besson, Guillaume Blanc, Sébastien Bonnard, Emmanuel Dhuisme, Virginie Duchêne, Marie-Christine Enshaïan, Claire Garnier, Vidal Garrido, Emmanuelle Hincelin, Laurence Labbe, Leslie Lechevallier, Jean-Paul Mercier-Baudrier, Stéphanie Molins, Jérôme Monnier, Stéphanie Nisole, Erol Ok, Beatrice Paasch, Mélanie Parmentier, Laurent Passelergue, Emilie Philippot, and Hughes Terrien.

The Paris office of the Picasso Administration was an essential resource for the efforts of our team. Claude Ruiz-Picasso, head of the Picasso Administration, generously supported the complex preparations for this exhibition. Profound thanks are due to Christine Pinault, whose sage advice and unfailing good cheer provided invaluable benefit to our working process.

All of our colleagues at The Museum of Modern Art provided extraordinary support for this undertaking. Director Glenn D. Lowry was an unwavering advocate from the outset, and we relied at crucial moments on his thoughtfulness and sage advice. Ramona Bronkar Bannayan, Senior Deputy Director, Exhibitions and Collections, unblinkingly oversaw a vastly complicated set of organizational issues. Her faith enabled us to surmount the many challenges inherent to such an ambitious undertaking. We also wish to extend warm thanks to Kathy Halbreich, Associate Director; Peter Reed, Senior Deputy Director, Curatorial Affairs; Todd Bishop, Senior Deputy Director, External Affairs; and James Gara, Chief Operating Officer. As ever, we are grateful for the extraordinary support of the Museum's Board of Trustees, led by Co-Chairmen Jerry I. Speyer and Leon Black and President Marie-Josée Kravis.

This exhibition was managed by our outstanding exhibitions coordinator, Randolph Black, who carefully stewarded the project through a forest of intricate negotiations. In the Department of Exhibition Planning and Administration, we also thank Jennifer Cohen, Erik Patton, Sarah Stewart, and Jaclyn Verbitski. Lana Hum, Director of Exhibition Design and Production, worked closely with us in planning the installation in the Alfred H. Barr, Jr. Painting and Sculpture Galleries on the Museum's fourth floor. We benefited mightily from Lana's ideas and enjoyed every minute of working with her. In the same department, Peter Perez and Harry Harris also deserve our warm thanks. In the Department of Collection Management and Exhibition Registration, Stefanii Ruta-Atkins, Head Registrar, and Rebecca Myles, Susan Palamara, and Jennifer Wolfe were exceptional in their efficiency and ingenuity as they solved one problem after another. We are grateful to Rob Jung and Sarah Wood and our excellent team of preparators. Lynda Zycherman, Sculpture Conservator, was a crucial partner in the preparation of this exhibition. Her collaborative spirit, expertise, and relentless curiosity contributed significantly to our understanding of Picasso's materials and methods. In the Department of Conservation we also extend our deep thanks to Jim Coddington, Chief Conservator, and Eugene Albertelli, Anni Aviram, Roger Griffith, Ana Martins, Chris McGlinchey, Ellen Moody, and Erika Mosier.

In the Department of Painting and Sculpture, several people deserve special mention in addition to the exhibition team. These are Francesca Dolnier, Lily Goldberg, Danielle Johnson, Danielle King, Stephanie Kingpetcharat, Talia Kwartler, Cara Manes, Cora Rosevear, and Janet Yoon. We also are grateful for the help of interns Kaysie Hawke, Kylie King, and Ashley Park. In addition, we wish to recognize the contributions of Quentin Bajac and Sarah Meister in the Department of Photography and Christophe Cherix and Kathy Curry in the Department of Drawings and Prints. We thank Wendy Woon, Deputy Director for Education, and Sara Bodinson, Cari Frisch, Pablo Helguera, Jenna Madison, Mary Malaythong, Elizabeth Marguiles, Samantha Rowe, and Jess Van Nostrand in the Department of Education; in the Departments of Library and Archives, Milan Hughston, Chief of Library, and Michelle Elligott, Chief of Archives, and Thomas D. Grischkowsky,

Michelle Harvey, David Senior, Elisabeth Thomas, and Jenny Tobias; Patty Lipshutz, General Counsel, and Nancy Adelson and Dina Sorokina in the Department of the General Counsel; in the Department of Graphic Design and Advertising, H. Y. Ingrid Chou, Claire Corey, Joceyln Meinhardt, Wendy Olson, Althea Penza, JiEun Rim, and Damien Saatdjian; in the Department of Communications, Kim Mitchell, Chief Communications Officer, and Margaret Doyle, Tina Adlaf Hlebec, and Paul Jackson; in the Department of Exhibition and Program Funding, Lesley Cannady, Claire Huddleston, Bobby Kean, Sylvia Renner, Jessica Smith, Lauren Stakias, and Anna Luisa Vallifuoco; in the Department of Imaging and Visual Resources, Erik Landsberg, Director, and Paul Abbey, Peter Butler, Thomas Griesel, Robert Kastler, Jonathan Muzikar, Roberto Rivera, and John Wronn; in the Department of Collection and Exhibition Technologies, Ian Eckert, Manager, and Leslie Davis, Allison LaPlatney, and Kathryn Ryan; in the Department of Special Programming and Events, Maggie Lyko, Director, and Pamela Duncan; LJ Hartman, Director of Security; and Tunji Adeniji, Director of Facilities and Safety.

We are fortunate that the Museum's collection of Picasso's work provided the focus of study for this year's Museum Research Consortium (MRC), headed by Leah Dickerman, Marlene Hess Curator, Department of Painting and Sculpture, and supported by The Andrew W. Mellon Foundation. We thank faculty members Bridget Alsdorf, Emily Braun, Thomas Crow, Noam Elcott, Hal Foster, David Joselit, Branden Joseph, Kobena Mercer, Robert Slifkin, and Sebastian Zeidler; fellows Rebecca Lowery, Kristin Poor, Lauren Rosati, Sam Sackeroff, and Rachel Silveri; as well as all the participating students. Jason Dubs and Jennifer Harris gracefully facilitated all MRC programming.

The preparation of this exhibition catalogue has been a herculean task, one that could not have been accomplished without the generous advocacy of Publisher Christopher Hudson and the supreme dedication demonstrated by every member of the Department of Publications. David Frankel, Chul R. Kim, and Marc Sapir have guided the project with characteristic thoughtfulness and tenacity; they have our warm admiration. We cannot overstate our gratitude to editor Rebecca Roberts, who provided thoughtful advice and revisions with rigor, patience, and deeply appreciated good humor. We also thank our team of auxiliary editors Thomas Fredrickson, Nancy Grubb, Alexander Provan, Sarah Resnick, and Elizabeth Smith, as well as proofreaders Aimery Dunlap-Smith and Lynn Scrabis. Matthew Pimm deftly handled image production for more than five hundred plates and illustrations. We also thank Genevieve Allison, Cerise Fontaine, Hannah Kim, Bryan Stauss, and Makiko Wholey. We owe the elegant design of this catalogue to Mark Nelson and David Zaza of McCall Associates, assisted by Michelle Nix and Marijane Kubow. The design team worked under tremendous pressure to produce a catalogue that shows no sign of that; we are deeply grateful for their outstanding work.

We have saved until the end our words of appreciation for the core members of our exhibition team. Their dedication has reached far beyond what we ever could have reasonably expected, and their intelligence and creativity have enriched every aspect of the exhibition and this catalogue. We cannot begin to express our admiration and gratitude for the work of Luise Mahler, Assistant Curator. Her research skills, creativity, and exacting standards are reflected on every page of this book and contributed immeasurably to the quality of the exhibition. Curatorial Assistant Nancy Lim has handled an unfathomable range of administrative details with extraordinary skill and has been an invaluable partner in all our aesthetic decisions. Like Luise, she has been a remarkable model of grace under pressure. We also thank Silvia Loreti for her help during the early stages of research; Rebecca Lowery for her valuable assistance with research and writing; and intern Hannah Garner for the efficiency and diligence with which she helped all of us. It has been a pleasure and a privilege to participate in the close teamwork of this remarkable group.

Finally, we reiterate Glenn Lowry's thanks to all those who made the exhibition financially possible. We gratefully acknowledge the exhibition's sponsor, Hyundai Card, and the major support provided by Monique M. Schoen Warshaw, Marie-Josée and Henry Kravis, Robert Menschel and Janet Wallach, Sue and Edgar Wachenheim III, Cornelia T. Bailey, and the MoMA Annual Exhibition Fund. The exhibition is supported by a generous indemnity from the Federal Council on the Arts and the Humanities; we thank Pat Loiko, especially, for her patience and support. We are honored by the support provided for this catalogue by The International Council of The Museum of Modern Art, the Jo Carole Lauder Publications Fund of The International Council of The Museum of Modern Art, and The Museum of Modern Art's Research and Scholarly Publications endowment established through the generosity of The Andrew W. Mellon Foundation, the Edward John Noble Foundation, Mr. and Mrs. Perry R. Bass, and the National Endowment for the Humanities' Challenge Grant Program.

Ann Temkin
The Marie-Josée and Henry Kravis
Chief Curator of Painting and Sculpture

Anne Umland
The Blanchette Hooker Rockefeller
Curator of Painting and Sculpture

PICASSO SCULPTURE
AN INTRODUCTION

ANN TEMKIN | ANNE UMLAND

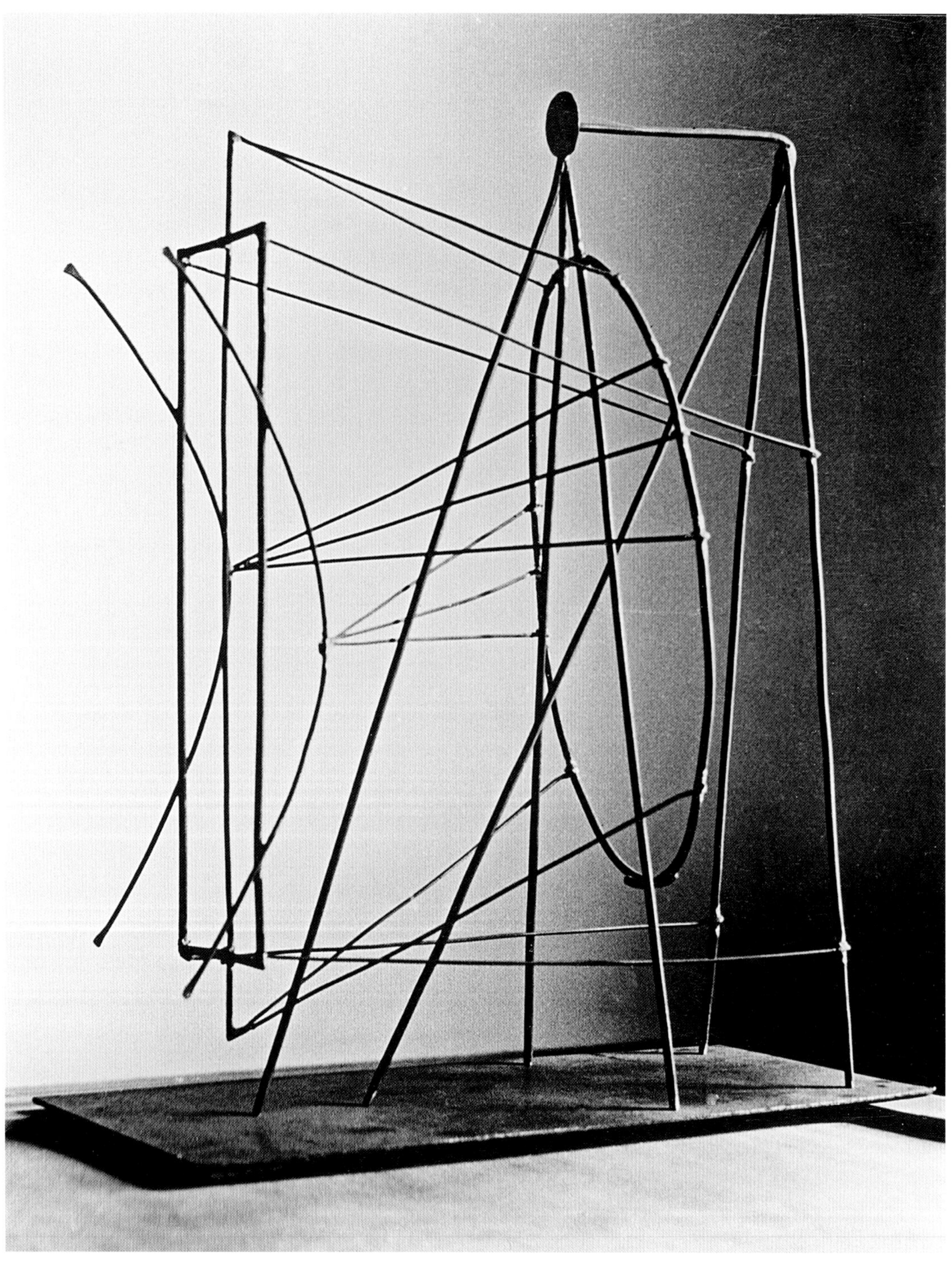

Figure (fall 1928). Paris, rue La Boétie, December 1932. Gelatin silver print, 11 ⅜ × 9 in. (29 × 22.8 cm). Photograph by Brassaï. *Musée national Picasso–Paris. Purchase, 1996*

PICASSO'S SCULPTURE has long been discussed as the least-known facet of the artist's protean career. In the first book devoted to the sculpture, published in 1949, Picasso's longtime dealer Daniel-Henry Kahnweiler felt obliged to open his text with a defense of the sculptures as more than Picasso's "violon d'Ingres," a French expression for an artist's hobby.[1] As recently as 2000, a sculpture retrospective at the Centre Georges Pompidou described its subject as "the best kept secret of the twentieth century."[2] Perhaps it is not surprising that Picasso himself contributed to this mythology, reportedly greeting the 1971 catalogue raisonné of the sculptures as the record of "an unknown civilization."[3] It is true that only in 1966, at age eighty-five, did the artist first agree to release for a comprehensive exhibition at the Petit Palais in Paris the dozens he had kept with him at home. It is true too that, even since then, exhibitions and books devoted to Picasso's paintings and works on paper have vastly outnumbered those addressing the sculptures.

Like all such myths, however, this particular one is only partially accurate. An emphasis on the sculptures' absence has eclipsed a rich body of evidence underscoring the vitality of their presence. This publication therefore approaches its subject from a different viewpoint: instead of asking why and how the sculptures remained a well-kept secret, we decided to investigate the possibility that these objects actually did have dynamic histories far more lively and complicated than the myth of secrets would suggest. Noted scholars have introduced such a revisionist view during this past decade.[4] Given the sculptures' relatively small number within Picasso's gargantuan output—the artist made approximately 700, as compared to approximately 4,500 paintings—the role they played is remarkably rich. Within this introductory overview, and in the detailed historical chronicle that follows, we set out to provide a history of Picasso's sculptural oeuvre that argues for its visibility and impact throughout the course of his long lifetime.

When Picasso was growing up in Spain, and studying under the watchful eye of his father, the painter José Ruiz y Blasco, becoming a sculptor was probably the last thing on his mind. He pursued a rigorous program of traditional academic study, first in La Coruña and then in Barcelona and Madrid. His goal was to master the art of painting, in accordance with the divisions between disciplines and the hierarchies of the times. Sculpture at the end of the nineteenth century in Europe was an art that required specialized techniques and training of a very different sort from painting: traditional materials such as bronze, marble, stone, and wood were hard and resistant; the tools and processes required to manipulate these materials were distinct and labor-intensive; and of course the act of creating an object in the round that occupies real space, and presents multiple points of vantage, is very different from that of representing a two-dimensional illusion of something, on a flat pictorial surface, using brushes and fluid paints.

Picasso proved preternaturally adept both as a draftsman and as a painter, rapidly surpassing the abilities of his father. Early drawings that he made in classes at La Coruña depict plaster casts of fragments of classical Greek and Roman sculptures and testify to his command of the pictorial techniques of shading, contouring, and chiaroscuro. Given their status as standard exercises assigned to all academic students, they cannot be interpreted as evidence of an early interest in sculpture on Picasso's part. Moreover, his first such drawings were based on lithographic plates from a drawing manual rather than the plaster casts themselves; in other words, Picasso initially studied classical sculpture only as translated into two dimensions. The dialogue between the pictorial and the sculptural, and the intermingling of conventions used for one with those used for the other, would prove to be constants in his work.

If Picasso tried his hand at sculpting during his student years, no traces remain of his efforts. As a child, he made cut-paper silhouettes that prefigure his Cubist constructions as well as his post–World War II sheet metal cutouts (fig. 1). Likewise, the crèche figurines he modeled and painted as a young boy presage an interest in ceramics and in polychromy that manifests itself, with varying degrees of intensity, throughout his sculptural oeuvre. Both these protosculptural pastimes have roots in craft traditions as opposed to the history of Western sculpture. Considered in relation to what was to come, they indicate how for Picasso sculpture would always be something deeply personal, highly improvisatory, often intimate in scale, and encompassing a vast range of styles,

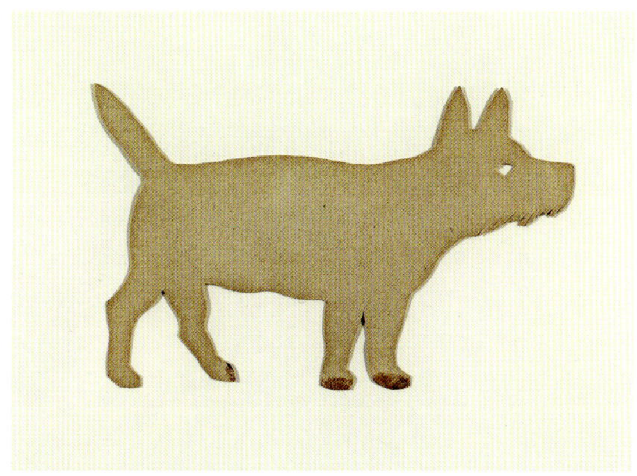

1. Pablo Picasso. *Dog*. Malaga, c. 1890. Paper, 2 ⅜ × 3 ⅝ in. (6 × 9.2 cm). Museu Picasso, Barcelona

materials, and techniques. He was no more likely to engage in typical sculptural practices such as modeling or carving than he was to produce works using tools as simple as a pair of scissors, skills as rudimentary as cutting and folding, and materials as humble, light, and easily accessible as whatever scraps of paper happened to be at hand.

Picasso's first true sculpture measures only some five inches high. This modest *Seated Woman* (pl. 1) was made in the Barcelona studio of Emili Fontbona, one of the young Picasso's many sculptor friends. It is from these individuals, rather than from any formal course of study, that Picasso learned the basics of modeling and how to shape a dense, heavy, wet material like clay to his own ends. After 1904, when he definitively moved to Paris, he continued to produce sculptures, albeit sporadically: between 1904 and late 1909, he created fewer than thirty, after which he made no sculptures for almost three years. These early sculptures, vastly outnumbered by his drawings and paintings, register a wide variety of influences. Among them were the ceramics and woodcarvings of Paul Gauguin; Edgar Degas's early, naturalistic figures; the impressionistic surfaces of Auguste Rodin and Medardo Rosso; and ancient Iberian stone carvings.

Most important, perhaps, was Picasso's discovery of African and Oceanic sculpture, which he studied with particular intensity during the summer of 1907. It was then, at the urging of his friend André Derain, that he paid a visit to the unrivaled collection of African art at the Musée d'Ethnographie du Trocadéro in Paris. The impact on his explosive masterpiece *Les Demoiselles d'Avignon* (1907) was immediate and decisive. The visit also seems to have prompted Picasso to turn in earnest to wood carving: the works he created between 1907 and early 1908 by chiseling into pieces of found wood are among his most direct homages not only to Gauguin but also to his memorable encounters within the museum's dusty rooms (see, for example, pls. 6–9).

Picasso was not content simply to look at sculpture from Africa and Oceania; like many of his peers, he wanted to own it. Although over the years he would prove to be an avid buyer and swapper of other artists' paintings and works on paper, in the sculptural realm he set his acquisitive sights almost exclusively on non-Western art and artifacts. Picasso's attraction to African and Oceanic sculptures was driven as much by his sense of these objects' original functions and roles as by their formal qualities. Understanding them as capable of exerting a potent talismanic force, he sought the same for his own sculptures. The unique charisma of much of his work in three dimensions testifies to this ambition; it also helps to explain his penchant for keeping his sculptures with him, a practice that began early on and became ever more pronounced throughout the course of the decades.

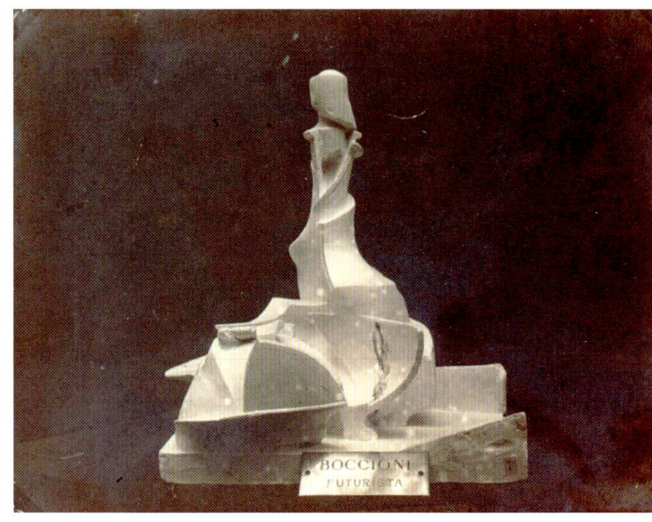

2. *Development of a Bottle in Space* (1912) by Umberto Boccioni as installed at the *Première exposition de sculpture futuriste du peintre et sculpteur futuriste Boccioni* (First exhibition of the Futurist sculpture of the Futurist painter and sculptor Boccioni), Galerie La Boétie, Paris, June 20–July 16, 1913. Private collection

Among Picasso's early sculptures, his 1909 *Head of a Woman* (pl. 11) was quick to become the most famous. Soon after its completion, the Paris art dealer Ambroise Vollard purchased the original clay version of this Cubist sculpture and that of four earlier works, including *The Jester* (pl. 3) and *Kneeling Woman Combing Her Hair* (pl. 5). Vollard subsequently had these sculptures cast in bronze and put them on display in his gallery on rue Laffitte, where collectors and dealers could order their own on demand. Among those who bought *Head of a Woman* were the American photographer Edward Steichen, acting on behalf of the photographer and gallerist Alfred Stieglitz; the Czech collector Vincenc Kramář; and the German dealer Alfred Flechtheim. By 1913, thanks to their purchases, bronze casts of *Head of a Woman* were on public display in cities as far-flung as New York, Prague, and Düsseldorf. In New York alone, the sculpture would have been seen by the eighty thousand visitors who attended the fabled Armory Show (officially, the *International Exhibition of Modern Art*) in February and March.

The most important audience for *Head of a Woman* was that of fellow artists upon whose work it would have a transformative effect. The Italian Futurist Umberto Boccioni, for example, traveled to Paris in 1912, and probably had an opportunity to see the bronze in Vollard's gallery at that time. When Boccioni's first sculpture exhibition opened in Paris in the summer of 1913, works such as his *Development of a Bottle in Space* (fig. 2) and *Unique Forms of Continuity in Space* (1913) made clear their debt to this predecessor; Picasso's example is felt both in the faceting of form and the opening up of a sculpture's core to the play of light. Similarly, works by other early Cubist sculptors working in Paris, such as Aleksandr

Archipenko, Henri Laurens, and Jacques Lipchitz, signal a keen awareness of Picasso's innovations.

Not atypically, what was a starting point for others marked an end of sorts for Picasso. After completing *Head of a Woman* in late 1909, he set aside his clay, bringing his first pioneering sculptural episode to a close. When more than two years later he again turned to working in three dimensions, it was to produce sculptures of a very different sort. This initiated what would become a consistent pattern in his practice as a sculptor: distinct periods of concentration, interrupted by intervals of greater or lesser duration, followed by works that bore no obvious relation to those that preceded them.

This holds particularly true for the group of objects Picasso created between the fall of 1912 and, with a few later exceptions, the outbreak in summer 1914 of World War I. During this brief yet extraordinarily generative period, he produced any number of landmarks within the history of twentieth-century sculpture: a cardboard *Guitar* that introduced space for the first time as a sculptural material (pl. 13); six uniquely polychromed bronze sculptures entitled *Glass of Absinthe* that incorporated commercially manufactured absinthe spoons (pls. 21–26); and painted wall reliefs that, like many works from this moment, hover between painting and sculpture, defying all attempts to categorize them. Today we take for granted that sculpture can include space as an integral element; that it can be made from any material and composed from disparate parts; and that it need not be imposing in size or take the human figure as its subject. This was far from the case in the fall of 1912.

Picasso's breakthrough came with the realization that he did not need particular tools or difficult-to-manipulate materials in order to work sculpturally. Many of his sculptures from these years have a notably improvisatory air. This is the result of Picasso's seizing upon whatever lay close at hand within his own studio—not those of his sculptor friends, where most of his earlier sculptures were made—and cobbling these things together using the simplest and most expedient of means. String, wire, pieces of paper and cardboard, wood scraps, and tin cans were cut, folded, glued, stitched, or otherwise assembled. The results were musical instruments and other still life subjects of an unprecedented sort.

As early as January 1913, news of the existence of such works reached an attentive audience in Berlin. The poet and critic Guillaume Apollinaire, Picasso's good friend and early champion, gave a lecture at the Galerie Der Sturm, excerpts of which were published the following month in the gallery's journal. Therein Apollinaire described how Picasso recently had "renounced ordinary paints to compose relief pictures made from cardboard, or papier collé."[5] Later that year, Apollinaire published four black-and-white photographic reproductions of

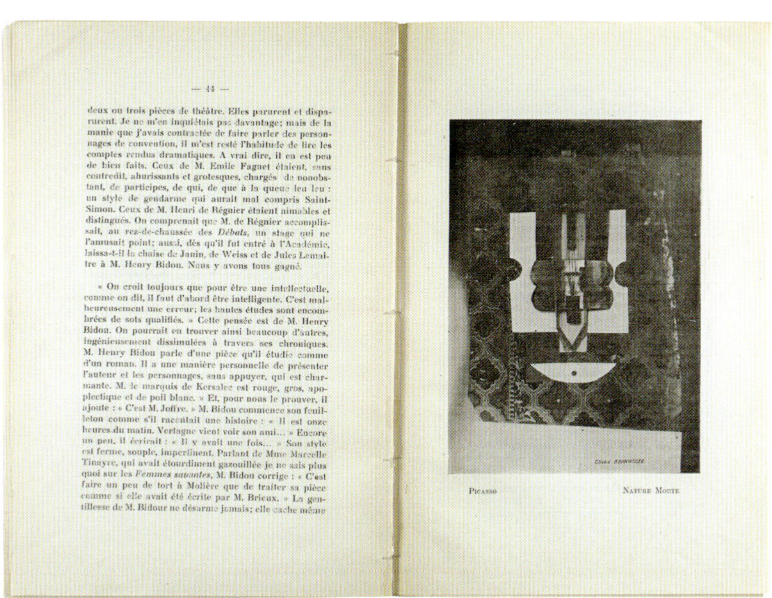

— 44 —

deux ou trois pièces de théâtre. Elles parurent et disparurent. Je ne m'en inquiétais pas davantage; mais de la manie que j'avais contractée de faire parler des personnages de convention, il m'est resté l'habitude de lire les comptes rendus dramatiques. A vrai dire, il en est peu de bien faits. Ceux de M. Emile Faguet étaient, sans contredit, ahurissants et grotesques, chargés de nonobstant, de participes, de qui, de que à la queue leu leu : un style de gendarme qui aurait mal compris Saint-Simon. Ceux de M. Henri de Régnier étaient aimables et distingués. On comprenait que M. de Régnier accomplissait, au rez-de-chaussée des *Débats*, un stage qui ne l'amusait point; aussi, dès qu'il fut entré à l'Académie, laissa-t-il la chaise de Janin, de Weiss et de Jules Lemaître à M. Henry Bidou. Nous y avons tous gagné.

« On croit toujours que pour être une intellectuelle, comme on dit, il faut d'abord être intelligente. C'est malheureusement une erreur; les hautes études sont encombrées de sots qualifiés. » Cette pensée est de M. Henry Bidou. On pourrait en trouver ainsi beaucoup d'autres, ingénieusement dissimulées à travers ses chroniques. M. Henry Bidou parle d'une pièce qu'il étudie comme d'un roman. Il a une manière personnelle de présenter l'auteur et les personnages, sans appuyer, qui est charmante. M. le marquis de Kersalec est rouge, gros, apoplectique et de poil blanc. » Et, pour nous le prouver, il ajoute : « C'est M. Joffre. » M. Bidou commence son feuilleton comme s'il racontait une histoire : « Il est onze heures du matin. Vertagne vient voir son ami... » Encore un peu, il écrirait : « Il y avait une fois... » Son style est ferme, souple, impertinent. Parlant de Mme Marcelle Tinayre, qui avait étourdiment gazouillée je ne sais plus quoi sur les *Femmes savantes*, M. Bidou corrige : « C'est faire un peu de tort à Molière que de traiter sa pièce comme si elle avait été écrite par M. Brieux. » La gentillesse de M. Bidour ne désarme jamais; elle cache même

PICASSO

NATURE MORTE

3. Picasso's *Nature Morte* (Still life) with *Violin* (Paris, 1912–13) reproduced in *Les Soirées de Paris*, no. 18 (November 15, 1913): 45. Photograph by Émile Delétang for Galerie Kahnweiler. The Museum of Modern Art Library, New York

Picasso's new constructions in the journal *Les Soirées de Paris* (fig. 3). The photographs were taken by Émile Delétang, a professional fine-art photographer often employed by Kahnweiler, Picasso's new dealer. The captions accompanying the four works attribute them to Picasso and identify each simply as a "Nature Morte" (Still life).[6] None of them survives today as pictured, testimony to the radically provisional character of Picasso's sculptural practice at this moment. Judging from the *Soirées* photographs and other, more intimate studio snapshots taken for his own private use, he treated constructions like *Violin* and the cardboard *Guitar* as repositionable elements that could be arranged in various ways within the studio. As such, these works offer material corollaries to the semantic mobility of Cubism's visual language of schematic signs.

The images in *Les Soirées de Paris* epitomize the strong symbiosis between the mediums of sculpture and photography that was as fundamental for Picasso as for many of his peers. Like Stieglitz's photographs of the 1909 *Head of a Woman*, published in *Camera Work* one year earlier, the photos of the constructions provide an early and revealing demonstration of the essential role played by photography in the dissemination, reception, and interpretation of Picasso's sculptural oeuvre. Copies of the French journal were distributed at the November 14, 1913, vernissage of the Salon d'Automne in Paris. Although Picasso notoriously refrained from exhibiting with the so-called Salon Cubists, the published photographs of his new constructions gave them a conspicuous if indirect presence

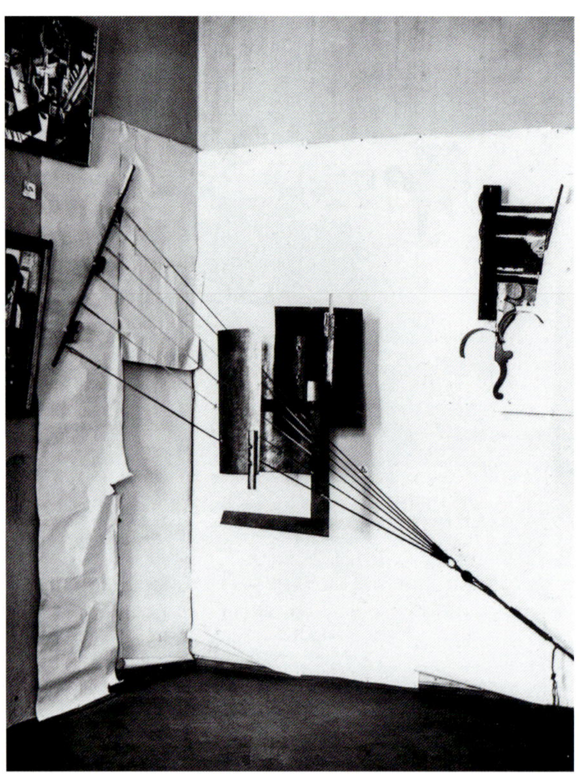

4. *Corner Counter-Relief, no. 132*, by Vladimir Tatlin, in the exhibition *Poslednyaya futuristicheskaya vystavka kartin: 0.10* (The last futurist exhibition of paintings 0.10), Khudozhestvennoe buro, Petrograd (now St. Petersburg), 1915. The Russian State Archive of Literature and Art (RGALI)

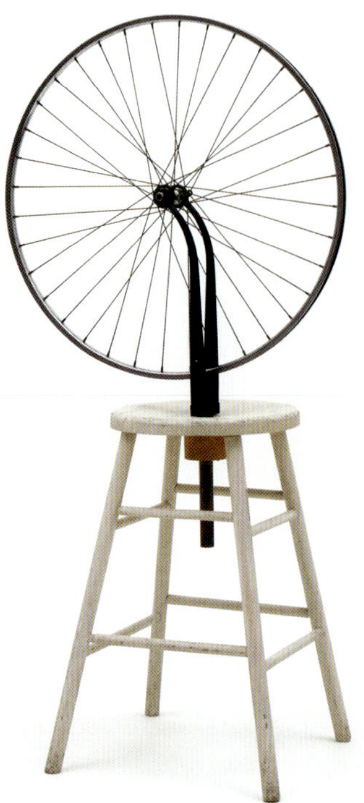

5. Marcel Duchamp. *Bicycle Wheel*. New York, 1951 (third version, after lost original of 1913). Metal wheel mounted on painted wood stool, 51 × 25 × 16 ½ in. (129.5 × 63.5 × 41.9 cm). The Museum of Modern Art, New York. The Sidney and Harriet Janis Collection

on this important occasion. Years later, the Surrealist leader André Breton recalled the lasting impression that the *Soirées* photographs of Picasso's new works had made on him as a young man. The power of his memories exemplifies the impact that Picasso's photographed constructions and sculptures would prove capable of exerting, even when the objects themselves remained with him in the studio.

For fellow artists, that studio was a magnet. In early 1914, the Russian artist Vladimir Tatlin visited, probably alerted by *Les Soirées de Paris* to Picasso's new work. Immediately upon returning to Moscow, Tatlin set about producing his own first series of relief constructions, taking Picasso's discoveries in a new, more radical direction. His *Corner Counter-Relief, no. 132* (fig. 4), which was first shown in December 1915, comprised various found materials, including sheet metal, copper, wood, and string, and was suspended across a corner space. Tatlin deliberately rejected any referent external to his chosen materials, relying solely on their own physical properties to determine his formal moves. Picasso, on the other hand, persisted in transforming his found materials into something, be it a musical instrument, a glass, or a guitar's sound hole. Even at its most simple and reductive, Picasso's art always has a nameable counterpart, a mimetic relationship to things that exist in the world.

During the spring of 1914, Picasso literally assimilated a bit of reality into his work. It took the form of a mismatched set of six cheap metal absinthe spoons, each of which he laid across the rim of a small bronze sculpture of a glass and topped with an indissoluble bronze sugar cube. A hidden bronze pin held the three components (glass, spoon, and sugar cube) together. This *Glass of Absinthe* was Picasso's first and only Cubist sculpture to be editioned by Kahnweiler (pls. 21–26). Although, conventionally, works within a bronze edition look the same, Picasso decorated the surface of each of his six small bronze sculptures differently, using oil paint and, in one instance, sand. Working against tradition, he applied his skills as a painter to make each of his sculptures unique.

Just a year before Picasso used paint and ready-made spoons to create a new, audaciously hybrid form of bronze sculpture, a slightly younger artist named Marcel Duchamp had placed a bicycle wheel atop a kitchen stool in his studio and set it spinning, dispensing entirely with artist's materials to create what he would later pronounce a "readymade" (fig. 5). Picasso's positioning of his absinthe spoons represents an alternative approach: although the spoons remain physically unaltered, and in this sense are comparable to Duchamp's bicycle wheel, Picasso inserted them into a narrative context and asked them to play dual roles, as representations and as the things themselves. The complex interplay between the found objects and the marks and shapes created by Picasso's own hand prove that, for the Spaniard, the magic of making was foremost. But like Duchamp, Picasso decisively revoked the insularity of the art object, forty years before the American Robert Rauschenberg would invoke the concept of working in the "gap" between life and art.[7]

Picasso's interest in creating works that incorporated real space and everyday objects found a new outlet when, in 1916, he became intensely engaged in designing costumes, curtains, and sets for the theater and ballet. Although the catalogue raisonné of Picasso's sculpture includes some of his designs for the theater, implying that they should be considered as part of his sculptural practice, the two bodies of work stand distinctly apart. Costumes like those he made for Erik Satie and Jean Cocteau's ballet *Parade*, for example, despite the garments' Cubist syntax, constructed volumes, and heterogeneous materiality, were made to come alive only when they were worn and moved about in onstage amid music and dance (fig. 6). During his immersion in the world of theater, Picasso set aside the making of sculpture per se.

In 1924, the year of his final major stage designs, Picasso created his first important postwar construction: a monumental sheet metal *Guitar* measuring almost four feet tall (pl. 29). This work's subject, materials, and techniques are fundamentally retrospective in character. They reprise those of Picasso's earlier Cubist constructions, now with a somber grisaille palette that hints at the profound changes in Picasso's life and art since the heady days of his first *Guitar* works (pls. 13, 14). In this sense, the 1924 *Guitar* marks more an end than a beginning. Four more years would pass before Picasso returned to sculpture.

An image of Picasso's 1924 *Guitar* was first published by the young poets and writers who, in October that same year, rallied to the call of Surrealism. It appeared in the pages of the inaugural issue of the Surrealists' newly minted journal, *La Révolution surréaliste*, where it illustrated a text on dreams by Pierre Reverdy. That same issue included a portrait photograph of Picasso by the Surrealist photographer Man Ray, set within a grid of photos of the group's members surrounding an image of the anarchist Germaine Breton. The implication was that the celebrated artist shared the young group's radical politics and its disdain for law and order; whether Picasso actually had granted permission to use his portrait in such a way is unknown. In any event, he seems to have done little during the 1920s and early 1930s to discourage his appropriation by the Surrealists, and later even claimed that he and Apollinaire had coined the term "Surrealism." Picasso welcomed Breton into his studio on multiple occasions, and allowed him to broker the sale of *Les Demoiselles d'Avignon* to the couturier and collector Jacques Doucet. It would have been difficult not to appreciate the energizing attention of a new generation of devotees who proclaimed their "profound and total admiration"[8] for him and acknowledged they would "merely follow where Picasso has gone before and will go again."[9]

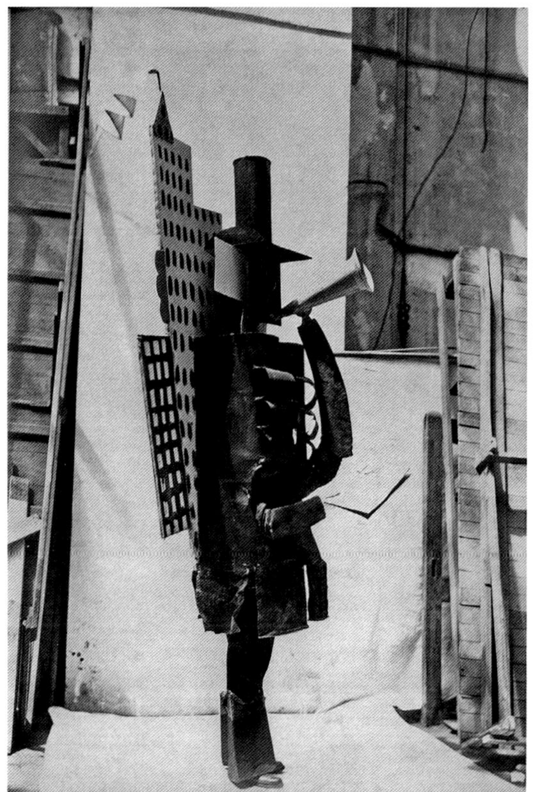

6. Costume designed by Picasso for the American Manager in the ballet *Parade*, 1917. Photograph by Harry Lachmann. Bibliothèque nationale de France, Paris

The powerful impact of Surrealism on Picasso's own work is undeniable, evidenced in the realm of sculpture as much or more than any other. Two small objects created in 1928, *Metamorphosis I* and *Metamorphosis II* (pls. 30–31), announce the artist's reengagement with sculpture which, over the course of the next six years, would produce the most highly eroticized objects within his sculptural corpus. On several counts, the two works entitled *Metamorphosis* are harbingers of things to come. The plaster with which Picasso modeled *Metamorphosis I* and *Metamorphosis II* would become, by 1931, his material of choice. In contrast to the elliptical anthropomorphism of his Cubist still life subjects, the distended shapes and swelling volumes of these two objects are explicitly figurative and physical. They introduce a formal vocabulary of volumetric distortion that Picasso would soon develop to create his first truly large-scale sculptures.

Also in 1928, working in close collaboration with the Catalan sculptor Julio González, Picasso produced a series of

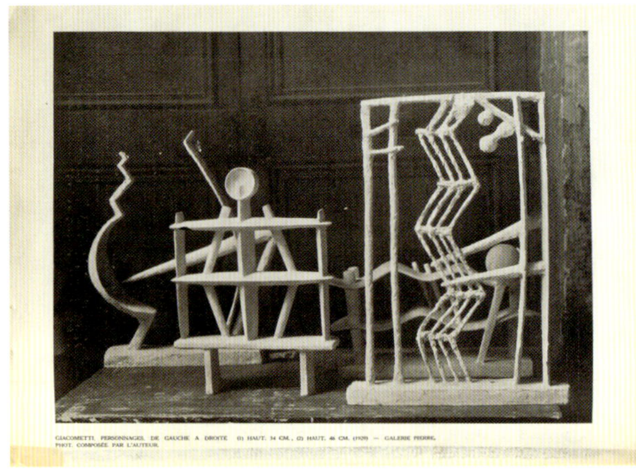

7. Open-form sculptures by Alberto Giacometti reproduced in *Documents*, no. 4 (1929): [214]. Left to right: *Man and Woman*, *Man (Apollo)*, *Reclining Woman Who Dreams*, and *Three Figures Outdoors*, all 1929. Photograph by Marc Vaux. Courtesy Bibliothèque Kandinsky, Paris

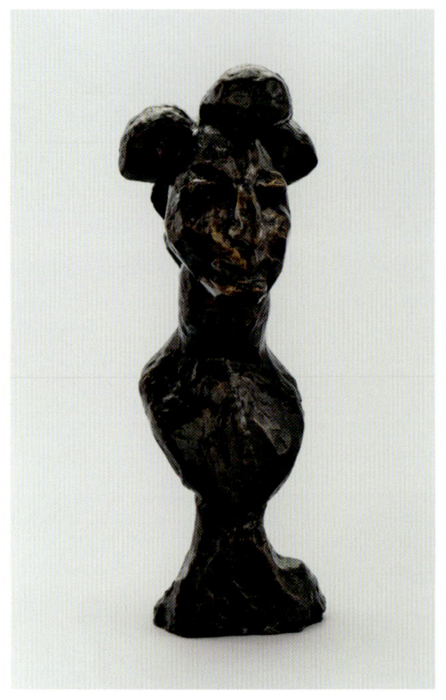

9. Henri Matisse. *Jeannette (IV)*. April–September 1910 or February–mid-July 1911. Bronze, 24 ⅛ × 10 ¾ × 11 ¼ in. (61.3 × 27.4 × 28.7 cm). The Museum of Modern Art, New York. Acquired through the Lillie P. Bliss Bequest

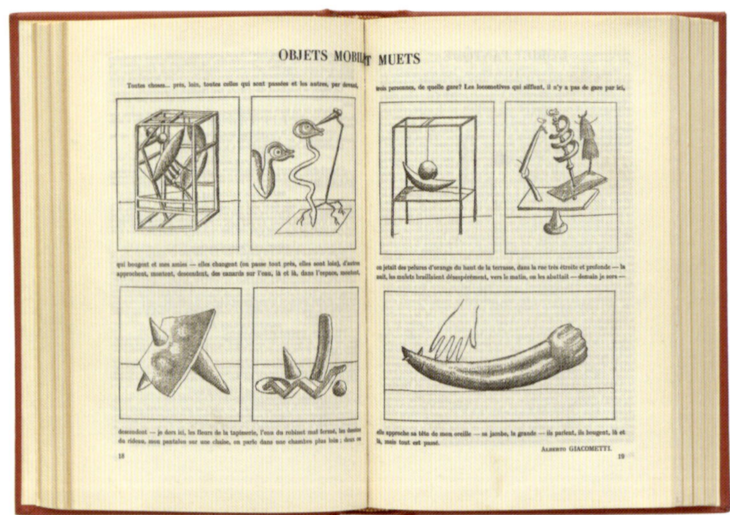

8. Alberto Giacometti, illustrated essay "Objets mobiles et muets" (Mobile and mute objects), *Le Surréalisme au service de la révolution*, no. 3 (1931): 18–19

nearly transparent constructions; Kahnweiler later dubbed these radical works "drawings in space" (pls. 34–36).[10] Physically, they comprise nothing more than thin iron wires welded together; the wires define the boundaries of bodies whose primary substance is air. These openwork sculptures, preceded by drawings for *Metamorphosis I* and *Metamorphosis II*, were among the early proposals Picasso submitted to a committee responsible for a memorial to Apollinaire, who had died at age thirty-eight in 1918. Each design was rejected in turn, as were subsequent ones. One might argue that the serial rebuffs of the Apollinaire memorial commission deserve much of the credit for Picasso's deepening engagement with sculpture. His purchase in June 1930 of the Château de Boisgeloup, a country manor some forty miles north of Paris, also played a decisive role. The vacant stables on the Boisgeloup property provided an ideal setting for Picasso to set up a sculpture studio for the first time in his career, and to dedicate himself to making sculpture in the round.

Between 1928 and 1934, Picasso created more than ninety sculptures, ranging widely in technique, materials, and iconography. This diverse body of work encompassed new forms of welded metal assemblage, the result of his collaboration with González; finger-slender carved wood figures; voluptuously modeled and carved plasters; and, from 1933 on, uniquely imprinted plaster-and-found-object figures that reinvent classical themes. These new sculptures were reproduced in contemporary periodicals with notable alacrity. *Cahiers d'Art*, launched in 1926 by the publisher, art critic, and gallerist Christian Zervos, played a significant role in this regard. Zervos was the first to publish images of Picasso's new *Metamorphosis* sculptures in 1928, followed early the next year by a photograph of one of the series of small welded-iron "drawings in space" (pl. 34). Such signals of Picasso's activity would have been important to the younger artists working in Paris. It seems likely that the Swiss sculptor Alberto Giacometti, in particular, studied reproductions of Picasso's *Metamorphosis* plasters and first openwork constructions with deep interest.

Photographs of Giacometti's own "perforated" sculptures were published in the dissident Surrealist journal *Documents* in the fall of 1929 (fig. 7).[11] As pictured in *Documents*, the linear

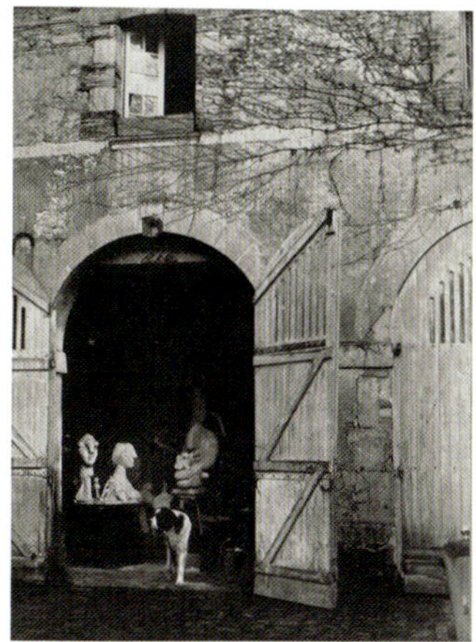

L'ATELIER DE SCULPTURE

DANS L'INTÉRIEUR DE CET ATELIER PHOTOGRAPHIÉ DE JOUR ET DE NUIT, SE TROUVENT LES SCULPTURES EXÉCUTÉES AU COURS DE CES DERNIÈRES ANNÉES : LES STATUES MÉTALLIQUES, LES CONSTRUCTIONS EN FIL DE FER, LES SCULPTURES EN BRONZE DORÉ, LA SÉRIE DES TÊTES MONUMENTALES, LES PETITES STATUES DE PLATRE, L'OISEAU, LA GÉNISSE ET LE COQ.

(Photographies exécutées par Brassaï.)

10. View of Picasso's studio at Boisgeloup reproduced in André Breton, "Picasso dans son élément" (Picasso in his element), *Minotaure* 1, no. 1 (June 15, 1933): 15. Photograph by Brassaï. The Museum of Modern Art Library, New York

sculpture est assujettie au devenir de ce figuier. Et cela est si vrai qu'on peut constater devant une autre image qu'elle a déserté le voisinage du figuier mort, dont les racines saillent de la terre, s'arc-boutent et se mêlent inextricablement dans une convulsion suprême, qui n'est plus que la grimace de l'étreinte. La lignification totale de la tige, gainée à son extrémité d'une corne de bœuf, la disparition des feuilles compensée, par contraste, par l'imperceptible frémissement d'un petit plumeau rouge, sont exploitées on ne peut plus contradictoirement avec tout ce qu'a pu faire naître le sentiment de la vie réelle de l'arbuste. Mais cette idée même de support, de soutien, avec toute la valeur encore une fois justificative qui s'y attache, cette idée en se réfléchissant sur elle-même exige encore sa réciprocité : si la sculpture prend appui sur la plante, il n'est pas interdit non plus que des objets aussi hétéroclites qu'on voudra reposent sur elle (aussi bien est-il d'un intérêt douteux de se demander si le lierre a été fait pour le mur ou le mur pour le lierre) et ces objets, en eux-mêmes, ne seront jamais trop humbles, jamais trop futiles — toque de vizir de pacotille, petits « Micky » ou ouistitis des fêtes foraines, joujoux de clinquant — pour attenter à la dignité de ce personnage en fonte, qui ne sait apparemment trop quoi faire de son pied, — au demeurant simple forme métallique de cordonnier. A qui se croirait encore autorisé à mettre en doute la démarche toujours dialectique de cette pensée, je pense qu'il me suffira de rappeler comment, lors de son exposition de juin dernier aux galeries Georges Petit, Picasso avait fait en sorte d'opposer, d'un mur à l'autre d'une longue salle, les deux grandes ferronneries dont on peut voir ici d'autre part la reproduction photographique — ferronneries dont l'une apparaissait couverte de rouille et l'autre fraîchement ripolinée de blanc, — manifestant assez clairement que sous ces toilettes extrêmement dissemblables il désirait qu'au passage des visiteurs elles *se répondissent*. Entre ces deux statues, indiscutablement jumelles, s'échangeaient toutes les considérations, d'une philosophie légèrement ironique, qui sont de mise dès qu'on se laisse aller à agiter le problème de la destinée.

Si, comme on l'a vu, Picasso peintre n'a pas le préjugé de la couleur, il faut bien s'attendre à ce que Picasso sculpteur n'ait pas le préjugé de la

C'est avec une complaisance à cet égard très

ficative et charmante qu'il attire l'attention sur

menues imperfections que tirent de leur

originelle — désobéissances du ciseau, accidents

bois — les grêles petits personnages, reproduits

part, qui reviennent tout dorés de chez le

Ces imperfections, on ne peut nier, d'ailleurs,

lui elles deviennent autant

perfections sensibles. Le bois,

fil de fer, le plâtre sont ici

ployés tour à tour,

ment, par un homme dont

besoin de concrétisation

instantanément de sa

tion même ; qui est, comme

les grands inventeurs,

d'une sollicitation continue ;

qui il est totalement inutile

sans doute aussi, totalement

possible de se prévoir.

aimantation élective, qui

toute élaboration préalable,

cide seule, par le truchement

la substance qui se trouve

ralement *sous la main*, de

venue d'un corps ou d'une

Cette matière est

aimée pour elle-même,

seulement comme matière

général, tout à fait en dehors

la considération de ses états

ticuliers, elle est aimée

dans ces *Fêtes de la Faim*

Rimbaud :

Si j'ai du goût, ce n'est guère
Que pour la terre et les pierres.
Dinn ! dinn ! dinn ! dinn !
Le roc, les charbons, le fer.

Mais pourquoi, dira-t-on,

le plâtre ? Pourquoi

nuerions-nous à manger

bouillie classique du plâtre

Une sorte de chœur

autour de moi, dans lequel

reconnais les voix séduites

irritées des jeunes générations : assez de plâtre,

grand affamé qu'est Picasso pourrait se

de gâcher le plâtre. La vérité est pourtant, je

bien, que ce soit là leur sens dialectique et

le sien qui soit pris en défaut. L'objet extérieur,

que j'ai tenté de le définir visuellement comme

duit de la manifestation dans la toute-lumière

principe de l'obscurité, manifestation qui trouve

surface à se mesurer par la couleur, demande à

que, privé du secours de cette couleur si l'on

au volume, on puisse y suppléer par l'affirmation

rapports d'ombre et de lumière satisfaisants, de

LA GRANDE STATUE.

16

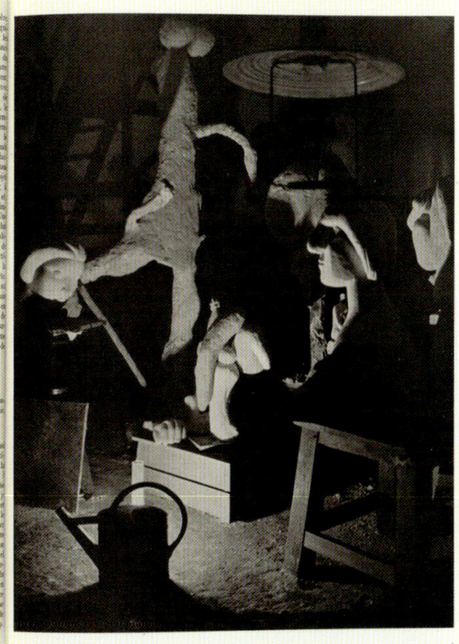

11. Views of Picasso's studio at Boisgeloup in December 1932 reproduced in André Breton, "Picasso dans son élément" (Picasso in his element), *Minotaure* 1, no. 1 (June 15, 1933): 16–17. Photographs by Brassaï. The Museum of Modern Art Library, New York

elements of Giacometti's sculptures were thicker than those of Picasso's, the result of their being fabricated in plaster; they were also, generally speaking, more planar; and their forms were more abstract and stylized. Yet the similarities are strong enough to suggest that, at the very least, Giacometti would have been keenly attentive to Picasso's new work. The conscious staging of his plasters in this *Documents* photograph makes explicit the radical implications of Picasso's welded iron structures. Works that can be seen through are easily confused with their surroundings, blurring distinctions between outside and in, proximity and distance. Giacometti would exploit these ambiguities to powerful psychic effect in his subsequent work.

Giacometti's sculpture, in turn, caught Picasso's own eye. The older artist made an unannounced visit to the Swiss sculptor's first solo exhibition in Paris, at the Galerie Pierre Colle in May 1932. By that point, Giacometti had come to be recognized as Surrealism's leading sculptor. His illustrated essay of 1931, "Objets mobiles et muets" (Mobile and mute objects) included drawings of imaginary and actual works that articulated a new libidinal territory for object making, filling it with intimations of fetishism, frustrated desire, and erotic frisson (fig. 8). Whereas in later years Picasso would take pains to distinguish his art from that of the Surrealists, at this point the group's interest in "mad love" and "convulsive beauty," along with Giacometti's sexually suggestive abstract objects, find echoes in Picasso's own profoundly sensual sculptures of the early 1930s.[12]

On June 15, 1932, a major retrospective of Picasso's work opened at the Galeries Georges Petit in Paris, selected and installed by the artist. While the exhibition featured more than 230 paintings, Picasso chose to include only seven sculptures. Four of these were Vollard bronzes dating from before the First World War, and three were recent assemblages made in collaboration with González. Picasso decided to show the sculpture *Woman in the Garden* in two versions: his original iron version painted white (pl. 41), and a bronze painstakingly executed by González in 1931–32. But the plasters of the previous year or two remained in the Boisgeloup studio, unseen. Visitors to his retrospective could be forgiven for assuming that sculpture was merely a small component of his current practice.

The inaugural issue of the new luxe periodical *Minotaure*, published in June 1933, offered a powerful counterargument to any such assumption. Over the course of twenty-two pages, it detailed a densely populated world of sculpture created by Picasso over the past five years. Captured in photographs taken by the Hungarian artist Brassaï, almost none of the works had been seen before. The calculated result of this presentation was to establish in one fell swoop Picasso's clear place, at age fifty-two, within an elite group of artists recognized as painter-sculptors. Its members included, most pertinently, the towering Renaissance master Michelangelo and Picasso's formidable friend Henri Matisse (fig. 9). The praise accorded a 1930 exhibition of Matisse's sculpture would not have escaped Picasso's fiercely competitive eye.

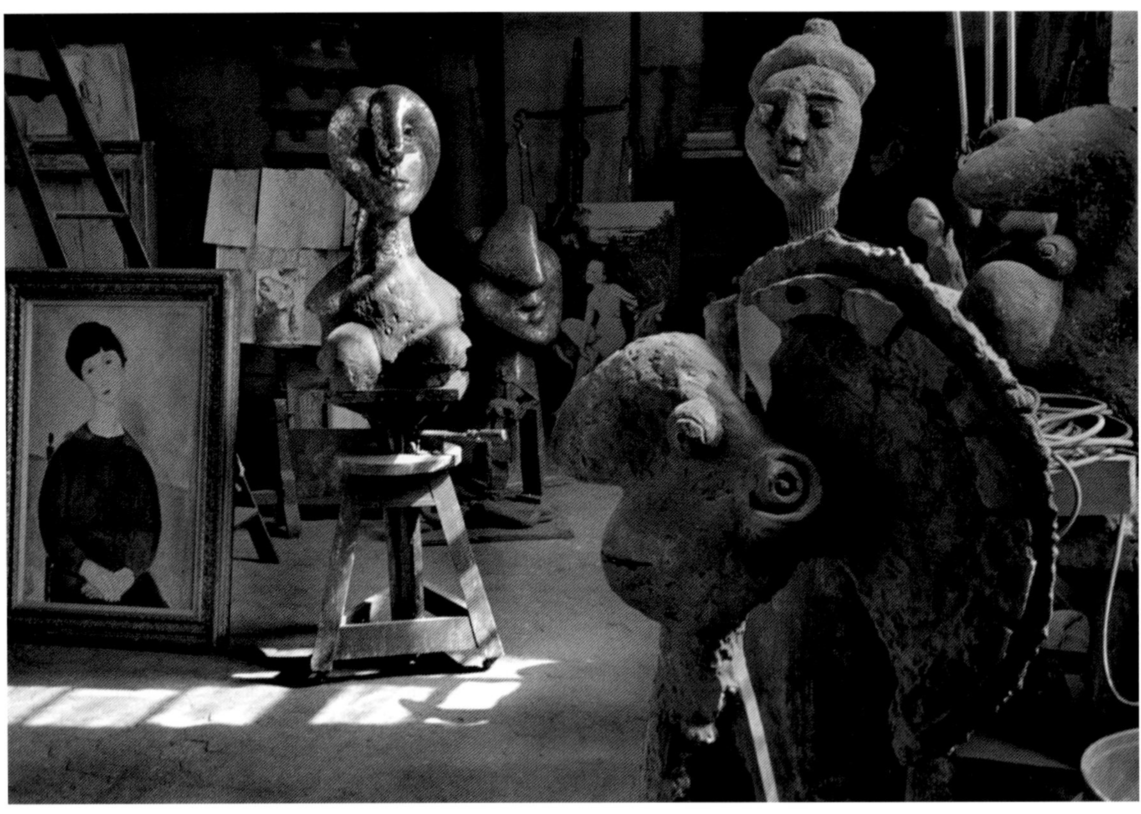

12. View of Picasso's studio at 7, rue des Grand-Augustins, Paris, 1944. Photograph by Henri Cartier-Bresson. Magnum Photos

The *Minotaure* article included an image prominently labeled "L'Atelier de sculpture" (The sculpture studio), which pictured the Boisgeloup stable doors invitingly flung open (fig. 10). A series of dazzling white plaster sculptures of varying dimensions can be glimpsed within a dark interior. Immediately following this page was a close-up of an exceptionally tall figure surrounded by smaller works on sculptor's tables; next, the camera took the visitor even further into the studio, approaching the same objects from a slightly different angle and revealing more within the room (fig. 11). The theatrical night lighting makes this photograph among the most indelibly memorable of Brassaï's Boisgeloup images. The placement on the floor of a single light source—perhaps borrowed from the suspended lantern fixture that appears at center foreground—set off a powerful play of light and shadow that dramatized Picasso's new approach to sculpting the human form. Noses, mouths, and eyes doubled as male and female sexual organs, with surfaces that simultaneously conjured the softness of flesh and the unforgiving hardness of bone. Prominently on display was Picasso's love of visual punning, along with his remarkable ability to render the familiar deeply strange. Years later, scholars identified the subject of these works as Marie-Thérèse Walter, a young woman Picasso met in 1927 who became his secret mistress and muse.

Picasso continued to create sculptures in his Boisgeloup studio throughout 1934, exploring the process of imprinting plaster using everyday objects and materials. The narrow ridges of corrugated cardboard, for example, served to articulate the figures of *Woman with Leaves* (pl. 75) and *The Orator* (pl. 76). He also used plaster to bind together a variety of these found objects, combining the expedient solutions of bricolage with those of conventional modeling to create a new form of assemblage in works such as *The Reaper* (pl. 74). A relatively undistinguished set of images including a number of this second generation of Boisgeloup works, taken by the studio Bernès, Marouteau & Cie, was published in *Cahiers d'Art* in 1935. By then Picasso's own intense focus on sculpture had dissipated, bringing this prolonged and groundbreaking episode of sculptural productivity to a close.

In January 1937, Picasso began work in a new studio at 7, rue des Grand-Augustins in Paris. There he would paint *Guernica*, his epic anti-Fascist and antiwar masterpiece, provoked by the German bombing of the eponymous Basque town in his native Spain. This work went on display in Paris that July as a centerpiece of the Spanish Pavilion at the World's Fair, bringing to the fore, as art historian T. J. Clark has written, the "issue of Picasso's contact as a citizen with the events of the twentieth century."[13] *Guernica*'s vast fame has effectively

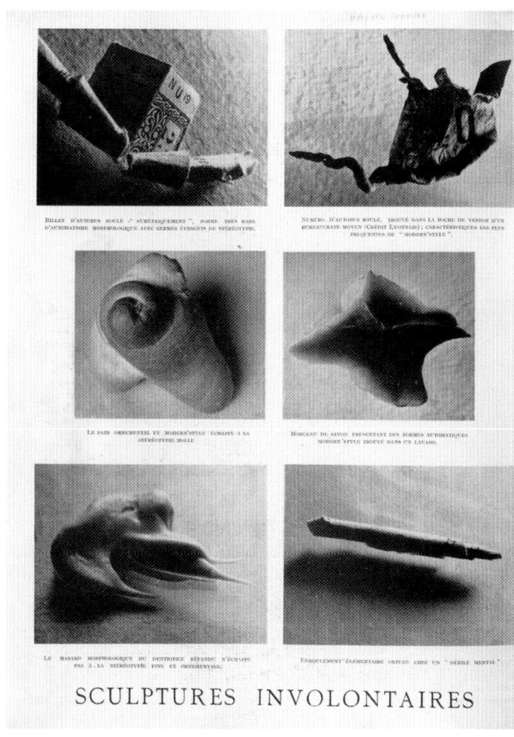
SCULPTURES INVOLONTAIRES

13. "Sculptures involontaires" (Involuntary sculptures), *Minotaure*, no. 3–4 (December 1933): 67. Photographs by Brassaï, captions by Salvador Dalí. The Museum of Modern Art Library, New York

overshadowed the fact that it was not the only work Picasso chose to exhibit at the Spanish Pavilion. Also on display were five of his Boisgeloup sculptures, which the artist had cast in cement and bronze specifically for this occasion. The cement version of his monumental *Head of a Woman* (pl. 56) greeted visitors at the staircase of the Spanish Pavilion (see fig. 2 on p. 305) and was repeatedly featured in the flurry of press surrounding the Pavilion's highly politicized displays.

On September 3, 1939, following Germany's invasion of Poland, France declared war on Germany, and World War II began. Two months later, in the still neutral United States, The Museum of Modern Art opened its first Picasso exhibition, *Picasso: Forty Years of His Art*, organized by the Museum's founding director, Alfred H. Barr, Jr. Barr had established a relationship with Picasso in 1930, hoping as early as then to present a retrospective of the artist's work. Nine years and many disappointments later, Barr had managed to purchase *Les Demoiselles d'Avignon* and to secure the loan of *Guernica* for the 1939 retrospective exhibition, timed to commemorate the tenth anniversary of the Museum and the opening of its new International Style building. Barr's efforts in the realm of sculpture were notably less successful. Despite repeated entreaties, and the reported willingness of the artist to have bronze casts made of recent works for the show, Barr was able to include only five sculptures in the round, all bronzes dated no later than 1914, in the company of some 160 paintings.

Picasso remained in Paris during the dark years of the German occupation. He was under constant surveillance and, as an artist denounced by the Nazis as "degenerate," he was forbidden to exhibit or publish his work. Worried about the safety of the sculptures he had left behind at Boisgeloup and at the Valsuani foundry in Paris (a feared target of Allied bombing), Picasso took pains to have them gathered together and brought to the relative safety of the rue des Grands-Augustins studio. It was at this moment that his penchant for cohabiting with his sculptures, past and present, became pronounced. In 1940, after a six-year hiatus from making sculpture, Picasso repurposed as a sculpture studio the rue des Grands-Augustins bathroom, as it was the only space he was able to heat. This became the center for a new period of intense sculptural activity. The imposing population of naturalistic human and animal figures that he created shares a sobriety of tone utterly in keeping with the wartime context in which they were made. Picasso cast into bronze a number of these new works, including *Cat* (pl. 81), *Death's Head* (pl. 82), and *Bull's Head* (pl. 88), despite strict prohibitions against such expenditure of precious metal. During the Occupation he managed to have several of his major Boisgeloup sculptures converted to bronze as well (fig. 12). Picasso thereby transformed the use of one of sculpture's most traditional materials—bronze—and processes—casting—into radically resistant acts. The resulting works, frequently unique casts, kept him company during the war years: totemic sentinels on duty until the danger had passed.

Beginning in September 1943, at Picasso's request, Brassaï began to photograph his sculptures surreptitiously, in preparation for a monograph devoted to the sculptural oeuvre. Brassaï's clandestine enterprise continued throughout the Occupation, equally addressing objects of major and seemingly minor importance. A decade earlier, in December 1933, the Hungarian's photographs of castaway objects such as a torn and rolled bus ticket, a used sliver of soap, and a blob of toothpaste had been published in *Minotaure* as "Sculptures involontaires" (Involuntary sculptures) (fig. 13). Looking at those images' dramatically lit and enlarged subjects, dignified by what Brassaï modestly described as his "way of seeing,"[14] it is easy to imagine how sympathetic that viewpoint must have been to Picasso's own profoundly democratic gaze, ever alert to the sculptural potential of things in the world. It also is easy to imagine how, during Picasso's three years of enforced isolation, the time spent gazing back at his sculptures through the sensitive lens of his friend might have helped to inspire the sculptural renaissance soon to come.

The postwar period brought two parallel developments in the narrative of Picasso's sculpture. His work in three dimensions blossomed into a foremost aspect of his practice, as Picasso again reinvented his methods and materials and became more prolific as a sculptor than ever before. This expanded output developed in tandem with the sculptures' higher visibility in terms of collections, publications, and exhibitions. During the postwar decades, Picasso's sculptures gradually became available to anyone who was interested, not only to the familiars of his studio or his galleries. *Les Sculptures de Picasso*, with an introduction by Kahnweiler and photographs by Brassaï, finally was published in 1949. It appeared in English later that year; David Sylvester, a young art historian who in coming decades would become one of Britain's greatest art critics, translated Kahnweiler's text. In 1951, the first exhibition devoted to a survey of Picasso's sculpture in tandem with drawings took place at the Maison de la pensée française, a cultural space in Paris run by the Communist Party. The cover of its small catalogue featured a pebble on which Picasso had incised a face (one of a large group of these he made after the war) and a sketch for *Man with a Lamb* (pl. 87), deceptively modest indicators of the exhibition's many revelations (fig. 14).

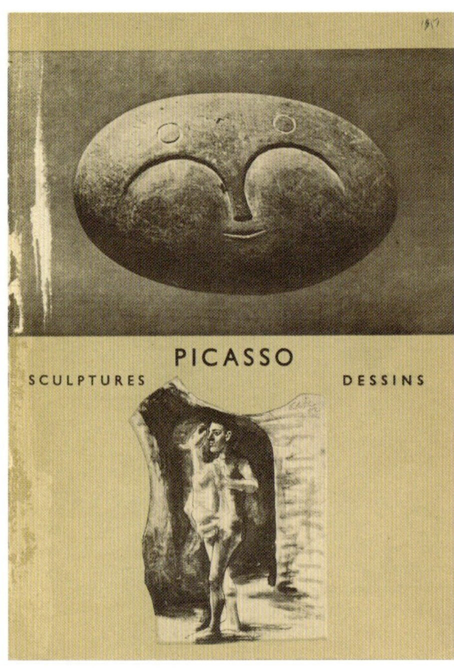

14. Front cover of the exhibition catalogue *Picasso: Sculptures, dessins* (Picasso: Sculptures, drawings) (Paris: Maison de la pensée française, 1950)

Picasso spent most of the last quarter century of his life at a succession of homes on the French Riviera. Since leaving Spain for good, forty years earlier, he had lived primarily in Paris, despite productive summer sojourns elsewhere. Picasso's decision to remain in the city during the war gave him the status of a hero after the Liberation. But now that he was free to come and go as he pleased, the Riviera, a favorite destination since the 1920s, would become his main base of activity. It formed the sole setting for the making of sculpture for the remainder of his career.

There were many possible reasons for this geographic shift. The Liberation did not immediately bring an end to wartime's many privations, and Paris's lights remained dimmed both literally and figuratively. The city was no longer the same international mecca that it had been at the beginning of the century, when as a Spaniard Picasso would have felt no more a foreigner than countless other artists from all over the world. Artistically, Paris now belonged to a new avant-garde generation, one for which Picasso was an old master rather than a fellow participant. The irrepressibly diaristic nature of his art was firmly out of step with the growing prevalence of abstraction.

Indeed, the sculptures of the 1950s, like the paintings, make manifest the extreme cross-fertilization of Picasso's life and his art. Throughout his career, the people and things around him were the essential fuel for his art making. The sculptures of the late 1940s and 1950s make clear that Picasso was again a family man: his companion Françoise Gilot's pregnancies in 1947 and 1949 bring about pregnant women (pls. 114–15); children's toys find their way into artworks (pl. 116); and even the neighborhood goats earn a sculptural counterpart (pl. 119). Domestic still life scenes that fill Picasso's paintings of the time take three-dimensional form as well (pls. 123–25).

As importantly as life directed art, art directed life. Picasso's move south was largely motivated by his insatiable appetite for work. Due to his newfound passion for making ceramics, in 1948 he purchased a house in the village of Vallauris, his first property on the Riviera. Vallauris had been a thriving ceramics center for centuries but by this time was suffering a deep decline. The enterprising couple Georges and Suzanne Ramié invited Picasso to experiment at their Madoura workshop when he was staying in Antibes in summer 1946. It was a felicitous match: the artist eagerly took to the challenge of clay, working closely with the Ramiés' master potters. Picasso used his inexperience as an advantage and thrived on flouting conventional rules of the process. The Ramiés often remarked that an apprentice who worked like Picasso would never find a job, a judgment that could be applied to much of his career. Over the next two decades Picasso would produce thousands of ceramic pieces, either designated as unique objects or for reproduction in quantities allowing widespread distribution.

Picasso maintained an uncharacteristically spartan environment within La Galloise, his modest villa in Vallauris. For the inevitable chaos of work he purchased a former perfume factory, which he divided into separate studios for painting

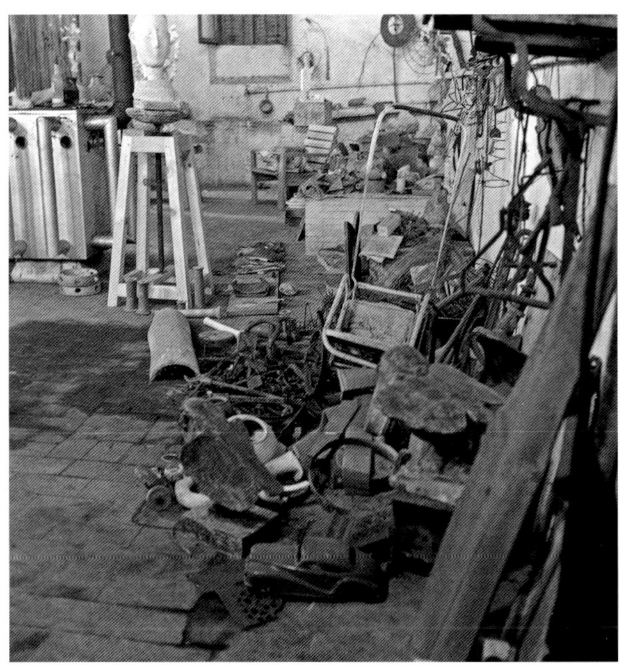

15. The junk pile at Le Fournas, Vallauris, 1953. Photograph by Edward Quinn

and sculpture. Assemblage became his primary mode of operation, and the sculpture studio became the site of an escalated engagement in the game of metamorphosis. The fortuitous convenience of a junk heap near his studio provided the engine for his sculptural activity, as Picasso's ragpicking proclivities rose to new heights (fig. 15). The *Woman with a Baby Carriage* (pl. 118) happens to be chauffeuring a baby, but Gilot's memoir offered another view on the subject: walking from the house to the studio with Picasso, she'd push an old pram so that Picasso could toss in his finds along the way.[15]

On the surface, the resolutely autobiographical cast of Picasso's postwar art distinguishes it from the art-historical moment in which it was situated. But at a deeper level, his postwar commitment to a new beginning was firmly in sync with the zeitgeist. After the end of World War II, the need for a reinvention of art de novo took hold of artists in Europe and the Americas across the stylistic spectrum. The attraction to the so-called primitive, which had first presented itself as a model at the beginning of the century, returned with fresh urgency in the wake of the atom bomb and the Holocaust. Inevitably, chosen models of primitive art differed from those a half century earlier, as a search for fresh origins shaped the work of artists two, three, and four decades Picasso's junior.

Picasso's move to the Riviera can be read in part as an effort to shake off a self that virtually personified modern art. The ceramics that lured him to return and to stay in the south were an ancient and elemental realm of making that preceded the very concept of "art." While the postwar assemblage-based sculptures do not evoke Oceanic and African art in the way his woodcarvings of 1907–08 do, they share a character that is assertively primitive, meant in the dictionary's sense of "seeming to come from an early time in the very ancient past."[16] In the sculptures' original states, prior to being cast in bronze, there is little of the professional about them in modern Western terms; their material heterogeneity has a closer precedent in African masks and figures that harbor nails, shells, and beads. For Picasso, junkyard finds associated sculpture with ordinary reality, just as utilitarian function associated ceramics with the everyday. Talismanic power resides within an art meant to be utterly familiar and accessible, rather than mysterious or imposing.

This deliberately unprofessional quality was one dimension, among many, of the postwar version of primitivism. Scholarly and critical attention to sculpture at the time viewed it as a field of opportunity potentially richer than that of painting. The American art critic Clement Greenberg observed that,

> To painting, no matter how abstract and flat, there still clings something of the past simply because it is painting and painting has such a rich and recent past.... The new sculpture has almost no historical associations whatsoever—at least not with our own civilization's past—which endows it with a virginality that compels the artist's boldness and invites him to tell everything without fear of censorship by tradition. All he need remember of the past is cubist painting, all he need avoid is naturalism.[17]

Picasso would have disagreed with both halves of the last sentence, but his work of the next few years offered robust support for Greenberg's argument. The search for innocent beginnings engaged countless artists in Europe and the Americas in the years following World War II and took countless forms. Jean Dubuffet, twenty years Picasso's junior, was perhaps the most explicit in his program. Inspired by what he dubbed *l'art brut*—work made by asylum inmates as well as that of children—Dubuffet championed an anticultural position, extolling the viewpoint of "primitive man" for whom "the notion of beauty is specious" (fig. 16).[18] Picasso's total lack of interest in manifesto or theory places him at an opposite pole from Dubuffet. Yet one might say that the role of the outsider was exactly that which the postwar Picasso cultivated, despite the fact that he had by this time achieved levels of fame and wealth theretofore unfathomable for an artist. The father of two young children, he flaunted the mischievous quality of his

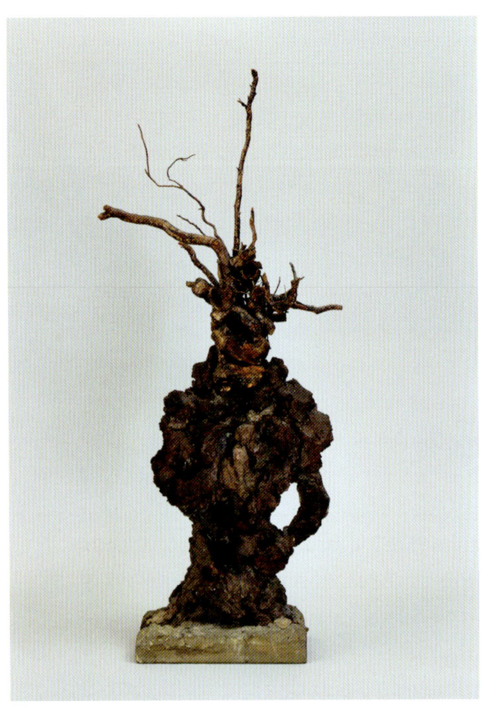

16. Jean Dubuffet. *The Magician*. September 1954. Slag and grapevines, 43½ × 19 × 8¼ in. (109.8 × 48.2 × 21 cm) including slag base. The Museum of Modern Art, New York. Gift of Mr. and Mrs. N. Richard Miller and Mr. and Mrs. Alex L. Hillman and Samuel Girard Funds

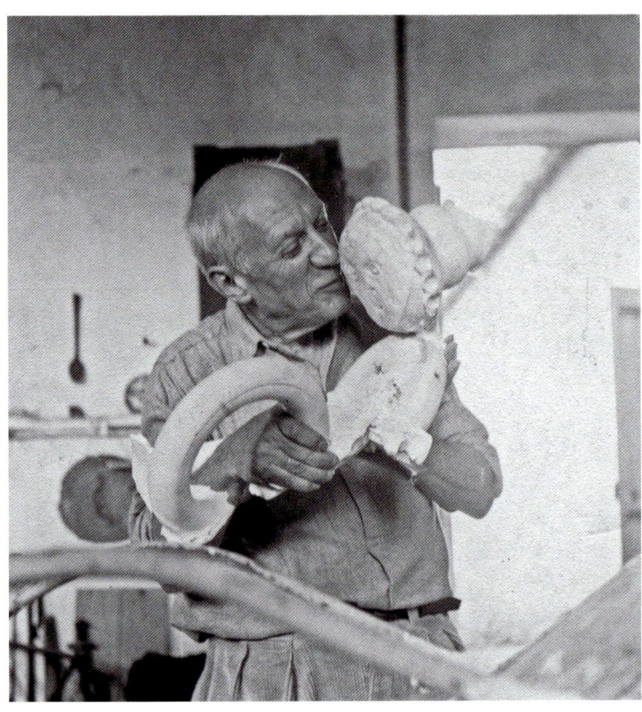

17. Picasso with the baby from his sculpture *Woman with a Baby Carriage* (1950–[54]), Vallauris, 1954. Photograph by Lee Miller

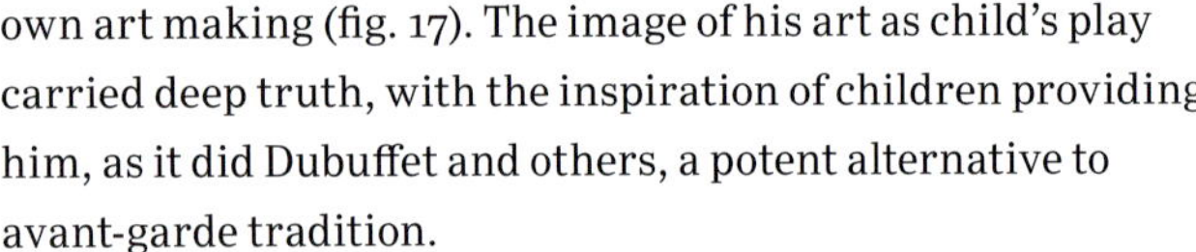

own art making (fig. 17). The image of his art as child's play carried deep truth, with the inspiration of children providing him, as it did Dubuffet and others, a potent alternative to avant-garde tradition.

During his later years, Picasso lived amid his sculpture in an astonishing way. When in 1955 he quit Vallauris and moved to Cannes, he summoned his earlier works from Paris to join him. Once again he was able to live and work in the same building, a situation best suited to the indivisibility of his life and art. The villa in Cannes, named La Californie, and the two residences that followed—the Château de Vauvenargues (1958) and Notre-Dame-de-Vie in Mougins (1961)—were destined to spill over with sculpture inside and out. Despite their varying styles, sizes, and levels of grandeur, each home became a place where Picasso could easily cohabit with his three-dimensional creations. Whereas he mostly sent new paintings to exhibitions and dealers, and stacked scores of older ones in closed rooms, his sculptures remained an integral part of the environment, as they had been at rue des Grands-Augustins.

We know this so well because of the ample evidence provided by countless photographs of Picasso's later residences. Virtually every significant photographer of the period—Henri Cartier-Bresson, Robert Doisneau, and Irving Penn, to name just a few—arrived at the artist's door, determined to capture with a camera the essence of his genius. In particular, the American photojournalist David Douglas Duncan developed a close relationship with Picasso, spending several months of 1956 at La Californie, and publishing in 1958 *The Private World of Pablo Picasso*. Douglas exposes the untamable clutter the artist nurtured even, or especially, within a grand home built for elegant living. Notwithstanding his fantastic wealth, Picasso created a habitat true to the romantic myth of the bohemian artist. Bronzes offhandedly surrounded the villa's front steps and filled the entrance hall. Further inside, the sculptures mixed with lamps, clocks, African objects, dried flowers, books, packages, and paintings leaning everywhere (including against sculptures). Duncan's photographs portray the bronze-filled garden behind the house as a playground for the household animals; one famous image shows Picasso's pet goat tethered with a metal chain to the tail of the *She-Goat* she had inspired (fig. 18).

The pleasure Picasso took from this environment brought with it a complete lack of desire to release the sculptures for exhibition or sale, a source of great vexation for art dealers and curators. The publication of Kahnweiler's monograph on the sculptures in 1949 only intensified the eagerness to present these objects to the public. At The Museum of Modern Art, Barr tried to convince the artist that the show *Picasso: 75th Anniversary Exhibition*, to be presented in summer 1957,

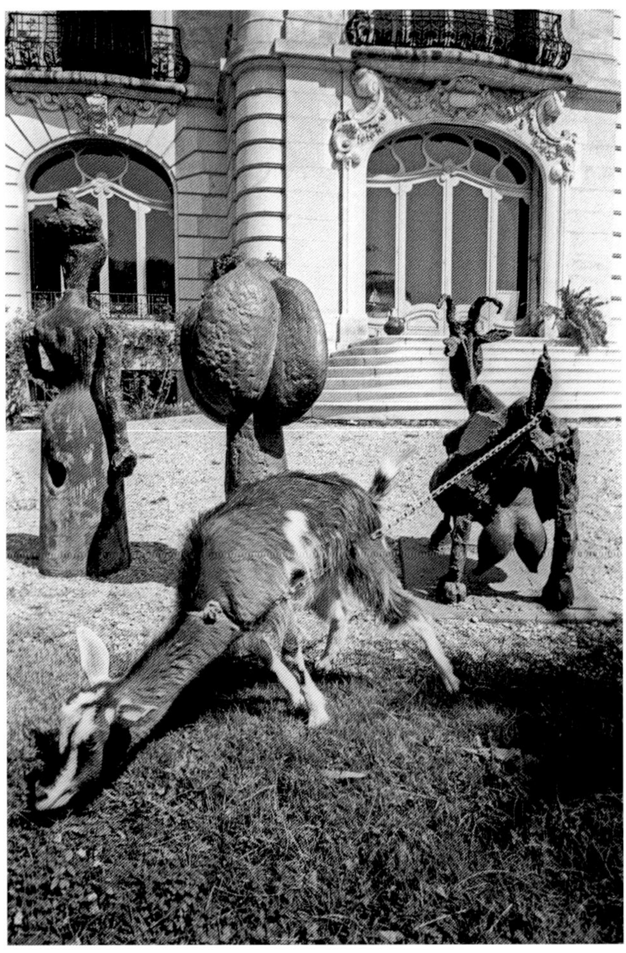

18. The goat Esmeralda tethered to Picasso's *She-Goat* (1950) at La Californie, Cannes, 1957. Photograph by David Douglas Duncan. Photography Collection, Harry Ransom Center, The University of Texas at Austin

would be an opportunity "to give the sculpture a special and conspicuous attention."[19] He implored Picasso to lend sculptures from his own collection for the galleries and the newly opened Abby Aldrich Rockefeller Sculpture Garden. Unmoved, the artist would not relinquish them.

Fortunately Barr had been busy building the Museum's own collection of sculptures beyond the single 1909 *Head of a Woman* purchased in 1940. In the spring of 1956, as Barr renewed his efforts, Kahnweiler explained that Picasso was always eager for the Valsuani foundry to cast his new sculptures and that he did not want to impede their progress by having them return to previous creations.[20] Thus, Barr had no luck with *Death's Head* (pl. 82), which he desired "almost more than anything";[21] *She-Goat;* or *Man with a Lamb*, which had gone to the collector R. Sturgis Ingersoll in Philadelphia. But he did manage to purchase *Goat Skull and Bottle* (pl. 123), *Pregnant Woman*, and *Head of a Woman* from Kahnweiler, and reinforced these with *Baboon and Young* (pl. 116) bought from the New York dealer Sam Kootz. In October 1956, trustee Louise Reinhardt Smith purchased *Glass of Absinthe* (pl. 25) as a gift to the Museum; with the other acquisitions and a few outside loans, it would make the case for Picasso as a sculptor within the seventy-fifth-anniversary exhibition.

One would love to know what Picasso's sculptures suggested to young New York artists in the late 1950s. The combinatory method of assemblage and the notion of art made in the midst of the everyday dovetailed closely with the thinking of the generation that followed the Abstract Expressionists. *Glass of Absinthe*, with its actual spoon and painted bronze glass, liqueur, and sugar cube, was startlingly up to date forty years after it was made. Jasper Johns's *Painted Bronze* of 1960 (fig. 19), routinely linked to Duchamp's readymades, is actually a far closer descendant of Picasso's *Glass* in both sensibility and materiality. Picasso's recent sculptures, employing real elements such as colanders, cake molds, baskets, screws, and nails, anticipated by merely a few years Robert Rauschenberg's Combines, which integrated painting and sculpture, art and life, with no thought as to genre or medium. The crucial difference was that whereas Picasso's 1950s sculptures transformed his raw materials into elements of human or animal figures, or even bouquets, the Americans let heterogeneous items stand on their own rather than in the service of visual metaphor. In 1959, the year that Barr finally managed to acquire *She-Goat* for the Museum, Rauschenberg completed four years of work on *Monogram*, a Combine in which a taxidermied Angora goat, a rubber tire around its neck, stands atop a painting laid flat (fig. 20). Nearly fifty years Picasso's junior, Rauschenberg was extending the assemblage mentality in a way that one can imagine both interesting and enraging his predecessor.

Picasso's choice of casting his assemblages in the time-honored and durable medium of bronze effectively disguised for many years the radicalness of his method. It is probably due to their existence as bronzes, for example, that these recent sculptures were not featured in *The Art of Assemblage*, the landmark exhibition held at MoMA in 1961. Although the catalogue essay acknowledged that the 1950s assemblages were "as youthfully iconoclastic as a work by any artist under thirty,"[22] the show represented Picasso with only two papiers collés and one Cubist construction. For decades to come, the bronze casts served exclusively to represent this body of work, as Picasso did not release the originals for sale or exhibition. Even the 1971 catalogue raisonné of the sculpture enumerated the original assemblages but reproduced the bronze versions. It was only with the settlement of Picasso's estate in the 1980s and the distribution of works to the Musée national Picasso–Paris and the artist's heirs that these objects came into circulation, and their form and meaning could begin to be studied.

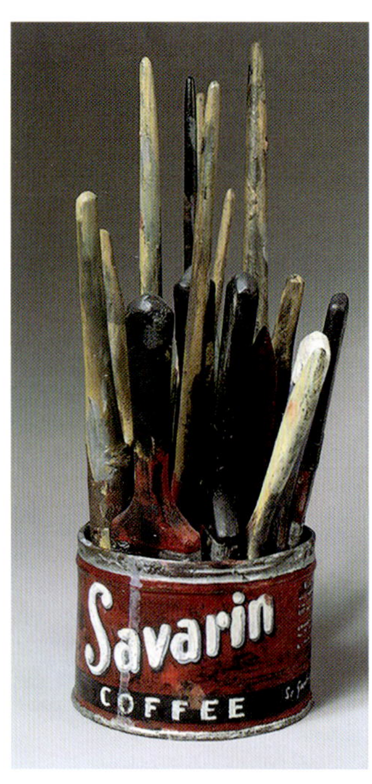

19. Jasper Johns. *Painted Bronze.* 1960. Oil on bronze, 13½ × 8 in. (34.4 × 20.3 cm) diam. The Museum of Modern Art, New York. Promised gift of Marie-Josée and Henry R. Kravis in honor of David Rockefeller

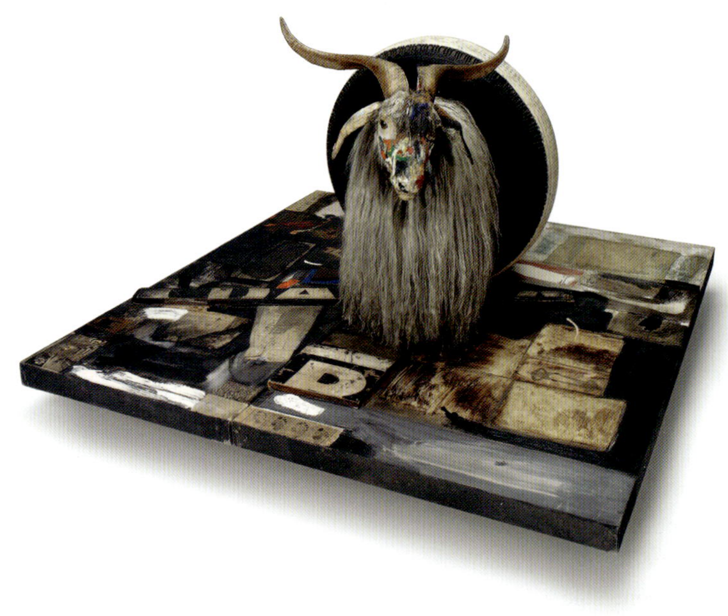

20. Robert Rauschenberg. *Monogram.* 1955–59. Combine: oil, paper, fabric, printed paper, printed reproductions, metal, wood, rubber shoe heel, and tennis ball on canvas with oil on Angora goat and rubber tire on wood platform mounted on four casters, 42 × 63¼ × 64½ in. (106.7 × 160.7 × 163.8 cm). Moderna Museet, Stockholm. Purchase 1965 with contribution from Moderna Museets Vänner/The Friends of Moderna Museet

Picasso's own assessment of the originals, and their position vis-à-vis the bronze casts, remains unknowable. The possible answer could lie anywhere between two poles: that he saw the originals as maquettes that became finished works of art only when cast in bronze, or that he preferred the originals as finished works and merely accepted the bronzes as an inevitable compromise, given the danger and difficulty of transporting the originals. Various remarks suggest that he welcomed the disjunction between the uniform material of the bronze sculpture and the heterogeneous nature of its construction, and his decision to paint many of the bronzes certainly reflects his commitment to those versions as unique and important objects. At the same time, his careful preservation of the original assemblages indicates that they held real value for him.

The present exhibition differs from those during Picasso's lifetime most strongly in its inclusion of many originals, reflecting a curatorial aesthetic shaped by the art of the intervening decades. Extreme fragility has made transport impossible in many cases, such as that of *She-Goat* of 1950 or *Female Bather Playing* of 1958. But where possible, for the modeled figures made in Boisgeloup as well as the postwar assemblages, the priority has been to present the direct products of Picasso's hand and to make manifest the materiality of his touch. From a twenty-first-century viewpoint, these works in their original form have a startling contemporaneity. Their unalloyed enthusiasm for the banal and their seemingly amateurish assembly resonate closely with a present-day attraction to humble materials, ordinary objects, and technical approaches that show no evidence of skilled training.

Picasso carried out his final experiments in assemblage at La Californie, in the mid-1950s. He left behind the robust three-dimensionality of the Vallauris sculptures and instead adopted a planar format that harked back to the Cubist constructions and theater figures of the 1910s. Wood again became the dominant material: old lumber, dowels, furniture fragments, and even picture frames compose six magisterial *Bathers* (pls. 128–33), as well as several smaller sculptures. By the time the 1950s drew to a close, however, Picasso had made his last assemblage. True to the rigorously episodic nature of his sculptural career, when he was finished he made a clean break. Next, he would again leapfrog ahead to a way of working that anticipated the proclivities of artists far younger than he: sculpture that would be made of a commercial material and fabricated by workers who otherwise had no experience with art. The material was thin sheet metal, which was manufactured for purposes ranging from industrial parts to lighting fixtures and furniture.

As had been true for ceramics, Picasso's sheet metal adventure was instigated by the enthusiasm of a facilitator. In this case, an entrepreneur named Lionel Prejger, who had recently acquired the Société Tritub sheet metal firm, proposed the collaboration to Picasso. As a champion bricoleur Picasso already knew Prejger from his ownership of demolition and scrapyard businesses in Cannes, and he also had had works fabricated at Tritub a few times in the 1950s. There a workman named Joseph-Marius Tiola had become Picasso's expert accomplice. In this new arrangement, Picasso drew and cut paper and cardboard maquettes, usually of a human face or figure. Prejger would pick them up from the artist's house and return the next day with one-to-one-scale versions made in sheet metal. Picasso would sometimes add further painted details, integrating painting and sculpture much as he had done in his ceramics. The borderline between the two practices was further blurred by the fact that many of the sheet metal sculptures had direct parallels in the motifs of contemporaneous paintings.

The period of sheet metal sculptures was the most densely concentrated episode of sculpture making of Picasso's career. Like the ceramics, these were quick, often whimsical, and primarily modest in scale. They fit perfectly with Picasso's hyperkinetic pace; like his paintings of that moment, these were not objects to be fussed with or labored over, as the assemblages had been, but rather speedily invented and completed. Between 1960 and 1961, Picasso made more than one hundred unique figures, a marathon that came to a close only when Prejger moved to Paris in autumn 1961. No book or show provided a culmination to the episode; instead dense clusters of sheet metal works filled the spaces at Picasso's home in Mougins.

In the realm of sculpture, the conclusion of Picasso's career stands as the polar opposite of the beginning. What initially had been a primarily private endeavor now became public: in 1966 and 1967 comprehensive exhibitions of the sculpture in Picasso's collection were presented to widespread acclaim in Paris, London, and New York. And what first had been a body of work unassuming in scale now grew to become enormous, as the sheet metal sculptures gained new life via monumental enlargements in concrete and Cor-Ten steel erected in Europe and the United States. Although the prolific final years of his life included no physical making of new sculpture, it is during this period that Picasso the sculptor became a well-known entity for the first time.

In November 1966 in Paris, a one-thousand-work, three-venue exhibition in honor of the artist's eighty-fifth birthday inaugurated the era of the museum blockbuster. Paintings were shown at the Grand Palais; sculpture, ceramics, and drawings a short walk away at the Petit Palais; and prints at the Bibliothèque national. Working with curator Jean Leymarie, Picasso finally had been convinced to send nearly two hundred sculptures to Paris. Less than two months before the exhibition's opening, the British writer and curator Roland Penrose reported that "Picasso had completely come round to the idea of the sculptures going to Paris and kept on producing new pieces from dark corners in his enthusiasm. In all when he left there were over 180 items varying of course very much in size but all of great interest, including cubist reliefs of 1914 which he had formerly discarded as hopelessly damaged and now is putting together again."[23]

Leymarie's success was fortunate for Penrose and Barr, who had joined forces in 1965 to try to organize a sculpture show for the Tate Gallery and The Museum of Modern Art. After the exhibition opened at the Petit Palais, Picasso was persuaded to let the sculptures travel to London in spring 1967, and eventually he agreed to an autumn showing in New York. MoMA's director, René d'Harnoncourt, was responsible for the installation, for which he prepared, as usual, by drawing the objects in the show (fig. 21). The exhibition opened in a Manhattan art world at "a moment when sculpture [was] all the rage," according to art critic Hilton Kramer of the *New York Times*. In fact, Picasso's person- and thing-based visions were utterly foreign to the fiercely abstract Minimalist sculpture filling New York galleries. Yet the exhibition awed the critics. Kramer wrote that it "persuades us for the first time that Picasso would have to be considered one of the great

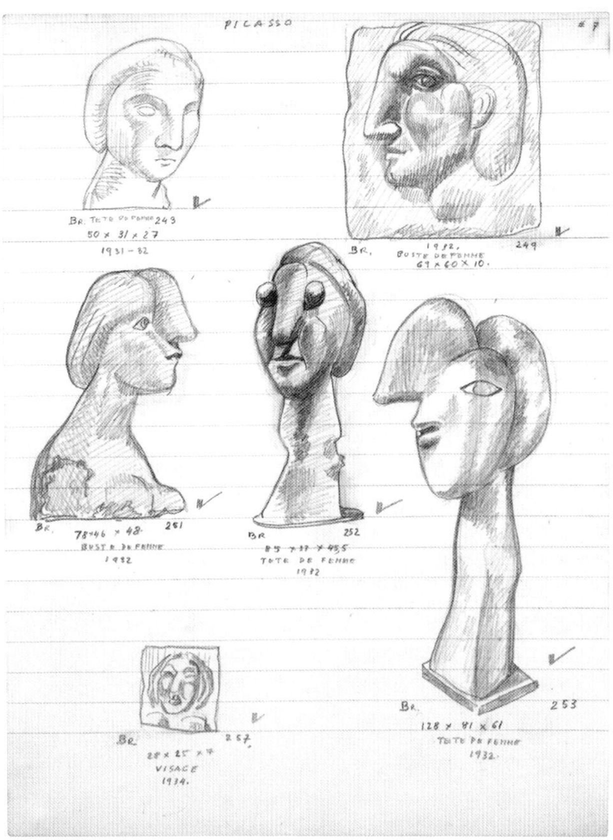

21. Sketches by René d'Harnoncourt for the exhibition *The Sculpture of Picasso* at The Museum of Modern Art, 1967. René d'Harnoncourt Papers, The Museum of Modern Art Archives, New York

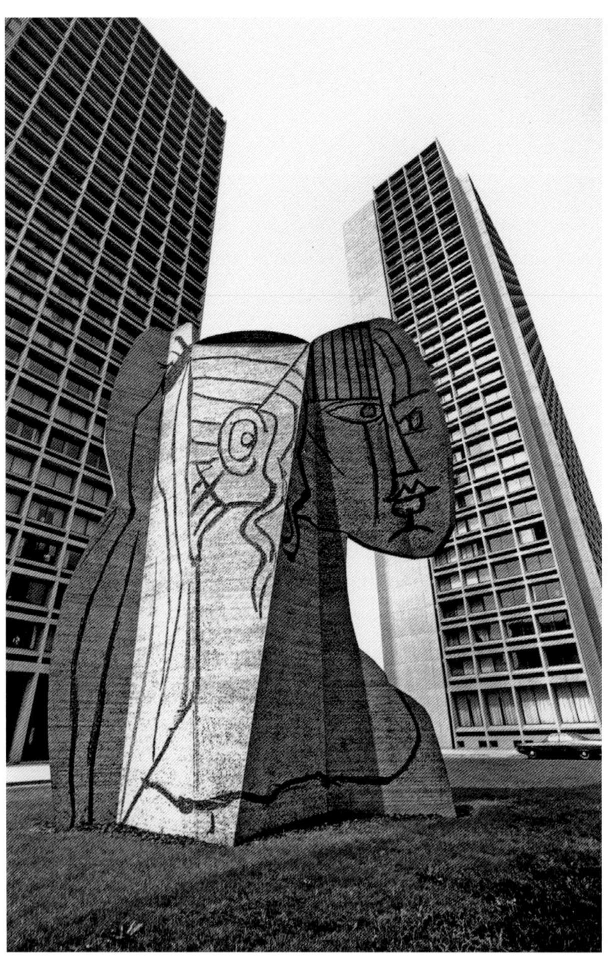

22. *Head of Sylvette* (1954) enlarged in concrete, cement, and granite, executed by Carl Nesjar and installed at New York University's Silver Towers apartment buildings, September 24, 1968. Photograph by Dean Brown. Courtesy New York University Archives

artists of the century even if he had never painted a single picture and indeed, it may persuade some that he is a greater sculptor than a painter."[24]

Not only exhibitions, but books too had recently provided new insight into the role of sculpture in Picasso's work. Françoise Gilot's 1964 *Life with Picasso* enraged the artist and his friends with its forthright recounting of a life together gone sour. But Gilot described Picasso's working process in precise eyewitness detail and with the sharp insight of a fellow artist. Brassaï's *Conversations with Picasso*, also published in 1964, drew on the author's intimate experience with the sculptures as the one person Picasso trusted to photograph them during the war years. Working from notes he had written at the end of each day, Brassaï wrote about the sculptures with deep familiarity and affection.

By the mid-1960s the idea of Picasso as sculptor was becoming visible even to those people who would never step inside an art museum or read an art book. From the comfortable seclusion of his home in Mougins, Picasso became a prominent figure in a modern heyday for the creation of public sculpture in European and American cities. The urban redevelopment brought on by the postwar economic boom united with populist sensibilities to produce widespread demand for architecturally scaled works that would enrich the contemporary cityscape and enhance civic culture. In the early days of this renaissance of public sculpture, the clients were prominent businessmen and architects who were themselves devotees of modern art, and who wished to add the luster of a famous name to a given building project. Private developers and donors sought out modern artists such as Alexander Calder, Henry Moore, Jean Dubuffet, Isamu Noguchi, and, ideally, Picasso himself.

Picasso's small-scale, autobiographical, and utterly nonsymbolic sheet metal cutouts might seem the least obvious candidates for public monuments. But these became the basis for such commissions thanks to a long-term collaboration with a young Norwegian artist named Carl Nesjar, who convinced Picasso that he could translate his designs into engraved concrete ideal for large-scale outdoor purposes. Picasso responded enthusiastically, having harbored dreams of monumental works as long ago as the late 1920s. Pre-existing sheet metal sculptures formed the basis for more than twenty concrete enlargements in cities as far-flung as Marseille, Stockholm, Rotterdam, and New York. For example, Picasso responded to the architect I. M. Pei's commission for a sculpture outside a new housing complex at New York University with a 1954 *Head of Sylvette*, executed by Nesjar in autumn 1968 (fig. 22).

Picasso's one late sculpture specifically made for an outdoor site was a *Head* for the Chicago Civic Center plaza, a project spearheaded by William E. Hartmann, the Skidmore, Owings & Merrill architect in charge of the new public space. Expertly supported by Penrose, this commission prompted the artist to make new drawings in 1964 and produced an intensive exchange with the architects over the course of the next three years. Tiola produced from Picasso's studies two forty-one-inch sheet metal maquettes for what would be a fifty-foot sculpture produced by U.S. Steel in Gary, Indiana. Thousands of Chicagoans turned out to celebrate its dedication at the plaza in August 1967 (fig. 23).

As is true of the concrete monuments, the sculpture in Chicago has received relatively little discussion by art historians; its significance has been read as more sociocultural than aesthetic. But it is manifestly the case that here Picasso remained his experimental self in matters of both form and content. The *Head* harks back to the sheet metal *Guitar* of 1914 and to the 1928 studies for a monument to Apollinaire in its bold engagement of negative space and its network of interpenetrating planes and rods. It also speaks directly to the paintings of Picasso's wife, Jacqueline, that issued from his studio on an almost daily basis. Picasso's pleasure in the assignment is evident in his decision to decline a fee and to donate the maquette to the Art Institute of Chicago. At this point, his payment was the opportunity to do work that was brand new to him and that situated the octogenarian in the here and now as opposed to the annals of art history.

To the end, Picasso's sculpture represents in the extreme the reinvention that characterized his work in every medium. He changed the language of his painting throughout the decades, but paint and canvas remained a constant. In contrast, each return to sculpture brought a fresh start technically and materially. From the Cubist years onward, he questioned the definition of sculpture as even he himself had most recently defined it. The history of art includes pioneering sculptors—Constantin Brancusi to name just one—who transformed nineteenth-century sculpture into that of the twentieth. But Picasso's radicality was of another order, one that must be considered in terms of revolution rather than evolution.

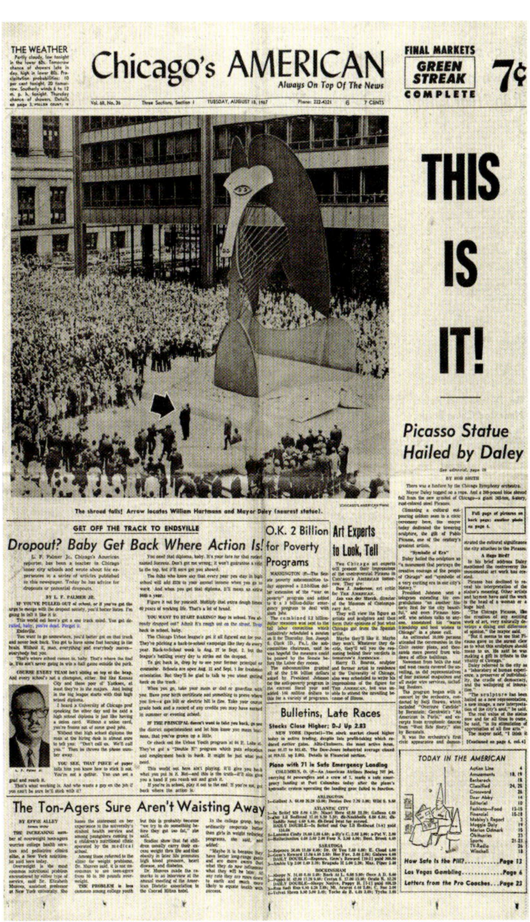
THE WEATHER

Chicago's AMERICAN

Always On Top Of The News

FINAL MARKETS GREEN STREAK COMPLETE

7¢

TUESDAY, AUGUST 15, 1967

THIS IS IT!

Picasso Statue Hailed by Daley

The shroud falls! Arrow locates William Hartmann and Mayor Daley (nearest statue).

GET OFF THE TRACK TO ENDSVILLE

Dropout? Baby Get Back Where Action Is!

O.K. 2 Billion for Poverty Programs

Art Experts to Look, Tell

Bulletins, Late Races

Stocks Close Higher: D-J Up 2.83

Plane with 71 in Safe Emergency Landing

The Ton-Agers Sure Aren't Waisting Away

TODAY IN THE AMERICAN

How Safe Is the Pill?..........Page 13

Las Vegas Gambling..........Page 6

Letters from the Pro Coaches...Page 23

23. The front page of *Chicago's American*, August 16, 1967, covering the unveiling of Picasso's *Richard J. Daley Center Sculpture* on August 15, 1967, at the Chicago Civic Center (now the Richard J. Daley Center), Chicago

Throughout his life, Picasso approached sculpture less as a sculptor than as an artist. In so doing, he was unburdened by any legacies of process and method and anticipated a present-day situation in which the boundaries have blurred between painting, sculpture, and other genres.

In certain ways, attention to the sculpture provides a view of Picasso allied more closely to fact than to legend. For example, Picasso's achievement has been largely framed in terms of the individualistic Romantic genius, despite his vital partnership with Georges Braque during the Cubist years. The sculptural oeuvre reveals him as a lifelong collaborator, intensely and willingly reliant on fellow artists and artisans. It also is with sculpture that we discover a Picasso deeply attached to the seemingly inconsequential and even amateurish object, unassuming in everything but its talismanic ambitions. Another Romantic concept long associated with Picasso—the masterpiece—is brought boldly into question as the foremost shaper of an artist's identity.

A focus on the sculpture leaves aside, for the moment, the fascinating back and forth between two and three dimensions within Picasso's oeuvre. What is gained instead is the startling clarity of the centrality of this work within the history of modern sculpture. The proportion of iconic milestones within his concise sculptural corpus is astonishingly high. One might say that Picasso's sculpture stands apart from the paintings and works on paper in the remarkable efficiency with which it accomplished its many reinventions and redefinitions. But in its ongoing dance between the private and the public, the intimate and the monumental, the experimental and the definitive, the sculpture reveals itself as a quintessential rather than exceptional aspect of Picasso the artist.

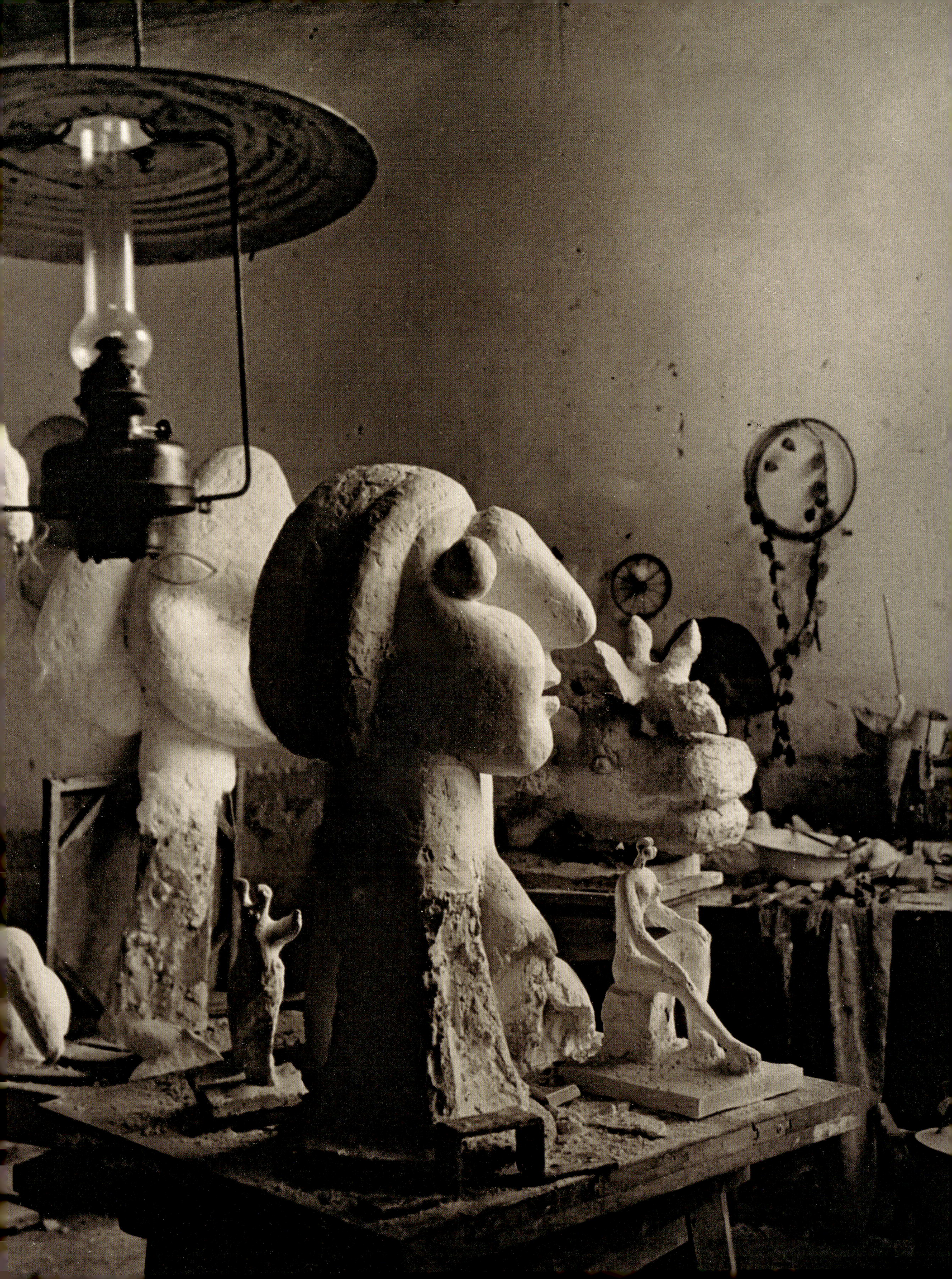

Rebecca Lowery. Diana Widmaier Picasso, author of the catalogue raisonné of Picasso's sculpture now in preparation, generously provided archival materials and information for this chronology.

CHAPTER 1

BEGINNINGS 1902–1906

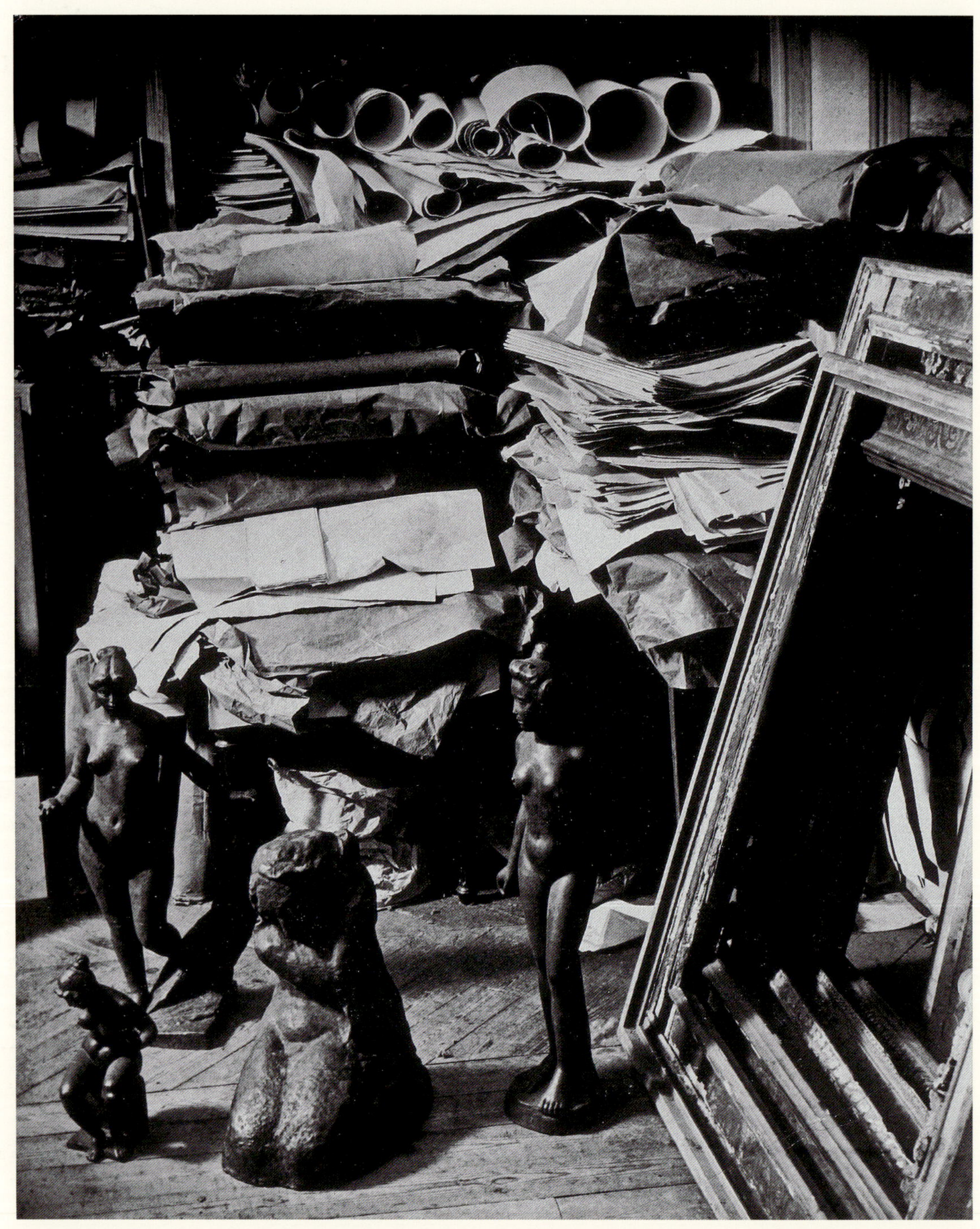

A corner of Ambroise Vollard's stockroom, with a bronze cast of Picasso's *Kneeling Woman Combing Her Hair* (1906) and sculptures by Aristide Maillol and Auguste Rodin, Paris, 1934. Photograph by Brassaï. Private collection

PICASSO COMPLETED his first sculpture—*Seated Woman* (pl. 1), a small work modeled in clay—before late October 1902. He was just twenty years old and living in Barcelona, although he had traveled to Paris several times. Picasso was the son of an artist, and his formal training had been confined to drawing and painting. He did, however, have many friends who were sculptors, including the Basque artist Francisco "Paco" Durrio y Madrón, who was a disciple of the Post-Impressionist artist Paul Gauguin. The archaized forms of Gauguin's ceramic and wood sculptures and his keen interest in non-Western art would have an early and decisive impact on Picasso. The work of the late-nineteenth-century French sculptor Auguste Rodin was also much discussed in Picasso's Barcelona circles, and the expressive poses, animated surface effects, and psychological intensity of Rodin's monumental figure sculptures offered another powerful example of what modern sculpture could be. Picasso's 1903 *Head of a Picador with a Broken Nose* (pl. 2) is among his most Rodinesque works, with its emphasis on surface and the strong contrasts of light and shadow that dramatize its subject's disfigured physiognomy. Such contrasts and the work's expressive traces of process would continue to animate Picasso's sculptural production even as he left Rodin's mode of figuration far behind.

The intensity of Picasso's ambition as a young artist is impossible to overestimate. By 1904 Barcelona had come to seem too provincial, and in April of that year he moved permanently to Paris, the center of the art scene. Ambroise Vollard, the first dealer to take an interest in Picasso's sculpture, also made him keenly aware of the model of the painter-sculptor, an artist who excelled in both fields of creativity. From his earliest attempts at sculpting, there was a constant back and forth between Picasso's work in two dimensions and in three. *Seated Woman*, for example, bears a strong resemblance to the melancholic, down-and-out figures that populate the artist's Blue Period paintings and drawings. Similarly, *The Jester* (pl. 3), the first sculpture Picasso is known to have completed following his move to Paris, is intimately related to his contemporaneous Rose Period paintings, which picture the itinerant circus performers known as saltimbanques.

The Jester, a bust of a young man in a pointed cap, is rumored to have begun as a portrait of the poet and critic Max Jacob or, possibly, of another treasured confrère, the poet, playwright, and critic Guillaume Apollinaire. Ultimately, resemblance to any one individual was subsumed into a more generalized, universal form, but in his sculptures as in his paintings, the people around Picasso would continue to have an impact. Their presence is felt in a lingering residue of likeness that persists throughout the artist's sculptural oeuvre.

Picasso's early three-dimensional works were realized in the studios of sculptor friends. In keeping with his status as a self-taught sculptor, he owned none of the specialized tools and equipment traditionally used to work with materials like clay, plaster, and stone. Among the many breakthroughs of Picasso's Cubist years was the realization that he didn't need those things; he could construct sculptures using light, inexpensive materials like paper, cardboard, and wood and the most rudimentary of craft techniques. During his first years in Paris, however, this breakthrough was yet to come. He modeled his sculptures in clay and fired two of them—*Head of a Woman (Fernande)* (pl. 4) and *Kneeling Woman Combing Her Hair* (pl. 5)—in his friend Durrio's kiln.

Head of a Woman (Fernande) is Picasso's first life-size sculpted portrait of his companion Fernande Olivier. *Kneeling Woman Combing Her Hair* is a relief sculpture, not modeled in the round, and it relates closely both to the wall and to Picasso's 1906 paintings and drawings of the same theme. As with so much of his three-dimensional work still ahead, he forced the sculpture to perform in a way that is aligned with painting, creating a distinctively hybrid form. The traces of color found on the terracotta original of *Kneeling Woman Combing Her Hair* are further evidence of Picasso's determination to defy conventional distinctions between painting and sculpture. Had he trained as a sculptor, he might have been less inclined to violate the genre's academic norms.

Vollard purchased five of Picasso's earliest clay sculptures, including *The Jester*, *Head of a Woman (Fernande)*, and *Kneeling Woman Combing Her Hair*, and used them to issue editions in bronze. As a result, these works led a far more visible public life than many of Picasso's subsequent works in three dimensions, and for decades they played a disproportionately important role in perceptions of his accomplishments as a sculptor.

PRELUDE, 1892–1901: As a young man, Picasso's goal was to become a painter. He did not study sculpture and, at first, showed little interest in the medium. He took art classes at the Instituto da Guarda, in La Coruña, from 1892 to 1894; at the Escola Provincial de Belles Artes (better known as "La Llotja"), in Barcelona, beginning in 1895; and, finally, at the Academia de San Fernando, in Madrid, from 1897 to 1898. At these institutions Picasso received rigorous training in drawing the human body: at the Instituto da Guarda, copying lithographic plates drawn after plaster casts (figs. 1, 2), and at La Llotja, practicing life drawing.[1] These skills would later prove pivotal in his visualizing of mass and volume in three dimensions. During these years of training, he saw little of modernism. The relative isolation of the classes in La Coruña, Barcelona, and Madrid prevented Picasso from engaging with these new ideas until the end of 1899, when he joined the circle of artists at Els Quatre Gats café in Barcelona. Ramón Casas y Carbó, Santiago Rusiñol, and Miguel Utrillo formed the core of the Quatre Gats group, and it was through these artists that Picasso first encountered the work of Edgar Degas.[2] This may have included an introduction to Degas's sculpture and thus to the new category of "painter-sculptor" that had emerged in the nineteenth century—a group that included Degas, Honoré Daumier, and Paul Gauguin. Picasso took an interest in the ambitions of this new breed of artist, who worked with sculpture alongside painting and drawing.

On his first trip to Paris, in late October 1900, Picasso became personally acquainted with French modernism through a visit to the Exposition Universelle.[3] On October 25, he and his friend and traveling companion Carles Casagemas, a painter and poet, wrote to Ramon Reventós back in Barcelona, "Here there are real teachers everywhere. Soon the Exposition will close and we still haven't seen more than the painting section."[4] The largest and most spectacular fair of its kind at the time, the Exposition featured numerous venues dedicated to contemporary art. It also coincided with other exhibitions, including a grand retrospective of the work of French sculptor Auguste Rodin in the pavilion at the place de l'Alma (fig. 3).[5] It is not known for certain that Picasso saw this exhibition, but a quickly drawn portrait of Rodin on a sheet full of sketches he made that year suggests that he encountered the artist or his work in the stimulating milieu of the Exposition and its environs (fig. 4). He must also have seen an article on the sculptor by Joaquim Cabot i Rovira published in *Pèl & Ploma* in January 1901: by the following year, the image of Rodin's *The Thinker* (1880) that accompanied the text had been fixed to a wall in his studio (fig. 5).[6]

EARLY 1902: Back in Barcelona in early January, after a second trip to Paris, Picasso settled in a studio at 10 Carrer Nou de la Rambla. There he was among sculptors such as Emili Fontbona, Manolo, and Francisco "Paco" Durrio y Madrón; he had met others, including Aristide Maillol, as early as 1900 or 1901. In addition, he had witnessed the innovations Rodin brought forth in sculpture—asymmetry and blurring, among them—and he might have been aware of the work of Italian sculptor Medardo Rosso, who used similar techniques.

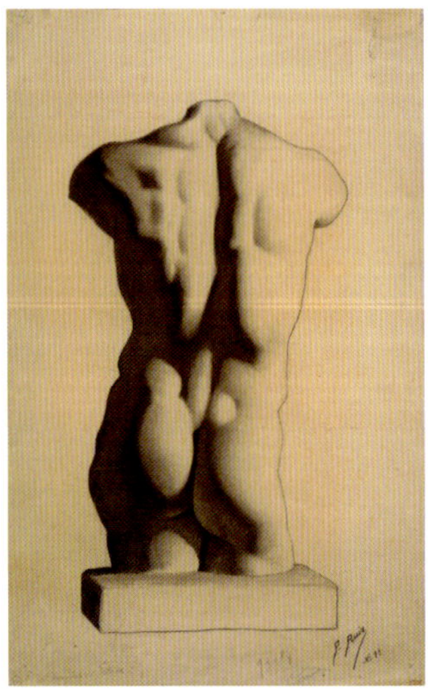

1. Pablo Picasso. *Academic Study of an Antique Plaster (A Hercules by Phidias)*. La Coruña, 1893–94. Charcoal and pencil on paper, 19 5/16 × 12 7/16 in. (49 × 31.5 cm). Musée national Picasso–Paris. Dation Pablo Picasso

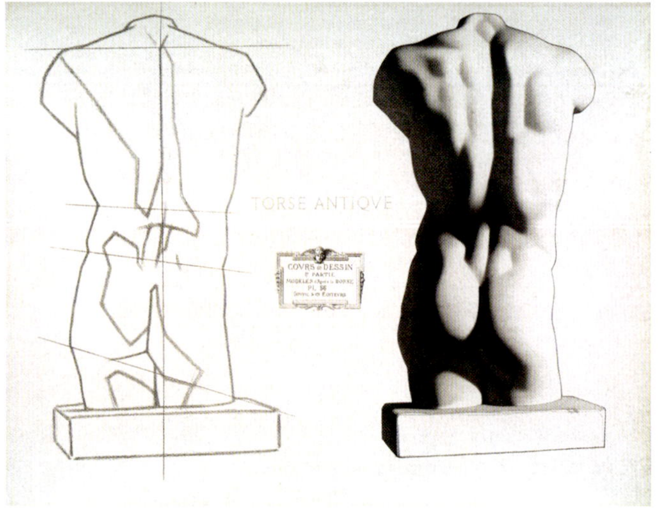

2. Charles Bargue, with the collaboration of Jean-Léon Gérôme. Plate 56 from *Cours de dessin* (Drawing course). Paris: Goupil et Cie, 1868

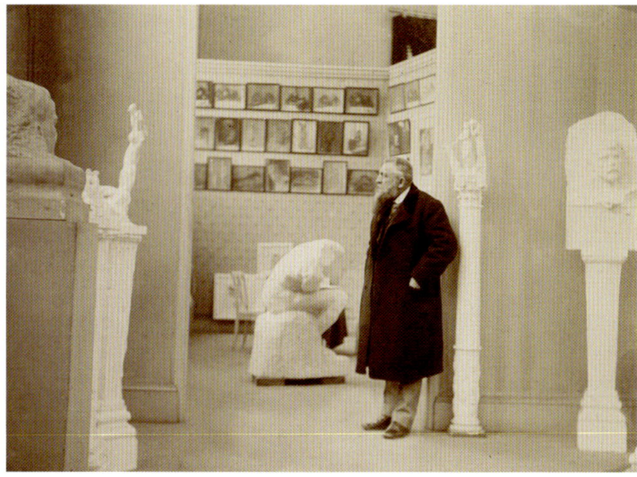

3. Auguste Rodin in the retrospective of his work at the place de l'Alma, with *Torso of Ugolino* at center, Paris, 1900. Musée Rodin, Paris

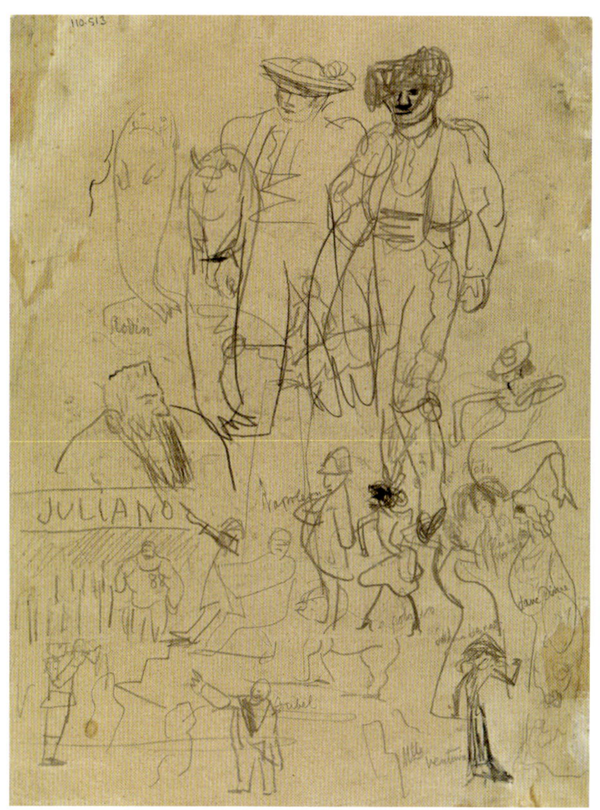

4. Pablo Picasso. *Bullfighter and Picador, and Various Caricatures*, with a sketch of Rodin at center left. Barcelona, 1900. Graphite pencil on paper, 10 5/16 × 8 1/4 in. (26.2 × 20.9 cm). Museu Picasso, Barcelona. Gift of Pablo Picasso

SPRING 1902: Under the title "Renacimiento de la escultura" (Renaissance of sculpture), the Madrid review *La lectura* printed a revised version of Edmond Claris's study "De l'impressionnisme en sculpture: Auguste Rodin et Medardo Rosso" (On Impressionism in sculpture: Auguste Rodin and Medardo Rosso), which had been published in *La Nouvelle Revue* the previous June.[7] Claris had asked artists, critics, and collectors for their opinions on the critique of sculpture advanced by Charles Baudelaire and posed the question, "Can and should sculpture compete with painting?" In a reply to this text, published in May 1902, Rosso advocated for the painter-sculptor, declaring that "art is indivisible"; for him, painting and sculpture were not opposites, but rather two parts of a cohesive effort.[8]

***SEATED WOMAN*, 1902**

Picasso and Fontbona had both attended regular gatherings at Le Zut, a Parisian artists' hangout on place Ravignan in Montmartre, in fall 1901, and back in Barcelona they developed a closer bond.[9] It is not known when Picasso first sought Fontbona's advice on how to model in clay, but he made *Seated Woman* (pl. 1) in that material sometime between January and late October 1902 at the Fontbona family residence on Carrer Padua, in Sant Gervasi.

Like all of Picasso's early sculptures, *Seated Woman* is closely related to the paintings and drawings the artist worked on at the same time. During his childhood, Picasso had modeled many crèche figures, which he would later recall in relation to *Seated Woman*.[10] Crèche figures can be arranged in a variety of settings and combinations; similarly, the motif of *Seated Woman* moved freely between the artist's paintings and sculpture. Picasso had been preoccupied with the huddled female

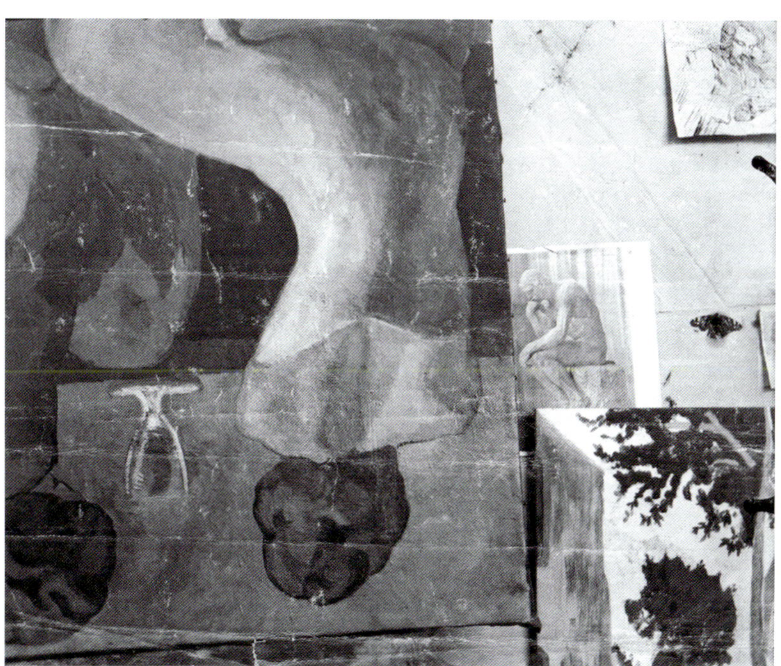

5. Picasso's studio at 10 Carrer Nou de la Rambla, with the artist's painting *Two Women at a Bar* (1902) upside down in the foreground and a reproduction of *The Thinker* (1880), by Auguste Rodin, fixed to the wall, Barcelona, 1902. Musée national Picasso–Paris

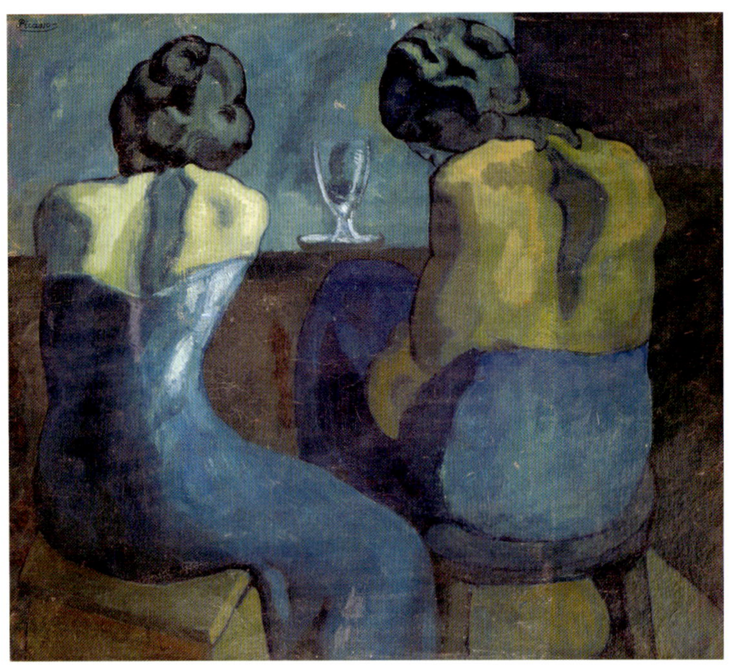

6. Pablo Picasso. *Two Women at a Bar.* Barcelona, 1902. Oil on canvas, 31½ × 36 in. (80 × 91.4 cm). Hiroshima Museum of Art, Hiroshima City, Japan

figures that populate his Blue Period paintings of 1901, and in January 1902 he had further developed these figures in a series of portrayals of women (fig. 6), who, in their introverted poses, resemble *Seated Woman*. At the Instituto da Guarda, Picasso had learned how to represent bodies in space in two dimensions, a process he inverted by applying his painterly imagination to sculpture. *Seated Woman* marks the beginning of Picasso's lasting dialogue with sculpture, in which he sought to advance his pictorial ideas of mass and volume in three dimensions.

For a long time, Picasso's first sculpture remained unknown. Although a number of the artist's early sculptures were publicized and exhibited prior to World War II, *Seated Woman* was not included in the catalogue raisonné of the artist's work by Christian Zervos or presented in the artist's first retrospective exhibition, held in Paris and Zurich in 1932. When a bronze cast of *Seated Woman* was shown for the first time, in an exhibition organized by the Buchholz Gallery in New York in late 1942, it was dated 1905.[11] Seven years later, in *Les Sculptures de Picasso*, the first book-length study of the artist's sculpture, *Seated Woman* was dated 1899.[12] The book, which included a text by Daniel-Henry Kahnweiler, was the first comprehensive presentation of Picasso's three-dimensional objects to an international audience. Among its more than two hundred black-and-white images is the earliest known reproduction of *Seated Woman*—a photograph of a bronze cast of the work—which had been chosen to represent the artist's sculptures of this period. In the early 1960s, when Picasso retroactively assigned dates to his first sculptures, he explained that *Seated Woman* had not been made before 1900. This led John Richardson, organizer of the 1962 New York exhibition *Picasso: An American Tribute*, to date the sculpture to 1901.[13] In 1971, Werner Spies, in his catalogue raisonné of Picasso's sculpture, established the date of 1902 for the work, based on comparison with contemporaneous paintings of women in very similar poses.[14]

Like the majority of the artist's works in three dimensions, the original clay *Seated Woman* figure would remain in Picasso's personal collection until the end of his life. It entered the Musée national Picasso–Paris, through the Dation Picasso, in 1979.

EARLY FALL 1902: On September 25, an exhibition presenting nearly 1,900 artifacts from the Catalan region of Spain opened at the Palau de Belles Artes in Barcelona, including Romanesque and Gothic sculpture as well as works by El Greco and Francisco de Zurbarán.[15] Picasso might have visited the show with his artist friend Vidal Ventosa, who had studied sculpture at La Llotja and awakened Picasso's interest in the rich Romanesque culture of Catalonia.[16]

OCTOBER 19, 1902: Picasso left for Paris on the express train from Barcelona with Josep Rocarol, with whom he had shared the Carrer Nou de la Rambla studio, and Julio González. Their departure was reported the next day in the Barcelona newspaper *El Liberal*.

MID-JANUARY 1903: The artist returned to Barcelona, where he continued to make paintings and sculpture.

***HEAD OF A PICADOR WITH A BROKEN NOSE*, 1903**

Picasso modeled two masks—*Head of a Picador with a Broken Nose* (pl. 2) and *Mask of a Blind Singer*—sometime in 1903.[17] Each work depicts a face marked by physical deformation; *Head of a Picador*, created in clay in Fontbona's studio, is nearly life-size.[18] The sculpture may have been a tribute to Rodin's portrait mask *Man with a Broken Nose* (1863–64); it might also have been inspired by the glazed ceramic *Mask of a Savage*, of 1894, by Gauguin. *Mask of a Savage* (Musée Léon-Dierx, Saint-Denis) had entered the stock of the dealer Ambroise Vollard sometime after May 1902, and Vollard quickly had the ceramic mask cast in bronze (fig. 7).[19] Vollard had shown Picasso's work in his Paris gallery in summer 1901, and he was familiar to the young artist as a dealer of sculptures by Degas, Gauguin, Maillol, and Rodin.[20] It is not known whether Picasso saw Gauguin's sculpture at Vollard's

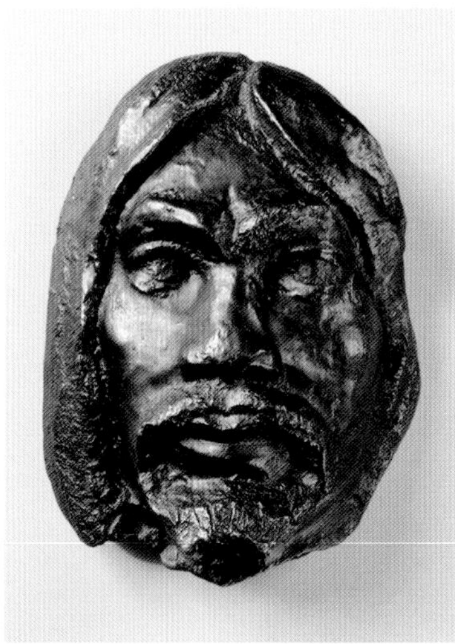

7. Paul Gauguin. *Mask of a Savage*. 1894. Bronze, first cast spring 1902, 9 ⅞ × 7⅛ × 4 ¾ in. (25 × 18 × 12 cm). Musée d'Orsay, Paris

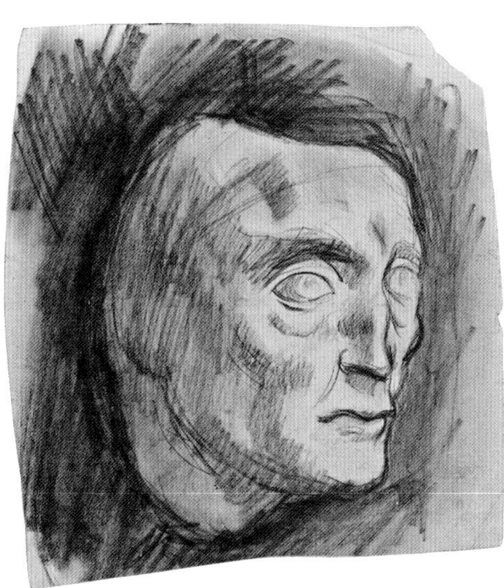

8. Pablo Picasso. *Picador with Broken Nose*. Barcelona, 1903. Pencil on the back of an illustration, 5 ¾ × 5 ½ in. (14.5 × 14 cm). Private collection. Courtesy Fundación Almine y Bernard Ruiz-Picasso para el Arte, Brussels

gallery, but the formal similarities between it and his work and the close proximity in date and milieu suggest that he encountered it. Unlike *Seated Woman* or *Mask of a Blind Singer, Head of a Picador* has no direct visual parallel in Picasso's work except in drawings, one of which is a rendering of the sculpture itself (fig. 8).

A bronze cast of *Head of a Picador* was made early on. It belonged to the writer and collector Gertrude Stein, who acquired it with her brother Leo Stein. The Steins had met Picasso through the French writer Henri-Pierre Roché, probably on May 9, 1905, the earliest date at which they would have acquired it.[21] Gertrude kept the sculpture when she and Leo split their collection in 1913–14. On July 9, 1925, the Baltimore-based sisters Dr. Claribel Cone and Etta Cone purchased the sculpture from Gertrude Stein for 5,000 French francs (fig. 9).[22] At that time, the work was titled *Mask* and dated to 1905, based on the markings "Picasso / 04 / 1905" incised on the lower left side of the cast, probably denoting the casting date. Fine mold lines indicating the sand-casting process are visible on each side of the face. In addition, along the subject's upper left hairline there is a rough, ragged piece of metal that distinguishes this bronze from later casts. Called "flashing," this is the result of metal flowing into a crack in the mold during casting.[23] Mold lines and flashing are normally chased off or repaired after the bronze is cast; there is no way of knowing what role Picasso played in the production of this early work, or whether it was he who requested that these details be retained.

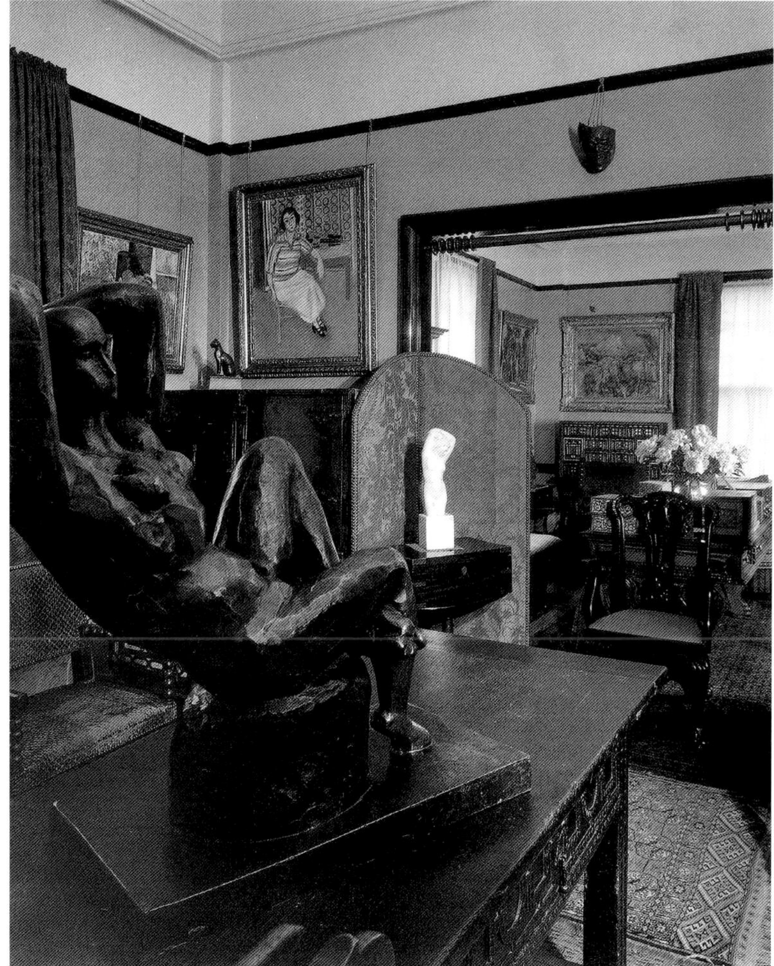

9. Claribel and Etta Cone's apartment, with Picasso's *Head of a Picador with a Broken Nose* on display over the doorframe, Baltimore, 1941. Claribel and Etta Cone Papers, Archives and Manuscript Collections, Baltimore Museum of Art

It is also not known who commissioned or produced the cast. Although the bronze formed part of the renowned Stein collection, it was not widely known that Picasso, or someone acting in his stead, had issued *Head of a Picador* in bronze. In his 1928 monograph on the artist, André Level declared that "a number of Picasso's sculptures, including a mask of a picador with broken nose, have not been editioned."[24] Fernande Olivier, Picasso's companion from 1904 to 1912, associated the mask with Vollard, but apart from this there is no evidence that the dealer was involved with this work.[25]

The cast gained some exposure in 1930, when it was included in a memorial exhibition for Dr. Cone at the Baltimore Museum of Art.[26] Outside the United States the sculpture would remain largely invisible until 1960, when Kahnweiler, then Picasso's dealer, commissioned an edition of eight bronzes. According to Kahnweiler, the clay model resurfaced in Paris around 1959 in one of Picasso's closets, as the artist was moving belongings from 7, rue des Grands-Augustins to southern France.[27] Records in the archives of the Valsuani foundry, in Paris, suggest that the newly commissioned bronzes were cast there in August 1960.[28] The Hamburger Kunsthalle acquired a cast from Kahnweiler in 1961, during its presentation in an exhibition at the Kunsthalle Bremen.[29] In 1962 a bronze was also included in a Picasso sculpture exhibition at the Otto Gerson Gallery in New York.[30]

AUGUST 10, 1903: Three drawings by Picasso, including a sketch of Rodin's portrait bust *Jules Dalou* (1883), were reproduced on the front page of *El Liberal* with a review of the 1900 Exposition Universelle (fig. 10).[31] The sketch, made in 1903 (Museu Nacional d'Art de Catalunya, Barcelona), was likely drawn from a reproduction of Rodin's work published at the time of Dalou's death, in April 1902.[32] Picasso might have seen the sculpture in Paris three years earlier, as it was shown in both the Exposition and Rodin's retrospective at the place de l'Alma.[33]

MID-APRIL 1904: Picasso left Barcelona to definitively relocate to France. The artist's departure was announced on March 24 in *El Liberal*, and he arranged for a brief notice to appear in the newspaper on April 11 and 12: "The artists Messrs. Sebastià Junyer Vidal and Pablo Ruiz Picasso are leaving on today's express for Paris, where they propose to hold an exhibition of their latest works."[34] In Paris, Picasso took over the studio of his friend Paco Durrio in the Bateau-Lavoir building, at 13, rue Ravignan, where he would remain until fall 1909. Durrio, a Basque sculptor and ceramicist Picasso had met together with Jaime Sabartés in fall 1901, moved to a less developed part of Montmartre, known as the Maquis, where he could install a kiln, setting up what he called a "cuisine atelier."[35]

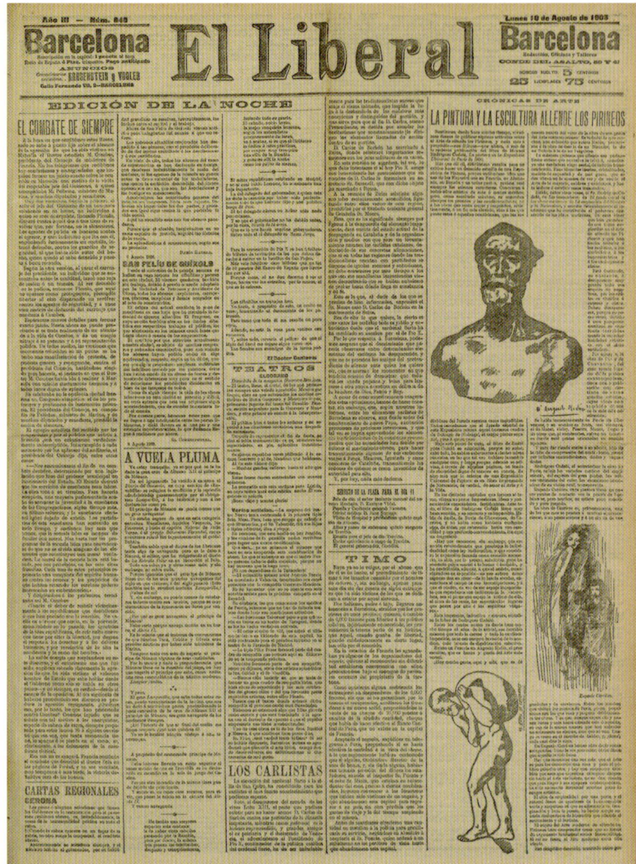
Barcelona
El Liberal
Barcelona
EDICIÓN DE LA NOCHE
EL COMBATE DE SIEMPRE
A VUELA PLUMA
TEATROS
TIMO
LOS CARLISTAS
CARTAS REGIONALES
CRÓNICAS DE ARTE
LA PINTURA Y LA ESCULTURA ALLENDE LOS PIRINEOS

10. The front page of *El Liberal*, featuring a sketch by Picasso of Auguste Rodin's bust *Jules Dalou* (1883), August 10, 1903. Arxiu Històric de la Ciutat de Barcelona

SEPTEMBER 1904: The Musée du Louvre presented its collection of Iberian sculptures from Cerro de los Santos and Osuna in Andalusia.[36] The influence of this close encounter with the ancient art of his homeland would become visible in Picasso's work in 1906—in the paintings *Woman Plaiting Her Hair* (see fig. 18) and *Two Nudes* (The Museum of Modern Art New York), among numerous examples.

OCTOBER 15–NOVEMBER 15, 1904: The annual Salon d'Automne at the Grand Palais featured two plaster sculptures by Matisse: a study for *The Serf* (1900–1903) and *Madeleine I* (1901).[37] This was the first time the artist's sculpture was exhibited publicly. It is not known whether Picasso attended the Salon, but the event reliably attracted members of Paris's avant-garde circles.

FEBRUARY 24–MARCH 6, 1905: Numerous recent paintings, drawings, and prints by Picasso featuring images of harlequins, acrobats, and circus performers were presented in a group exhibition organized by the art critic Charles Morice at the Galerie Serrurier, at 37, boulevard Haussmann.[38]

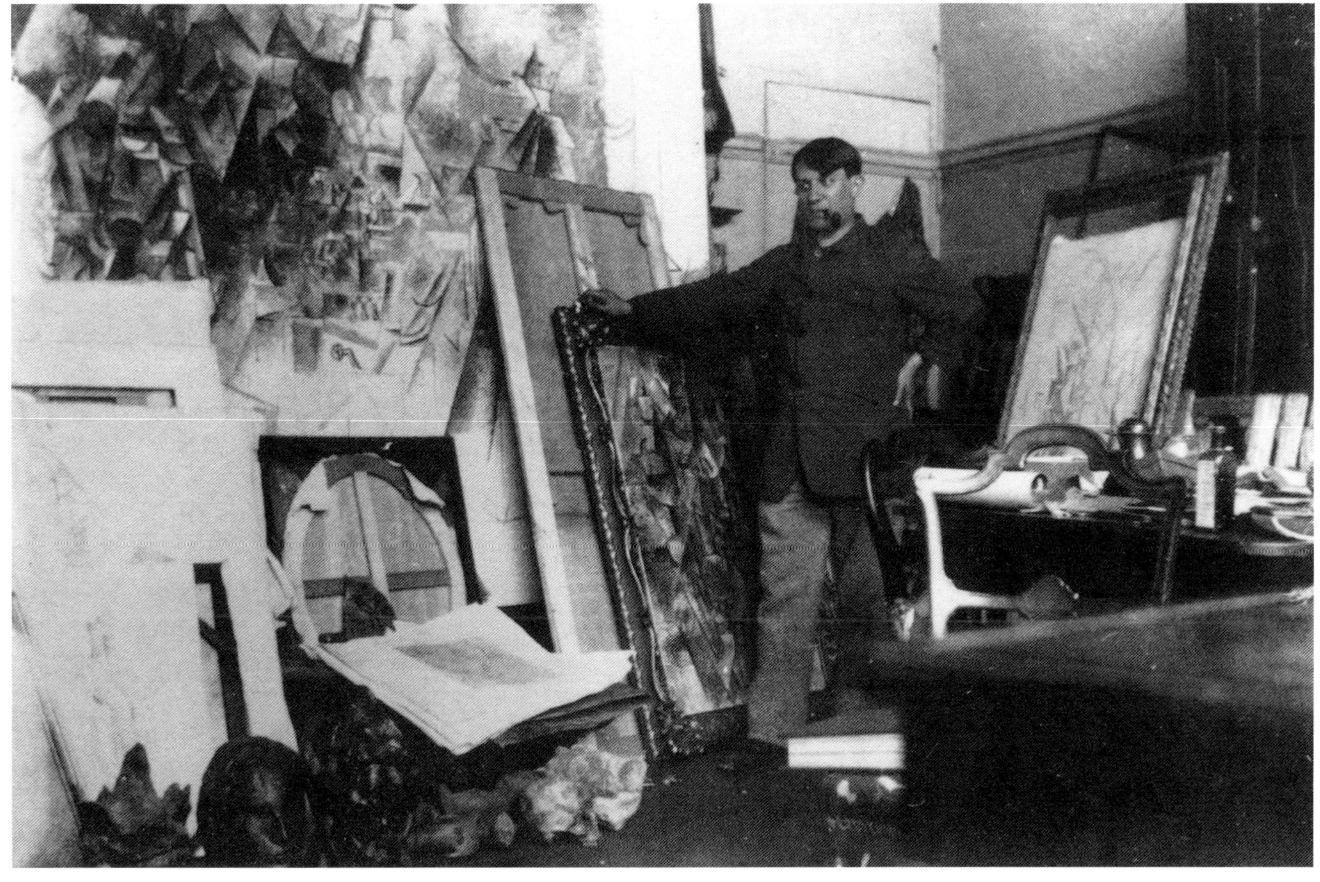

11. Picasso in his studio at 11, boulevard de Clichy, with bronze casts of *The Jester*, *Head of a Woman (Fernande)* (1906), and *Head of a Woman* (1909) in the foreground, Paris, early 1911. Archives Quentin Laurens, Paris

Picasso's works resonated with his new friend Guillaume Apollinaire, a poet and art critic whose review of the show would be published in his journal *La Revue immoraliste* in April.[39]

THE JESTER, 1905

Picasso made *The Jester* (pl. 3), a harlequin head modeled in clay, over the course of a few days. Shortly before, the artist had visited the Cirque Médrano with the poet Max Jacob, and according to Kahnweiler it was the figure of Jacob that inspired the sculpture.[40] In old age, Picasso would recall that "Jacob had invented a little to add to it," perhaps a reference to the jester's cap, which ultimately transformed the figure from a likeness of the poet into a head of a harlequin.[41] Apollinaire shared the artist's enchantment with the circus theme, an interest that is also reflected in his poetry; he, too, might have been a source of inspiration for *The Jester*.[42] A large retrospective of Rodin's work presented at the Musée du Luxembourg that spring could have been another stimulus; the pinched and pulled quality of the figure's flesh and pointy cap is highly reminiscent of Rodin's surface textures.

Vollard would purchase the clay sculpture from the artist in 1910, together with four others: *Head of a Woman (Fernande)* (1906; pl. 4), *Kneeling Woman Combing Her Hair* (1906; pl. 5), *Bust of a Man* (1906), and *Head of a Woman* (1909; pl. 11).[43] Between 1910 and his death in 1939, Vollard ordered an unknown number of casts of these sculptures; his practice, Una Johnson writes, "was to keep in his shop [at 6, rue Laffitte] an example of each of the bronzes. When a collector or dealer wished to obtain one, Vollard would order a cast made."[44] It is likely that he used a variety of foundries, as the bronze casts of *The Jester* differ greatly in their patinas—some are green, while others are brown or black.[45] Vollard gave Picasso an artist's proof of each sculpture he published, some of which the artist kept on view in his studio (fig. 11). Vincenc Kramář, a Czech art historian and collector of Cubism, saw a cast of *The Jester* in spring 1912, when he visited Picasso's studio on rue Ravignan. Among his travel notes from that trip is a quick sketch of the sculpture, next to which he wrote, "Too much literature and not enough sculpture," likely expressing the opinion that the work was rich in concept but lacking in its execution (fig. 12).[46]

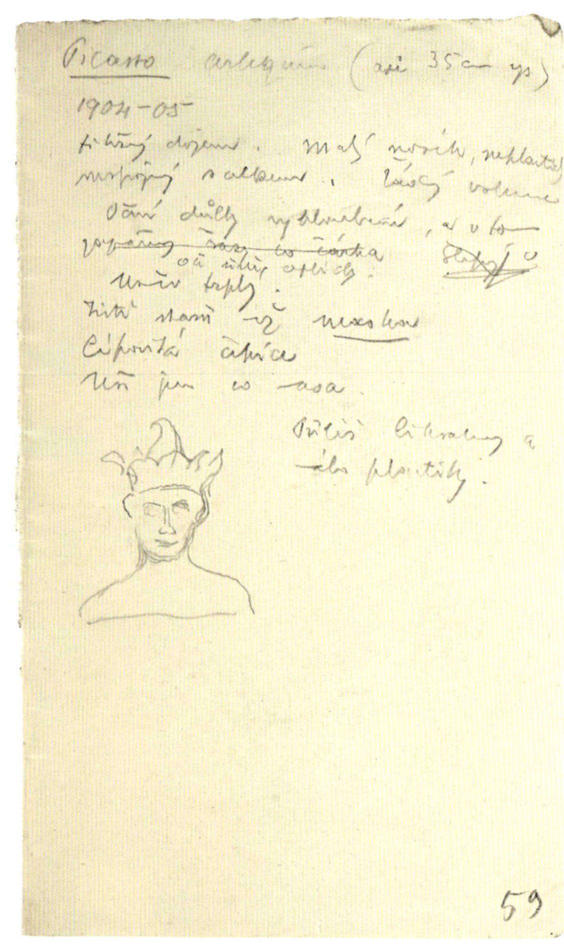

12. Sketch and notes by Vincenc Kramář in his Paris travel notebook, 1912. Archives Vincenc Kramář, Institute of Art History, ASRC, Prague

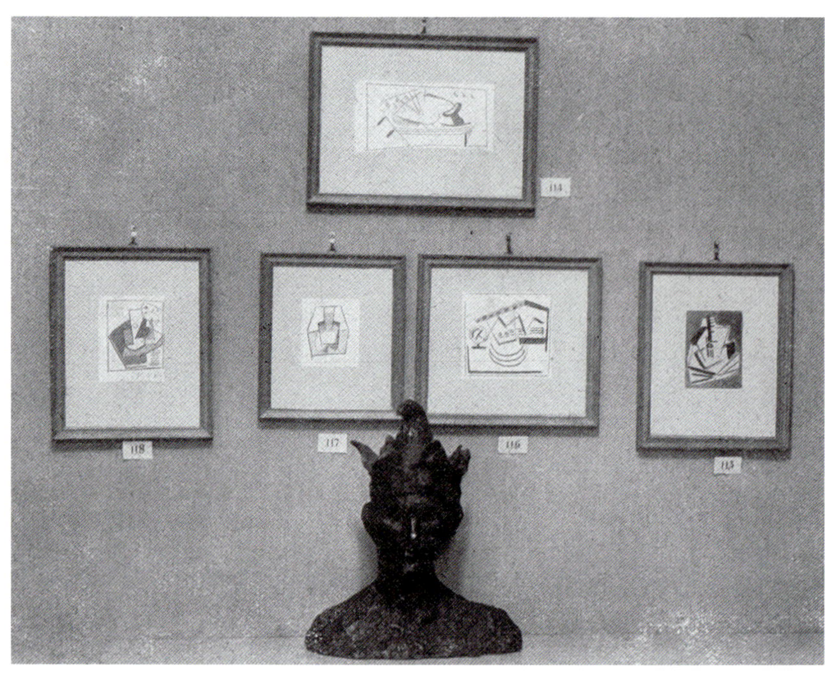

13. View of the 1927 exhibition of Picasso's work at Galerie Alfred Flechtheim, Berlin, with *The Jester* at center

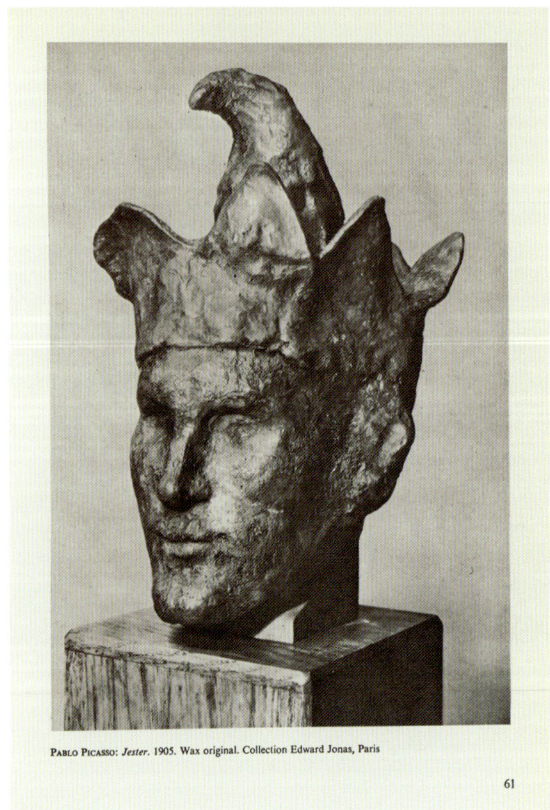

PABLO PICASSO: *Jester*. 1905. Wax original. Collection Edward Jonas, Paris

61

14. Fragment of *The Jester* reproduced in Andrew C. Ritchie, *Sculpture of the Twentieth Century* (New York: The Museum of Modern Art, 1952), p. 61

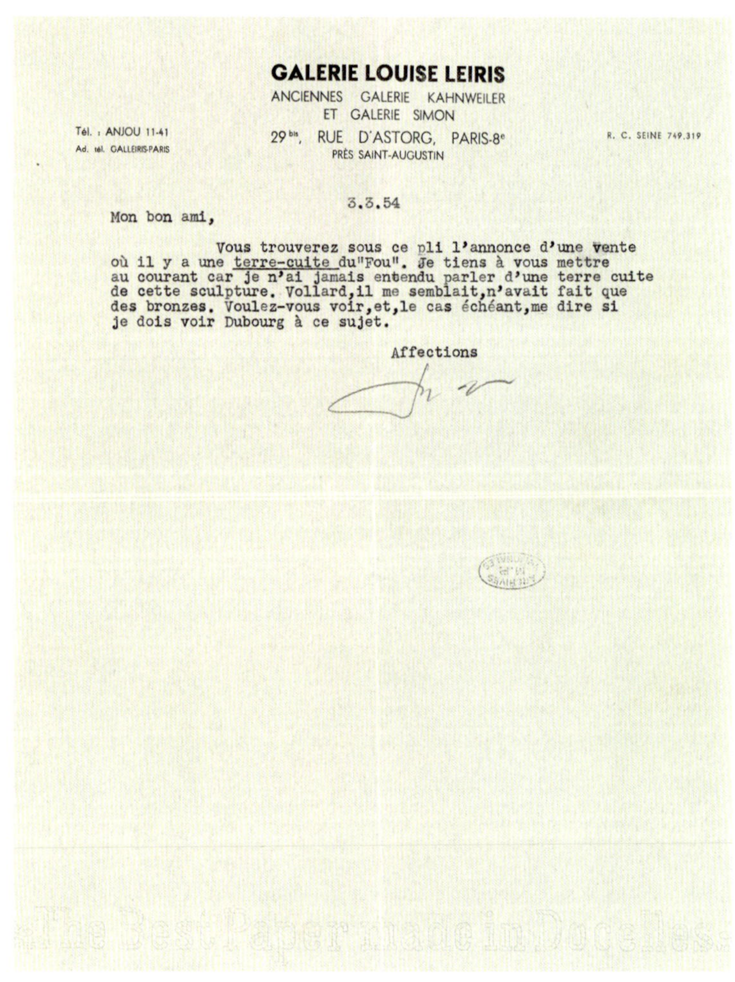

GALERIE LOUISE LEIRIS
ANCIENNES GALERIE KAHNWEILER
ET GALERIE SIMON

Tél. : ANJOU 11-41
Ad. tél. GALLERIS-PARIS

29 bis, RUE D'ASTORG, PARIS-8e
PRÈS SAINT-AUGUSTIN

R. C. SEINE 749.319

3.3.54

Mon bon ami,

Vous trouverez sous ce pli l'annonce d'une vente où il y a une terre-cuite du"Fou". Je tiens à vous mettre au courant car je n'ai jamais entendu parler d'une terre cuite de cette sculpture. Vollard,il me semblait,n'avait fait que des bronzes. Voulez-vous voir,et,le cas échéant,me dire si je dois voir Dubourg à ce sujet.

Affections

15. Letter from Daniel-Henry Kahnweiler to Picasso, informing the artist of the upcoming sale of a fragment of *The Jester*, March 3, 1954. Picasso Archives, Musée national Picasso–Paris

A bronze cast of *The Jester* was included in the 1913 inaugural show at Galerie Alfred Flechtheim in Düsseldorf; this is the earliest known public exhibition of the work.[47] It was presented again in Flechtheim's gallery in Berlin in 1927, as documented in a rare installation photograph published in *feuilles volantes*, a supplement of the French art journal *Cahiers d'Art* (fig. 13).[48] A different cast of *The Jester* was donated by Vollard to the Musée d'art moderne de la Ville de Paris in 1937 (see pl. 3).

The material in which Picasso made this sculpture has sometimes been identified as wax, rather than clay. A fragment of the object (only the head remained) was described as wax in Andrew C. Ritchie's 1952 study *Sculpture of the Twentieth Century* (fig. 14) and as "terracotta original coated with varnished wax" in a French auction catalogue in 1954, when it was offered for sale by the dealer Édouard Jonas.[49] Kahnweiler was surprised to learn of the existence of the clay sculpture. On March 3, 1954, he wrote to the artist, "I need to update you as I have never heard of a clay version of this sculpture. Vollard, it seemed to me, had only made bronzes. Do you want to see for yourself and, if necessary, tell me if I need to consult [Jacques] Dubourg regarding this" (fig. 15).[50] Kahnweiler pursued the fragment at auction without success. It was sold to an unidentified bidder for 410,000 French francs.[51]

SPRING 1906: Picasso met Matisse sometime before the opening of the Salon des Indépendants, which launched on March 20. Gertrude and Leo Stein acted as intermediaries.[52] Both artists were regular invitees to the Saturday evening salon at the Steins' apartment, at 27, rue de Fleurus.

HEAD OF A WOMAN (FERNANDE), 1906

Picasso modeled *Head of a Woman (Fernande)* (pl. 4), his first life-size sculpted portrait of Olivier, in clay in Durrio's studio in the Maquis and subsequently fired it in Durrio's kiln. Picasso had consulted with Durrio about making more elaborate sculpture, and it might have been the latter who advised the artist to press "fine tulle . . . into the surface of the moist clay to evoke the porous texture of skin."[53] A similar emphasis on the texture of the left side of Olivier's face is evident in a related charcoal drawing, in which Picasso employed hatched lines and stumping to animate his companion's skin and hairline (fig. 16).[54] As in *The Jester*, the artist's process is clearly visible in the finished work. Using his fingers, a sculptor's knife, and scraping tools, he worked quickly to model the textured hair, from which the smoother face and neck emerge—a technique reminiscent of contemporaneous sculptures by Rodin and Rosso. The work of Degas—in particular his head of the ballerina Mathilde Salle (fig. 17), which he modeled in 1892 but left unfinished—looks forward to Picasso's choice of a dynamic surface treatment and unfinished look; the French artist was known for his love of *non finito* and for his use of found materials, including cloth, rags, ribbon, satin shoes, and a muslin tutu, in his sculptures.[55]

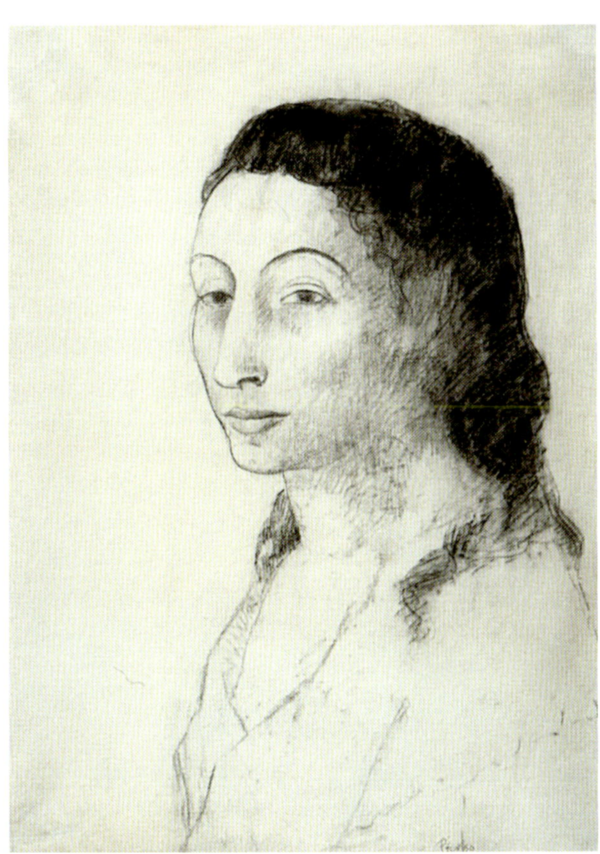

16. Pablo Picasso. *Fernande Olivier*. Gósol, 1906. Charcoal with stumping on laid paper, 24 × 18 ⅟₁₆ in. (61 × 45.8 cm). Art Institute of Chicago. Gift of Hermann Waldeck

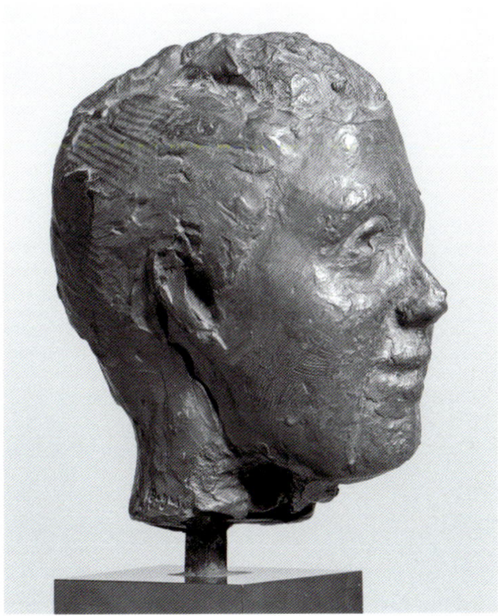

17. Edgar Degas. *Head of a Woman (Mlle Salle)*. 1892. Bronze, cast after 1919, 10 ⅟₁₆ × 6 × 7 ⁹⁄₁₆ in. (25.5 × 15.3 × 19.2 cm). Museum of Fine Arts, Boston. Bequest of Margarett Sargent McKean

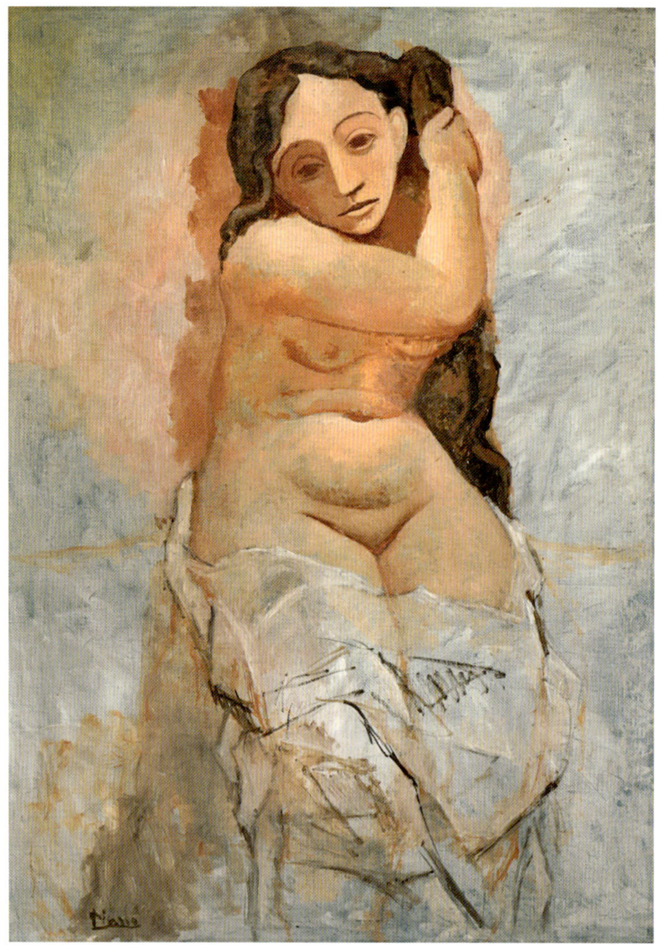

18. Pablo Picasso. *Woman Plaiting Her Hair*. Paris, late summer or fall 1906. Oil on canvas, 50 × 35 ¾ in. (127 × 90.8 cm). The Museum of Modern Art, New York. Florene May Schoenborn Bequest

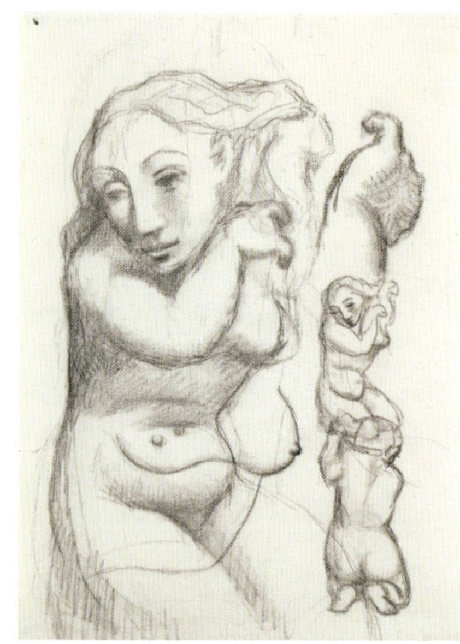

19. Pablo Picasso. Study for *Kneeling Woman Combing Her Hair*. 1906. Pencil on paper, 11 ⅞ × 8 ⅝ in. (30.2 × 21.9 cm). Hamburger Kunsthalle. Sammlung Hegewisch

Head of a Woman (Fernande), like *The Jester*, would be editioned in bronze by Vollard beginning in 1910 and first exhibited, as a cast, in the 1913 inaugural show at Galerie Alfred Flechtheim in Düsseldorf. In 1937 Vollard would give a cast of the work (pl. 4), along with *The Jester*, to the Musée d'art moderne de la Ville de Paris.

MAY 21, 1906: Picasso and Olivier arrived in Barcelona. They subsequently traveled to Gósol, a small village near Andorra, in the Pyrenees, where they spent June and July. This period in Picasso's work was defined by motifs inspired by Iberian sculpture, examples of which had been on view at the Louvre in fall 1904.

***KNEELING WOMAN COMBING HER HAIR*, 1906**

Picasso began *Kneeling Woman Combing Her Hair* (pl. 5) in Durrio's studio, after his return to Paris from Spain. When the figure was finished, he fired it in his friend's kiln, transforming the soft clay into terracotta. The sculpture, formerly dated to 1905 and once known as *La Coiffure*, shares its motif with the paintings and drawings of women arranging their hair that Picasso executed in Gósol that summer and in Paris in the late summer and fall (fig. 18).[56] Unlike *Seated Woman*, *The Jester*, and *Head of a Woman (Fernande)*, which were modeled in the round, the sculpture is hollow and is intended to be seen only from certain viewpoints. A preparatory drawing includes a sketch of the figure's back (fig. 19), showing that Picasso first conceived of the female figure from multiple viewpoints. Preoccupied by the frontal and side views, in the end he treated the sculpture like a painting by relating it to an imaginary wall.[57]

Firing the sculpture allowed Picasso to exploit the use of surface glazes and further "blur the distinction between painting and sculpture."[58] Picasso had encountered glazed stoneware by Gauguin at Vollard's gallery, and he learned the technique at Durrio's studio.[59] Durrio had met Gauguin as early as 1893 and had become his disciple. He presided over a considerable collection of Gauguin's paintings, works on paper, and woodcuts, which he had been asked to care for when the artist left for Tahiti in June 1895.[60] Picasso's terracotta figure

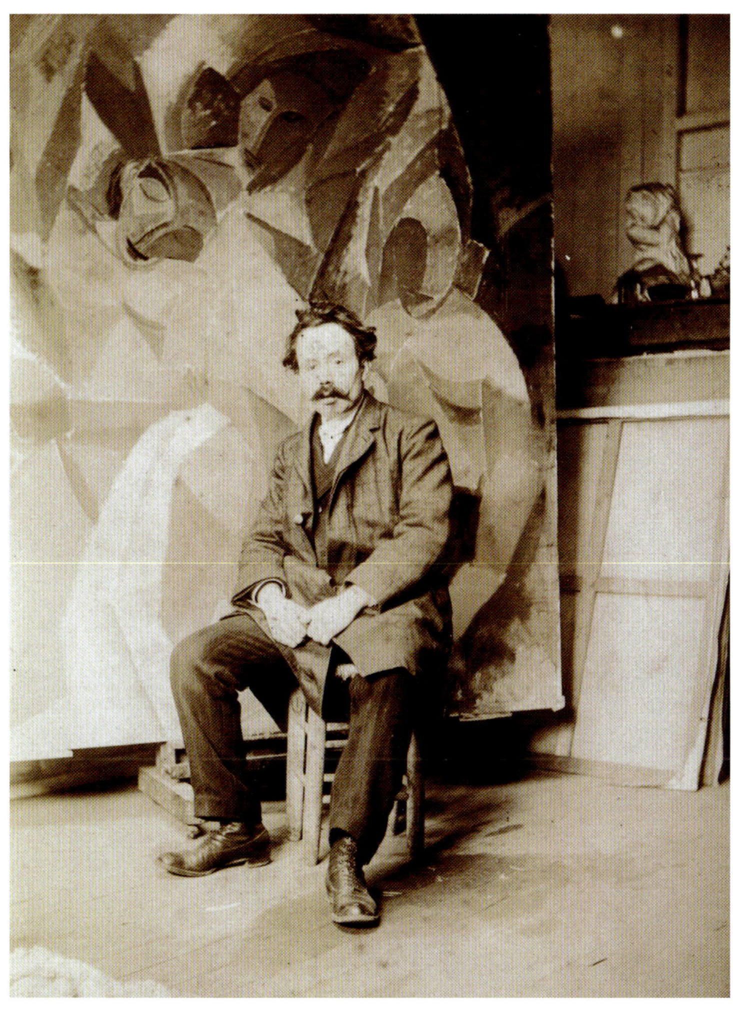

20. Sebastià Junyer Vidal in front of Picasso's unfinished painting *Three Women* (1908; State Hermitage Museum, St. Petersburg) in the artist's Bateau-Lavoir studio, Paris, spring–summer 1908. The original terracotta sculpture of *Kneeling Woman Combing Her Hair* is on the mantelpiece at right. Photograph by Picasso. Musée national Picasso–Paris

features traces of glaze, indicating that it once had color. A slender wooden figure Picasso had carved in Gósol over the summer (see fig. 2 on p. 52) also bears traces of color—black and red—and he would go on to explore polychrome sculpture throughout his career.

A photograph by Picasso from spring–summer 1908 shows the painter Sebastià Junyer Vidal in the artist's Bateau-Lavoir studio with *Kneeling Woman Combing Her Hair* (fig. 20), indicating that visitors saw it early on.[61] In 1910 Vollard purchased this work, along with four other early sculptures, all of which he would edition in bronze.

In 1928 a photograph of a bronze cast of the sculpture was published for the first time in Level's Picasso monograph (fig. 21) and in Zervos's essay "Sculptures des peintres d'aujourd'hui" (Sculptures by today's painters), in *Cahiers d'Art*.[62] In 1932 Picasso chose to include *Kneeling Woman Combing Her Hair,* together with *The Jester* and *Head of a Woman (Fernande),* in his first retrospective, held at the Galeries Georges Petit in Paris and subsequently at the Kunsthaus Zürich.

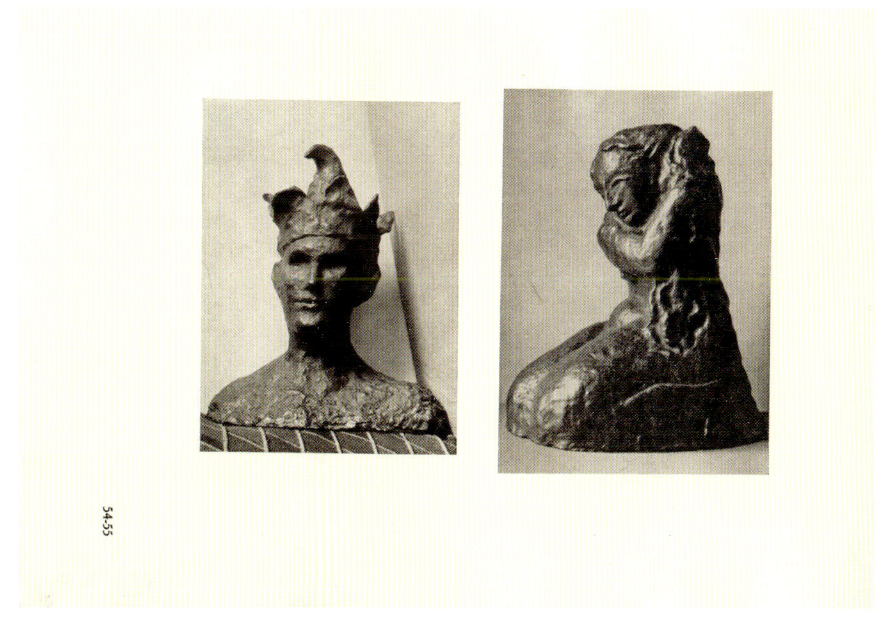

21. Bronze casts of *The Jester* and *Kneeling Woman Combing Her Hair* reproduced in André Level, *Picasso* (Paris: Éditions G. Crès et Cie, 1928), plates 54 and 55

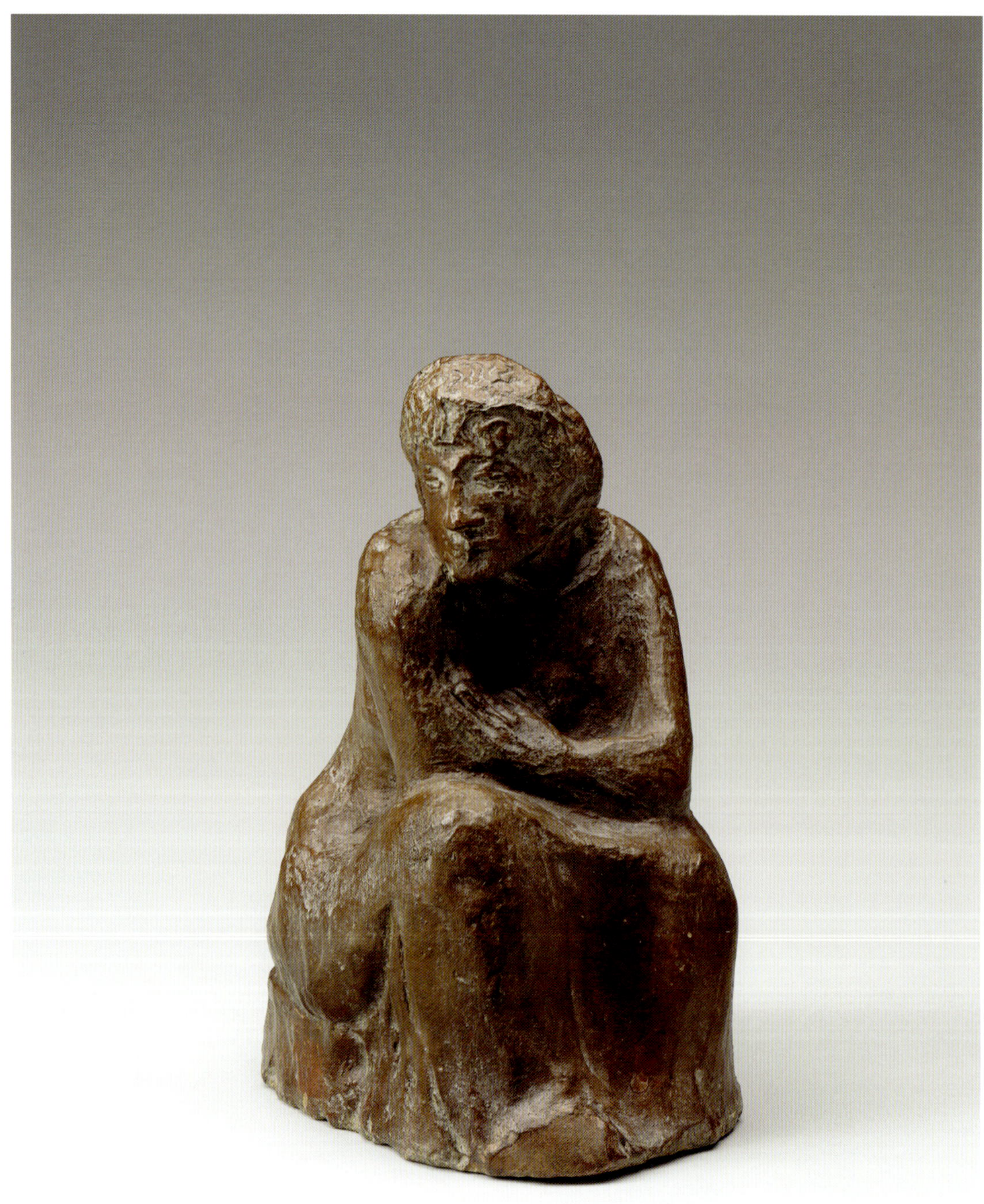

1. **SEATED WOMAN.** Barcelona, 1902
Unfired clay
5 11/16 × 3 3/8 × 4 1/2 in. (14.5 × 8.5 × 11.5 cm)
Musée national Picasso–Paris. Dation Pablo Picasso

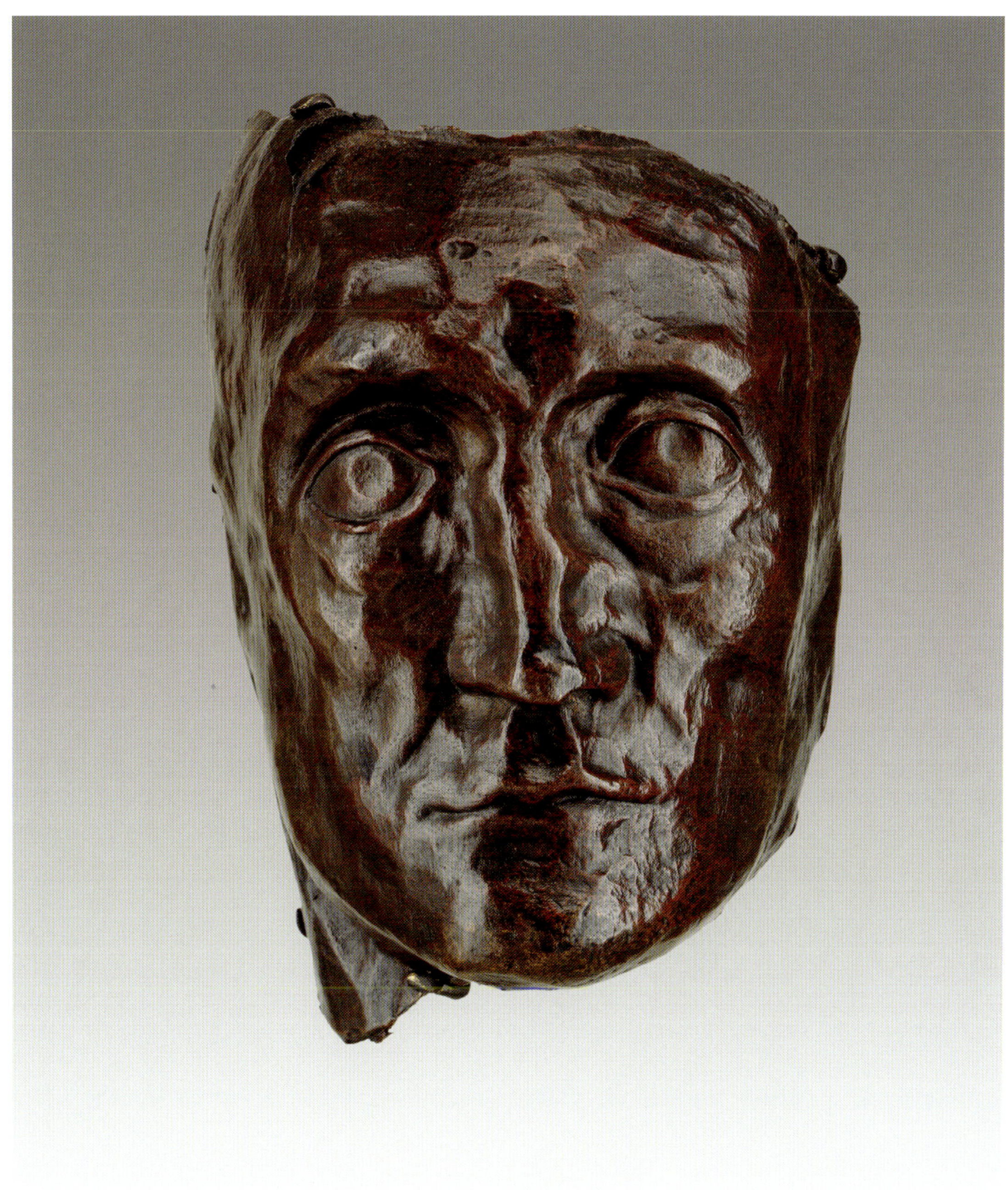

2. **HEAD OF A PICADOR WITH A BROKEN NOSE.** Barcelona, 1903
Bronze, cast by July 1925
Approx. 7 11/16 × 5 11/16 × 4 1/2 in. (19.6 × 14.5 × 11.4 cm)
Baltimore Museum of Art. The Cone Collection, formed by
Dr. Claribel Cone and Miss Etta Cone of Baltimore, Maryland

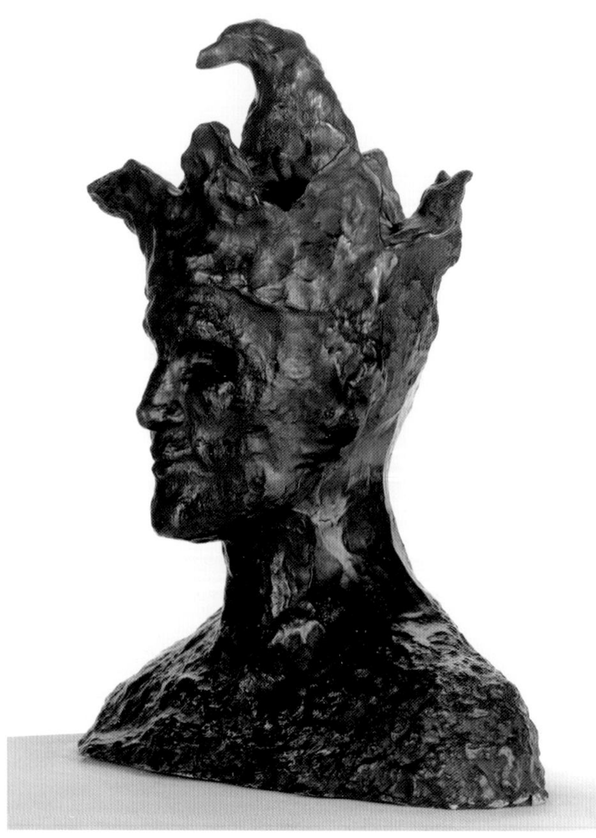

3. **THE JESTER.** Paris, 1905
Bronze, cast between 1910 and 1937
16 5/16 × 14 9/16 × 9 in. (41.5 × 37 × 22.8 cm)
Musée d'art moderne de la Ville de Paris. Gift of Ambroise Vollard

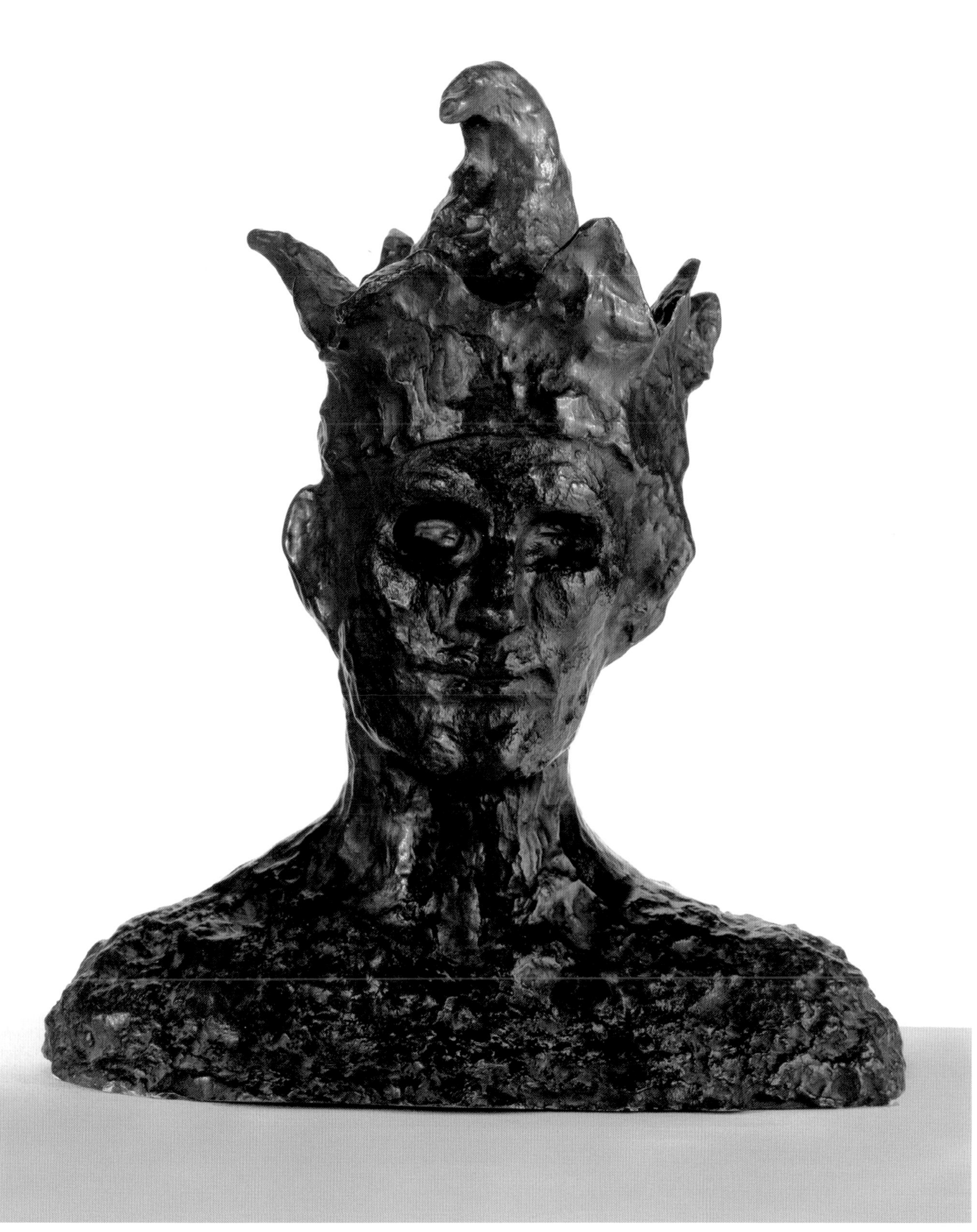

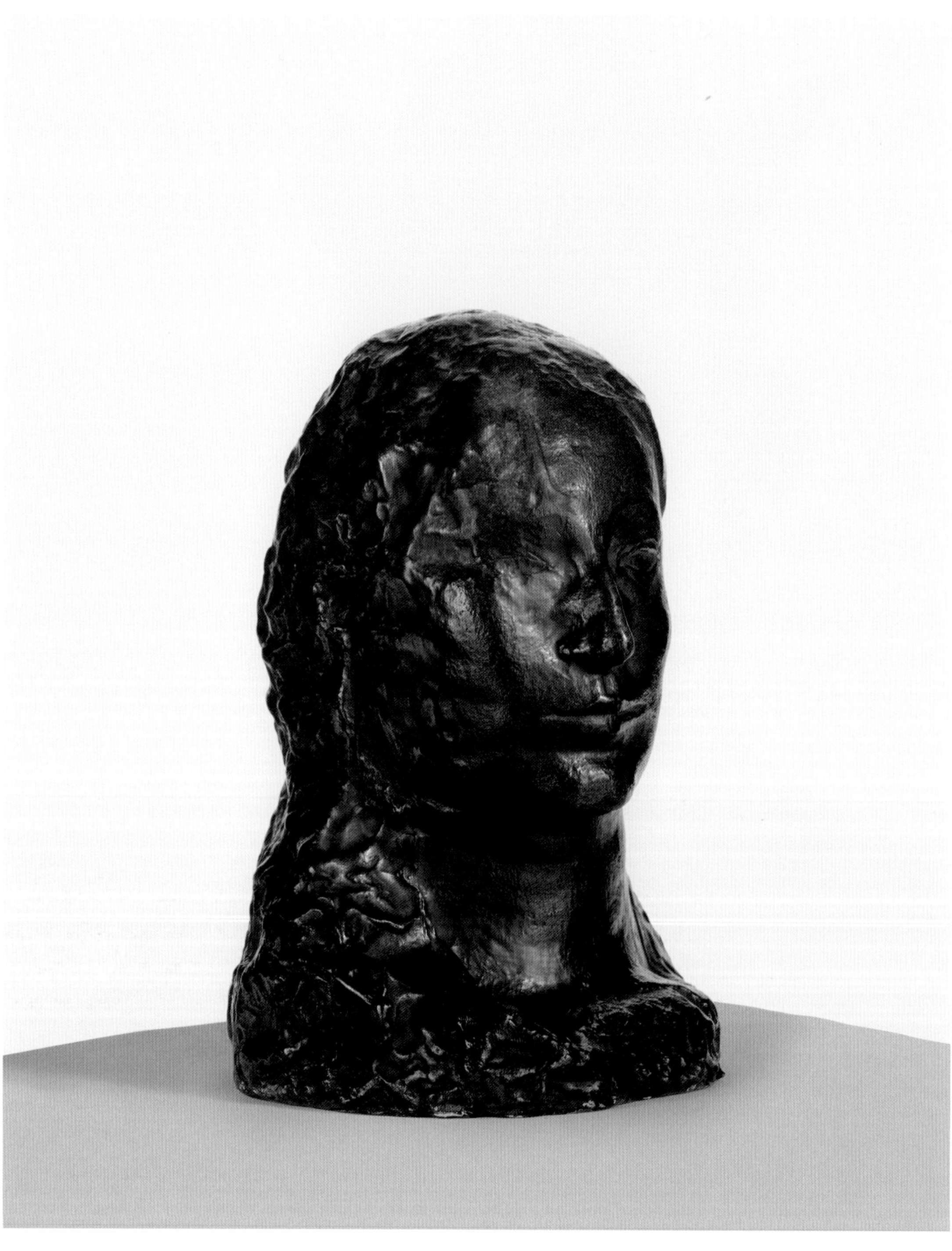

4. **HEAD OF A WOMAN (FERNANDE).** Paris, 1906
Bronze, cast between 1910 and 1937
13 ¾ × 9 ⁷⁄₁₆ × 9 ¹³⁄₁₆ in. (35 × 24 × 25 cm)
Musée d'art moderne de la Ville de Paris. Gift of Ambroise Vollard

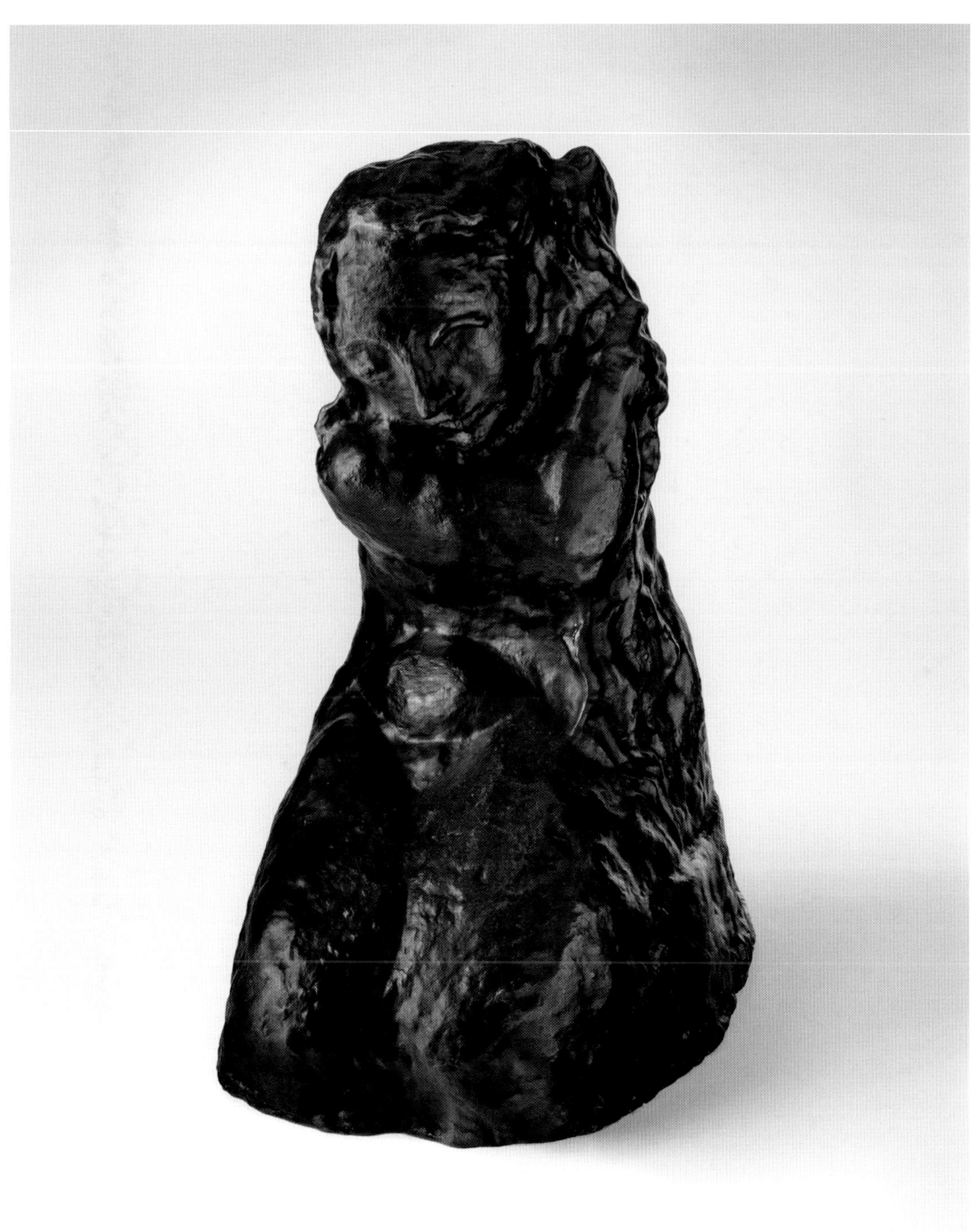

5. **KNEELING WOMAN COMBING HER HAIR.** Paris, 1906
Bronze, cast between 1910 and 1939
16 ⅝ × 10 $^{3}/_{16}$ × 12 ½ in. (42.2 × 25.9 × 31.8 cm)
Hirshhorn Museum and Sculpture Garden, Smithsonian Institution,
Washington, D.C. Gift of Joseph H. Hirshhorn

CHAPTER 2

WOOD CARVING AND THE FIRST CUBIST SCULPTURES 1907–1909

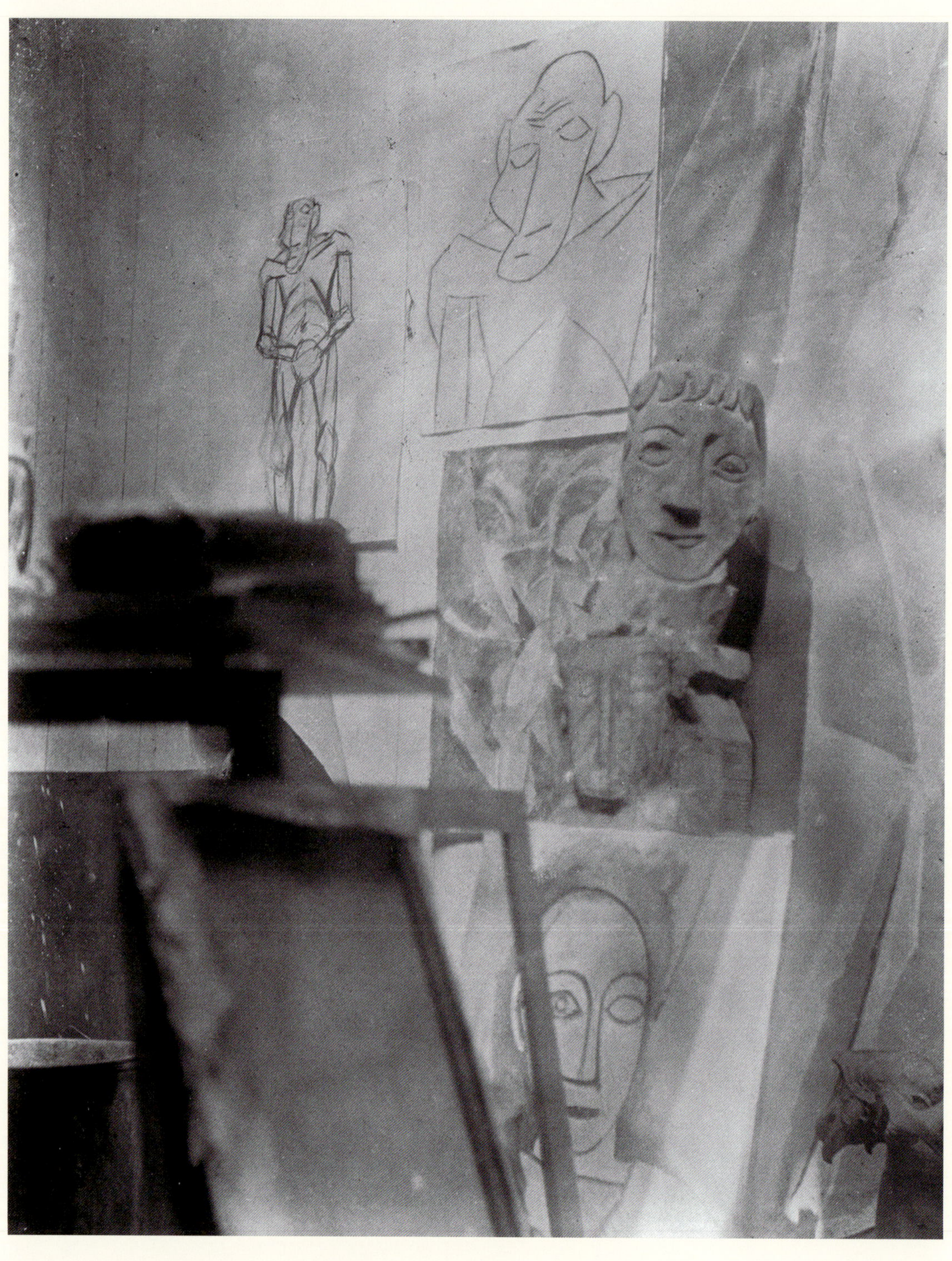

Artworks in Picasso's Bateau-Lavoir studio, with the sculptures *Head* (1907) and *Figure* (1908) stacked at center right, Paris, spring 1908. Photograph by the artist. Musée national Picasso–Paris

BETWEEN 1907 AND 1909 Picasso altered not only his own path as an artist but also the course of twentieth-century art. In the methodical yet startlingly dramatic elucidation of Cubism, Picasso and his friend Georges Braque invented a new language for modern painting. Its ramifications extended around the world and changed forever the relationship between visual experience and pictorial representation.

Although Cubism was elaborated primarily in paintings and drawings, a sculptural perspective propelled its fundamental researches. Picasso biographer and scholar Roland Penrose wrote that while the Cubist artist acted as a painter, "he thought as a sculptor."[1] Similarly, the photographer Brassaï observed of Picasso's Cubism that "sculpture was lurking like a virtuality deep within his paintings themselves."[2] Analytic Cubism translates three-dimensional objects and figures into two-dimensional space by simultaneously providing multiple viewpoints; this is essentially a sculptural solution to a painterly problem. Gazing at an early Cubist painting, one almost feels Picasso turning, segmenting, and carving the subject that will materialize from his colored lines and planes.

This is first true in the works of 1906–07, when Picasso's keen interest in Iberian and then African sculptures made its presence fully felt in his art. The epochal painting *Les Demoiselles d'Avignon*, made in summer 1907 after months of preparatory study, explicitly acknowledges these catalysts to a new way of seeing, particularly in the disjunctive African mask–like heads of three of its five protagonists. The paintings of the year following *Les Demoiselles d'Avignon* could almost be portrayals of wooden sculptures, so solid and blocky are the forms they depict; even their palettes evoke the hues of rich woods, together with forest greens. Figural drawings feature colored hatchings and schematized forms that suggest nothing so much as a carver working with a knife.

Only a handful of sculptures accompany these innovations; it was Western painting, not sculpture, that Picasso was then intent on reinventing. In 1907 and early 1908 Picasso set knife to wood to make fewer than ten surviving sculptures, all but one less than twenty inches tall (pls. 6–9). Described by an American journalist who visited Picasso's studio as "hideosities," these works conjure female heads or figures from salvaged chunks of wood. Their closest precedents in French art are Paul Gauguin's turn-of-the-century carvings inspired by his stays in the South Pacific. Some of Picasso's objects are freestanding, while others require support; some are strictly frontal, while others operate fully in the round. The one large-scale work is a standing figure in the flat-topped form of a caryatid. Carved from an old oak beam, it is manifestly unfinished. The figure's face is present only as painted red lines, traces of which also remain within the roughly hewn contours of torso, arms, and legs.

During the course of 1909, Picasso and Braque developed the Cubist language in a direction inspired by the paintings of Paul Cézanne. The Catalonian village of Horta de Ebro (present-day Horta de Sant Joan), where Picasso spent the summer, provided a rocky hilltop terrain that physically incarnated the structural system he was beginning to craft in his painting. Picasso's landscape paintings portray the rugged topography in accumulations of planes in which light and shadow articulate depth and relief, solid and void. Fifteen portrait paintings of the artist's companion, Fernande Olivier, share the luminous solidity of the landscapes. These were followed by one sculpture, made after Picasso returned to Paris that autumn: *Head of a Woman* (pl. 11), modeled in clay in the studio of the Spanish sculptor Manolo and cast in bronze in 1910. Uncannily close to the drawings and paintings that preceded it, the angular sculpture reimagines the rounded form of a turning head, the curved features of a face, and the soft shape of pulled-back hair. It is as if the sharp inclines and steep ridges of the portraits had transformed themselves into three dimensions. The model for the sculpture was, in effect, the Olivier created by the paintings of the summer and not the flesh-and-blood woman with whom Picasso shared his life.

Other than a small, unresolved *Head*, only the life-sized plaster *Apple* (pl. 10) joins *Head of a Woman* in returning Picasso's painterly investigations full circle to sculpture. Although facsimiles of fruit are abundant in the realm of the decorative arts, surely this is an apple's first appearance as sculpture qua sculpture. Its modest size and quotidian subject belie its magical presence. Most simply, the work re-creates an apple, its rounded body and shiny, smooth surface transformed into a blocky aggregate of matte, jagged planes. But at the same time the whole conveys a strong sense of topography; this small apple could also be the hilltop village of Horta de Ebro, birthplace of Picasso's Cubist language of 1909.

SPRING 1906: Picasso, Guillaume Apollinaire, Max Jacob, and the poet and critic André Salmon were in the habit of meeting Henri Matisse for dinner on most Thursday evenings. Jacob would later report, "I think it was at Matisse's that Picasso saw Negro sculpture, or at least was struck by it, for the first time."[1] Matisse, on the other hand, recalled that he had introduced Picasso to African sculpture at Gertrude Stein's apartment.[2] Matisse and Stein probably each had a share in the artist's first encounter with these objects, which both of them collected. Matisse eloquently summarized the attraction African sculpture held for the diverse group of avant-garde artists and intellectuals who were then looking for inspiration outside their own culture: "Compared to European sculpture, which always took its point of departure from musculature and started from the description of the object, these Negro statues were made in terms of their material, according to invented planes and proportions."[3] Beginning in summer 1906, Picasso's acquaintance with African and Oceanic artifacts, together with his continued interest in Iberian sculpture and the work of Paul Gauguin, would inspire him to move from working in clay and ceramic to experimenting with the direct carving of wood, stone, and plaster.

LATE APRIL 1906: Picasso saw a collection of works by Gauguin belonging to the French painter, designer, and potter Gustave Fayet on or around April 23, 1906.[4] Fayet, who was one of Picasso's first patrons, had moved to Paris from Béziers in 1905. He owned numerous wooden sculptures and ceramics by Gauguin, in addition to paintings and works on paper.[5] Fayet's collection included the partly enameled stoneware deity figure *Oviri*, which Gauguin had made in 1894 and left with his patron before returning to Tahiti in June 1895 (fig. 1).[6]

LATE SPRING–SUMMER 1906: Picasso and Fernande Olivier arrived in Barcelona on May 21, 1906. They subsequently traveled to Gósol, in the Pyrenees, where they spent the months of June and July. During their stay Picasso created his first wooden sculptures, and he repeatedly requested materials and tools from the sculptor Enric Casanovas in Barcelona. On June 27 Picasso wrote to his friend, "I continue working and this week they brought me a piece of wood and I'll begin something. Tell me a few days before you come so that I can answer you, because I may want you to bring some *eynas* [*sic*; chisels] to work the wood."[7] Having not received a reply, he sent another letter in July: "Could you send me in the same package two or three small *eines* to work in wood?"[8] Casanovas did not visit, and it is not known if the tools arrived. A typhoid outbreak forced the couple to make a sudden departure from the village; they returned to Paris in August.

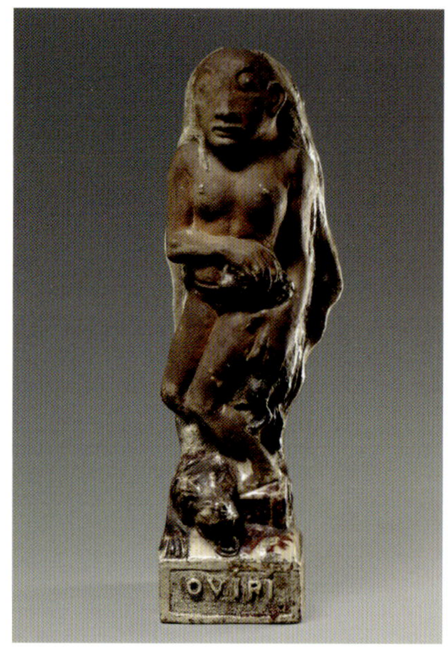

1. Paul Gauguin. *Oviri*. 1894. Partially enameled stoneware, 29 9/16 × 7 1/2 × 10 5/8 in. (75 × 19 × 27 cm). Musée d'Orsay, Paris

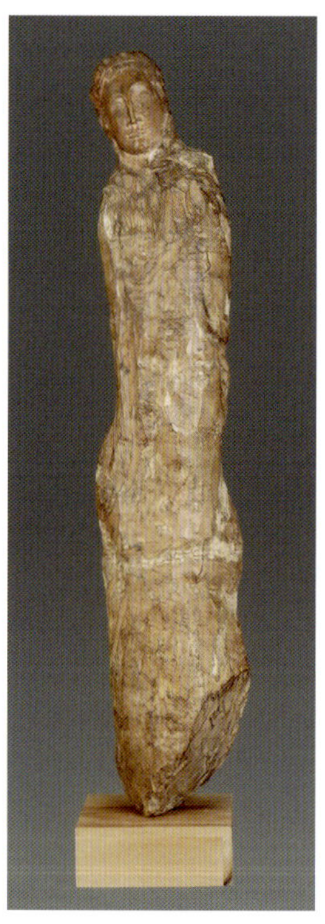

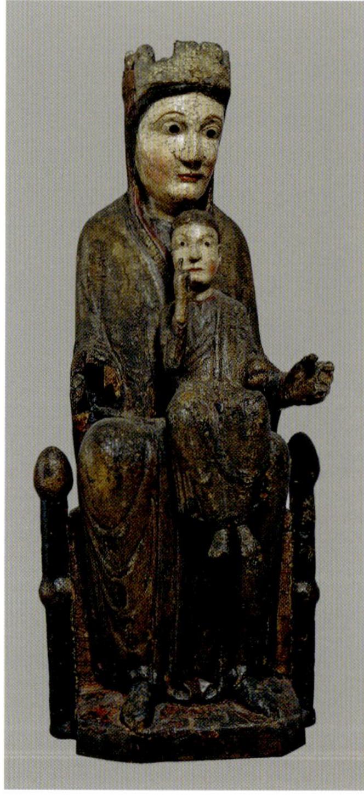

2. Pablo Picasso. *Bust of a Woman (Fernande)*. Gósol, summer 1906. Carved wood with traces of red and strokes of black paint, 30 5/16 × 6 11/16 × 6 5/16 in. (77 × 17 × 16 cm). Musée national Picasso–Paris. Dation Pablo Picasso

3. Gósol Madonna. From the church of Santa Maria in the castle of Gósol (Berguedà), Spain. 1150–99. Polychrome woodcarving with remains of varnished metal plate, 33 11/16 × 15 9/16 × 12 5/8 in. (85.5 × 39.5 × 32 cm). Museu Nacional d'Art de Catalunya, Barcelona

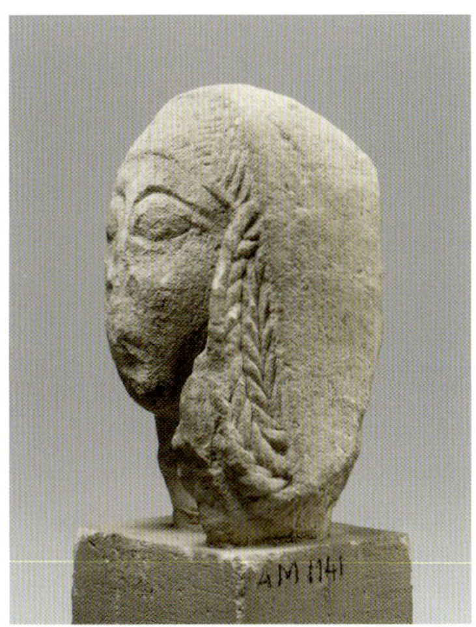

4. Head of a woman. Iberian sculpture from Cerro de los Santos, Spain. 400–200 BCE. Stone, 18 ⅛ × 10 ⅝ × 6 ¹¹⁄₁₆ in. (46 × 27 × 17 cm) Musée d'Archéologie nationale, Saint-Germain-en-Laye, France

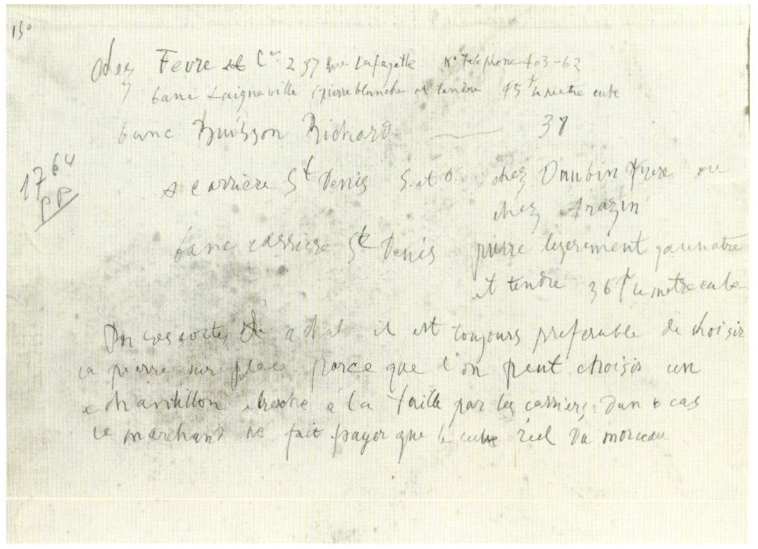

6. Notes by Picasso regarding stone available from quarries near Paris on the inside front cover of his notebook of March–July 1907. Musée national Picasso–Paris

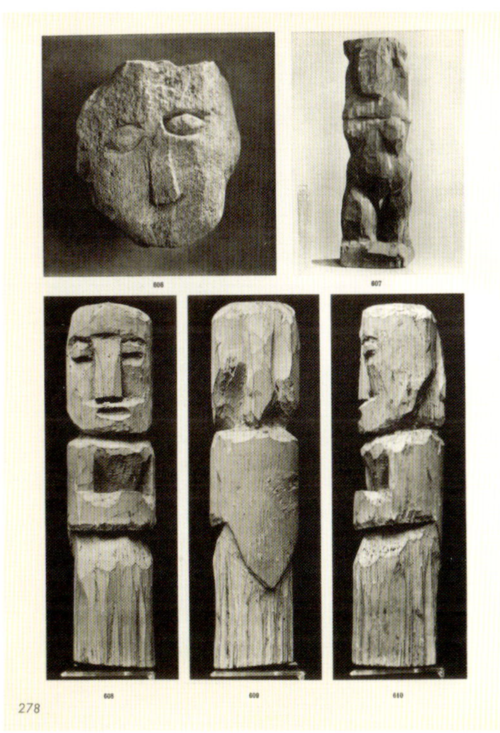

5. Picasso's stone *Head*, top left, reproduced in Christian Zervos, *Pablo Picasso*, vol. 2, part 2 (Paris: Éditions "Cahiers d'Art," 1942), plate 278, no. 606

Close inspection of *Bust of a Woman (Fernande)* (fig. 2) reveals that the artist whittled a found piece of wood with a simple knife, and then applied color. One stimulus for this might have been the Gósol Madonna (fig. 3), a twelfth-century polychrome wooden statue with stylized features that Picasso likely saw that summer.[9]

OCTOBER 6–NOVEMBER 15, 1906: Woodcarvings and ceramic sculptures were among the 227 objects presented in a retrospective of Gauguin's work at the fourth Salon d'Automne.[10] Picasso had already shown considerable interest in Gauguin, and the woodcarvings he would work on following the exhibition have much in common with *Oviri*, which was among the sculptures on view. Fayet, Picasso's friend Paco Durrio, and the dealer Ambroise Vollard were among the most generous lenders to the exhibition.[11]

MARCH 1907: Picasso purchased one of two Iberian stone heads that Géry Pieret, Apollinaire's sometime secretary, had stolen from the Louvre earlier that month (fig. 4).[12] Pieret also left the second head at the Bateau-Lavoir studio, although the artist had refused to buy it.[13]

Four years later, this purchase would involve Apollinaire and Picasso in what has come to be known as "l'affaire des statuettes." Following the theft of the *Mona Lisa* from the Louvre on August 21, 1911, Pieret, in hope of a reward, contacted the *Paris-Journal* newspaper with an account of the earlier burglary and sale of the statuettes. The paper began reporting the story on August 29. To avoid implication in a crime he had not committed, Apollinaire convinced Picasso to "get rid of the compromising objects immediately," Olivier later wrote.[14] On September 5, Apollinaire, who had been providing Pieret with on-and-off support, submitted the stolen goods to the newspaper's editors. He was subsequently arrested, and police investigations ensued that also involved Picasso. This episode caused a brief scandal, but their names were ultimately cleared.

During this period Picasso attempted to carve a small stone head (fig. 5), but the material, difficult to work with, may not have provided the immediate gratification the artist

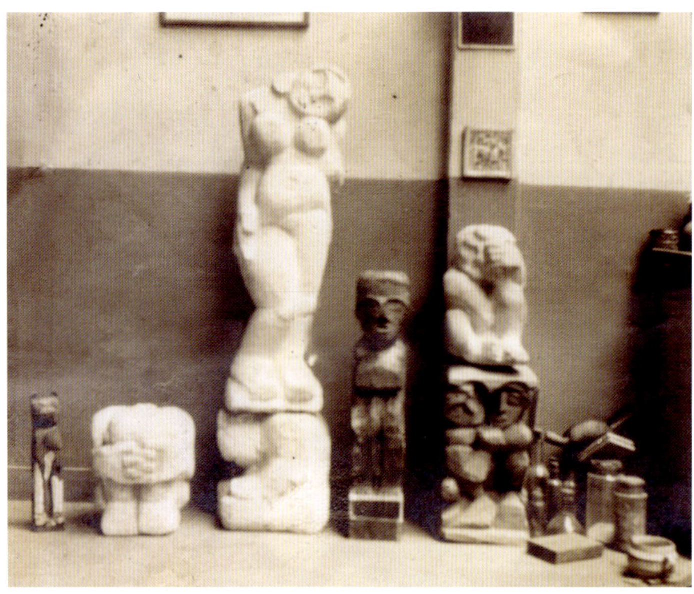

7. André Derain's studio at 22, rue de Tourlaque, with *Crouching Figure* and *Standing Female Nude* (second and third from left, respectively), Paris, spring–summer 1908. Photograph by Gelett Burgess. Archives Taillade

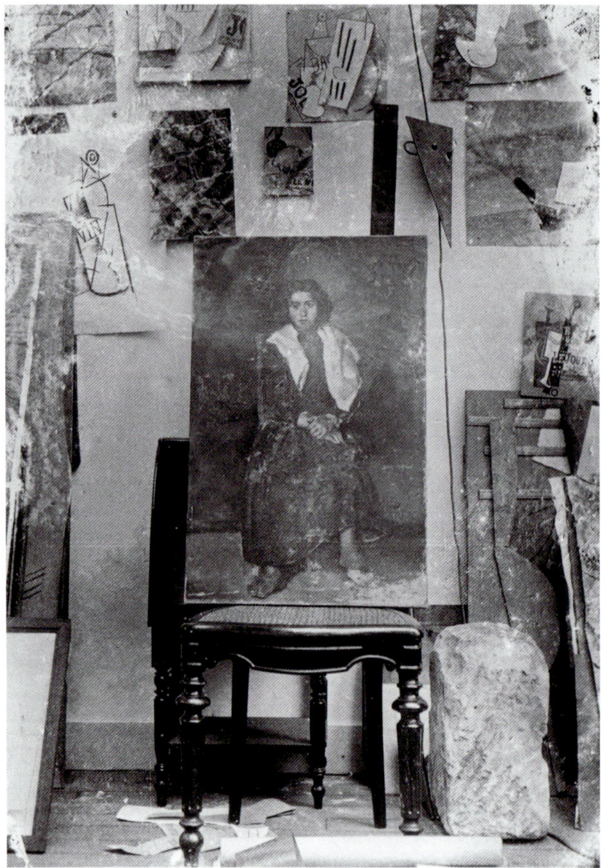

8. Picasso's studio at 5 *bis*, rue Schoelcher, with a partially carved and chiseled block of stone next to the artist's painting *Girl with Bare Feet* (early 1895; Musée national Picasso–Paris), Paris, spring 1908. Photograph probably by the artist. Musée nationale Picasso–Paris

sought; he gave up and switched to wood.[15] However, he made detailed notes in his imperfect French about the types of stone available at quarries north of Paris (fig. 6).[16] He described a "white, tender stone [for] 45 francs per cubic meter" at the stone reserve in Laigneville and a "slightly yellowish and soft stone [for] 36 francs per cubic meter" at a quarry in Saint-Denis.[17] Picasso also carefully wrote down the following instructions: "For such purchases it is always preferable to select the stone on site for fear that it is chipped while being cut at the quarry."[18] The family of André Derain lived near the quarries, and it seems plausible that Picasso obtained the information from him. Derain had been in regular contact with the Spanish artist since 1906, when he moved into an atelier within walking distance of the Bateau-Lavoir.[19] Like Matisse and Gauguin, Derain was a painter-sculptor as well as a fervent collector of non-Western art. He had developed an interest in African art on visiting the anthropological collection of the British Museum during three trips to London in 1906 and had purchased a Fang mask as early as the summer of that year.[20] In 1907 Derain made a stone carving, titled *Crouching Figure*, that might have inspired Picasso to experiment with the medium (fig. 7). A partially carved and chiseled block of stone is visible in a photograph taken a few years later at Picasso's rue Schoelcher studio (fig. 8).

MAY OR JUNE 1907: At Derain's urging, Picasso visited the Musée d'Ethnographie du Trocadéro (fig. 9). His encounter there with sculpture from the African continent and Oceania would have a deep and lasting effect on his work, and it directly influenced *Les Demoiselles d'Avignon* (The Museum of Modern Art, New York), which Picasso completed that July. Thirty years later, in an exchange with André Malraux, Picasso would recall,

> When I went to the old Trocadéro, . . . I was all alone. I wanted to get away. But I didn't leave. I stayed. I stayed. I understood something very important: something was happening to me, wasn't it? The [African] masks weren't like other kinds of sculpture. Not at all. They were magical things. And why weren't the Egyptian or the Chaldean pieces [magical]? We hadn't realized it. Those were primitive [archaic], not magical things. The Negro pieces were intercessors. . . . All alone in that awful museum, the masks, the Red Indian dolls, the dusty mannequins. *Les Demoiselles d'Avignon* must have come to me that day.[21]

SUMMER 1907: Picasso turned in earnest to wood carving. He had become well acquainted with Gauguin's work and was, Marilyn McCully writes, "keen to understand, if not appropriate, the stylistic means by which Gauguin had transformed 'primitivism' in his own art."[22] In addition, his imagination and vision had been transformed through his experience at the Trocadéro. Picasso carved and incised the material, retaining the structure, shape, and rough quality of the pieces of wood he had selected, much as the makers of the museum's African spirit figures, masks, and statues had done.

***HEAD*, 1907**

To make the large *Head* of 1907 (pl. 9), Picasso carved and then painted a fragment of beech wood. The sculpture's distinct facial features—the carefully outlined strands of hair across the forehead, the heavy-lidded eyes, the large ears—have often been noted as closely resembling the Iberian stone head of a man Pieret had left with Picasso in March. Yet the artist was careful not to imitate. He worked in another medium, and he applied color. He had abandoned his earlier carving in stone, but here he persevered, encouraged, perhaps, by the African masks he had encountered at the Trocadéro. *Head* is closely related to the three masked figures Picasso had repainted in *Les Demoiselles d'Avignon* after his visit to the museum.

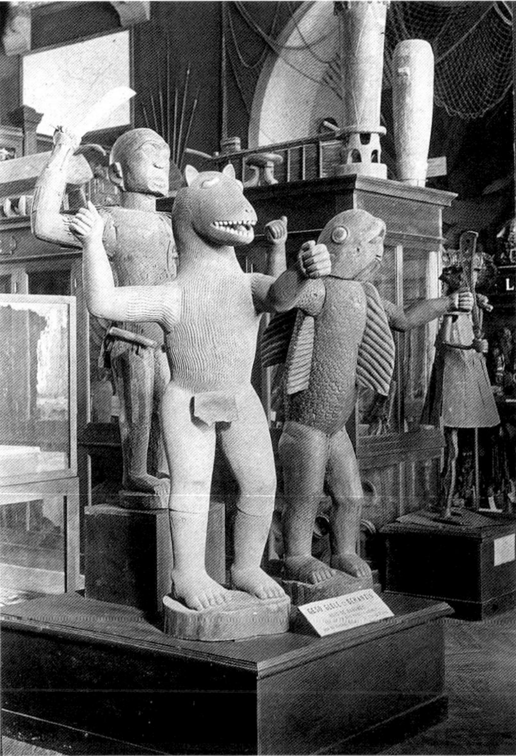

9. A gallery at the Musée d'Ethnographie du Trocadéro, with standing Fon sculptures, Paris, 1895. Musée du quai Branly, Paris

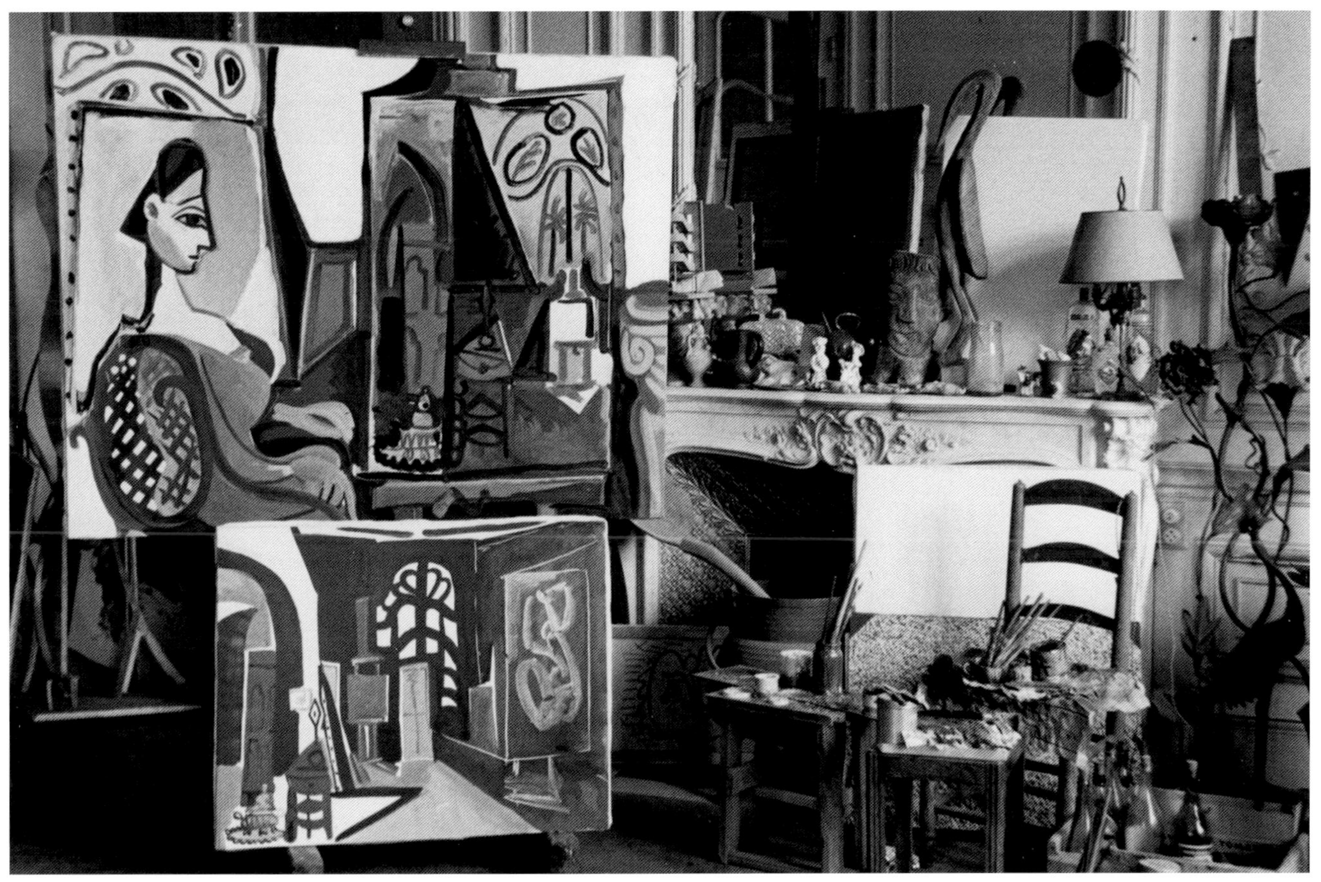

10. Artworks at Picasso's villa La Californie, with *Head* on the mantelpiece at center, Cannes, c. 1955. Photograph by Roland Penrose. Picasso Archives, Musée national Picasso–Paris

Head, like most of the artist's early woodcarvings, would not be exhibited during his lifetime. But it was prominently displayed in Picasso's Bateau-Lavoir studio shortly after it was made, placed on top of the large oak *Figure* of early 1908 (see p. 50). In the company of other recent works, the carvings seem to embody the talismanic nature Picasso bestowed on his sculptures. He considered them his intimates and they moved with him from residence to residence and studio to studio. About five decades later, *Head* would be photographed sitting on a mantelpiece at the artist's villa La Californie, in Cannes (fig. 10).

FIGURE AND *DOLL*, 1907

Picasso made *Figure* and *Doll* from single pieces of recycled wood (pls. 7, 6).[23] In carving them he again followed the shape of the material but allowed the whittling process to remain visible. In *Figure*, which features a masklike face with a long, geometricized nose, Picasso "retain[ed] the curve and rough quality of the lower part of the wood," Marilyn McCully points out.[24] For *Doll* he transformed a turned chair leg into a small, saucer-eyed figurine with a blocky nose and plump lips, adding brass pins for the eyes.[25] The majority of the African and Oceanic sculptures he had seen were made from pieces of found wood with added materials like feathers, string, hair, and metal.

Picasso made *Doll* as a toy for Germaine "Mémène" Fornerod, the daughter of a friend from his early years in Paris.[26] The small sculpture would reenter his life in the mid- to late 1950s, when Germaine's mother, Antoinette, wrote to Picasso. He authenticated the work and, in 1961, helped her sell *Doll* to the Galerie Louise Leiris in Paris. Three years later, he agreed to have an edition of twelve bronzes made. It is the only wood-carving among the seven figures he produced in this period that was cast in bronze.

FIGURE, 1908

In early 1908 Picasso made by far the largest of the wooden figures he carved during this period. Historically, the work has been dated to 1907, but Elizabeth Cowling argues that *Figure* (pl. 8) is closely related to a vibrant gouache-and-pastel drawing Picasso made in spring 1908 (fig. 11).[27] Unlike his earlier woodcarvings, which more closely resemble the African or Oceanic artifacts he admired and collected, *Figure* bridges two distinct traditions: the sculpture's motif of a standing woman carrying weight on her head echoes Greek caryatid figures, and the distribution of weight on one leg reveals the influence of African Fon sculpture, which the artist had likely encountered at the Trocadéro.[28] Red lines marked on the face and body are clues to where Picasso would have next carved the oak figure had he continued to work on the piece. Durable and hard, oak is a demanding material to hew, requiring expert skill and a set of iron tools, including axes, chisels, and gouges, that must be sharpened regularly. Cowling and other scholars agree that he may have left the object unfinished in part because the work did not proceed as quickly as he had hoped.[29]

Close examination of the back and left side of the sculpture reveal that Picasso began with "a large rectangular block with an almost square base" bearing a railway label.[30] The now torn label, showing some red paint, reads "Chemin de fer de l'Ouest—Destination Paris, Saint Lazare—exp.[edition] bagages." It is possible that he began carving *Figure* while vacationing in La Rue-des-Bois, the small French village where he and Olivier rented a cottage in August 1908, and later had the block shipped to Paris.[31] While there, the artist completed a series of paintings and drawings of their heavyset landlady, Madame Putnam.[32] The sculptural emphasis and simplified features in these works resonate with the hefty figure and rough surface of Picasso's large woodcarving. Derain, together with Apollinaire, visited La Rue-des-Bois for several days. The close rapport between the two artists at this period supports Cowling's idea that *Figure* may have been Picasso's response to Derain's *Standing Female Nude* (Centre Pompidou, Paris), a stone figure of similar height, pose, and reduced outline, albeit more resolved, made in fall 1907.[33] Derain's sculpture is pictured in a photograph taken by the American journalist Gelett Burgess during his visits to the artist's studio in spring–summer 1908 (see fig. 7, third from left).[34]

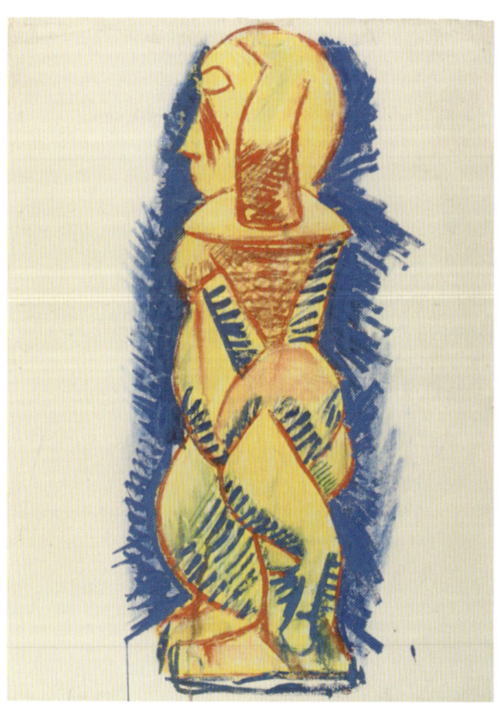

11. Pablo Picasso. *Standing Nude in Profile*. Spring 1908. Gouache and pastel, 24 5/8 × 18 5/16 in. (62.5 × 48 cm). Musée national Picasso–Paris

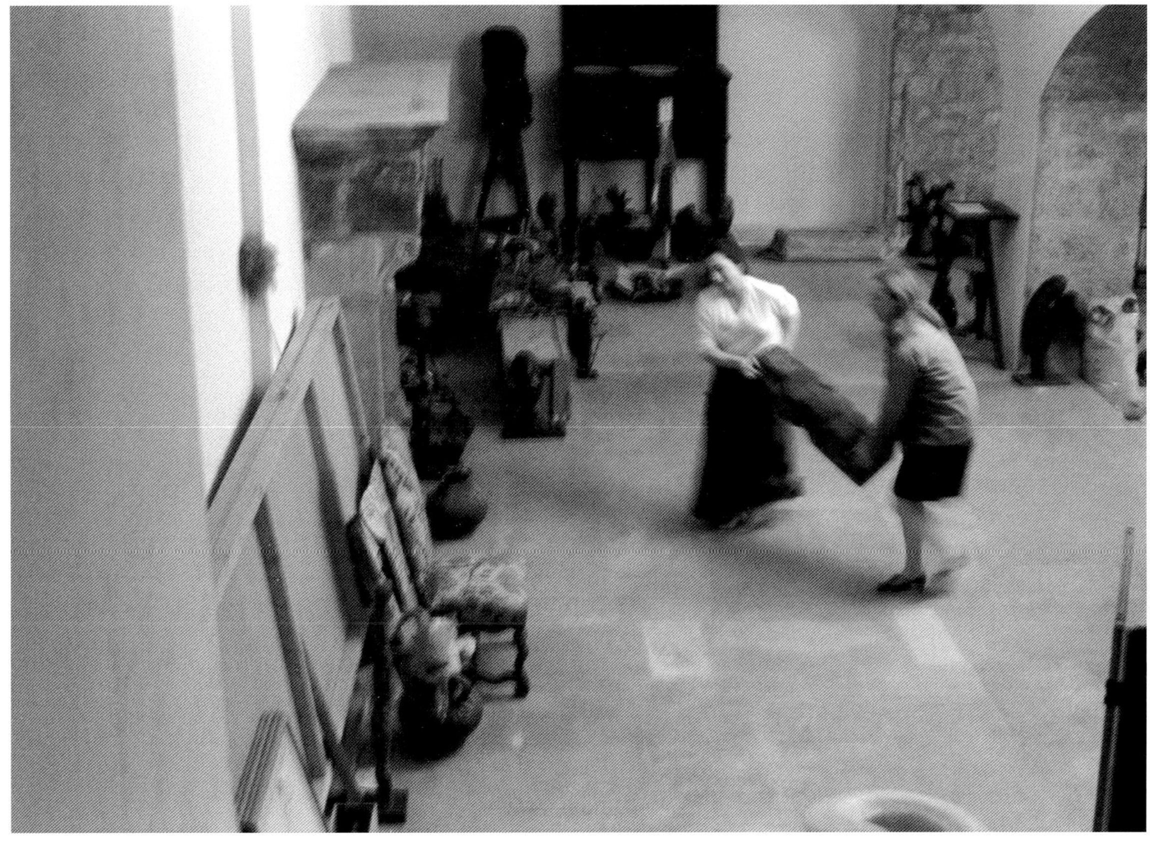

12. Picasso's studio at Notre-Dame-de-Vie, with the artist's wife, Jacqueline Picasso (left), and the curator and gallery director Joanna Drew carrying *Figure*, Mougins, January 1968. Photograph by Lee Miller. The Lee Miller Archives, London

Figure and a bronze cast of *Doll* would be the only works to represent Picasso's wood carving from this period in the historic exhibition *Hommage à Pablo Picasso*, at the Petit Palais, Paris, in 1966, and the subsequent exhibitions of his sculptures at the Tate Gallery, London, and The Museum of Modern Art.[35] A photograph records the return of *Figure* to the artist's studio at Notre-Dame-de-Vie in Mougins in January 1968 (fig. 12).

APRIL 29, 1908: The American author and journalist Inez Haynes Irwin visited Picasso's Bateau-Lavoir studio, where she saw recent works by the artist as well as the artifacts he was collecting. While Haynes Irwin found Picasso to be "a darling," his art impressed her less. Among the various objects she would later recall were "a mask from the Congo and some totem-pole like hideosities that he [Picasso] made himself."[36] Also that spring, Burgess visited Picasso, Derain, and other artists for an article on "The Wild Men of Paris."[37] Burgess chose to photograph Picasso surrounded by the sculptures he had collected—including works from the Congo, Gabon, and New Caledonia—rather than in front of his own work (fig. 13).[38]

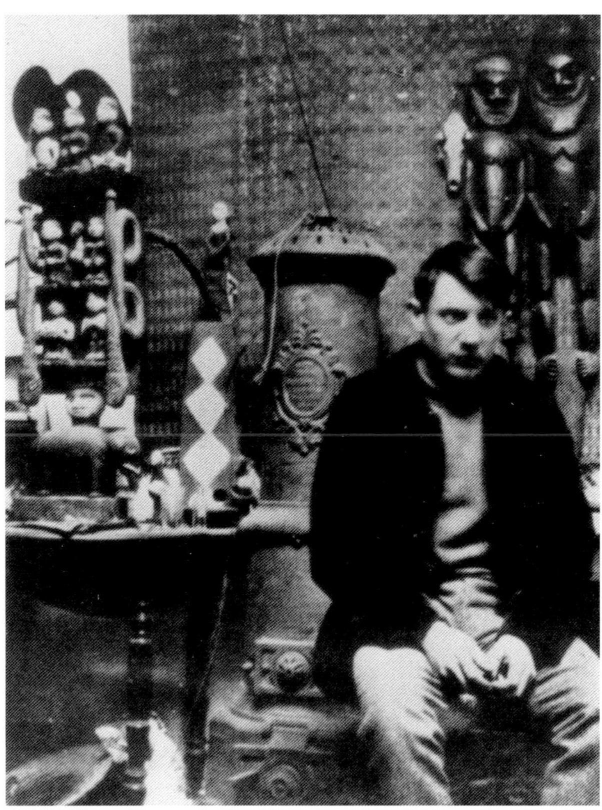

13. Picasso in his Bateau-Lavoir studio, Paris, May–July 1908. Photograph by Gelett Burgess. Musée national Picasso–Paris

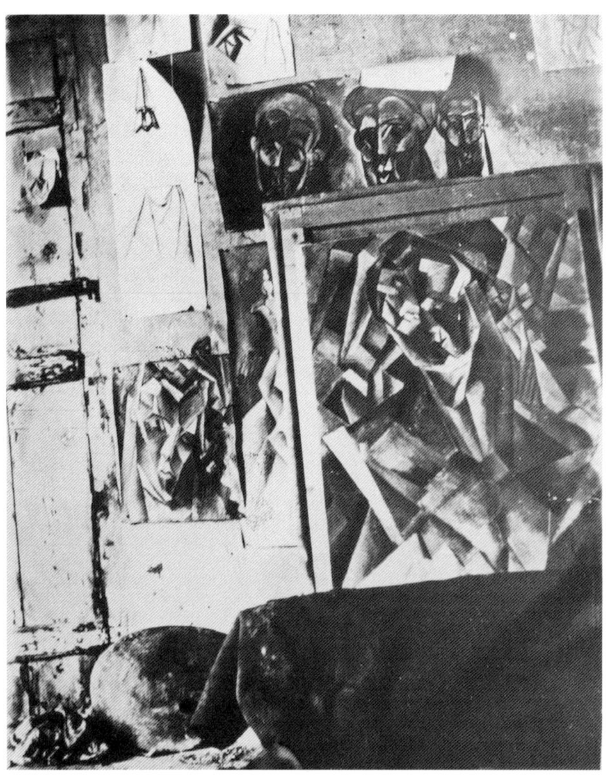

14. Picasso's studio in Horta de Ebro, Spain, with studies of facial features, such as a nose, an eye, and a neck, pinned to the wall (top left) and the paintings *Head of a Woman in a Mantilla* (bottom left; current location unknown) and *Seated Woman* (stretched, at right; private collection) among others, summer 1909. Photograph by the artist. Private collection

FALL 1908: Picasso and Georges Braque began the close partnership that would lead to the invention of Cubism. The two artists had met the previous spring and by fall 1908 each had developed a pictorial language that broke its subjects into planes and facets. Both men were engaged in an artistic dialogue with the work of Paul Cézanne, a preoccupation reflected not only in Picasso's paintings but also in the Cubist sculptures that would follow.

FALL 1909: Picasso and Olivier returned to Paris from a four-month stay in Barcelona and Horta de Ebro (present-day Horta de Sant Joan) around September 11. Shortly after, they moved into a new apartment at 11, boulevard de Clichy, leaving behind the Bateau-Lavoir abode they had shared since 1905. Picasso made no sculptures in Horta de Ebro, but the two-dimensional works he produced there have an architectonic, constructed quality and a distinct sculptural emphasis (fig. 14).

***HEAD OF A WOMAN*, FALL 1909**

In the weeks that followed his return to Paris, Picasso immersed himself in analyzing and condensing the images he had made in Horta de Ebro, eventually translating them into a synthesized form in sculpture. Modeled in clay in the studio of the Spanish sculptor Manolo in late September or early October 1909, *Head of a Woman* (pl. 11) is traditionally considered Picasso's first Cubist sculpture; it represents an initial, concentrated effort to realize Cubist principles in three dimensions.[39] To achieve this, Picasso fragmented Olivier's natural features into multiple abstract elements and then constructed an entirely new image of her from these pieces. Julio González would report in 1936 that Picasso thought of the Cubist segmentation of form in his early paintings as a reversible building exercise. According to González, Picasso declared that it would suffice "to cut up these paintings . . . —the colors only being in the end indications of different viewpoints, planes sloping one way or another—and then to assemble them according to the cues given by color, in order to find [himself] in the presence of a 'sculpture.'"[40] Another source of inspiration may have been the *écorchés* or flayed figure models used by artists to study musculature under the skin.[41] Years later, discussing *Head of a Woman* and the development of the Cubist language in three dimensions, Picasso would tell Roland Penrose, "I thought that the curves you see on the surface should continue into the interior. I had the idea of doing them in wire . . . [but] it was too intellectual, too much like painting."[42] He would not explore his ambitions of opening up the solid mass of his sculpture until 1912, when he created his first Cubist cardboard constructions (see pl. 13).

Vollard would buy *Head of a Woman* in 1910, along with four other clay sculptures, including *The Jester* of early 1905 (pl. 3). Valerie J. Fletcher suggests that this purchase took place "in or soon after September 1910," in time for an exhibition of the artist's work that the dealer had just announced.[43] The show opened on December 20, 1910, and ran through February 1911, but due to the lack of a catalogue or other documentation and the silence on the subject in reviews, it is not known whether any of Picasso's sculptures were exhibited. However, Vollard did begin the process of casting the works in bronze shortly after his purchase. Fletcher writes that Picasso visited a foundry to review a plaster cast of *Head of a Woman*, probably in fall 1910, and reworked areas, especially along the neck, with a knife in order to "reduce the modeled aspect and to make the angles more acute" (fig. 15).[44] In other areas, such as the face and hair, Picasso preserved the traces of his touch. Between 1910 and his death in 1939, Vollard would use this "master" plaster cast to issue an unnumbered edition of bronzes.[45]

The Czech art historian Vincenc Kramář was likely the first to acquire a bronze cast of *Head of a Woman*; he paid Vollard 600 French francs for the work on May 26, 1911.[46] He was followed by the American photographer and art dealer

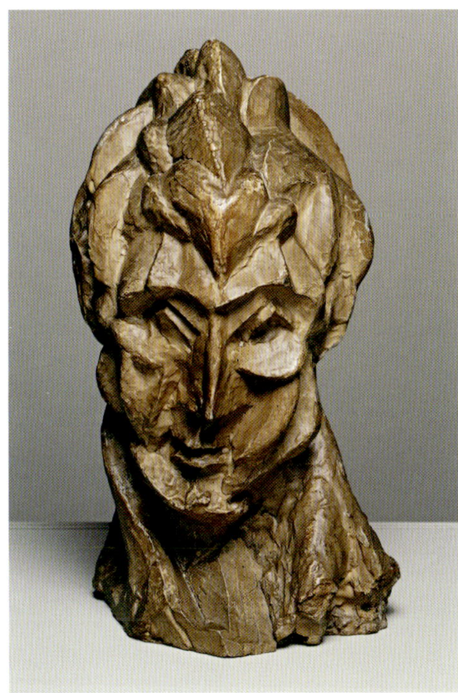

15. Pablo Picasso. *Head of a Woman*. Paris, 1909. Plaster, cast as early as late 1910, 16 ½ × 10 × 11 ½ in. (41.9 × 25.4 × 29.2 cm). The Latner Family Collection, Toronto. On long-term loan to Tate, London

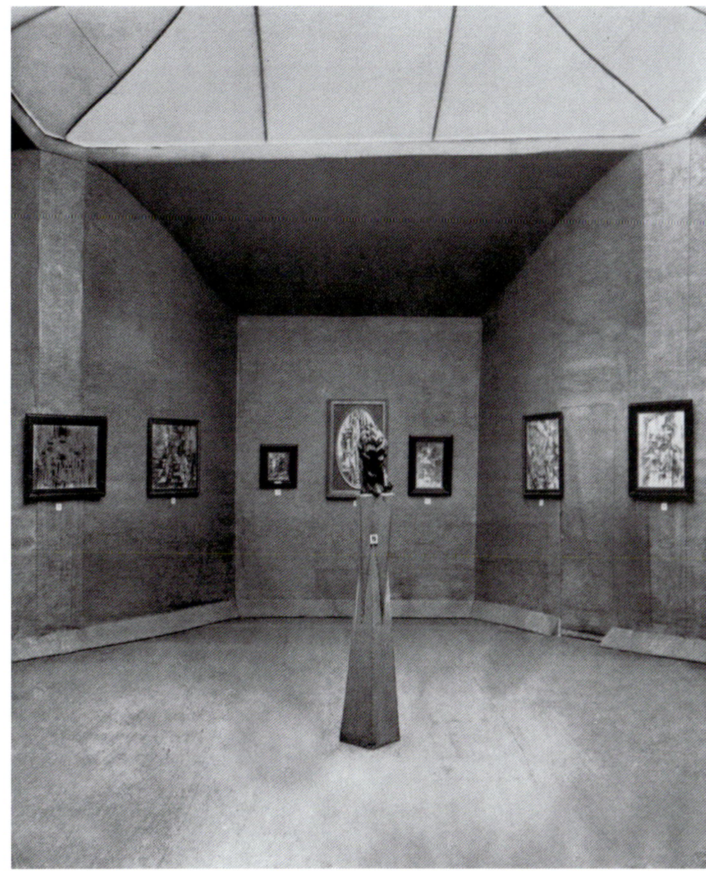

16. View of the *Third Exhibition of the Skupina Výtvarných Umělců* (Group of fine artists), with a bronze cast of *Head of a Woman* on the plinth at center, Obecní Dům Města, Prague, May–June 1913

Alfred Stieglitz, who purchased a bronze from Vollard on January 15, 1912, with the help of the photographer Edward Steichen (pl. 11).[47] Larger audiences in Eastern Europe and the United States would see both casts shortly thereafter: Stieglitz's was included in the *International Exhibition of Modern Art*—known as the Armory Show—in New York in spring 1913, and Kramář's was exhibited in Prague in early summer that same year, in the *Third Exhibition of the Skupina Výtvarných Umělců* (Group of fine artists) (fig. 16). Another bronze cast of *Head of a Woman* was presented in the inaugural show at Alfred Flechtheim's gallery in Düsseldorf that same year.[48] Vollard kept a cast of the sculpture on view in his Paris gallery to show to his customers, among whom it became a sensation.[49] A letter from the Czech painter Emil Filla to Kramář dated April 25, 1913, confirms that *Head of a Woman* was on view in the gallery that year.[50] The sculpture was also disseminated early on by way of reproductions. Stieglitz's photographs of his cast were included in a special issue of his journal *Camera Work* in August 1912 (fig. 17). Kramář's cast was reproduced in an installation photograph that accompanied a review of the 1913 Prague exhibition in the avant-garde Czech art journal *Umělecký měsíčník* (fig. 18).

By 1913 the sculpture had entered the discourse on both Picasso's work and modern sculpture in general. In his review of an exhibition of Futurist sculpture by the Italian painter and sculptor Umberto Boccioni, Apollinaire recalled

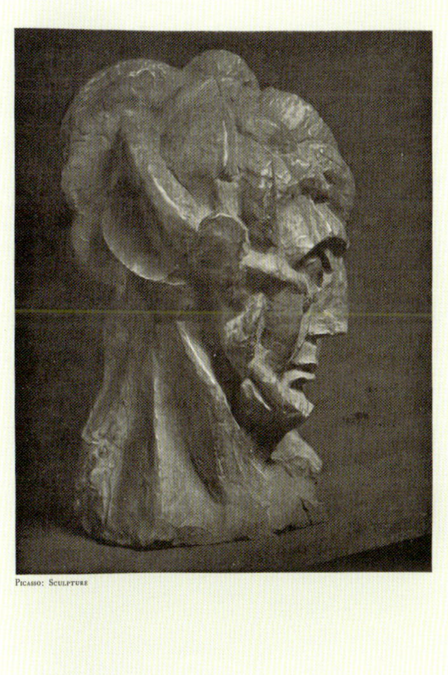

17. Bronze cast of *Head of a Woman* reproduced in *Camera Work*, special issue (August 1912): 44. Photograph by Alfred Stieglitz

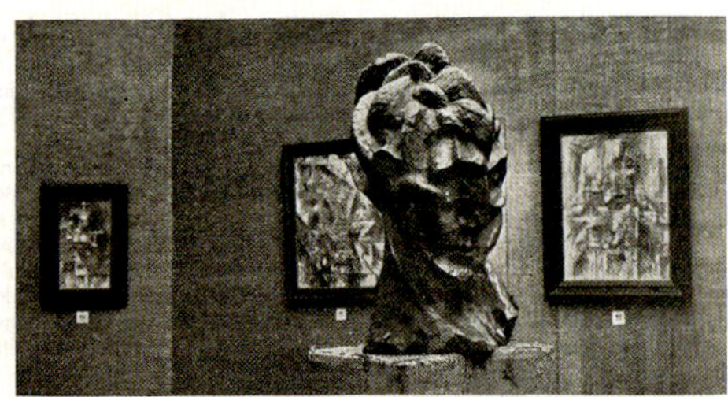

III. Výstava Skupiny v Obecním domě.
Z oddělení francouzského umění.

krajiny, postavy i zátiší pod jižním nebem. Podstatným prvkem, k němuž obrací Mattise celý soubor svého úsilí a zkušenosti, jest silná a čistá barva. Jest neuvěřitelno, jakými jednoduchými prostředky podařilo se mu rozvinouti veškeru nádheru jihu. Nepodává duši krajiny, věcí a lidí, pouze jejich vnějšek, ale tak mistrně a pregnantně, že chceme vysloviti již slovo „virtuosita", jež vyjadřuje již zároveň určitý chlad a vypočítavost. Obrazy určeny jsou konečně pro hudební sál, takže jest ospravedlněn jejich ryze dekorativní ráz. Viktor Wallerstein, Berlín.

K. Coellen: Nové malířství.

(Dokončení.)

Čistý lyrism, k němuž Matisse dospěl přes Gauguina, je prvním a nejbezprostřednějším způsobem nazírání, který navazuje na přírodu mohl splniti nové snažení po zduchovnění: duchovní podstata věcí musila zde být odhalena ve svém stavu jevícím se na věcech a v hodnotě toho stavu, t. j. jako citová oblast, jíž věci jsou neseny. Modernímu člověku nutně vše připadalo jako mimolidská, objektivní oblast mysli, která rozmanitostí věcí získává rozmanitost své hodnoty; v malířství, ve vytváření vnějšího prostoru, byla ona oblast nejdříve umělecky odkryta. Leč byla pouze povrchovým zjevením duchovního světa, kdežto romantik je puzen až k základům. Chce víc než odůvodnit pouhý stav, chce, jako usiloval van Gogh po původu sil, projeviti zákon, původní zákon tohoto duchovního, jeho vnitřní podstatu; chce zdůvodniti a uzpůsobiti živoucí aktivitu, v níž se ona citová oblast rodí.

Z této umělecké vůle, která přirozeně působí jen jako zvláštní způsob nazírání, povstává dílo Pabla Picassa. A povstává v podivuhodné důslednosti jako forma, která byla nazvána kubismus. Nikde v tomto celém vývoji malířského stylu nejeví se tak jasně jako u Picassa, že práce a dobytí je

192

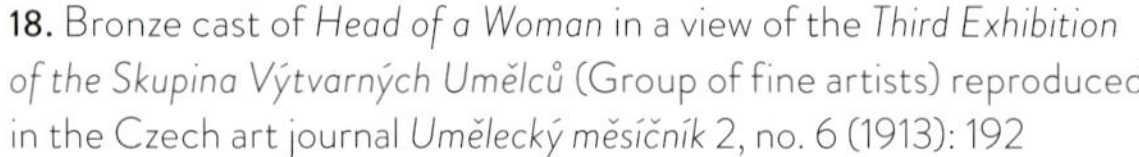

18. Bronze cast of *Head of a Woman* in a view of the *Third Exhibition of the Skupina Výtvarných Umělců* (Group of fine artists) reproduced in the Czech art journal *Umělecký měsíčník* 2, no. 6 (1913): 192

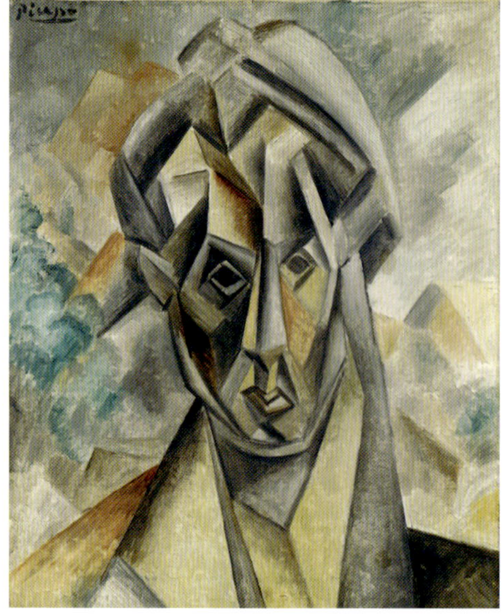

19. Pablo Picasso. *Head of a Woman (Fernande Olivier)*. Horta de Ebro, summer 1909. Oil on canvas, 25 9/16 × 21 7/16 in. (65 × 54.5 cm). Städelscher Museums-Verein eV, Frankfurt am Main

having observed the same dynamism in *Head of a Woman* three years prior, describing it as "a bronze in which [Picasso] concentrated the greatest possible quantity of light."[51] A year later, the Russian literary critic and poet Ivan A. Aksenov discussed the work in the context of the artist's development and, in particular, the invention of Cubism. Perhaps by mistake, Aksenov referred to the sculpture as "a cycle of wax heads" in a manuscript, dated June 1914, that would be included as an appendix in his 1917 monograph on Picasso, published in Moscow.[52] Over the next decades, *Head of a Woman* would become one of Picasso's most famous sculptures.

Many different titles have been assigned to this work, including some that identify the subject as a man. The receipt Vollard issued to Kramář gives the title as *Tête d'homme* (Head of a man); in the dealer's files the work is described as *Buste* (Bust), *Tête* (Head), or *Tête de femme* (Head of a woman).[53] In 1913 the sculpture appeared under at least three different titles: *Bust* at the Armory Show, *Hlava* (Head) in the catalogue for the Prague exhibition, and *Frauenkopf* (Female head) in the Galerie Flechtheim catalogue.[54] The catalogues for the 1932 retrospective of Picasso's work, presented in Paris at the Galeries Georges Petit and then at the Kunsthaus Zürich, refer to the work as *Buste d'homme* and *Männerbüste* (Bust of a man).[55]

Contradictory interpretations of the gender of Picasso's subjects were common in the reception of his early Cubist sculptures. In the case of *Head of a Woman*, determination of the subject's gender may depend upon viewpoint: the forward-tilted head, full lips, right eye, and cheekbone are typically feminine, while the left eye and cheek, full right profile, and back may read as masculine. This ambiguity is also apparent in a number of the paintings and drawings that Picasso made of Olivier at Horta de Ebro that summer. While a great number of them portray her in domestic settings that include feminine attributes such as flowers and fruit or depict more of her body, including her breasts, the paintings that lack these details are relatively ageless and sexless (fig. 19). Jeffrey Weiss distinguishes between the portraits of Olivier made during the summer and the images of women Picasso created in spring 1909 and fall 1909–winter 1910, before and after his stay at Horta de Ebro.[56] In the second category, which includes *Head of a Woman*, Picasso isolated elements and features associated with Olivier to create images that do not depict her as an individual, but rather as a female type. The anatomical characteristics portrayed in the sculpture are closer to the solutions Picasso had previously worked out in two dimensions. Aksenov, who probably saw Picasso's depictions of Fernande in spring 1914, wrote that the similarity between *Head of a*

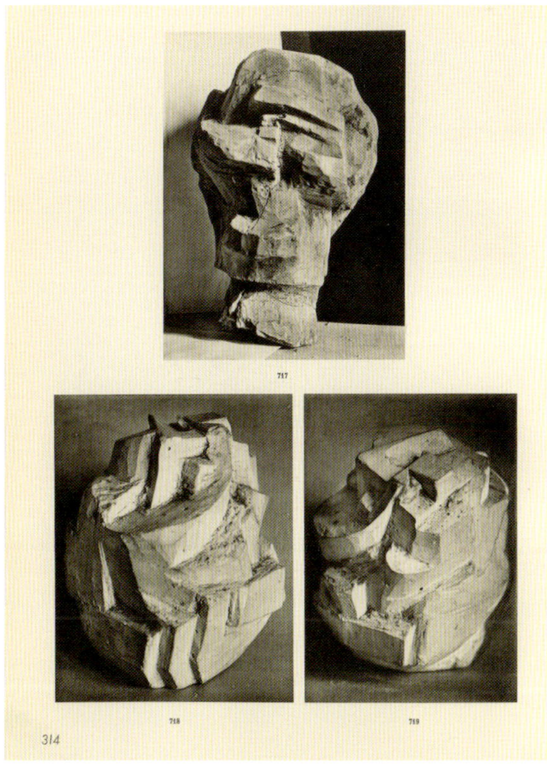

20. *Head* (top) and *Apple* (bottom) reproduced in Christian Zervos, *Pablo Picasso*, vol. 2, part 2 (Paris: Éditions "Cahiers d'Art," 1942), plate 314, nos. 717–19

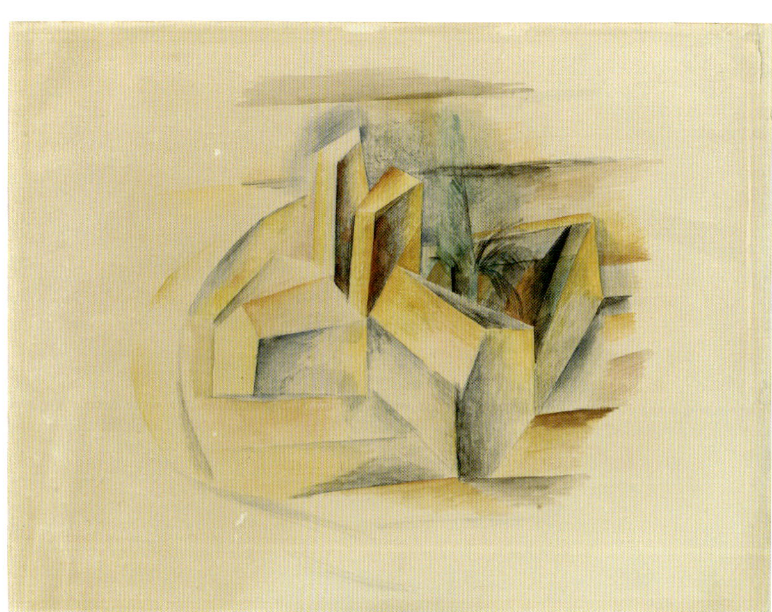

21. Pablo Picasso. *The Mill at Horta*. Horta de Ebro, summer 1909. Watercolor on paper, 9 ¾ × 15 in. (24.8 × 38.2 cm). The Museum of Modern Art, New York. The Joan and Lester Avnet Collection

Woman and the two-dimensional works "amounts almost to copying."[57] The connection between Olivier and the sculpture was not made until after Picasso's death.[58]

APPLE, FALL–WINTER 1909

Picasso engaged in two smaller sculptural projects, creating *Apple* (pl. 10) and *Head* (private collection).[59] While *Apple* is known only as a plaster, *Head* is documented as having been modeled in clay.[60] There is little evidence as to where Picasso made these sculptures, but he may again have worked at Manolo's studio. When *Apple* and *Head* were reproduced for the first time, in 1942 in Christian Zervos's catalogue raisonné of the artist's work, they were dated to 1910 (fig. 20).[61] Since then, art historians have argued convincingly that Picasso made the small sculptures around the same time as *Head of a Woman*.[62]

Picasso used a knife and other cutting tools to create and sharpen *Apple*'s edges and ridges, emphasizing its Cubist faceting, much as he had revised the "master" plaster cast of *Head of a Woman* and not unlike the way in which one might slice into an actual apple. The ridges and voids echo the architectural thrusts of the earlier work but also resemble the landscape of Horta de Ebro, with its cluster of small cubic houses, which Picasso had painted with intensity that summer (fig. 21). The size of a large apple, the sculpture could easily be held and turned in one hand, allowing for light to interact with its structure. In its relationship to the artist's drawings and paintings, the sculpture illustrates his drive to find a pictorial language applicable to representation in both two and three dimensions. The choice of the apple as motif—an iconic subject of Cézanne's paintings—attests to the artist's ongoing dialogue with the French painter during Cubism's formative years.

Apple remained largely unknown until after Picasso's death. It was exhibited in 1979–80 at the Grand Palais, Paris, as part of a selection of Picasso's work received by the French state in lieu of inheritance taxes.[63]

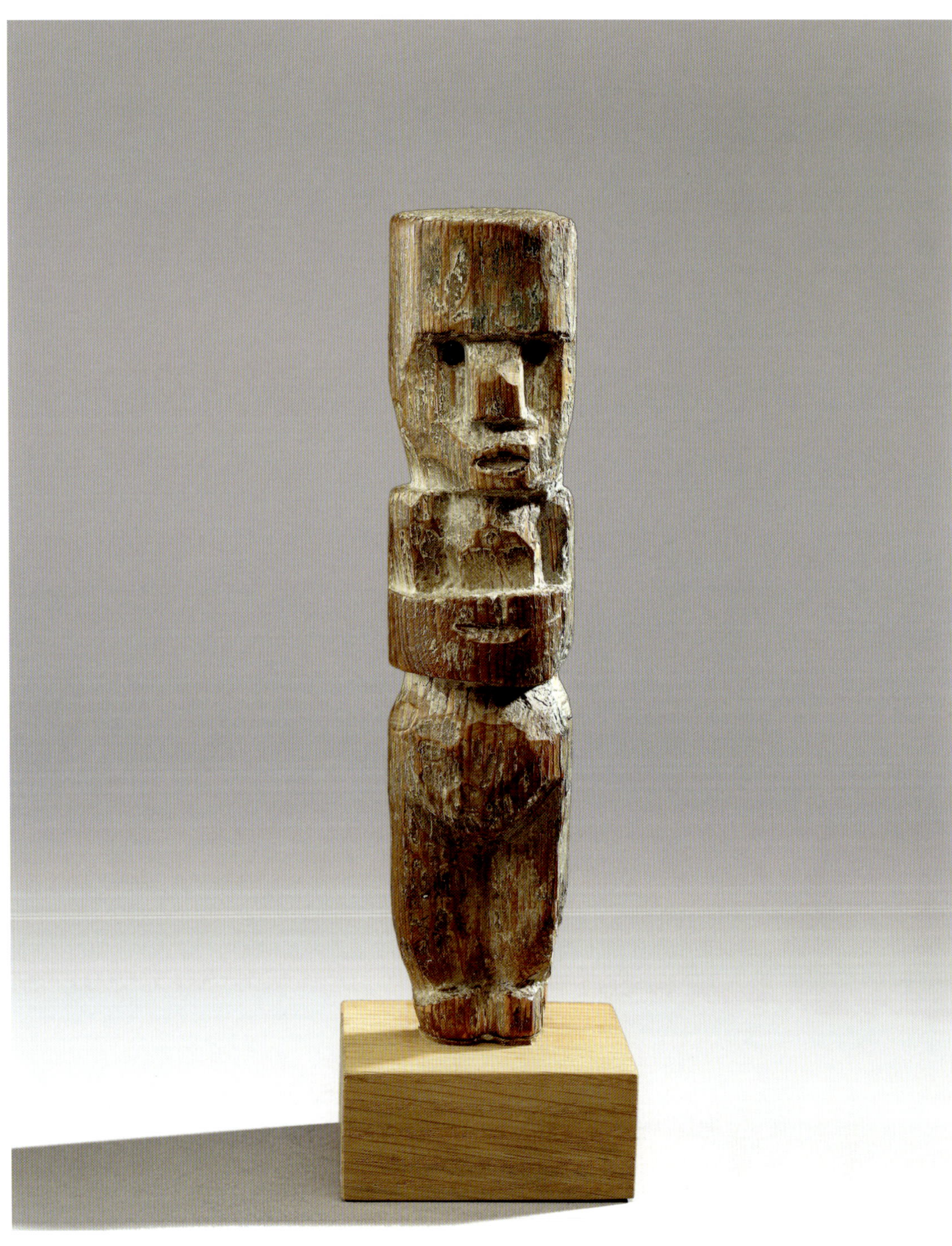

6. DOLL. Paris, 1907
Wood, brass pins, and traces of oil paint and gesso
9 ¼ x 2 3/16 x 2 3/16 in. (23.5 × 5.5 × 5.5 cm)
Art Gallery of Ontario, Toronto. Purchase

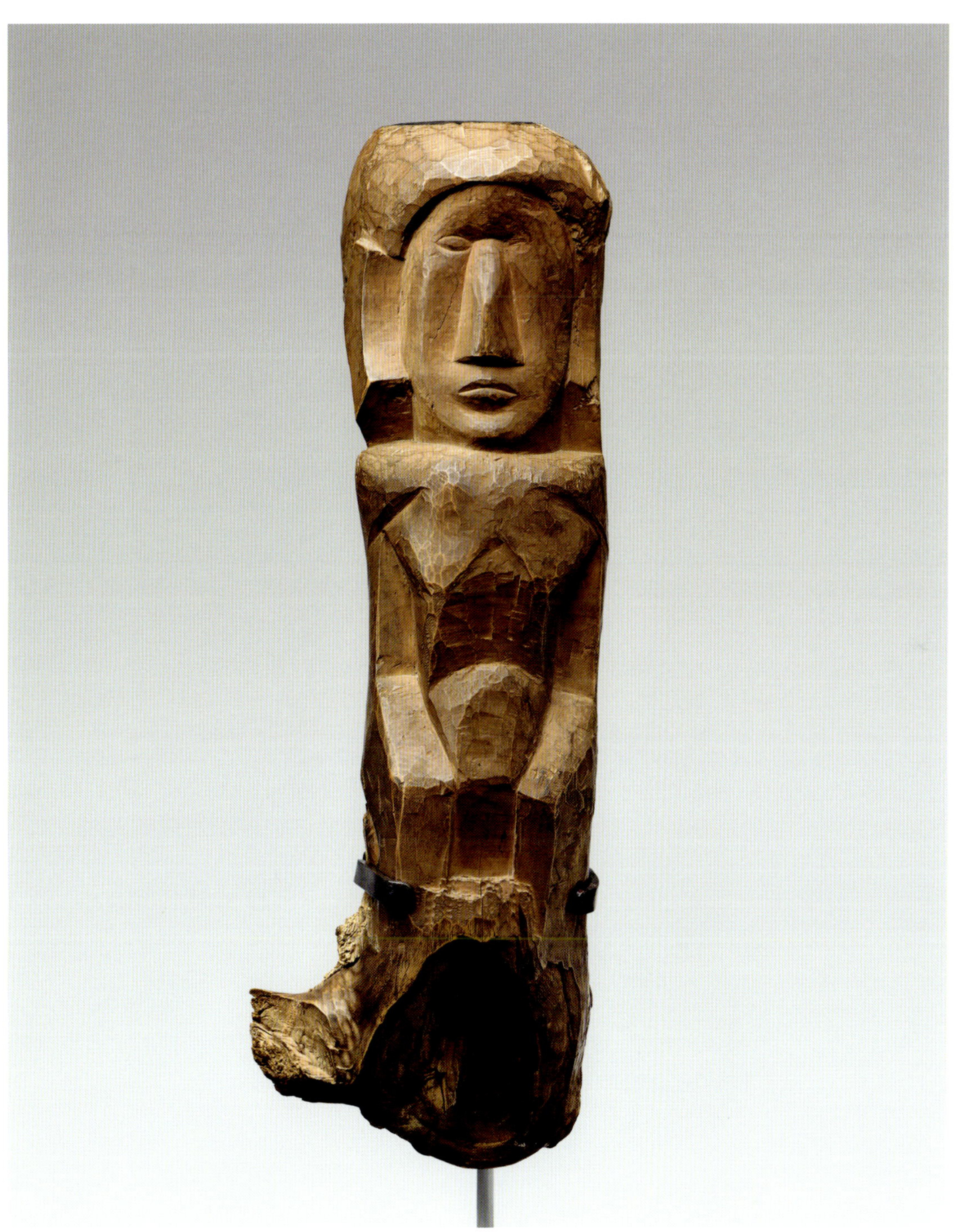

7. **FIGURE.** Paris, 1907
Boxwood with pencil and traces of paint on top of the head
13 ⅞ × 4 ¹³⁄₁₆ × 4 ¾ in. (35.2 × 12.2 × 12 cm)
Musée national Picasso–Paris. Dation Pablo Picasso

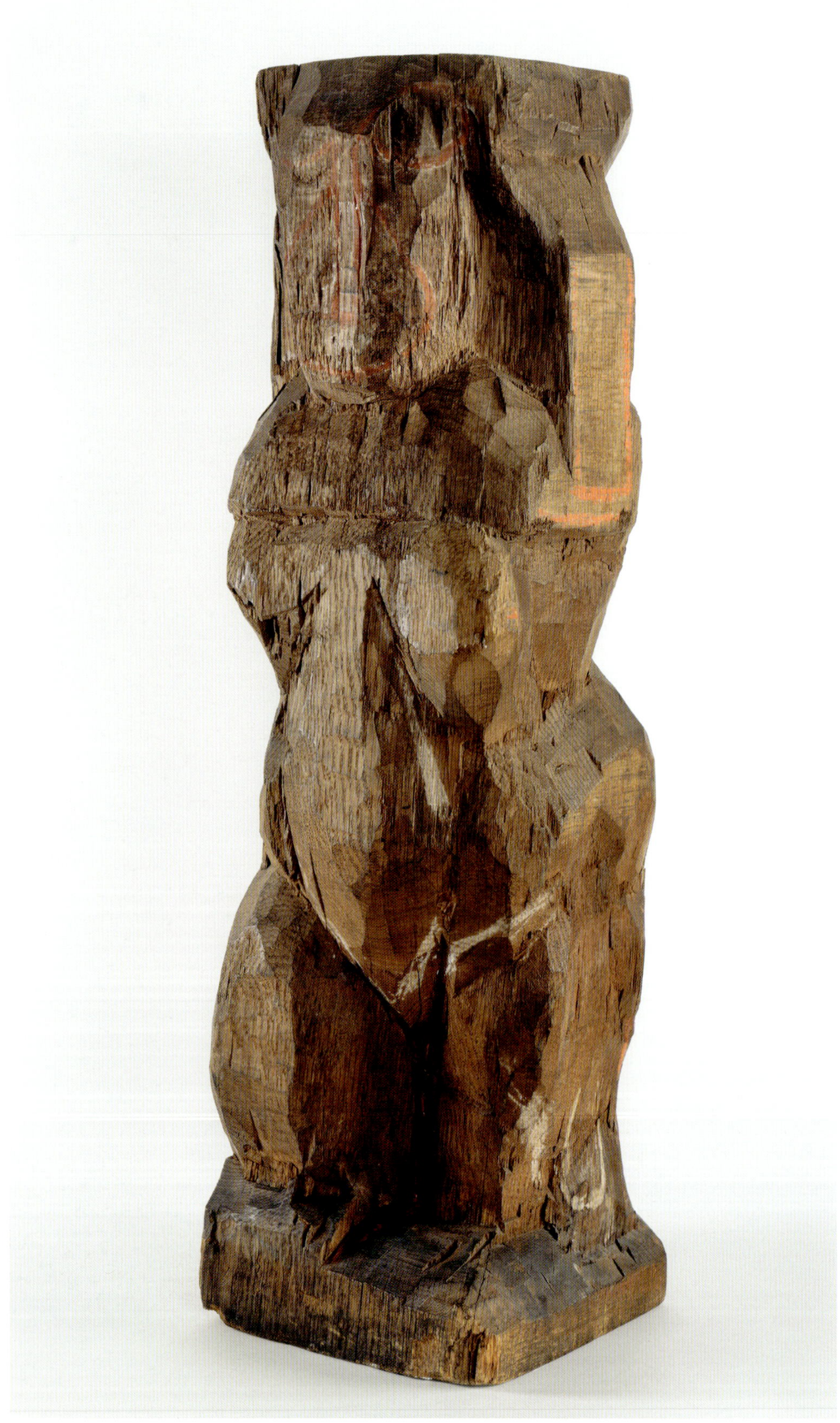

8. **FIGURE.** Paris, 1908
Oak with painted accents
31 11/16 × 9 7/16 × 8 3/16 in. (80.5 × 24 × 20.8 cm)
Musée national Picasso–Paris. Dation Pablo Picasso

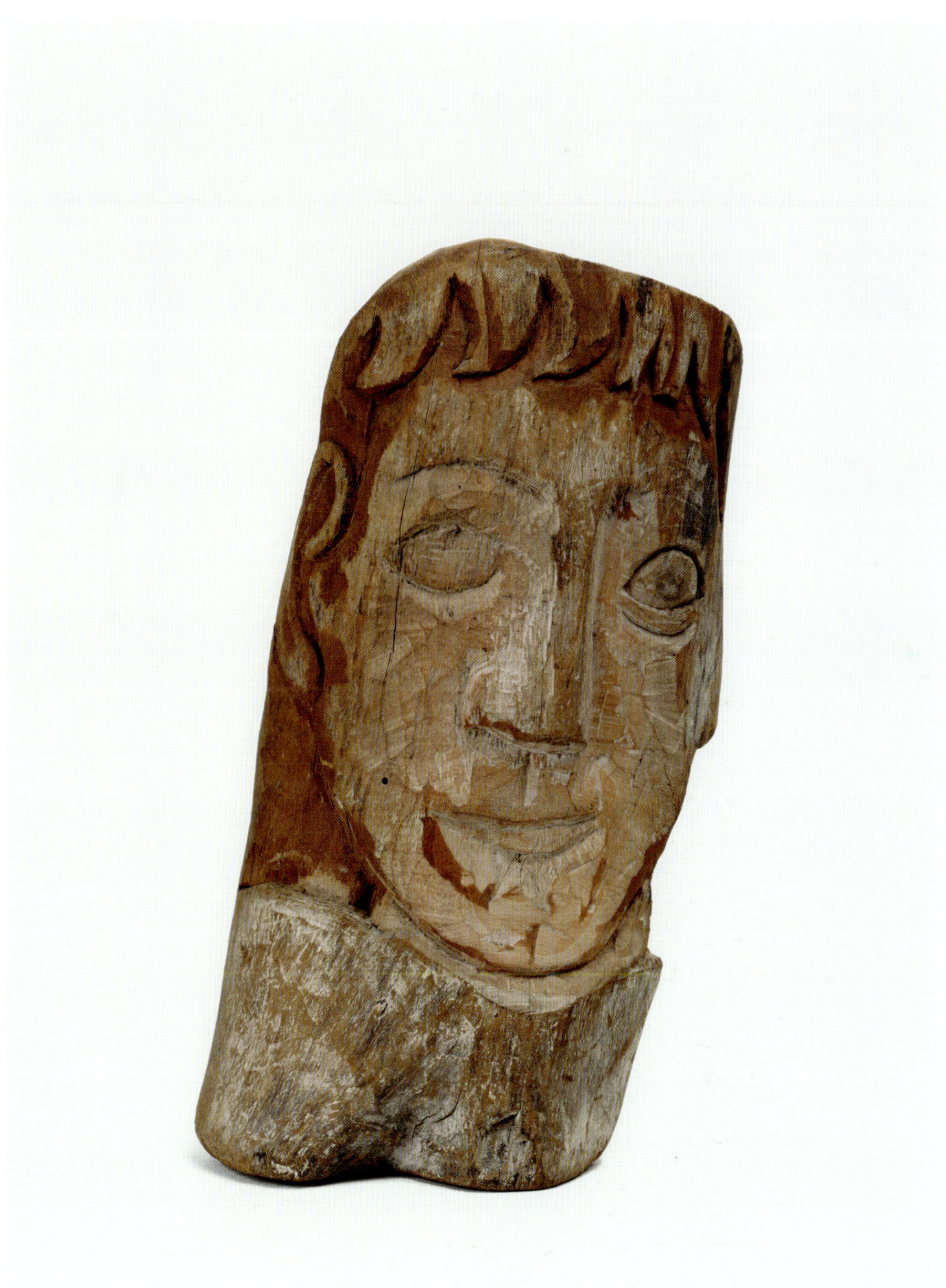

9. **HEAD.** 1907
Beech, partially painted
14 9⁄16 × 7 7⁄8 × 4 3⁄4 in. (37 × 20 × 12 cm)
Musée national Picasso–Paris. Dation Jacqueline Picasso

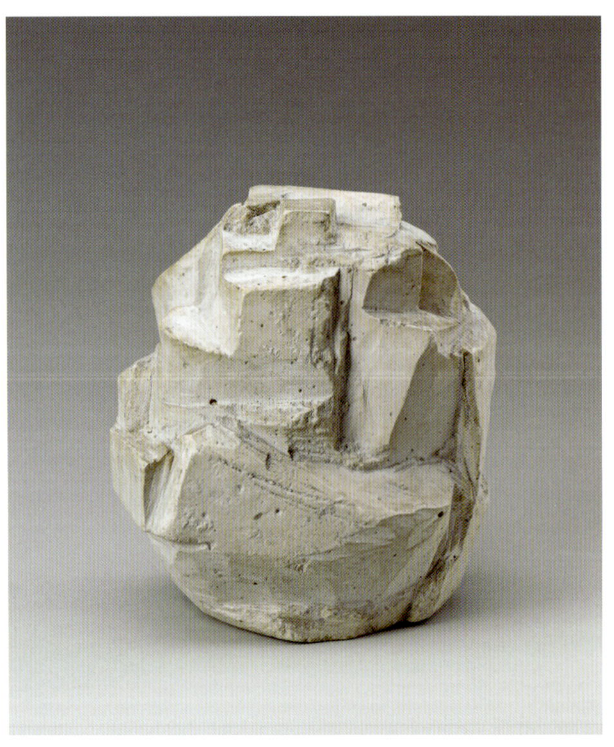

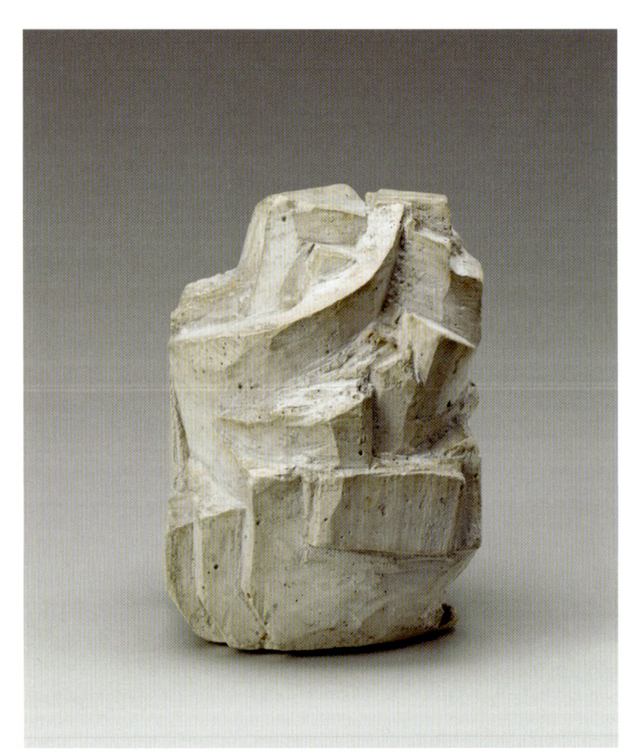

10. **APPLE.** Paris, fall–winter 1909
Plaster
4⅛ × 3 15/16 × 2 15/16 in. (10.5 × 10 × 7.5 cm)
Musée national Picasso–Paris. Dation Pablo Picasso

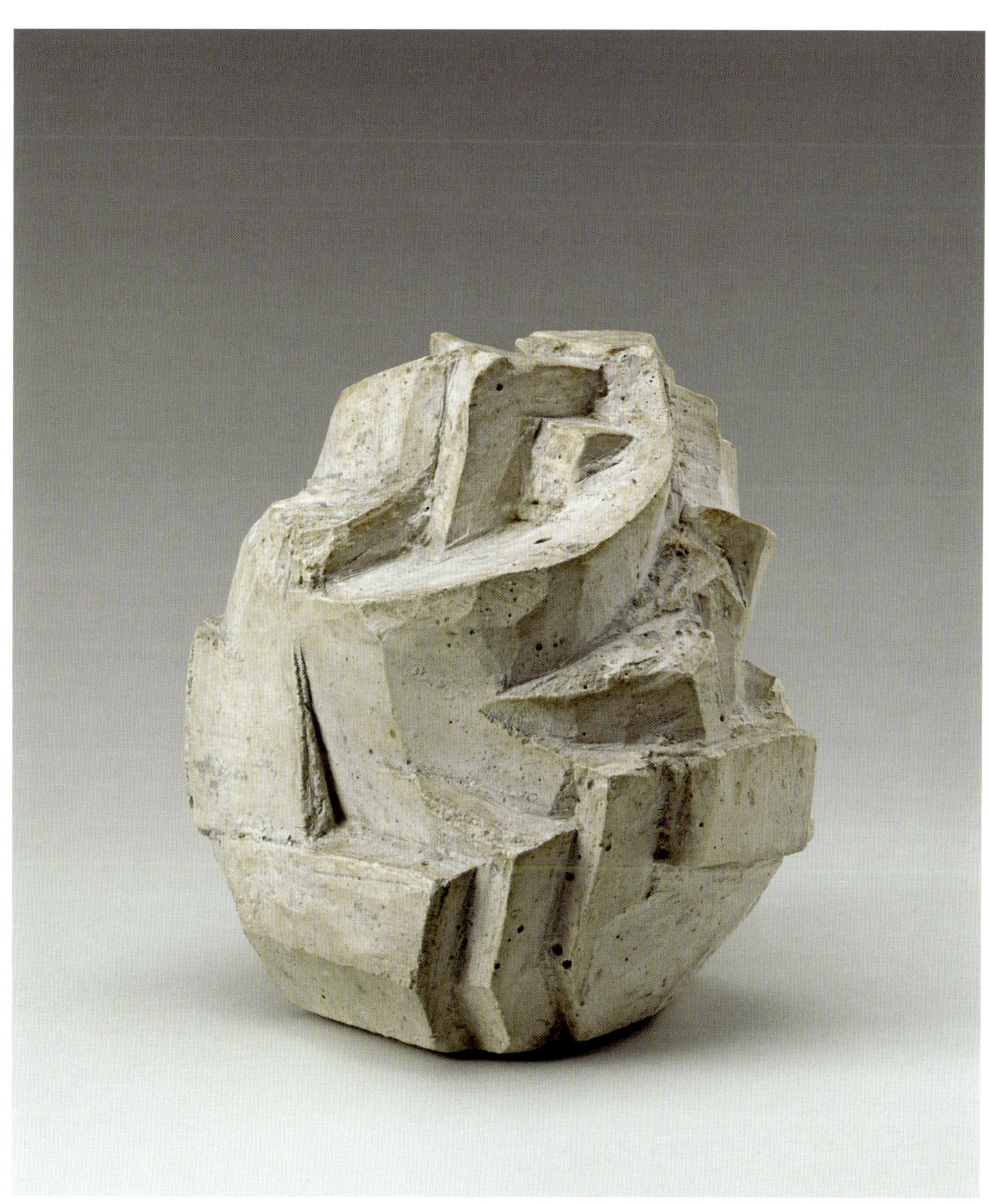

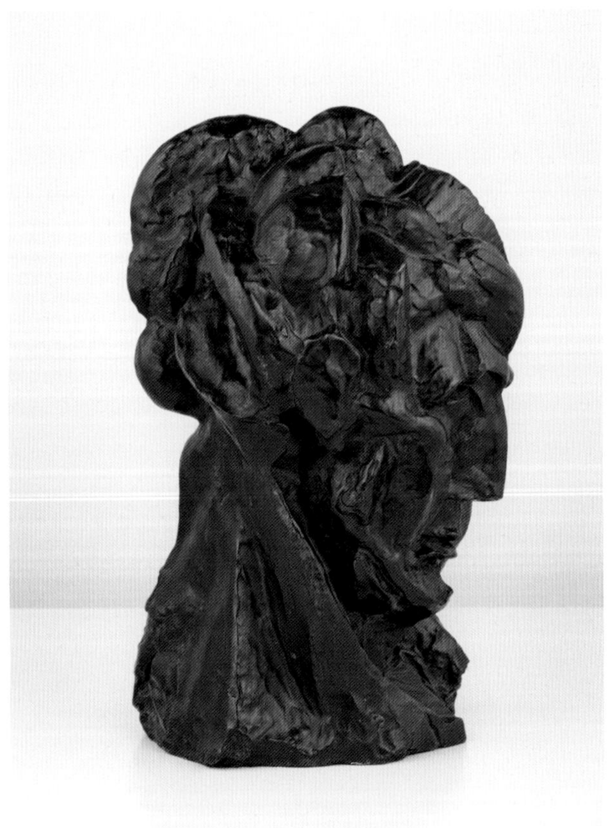

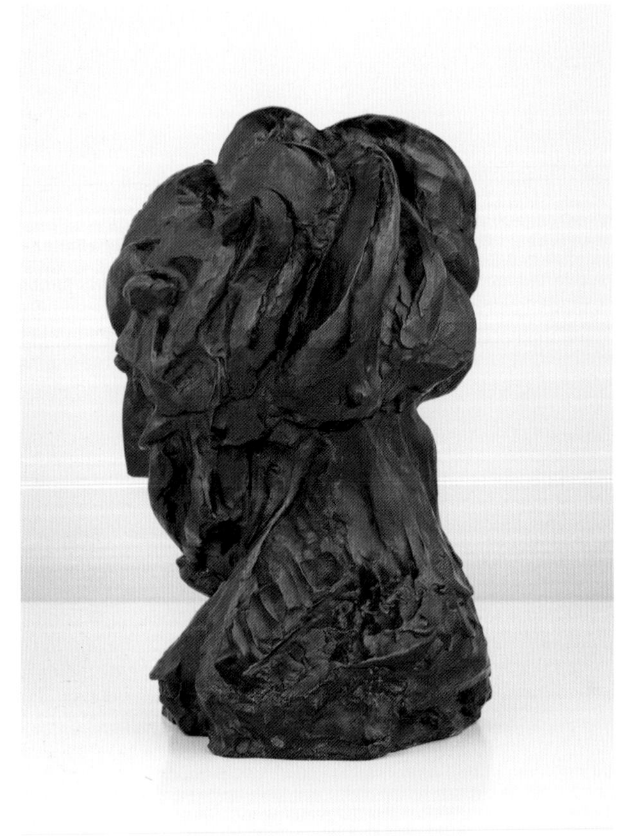

11. **HEAD OF A WOMAN.** Paris, fall 1909
Bronze, cast between 1910 and 1912
16 ¼ × 9 ¾ × 10 ½ in. (41.3 × 24.7 × 26.6 cm)
The Art Institute of Chicago. Alfred Stieglitz Collection

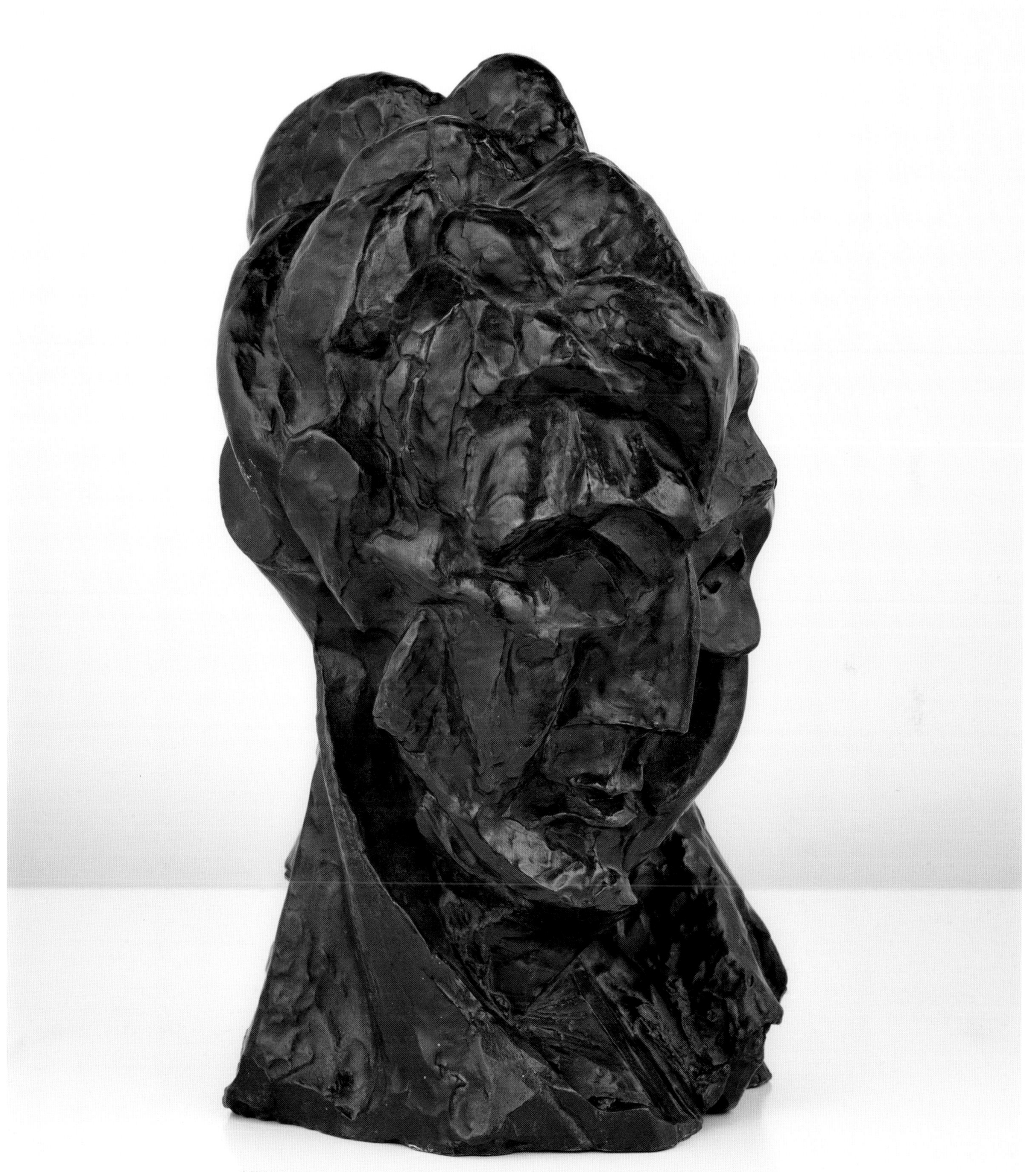

CHAPTER 3

REINVENTING SCULPTURE: THE CUBIST YEARS 1912–1915

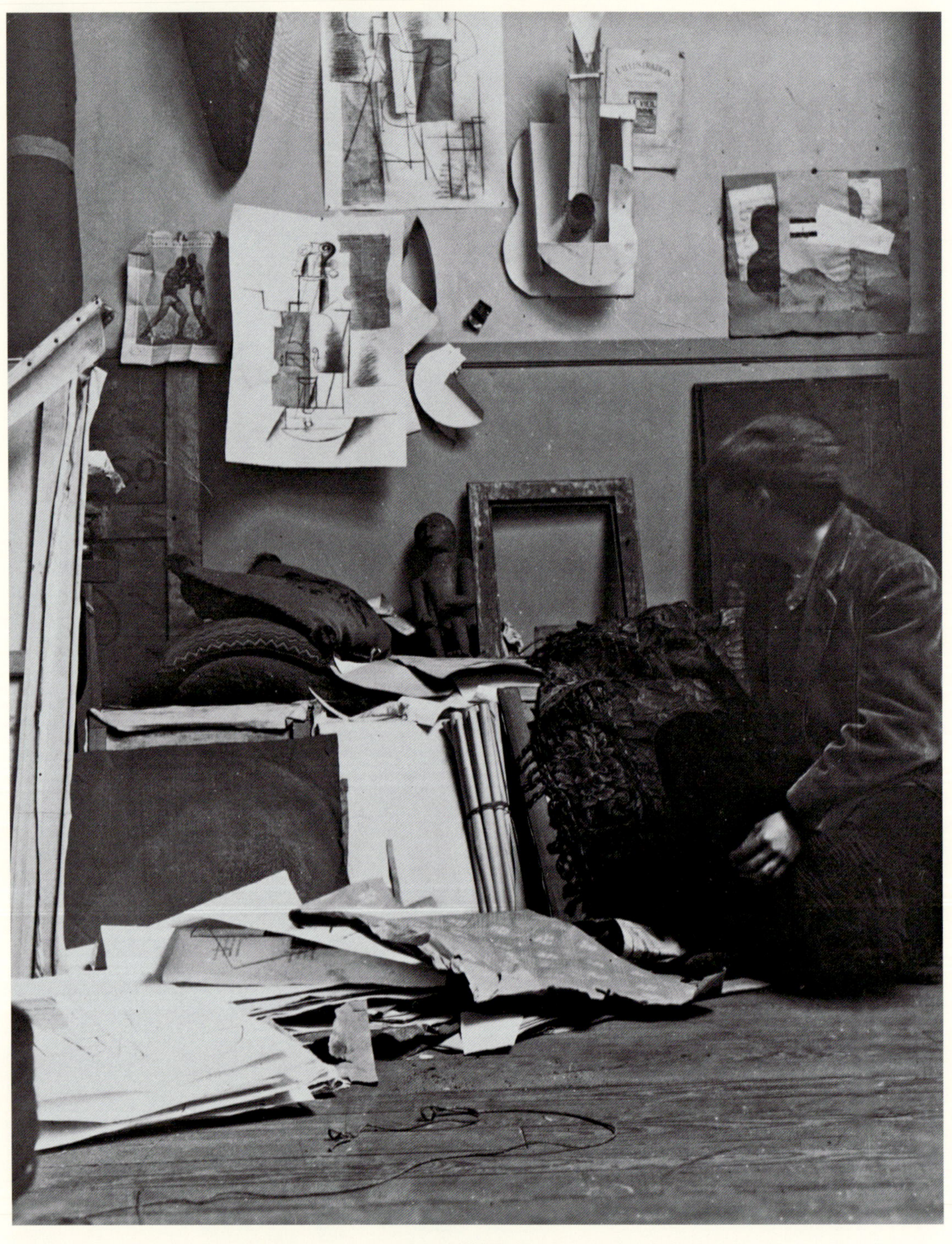

Picasso with an installation of works in his studio at 242, boulevard Raspail, Paris, December 1912 [or February 1913]. Archives Olga Ruiz-Picasso. Courtesy Fundación Almine y Bernard Ruiz-Picasso para el Arte

PICASSO SPENT the late summer of 1912 in Sorgues, in the South of France, with his good friend and collaborator, the artist Georges Braque. There, in addition to painting, he produced a number of pen-and-ink drawings of guitarists composed of tenuously connected spheres, rectangular planes, and cylinders. That he had not been tempted to sculpt for some three years suggests that, on some level, Picasso had found working with materials like clay and plaster unsatisfying. His drawings announce a fresh engagement with the making of three-dimensional objects, in the form of imaginary constructions. They may coincide with Braque's work on a series of paper sculptures (now lost) and with a trip the two artists made in late summer to Marseille, looking for African art to acquire. Among the works Picasso purchased, he would later single out a Kru mask—whose protruding cylindrical eyes double as recessive eye sockets—as having been crucial to the conception of the sculptures he would make that fall.

Picasso returned to Paris in September 1912. On October 9 he wrote to Braque and reported that he was "in the process of imagining a guitar."[1] These words announce his opening salvo in what would become a radical overhaul of the tradition of sculpture: a paperboard, string, and cardboard *Guitar* (pl. 13), unlike any musical instrument or work of art ever seen before. This breakthrough came with his decision to incorporate commercially produced materials, artisans' techniques, and simple craft processes into the making of three-dimensional objects. The result was a revolutionary new conception of sculpture as something constructed from separate components, not modeled or carved.

The multipart open structure of *Guitar* allowed Picasso to introduce negative space into sculpture's customary solids for the first time. Its humble still life subject was also a first. Instead of the imposing and heroic figures of traditional French sculpture, he proposed a musical instrument that was intimate in scale, inherently volumetric, and designed to be touched, played with, or otherwise manipulated. In a letter written to one of Picasso's collectors in December 1913, his dealer, Daniel-Henry Kahnweiler, described constructions like *Guitar* as "sculpture studies made of paper, pieces of wood, etc., . . . on which [Picasso] of course continues to work."[2] His words capture these works' provisional character, which was manifested by Picasso's deliberate rejection of careful execution in favor of irregularly cut contours, improvised methods of assembly, and raw, unfinished surfaces.

Sometime in January or February 1914, Picasso decided to translate his cardboard *Guitar* into sheet metal, reiterating its fragile papery parts in a more fixed form (pl. 14). Up to this point, his three-dimensional works had taken the hybrid form of *tableaux-objets* or *tableaux-reliefs*, falling somewhere between painting and what Kahnweiler characterized as "true" sculpture in the round.[3] Beginning in the spring of 1914, Picasso's interest in working with the more stable material of metal coincided with an impulse to make freestanding sculptures. One such work represents a single glass, cobbled together from cut-and-painted tin, nails, and wood (pl. 17); another, a remarkably elaborate still life composition depicting a bottle, a glass, and a piece of newspaper, was cut with metal shears from a dried-milk tin (pl. 16). Most astonishing of all is *Glass of Absinthe* (pls. 21–26), six bronze casts produced at a foundry, as any traditional bronze sculpture would have been, each of which thoroughly, and very humorously, upends and reinvents the fundamental characteristics of this ancient art form.

With *Glass of Absinthe*, Picasso set himself the seemingly impossible task of representing in sculpture things that are transparent. These works take as their subject a glass and its liquid contents. The latter is identified as absinthe, a clear liqueur, by the artist's inspired decision to incorporate a real-life metal absinthe spoon into his work of art. The perforations in these found spoons constitute one form of transparency; the diffuse polka-dot patterns that Picasso painted on some of the casts supply another; and the cuts he made into his glasses' paradoxically opaque contours, revealing their interior views, represent a third. Here the revolution announced by Picasso's decision to open up the volumes of his *Guitar* to light and shadow, incorporating space as a sculptural material, is taken a step further. His *Glass of Absinthe* sculptures swallow up real objects, transforming them from things of use into elements worthy of contemplation. This operation would remain a constant in Picasso's sculpture practice, the result of his exceptional openness to the sculptural potential of objects in the world.

The historical significance of Picasso's *Glass of Absinthe*, along with that of his Cubist constructions, cannot be overestimated. With them, the development of his own sculpture, and that of sculpture in the twentieth and twenty-first centuries, was forever changed.

LATE AUGUST–SEPTEMBER 1912: During these months, Picasso and Georges Braque worked in Sorgues, near Avignon in southern France. They wrote almost daily to Daniel-Henry Kahnweiler, their dealer in Paris, about their current work. Braque, who had arrived in late July—early August, started to make three-dimensional objects using paper. In one of his letters to Kahnweiler, on or after August 24, he wrote, "I am working well and taking advantage of my stay in the country to do things that cannot be done in Paris, such as paper sculpture, something that has given me much satisfaction" (fig. 1).[1]

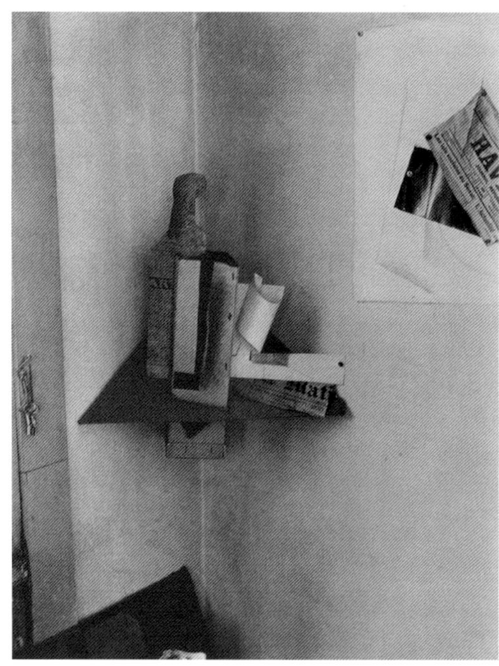

1. The only documented paper sculpture by Georges Braque, photographed in the artist's studio at the Hôtel Roma, 101, rue Caulaincourt, Paris, on or after February 18, 1914. Archives Quentin Laurens, Paris

SEPTEMBER 18, 1912: Picasso received by mail from Gertrude Stein the August 1912 special issue of Alfred Stieglitz's journal *Camera Work*, with her 1909 word-portrait "Pablo Picasso." Her text was accompanied by illustrations of the artist's work, including two views (front and right profile) of his first Cubist sculpture, *Head of a Woman* of 1909 (see fig. 17 on p. 59).[2] One of Stein's passages reads, "Something had been coming out of him, certainly it had been coming out of him, certainly it was something, certainly it had been coming out of him and it had meaning, a charming meaning, a solid meaning, a struggling meaning, a clear meaning."[3] Unable to read her text in English, Picasso responded: "I'll have someone translate it. In any case, the reproductions are very beautiful. I thank you for all that, and for your dedication."[4]

LATE SEPTEMBER 1912: Picasso moved to 242, boulevard Raspail with his girlfriend Marcelle Humbert, known as Eva Gouel.

SEPTEMBER 30, 1912: Umberto Boccioni's *Manifesto tecnico della scultura futurista* (Technical manifesto of Futurist sculpture)—dated April 11, 1912, but first issued as a leaflet around September that year—appeared in the newspaper *L'Italia* and soon after was translated into French and English.[5] In typical Futurist fashion, Boccioni declared, "Destroy the literary and traditional dignity of marble and bronze. Reject the idea that one material must be used exclusively in the construction of a sculptural whole. Insist that even twenty different types of material can be used in a single work of art in order to achieve its plastic feeling. To mention a few examples: glass, wood, cardboard, iron, cement, hair, leather, cloth, mirrors, electric lights, and so on."[6] For Boccioni, such everyday materials revitalized what he rejected as outdated ideas in sculpture.

OCTOBER 6, 1912: Boccioni's manifesto of Futurist sculpture appeared, in French, in the Paris journal *Je dis tout*.

OCTOBER 9, 1912: In a letter to Braque, who was still in Sorgues, Picasso wrote: "I'm using your latest papery and powdery procedures. I'm in the process of imagining a guitar and I'm using a bit of earth on our dreadful canvas."[7] The "procedures" Picasso referred to are those of papier collé, constructed paper sculpture, and paint mixed with sand, sawdust, and other grainy particles. The guitar Picasso was then "imagining" corresponds to the paper construction now in the collection of The Museum of Modern Art, New York (pl. 13).

STILL LIFE WITH *GUITAR* (VARIANT STATE), ASSEMBLED BEFORE NOVEMBER 15, 1913

Picasso began to construct his first open-form *Guitar* around October 1912, using thin paperboard, paper, brown-paper tape, string, and painted wire (pl. 13).[8] Satisfied with the progress he had been making on the sculpture and on other recent drawings and papiers collés, Picasso would document his recent work either that December or in February 1913. A series of at least four photographs taken at his studio at 242, boulevard Raspail in Montparnasse constitutes the earliest known visual record of *Guitar*, which was hung on a wall like a real guitar (fig. 2).[9] By juxtaposing his first open-form construction (a relief sculpture) with his current works on paper, Picasso captured the way the various papier collé elements resonated with the projecting planes of cut paperboard that he used to construct space and create depth. A less densely populated installation view of *Guitar* next to the artist's *Head of a Man* (1912; Leonard A. Lauder Cubist Trust) and

Violin (1912; Centre Pompidou, Paris) is particularly revealing in terms of Picasso's various modes of depicting depth (see p. 70). In this image—which may be the first in the series, for it records an early stage of Picasso's installation of recent works on the wall—*Guitar* hangs in close proximity not only to the papiers collés but also to other printed matter and an unidentified African or Oceanic mask.

A few months later, Picasso transferred *Guitar* to his new studio at 5 *bis*, rue Schoelcher, where the paper sculpture was photographed in an altered state (see fig. 3). Its semicircular cardboard tabletop sits on a makeshift pedestal made of a folded-paper triangle tacked to the wall and surrounded by other flat paper objects.[10] He had assembled this provisional still life from different kinds of paper, as well as a piece of wooden molding.[11]

After the artist's death in 1973, *Guitar* entered the collection of The Museum of Modern Art, where it joined the 1914 sheet metal *Guitar* (pl. 14) as a gift from Picasso. The 1912 sculpture—which had been dismantled, probably in 1916, and kept in a paper box—arrived in New York in the suitcase of chief curator William Rubin on September 9, 1973.[12] After being held for two years by the customs authorities, the sculpture was transferred to the Museum on or around October 21, 1975. The cardboard sculpture was assembled again, for the first time since about 1916, in conjunction with the retrospective of the artist's work organized by Rubin at the Museum in 1980.

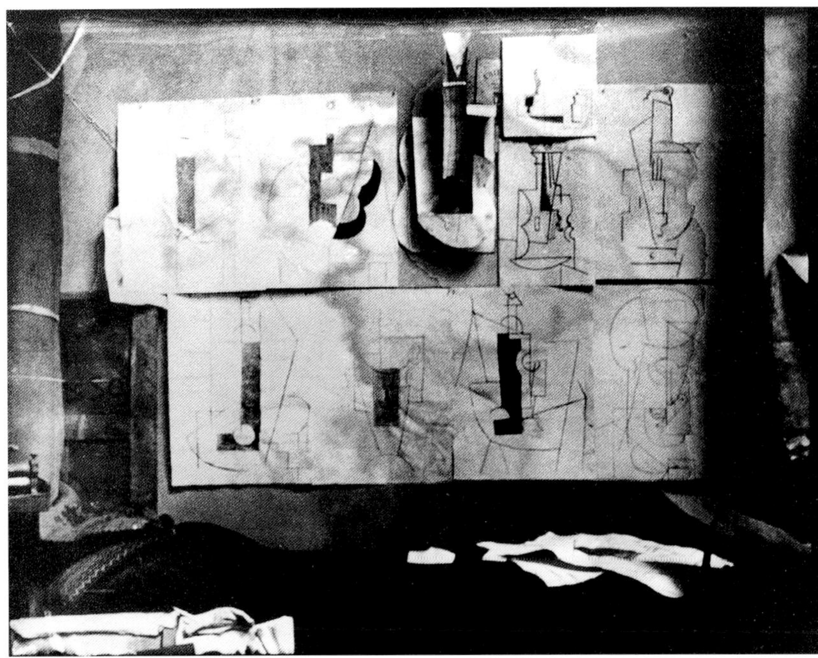

2. Recent drawings, papiers collés, and an early variant of the cardboard *Guitar* installed at Picasso's studio at 242, boulevard Raspail, Paris, mid-December 1912 or February 1913. Photographer unknown, possibly the artist. Picasso Archives, Musée national Picasso–Paris

DECEMBER 18, 1912: Picasso and Kahnweiler agreed to sign a three-year contract that gave the dealer the exclusive right to choose from the artist's complete production.[13] Picasso—with his radically new cardboard *Guitar* no doubt fresh in his mind—underlined the word *escultures* in the contract and stipulated that "sculptures and engravings were subject to debate" between him and Kahnweiler and not subject to the standard pricing otherwise outlined in the contract.[14] Two years before, the dealer had missed the opportunity to purchase a number of Picasso's earlier sculptures, including the Cubist *Head of a Woman* (pl. 11). Now that he and the artist had decided to work together and Picasso was making three-dimensional objects again, the category of sculpture received particular attention.

JANUARY 1913: Picasso's friend Guillaume Apollinaire presented the first public lecture to include a discussion of Picasso's recent paper constructions, at Herwarth Walden's Galerie Der Sturm in Berlin. He declared, "At times Picasso has renounced ordinary paint to compose relief pictures made of cardboard, or papiers collés; he was guided by a plastic inspiration, and these strange, coarse, and mismatched materials were ennobled because the artist endowed them with his own delicate and strong personality."[15] The following month the lecture was published as "Die moderne Malerei" (Modern painting) in the journal *Der Sturm*.

FEBRUARY 17–MARCH 15, 1913: Alfred Stieglitz's cast of *Head of a Woman* of 1909 (see pl. 11) was the only sculpture by Picasso to be presented in the *International Exhibition of Modern Art* (known as the Armory Show) at the Armory of the Sixty-ninth Regiment in New York. It would not travel to the exhibition's subsequent venues in Chicago and Boston.

MAY–JUNE 1913: Vincenc Kramář's cast of *Head of a Woman* of 1909 was included in the *Third Exhibition of the Skupina Výtvarných Umělců* (Group of fine artists), organized in Prague by the Mánes Association (see fig. 16 on p. 59).

JUNE 20–JULY 16, 1913: In Paris, Galerie La Boétie presented a series of eleven "plastic ensembles" in the first exhibition of Futurist sculpture by Boccioni, who called himself a "painter-sculptor."[16] As announced in his manifesto, the show included a number of plaster constructions that combined multiple mediums. In order to realize his idea of a plastic ensemble, Boccioni used metal spurs and a thin, upright plane coated with lumpy plaster to create space in the form of a building around the figure in *Antigraceful* (1913; variant state, Galleria nazionale d'arte moderna, Rome)—a sculpted plaster head that echoes Picasso's 1909 *Head of a Woman*.[17] In *Fusion of a Head and a Window* (1913) and *Head + House + Light* (1912 or 1913), Boccioni combined parts of a wooden easel, a segment of a balustrade, metal bars, wire, glass, and horsehair to create two outward-projecting plaster constructions that evoke the fusing of matter.[18] Even though Picasso was not in Paris when the show opened, one can assume that Apollinaire's review published in *L'Intransigeant* on June 21, in which the critic related Boccioni's sculptural enterprise to Picasso's 1909 *Head of a Woman*, would have encouraged the artist to visit the exhibition before it closed.[19] Filippo Tommaso Marinetti, the founder of Italian Futurism, mistakenly recalled greeting Picasso in Boccioni's presence during the opening at the gallery.[20] The occasion that Marinetti was remembering may instead have been Boccioni's "Conférence contradictoire" (An opposing lecture) on Futurist sculpture, which had been promoted in the catalogue and was held at the gallery on the evening of June 27.

***MANDOLIN AND CLARINET*,[21] [FALL 1913]**
After a brief stay in Céret, in southern France, Picasso found a new studio space at 5 *bis*, rue Schoelcher in Montparnasse on August 19, 1913.[22] He and Braque had been experimenting with paper sculptures and constructions since 1912, but now Picasso began using more durable materials. He moved to his new studio in early October and began a series of still life relief constructions. *Mandolin and Clarinet* (pl. 12), of uncertain date, is one of three such constructions.[23] To make these, Picasso quickly put together scraps of found or recycled wood, some of which he had sawed to the desired shape. As with many of his other wooden reliefs created between 1913 and 1915, he was careful not to tidy up his crude process. Picasso was eager for the sculpture's construction to remain legible—not least, to contradict the convention of refinement in sculpture.

Boccioni's recent work would have resonated closely with Picasso's drive to expand the possibilities for sculpture. But rather than modeling his still life sculptures in the round, as Boccioni did, he decided to flatten them, pushing them back into the painterly realm. Indeed, photographs taken around this time at his studio show that Picasso had constructions similar to *Mandolin and Clarinet* hanging on a wall or propped up on an easel.[24] In November 1917, the Danish artist Axel Salto wrote about a visit to the artist's Montparnasse studio. His article in the avant-garde journal *Klingen*, which he had founded, stated:

> On an easel in the middle of the room, among pots of Ripolin enamel paint, there hung a square box without a lid, containing some bits of wood fixed at an angle to the bottom and sides; another piece of wood, like the handle of an awl, was fastened so as to cast a shadow on the inside of the box. This produced an interplay of light and shade, angles and planes, in the little world within; here and there the effect was varied with stuck-on sand or bits of newspaper. This work had been created by Picasso with the utmost *objectivity*, taking precise account of the character of the materials and the balance of the planes in relation to one another. His method of work, in which German aestheticians are so interested, is marked by a determined attempt to establish as concretely as possible the extent of the decorative elements of a picture, their material value and location in space. He strives to reduce the "picture" to its simplest forms. Such experiments have been taken up by grateful imitators and developed into a philosophy.[25]

The work described by Salto might have been *Bottle and Guitar* (destroyed), a construction made by Picasso in the fall of 1913, which featured a thin wooden rod with a right angle, attached to a boxlike support (see work at center in fig. 13).[26]

NOVEMBER 15, 1913: The journal *Les Soirées de Paris* devoted an entire issue (no. 18) to Picasso. This issue relaunched the publication after a hiatus of four months; its new format now included photographic reproductions. Apollinaire and his coeditors, Baroness Hélène d'Oettingen and Serge Férat (who together used the pseudonym Jean Cérusse), chose to illustrate one painting and four Cubist constructions (all titled *Nature morte*), interspersed throughout the issue as full-page plates.[27] Kahnweiler provided the images used for printing. Among them was a photograph of the temporary still life arrangement that featured the cardboard *Guitar* as its centerpiece (fig. 3).

The journal's revised layout and the inclusion of Picasso's current work are said to have caused an uproar and resulted in numerous canceled subscriptions, but Blair Hartzell has provided a more nuanced picture.[28] She demonstrates that the editorial reorganization and higher price resulted in some cancellations, but the number of subscriptions from the avant-garde audience increased following the publication of the Picasso issue. The publication of the November issue coincided with the opening of the 1913 Salon d'Automne, during which copies of the journal were handed out to those attending the vernissage.[29] Kahnweiler not only dispatched one copy to Kramář, one of his most loyal clients and a pioneering collector of Cubism, but also felt compelled to explain

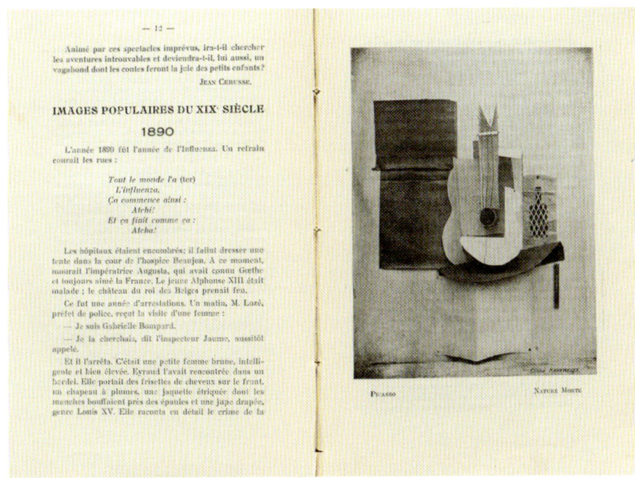

— 12 —

Animé par ces spectacles imprévus, ira-t-il chercher les aventures introuvables et deviendra-t-il, lui aussi, un vagabond dont les contes feront la joie des petits enfants?

JEAN CERUSSE.

IMAGES POPULAIRES DU XIX SIÈCLE

1890

L'année 1890 fût l'année de l'Influenza. Un refrain courait les rues :

Tout le monde l'a (ter)
L'influenza.
Ça commence ainsi :
Atchi!
Et ça finit comme ça :
Atcha!

Les hôpitaux étaient encombrés; il fallut dresser une tente dans la cour de l'hospice Beaujon. A ce moment, mourait l'impératrice Augusta, qui avait connu Gœthe et toujours aimé la France. Le jeune Alphonse XIII était malade ; le château du roi des Belges prenait feu.

Ce fut une année d'arrestations. Un matin, M. Lozé, préfet de police, reçut la visite d'une femme :

— Je suis Gabrielle Bompard.

— Je la cherchais, dit l'inspecteur Jaume, aussitôt appelé.

Et il l'arrêta. C'était une petite femme brune, intelligente et bien élevée. Eyraud l'avait rencontrée dans un bordel. Elle portait des frisettes de cheveux sur le front, un chapeau à plumes, une jaquette étriquée dont les manches bouffaient près des épaules et une jupe drapée, genre Louis XV. Elle raconta en détail le crime de la

PICASSO — NATURE MORTE

3. Still life with *Guitar* reproduced in *Les Soirées de Paris*, no. 18 (November 15, 1913): 13

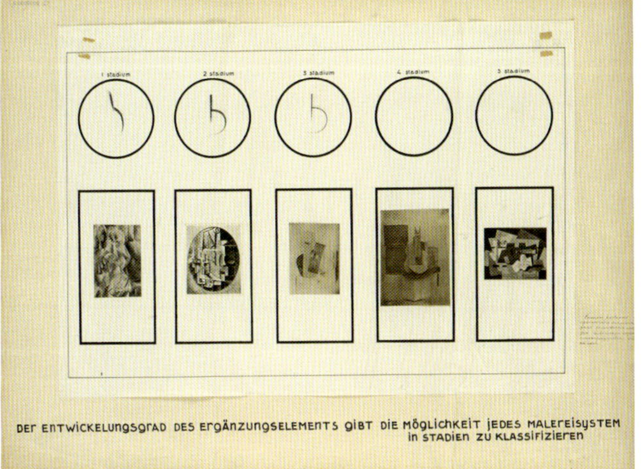

4. Kazimir Malevich. *Analytical Chart*. 1924–27. Cut-and-pasted printed paper, gelatin silver prints, ink, and crayon on paper with ink and pencil on paper, 28 ½ × 38 ¾ in. (72.4 × 98.4 cm). The Museum of Modern Art, New York. 1935 Acquisition confirmed in 1999 by agreement with the Estate of Kazimir Malevich and made possible with funds from the Mrs. John Hay Whitney Bequest (by exchange)

to him the nature of the published objects. In a letter dated December 4, 1913, Kahnweiler wrote, "The things reproduced therein are not new works, i.e. not things specifically designated for sale or exhibition, but sculpture studies made of paper, pieces of wood, etc., which Picasso considers as studies only, and on which he of course continues to work."[30]

The dissemination of *Les Soirées de Paris* across Europe, the United States, and beyond marked the first time that Picasso's constructions were seen outside his studio, offering immediate access to some of his most revolutionary works of the period. A decade later, Kazimir Malevich would paste reproductions of Picasso's Cubist constructions, including the *Soirées* image of the still life with *Guitar* as comparative images in his *Analytical Charts* of 1924–27 (fig. 4). In 1961, André Breton would recall:

> I rediscover my youthful vision when I call to mind my first encounter with Picasso's work, at second hand, through an issue of Apollinaire's *Soirées de Paris* which included rather hazy reproductions of five of his latest still lifes (the date was 1913). Four of them were composed of an assemblage of materials of a residual nature such as slats, spools, discarded fragments of linoleum, lengths of string, all borrowed from everyday life. The initial shock provoked by an entirely new visual experience was succeeded by an awareness of the incomparable balance achieved by these works, which were thus endowed, willy-nilly, with an organic life that justified the necessity of their existence. Since then, nearly half a century has gone by. I gather, from what Picasso said to me one day, that these early constructions have long since been dismembered, but the image that remains of them suffices to demonstrate to what a degree they anticipate those forms of expression today which are most convinced of their own daring.[31]

LATE DECEMBER 1913: Around the Christmas holidays (December 24–26), the art dealer Alfred Flechtheim opened his gallery at Alleestraße 7 in Düsseldorf.[32] The inaugural exhibition included bronze casts of three of Picasso's early sculptures: *The Jester* of 1905, *Head of a Woman (Fernande)* of 1906, and *Head of a Woman* of 1909.[33] This was the first exhibition of Picasso's sculpture in Germany. None of his three-dimensional works or his most recent constructions had been included in his exhibitions at the Galerie Hans Goltz in 1912 and Heinrich Thannhauser's Moderne Galerie in Munich in late February 1913.

EARLY 1914: Working in the rue Schoelcher studio, Picasso entered another intense period of making collages and papiers collés; he also explored planar depth in various types of relief constructions and in his first freestanding sculptures since the 1909 *Head of a Woman*. By this time he had grown comfortable with the process of cutting—something he found extremely satisfying, judging by the number of papiers collés he was producing. The artist had moved from his paper-cutting practice to cutting specific shapes—such as a fluted glass, pipes, and wainscoting—from sheet metal, wood, and tin.

GUITAR, JANUARY–FEBRUARY 1914

Following the cardboard *Guitar* of fall 1912, Picasso made another *Guitar*, this time out of sheet metal, in January–February of 1914 (pl. 14).[34] Constructed from eight separate pieces of sheet metal, including a sound hole made of a section cut from a prefabricated metal cylinder and four strings of uncoated iron wire to hold it all together, *Guitar* was the first sheet metal sculpture created by the artist.[35] Whereas other tin and sheet metal sculptures of this period are painted, Picasso retained the dark gray (now rusty-brown) monochromatic surface of his ferrous *Guitar*, perhaps in a nod to the earlier, also monochrome *Guitar* of 1912.[36]

Guitar was first discussed in the final chapter, titled "El Guitare," of André Salmon's book *La Jeune Sculpture française* (New French sculpture).[37] Salmon wrote:

> When Picasso, leaving aside painting for a moment, was constructing this immense guitar out of sheet metal whose plans could be dispatched to any ignoramus in the universe who could put it together as well as him, I saw Picasso's studio, and this studio, more mind-blowing than Faust's laboratory, this studio which, according to some, contained no works of art, in the old sense, was furnished with the newest of objects. . . . Some witnesses, already shocked by the things that they saw covering the walls, and that they refused to call paintings because they were made of oilcloth, wrapping paper, and newspaper, said, pointing a haughty finger at the object of Picasso's clever pains: "What is it? Does it rest on a pedestal? Does it hang on a wall? What is it, painting or sculpture?" Picasso, dressed in the blue of Parisian artisans, responded in his finest Andalusian voice: "It's nothing, it's *el guitare*!"[38]

The sculpture would not be exhibited publicly until 1966, when it was included in the exhibition *Hommage à Pablo Picasso* (fig. 5). When the show continued on to The Museum of Modern Art, Nelson A. Rockefeller became interested in purchasing *Guitar*, with the understanding that it would eventually be given to the Museum. A series of negotiations led to an unexpected gift from the artist on February 8, 1971.

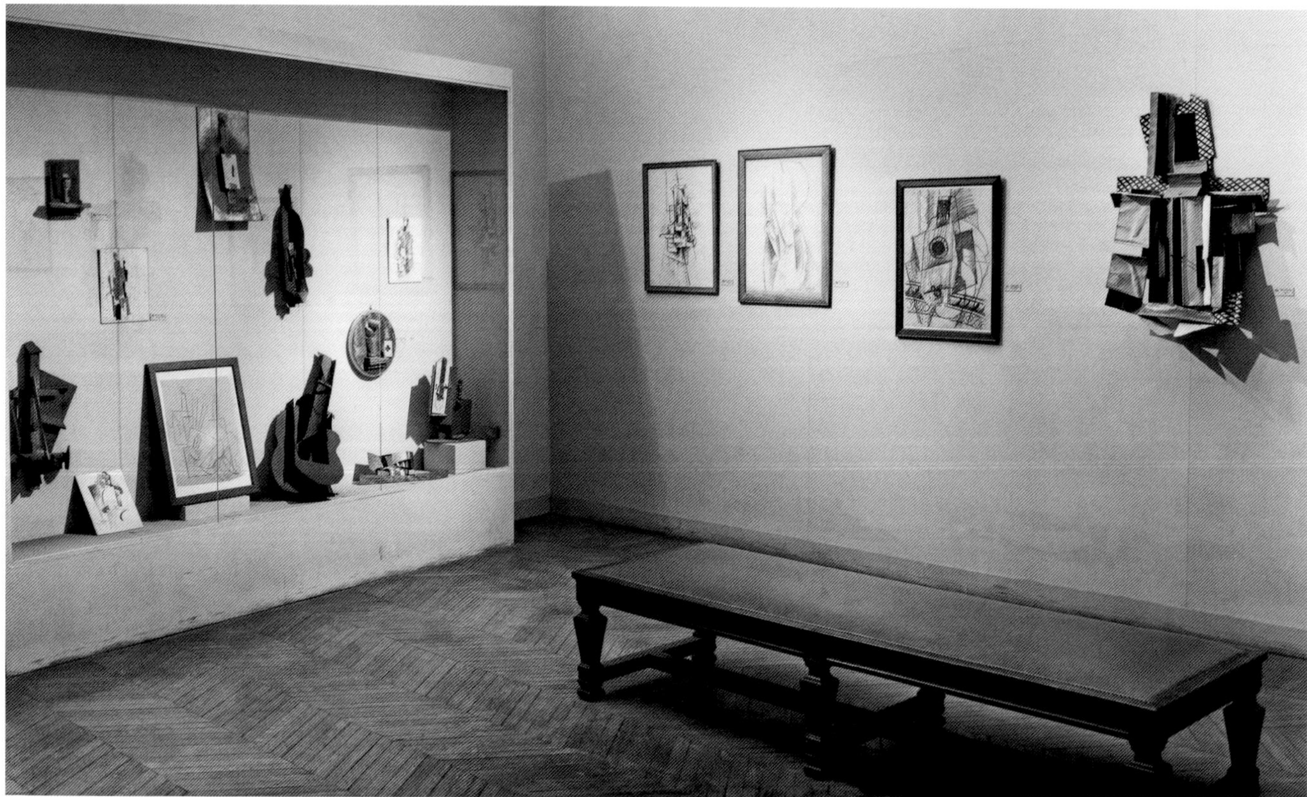

5. View of the exhibition *Hommage à Pablo Picasso* at the Petit Palais, Paris, November 19, 1966–February 12, 1967. In the vitrine, left to right: *Mandolin and Clarinet* ([fall 1913]) at bottom; *Glass and Dice* (variant state; spring 1914) at top; the sheet metal *Guitar* (January–February 1914) at bottom; *Violin and Bottle on a Table* ([fall] 1915) at bottom right; and on the right wall, at far right, *Violin* ([1915]). Archives Petit Palais. Musée des Beaux-Arts de la Ville de Paris

It received an unprecedented amount of coverage from television and print media, with a front-page article in the *New York Times* on February 11 declaring that the work had "virtually changed the course of sculpture in this century" (fig. 6).[39] The work was formally accessioned into the Museum's collection on March 9, 1971.[40]

LATE JANUARY 1914: The Ukrainian painter, designer, and sculptor Vladimir Tatlin left Russia to travel to Berlin and Paris. During his stay in the French capital, Tatlin met with Picasso at his rue Schoelcher studio; the exact dates of his visit are uncertain.[41] He would later recall seeing at the studio a "violin sawn up into pieces, hanging by threads on various planes."[42] Upon his return to Russia, Tatlin began to make three-dimensional constructions. He was outspoken in his admiration for the Spanish artist, and what he christened his "synthetic-static constructions" are greatly indebted to Picasso's contemporaneous sculptures made of wood, paper, cardboard, and metal.[43] *Painterly Relief ("Bottle")* (fig. 7), exhibited in Moscow at the end of 1914, is strikingly similar in its subject matter and use of mixed mediums to Picasso's still life with *Guitar* of 1913, published in *Les Soirées de Paris*.[44]

***STILL LIFE*, SPRING 1914**

Conceived as a relief sculpture depicting a worker's lunch on a table, *Still Life* (pl. 15) was assembled from found or roughly cut wood pieces of varying thickness that Picasso most likely painted after gluing and piecing together all the structural components.[45] It is one of the first Cubist constructions to include nontraditional materials, such as upholstery fringe, and another early example of the artist's use of nails as elements integral to the composition. Here, as Jackie Heuman observes, the dots of the salami are nail heads that the artist painted black.[46] Having received no formal training in sculpture, Picasso had no inhibitions about introducing materials that he thought of as meaningful. The composition of *Still Life* also closely relates to the painting *Glass, Newspaper, and Bottle* of the same period (fig. 8).[47] Like the sculpture, the painting shows a distinct separation between the vertically oriented still life and the horizontal emphasis of its environment. In both instances, the perception of depth is enhanced by shading and surface texture: the actual shade cast by the relief glass in the sculpture, and the use of paint mixed with sand in the painting. Seeing *Glass, Newspaper, and Bottle* juxtaposed with *Still Life* suggests that the sculpture should be perceived as a table rather than the shelf that it literally forms.[48]

Still Life is one of the few Cubist sculptures that Picasso would part with during his lifetime.[49] After its inclusion in the 1936 *Exposition surréaliste d'objets* (Surrealist exhibition of

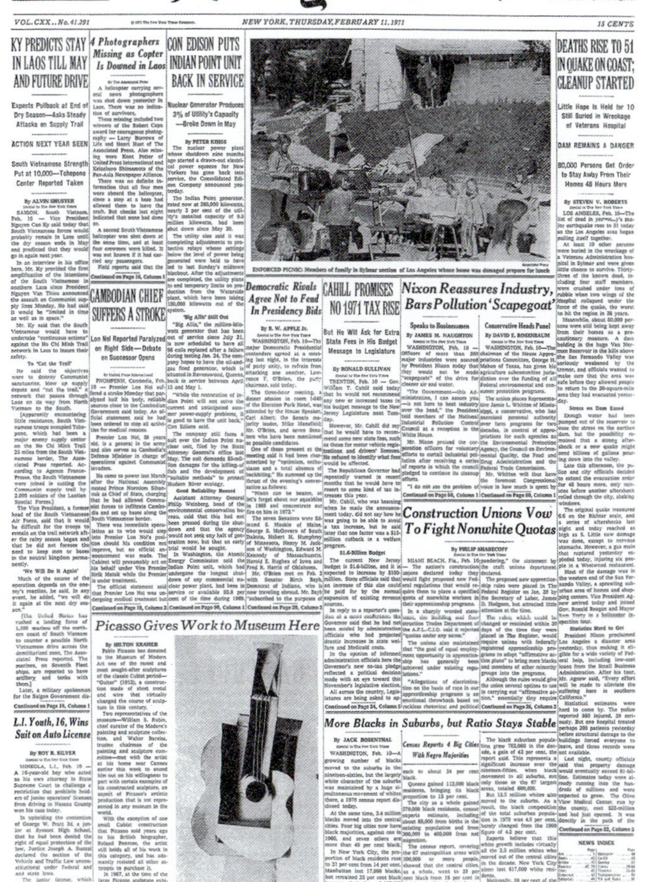

"All the News That's Fit to Print"

The New York Times

LATE CITY EDITION

VOL. CXX.. No. 41,391 — NEW YORK, THURSDAY, FEBRUARY 11, 1971 — 15 CENTS

KY PREDICTS STAY IN LAOS TILL MAY AND FUTURE DRIVE

Expects Pullback at End of Dry Season—Asks Steady Attacks on Supply Trail

ACTION NEXT YEAR SEEN

South Vietnamese Strength Put at 10,000—Tchepone Center Reported Taken

4 Photographers Missing as Copter Is Downed in Laos

CON EDISON PUTS INDIAN POINT UNIT BACK IN SERVICE

Nuclear Generator Produces 3% of Utility's Capacity —Broke Down in May

DEATHS RISE TO 51 IN QUAKE ON COAST; CLEANUP STARTED

Little Hope Is Held for 10 Still Buried in Wreckage of Veterans Hospital

DAM REMAINS A DANGER

80,000 Persons Get Order to Stay Away From Their Homes 48 Hours More

CAMBODIAN CHIEF SUFFERS A STROKE

Lon Nol Reported Paralyzed on Right Side—Debate on Successor Opens

Democratic Rivals Agree Not to Feud In Presidency Bids

CAHILL PROMISES NO 1971 TAX RISE

But He Will Ask for Extra State Fees in His Budget Message to Legislature

Nixon Reassures Industry, Bars Pollution 'Scapegoat'

Construction Unions Vow To Fight Nonwhite Quotas

Picasso Gives Work to Museum Here

By HILTON KRAMER

L.I. Youth, 16, Wins Suit on Auto License

More Blacks in Suburbs, but Ratio Stays Stable

6. The front page of the *New York Times*, featuring an article by Hilton Kramer about Picasso's gift of the sheet metal *Guitar* to The Museum of Modern Art, February 11, 1971

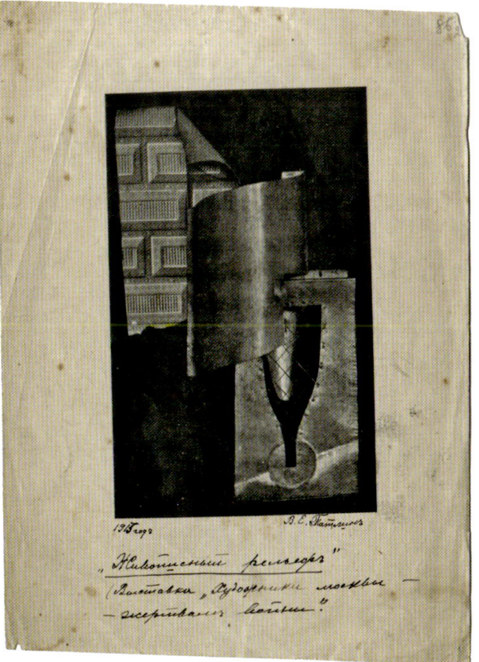

7. A reproduction of Vladimir Tatlin's relief construction *Painterly Relief ("Bottle")* (1914; destroyed) pasted onto paper upside down and inscribed by the artist

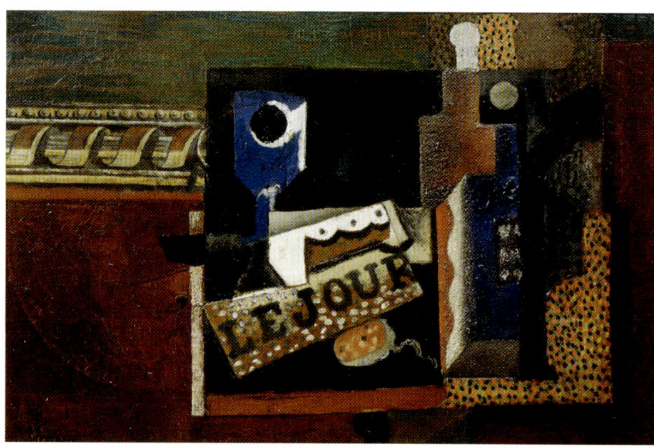

8. Pablo Picasso. *Glass, Newspaper, and Bottle*. Paris, 1914. Oil and sand on canvas, 14 ¼ × 24 in. (36 × 61 cm). Private collection, United States

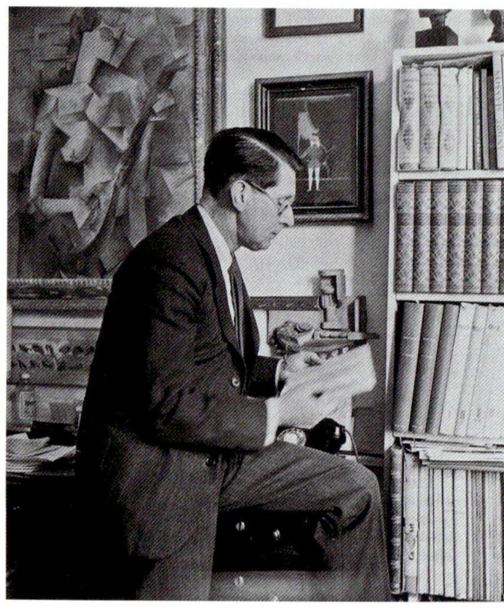

10. Roland Penrose at 11A Hornton Street, London, c. 1955, with Picasso's *Still Life* partially visible behind him. Photograph by Lee Miller. Lee Miller Archives, London

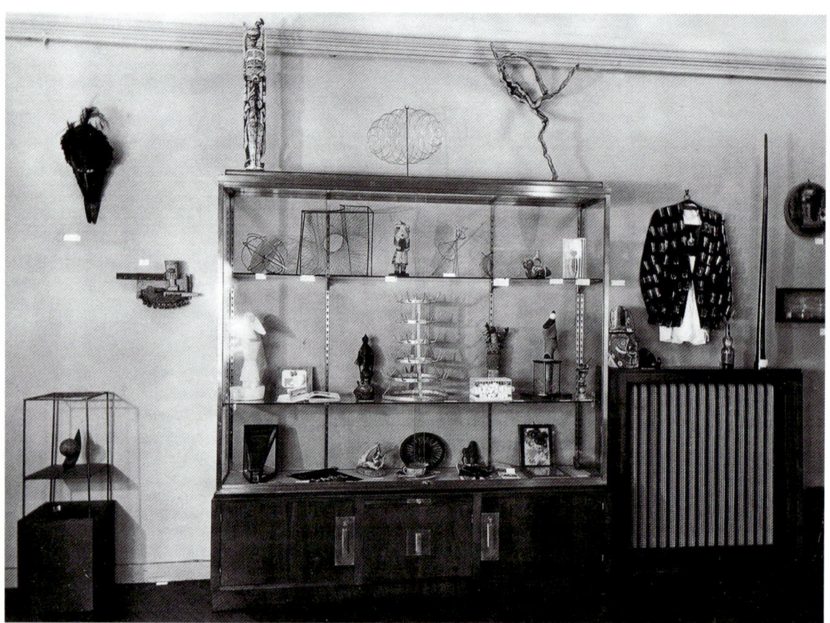

9. View of *Exposition surréaliste d'objets* (Surrealist exhibition of objects) at the Galerie Charles Ratton, Paris, May 22–29, 1936, with Picasso's Cubist construction *Still Life* hanging midwall on the left and *Glass of Absinthe* inside the vitrine on the middle shelf to the right (both spring 1914). Photograph by Man Ray. Guy Ladrière Archives, Paris

objects), organized by André Breton at the Galerie Charles Ratton in Paris (fig. 9), Picasso either gave or sold it to his friend the Surrealist poet Paul Eluard. Only two years later, in June 1938, the sculpture entered the collection of the English Surrealist painter and poet Roland Penrose, who would later be Picasso's biographer and the organizing director of the 1967 exhibition of his sculpture at the Tate Gallery, London, and The Museum of Modern Art (fig. 10). Beginning in the 1940s, Penrose lent *Still Life* to several sculpture and Surrealist exhibitions, making it accessible to the public at a time when other Cubist sculptures were stored away by the artist. When Picasso was preparing his sculptures for the monumental 1966 *Hommage à Pablo Picasso* show in Paris, a number of the Cubist constructions needed to be repaired. In a letter to Monroe Wheeler dated September 28, 1966, Penrose observed that Picasso "had formerly discarded [the Cubist reliefs] as hopelessly damaged and is now putting [them] together again."[50]

GLASS AND DICE (VARIANT STATE), SPRING 1914

Glass and Dice (pl. 18) was conceived as a simpler version of *Still Life* and constructed in much the same way as the larger relief. According to an early exhibition catalogue, a leather fringe, no longer present, hid the unpainted underside of the tabletop.[51] Unlike *Still Life*, in which the fluted glass casts its own shadow, Picasso used shading in *Glass and Dice* to create a perplexing effect: the glass cut from two pieces of wood projects into the viewer's space, but at the same time it recedes visually as a result of the painted shadow to its left. Picasso also explored this trompe l'oeil technique and doubled representation in his contemporaneous papiers collés and paintings.

GLASS, NEWSPAPER, AND DICE; *BOTTLE OF BASS, GLASS, AND NEWSPAPER*; AND *GLASS*, SPRING 1914

The newspaper depicted in the framed relief *Glass, Newspaper, and Dice* (pl. 19) is made from pieces of a can of dehydrated milk, as are the tin elements used in the freestanding sculptures *Bottle of Bass, Glass, and Newspaper* and *Glass* (pls. 16, 17). Paint now augmented the cutting and folding of thin metal

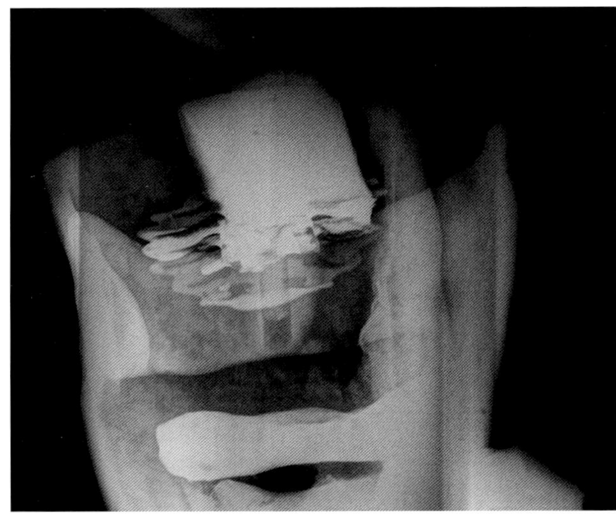

11. X-radiograph of the upper section of *Glass of Absinthe* (The Museum of Modern Art), showing the connection between the bronze sugar cube, the absinthe spoon, and the rim of the glass. X-radiograph taken and prepared by Lynda Zycherman, Conservator of Sculpture, The Museum of Modern Art, New York

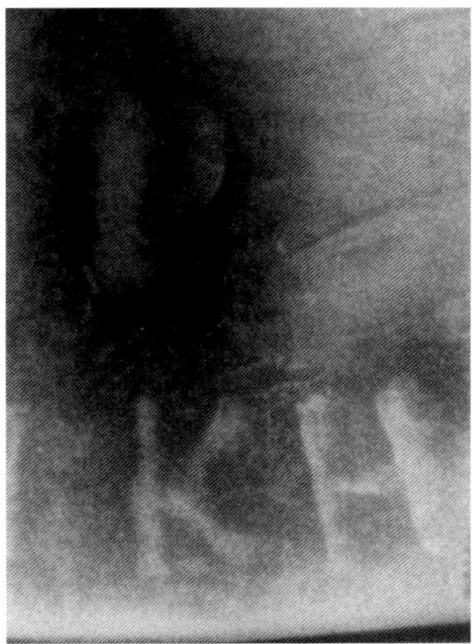

12. X-radiograph detail of the bottom cone of *Glass of Absinthe* (The Museum of Modern Art), showing both the exterior *P* and part of the interior marking in raised relief: *IIII HK*. The letter *K* faces backward, though it appears in the correct orientation in this image because the x-radiograph was taken through the exterior wall of the conical base. Image taken and prepared by Lynda Zycherman, Conservator of Sculpture, The Museum of Modern Art, New York

that Picasso had explored for the first time in the unpainted sheet metal *Guitar*. Of the two freestanding sculptures, *Bottle of Bass, Glass, and Newspaper* is more complex in its construction and decoration. Conceived as a high relief meant to be seen from the front, like the 1906 *Kneeling Woman Combing Her Hair* (pl. 5), the sculpture is not painted on the back. The paper label of the dried-milk tin ("COMPAGNIE FRANCAISE DU LAIT SEC") is visible along the rim of the sculpture's base. Picasso cut, bent, and folded the tin into four distinct sections; the resulting components were then carefully painted to animate the still life arrangement. The blue spots along the bottle's neck may indicate foaming bubbles; the gritty texture of the bottle's outer surface, which resulted from mixing sand into the paint, suggests condensation droplets.[52] All three works would be first published in 1942 in the second volume of Christian Zervos's catalogue raisonné.[53]

GLASS OF ABSINTHE, SPRING 1914

Picasso modeled *Glass of Absinthe* in wax, adding a real absinthe spoon (pls. 21–26). It was not the first time the artist introduced unconventional materials into his art, but as he later told Werner Spies, "the relation between the real spoon and the modeled glass" interested him, especially "in the way they clashed with each other."[54] It was the only Cubist sculpture to be editioned by Kahnweiler. In the spring of 1914, Kahnweiler had six bronze casts made, each of which Picasso decorated uniquely. They were assembled at the foundry, using a pin-shaft system to attach an absinthe spoon to each bronze glass.[55]

An x-radiograph of the upper section of one version shows that a pin—cast separately in bronze—penetrates the sugar cube, then passes through the spoon and a shaft along the rim of the glass to hold the three components together (fig. 11). It is not known which Parisian foundry Kahnweiler employed, as none of the bronzes is stamped with a foundry mark.[56] What is known is that Kahnweiler had each cast numbered—they are marked "0" through "V"—and had his initials, "HK," marked in high relief on the inside bottom cone of all but the first (fig. 12).[57] Kahnweiler's correspondence with Kramář indicates that Picasso must have received all six sometime in the spring and that he had finished painting all of them by June 1914. It is likely that Picasso first received the cast marked "0" (pl. 21) as an artist's proof for his review, and that the others followed shortly thereafter.[58] In a letter to Kramář dated July 3, Kahnweiler included thirty-five photographs of recent works by Picasso, among which were images of the five *Glass of Absinthe* casts he had recently acquired as part of his contract with the artist.[59] Kahnweiler wrote: "As you will see, among these works is a sculpture. It is a bronze painted with oil. There are five copies, each of course different."[60] One of these images was likely a picture taken by the photographer Émile Delétang for Kahnweiler that shows a cast Picasso had partially decorated with paint mixed with sand (pl. 22)—a technique he had tried on the cut-and-folded tin sculptures of the same period. In a letter of July 18, Kahnweiler sent additional photographs to Kramář, who had shown an interest in one of the casts.[61] However, Kramář would never acquire one. Kahnweiler closed

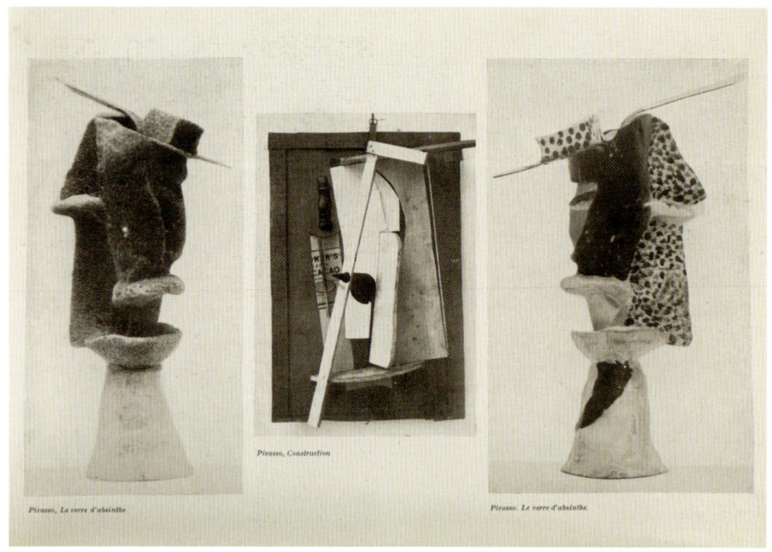

13. Two *Glass of Absinthe* casts reproduced at left and right in Christian Zervos, "Les Sculptures des peintres d'aujourd'hui" (Sculptures by today's painters), *Cahiers d'Art* (1928): 288. *Bottle and Guitar* (no longer extant) is at center.

his gallery for the summer, and after World War I broke out that August, as a German citizen he was forced into exile. His gallery remained closed.

Kahnweiler's photographs stayed in Kramář's possession and soon circulated among the avant-garde artists he knew in Prague. The earliest known publication to illustrate one of the *Glass of Absinthe* casts was Kahnweiler's *Der Weg zum Kubismus* (The rise of Cubism), published in Munich in 1920.[62] This was followed by Zervos's 1928 essay "Les Sculptures des peintres d'aujourd'hui" (Sculptures by today's painters), which included two of the six casts (fig. 13).[63] The earliest known exhibition to include one of the casts was the 1929 group show *Seit Cézanne in Paris* (Since Cézanne in Paris) at Flechtheim's Berlin gallery.[64] A different cast would be included in the 1936 Surrealist exhibition of objects organized by Breton (see fig. 9); that cast belonged to the French dealer Paul Rosenberg.

GLASS AND NEWSPAPER, SUMMER 1914

In late June, Picasso arrived in Avignon, in southern France. He lived in a rented house at 14, rue Saint-Bernard, remaining until mid-November because the onset of World War I prevented him from returning to Paris. Parallel to painting a series of predominantly green still lifes, Picasso took up work again on the small wooden constructions he had started to make in Paris that spring. As in *Glass, Newspaper, and Dice,* he used a small wooden box to frame his painterly relief *Glass and Newspaper* (pl. 20). Unlike the earlier work, which features a fluted wine glass, Picasso now adopted a rounder version of a glass, which Pierre Daix identified as "a veritable Avignon signature."[65]

DECEMBER 12, 1914: The stock of Kahnweiler's gallery at 28, rue Vignon was sequestered by the French government. With the outbreak of war, Kahnweiler had been declared an "enemy alien"; as such, his property was subject to confiscation.[66] Five of the six *Glass of Absinthe* casts were among the seized works, the only sculptures by Picasso known to have been affected.

Seven years later, Kahnweiler's confiscated stock would be put up for sale by the French government in a series of four auctions at the Hôtel Drouot in Paris. On June 14, 1921, the *Glass of Absinthe* casts sold for a fraction of their July 1914 value of 1,000 French francs (fig. 14).[67]

VIOLIN AND BOTTLE ON A TABLE, [FALL] 1915

One of two wooden constructions of the late Cubist period, *Violin and Bottle on a Table* (pl. 27) is reminiscent of the environments found in Boccioni's plastic ensembles. In Picasso's sculpture, the wainscoting extends away from the central representation, as in his earlier papiers collés. It thus creates a space surrounding the table, the musical instrument, and the bottle, which is both drawn (the body) and constructed (the neck). *Violin and Bottle on a Table* exemplifies Picasso's

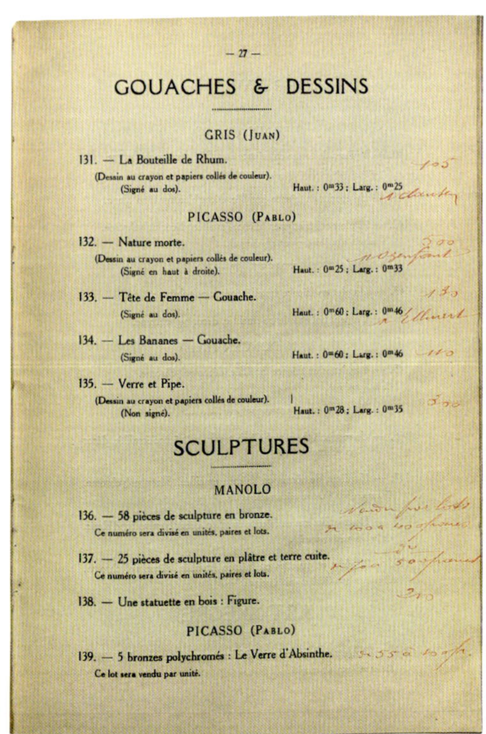
— 27 —

GOUACHES & DESSINS

GRIS (JUAN)

131. — La Bouteille de Rhum.
(Dessin au crayon et papiers collés de couleur).
(Signé au dos). Haut. : 0m33 ; Larg. : 0m25

PICASSO (PABLO)

132. — Nature morte.
(Dessin au crayon et papiers collés de couleur).
(Signé en haut à droite). Haut. : 0m25 ; Larg. : 0m33

133. — Tête de Femme — Gouache.
(Signé au dos). Haut. : 0m60 ; Larg. : 0m46

134. — Les Bananes — Gouache.
(Signé au dos). Haut. : 0m60 ; Larg. : 0m46

135. — Verre et Pipe.
(Dessin au crayon et papiers collés de couleur).
(Non signé). Haut. : 0m28 ; Larg. : 0m35

SCULPTURES

MANOLO

136. — 58 pièces de sculpture en bronze.
Ce numéro sera divisé en unités, paires et lots.

137. — 25 pièces de sculpture en plâtre et terre cuite.
Ce numéro sera divisé en unités, paires et lots.

138. — Une statuette en bois : Figure.

PICASSO (PABLO)

139. — 5 bronzes polychromés : Le Verre d'Absinthe.
Ce lot sera vendu par unité.

14. Annotated copy of the catalogue for the first Kahnweiler sequestration sale, at the Hôtel Drouot, Paris, June 13–14, 1921. Thomas J. Watson Library, The Metropolitan Museum of Art, New York

ability to imagine conventional everyday materials as meaningful objects in his sculpture: three nails have become pegs holding the instrument's strings at the top of the neck.

VIOLIN, [1915]

Violin (pl. 28) was assembled using four pieces of bent, cut, and folded sheet metal. To these Picasso added the top and bottom of a narrow tin box (the face of the violin); iron rings; and a few staples, which appear to hold the pieces together here and there. The elaborate multicolored paint surface—which Picasso applied before and after bending the sheet metal elements into shape—creates an even more hybrid category, hovering between painting and sculpture, than the earlier monochromatic *Guitars*.[68]

Unlike most of Picasso's Cubist constructions, *Violin* would enter the public sphere early on. In 1928 the sculpture was reproduced in André Level's monograph about Picasso.[69] *Violin* would be shown for the first time in the 1936 Surrealist exhibition at the Galerie Charles Ratton (fig. 15).[70] Breton boasted in a press release about having obtained for the exhibition a number of works from Picasso's studio that would be shown for the first time.[71]

GUITAR, 1924

In the mid-1910s, Picasso set aside the making of sculpture per se. His first important postwar construction was a monumental sheet metal *Guitar* (pl. 29), created in 1924, that measures almost four feet tall. It is closely related in scale, subject matter, and technique to Picasso's sheet metal *Guitar* (pl. 14) and *Violin* (pl. 28). But while these earlier works were composed from multiple pieces of metal, the 1924 *Guitar* is made from a single sheet, along with some wire and a tin-plate box.

Not long after it was made, *Guitar* was reproduced in the first issue of the journal *La Révolution surréaliste*. It accompanied Pierre Reverdy's text "Le Rêveur parmi les murailles" (The Dreamer amid the walls) (fig. 16). The illustration heralded the close association with Picasso that Surrealist writers and artists would cultivate in the years to follow. Picasso's Cubist constructions struck Breton as exemplary of the artist's ability to conjure the marvelous from the everyday. Like the 1915 *Violin* and other related works, *Guitar* was included in the 1936 Surrealist exhibition of objects at the Galerie Charles Ratton (see fig. 25 on p. 147).

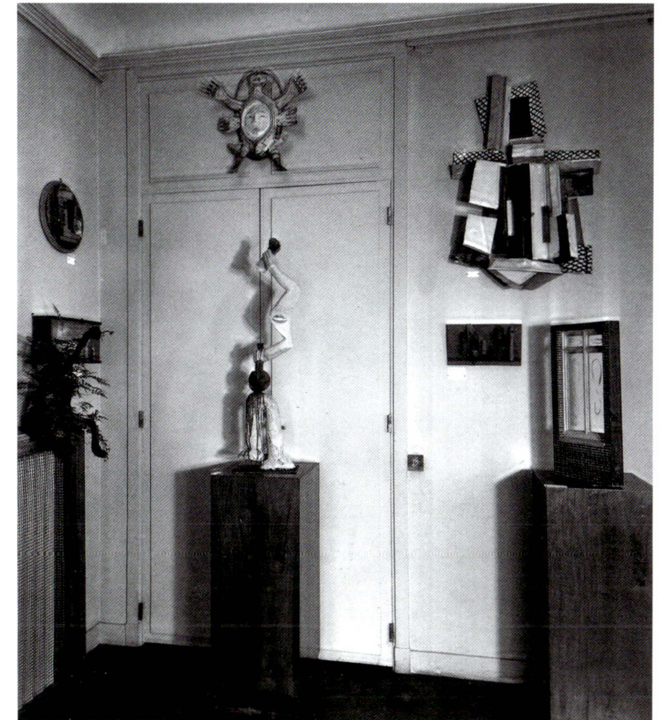

15. View of *Exposition surréaliste d'objets* (Surrealist exhibition of objects) at the Galerie Charles Ratton, Paris, May 22–29, 1936, with Picasso's *Glass, Pipe, and Playing Card* (summer 1914) and *Violin* ([1915]) installed at top of left wall and opposite at top right, respectively. Photograph by Man Ray. Guy Ladrière Archives, Paris

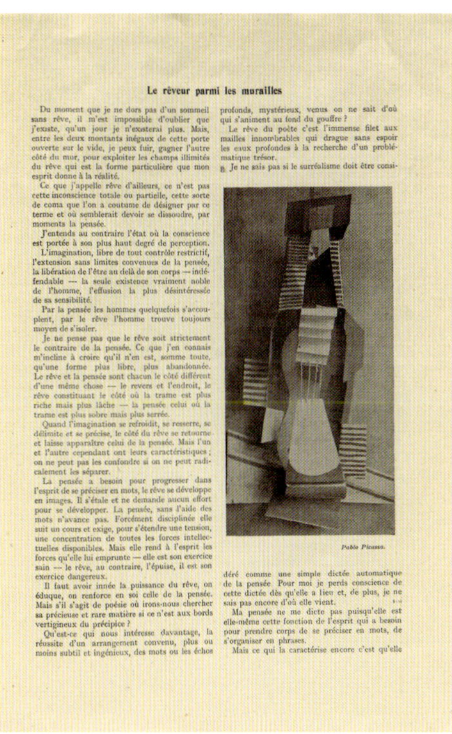

Le rêveur parmi les murailles

Du moment que je ne dors pas d'un sommeil sans rêve, il m'est impossible d'oublier que j'existe, qu'un jour je n'existerai plus. Mais, entre les deux montants inégaux de cette porte ouverte sur le vide, je peux fuir, gagner l'autre côté du mur, pour exploiter les champs illimités du rêve qui est la forme particulière que mon esprit donne à la réalité.

Ce que j'appelle rêve d'ailleurs, ce n'est pas cette inconscience totale ou partielle, cette sorte de coma que l'on a coutume de désigner par ce terme et où semblerait devoir se dissoudre, par moments la pensée.

J'entends au contraire l'état où la conscience est portée à son plus haut degré de perception.

L'imagination, libre de tout contrôle restrictif, l'extension sans limites convenues de la pensée, la libération de l'être au delà de son corps — indéfendable — la seule existence vraiment noble de l'homme, l'effusion la plus désintéressée de sa sensibilité.

Par la pensée les hommes quelquefois s'accouplent, par le rêve l'homme trouve toujours moyen de s'isoler.

Je ne pense pas que le rêve soit strictement le contraire de la pensée. Ce que j'en connais m'incline à croire qu'il n'en est, somme toute, qu'une forme plus libre, plus abandonnée. Le rêve et la pensée sont chacun le côté différent d'une même chose — le revers et l'endroit, le rêve constituant le côté où la trame est plus riche mais plus lâche — la pensée celui où la trame est plus sobre mais plus serrée.

Quand l'imagination se refroidit, se resserre, se délimite et se précise, le côté du rêve se retourne et laisse apparaître celui de la pensée. Mais l'un et l'autre cependant ont leurs caractéristiques ; on ne peut pas les confondre si on ne peut radicalement les séparer.

La pensée a besoin pour progresser dans l'esprit de se préciser en mots, le rêve se développe en images. Il s'étale et ne demande aucun effort pour se développer. La pensée, sans l'aide des mots n'avance pas. Forcément disciplinée elle suit un cours et exige, pour s'étendre une tension, une concentration de toutes les forces intellectuelles disponibles. Mais elle rend à l'esprit les forces qu'elle lui emprunte — elle est son exercice sain — le rêve, au contraire, l'épuise, il est son exercice dangereux.

Il faut avoir innée la puissance du rêve, on éduque, on renforce en soi celle de la pensée. Mais s'il s'agit de poésie où irons-nous chercher sa précieuse et rare matière si ce n'est aux bords vertigineux du précipice ?

Qu'est-ce qui nous intéresse davantage, la réussite d'un arrangement convenu, plus ou moins subtil et ingénieux, des mots ou les échos profonds, mystérieux, venus on ne sait d'où qui s'animent au fond du gouffre ?

Le rêve du poète c'est l'immense filet aux mailles innombrables qui drague sans espoir les eaux profondes à la recherche d'un problématique trésor.

Je ne sais pas si le surréalisme doit être considéré comme une simple dictée automatique de la pensée. Pour moi je perds conscience de cette dictée dès qu'elle a lieu et, de plus, je ne sais pas encore d'où elle vient.

Ma pensée ne me dicte pas puisqu'elle est elle-même cette fonction de l'esprit qui a besoin pour prendre corps de se préciser en mots, de s'organiser en phrases.

Mais ce qui la caractérise encore c'est qu'elle

Pablo Picasso.

16. *Guitar* reproduced in *La Révolution surréaliste* 1, no. 1 (December 1, 1924): 19

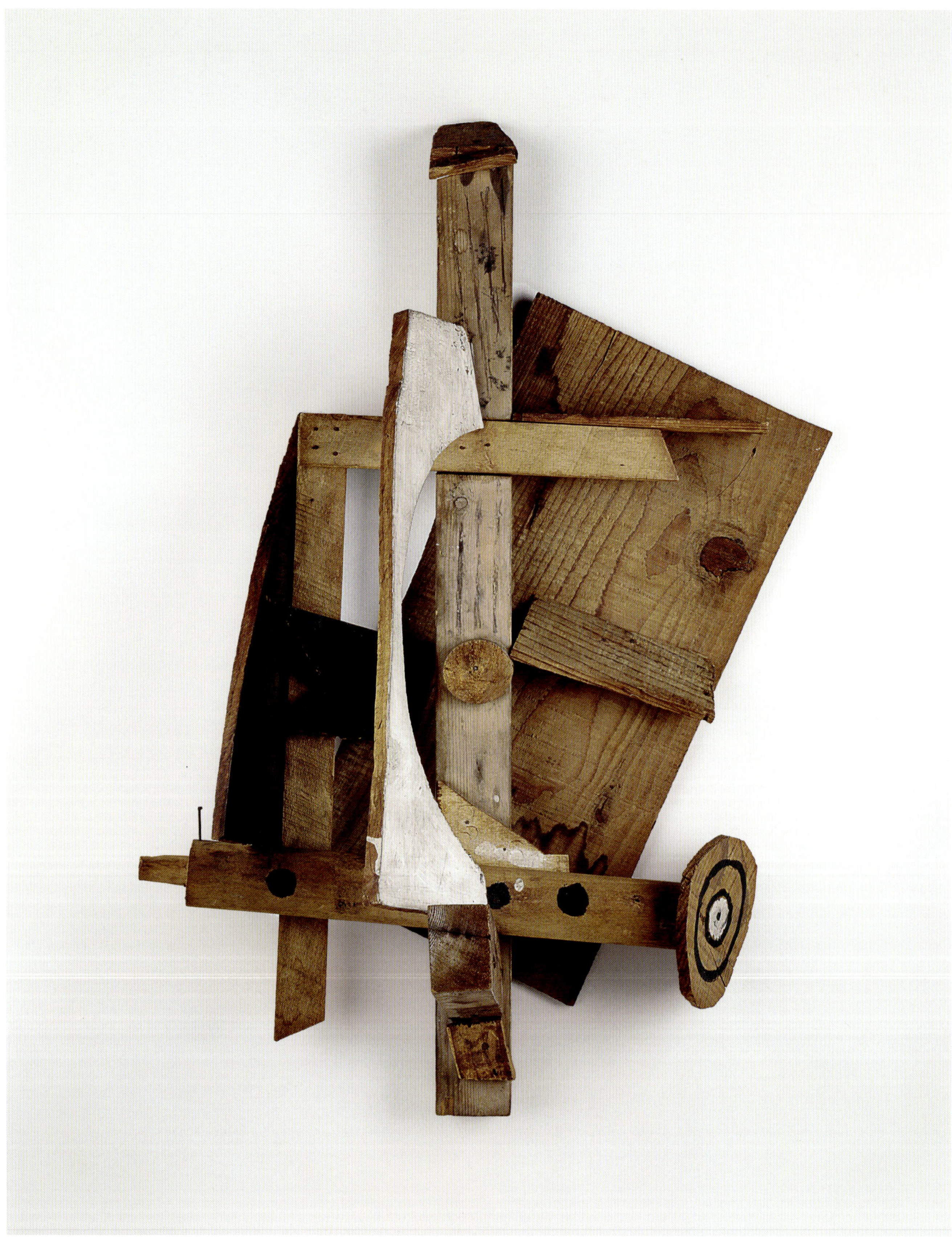

12. **MANDOLIN AND CLARINET.** Paris, [fall 1913]
Painted fir with pencil
22 13/16 × 14 3/16 × 9 1/16 in. (58 × 36 × 23 cm)
Musée national Picasso–Paris. Dation Pablo Picasso

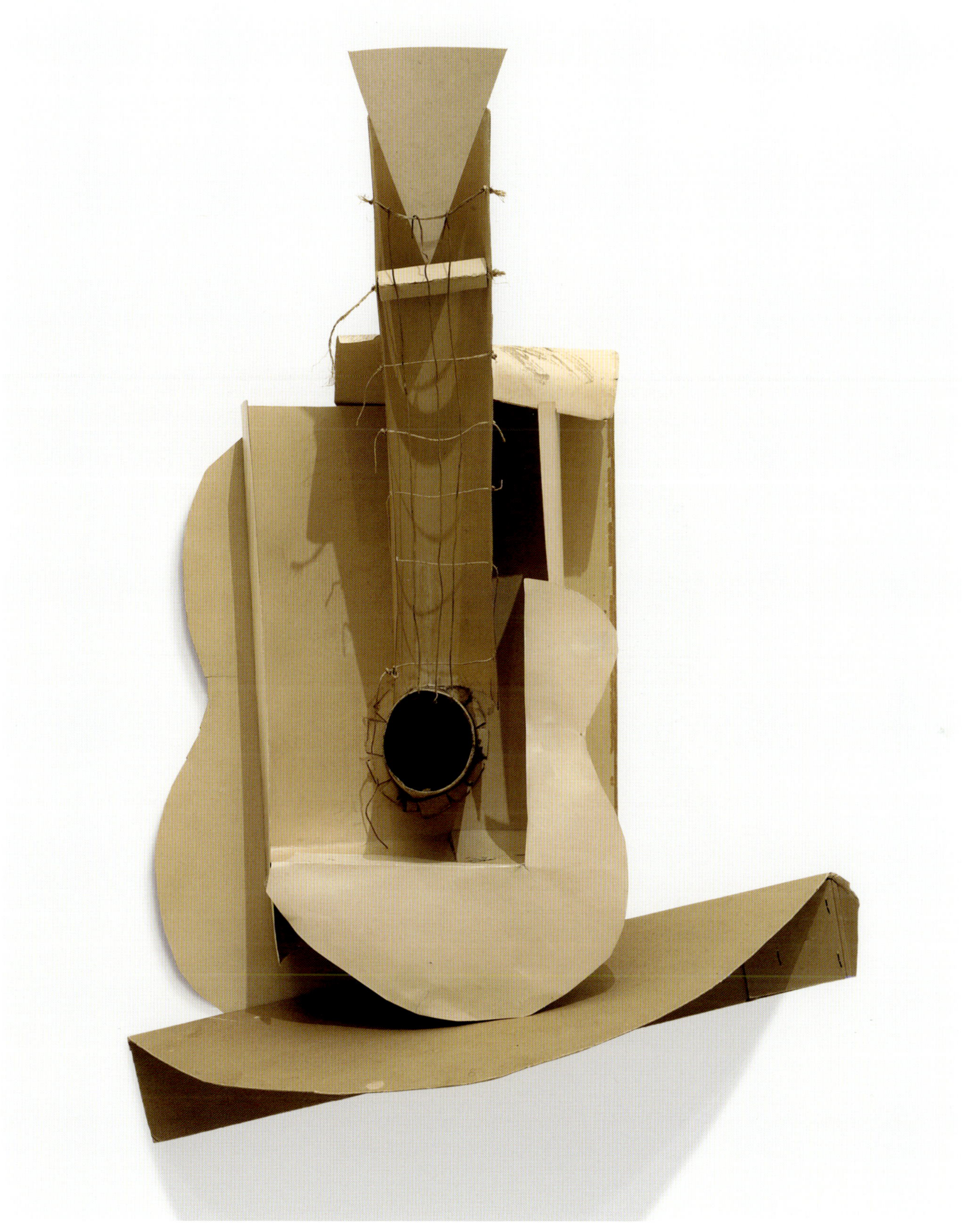

13. Still life with **GUITAR.** Variant state. Paris, assembled before November 15, 1913. Subsequently preserved by the artist
Paperboard, paper, thread, string, twine, and coated wire installed with cut cardboard box
Overall 30 × 20 ½ × 7 ¾ in. (76.2 × 52.1 × 19.7 cm)
The Museum of Modern Art, New York. Gift of the artist

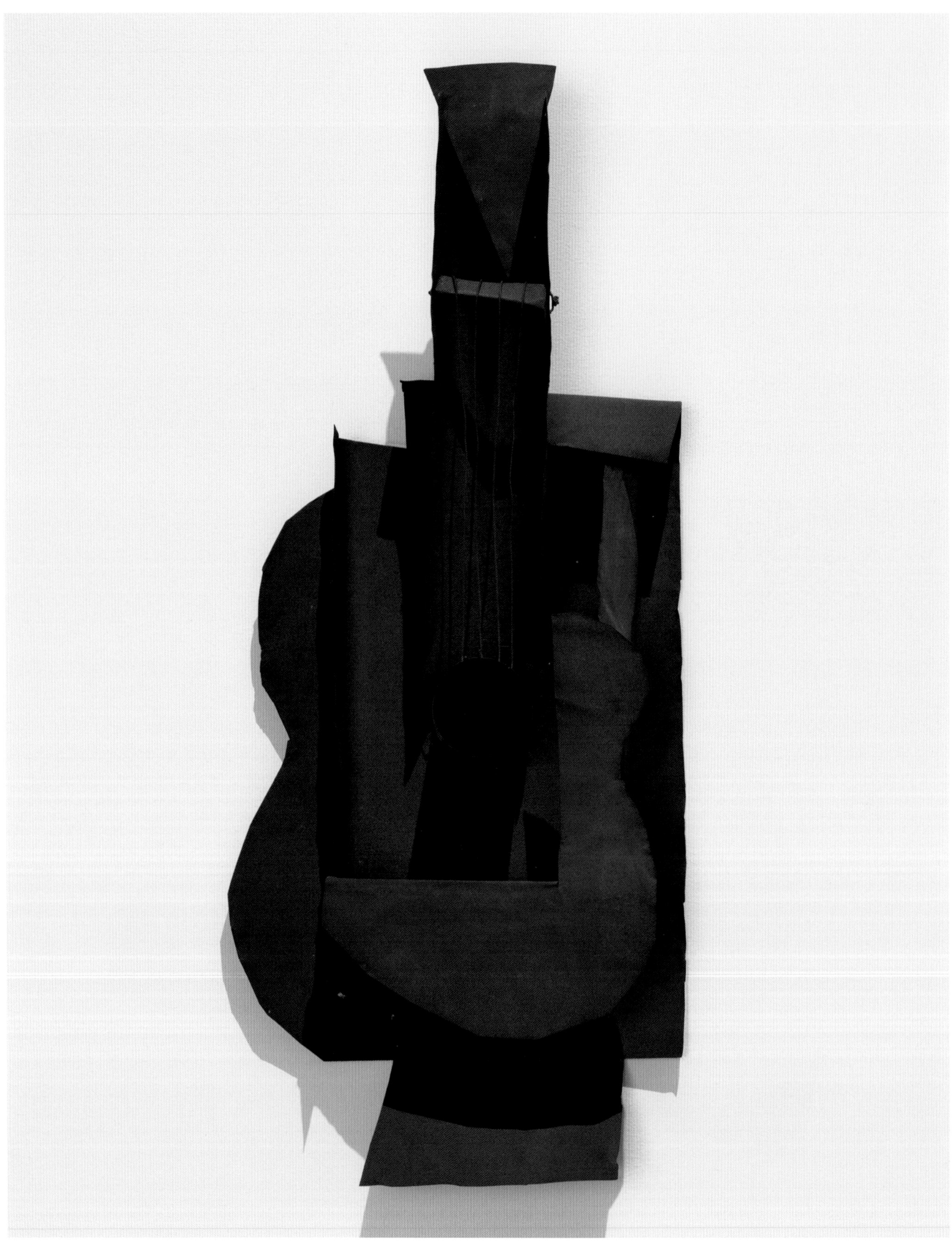

14. GUITAR. Paris, January–February 1914
Ferrous sheet metal and wire
30 ½ × 13 ¾ × 7 ⅝ in. (77.5 × 35 × 19.3 cm)
The Museum of Modern Art, New York. Gift of the artist

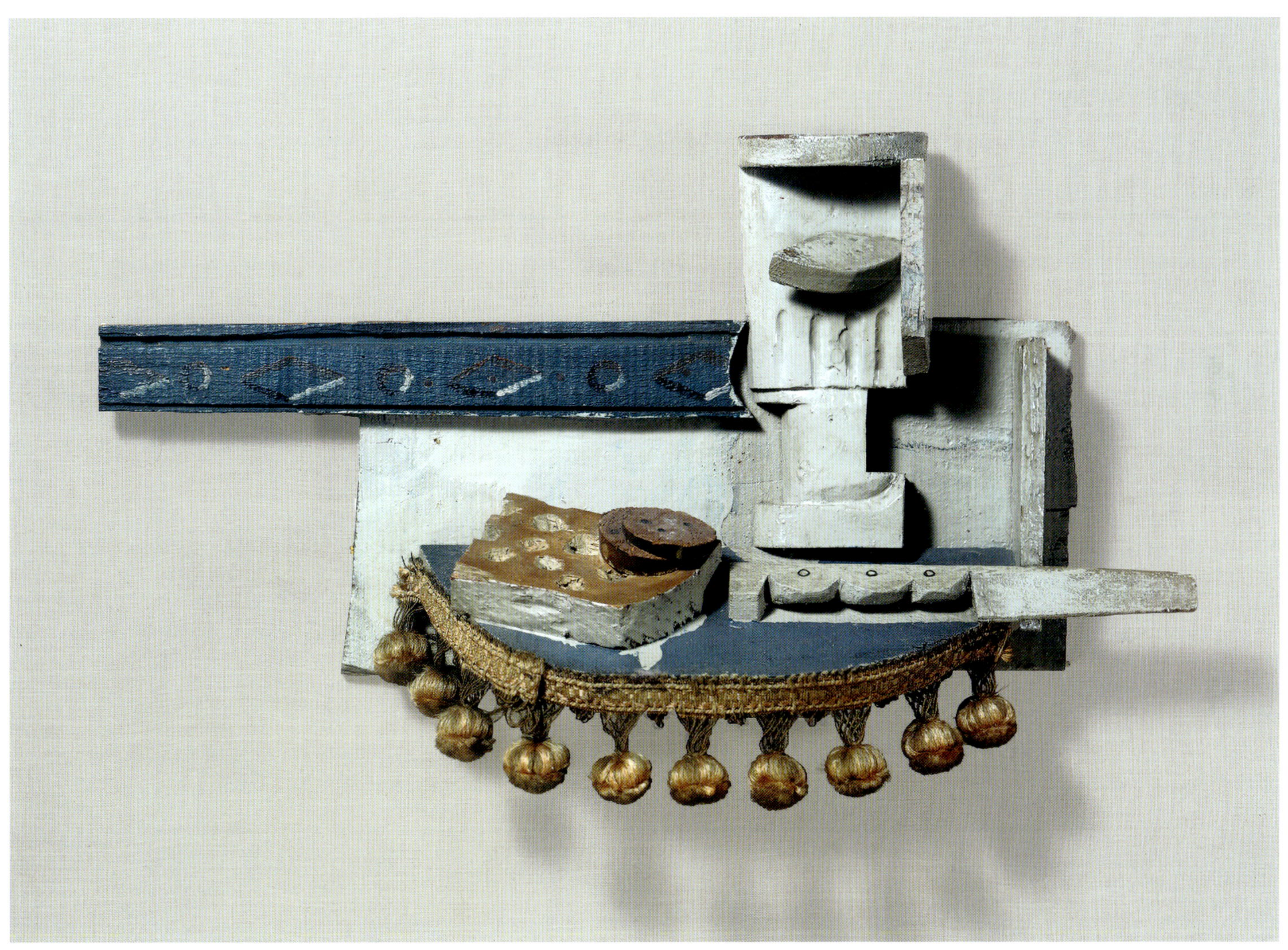

15. **STILL LIFE.** Paris, spring 1914
Painted pine and poplar, nails, and upholstery fringe
10 × 18 × 3⅝ in. (25.4 × 45.7 × 9.2 cm)
Tate. Purchase

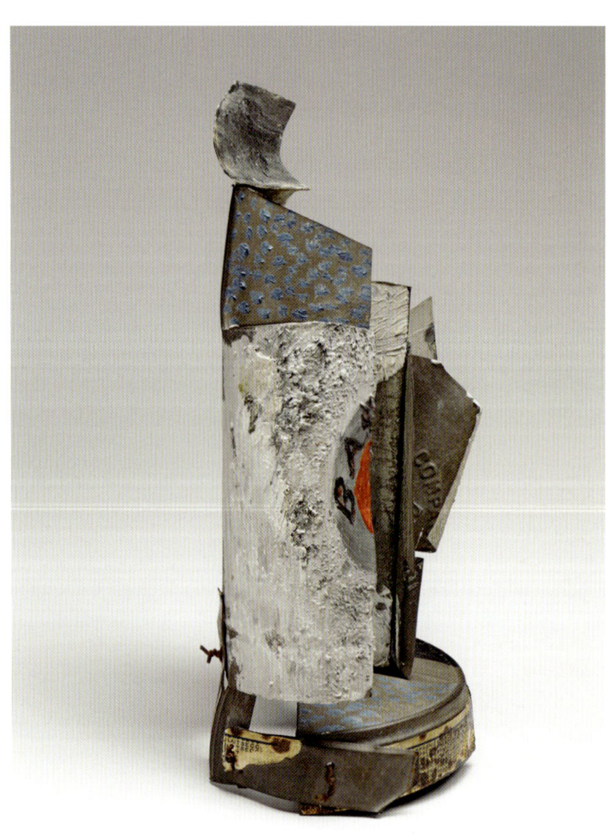

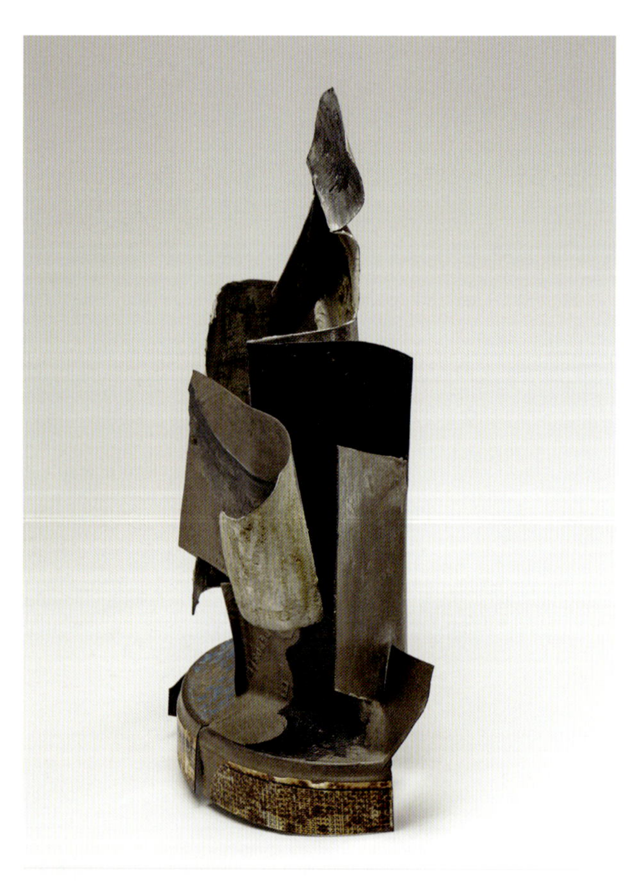

16. **BOTTLE OF BASS, GLASS, AND NEWSPAPER.** Paris, spring 1914
Painted tin plate, sand, iron wire, and paper
7 ⅞ × 5 ½ × 3 ⅜ in. (20 × 14 × 8.5 cm)
Musée national Picasso–Paris. Dation Pablo Picasso

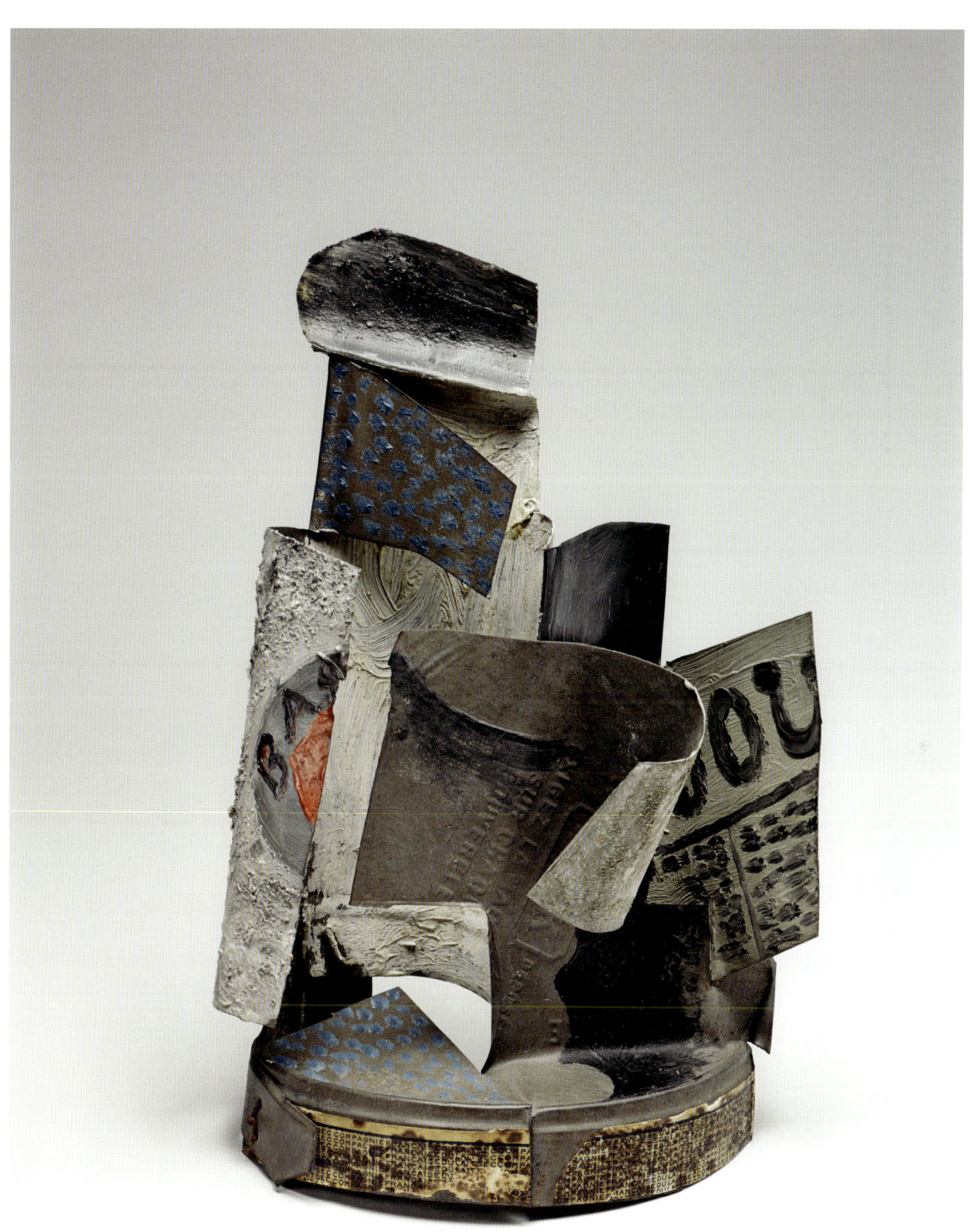
BA
OU

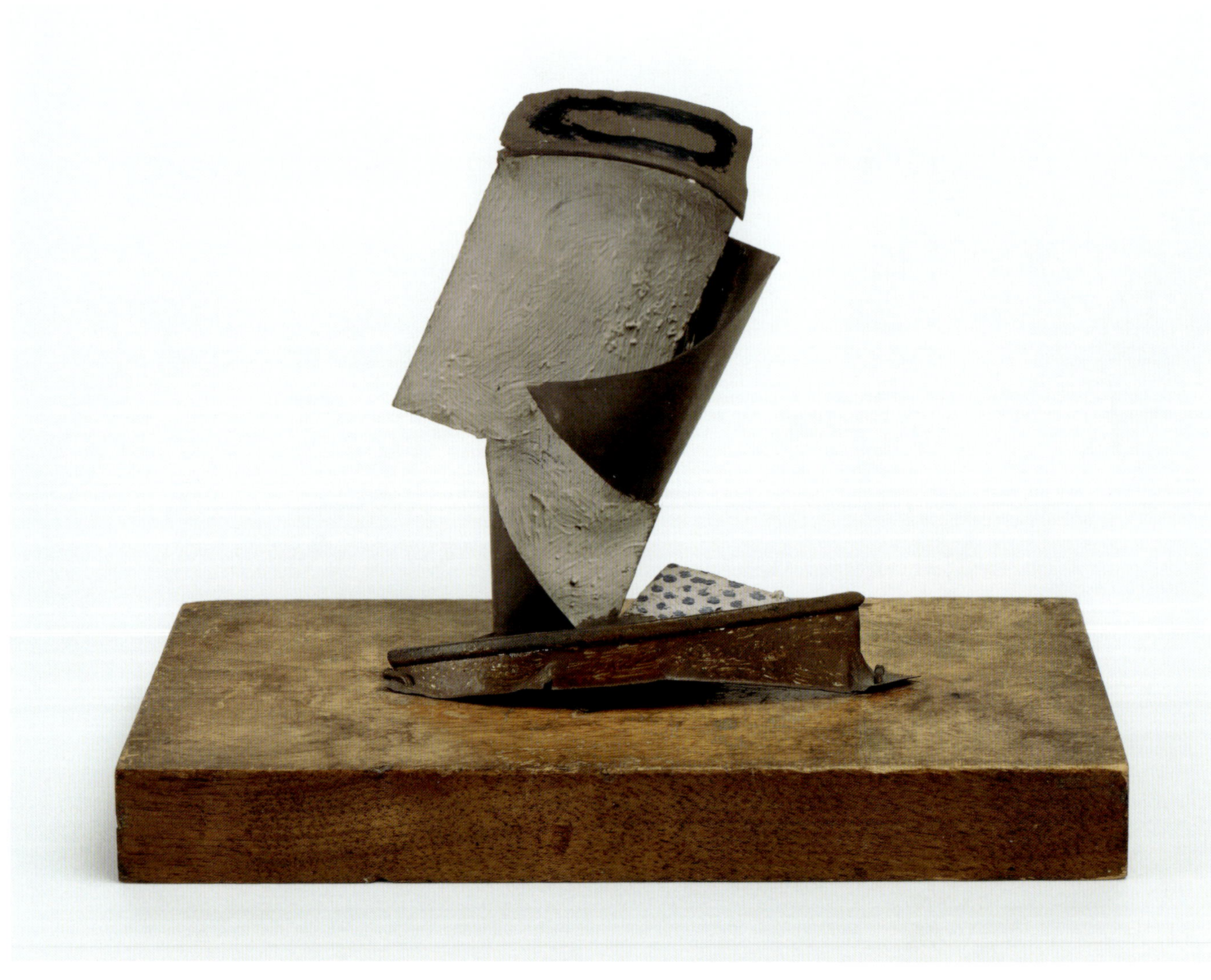

17. **GLASS.** Paris, spring 1914
Painted tin plate, nails, and wood
5 ½ × 7 ⅞ × 3 15/16 in. (14 × 20 × 10 cm)
Musée national Picasso–Paris. Dation Pablo Picasso

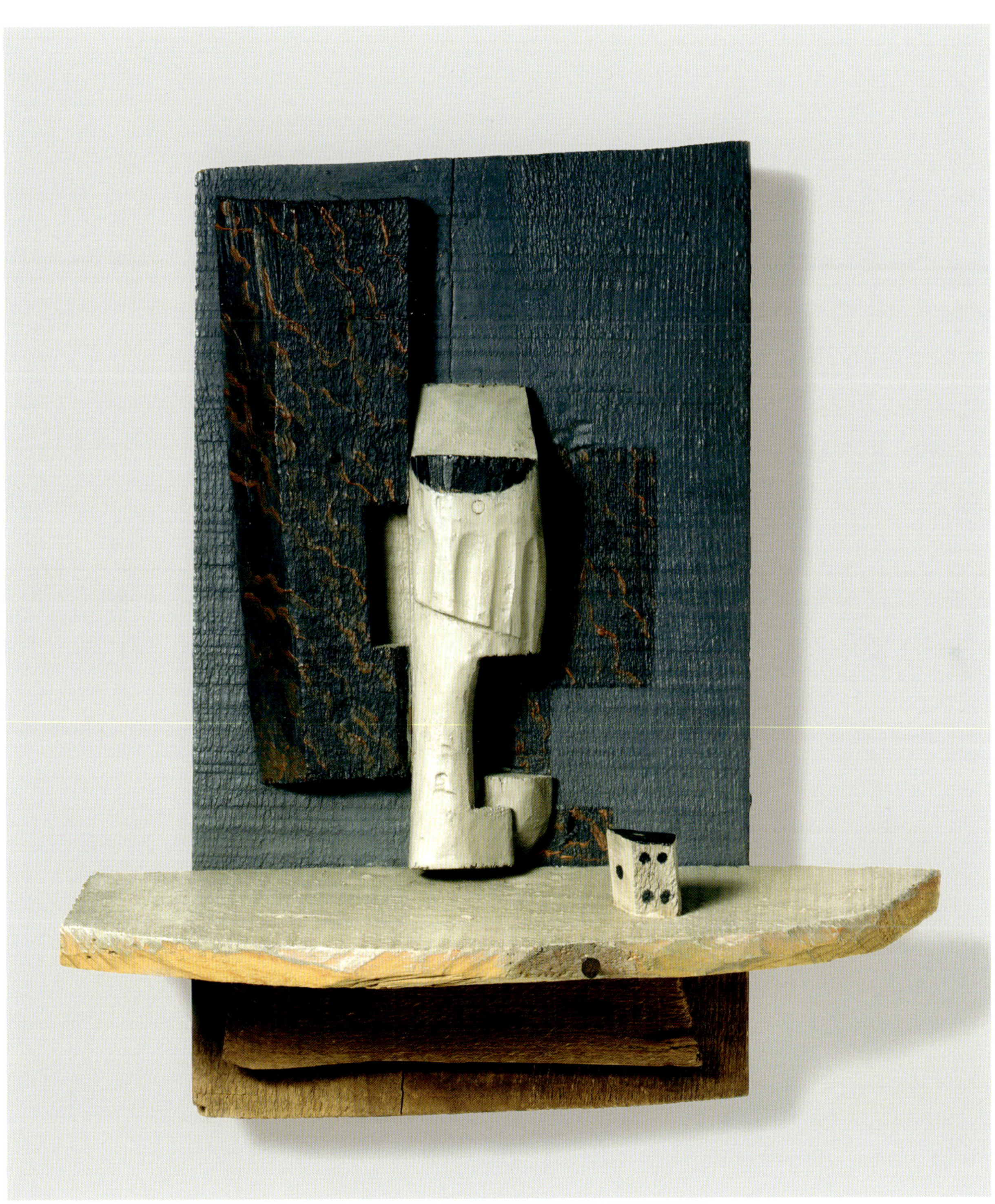

18. **GLASS AND DICE.** Variant state. Paris, spring 1914
Painted wood
9 1/4 × 8 5/8 × 1 7/8 in. (23.5 × 22 × 4.8 cm)
Private collection

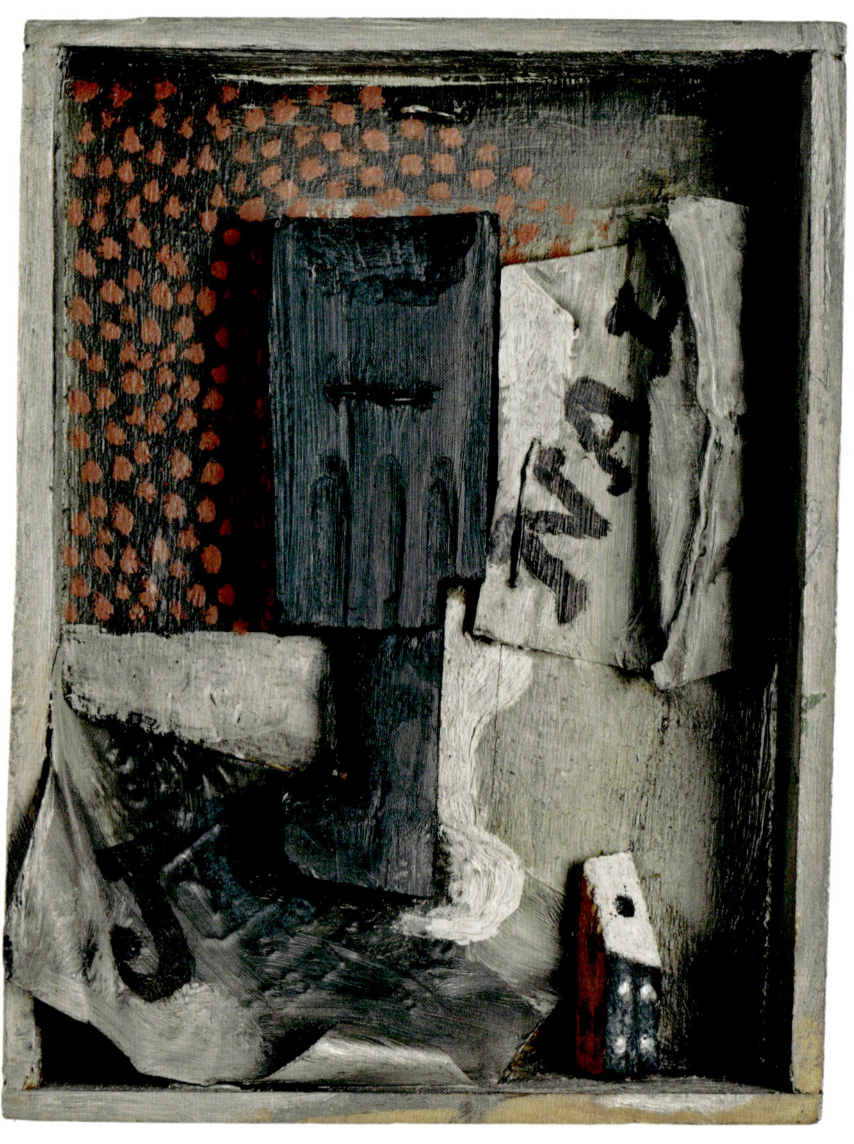

19. **GLASS, NEWSPAPER, AND DICE.** Paris, spring 1914
Painted fir and tin plate, iron wire, and oil on wood panel
6 ⅞ × 5 5⁄16 × 1 3⁄16 in. (17.4 × 13.5 × 3 cm)
Musée national Picasso–Paris. Dation Pablo Picasso

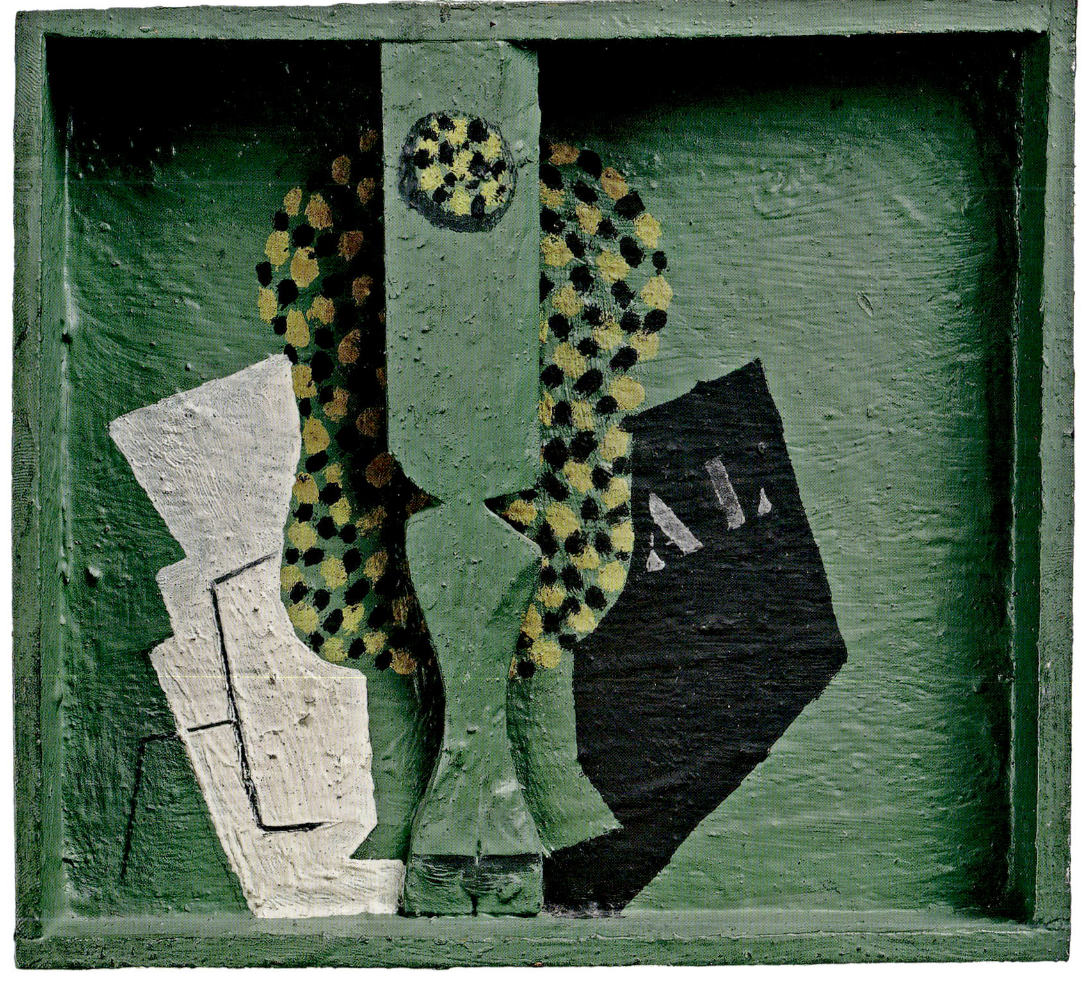

20. **GLASS AND NEWSPAPER.** Avignon, summer 1914
Painted wood, pencil, and oil on wood panel
6 1/16 × 6 7/8 × 1 3/16 in. (15.4 × 17.5 × 3 cm)
Musée national Picasso–Paris. Dation Pablo Picasso

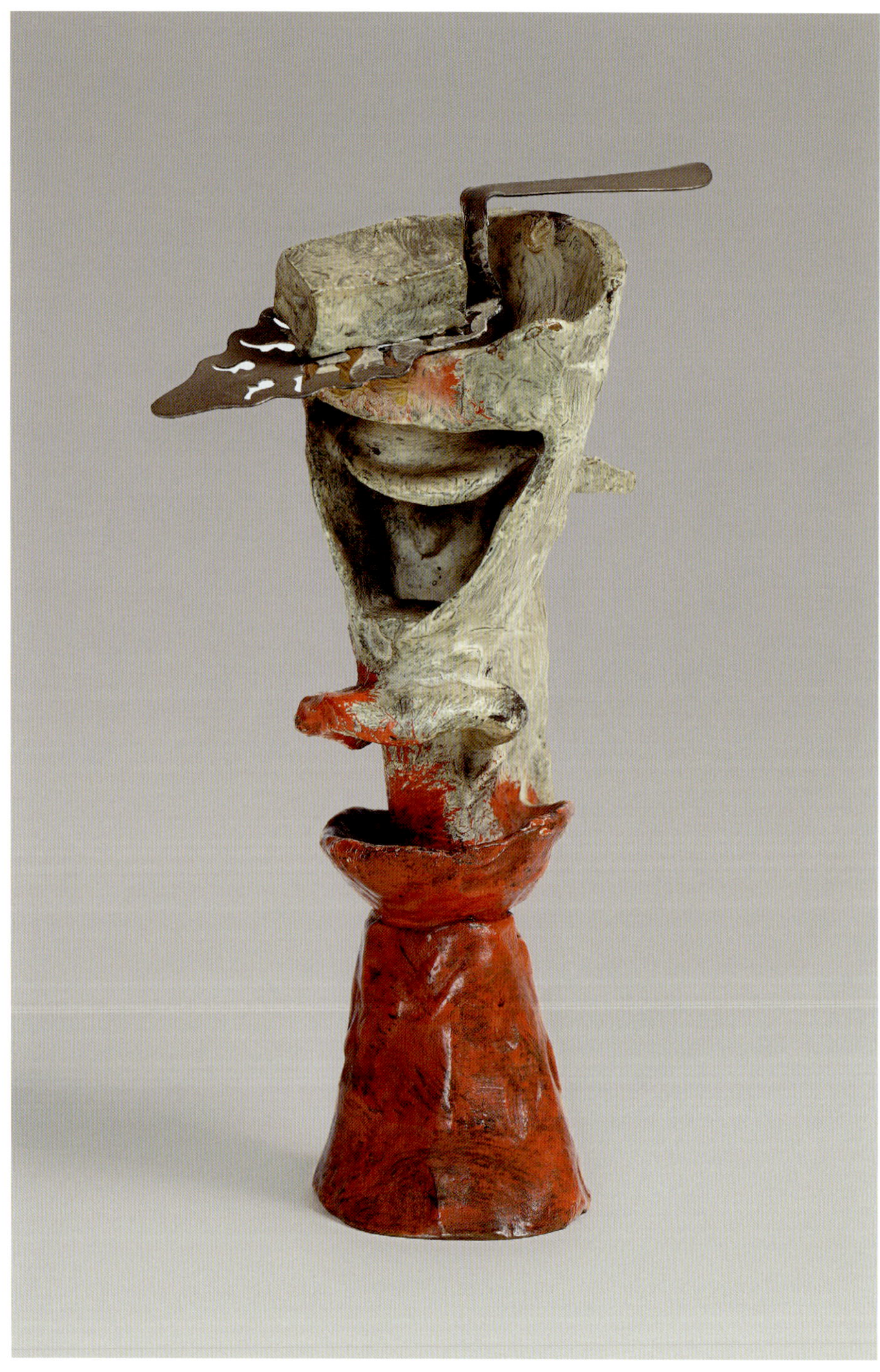

21. **GLASS OF ABSINTHE.** Paris, spring 1914
Bronze, painted in oil, and perforated white metal absinthe spoon
1 of an edition of 6 bronzes cast 1914, each uniquely treated
8 ¼ × 5 ½ × 2 ¾ in. (21 × 14 × 7 cm)
Private collection. Courtesy Fundación Almine y
Bernard Ruiz-Picasso para el Arte

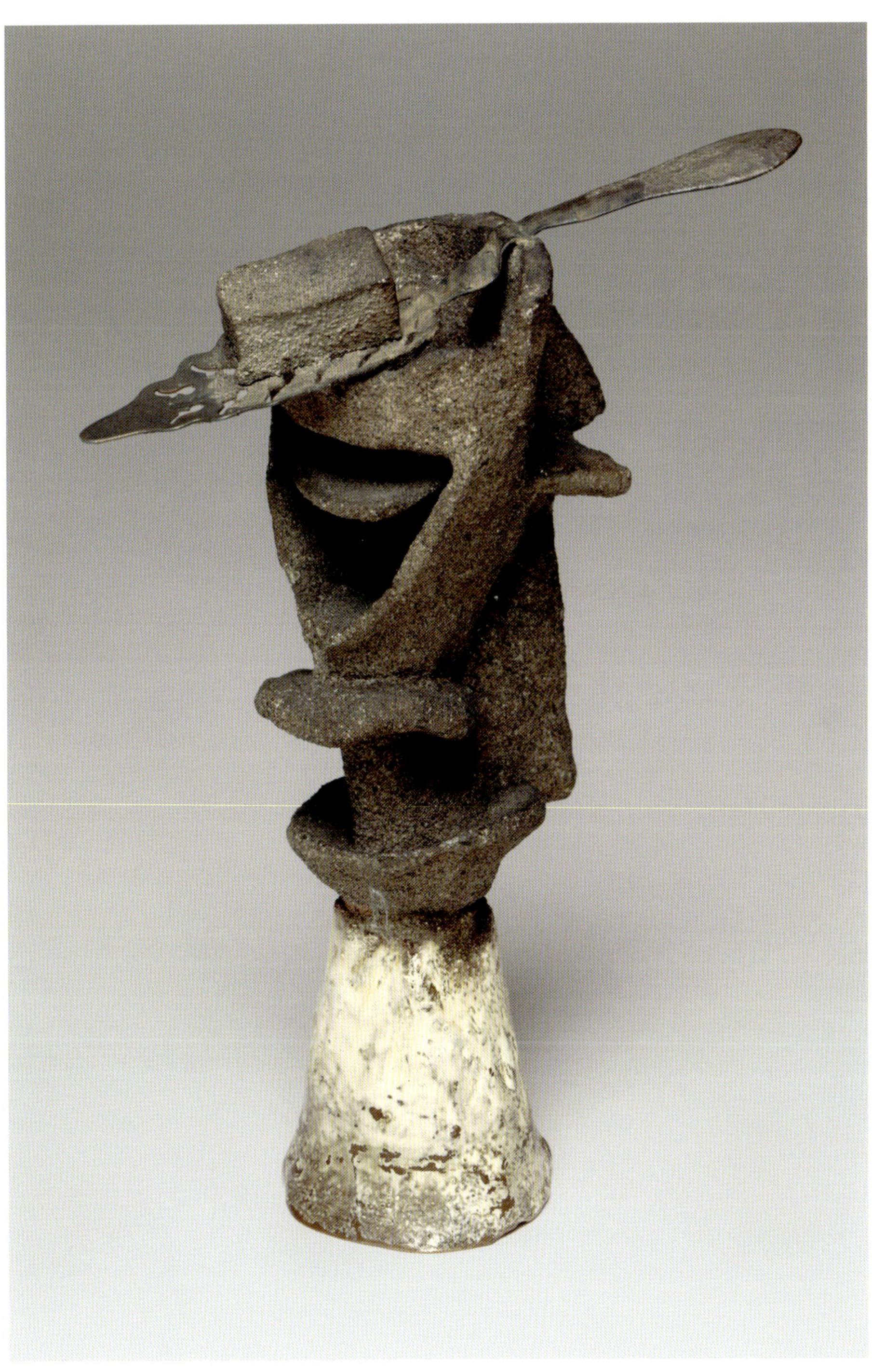

22. **GLASS OF ABSINTHE.** Paris, spring 1914
Bronze, painted in oil, and perforated white metal absinthe spoon
1 of an edition of 6 bronzes cast 1914, each uniquely treated
8 7/16 × 6 1/2 × 2 9/16 in. (21.5 × 16.5 × 6.5 cm)
Centre national d'art et de culture Georges Pompidou, Paris. Musée national d'art moderne/Centre de création industrielle. Donation Louise et Michel Leiris

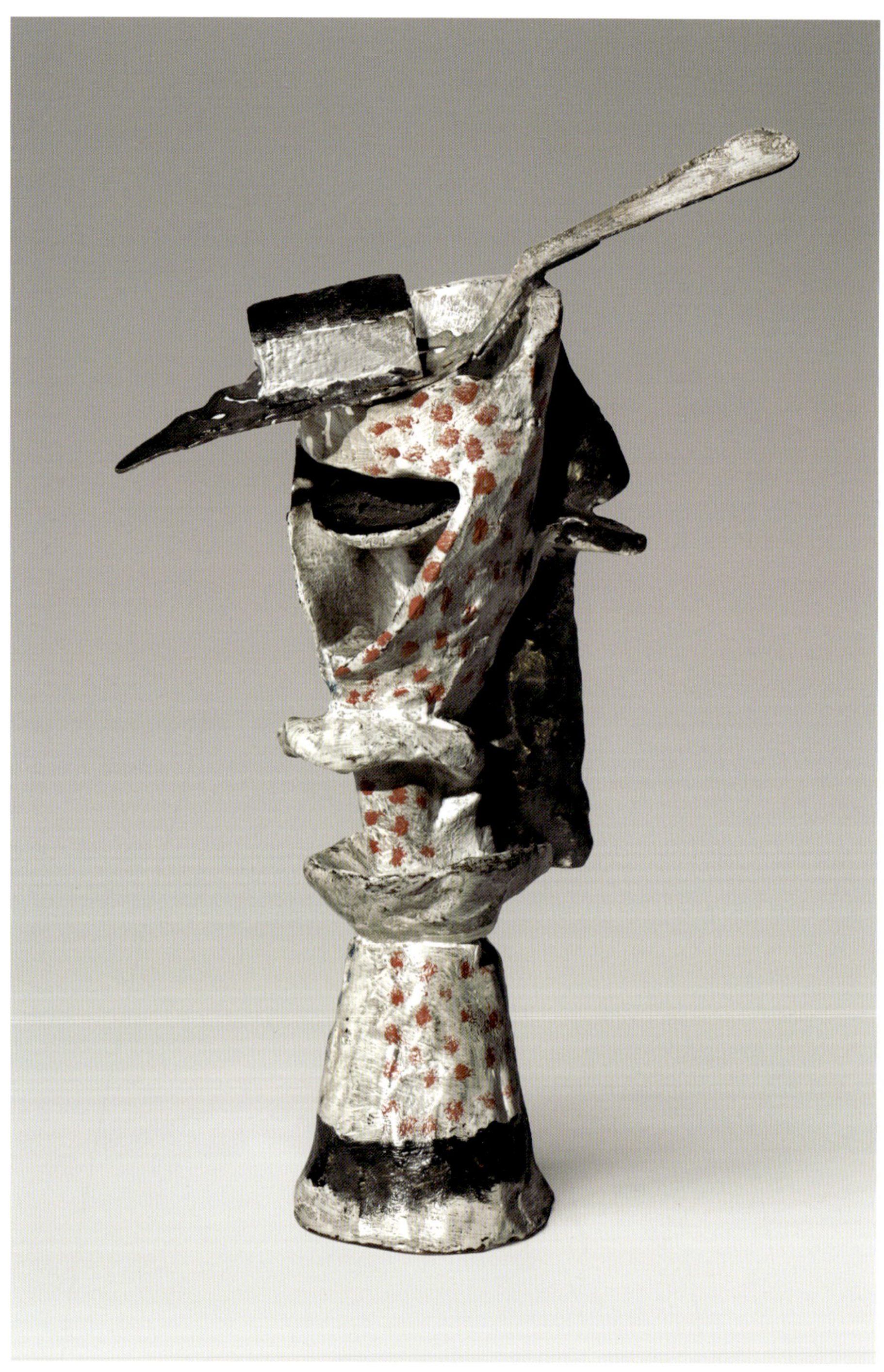

23. **GLASS OF ABSINTHE.** Paris, spring 1914
Bronze, painted in oil, and perforated white metal absinthe spoon
1 of an edition of 6 bronzes cast 1914, each uniquely treated
8 ⅞ × 4 ¾ × 3 ⅜ in. (22.5 × 12.1 × 8.6 cm)
Philadelphia Museum of Art. A. E. Gallatin Collection

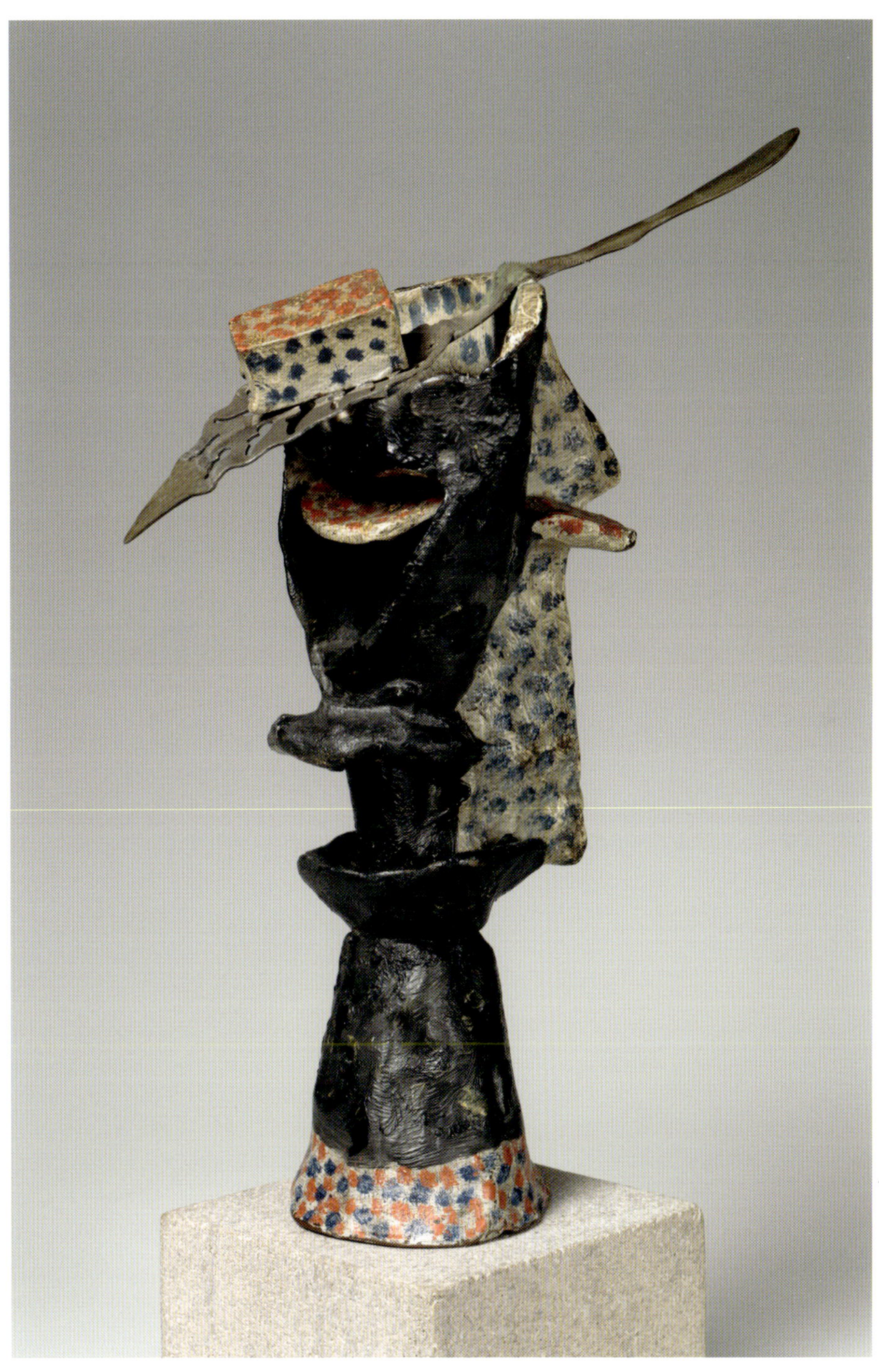

24. **GLASS OF ABSINTHE.** Paris, spring 1914
Bronze, painted in oil, and perforated white metal absinthe spoon
1 of an edition of 6 bronzes cast 1914, each uniquely treated
8 ⅞ × 5 × 2 ½ in. (22.5 × 12.7 × 6.4 cm)
Leonard A. Lauder Cubist Trust

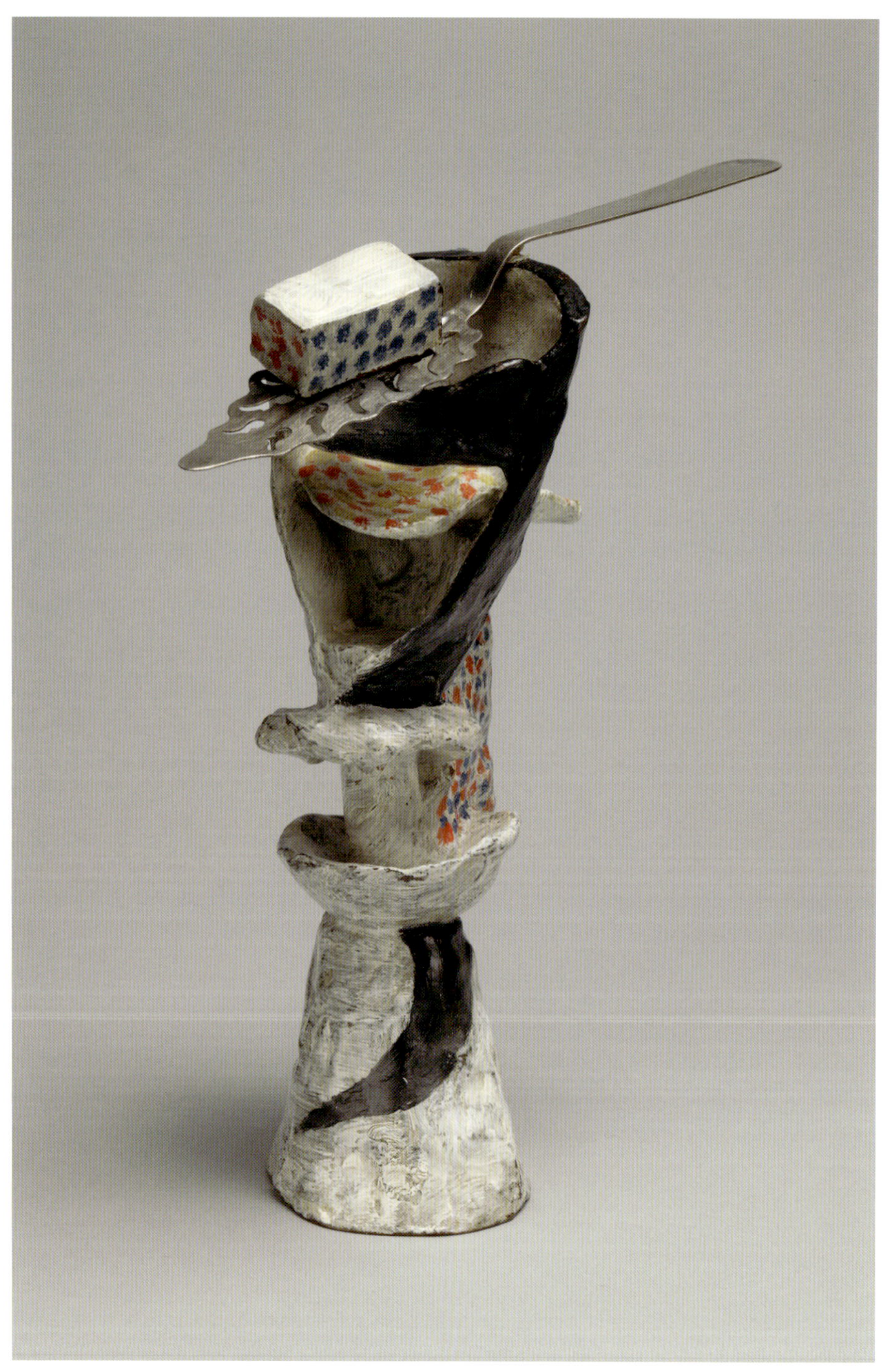

25. **GLASS OF ABSINTHE.** Paris, spring 1914
Bronze, painted in oil, and perforated white metal absinthe spoon
1 of an edition of 6 bronzes cast 1914, each uniquely treated
8 ½ × 6 ½ × 3 ⅜ in. (21.6 × 16.4 × 8.5 cm)
The Museum of Modern Art, New York. Gift of Louise Reinhardt Smith

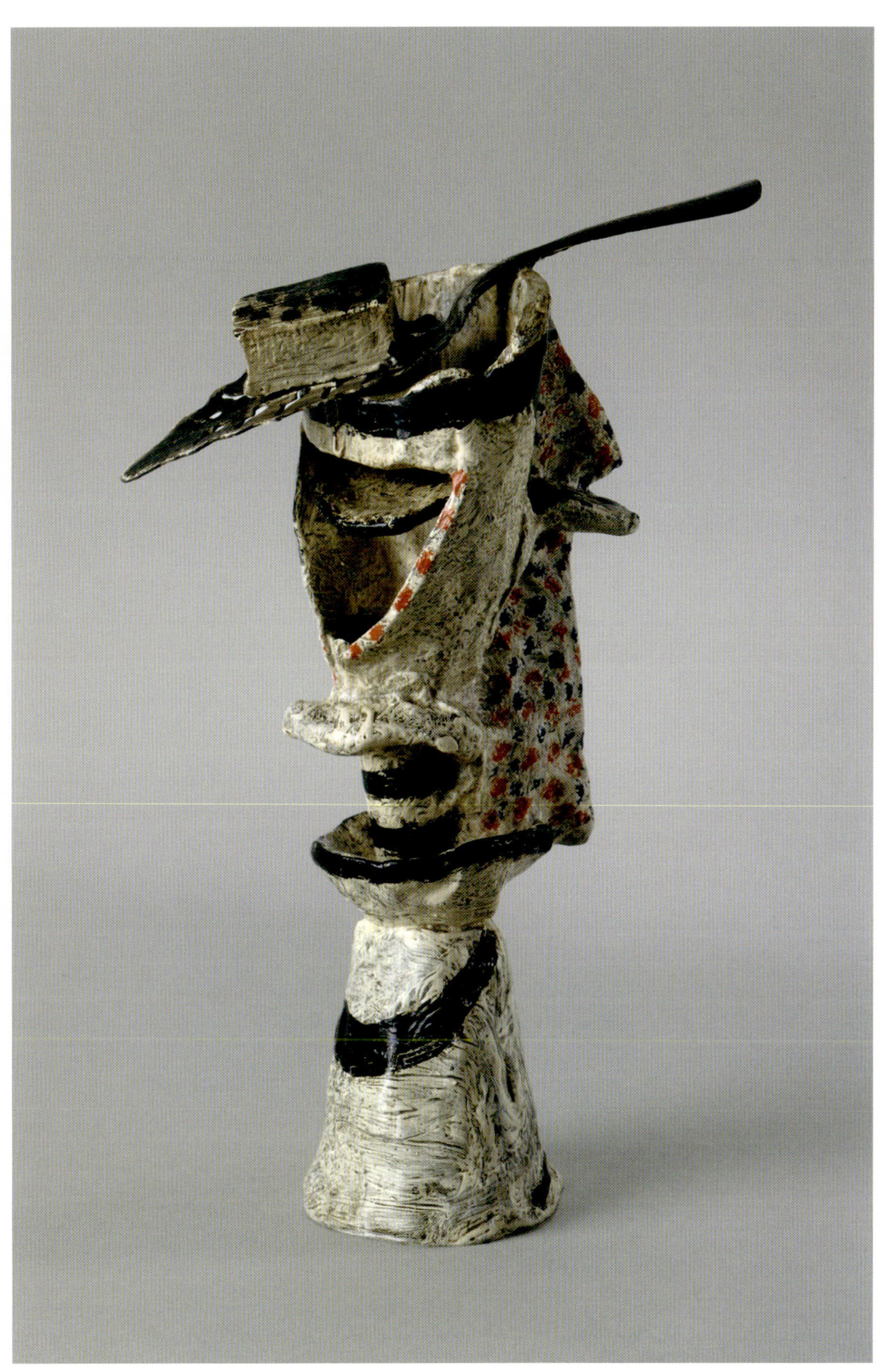

26. **GLASS OF ABSINTHE.** Paris, spring 1914
Bronze, painted in oil, and perforated white metal absinthe spoon
1 of an edition of 6 bronzes cast 1914, each uniquely treated
8 11⁄16 × 5 7⁄8 × 2 15⁄16 in. (22 × 15 × 7.5 cm)
Staatliche Museen zu Berlin, Nationalgalerie, Museum Berggruen

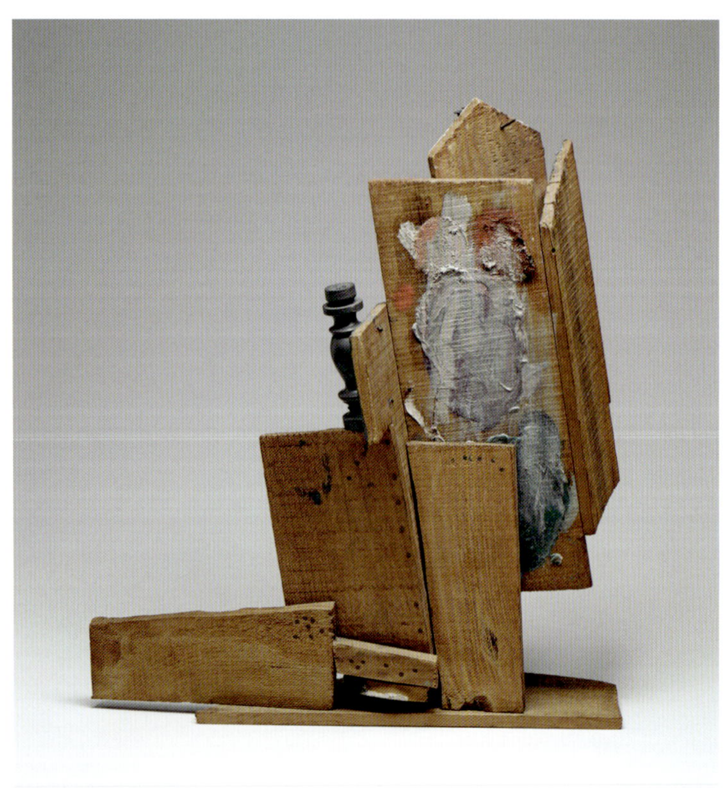

27. **VIOLIN AND BOTTLE ON A TABLE.** Paris, [fall] 1915
Painted fir, string, nails, and charcoal
$17\frac{11}{16} \times 15\frac{3}{4} \times 9\frac{1}{16}$ in. (45 × 40 × 23 cm)
Musée national Picasso–Paris. Dation Pablo Picasso

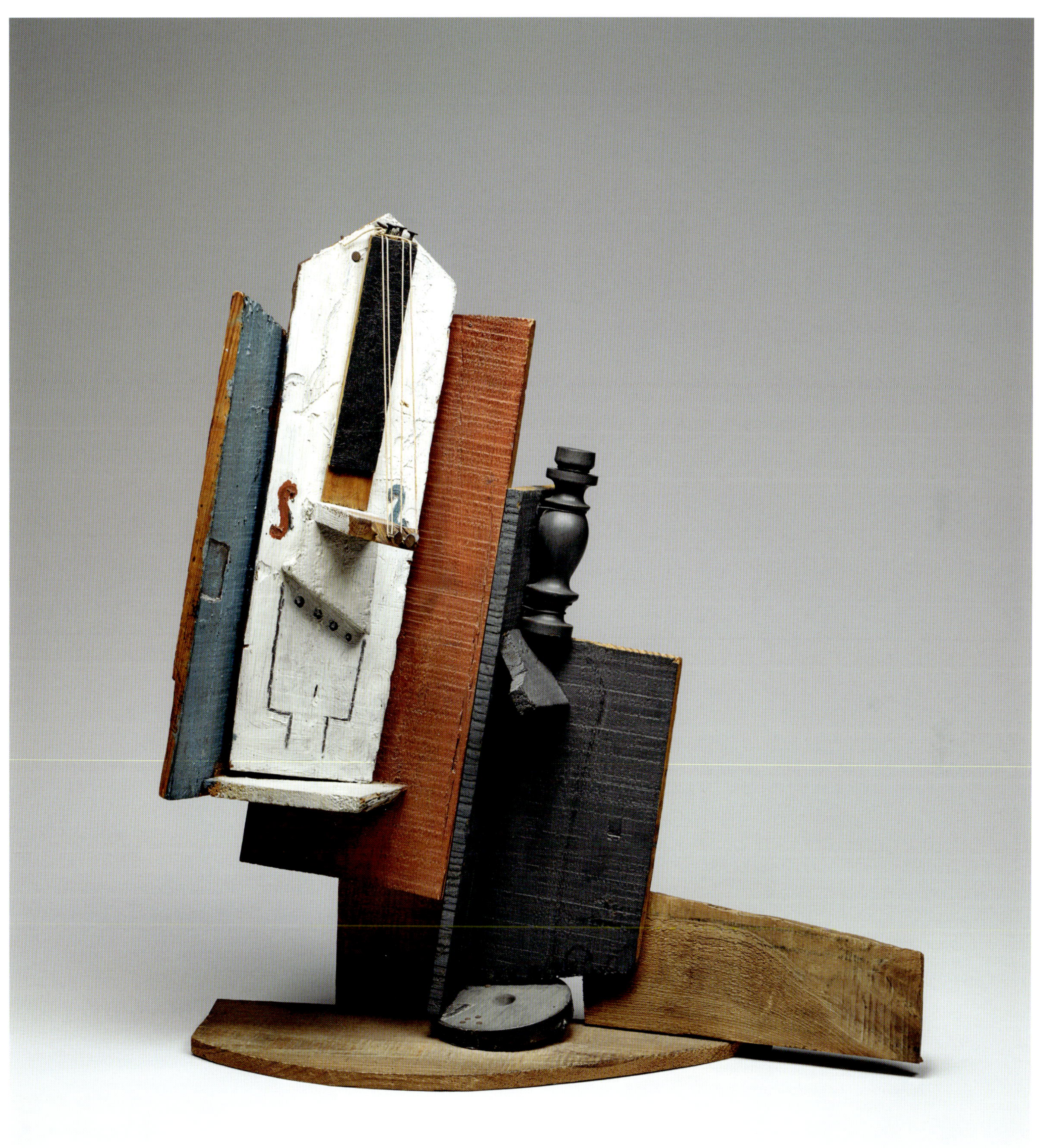

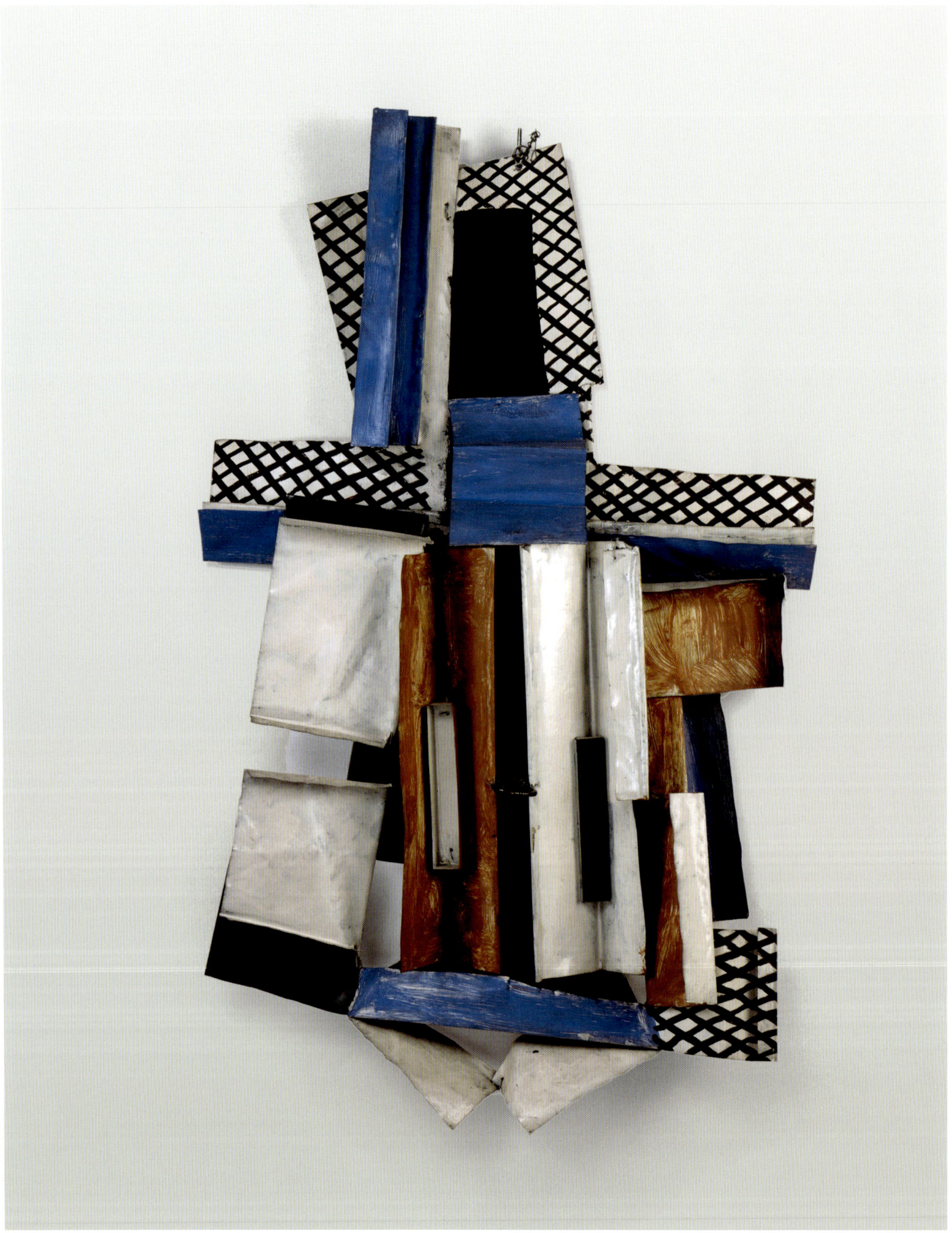

28. **VIOLIN.** Paris, [1915]
Painted sheet metal and iron wire
39 3/8 × 25 1/16 × 7 1/16 in. (100 × 63.7 × 18 cm)
Musée national Picasso–Paris. Dation Pablo Picasso

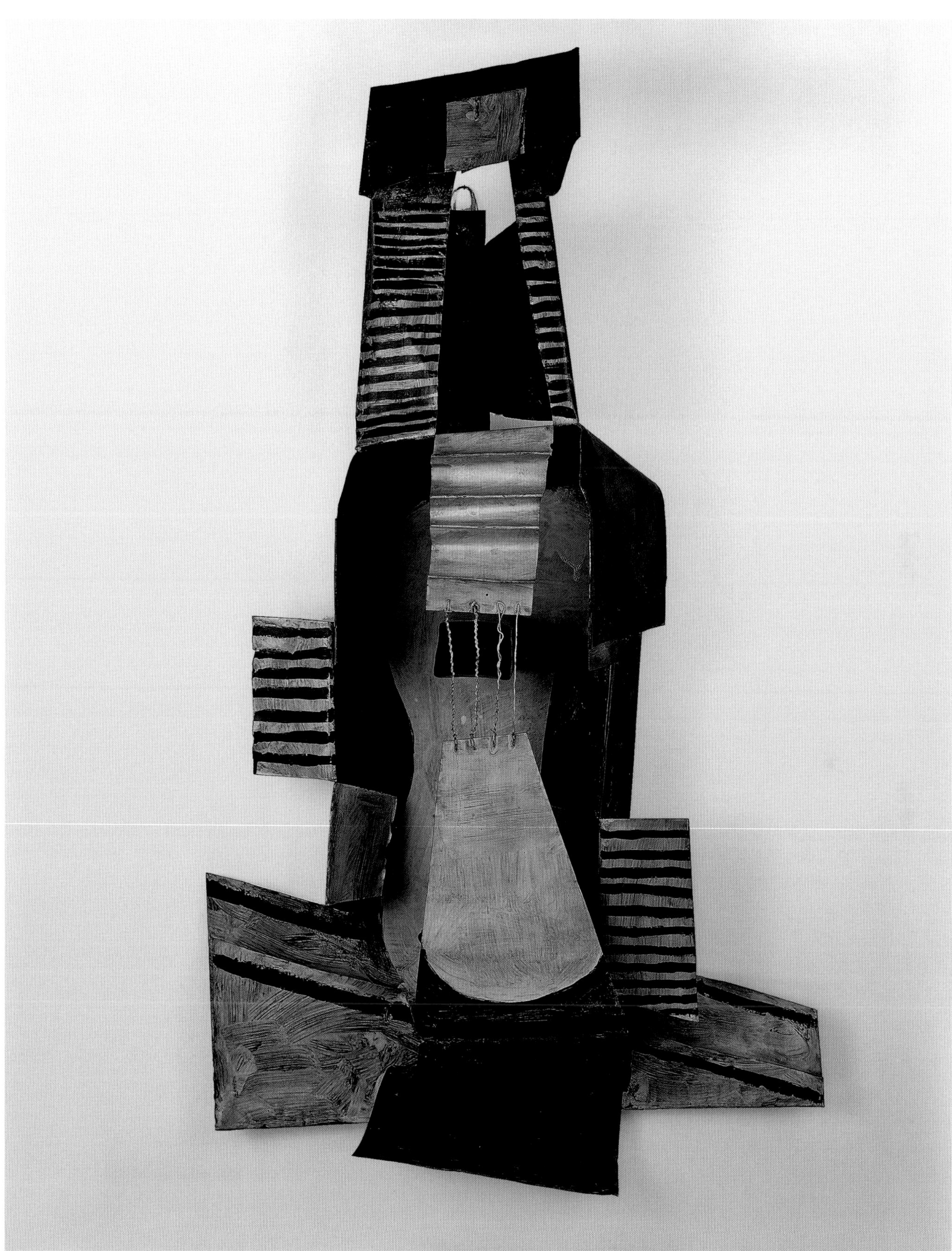

29. **GUITAR.** Paris, 1924
Painted sheet metal, painted tin box, and iron wire
43 11/16 × 25 × 10 1/2 in. (111 × 63.5 × 26.6 cm)
Musée national Picasso–Paris. Dation Pablo Picasso

CHAPTER 4

AROUND "THE MONUMENT TO APOLLINAIRE" 1927–1931

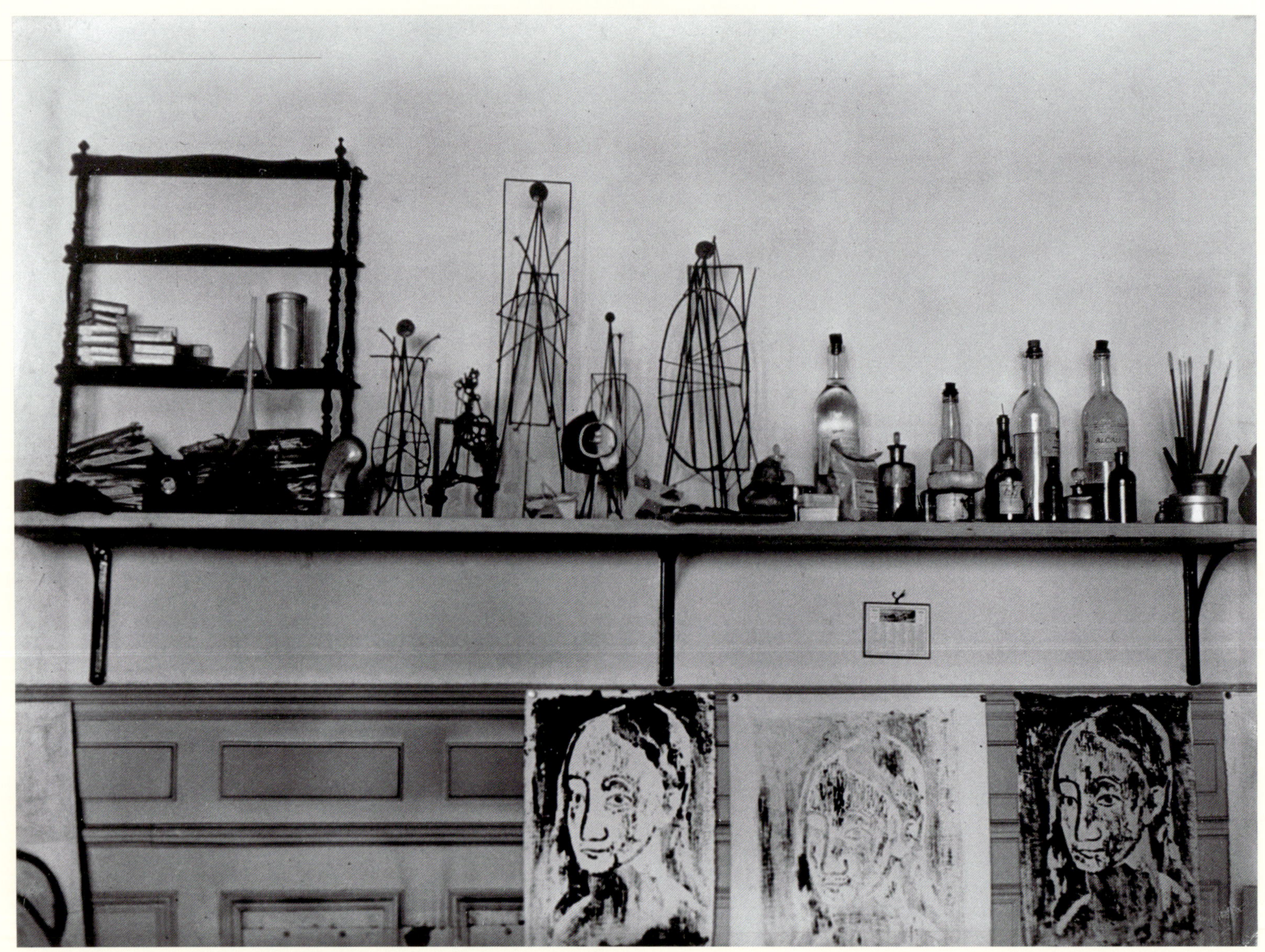

A shelf in Picasso's studio at 23, rue La Boétie, with the four *Figure* sculptures (1928), *Figure* ([1931]), and *Head* (1928), Paris, 1932. Photograph by Brassaï. Musée national Picasso–Paris

IN 1928 Picasso returned to the activity of sculpture after a fourteen-year hiatus that witnessed few interruptions. This new chapter, like all the phases of Picasso's sculpture making, was less a continuation of what preceded it and more the product of an entirely new set of imaginative concerns and formal hypotheses. It had its roots in a commission first announced at the end of 1920: the creation of a monument for the tomb of the poet and critic Guillaume Apollinaire, who had died in 1918 and was buried in Père Lachaise cemetery in Paris. Picasso's acceptance of the task paid homage to a writer who had been not only a close friend but also an early and eloquent champion of his work.

Commissions, whether public or private, often are fraught with discord and frustration, and the protracted saga of the Apollinaire memorial is no exception. Despite several rounds of effort, none of the multiple ideas that Picasso offered the memorial committee would be deemed acceptable. That failure belies—or perhaps confirms—the artistic importance of the drawings and sculptures that he imagined in relation to this project during the years 1927 to 1931. This profoundly varied set of works reflects an unexpectedly audacious level of formal and technical experiment even for Picasso. Bearing no reference to Apollinaire, Picasso's subjects all involved the human figure, either a head or an entire body, rendered in language that most viewers would not have recognized as figural. But their commonality ended there: the proposals encompassed thick, almost comically grotesque volumes of modeled plaster; diagrammatic wire constructions that Daniel-Henry Kahnweiler would christen "drawings in space";[1] and complex works in welded metal that anticipated the careers of many younger artists as well as Picasso's own ideas of thirty years later.

Picasso's return to sculpture was forecast in sketchbook activity that explores three-dimensional concerns with an intensity unmatched at any other phase of his career. For months before he again began to sculpt, he returned to it in his mind and in two-dimensional pencil, ink, and charcoal images. This ample body of sketchbooks begins with one made in Paris during the first half of 1927; thereafter the sketchbooks chronicle the artist's imagination as he worked most of the year in Paris and, during the summers, in Cannes (1927), in Dinard (1928 and 1929), and at his newly purchased château in Boisgeloup (1930). They prove how rapidly Picasso's imagination jumped from transparency to opacity, from a defiance of gravity to a celebration thereof, and from lines that stand in space as simply themselves to lines that evoke immense volume. Some of the drawings resulted in corresponding sculptures, others in paintings that seem populated by sculptures; and some live as sculptures only in sketchbook form.

This period of sculpture introduces a modus operandi that would remain important for Picasso the sculptor long after: collaboration. The sculptor's vocation often involves working with technicians who provide specialized tools and expertise and assistants who help with heavy or unwieldy forms. As a young man, Picasso had relied on sculptor friends to offer guidance and equipment. But he seems to have had little direct interaction with the workmen at the foundries who reproduced his early sculptures in bronze, and the Cubist constructions required no skill other than what Picasso could manage on his own with a bricoleur's eye and a handyman's implements. However, the sculptural realization of the 1928 line drawings for the monument to Apollinaire called for an expert in metal. Picasso found his solution in Julio González, whom he had known as a student in Barcelona and as a young émigré in Paris. Welcoming Picasso to his small metalworking studio in Montparnasse, González straddled the roles of tutor and assistant, at first translating into wire Picasso's line drawings of 1928 and eventually partnering with him on the complicated planes and angles of the constructions of 1929 to 1931.

According to several of Picasso's friends and colleagues, during this period the artist nurtured dreams of monumental creations that far exceed the parameters of a graveside sculpture and conjure the prospect of grand architectural scale. In the 1960s and 1970s, when Picasso became involved with outdoor sculpture, a wire construction conceived in homage to Apollinaire would be translated into larger versions. Meanwhile, in 1959, the Apollinaire committee installed Picasso's somber 1941 bronze *Head of a Woman* (pl. 80) outside the church of Saint-Germain-des-Prés in Paris. The resolution to this long tale thus occurred decades after Picasso first took up the challenge of a modern memorial and bore no trace of his bold experiments at that earlier moment. But Picasso's commitment to the call had accomplished the larger job of relaunching an intense involvement with sculpture that would continue to deepen over the next thirty-five years.

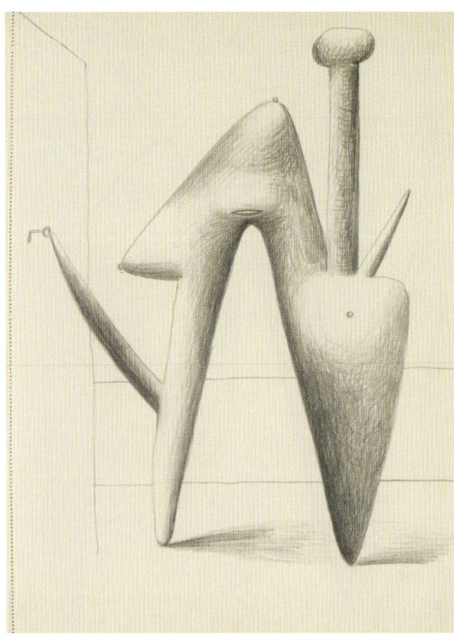

1. Pablo Picasso. Bather at the cabin, 1927. Sketchbook no. 015, sheet 21 recto. Graphite on paper, 11 13/16 × 9 1/16 in. (30 × 23 cm). Musée national Picasso–Paris

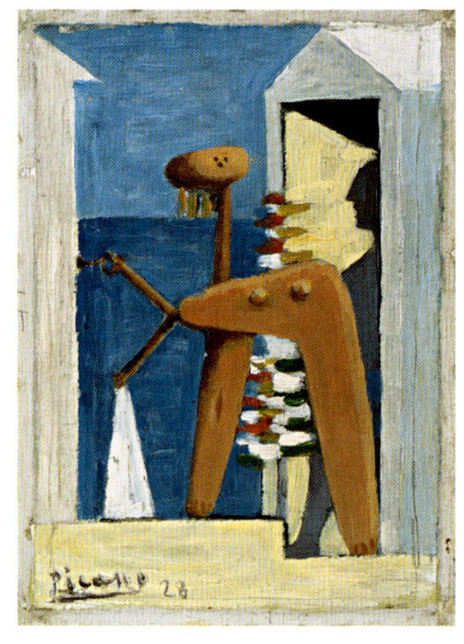

2. Pablo Picasso. *Bather and Cabin*. Dinard, August 1928. Oil on canvas, 8 1/2 × 6 1/4 in. (21.5 × 15.8 cm). The Museum of Modern Art, New York. Hillman Periodicals Fund

JULY–SEPTEMBER 1927: Picasso spent the summer in Cannes, at the Chalet Madrid on boulevard Alexandre III, with his wife, Olga Ruiz-Picasso, and their son, Paulo. The two sketchbooks he filled during that period feature several graphite drawings of androgynous bather figures whose monumental but elastic bodies are stretched and pulled into a host of sexually charged formulations. Often the bather holds a key and reaches to unlock a door (fig. 1), a theme developed in a number of paintings of this time (fig. 2). The intense eroticism of these compositions incarnates Picasso's desire for his young lover Marie-Thérèse Walter, who remained in Paris, where he had first met her in January. Toward the end of the second sketchbook, Picasso's drawings envisage three-dimensional networks of lines connected by points, harking back to sketchbook drawings he had made in Juan-les-Pins in summer 1924 (fig. 3). Now the linear networks formed standing figures, a concept that would materialize in wire sculptures the following year. The second sketchbook also contains a drawing of a work suggesting the influence of African and Oceanic masks and anticipating the sculptures in welded metal of a few years later.[1]

This pair of sketchbooks launched an intense dialogue between drawing and sculpture that would continue for three more years. They provide the first group of ideas that Picasso would consider in relation to a memorial sculpture for the grave of poet and art critic Guillaume Apollinaire. Apollinaire, a staunch defender of modern art and Picasso's close friend since 1905, had died of influenza on November 9, 1918. He was buried in Père Lachaise cemetery in Paris, where his plot was marked only by a wooden cross.

The goal of a monument had first been made public in December 1920, when French art critic Florent Fels announced in the pages of his avant-garde review *Action: Cahiers individualistes de philosophie et d'art* that a group of artists and intellectuals had formed a committee to create a memorial for Apollinaire. This announcement was followed by a flyer seeking donors for the project, which stated, "The model for the monument is a work by Picasso," despite the fact that no such work yet existed.[2] Shortly thereafter, notices were published in the periodicals *Mercure de France* and *L'Esprit nouveau*.[3] Fundraising continued over the next few years, with a highly successful auction of works donated by artists at the Hôtel Drouot on June 21, 1924 (a painting by Picasso fetched the highest price). The invitation to the exhibition preceding the auction, held at the Galerie Paul Guillaume, asserts that the profits "will be devoted entirely to the prompt execution of the funeral monument . . . for which Picasso has given the plan."[4] Two weeks after the fundraising auction, however, on Picasso's copy of a general letter to supporters describing the auction's success, committee member Serge Férat added an anxious handwritten note: "Have you thought about the plan??"[5] Three years later, in summer 1927, Picasso set to work in earnest.

FALL 1927: An article titled "L'Art nègre" (Negro art) in *Cahiers d'Art* reproduced a nineteenth-century Melanesian headdress mask from Picasso's collection, mistaking it as African. From the Torres Strait, it is made of painted sheet metal with shells and feathers.[6] The gently concave face, its striking features, and the decorative metal latticework that encircles the mask's

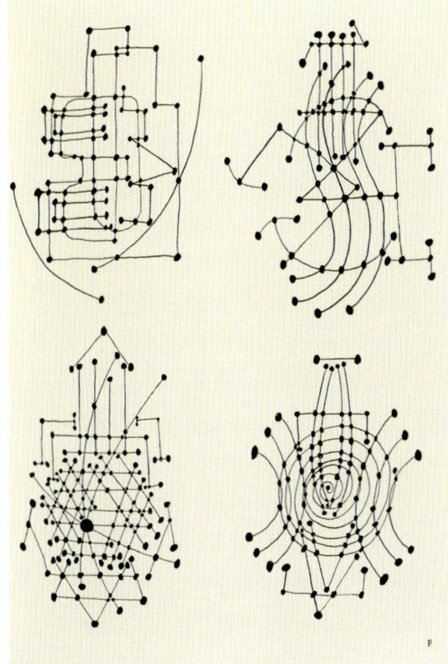

3. Pablo Picasso. Four studies of a guitar, Juan-les-Pins, [summer] 1924. Sketchbook no. 004, sheet 25 recto. Pen and india ink on paper, 12 ⅜ × 9 ¼ in. (31.5 × 23.5 cm). Musée national Picasso–Paris

lower half anticipate the bold direction Picasso's constructions would take over the next three years.

OCTOBER 16–NOVEMBER 10, 1927: The exhibition *Picasso: Pastelle, Aquarelle, Zeichnungen, Bronzen, usw., 1902–1927* (Picasso: pastels, watercolors, drawings, bronzes, etc., 1902–1927) took place at the Galerie Alfred Flechtheim in Berlin. It included four of the artist's early sculptures, including the 1909 *Head of a Woman* (pl. 11), but nothing made since then.

EARLY NOVEMBER 1927: Picasso invited the Apollinaire committee to his studio to see the sketchbooks he had produced in Cannes. Among the visitors was André Billy, one of the most conservative and outspoken members of the group. Writing in the *Journal littéraire*, the critic Paul Léautaud described Billy's reaction to the sketches they saw: "He told me there was recently a meeting at Picasso's for the monument to be placed on the tomb in Père Lachaise. He was there. Picasso produced a bizarre, monstrous, mad, incomprehensible, almost obscene thing, a sort of unidentifiable lump that looks as though it's got sexual organs sticking out of it here and there. He thinks that Picasso, in fact, still hasn't done anything for the monument and as he had the meeting with the committee, he produced any old thing from his folders."[7] Accordingly, seven years after Picasso had signed on to create a funerary monument for Apollinaire, nothing moved forward.

***METAMORPHOSIS I* AND *METAMORPHOSIS II*, 1928**

These two sculptures were modeled in plaster in early 1928 and thereafter each cast in a unique bronze (pls. 30, 31).

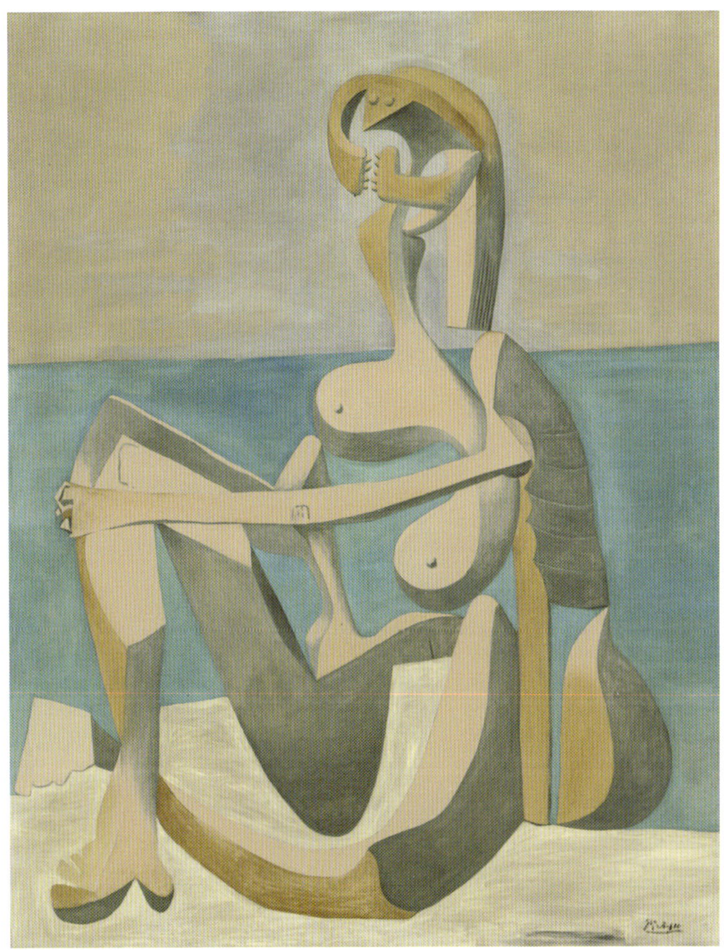

4. Pablo Picasso. *Seated Bather.* Paris, early 1930. Oil on canvas, 64 ¼ × 51 in. (163.2 × 129.5 cm). The Museum of Modern Art, New York. Mrs. Simon Guggenheim Fund

They were developed directly from the sketchbook drawings roundly rejected by the Apollinaire committee. While anatomical features identify them as androgynous personages, their distortions and exaggerations produce results at a far remove from an actual human body. Picasso approached the human subject as if to focus only on the information of sexual relevance: orifices, protuberances, swellings, slits, and curves. In both sculptures, elements suggesting an arm and a head reach upward and back, respectively, to meet and form a suggestive opening within the sculpture itself. The curving space between the two "legs," one of which is simply a gigantic foot, is similarly provocative. These two sculptures reflect a Picasso fully in sync with the climate of Surrealism and even predictive of the more sinister erotic charge its texts and imagery would assume at the turn of the decade, a development fully evident in Picasso's paintings as well (fig. 4).

The allusive title *Metamorphosis* was used by Daniel-Henry Kahnweiler in the 1949 monograph *Les Sculptures de Picasso*, although his basis for doing so is unknown; until then, reproductions merely stated *Sculpture* or *Composition*.[8]

MARCH 20–MAY 8, 1928: A sketchbook begun and finished on these dates, made in Paris, begins with the first ink drawings for the small painted brass and iron sculpture *Head* (pl. 32), which Picasso would complete in October.[9] Within that same sketchbook, a number of drawings from April further develop the concepts that would inform the linear networks of a set of sculptures titled *Figure* made that October (pls. 34–36) and the interpenetrating planes of *Woman in the Garden* (pl. 41) of the following spring (fig. 5).

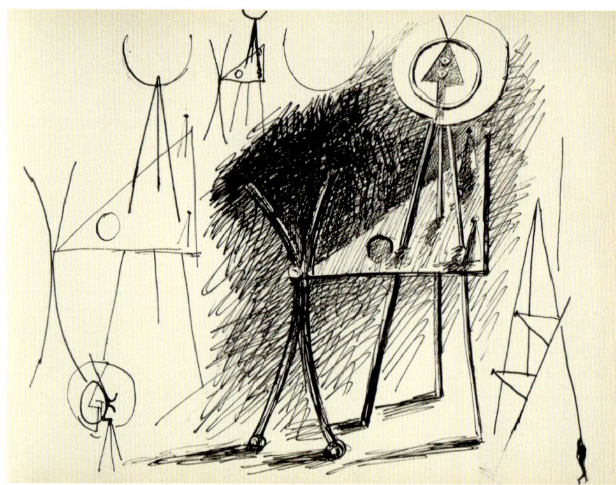

5. Pablo Picasso. Plans for a sculpture, Paris, 1928. Unnumbered sketchbook, sheet 47 recto. Pen and india ink on paper, 10 7/16 × 14 in. (26.5 × 35.5 cm). Musée national Picasso–Paris

MAY 13–14, 1928: On May 13 the artist and metalworker Julio González wrote to Picasso to tell him of his mother's death, and asked, "If as I believe you have the intention to give me work, could you be so kind as to advance me something."[10] Picasso replied the next day with condolences and a check. These notes are the first evidence of Picasso's decision to seek assistance in metalworking from González; the two had been friends in Barcelona and during Picasso's first years in Paris. González owned a metal workshop at 11, rue de Médeah in Montparnasse, where he made sculpture as well as decorative objects. In addition to the training he had received growing up in a family of metalworkers, he had learned oxyacetylene welding while employed at the metalworks of the Renault factories in Boulogne-sur-Seine in 1918.

JUNE 18–JULY 8, 1928: In Paris, Picasso filled a sketchbook with more than fifty drawings. Several begin to conceptualize the motif of a male-female pair of geometrically schematized standing figures. Other sketches use heavy modeling and shading to compose a monumental couple rendered as solid masses, as if they were made of stone. The last two sheets of the sketchbook present the two options, respectively, as if to demonstrate the comparison between the alternative modes of representation.[11] Picasso would work with González on sculptures of the former type that same year; he would embark on the latter type in plaster at the Château de Boisgeloup in 1931.

JULY 27, 1928: Picasso began another sketchbook while on vacation with his family in Dinard, at the Hôtel des Terrasses and the Villa des Roches. It continues the exploration of monumental, solid figures. On August 3, Picasso would switch his approach to begin a long series of linear sketches that would form the basis for sculptures made of wire rods (fig. 6); he experimented further with the same motif on August 12.

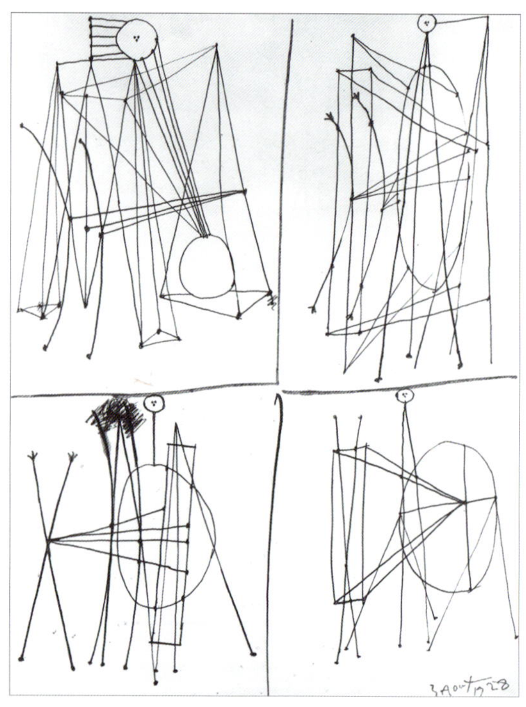

6. Pablo Picasso. Plans for a sculpture, Dinard, August 3, 1928. Sketchbook no. 1044, sheet 18. Pen and india ink and pencil on paper, 15 × 12 3/16 in. (38 × 31 cm). Private collection

FALL 1928: Picasso began his collaboration with González at his old friend's metalworking studio, striving for a satisfactory proposal for the monument to Apollinaire. His sketchbook drawings from the previous spring and summer provided fuel for the enterprise.

The journal *Cahiers d'Art*, founded in 1926 by Christian Zervos, featured an article by Zervos titled "Sculptures des peintres d'aujourd'hui" (Sculptures by today's painters). In it he observed, "The history of cubism is there to explain and

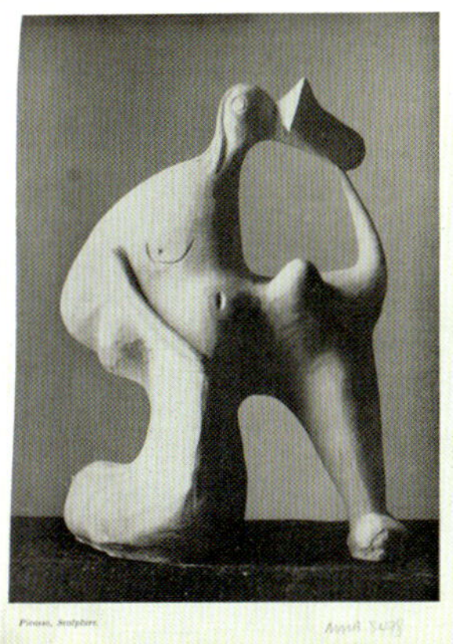
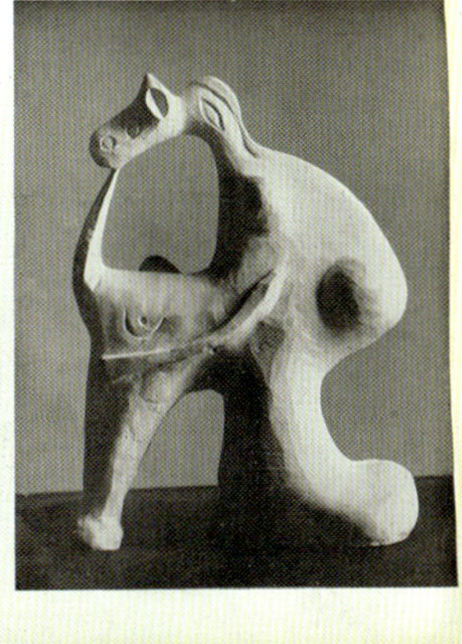

7. Two views (front and back) of the plaster original of *Metamorphosis II*, reproduced as "Sculpture" in Christian Zervos, "Sculptures des peintres d'aujourd'hui" (Sculptures by today's painters), *Cahiers d'Art*, no. 7 (1928)

justify the interpenetration of the two arts."[12] In the company of images of sculptures by Henri Matisse, Juan Gris, Georges Braque, and others were reproductions of three-dimensional works by Picasso: the early sculptures *The Jester* (pl. 3), *Kneeling Woman Combing Her Hair* (pl. 5), and *Head of a Woman* (pl. 11); two versions of *Glass of Absinthe* of 1914 (pls. 22, 25); a Cubist construction no longer extant;[13] and two views of the plaster *Metamorphosis II* (fig. 7). This constituted the most extensive published documentation of Picasso's sculptures to date.

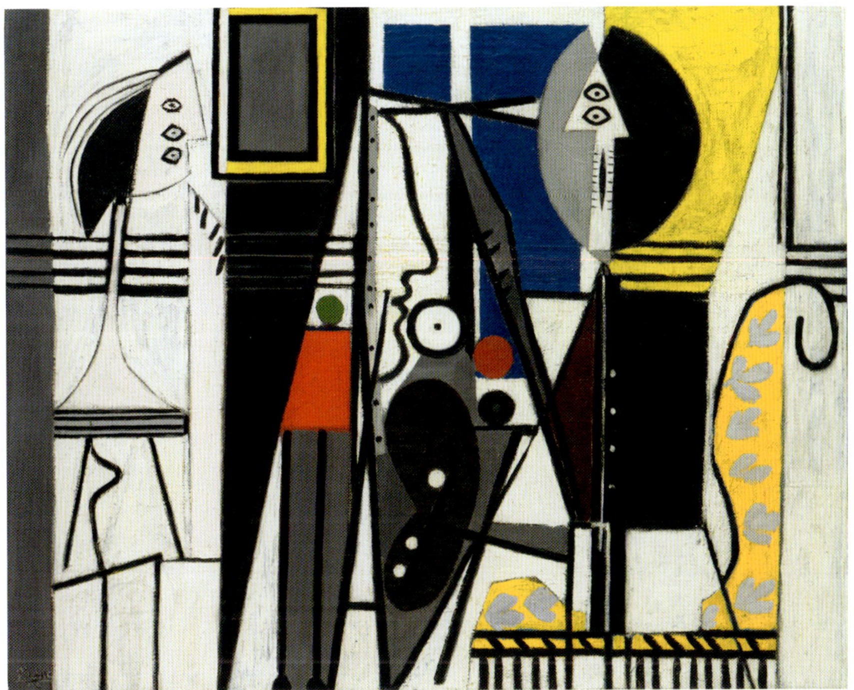

8. Pablo Picasso. *Painter and Model*. Paris, 1928. Oil on canvas, 51 ⅛ × 64 ¼ in. (129.8 × 163 cm). The Museum of Modern Art, New York. The Sidney and Harriet Janis Collection

***HEAD*, OCTOBER 1928**

Head (pl. 32) is thought to be the first collaboration between Picasso and González. Two versions were made, both of which unite planar brass elements with a simple tripod and open ring made of iron. The sculpture's black-and-white palette evokes a stark interplay of opposites that fuse at the site of the face; this same motif is evident in the 1928 *Painter and Model* (fig. 8). The angular arrangement at center, with its two eye- or mouth-like elements, also allows a reading of the head as two profiles kissing, an interpretation supported by preliminary sketchbook drawings. Elizabeth Cowling suggests that Picasso was thinking of a sculpture already adorning a grave in Père Lachaise cemetery: Constantin Brancusi's *Kiss* of 1911.[14]

On the second sheet of the sketchbook in which Picasso had conceived the sculpture in March, he envisaged *Head* as a majestic sculpture mounted on a half-sphere (fig. 9), which supports the idea that he was considering it at a larger size. The mounting also has been interpreted as a device that would put the work in motion.[15] A slightly larger version of *Head* was owned by Gertrude Stein and Alice B. Toklas (fig. 10; private collection); the smaller version would remain with the artist until his death.[16]

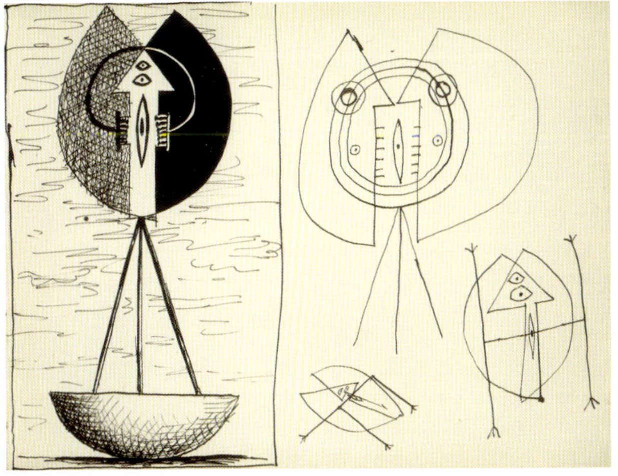

9. Pablo Picasso. Studies for *Head*, 1928. Unnumbered sketchbook, sheet 2 recto. Pen and india ink on paper, 10 7⁄16 × 14 ⅜ in. (26.5 × 36.5 cm). Musée national Picasso–Paris

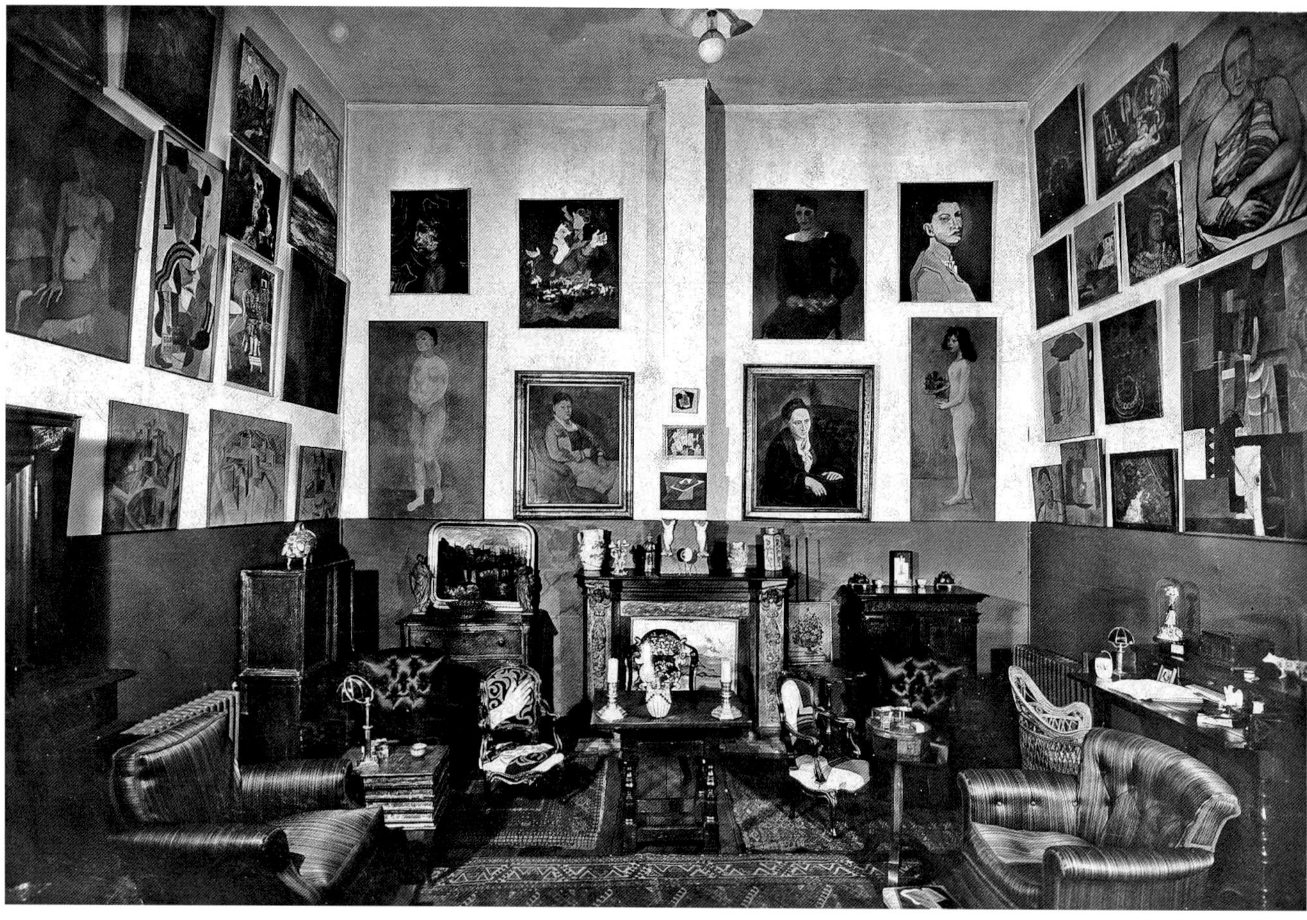

10. *Head* installed on the mantelpiece in the home of Gertrude Stein and Alice B. Toklas, 27, rue de Fleurus, Paris, 1933–34. The Metropolitan Museum of Art, New York. Gift of Edward Burns

FIGURE, _FIGURE_, AND _FIGURE_, FALL 1928

Picasso brought González the sketches he had made in August in Dinard with the wish that his drawings of linear networks be translated into iron. Four meticulously crafted sculptures resulted (pls. 34–36 illustrate three), presenting schematic configurations that suggest various stages in a game of cat's cradle.[17] In each, wire rods form a framework of long, slender lines that articulate a human figure and situate it within a spatial context. The soldering process replicates the heavy dots that reinforce the lines' meeting points in Picasso's sketches. It is these sculptures that would lead Kahnweiler to write of "drawings in space."[18] He would also describe them as a first step toward something that, until then, only architecture had achieved: the actual "creation of spaces."[19]

The four constructions vary in height from about 14 1/2 inches to about 23 1/2 inches and feature differing proportions and arrangements of straight and curved wires. A small, circular metal head incised with two eyes and a mouth rests directly atop long wires that define the body and extend down to the sheet metal base. Two arms and two legs are economically rendered with a single pair of rods situated in front of the body, assuming a unique position in each sculpture. The schematic hands and feet and the minimal details of the facial features endow these sculptures with a whimsical and even adorable quality that can obscure their formal complexity and sophistication.

The Apollinaire committee had no desire for the monument described by the *Figure* constructions. These small sculptures would remain with Picasso until his death. Late in his life they became the basis for enlargements, now in the collections of The Museum of Modern Art, New York, and the Musée national Picasso–Paris, that fulfilled his original vision of a majestic outdoor work (see fig. 23 on p. 262).

Picasso's conception of the monument to Apollinaire as a structure defined by voids as much as by solids is widely associated with Apollinaire's 1916 book *Le Poète assassiné* (*The Poet Assassinated*).[20] Reissued in 1926 and 1927, the quasi-autobiographical but fantastical tale casts the author as the character Croniamantal, Apollinaire's former lover Marie Laurencin as Tristouse Ballerinette, and Picasso as the Bird

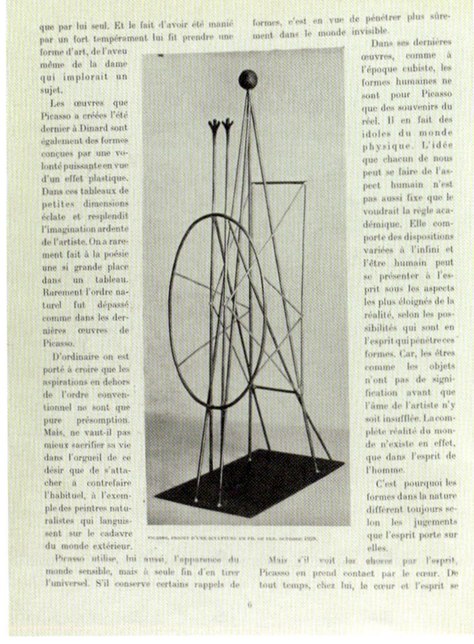

que par lui seul. Et le fait d'avoir été manié par un fort tempérament lui fit prendre une forme d'art, de l'aveu même de la dame qui implorait un sujet.

Les œuvres que Picasso a créées l'été dernier à Dinard sont également des formes conçues par une volonté puissante en vue d'un effet plastique. Dans ces tableaux de petites dimensions éclate et resplendit l'imagination ardente de l'artiste. On a rarement fait à la poésie une si grande place dans un tableau. Rarement l'ordre naturel fut dépassé comme dans les dernières œuvres de Picasso.

D'ordinaire on est porté à croire que les aspirations en dehors de l'ordre conventionnel ne sont que pure présomption. Mais, ne vaut-il pas mieux sacrifier sa vie dans l'orgueil de ce désir que de s'attacher à contrefaire l'habituel, à l'exemple des peintres naturalistes qui languissent sur le cadavre du monde extérieur.

Picasso utilise, lui aussi, l'apparence du monde sensible, mais à seule fin d'en tirer l'universel. S'il conserve certains rappels de formes, c'est en vue de pénétrer plus sûrement dans le monde invisible.

Dans ses dernières œuvres, comme à l'époque cubiste, les formes humaines ne sont pour Picasso que des souvenirs du réel. Il en fait des idoles du monde physique. L'idée que chacun de nous peut se faire de l'aspect humain n'est pas aussi fixe que le voudrait la règle académique. Elle comporte des dispositions variées à l'infini et l'être humain peut se présenter à l'esprit sous les aspects les plus éloignés de la réalité, selon les possibilités qui sont en l'esprit qui pénètre ces formes. Car, les êtres comme les objets n'ont pas de signification avant que l'âme de l'artiste n'y soit insufflée. La complète réalité du monde n'existe en effet, que dans l'esprit de l'homme.

C'est pourquoi les formes dans la nature diffèrent toujours selon les jugements que l'esprit porte sur elles.

Mais s'il voit les choses par l'esprit, Picasso en prend contact par le cœur. De tout temps, chez lui, le cœur et l'esprit se

PICASSO, PROJET D'UNE SCULPTURE EN FIL DE FER, OCTOBRE 1928.

6

11. *Figure* reproduced in Christian Zervos, "Picasso à Dinard, été 1928" (Picasso in Dinard, summer 1928), *Cahiers d'Art*, no. 1 (1929): 6

placer en évidence pour créer une valeur plastique en même temps qu'un prétexte de suggestion.

Il me serait difficile d'expliquer la raison pour laquelle les dernières œuvres de Picasso me laissent l'impression d'être plus qu'un profond regard sur la réalité, des contemplations mystiques. Il se pourrait que mon impression vienne du lyrisme véhément, tendu, violent, qui emporte les formes dans une agitation surnaturelle. Il n'est pas, en effet, d'exemple dans la peinture moderne, d'une tension si aiguë des formes groupées dans un style inouï. Romantisme, si l'on veut, mais un romantisme qui serait traversé par une fureur mystique. Ce qui explique d'ailleurs la grandeur de l'élément érotique de ses tableaux, érotisme qui nous émeut comme un sentiment religieux. L'érotisme des œuvres de Picasso nous apparait comme une exaltation par laquelle l'artiste subit la présence d'un sentiment universel. Pendant que des peintres insignifiants se complaisent dans une espèce de sensualité pornographique, Picasso franchit les barrières de la sensualité en imprégnant son érotisme de grandeur et d'universalité.

Il en est de même de tous les sentiments que Picasso exprime par la peinture.

Il emploie un langage spécial, comme une suite de métaphores qui expriment pleinement les sensations de l'amour, de l'air, de la lumière, de l'atmosphère maritime, de la joie de l'été. Sensations d'autant plus suggestives que les formes sont enveloppées dans les dernières œuvres de Picasso, d'une lumière irradiée et d'une troublante fulgurance.

Il est cependant des moments où Picasso suspend cette véhémence lyrique, et par dessus le tumulte des formes, il élève une figure symbolique et pure, dans toute la noblesse de la statique, une figure écrite en quelques traits très simples mais d'une plénitude qui se confond avec la statuaire. A tel point que Picasso sent, par moments, l'utilité de traduire ces formes par les moyens sculpturaux... A l'aide d'un fil de fer il écrit d'abord le dessin de sa sculpture, ensuite il l'agrandit pour le revêtir de plaques de fer forgé.

Ainsi les dernières œuvres de Picasso nous laissent voir qu'aujourd'hui comme naguère il sait passer des formes les plus pures et les plus statiques aux envolées lyriques les plus inattendues... C'est le vertige fait équilibre.

CHRISTIAN ZERVOS.

PABLO PICASSO, SCULPTURE, OCTOBRE 1928.

11

12. *Head* captioned "Pablo Picasso, sculpture, octobre 1928" in Christian Zervos, "Picasso à Dinard, été 1928" (Picasso in Dinard, summer 1928), *Cahiers d'Art*, no. 1 (1929): 11

of Benin. The last pages of the book virtually prescribe Picasso's future work on the author's funerary monument: the Bird of Benin and Tristouse discuss a memorial for Croniamantal, just murdered by an angry mob that included Tristouse. "'I ought to make a statue to him,' said the Bird of Benin. 'For I am not only a painter but also a sculptor.' 'That's right,' said Tristouse, 'we must raise a statue to him.'"[21] They ponder this further: "'A statue of what?' asked Tristouse. 'Marble? Bronze?' 'No, that's old fashioned. I must model a profound statue out of nothing, like poetry and glory.'"[22] The next day the Bird of Benin dug a trench in a clearing in the Meudon woods, and the following day workmen lined it with cement "so that the empty space had the form of Croniamantal, and the hole was full of his specter."[23] Thereafter, dirt was heaped atop the monument, a laurel tree planted above, and the Bird of Benin's work was complete.

NOVEMBER 11, 1928: Two days after the tenth anniversary of Apollinaire's death, Picasso started a new section in the sketchbook he had begun in Dinard on July 27, with a page inscribed with the address of his Paris studio: "23 R. La Boétie Paris 11 Novembre 1928."[24] There follow several sketches that conceptualize the beginnings of the welded metal sculptures of the next three years.

NOVEMBER 27, 1928: "Une Visite à Picasso" (A visit to Picasso), an article by the art critic and publisher E. Tériade, appeared in *L'Intransigeant*. Tériade was the first to identify Picasso's wire constructions as maquettes for the monument to Apollinaire, explaining that "Picasso can see these sculptures of masts and antennas enlarged, with pillars of iron or some other material."[25]

JANUARY 1929: An article by Zervos entitled "Picasso à Dinard, été 1928" (Picasso in Dinard, summer 1928) appeared in *Cahiers d'Art*. It reproduced twenty-three of the bather paintings the artist had made in Dinard the previous August (see fig. 2). It also illustrated two sculptures he had made in Paris in October: *Figure* (pl. 34) and *Head* (pl. 32), the former captioned "proposal for a sculpture in iron wire" (fig. 11) and the latter simply "sculpture" (fig. 12).[26] Zervos wrote of how the paintings' figures can blur into the realm of statuary "So much so that Picasso feels, at times, the usefulness of translating these forms through sculptural means."[27]

FEBRUARY 25, 1929: Picasso began a new sketchbook, which he would continue to use through January 12, 1930. It begins with preliminary drawings for the sculpture *Head of a Woman* of 1929–30 (pl. 40), conceptualizing such elements as the tripod base and the angled nose (fig. 13). The sketchbook thereafter ranges widely in its formal language and imagery, mirroring the inventiveness and diversity of the paintings and sculptures made during this fertile period of production.

***SEATED WOMAN* AND *SEATED WOMAN*, SPRING 1929**

During this period Picasso did not confine his sculptural activity to the metalwork collaborations with González.

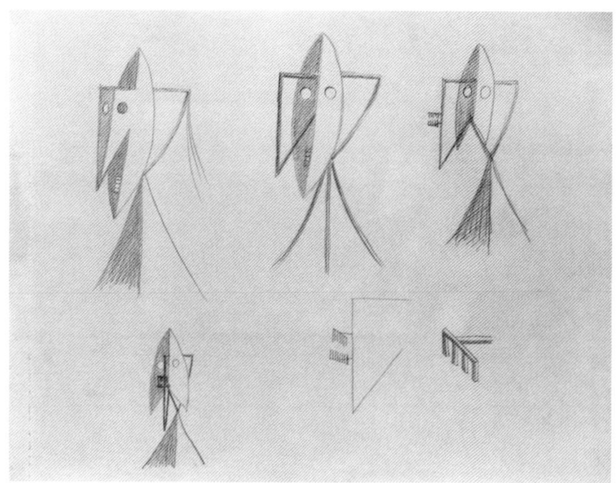

13. Pablo Picasso. Studies of a head for a sculpture project, 1929–30. Sketchbook no. 018, sheet 2 recto. Graphite on paper, 9 ¼ × 12 in. (23.5 × 30.5 cm). Musée national Picasso–Paris

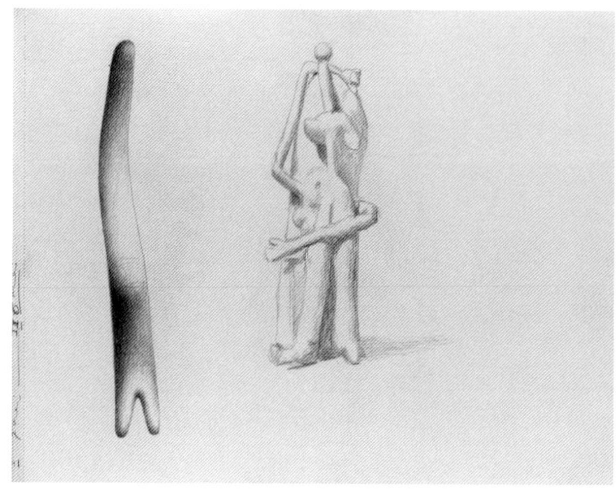

14. Pablo Picasso. Study of the sculpture *Seated Woman* with a detail of a leg, May 7 and 8, 1929. Sketchbook 018, sheet 38 recto. Graphite on Ingres paper, 9 ¼ × 12 in. (23.5 × 30.5 cm). Musée national Picasso–Paris

He occasionally turned to plaster modeling, as in these two seemingly pliable figures, both later translated into unique bronze casts (pls. 37, 38). These share little of the eroticism of the *Metamorphosis* figures and instead feel almost sedate, despite the startling elongation of their anatomies. Each corresponds to a sketchbook drawing that is so precise as to suggest that it followed rather than preceded the sculpture (fig. 14).

FALL 1929: Zervos's article "Projets de Picasso pour un monument" (Picasso's projects for a monument) was published in *Cahiers d'Art*, illustrated with ten drawings from Picasso's sketchbooks of July–December 1928 (begun in Paris, continued in Dinard, and finished in Paris). "It's not a series of simple drawings that we are presenting to our readers," Zervos began, "but rather studies for a monument that Picasso would like to realize."[28] He noted that Picasso's sketchbooks from 1927 had depicted "a series of monuments that the artist imagined spread over the length of the promenade de la Croisette."[29] The artist's desire to create monuments had persisted, Zervos wrote, and the 1928 drawings provided confirmation of the earlier research. Zervos explained that Picasso's monument would not be a solid mass like a pyramid but that "he rightly preferred to press his monument onto space and at the same time to penetrate it with that space itself. So that instead of entering into an antagonism with space, the monument could live in it."[30]

LATE 1929: Picasso visited Brancusi in his studio on the impasse Ronsin in Montparnasse, possibly for the first time and perhaps as a result of their individual friendships with González.[31] In temperament, the Romanian-born sculptor could not have been farther from Picasso: the former was a slow, patient craftsman who dedicated himself to a concise vocabulary of forms and themes; the latter was a restless experimentalist who placed no value on consistency. Picasso did not understand the attraction of carving marble. As he told Brassaï, "It seems strange to me that someone thought of making marble statues. I understand how you could see something in the root of a tree, a crack in the wall, in an eroded stone or pebble. But marble? It comes off in blocks and doesn't evoke any image. It does not inspire. How could Michelangelo have seen his *David* in a block of marble?"[32]

NOVEMBER 23–DECEMBER 24, 1929: The exhibition *Seit Cézanne in Paris* (Since Cézanne in Paris), organized by Alfred Flechtheim at his Berlin gallery, included bronze casts of four early sculptures: *The Jester* (pl. 3), *Head of a Woman (Fernande)* (pl. 4), *Head of a Woman* (pl. 11), and *Glass of Absinthe* (see pls. 21–26).

1930: Picasso and González worked together in González's studio on sculptures including *Head of a Man* (pl. 39), *Head of a Woman* (pl. 40), and *Woman in the Garden* (pl. 41), the latter two probably begun the previous year. These sculptures reveal the strong impact of the African and Oceanic objects that Picasso avidly collected and that were currently a major focus in Surrealist circles and in the pages of *Cahiers d'Art*. The commonalities include an enthusiasm for heterogeneous components; for example, Picasso's works employ pieces of scrap iron, using items that he and González found on foraging expeditions to junkyards.[33] Writing about these works in 1932, Zervos would note: "When working on his large metal figures, instead of kicking away the scraps of old iron littering the floor, Picasso carefully sifts through them and picks out pieces that nobody else would have bothered with, but that he can immediately use in his sculpture."[34]

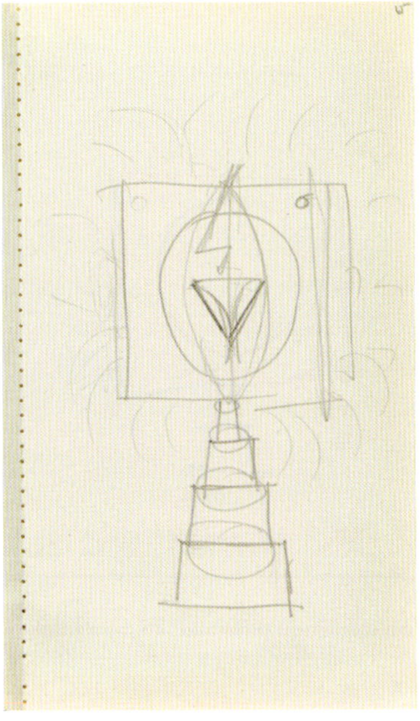

15. Pablo Picasso. Study for *Head of a Man*, July 1930. Sketchbook no. 020, sheet 15 recto. Graphite on paper, 6 11/16 × 4 1/8 in. (17 × 10.5 cm). Musée national Picasso–Paris

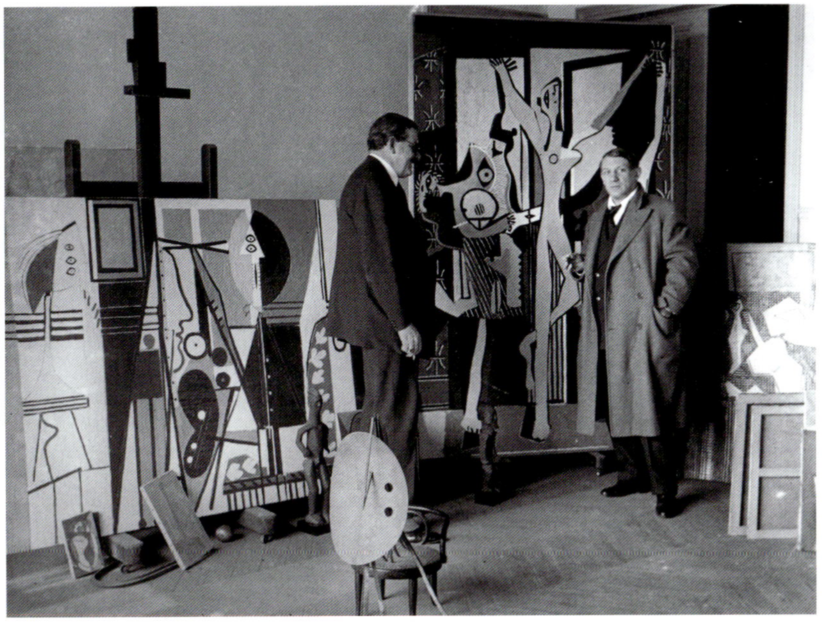

16. Picasso and a visitor in his studio with part of *Head of a Woman* in the foreground, Paris, [1928?]. Photograph by Albert Harlingue. Roger-Viollet/Parisienne de photographie

HEAD OF A MAN, 1930

This rugged sculpture (pl. 39) combines iron, brass, and bronze elements to form a strongly masklike head, characterized by the schematization and displacement of various anatomical elements. The long, lozenge-shaped mouth, for example, juts out from the head to which it belongs, much as the arms and legs of the wire *Figure* works of fall 1928 spring forward from the torsos. Viewed from different perspectives, the sculpture changes almost entirely; for example, only the profile view reveals that the back of the head is a shallow bronze dome. Contradictions abound: the right eye is a solid, and the left a void. Curved and welded metal sheets form the three progressively larger units composing the long neck, suggestive of a megaphonelike retractable stand (fig. 15).

Although this work acquired the title *Head of a Man* only after Picasso's death, and it has also been read as depicting a woman,[35] the male association is strongly supported by what appears to be a bristly moustache beneath the thin, pointing nose. The unified dark surface argues the case for it as a deliberate male pendant to the white-painted *Head of a Woman* made around the same time (pl. 40). The counterpoint between the two sculptures extends the black-white dialogue established in the left and right sides of *Head* of 1928 (pl. 32).

HEAD OF A WOMAN, 1929–30

While *Head of a Man* projects strength and solidity, this larger sculpture (pl. 40) is a lyrical celebration of lightness. Despite the weight and roughness of its metal elements, the airy composition is much in the spirit of the wire *Figure* works of fall 1928. *Head of a Woman* further develops the whimsical spirit that subtly informs those works, in large part due to its absurd combination of found elements—most notably the two colanders that form the head but equally suggest breasts or belly. The face is articulated by projecting beaklike lips, the nose is composed of an angular rod, and eyes and nostrils are connoted by two pairs of holes. A photograph taken in the artist's studio suggests that this was the portion of the sculpture with which Picasso began (fig. 16). As is true of *Head of a Man*, a profile view of the work reveals many surprises, such as the two cones behind the vertical pair of holes in the face and the metal springs that fly straight out in the manner of windswept hair. Whether the view is profile or frontal, Picasso's debt to African and Oceanic masks is highly evident, as is the sculpture's close relation to his drawings and paintings of the time.[36]

WOMAN IN THE GARDEN, SPRING 1929–30

Nearly seven feet tall, *Woman in the Garden* (pl. 41) was Picasso's final and most ambitious effort to create a memorial sculpture for Apollinaire. It is composed from a large number of salvaged metal elements, welded together and unified by an overall coating of white paint. The sculpture's disparate parts seem to flaunt their casual, almost accidental cooperation in composing a legible image. While preliminary drawings in

Picasso's sketchbooks provided a starting point, the improvisation inspired by found objects played an equally important role in the creation of this work and others of its moment. Just as the sketchbook drawings for *Head of a Woman* indicate nothing of colanders, for example, the drawings for *Woman in the Garden* show nothing of its large philodendron stems and leaves.

The sculpture's title encourages a reading of the ambiguous forms as a woman standing behind a table or seated in a chair. However, when Brassaï first saw the sculpture with Picasso in 1932, it was called "The Stag."[37] The tilting flat plane at center can indeed be read as a horizontal body, and the philodendrons as an exuberant tail.

JUNE 1930: Picasso bought the Château de Boisgeloup, near Gisors in Normandy, where he would settle the following spring. He began to work in Boisgeloup that summer (see Chapter 5).

OBJECT WITH PALM LEAF AND _COMPOSITION WITH GLOVE_, AUGUST 1930

During his summer holiday in the seaside town of Juan-les-Pins, Picasso created a series of eight sand reliefs, each set within the reverse side of a stretched canvas. The frames provided by the wooden stretchers can barely contain the objects with which Picasso filled the shallow space. *Object with Palm Leaf* (pl. 42) and *Composition with Glove* (pl. 43) are typical of the group in their combination of organic matter (twigs, leaves) and manufactured objects (small toys, a glove). Once the objects were satisfactorily arranged within the stretcher, the entirety was coated with coarse sand from the beach. This unified the disparate colors and textures of the materials, distilling an unruly assortment of forms and textures into an integrated whole.

NOVEMBER 15, 1930: The poet and critic André Salmon wrote to Picasso about a visit he had made to González's studio.[38] At this meeting, González had shown Salmon a sheet of bronze, a material under consideration for making a second, more durable version of *Woman in the Garden*. This note suggests that hope was still alive for the acceptance of the work by the Apollinaire committee.

DECEMBER 1930: The book *Pablo Picasso*, an illustrated study by Eugenio d'Ors, was published. Originally written in Spanish, Ors's text was simultaneously released in a French translation by Éditions des Chroniques du jour in Paris and in two English editions, by E. Weyhe in New York and A. Zwemmer in London.[39] The illustrations included a *Glass of Absinthe* (pl. 24) and the recently completed *Head of a Man* (pl. 39), reproduced for the first time. The caption calls the metal construction "Detail of a monument."[40]

FIGURE, [1931]

This compact personage (pl. 33) is characteristic of a set of contemporaneous works made of found metal elements and iron wire. Notwithstanding its diminutive size (just over ten inches tall), the sculpture has monumental stature, particularly as photographed by Brassaï close up and from below (see p. 294). Like far larger and more complex works such as *Woman in the Garden*, it explores the sculptural interrelationship of stasis and movement, of solid form and space.

Although it has been ascribed to the year 1931 since being designated as such in *Les Sculptures de Picasso* in 1949, there is compelling reason to place this sculpture earlier. Small-scale experiments such as this may just as well have stemmed from a moment closer to when González introduced Picasso to these materials. In "Picasso à Dinard, été 1928," published early in 1929, Zervos described how, during the writer's visit, "Picasso picks up a wire lying on the floor and proceeds to twist it while chatting. Without doing anything specific, after a few minutes, the wire sustained the imprint of a great sensitivity."[41]

SPRING 1931: At Picasso's request, González was working to make a version of *Woman in the Garden* in bronze, a material much better suited to prolonged outdoor display than painted sheet metal. Evidently the task was far more difficult than González had anticipated. In an express letter of April 2, 1931, he asked Picasso to stop by to give advice: "Yesterday I went to the ironmongers fair to buy a pair of larger hammers, because the 'casserole' has turned into a Titanic undertaking" (fig. 17).[42] González's bronze version would probably not be completed until 1932. The bronze and the painted white metal versions of *Woman in the Garden* would be shown that summer in Picasso's retrospective exhibition at the Galeries Georges Petit in Paris, placed at opposing ends of a long gallery (see fig. 16 on p. 141 and fig. 1 on p. 305). In his essay "Picasso dans son élément" (Picasso in his element), published the following year in the inaugural issue of the journal *Minotaure*, André Breton described this dark/light opposition as symptomatic of the dualistic nature of Picasso's artistic imagination.[43]

END OF 1931–EARLY 1932: González began writing "Picasso et les cathédrales" (Picasso and cathedrals), a manuscript devoted to the artist's sculptures (fig. 18). In it he described the creation of *Woman in the Garden* in 1931 as an improvisatory undertaking: "In spite of the thousands of studies, he took not a one the morning of the day he went to work at the forge; his hammer alone was enough to try to bring into being his monument to Apollinaire. He worked on it long months at a time and he finished it. He would often say, 'Once again I feel as happy as I was in 1912.'"[44] González went on to say that Picasso did not like the

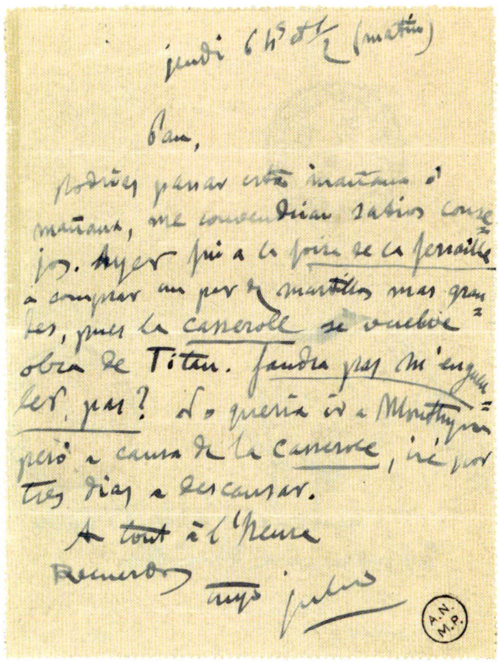

jeudi 6h et 1/2 (matin)

Pau,

podries pasar esta mañana ó
mañana, me convendria saber com
va. Ayer fui a la foire de la ferraille
a comprar un par de martillos mas grandes, pues la caserole se acaba =
obra de Titan. Faudra pas m'engueu-
ler, pas? Yo queria ir a Montlhéry =
però a causa de la caserole, iré por
tres dias a descansar.

A tout à l'heure

Recuerdos
tuyo Julio

A.N. M.P.

17. Express letter from Julio González to Picasso, April 2, 1931. Picasso Archives, Musée national Picasso–Paris

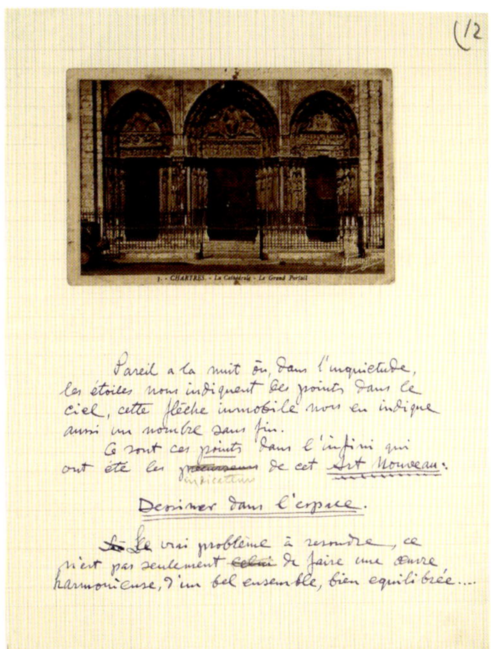

(12

1. - CHARTRES. - La Cathédrale - Le Grand Portail

Pareil a la nuit où, dans l'inquiétude,
les étoiles nous indiquent des points dans le
ciel, cette flèche immobile nous en indique
aussi un nombre sans fin.
Ce sont ces points dans l'infini qui
ont été les ~~précurseurs~~ indicateurs de cet Art Nouveau.

Dessiner dans l'espace.

~~Si~~ Le vrai problème à resoudre, ce
n'est pas seulement ~~celui~~ de faire une œuvre
harmonieuse, d'un bel ensemble, bien equilibrée....

18. Page 12 of Julio González's manuscript "Picasso et les cathédrales" (Picasso and cathedrals), late 1931–early 1932. Valencia/Julio González Archives, Paris

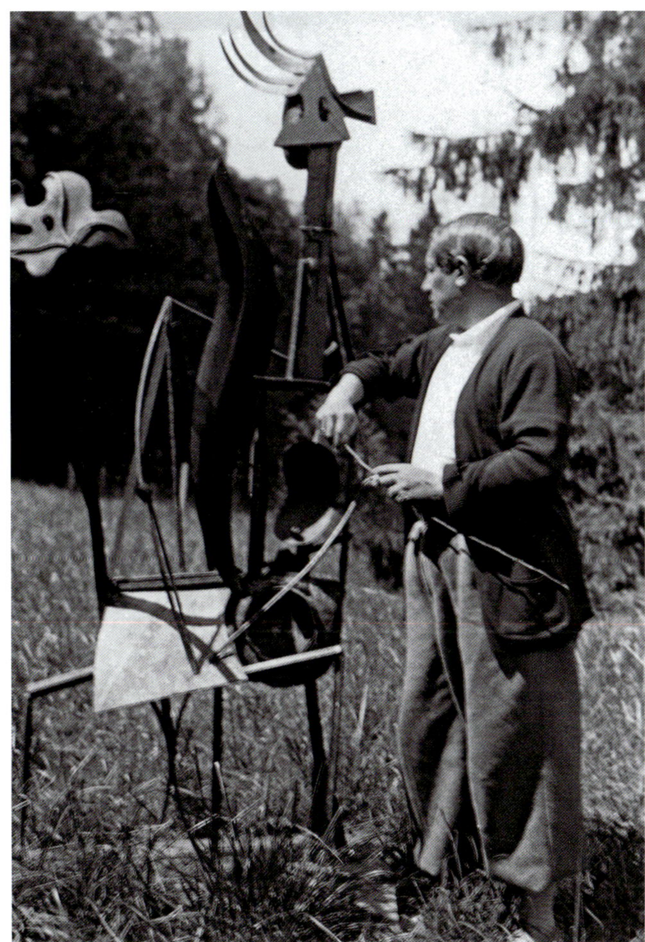

19. Picasso with the bronze version of *Woman in the Garden* in the garden at the Château de Boisgeloup, c. 1932. Picasso Archives, Musée national Picasso–Paris

idea of parting with the work, or sending it to "Père Lachaise in that collection of monuments where people seldom go. He wished that this monument would become the reliquary which would keep the ashes of the lamented poet and that he be authorized to place them near his house, in his garden."[45]

While the extraordinary notion of relocating Apollinaire's ashes remained just that, Picasso would indeed keep both versions of *Woman in the Garden* for the rest of his life (fig. 19). Evidently it, like his other designs, did not meet the favor of the Apollinaire committee. In November 1934, Salmon publicly announced that Picasso would present no further proposals for the memorial.[46] Subsequently, Serge Férat would design and order a granite monument, which would be placed on the tomb at Père Lachaise cemetery on September 5, 1935. Two decades after that, Picasso would fulfill his longstanding obligation by donating a bronze cast of a 1941 work, *Head of a Woman* (pl. 80), to be installed in honor of Apollinaire in the small square beside the Church of Saint-Germain-des-Prés in Paris (see fig. 6 on p. 185).

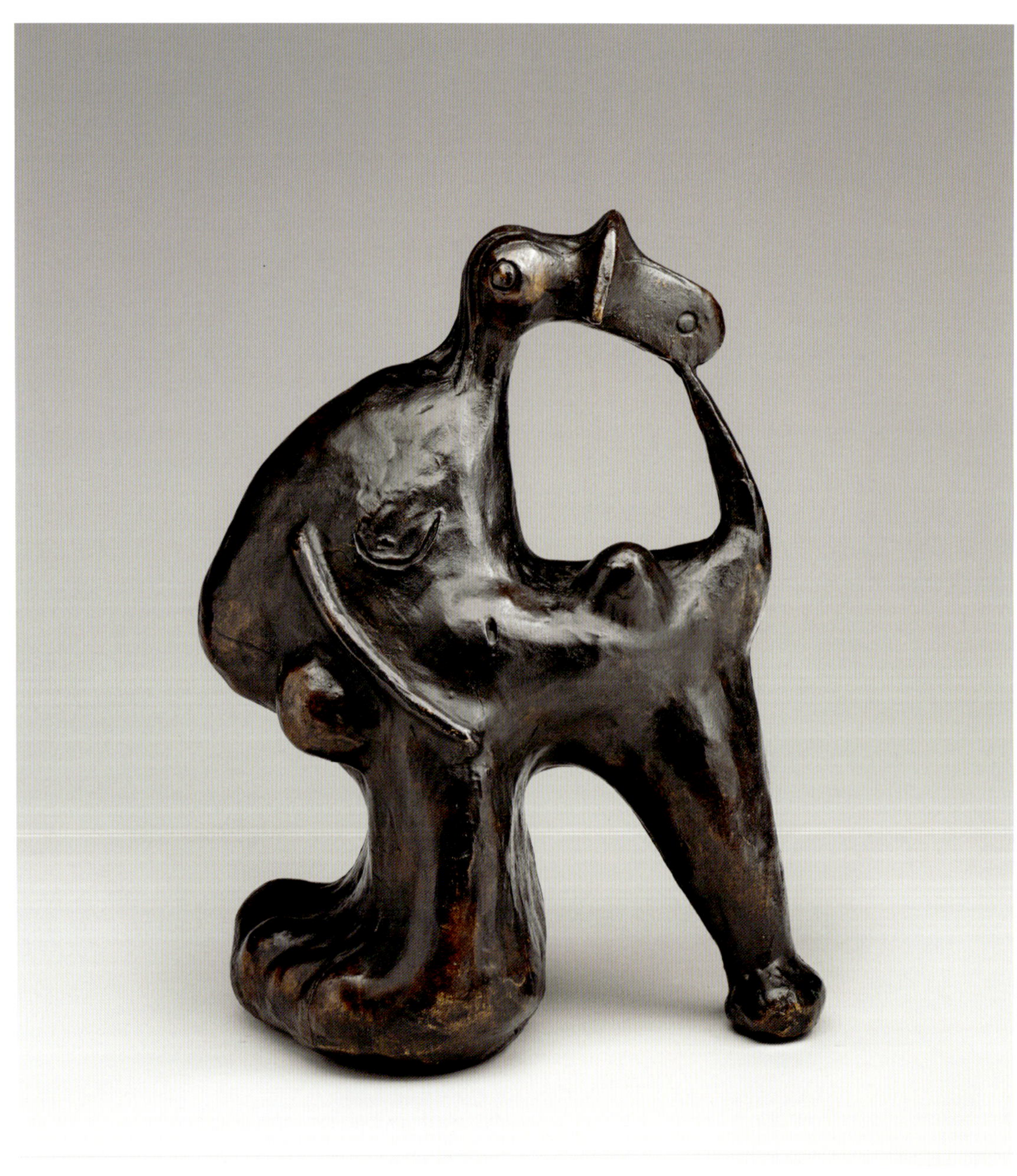

30. **METAMORPHOSIS I.** Paris, 1928
Bronze, unique, cast by October 1943
9 × 7 1/16 × 4 5/16 in. (22.8 × 18 × 11 cm)
Musée national Picasso–Paris. Dation Pablo Picasso

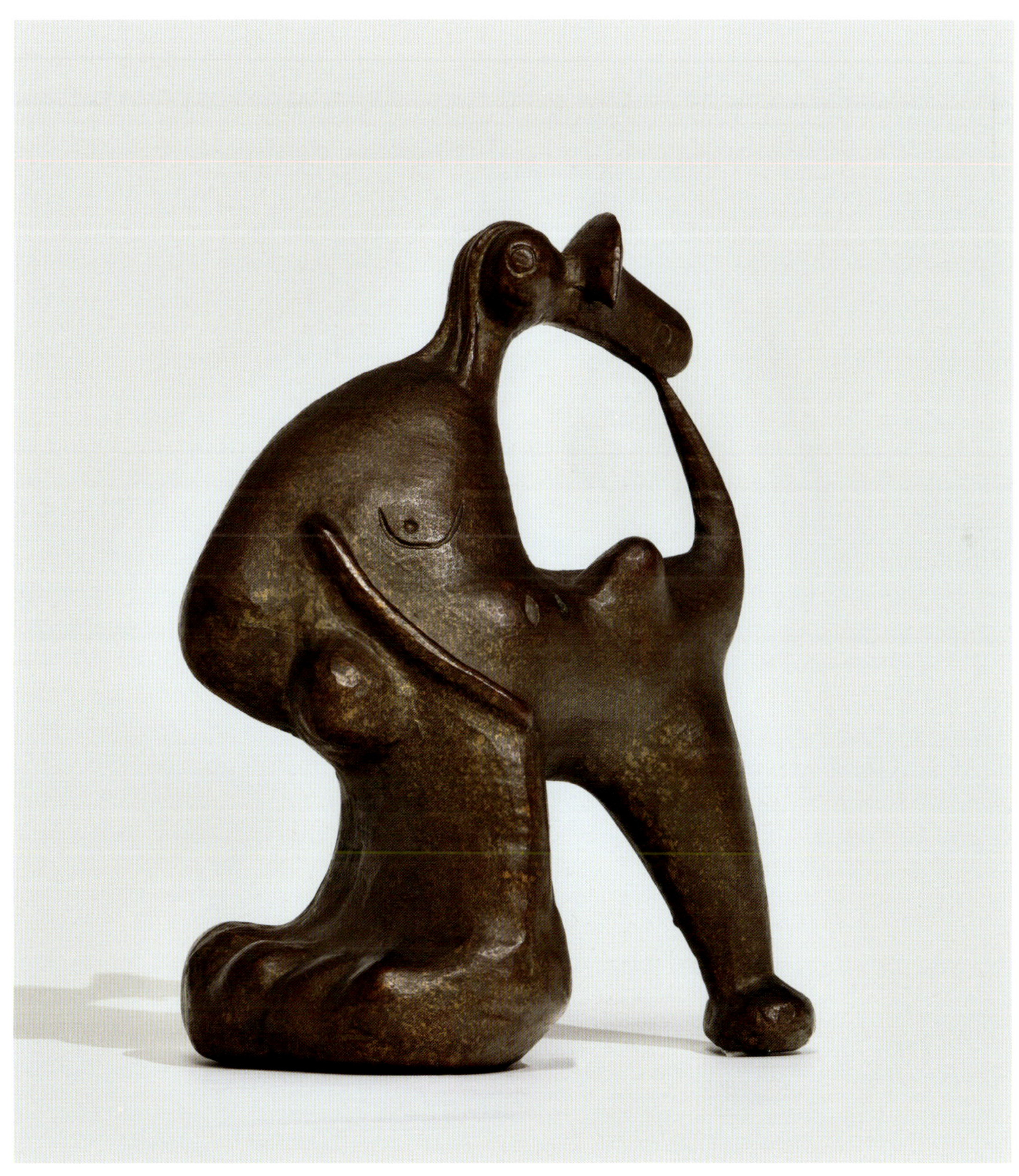

31. **METAMORPHOSIS II.** Paris, 1928
Bronze, unique, cast by October 1943
9 × 7 3/16 × 4 5/16 in. (22.8 × 18.3 × 11 cm)
Private collection. Courtesy Fundación Almine y Bernard Ruiz-Picasso para el Arte

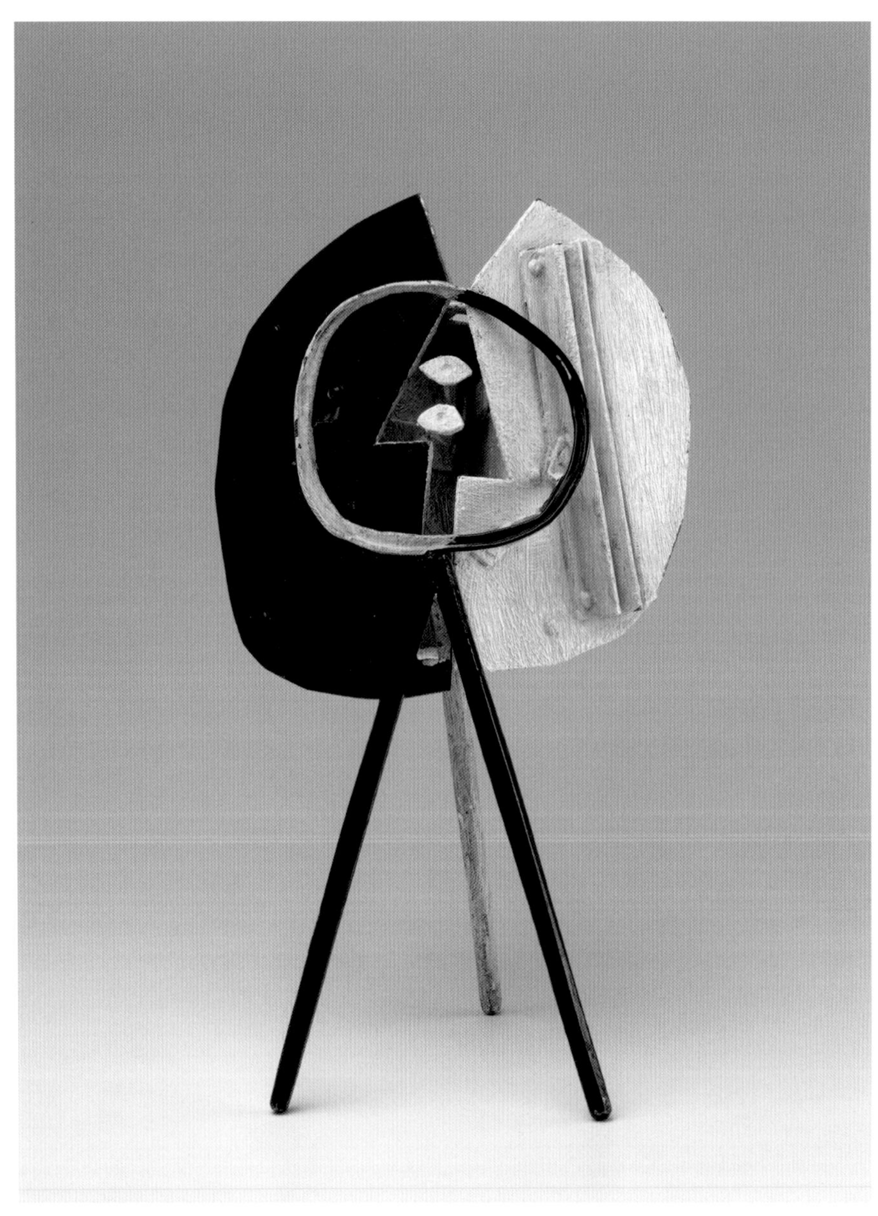

32. HEAD. Paris, October 1928
Painted brass and iron
7 1/16 × 4 5/16 × 3 3/4 in. (18 × 11 × 9.5 cm)
Musée national Picasso–Paris. Dation Pablo Picasso

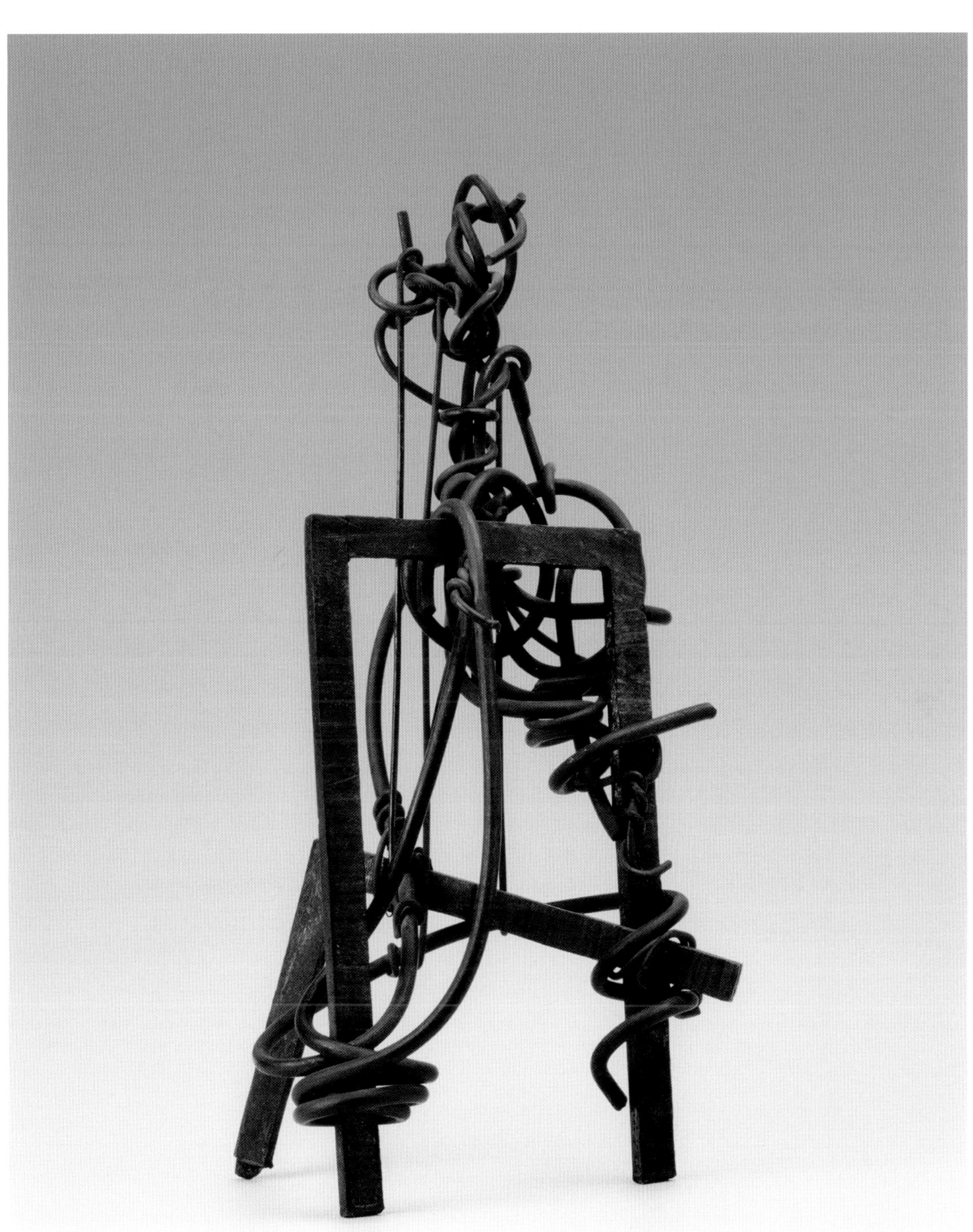

33. **FIGURE.** [1931]
Iron and iron wire
10 ¼ × 4 ¹⁵⁄₁₆ × 4 ⅜ in. (26 × 12.5 × 11.1 cm)
Musée national Picasso–Paris. Dation Pablo Picasso

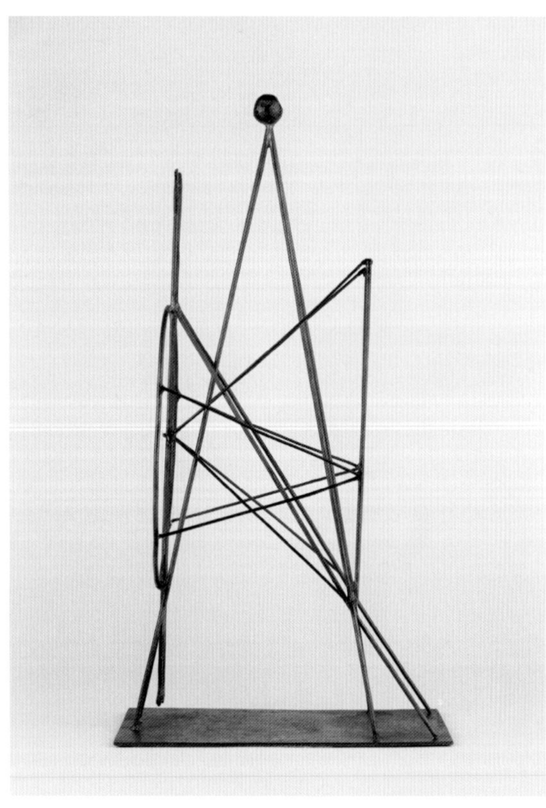

34. FIGURE. Paris, October 1928
Iron wire and sheet metal
14 ¾ × 3 ¹⁵⁄₁₆ × 7 ¹¹⁄₁₆ in. (37.5 × 10 × 19.6 cm)
Musée national Picasso–Paris. Dation Pablo Picasso; on long-term loan to the Centre national d'art et de culture Georges Pompidou, Paris. Musée national d'art moderne/Centre de création industrielle

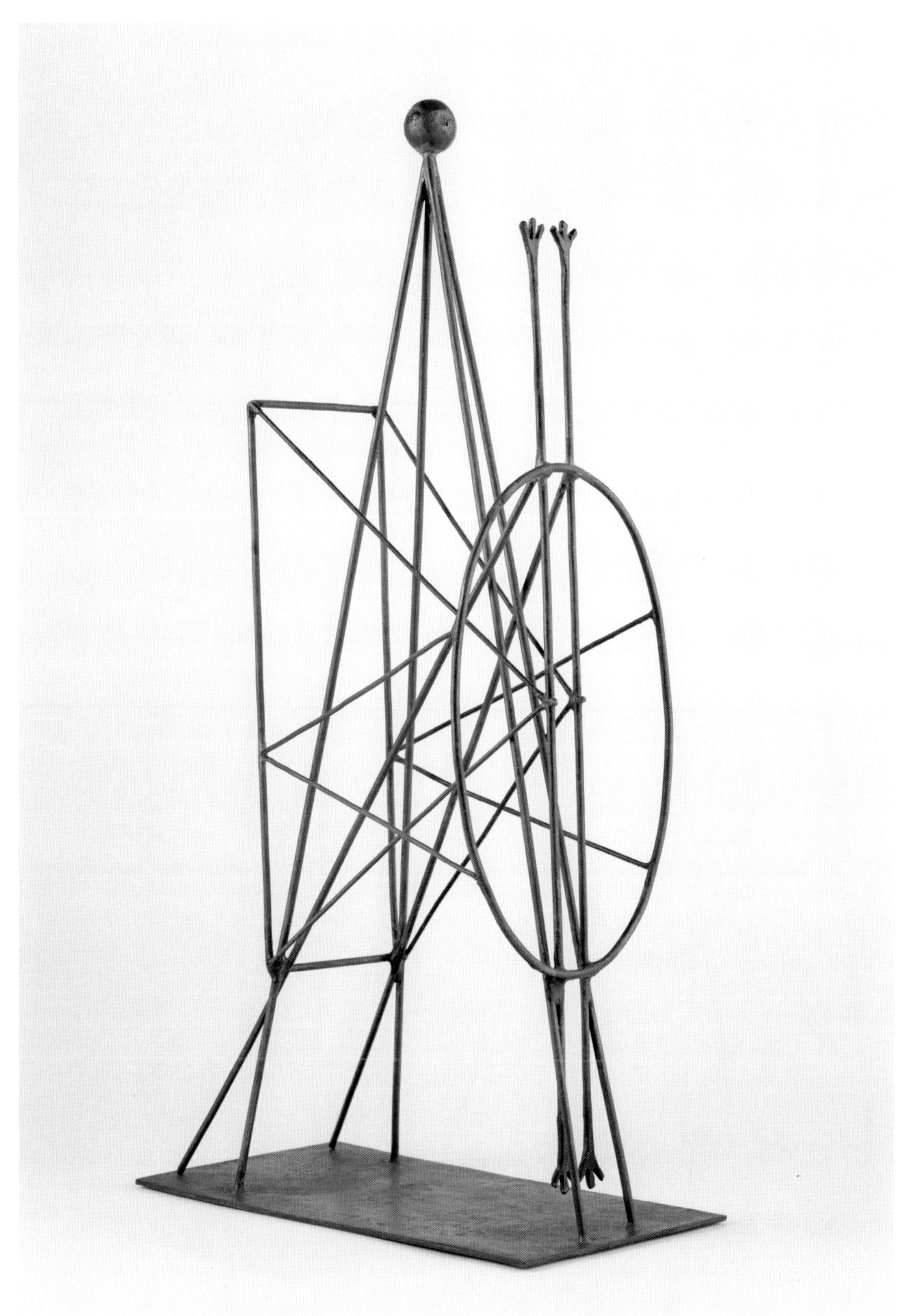

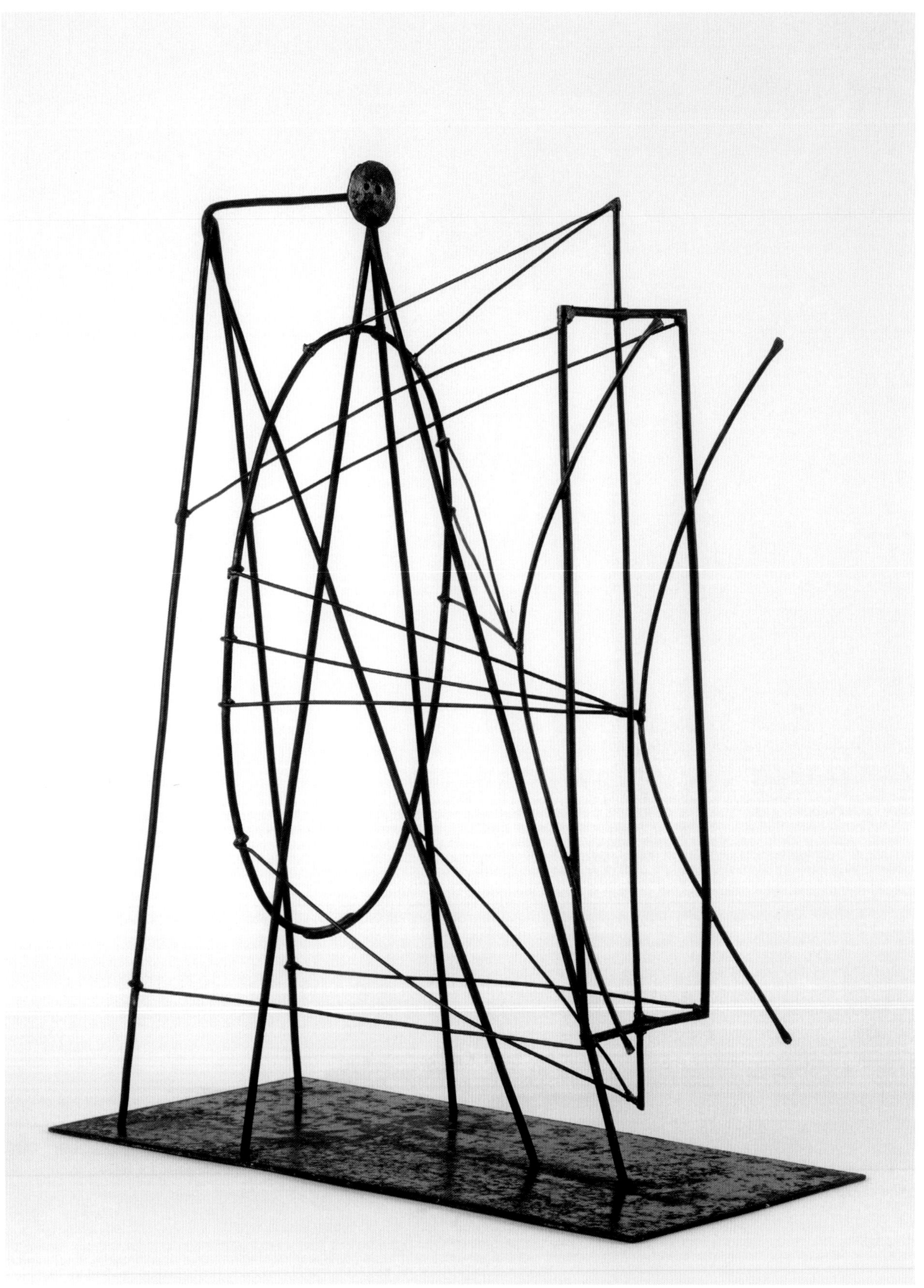

35. FIGURE. Paris, fall 1928
Iron wire and sheet metal
19 ⅞ × 7 5/16 × 16 1/16 in. (50.5 × 18.5 × 40.8 cm)
Musée national Picasso–Paris. Dation Pablo Picasso

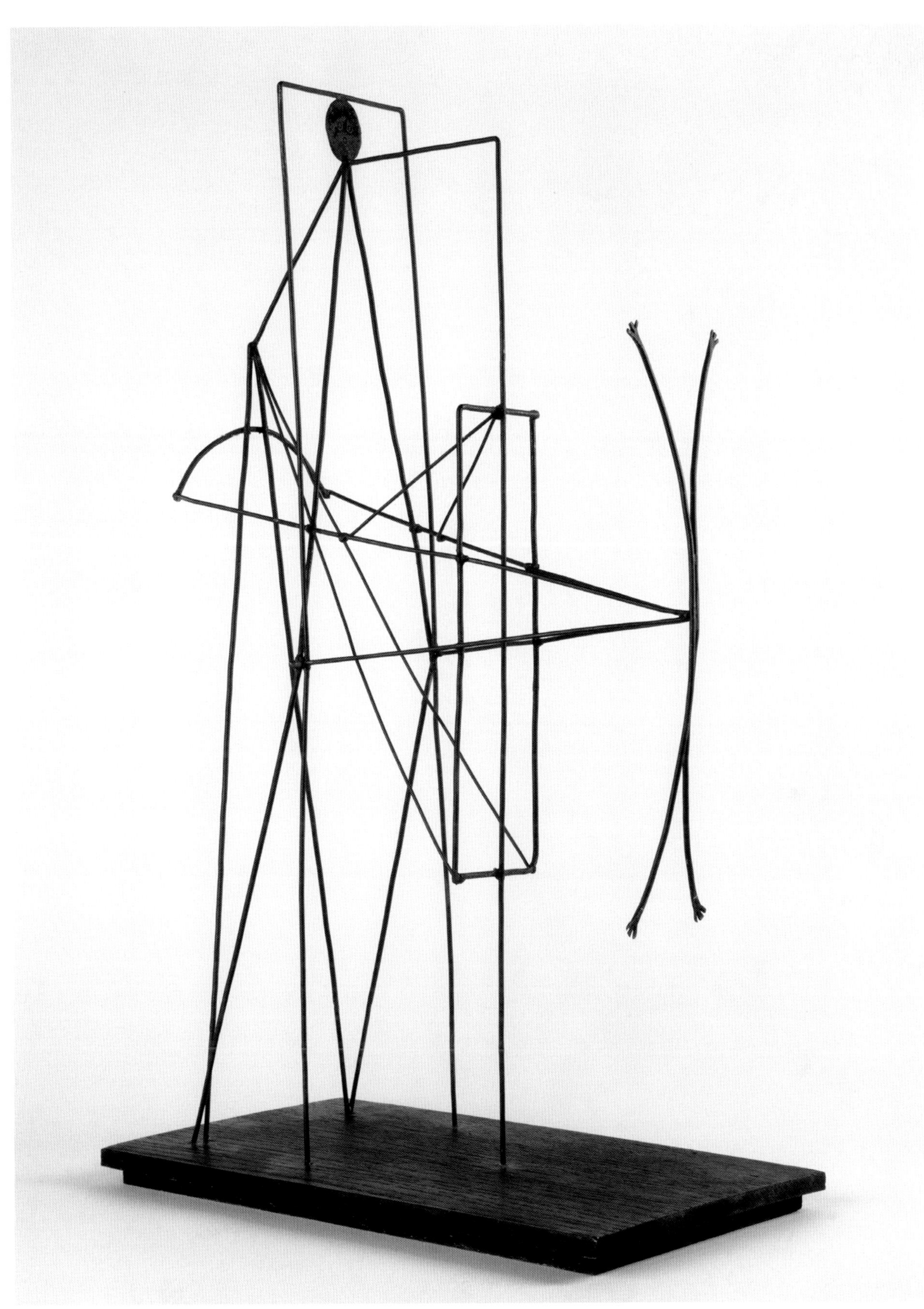

36. **FIGURE.** Paris, fall 1928
Iron wire and sheet metal
23 7/16 × 5 1/8 × 12 5/8 in. (59.5 × 13 × 32 cm)
Musée national Picasso–Paris. Dation Pablo Picasso

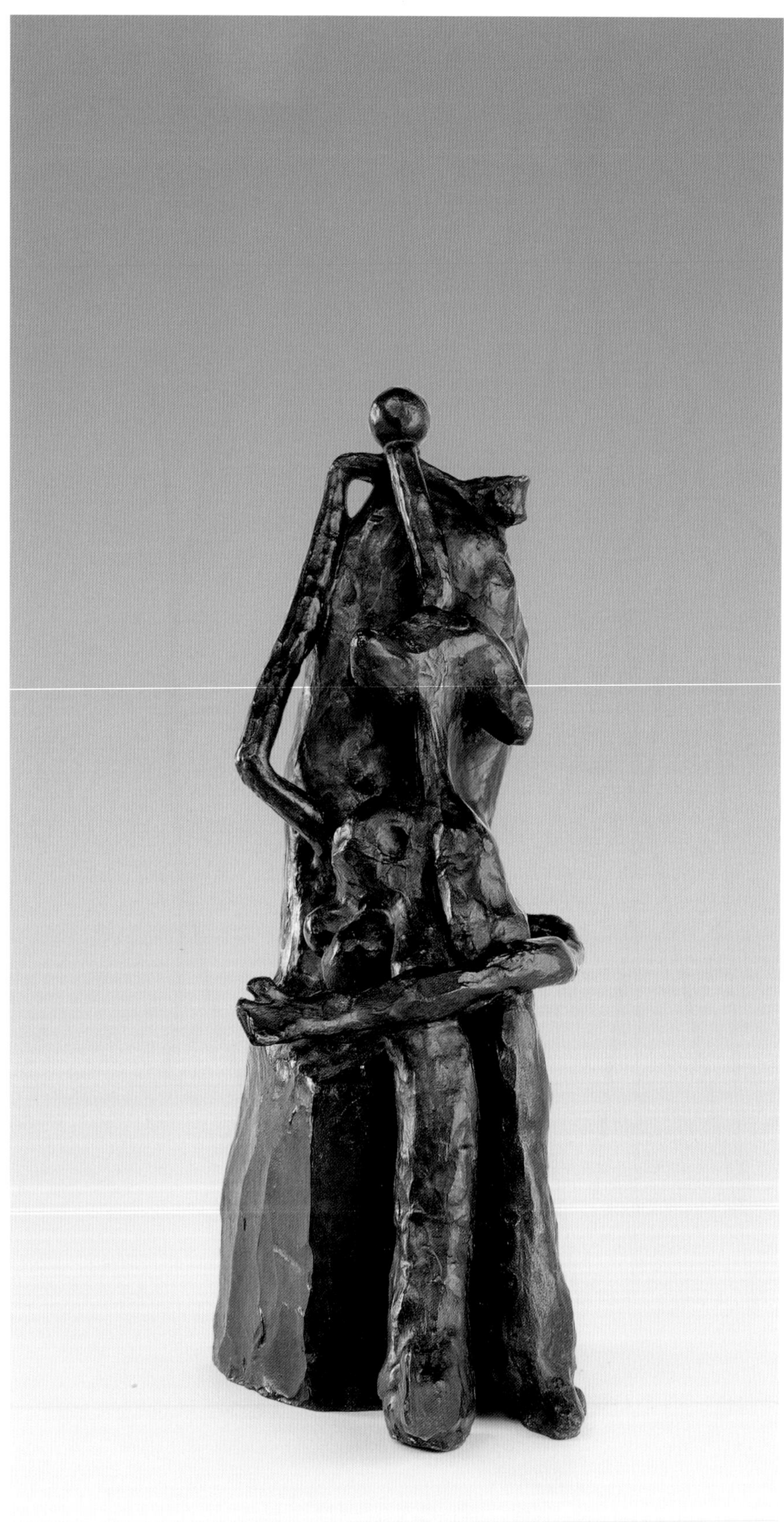

37. **SEATED WOMAN.** Paris, spring 1929
Bronze, unique, cast by 1943
16 ¾ × 6 ½ × 9 ¹³⁄₁₆ in. (42.5 × 16.5 × 25 cm)
Musée national Picasso–Paris. Dation Pablo Picasso

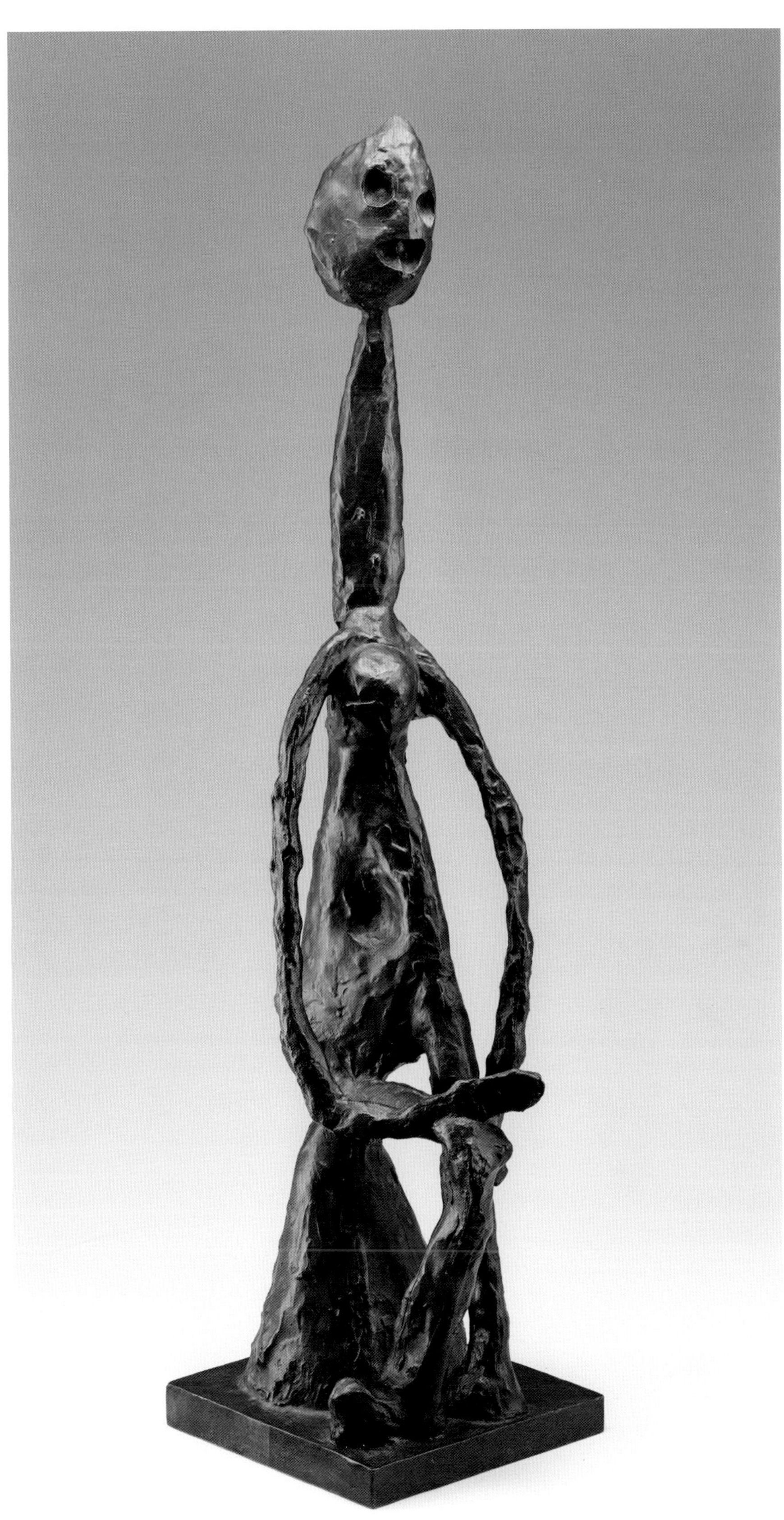

38. **SEATED WOMAN.** Paris, spring 1929
Bronze, unique, cast by 1943
31 11/16 × 7 7/8 × 8 11/16 in. (80.5 × 20 × 22 cm)
Musée national Picasso–Paris. Dation Pablo Picasso

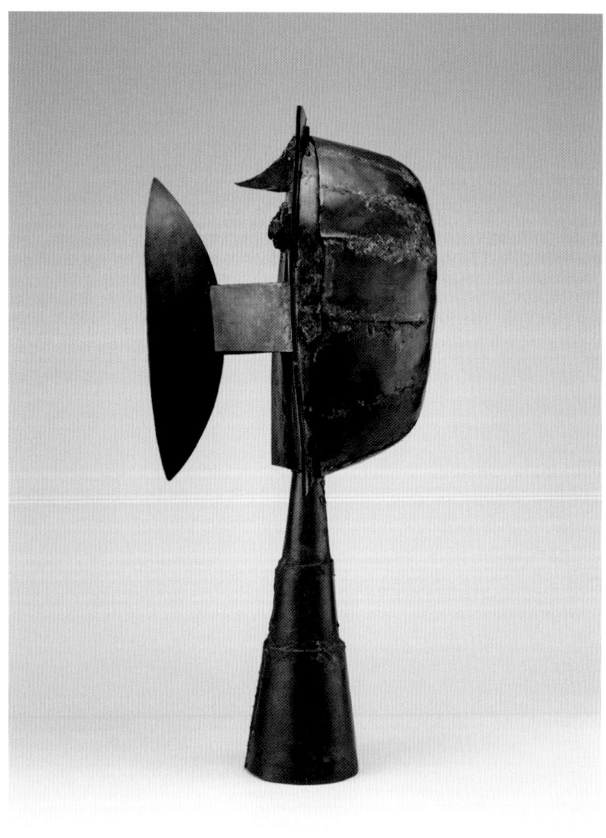

39. HEAD OF A MAN. Paris, 1930
Iron, brass, and bronze
32 7/8 × 15 3/4 × 14 3/16 in. (83.5 × 40 × 36 cm)
Musée national Picasso–Paris. Dation Pablo Picasso

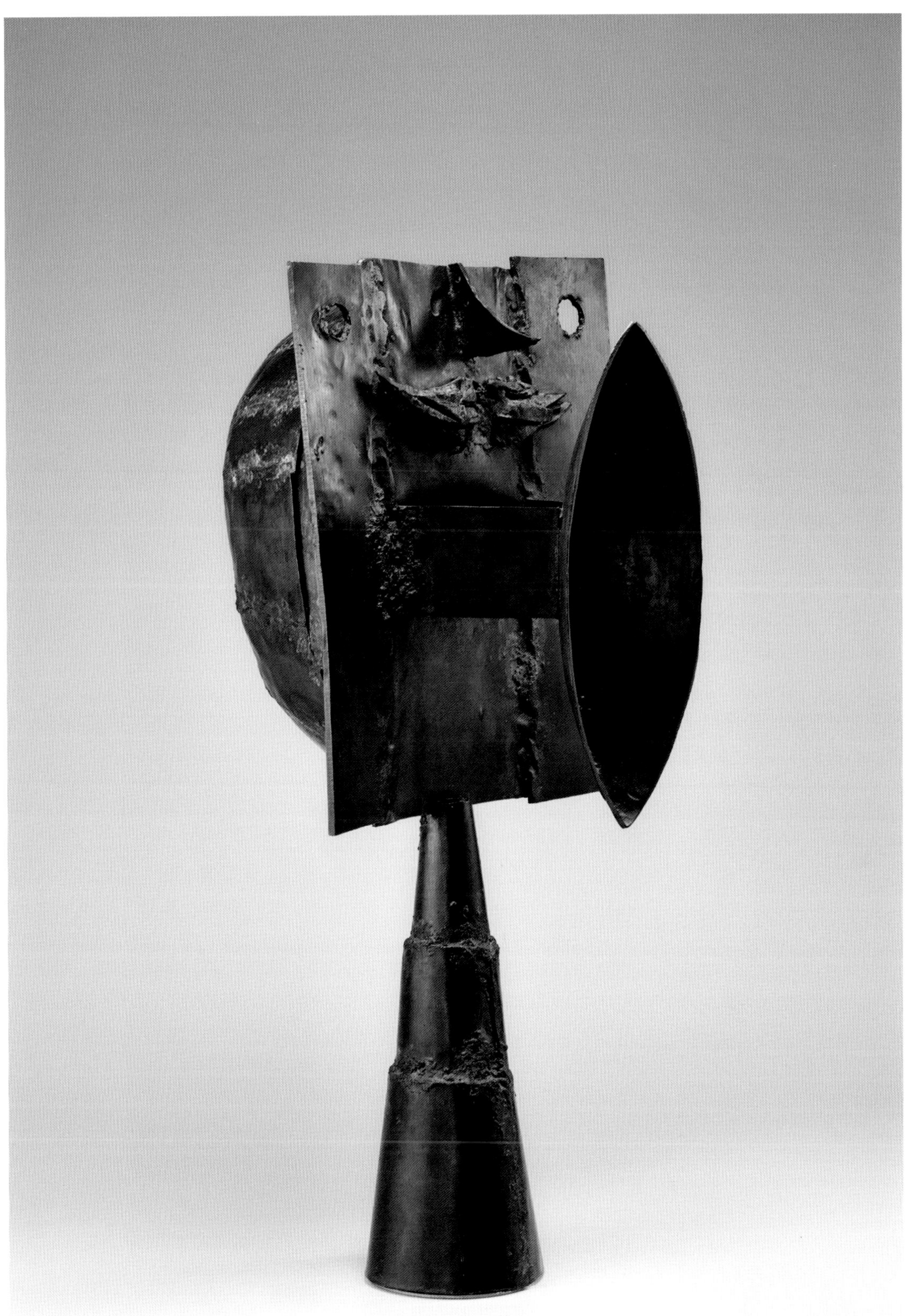

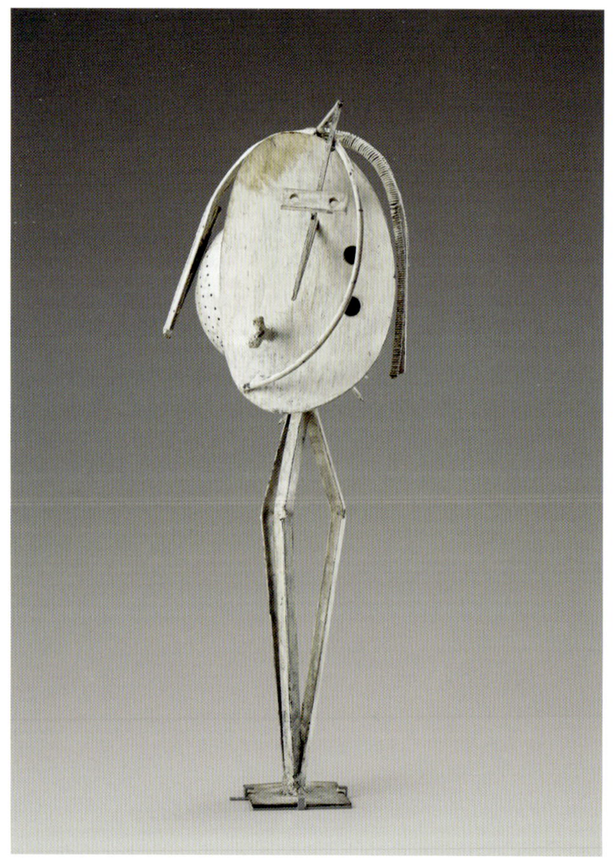

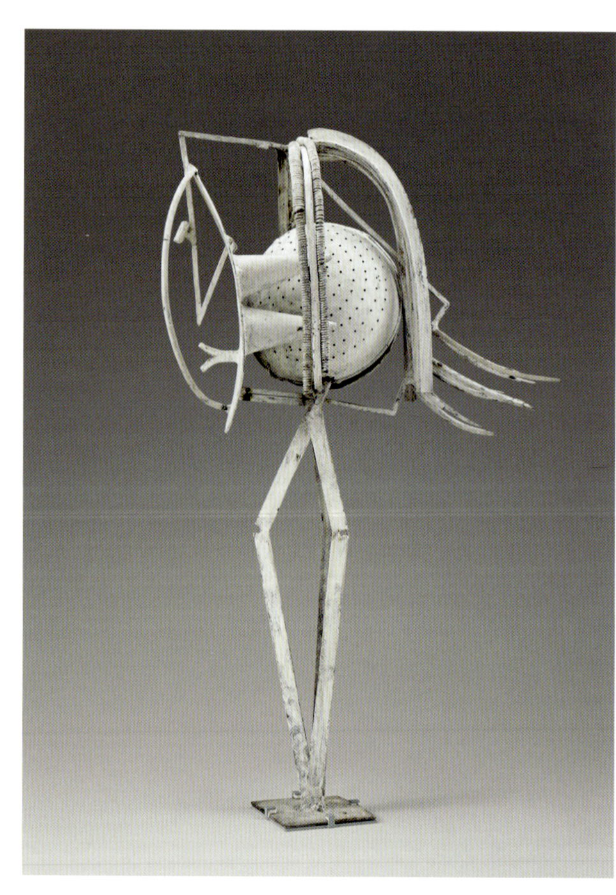

40. **HEAD OF A WOMAN.** Paris, 1929–30
Iron, sheet metal, springs, and metal colanders; all painted
39 ⅜ × 14 ⁹⁄₁₆ × 23 ¼ in. (100 × 37 × 59 cm)
Musée national Picasso–Paris. Dation Pablo Picasso

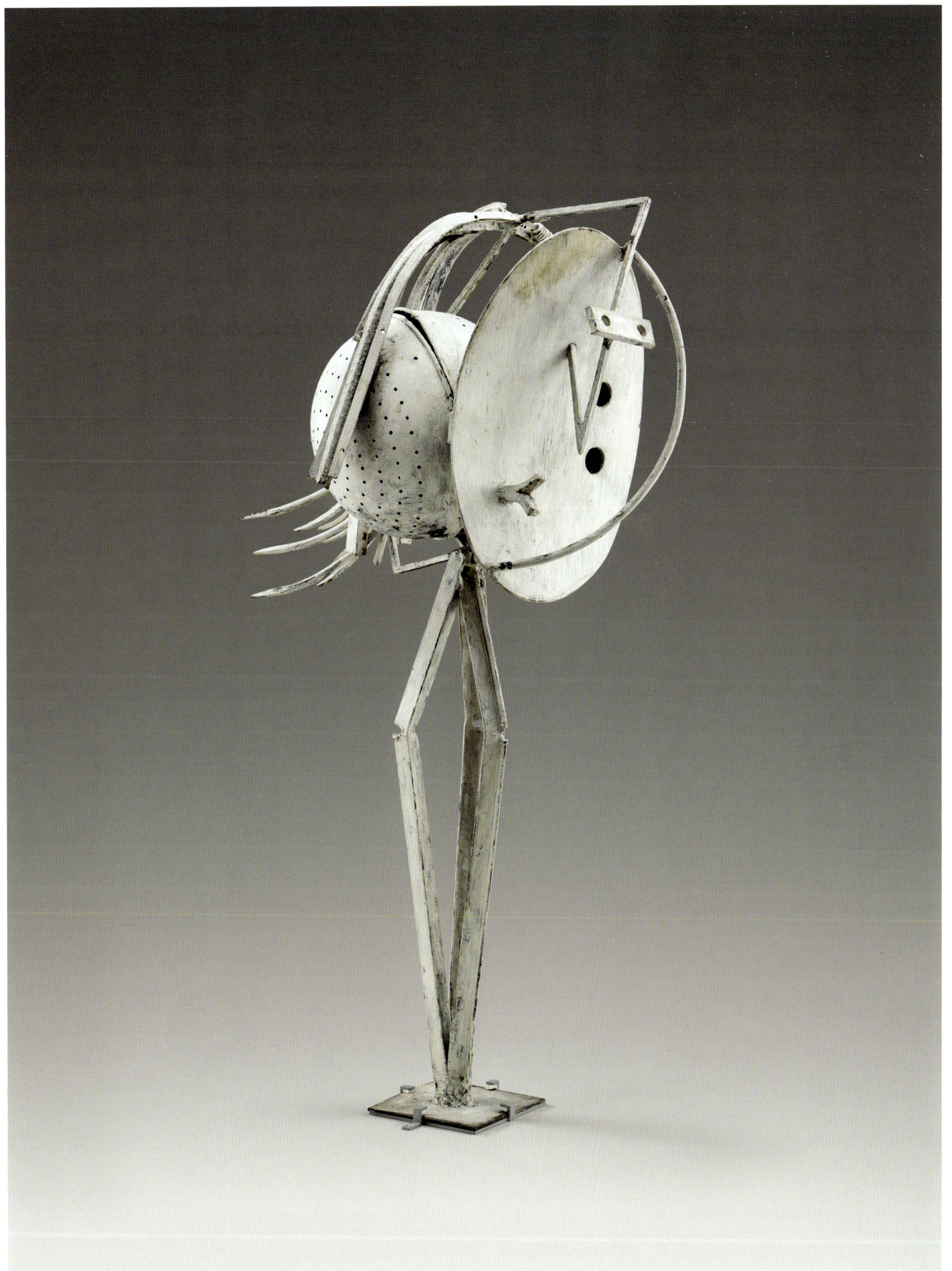

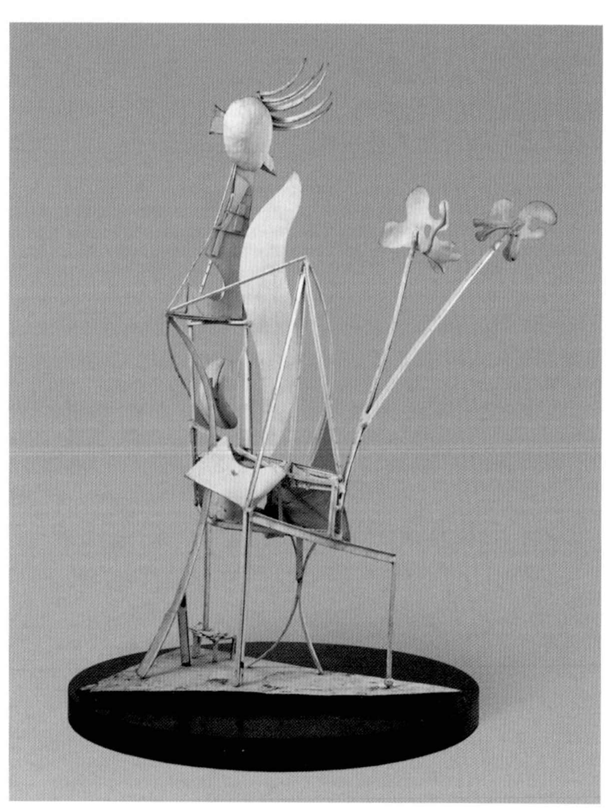

41. **WOMAN IN THE GARDEN.** Paris, spring 1929–30
Welded and painted iron
6 ft. 9⅛ in. × 46¹⁄₁₆ in. × 33⁷⁄₁₆ in. (206 × 117 × 85 cm)
Musée national Picasso–Paris. Dation Pablo Picasso

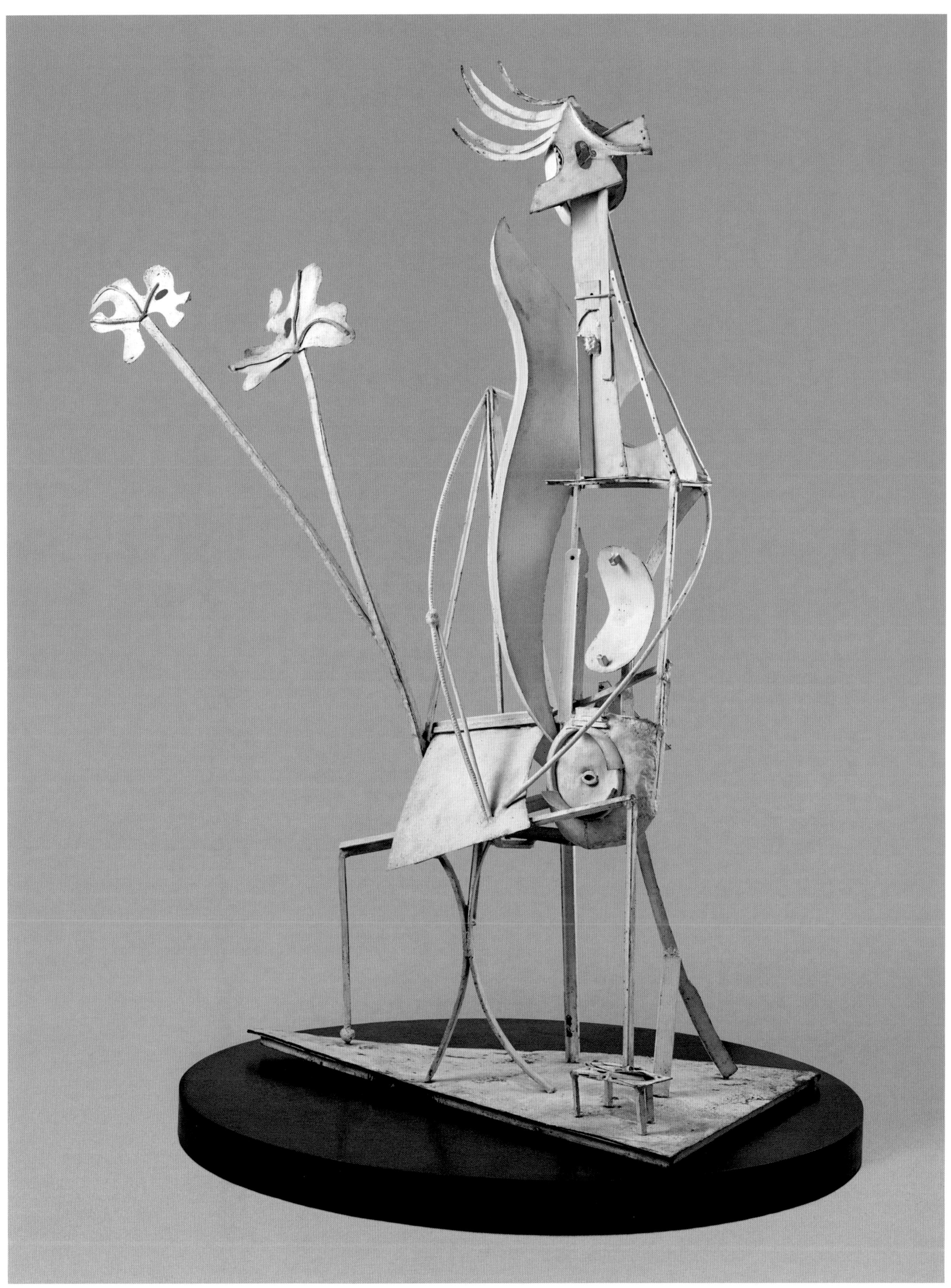

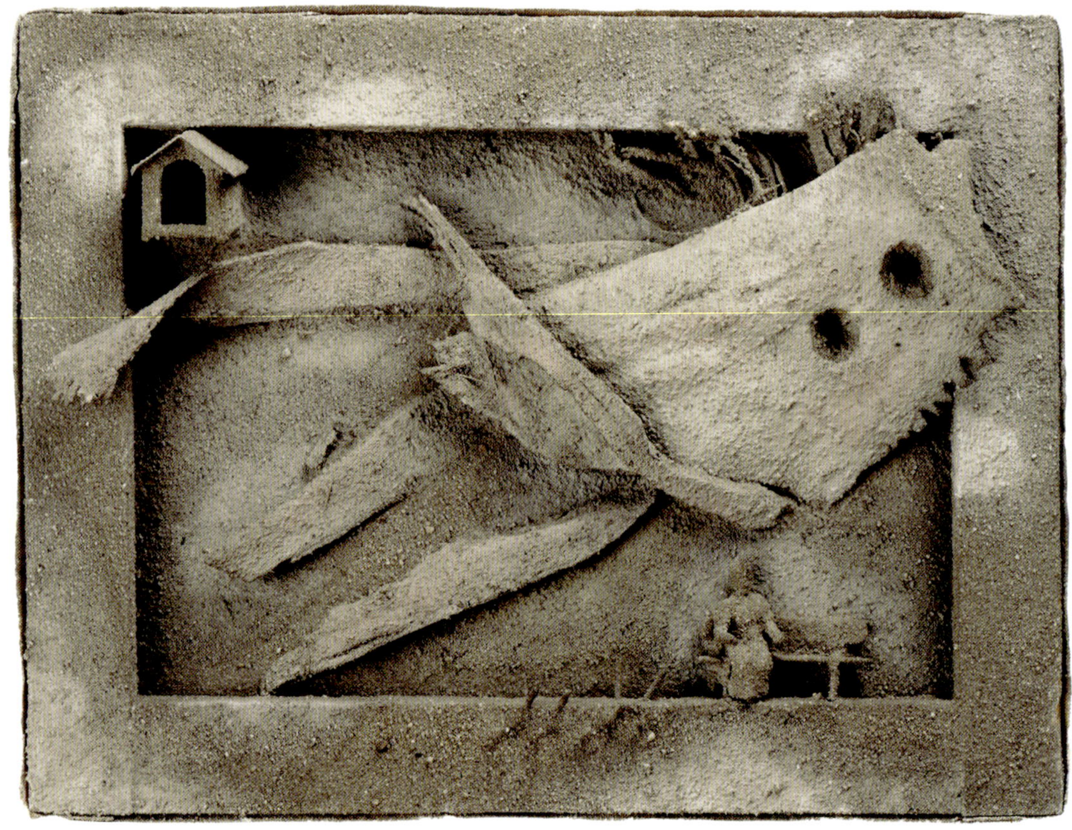

42. **OBJECT WITH PALM LEAF.** Juan-les-Pins, August 27, 1930
Cardboard, plants, nails, and objects sewn and glued to back of canvas and stretcher and coated with sand; sand partially painted
9 13/16 × 13 × 1 3/4 in. (25 × 33 × 4.5 cm)
Musée national Picasso–Paris. Dation Pablo Picasso

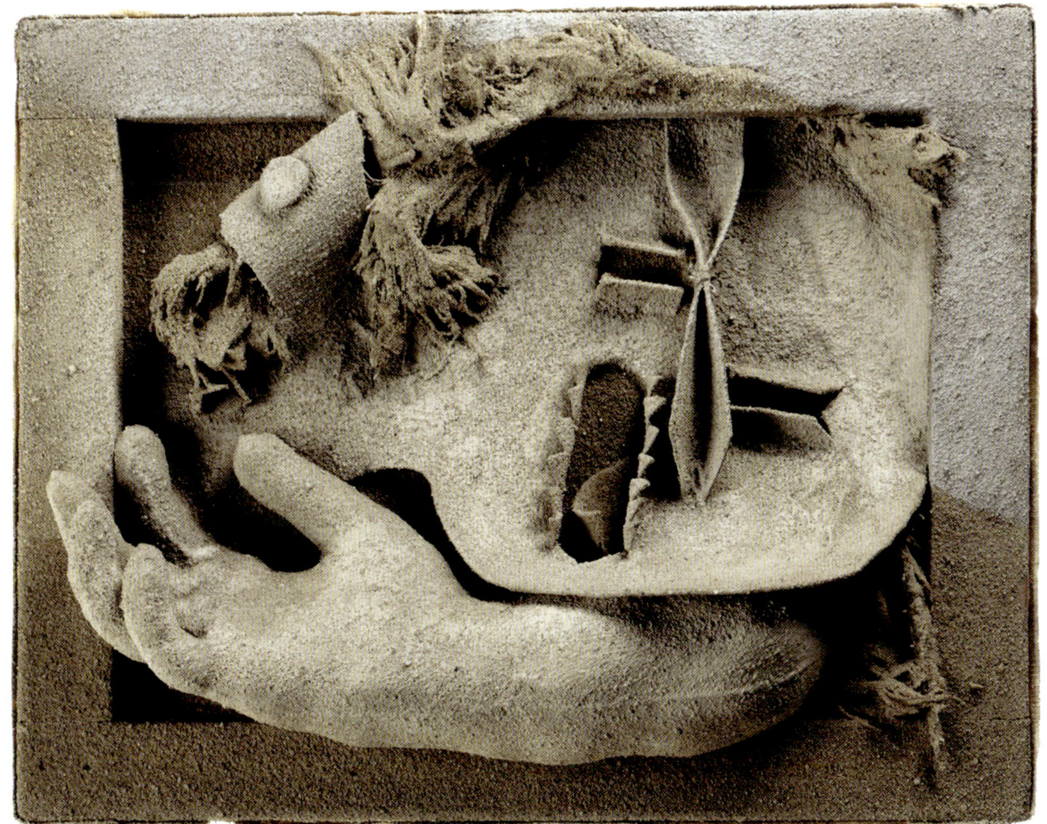

43. **COMPOSITION WITH GLOVE.** Juan-les-Pins, August 22, 1930
Glove, cardboard, and plants sewn and glued to back of canvas and stretcher and coated with sand; sand partially painted
10 13⁄16 × 14 × 3 1⁄8 in. (27.5 × 35.5 × 8 cm)
Musée national Picasso–Paris. Dation Pablo Picasso

CHAPTER 5

THE BOISGELOUP SCULPTURE STUDIO 1930–1937

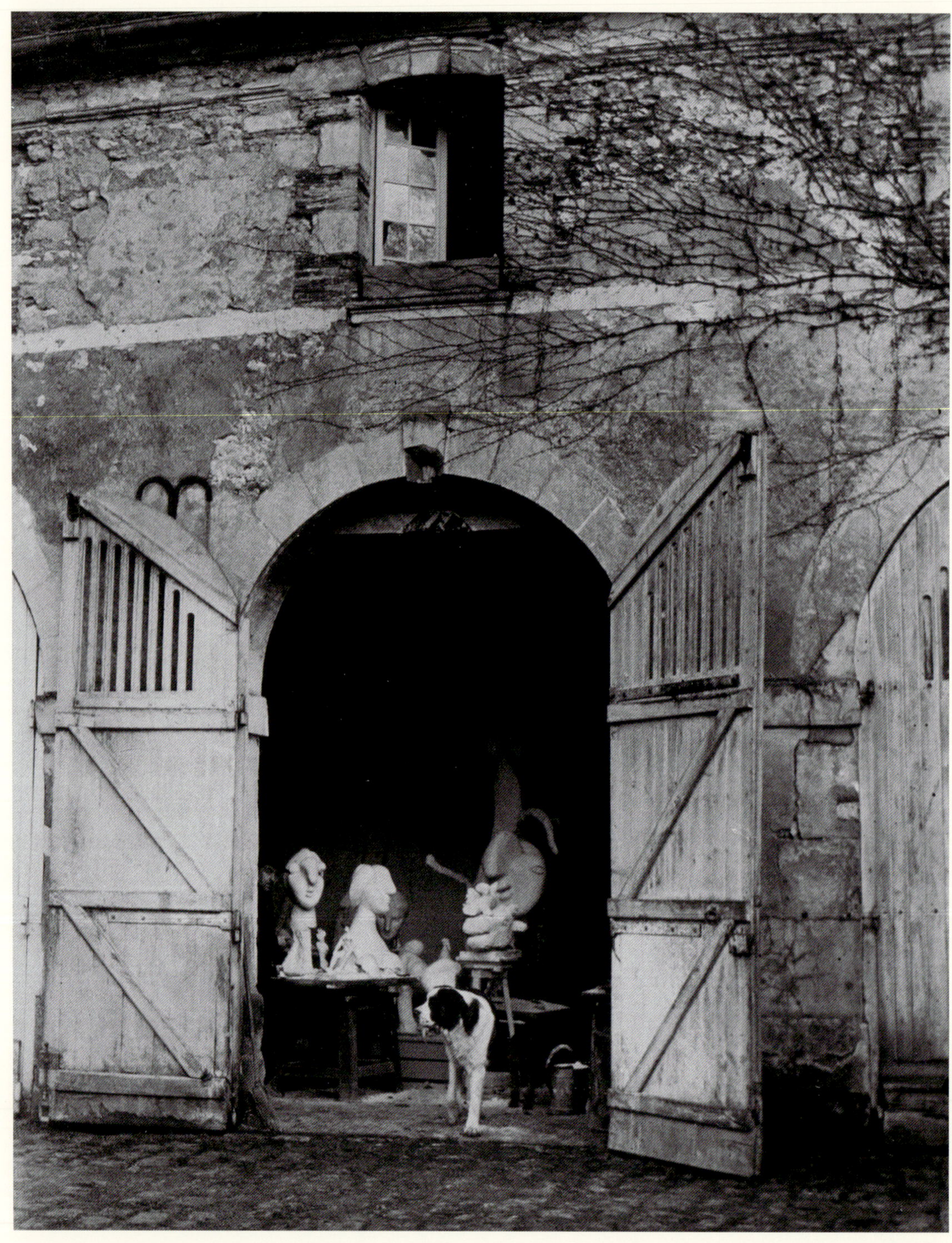

Picasso's sculpture studio at the Château de Boisgeloup, 1932.
Photograph by Brassaï. Musée national Picasso–Paris

IN JUNE 1930 Picasso purchased the Château de Boisgeloup, a property forty-five miles northwest of Paris, along the route to the Normandy coast. There, for the first time, he had enough space to set up his own sculpture studio, rather than having to rely on the cramped quarters of Julio González's metalworking shop or the facilities of other artist friends, as in earlier years. The converted stables of Boisgeloup provided him with a perfect environment within which to give free rein to his sculptural imagination. He embraced the building's lack of heat and electricity as catalysts to creativity, often working at night by the light of a single, large kerosene lamp.

The first sculptures Picasso made in Boisgeloup were delicately slender, carved wood figures (pls. 44–48), whittled from pieces of discarded painting stretchers and branches found on the forest floor. His signature Boisgeloup material, however, was luminous white plaster, which was relatively easy to obtain, dried quickly, and could be modeled, incised, carved, and added to over time. All were features that suited Picasso's improvisatory sensibility and ad hoc approach to making sculpture. He may also have welcomed plaster's association with casts of classical sculptures, which allowed him to situate his efforts within a centuries-old continuum, all the better to demonstrate the radically new character of his approach to sculpting the human form.

The sculptures Picasso created during his first two years in Boisgeloup are remarkably varied, despite their relative material unity. It was there that he produced his first truly monumental figures in the round, which ranged from smooth quasi-classical busts, to androgynous, simultaneously female and phallic heads, to an oddly exuberant figure almost ten feet tall. These imposing works were complemented by smaller frolicking bathers, strange birds and beasts, and anatomical fragments, notably eyes, along with an oversized hand. Mass, as opposed to empty space, plays the all-important role in Picasso's initial Boisgeloup sculptures; these were memorably photographed by the Hungarian artist Brassaï in December 1932 for publication in the new, deluxe Surrealist periodical *Minotaure* the following year. The biomorphic, swollen, and sexualized forms of Picasso's recent work provided a vivid, visual corollary to the Surrealist movement's embrace of irrationality and *l'amour fou* (mad love).

During this period, Picasso's drawing activity was closely intertwined with his work as a sculptor. In February and March 1933, he created a series of finely detailed pencil drawings collectively referred to as *An Anatomy* (pls. 59–66). In these works, wonderfully funny freestanding figures are built from combinations of imaginary objects, with firmly drawn contours and smoothly modeled forms that cast shadows on the ground. They spoof the newly found obsession of artists and poets in Surrealist circles with "symbolic" objects, while complementing Picasso's own heightened attentiveness to the sculptural potential of real objects lying around the studio and grounds of Boisgeloup.

Beginning in 1933, Picasso began to cast found objects in plaster and to incorporate them into his work. The eyes of his *Head of a Warrior* (pl. 68) began life as tennis balls; the folded pleats of the robe of *Woman with Leaves* (pl. 75) have their origins in a sheet of corrugated cardboard. Although Picasso famously had introduced real-life absinthe spoons into his *Glass of Absinthe* sculptures in 1914, here his found objects are forced to play multiple roles: as ghost-white representations of the things themselves, as the source of readymade textures and patterns, and as entirely other things, demonstrating Picasso's extraordinary ability to conjure the marvelous from the everyday.

Picasso's burst of sculptural productivity at Boisgeloup lasted for approximately four years. He was forced to leave the premises for good in 1936, as part of a separation agreement with his wife, Olga Ruiz-Picasso. Many have remarked on the resemblance between the features of his Boisgeloup busts and figures and those of Marie-Thérèse Walter, his secret lover during this same period. They are hardly, however, literal depictions. In April 1937, coincident with the Nazis' saturation bombing of the Spanish town of Guernica, Picasso selected five of his Boisgeloup women to accompany his as yet unrealized antiwar mural *Guernica* as part of the Spanish Pavilion in that summer's World's Fair in Paris. Among these five sculptures were cement casts of the monumental *Woman with Vase* (pl. 67) and *Head of a Woman* (pl. 56), which were positioned outside the pavilion. In this context, far from the sheltered world of Boisgeloup, these works were called upon to play the symbolic role of intercessor figures, as if to protect Picasso and others from the political evils that threatened not only Spain but all of Europe on the eve of World War II.

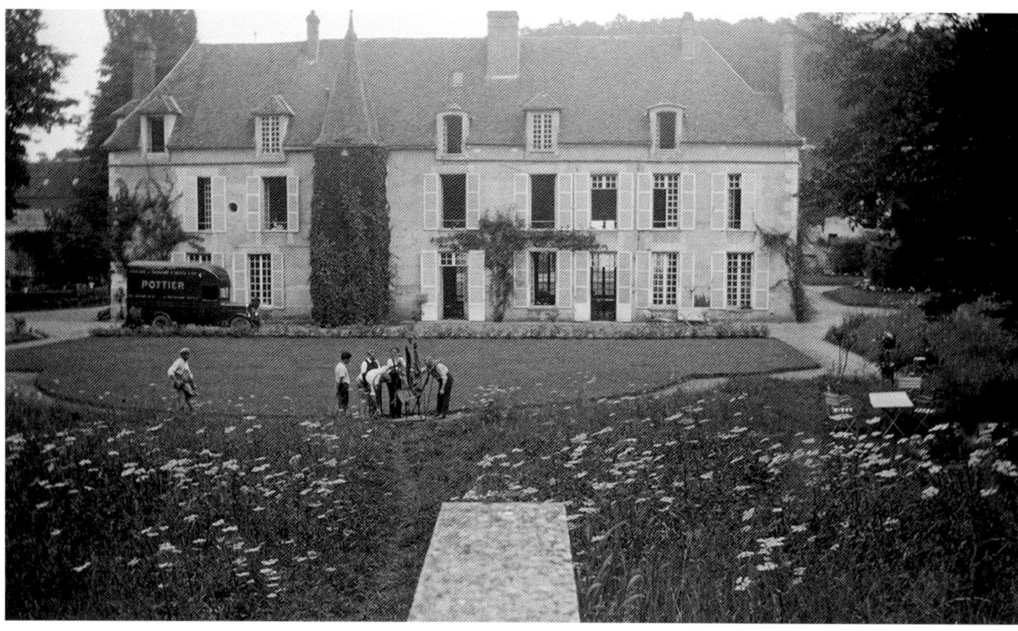

1. The Château de Boisgeloup, with Picasso and workers installing *Woman in the Garden* (spring 1929–30) outside, c. 1932. Archives Olga Ruiz-Picasso. Courtesy Fundación Almine y Bernard Ruiz-Picasso para el Arte

JUNE 10, 1930: Picasso bought the seventeenth-century Château de Boisgeloup from Léon Louis Joseph Renard and Jeanne Marie Georgette Weibel (fig. 1).[1] Daniel-Henry Kahnweiler's brother-in-law, the painter Elie Lascaux, had alerted him to this opportunity. About forty-five miles from Paris and near Gisors in Normandy, the secluded château lacked modern comforts but provided an abundance of space that Picasso's Paris studio did not. Before the end of the year the artist would convert one of the large stables into a sculpture studio, which he would continue to use until late 1936 (see p. 132). The photographer Brassaï, who would become Picasso's intimate in the early 1930s, later speculated, "I imagine that, when he visited the property for the first time, it was less the little castle that appealed to him than these vast empty outbuildings to be filled."[2]

JUNE 12–LATE JULY 1930: A sculpture exhibition by Henri Matisse was organized by Pierre Loeb at his Galerie Pierre in Paris. In a review of the exhibition published in *Cahiers d'Art* that year, Christian Zervos, who followed the sculpture practice of both artists closely, remarked on their similarity:

> Matisse and Picasso attach considerable importance to sculpture. With them it is no mere pastime. It is even more than a sort of effective way of disciplining the mind, encouraging or checking spontaneous impulses. It allows artists to achieve what the limitations of painting prevent. Every now and again, Matisse devotes the best part of his time to sculpture. And lately I saw Picasso in a state of extraordinary excitement because he had just begun to realize his new sculptural vision. "Since the Demoiselles d'Avignon," he confided, "I have never been so thrilled as I am with my new sculptures."[3]

In the exhibition Matisse presented his 1910–16 Jeannette series—five bronze busts—which Picasso would certainly remember when sculpting his own heads at Boisgeloup the following year (see fig. 9 on p. 18). These plaster sculptures are generally considered to be, in part, Picasso's response to the work of Matisse.[4]

SEATED WOMAN AND FOUR SCULPTURES TITLED _STANDING WOMAN_, SUMMER 1930

While working on his proposals for a monument to the poet Guillaume Apollinaire (see Chapter 4), Picasso embarked on another, more modest sculpture project, carving sixteen statuettes from thin slabs of scavenged wood and "fragments of canvas stretchers" he had found in his Boisgeloup studio (pls. 44–48).[5] Picasso had first engaged in wood carving in 1906, when he produced a small group of elongated figures during his stay in Gósol, Spain. In the summer of 1930 he may have whittled the seated and standing figures as a reprieve from the large-scale welded objects he had lately been working on.[6] Scholars suggest diverse sources of inspiration for these works, including the Etruscan bronzes illustrated

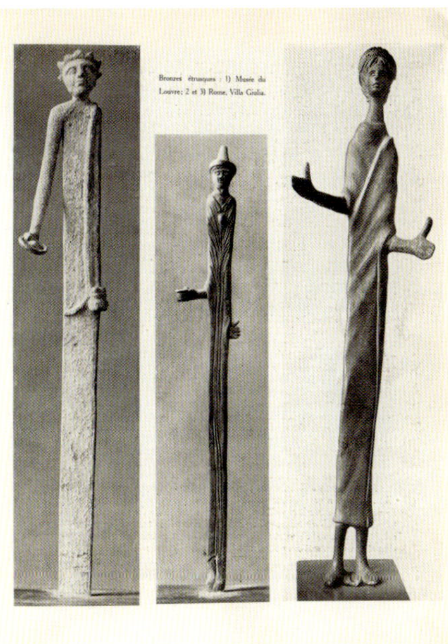

2. Etruscan sculpture reproduced in *Documents* 2, no. 4 (1930): 225

earlier in the year in the avant-garde magazine *Documents* (fig. 2).[7] The shape and form of the material itself, which naturally limited Picasso's options in depicting mass and volume, posed a stimulating artistic challenge. Using a small penknife, as the artist Julio González would later recall, Picasso followed "the planes and the dimensions of every piece [of wood], each one suggesting a different figure to him."[8] Naturally occuring grooves double as drapery of a woman's dress; a whorled knot becomes her gently bent knee. Because Picasso wanted to retain the vivid material character of wood, he incorporated the knots, fiber, and grain as formal elements of the sculptures rather than smoothing them away.

NOVEMBER 1930: His new sculpture studio at Boisgeloup inspired Picasso to think on a large scale, and by early November he had begun a set of preparatory drawings for a grand standing figure he would subsequently model in plaster. Titled *Tall Figure* (also known as *Large Statue*), the sculpture depicts a woman about ten feet tall, in mid-stride.[9] While it is not known when Picasso completed the work, a photograph taken in late 1930 shows what looks like the finished *Tall Figure* by itself in an otherwise empty workspace (fig. 3).[10] Working conditions were rudimentary: there was no electricity and no heating. The sculpture studio was lit by a simple kerosene lamp hanging from the ceiling at the center of the space. Tools, harnesses, and podiums would gradually populate the studio to accommodate the production of a vast array of voluminous plaster sculptures.

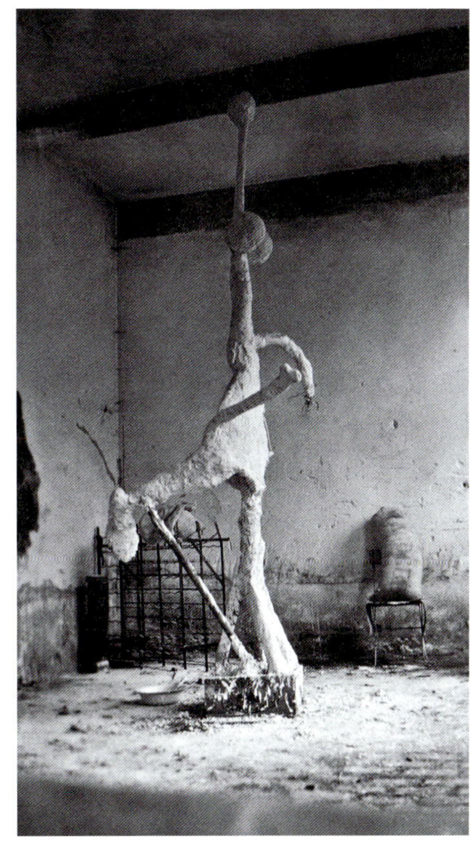

3. Picasso's sculpture studio at the Château de Boisgeloup, with *Tall Figure*, c. late 1930. Archives Olga Ruiz-Picasso. Courtesy Fundación Almine y Bernard Ruiz-Picasso para el Arte

DECEMBER 19–20, 1930: Picasso decided to have the delicate wooden statuettes he had made in the summer cast in bronze. Because of their height and slenderness, they required the support of a base in order to stand. At this time Picasso was collaborating with González on welded metal sculptures (see Chapter 4); brief messages exchanged between the two artists indicate that Picasso had arranged for González to help him with this new challenge as well. On December 19, González wrote, "Pablo: The first three small pedestals are promised for tomorrow at 10" (fig. 4). A short note sent the next day states, "You now have your six small pedestals in my studio."[11]

EARLY 1931: Picasso continued to work with González on sculptures prompted by the commission for a monument to Apollinaire.

FEBRUARY 16, 1931: González wrote again to Picasso about the bases he had made for the statuettes: "The twelve marble [pedestals] are ready for you. I will be in my studio every day until Friday."[12] Photographs taken in December 1932 by the photographer Brassaï at the artist's Paris studio, on rue La Boétie, show a bronze *Seated Woman* on a dark, square

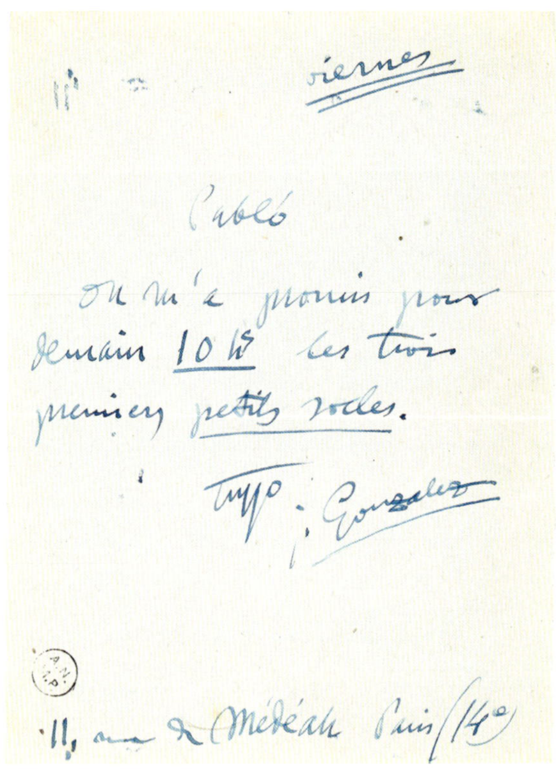

viernes

Pablo

On m'a promis pour demain 10 h les trois premiers petits socles.

Tuyo J. González

11, rue de Médéah Paris (14e)

4. Note from Julio González to Picasso, December 19, 1930. Picasso Archives, Musée national Picasso–Paris

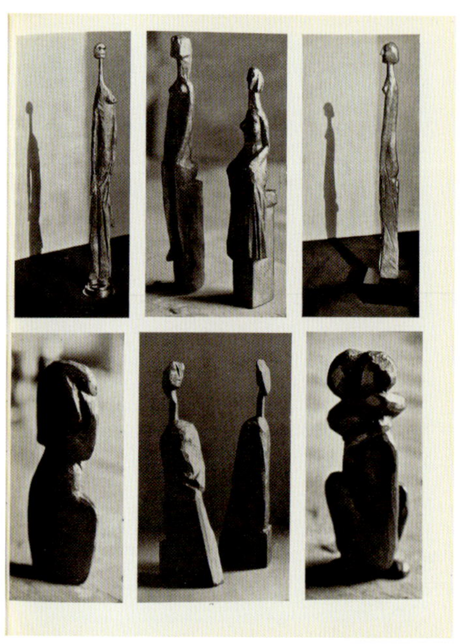

5. Bronze casts of several of Picasso's wooden statuettes of summer 1930 (top row) reproduced in André Breton, "Picasso dans son élément" (Picasso in his element), *Minotaure* 1, no. 1 (June 1933): 23

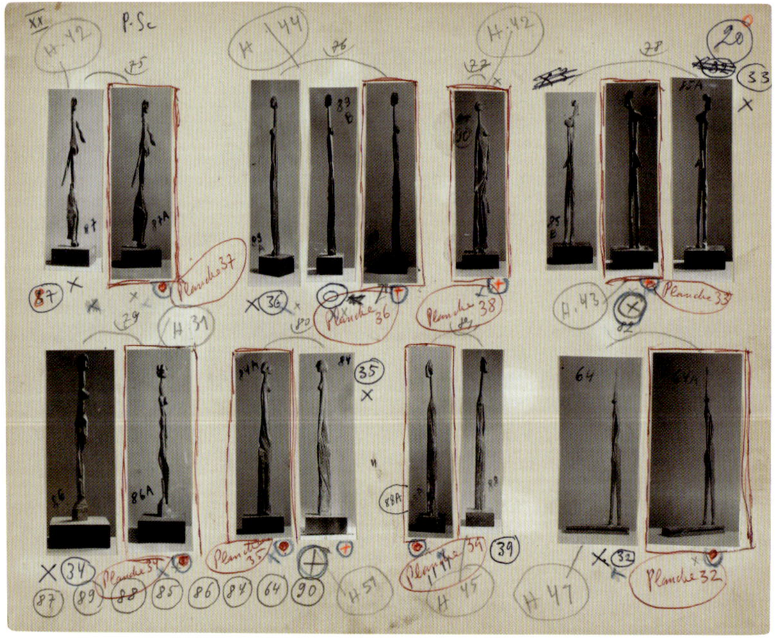

6. Brassaï. *Picasso's Sculptures: Contact Sheet 20*. Paris, [1946–late 1948]. Seventeen gelatin silver prints glued on cardboard, with annotations by the photographer, 9 7/16 × 12 5/8 in. (24 × 32 cm). Centre Georges Pompidou, Paris

plinth and a bronze *Standing Woman* on a small, shiny round base (fig. 5).[13] This would be the first time Brassaï photographed Picasso's work.

In 1943 Picasso would select Brassaï as photographer for the first monograph solely dedicated to his sculpture, *Les Sculptures de Picasso*.[14] On October 25 of that year, Brassaï photographed the tall statuettes again, this time at the artist's studio at 7, rue des Grands-Augustins (fig. 6). He would later describe the experience:

> Picasso wants to show me the display case, or, as [Jaime] Sabartés calls it, the "museum." It is a large metal and glass cabinet, locked, placed in a little room adjoining the studio. To open it, he takes out his voluminous set of keys. About fifty statuettes are piled up in it, along with wood he has sculpted, stones he has engraved, and other curious or rare objects [fig. 7].[15]

SPRING 1931: Picasso moved from Paris into the Château de Boisgeloup, renovations having been completed. He immediately embarked on an intensive campaign devoted to modeling sculptures in plaster, working in the converted stables. Marie-Thérèse Walter, the artist's mistress, would serve as the inspiration for this extraordinary phase of his sculptural work. Picasso recorded the development of the plaster sculptures in a series of photographs taken from March through July.[16]

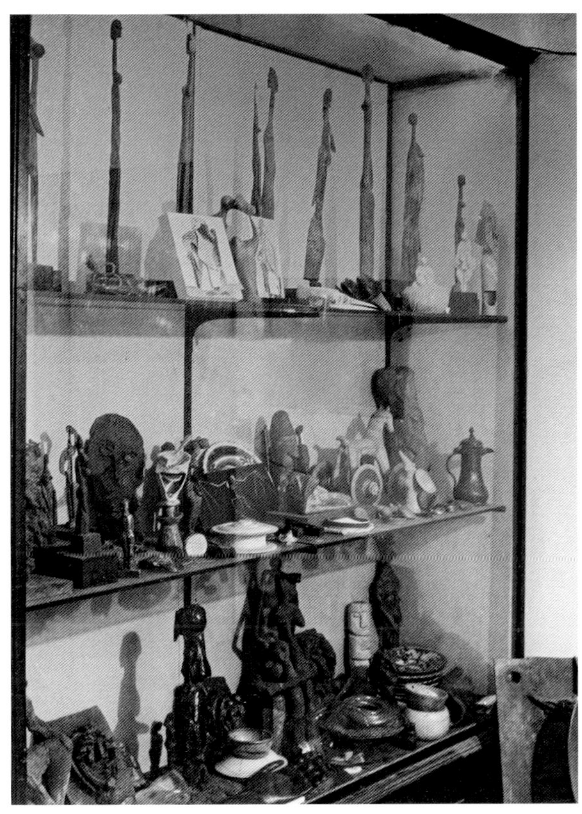

7. The "museum" in Picasso's studio at 7, rue des Grands-Augustins, Paris, on or after October 25, 1943. Photograph by Brassaï. Musée national Picasso–Paris

***BUST OF A WOMAN* AND *HEAD OF A WOMAN*, 1931**

Though they are stylistically distinct, *Bust of a Woman* (pl. 50) and *Head of a Woman* (pl. 49) were initially a very similar pair. Picasso's photographs from the studio indicate that he probably began modeling these plasters in March 1931, working on improvised stands that could serve as turntables (figs. 8–10). On June 13 he made a drawing of the Boisgeloup sculpture studio that depicts both works, completed.[17]

Both the figures initially had very long columnar necks and shared the bulbous facial features retained in *Head of a Woman*. Picasso posed the two works for the camera in a wide variety of configurations, often overlapping or abutting them, perhaps even seeking a way to join them together (fig. 11). He may have been attempting to work out, in three dimensions, a path to the multiple simultaneous perspectives that are his pictorial signature. However, the two sculptures remained separate and grew more dissimilar, though from the back their thick masses of hair remained alike in shape and size. Picasso made the most alterations to *Bust of a Woman*, replacing the subject's spherical eyes with more naturalistic, incised features, joining the large nose in a graceful swoop to the left side of her hair, and connecting the ridge of her right eyebrow with the hair on that side. He shortened her long neck with

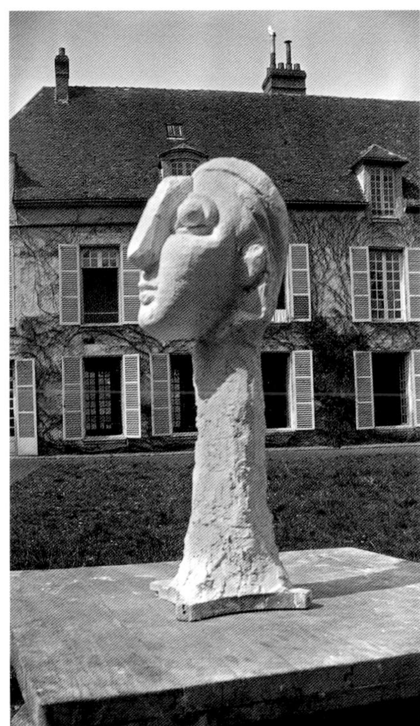

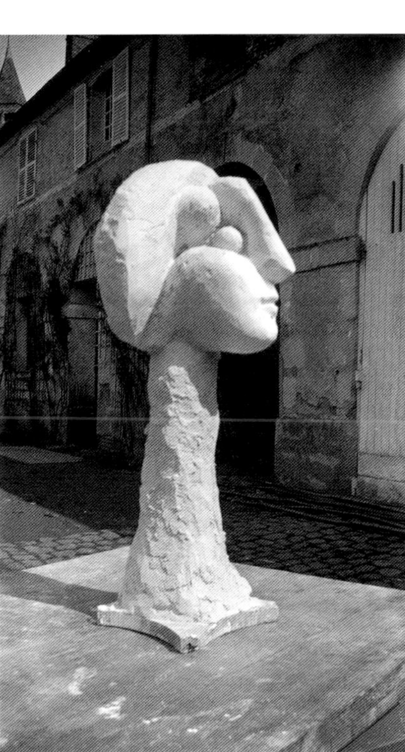

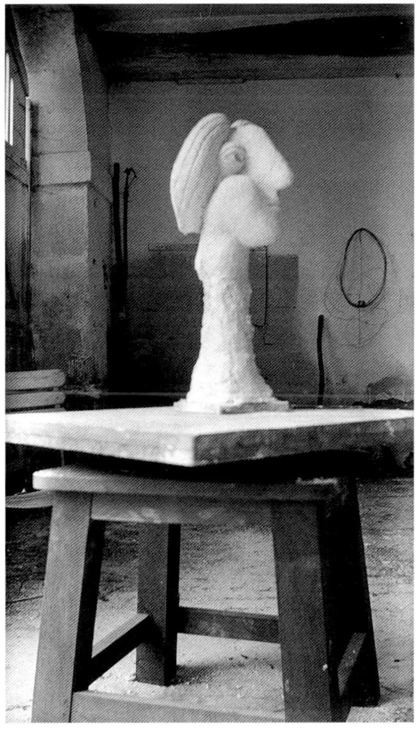

8–10. *Bust of a Woman* in progress at the Château de Boisgeloup, 1931. Archives Olga Ruiz-Picasso. Courtesy Fundación Almine y Bernard Ruiz-Picasso para el Arte

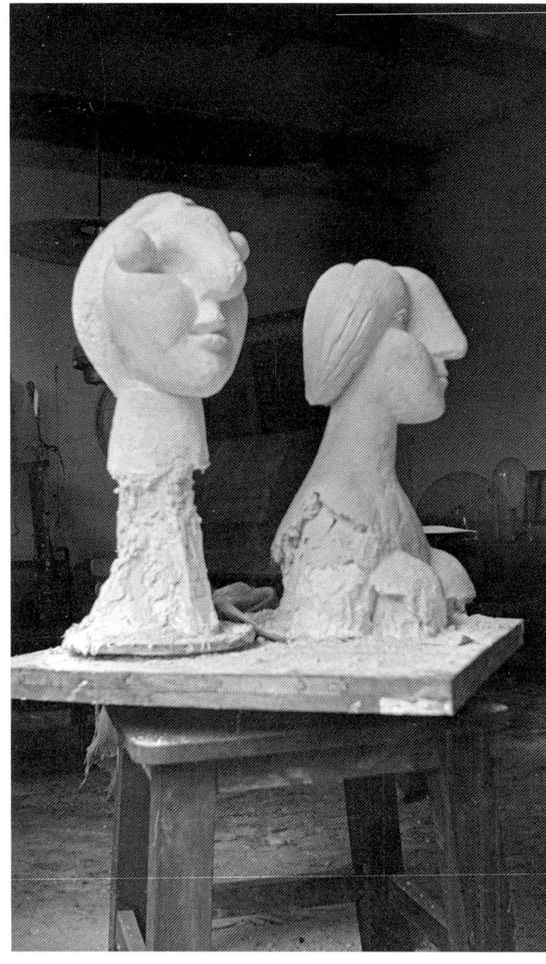

11. *Head of a Woman* (left) and *Bust of a Woman* (right) in progress in Picasso's sculpture studio at the Château de Boisgeloup, 1931. Archives Olga Ruiz-Picasso. Courtesy Fundación Almine y Bernard Ruiz-Picasso para el Arte

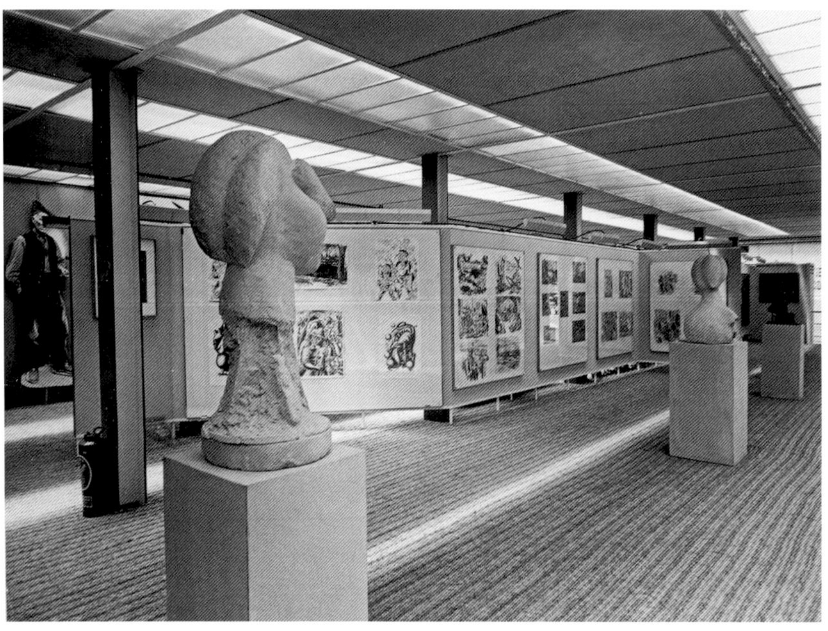

12. View of the Spanish Pavilion at the World's Fair, with cement casts of *Head of a Woman* (foreground) and *Bust of a Woman*, Paris, 1937. Photograph by Roness-Ruan. Fonds Cahiers d'Art, Bibliothèque Kandinsky, Paris

sloping shoulders and added ball-like breasts to her chest. Elizabeth Cowling notes that the sculpture's rutted surface is an artifact of this process: Picasso added plaster as he altered the form, then carved and sanded it to create a unified whole.[18]

Both *Bust of a Woman* and *Head of a Woman* would be cast in cement and displayed at the Spanish Pavilion at the 1937 World's Fair in Paris (fig. 12). A unique bronze cast of *Bust of a Woman* would be made at an unknown foundry by 1944. *Head of a Woman* would be cast in bronze three times, twice at the Valsuani foundry in Paris in 1973.

HEAD OF A WOMAN AND _BUST OF A WOMAN_, 1931

The radically segmented *Head of a Woman* (pl. 51) is the most abstract of Picasso's Boisgeloup female figures, although the fundamental eroticism of its forms is startlingly clear. After considering different arrangements, Picasso ultimately settled on four plaster elements that fit together like pieces of a puzzle. A long arc—a cascade of hair—falls over a head composed of two parts: the orb of a face with a phallic nasal projection, and a spherical eyeball. The ensemble rests on a femurlike vertical form that at first suggests a neck but may also be seen as an arm and closed fist upon which the woman rests her cheek, as Walter does so often in Picasso's paintings of her. A wire armature runs through this form to the parts of the head, fastening them in place.[19]

According to John Richardson, *Bust of a Woman* (pl. 52) predates *Head of a Woman* slightly: it appears earlier than the latter work in Picasso's photographs of these sculptures at Boisgeloup.[20] It, too, was fashioned around a wire armature, this time with gauze wrapped around the middle, creating bulk onto which the plaster was applied. This form, more solid than *Head of a Woman*, veers away from naturalism in a different fashion: male and female sexual characteristics come together in a compacted, almost totemic mass. Unique bronze casts of these two sculptures would later be made at the Robecchi foundry in Paris.

JUNE 7, 1931: A letter sent by Picasso's mother, Doña María, indicates that the artist had been working at the Boisgeloup sculpture studio for at least three months. While chastising her son for not finding time to write to her, Doña María was pleased to know that he had found a large space and felt confident that this would enable him to create innovative work. She wrote, "I am enthusiastic to learn that you are working on sculptures, but since you are too lazy to write, I will never know what you are really doing. But in any case, I already know that it will be good and different from everything else."[21]

***HEAD OF A WOMAN*, 1931**

In addition to his monumental freestanding heads and busts, Picasso created two plaster reliefs showing Walter's left and right profiles. One of these, *Head of a Woman* (pl. 55), was executed either just before or after his visit to Juan-les-Pins in August.[22] The relief format, intended for display against a wall, points to the close interdependence of Picasso's paintings and sculptures of this period. Picasso may have built the sculpture up in layers of plaster or carved it out of a mound.[23] There is a unique bronze cast of this work, likely created during the Occupation of Paris in the 1940s.

JULY 1931: Picasso visited the exhibition *Degas: Portraitist, Sculptor* at the Musée de l'Orangerie in Paris (July 1–November 11). The show featured more than 250 works in all mediums, including a set of bronze casts given to the French state by the A. A. Hébrard foundry.[24] This was not the first time that the artist saw Degas's sculpture, but the timing was propitious for a firsthand reacquaintance.

AUGUST 1931: Picasso spent the month at a villa in Juan-les-Pins. During this sojourn he made several sketches for sculptures that he would realize upon his return to Boisgeloup in September.

***RECLINING BATHER* AND *BATHER*, 1931**

Picasso's August studies for *Reclining Bather* (pl. 54) show a woman resting her head on her hand or arm and were interlinked with several sketches for *Head of a Woman* (pl. 51).[25] When Picasso created the recumbent figure in plaster, it possessed the spirit of a sculpture "in which all the parts were movable."[26] Long curved legs connect to an eggplant-shaped torso, encircled by arms that support the head and rise up to become breasts. Picasso continued the theme of seaside recreation with the plaster *Bather* (pl. 53) after making several studies in early October. The figure's substantial, muscular torso and legs spiral up from the rippled surface of the base, suggesting the pull of sand and sea. The diminutive head and arms recall the form of the Venus of Lespugue figurine—a Paleolithic fertility symbol discovered in the foothills of the Pyrenees in 1922—of which Picasso owned two plaster casts.[27] These two sculptures are unique bronze casts. The bronze *Bather*, cast at the Valsuani foundry, would be exhibited in the Spanish Pavilion at the World's Fair in Paris in July 1937.

***HEAD OF A WOMAN*, 1931–32**

Picasso began *Head of a Woman* (pl. 56) sometime late in 1931. He made studies for the sculpture on December 5, 1931 (fig. 13), and continued to work on it over the coming year. Of all the

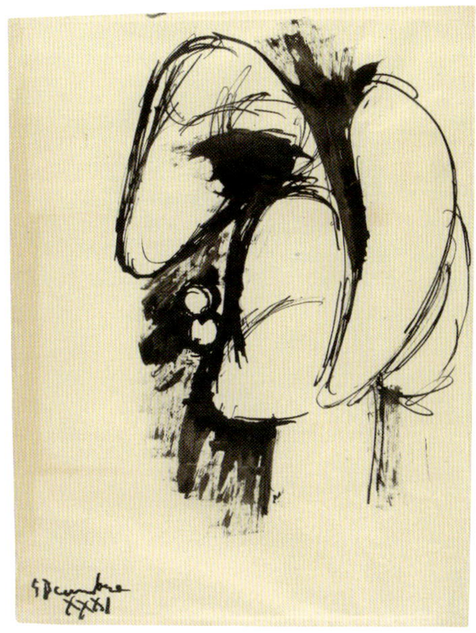

13. Pablo Picasso. Study for *Head of a* Woman. December 5, 1931. Charcoal and Chinese ink on vellum paper, 12 13/16 × 10 1/8 in. (32.5 × 25.7 cm). Musée national Picasso–Paris

Boisgeloup plaster heads, it has the most exaggerated proportions, and at over fifty inches tall it towered over its studio companions. *Head of a Woman* is simultaneously regal and cartoonlike in appearance, with an engorged nose, extended neck, and pneumatically modeled facial features that demonstrate Picasso's love of visual punning. The inherent luminosity of plaster complements the work's metaphoric character; it looks different from every angle, with swollen contours poised on the brink of perpetual change.[28]

Picasso seemed to understand that this work was a masterpiece; images of it soon found their way into other mediums, appearing in the artist's paintings and prints, where the sculpture figured as an object of admiration and even devotion (see fig. 18). In addition to the plaster original, *Head of a Woman* exists as a plaster proof, a unique bronze, and a cement version made for exhibition outside the Spanish Pavilion at the Paris World's Fair in 1937 (see fig. 2 on p. 305). The plaster proof would be given by Jacqueline Picasso, the artist's widow, to The Museum of Modern Art, New York, in 1982.

***BIRD*, 1931–32, AND *COCK*, 1932**

At Boisgeloup, Picasso created several works on the theme of birds, reflecting his countryside environs. By late 1932 he had completed a little bird with open wings (pl. 57) and a majestic cock (pl. 58), whose feathery plumage would especially impress Brassaï when he photographed both sculptures during his visit in December.[29] The rooster had been a recurring subject in Picasso's paintings and drawings, but *Cock* marks the first time the artist approached it in three dimensions (fig. 14). Picasso modeled both sculptures in plaster,

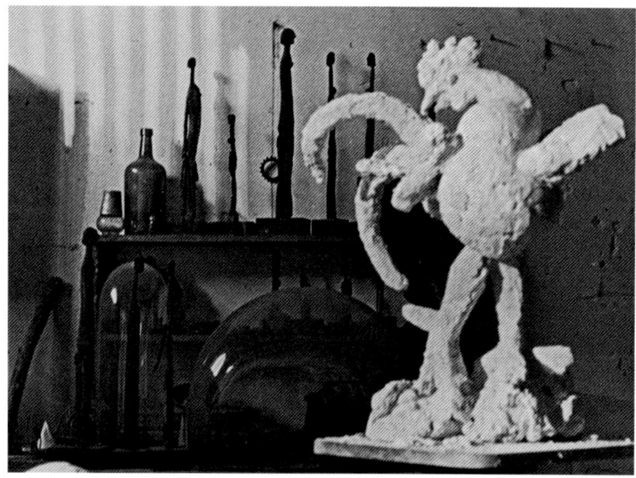

14. Picasso's sculpture studio at the Château de Boisgeloup, with the plaster *Cock* in front of bronze casts of the artist's wooden statuettes of summer 1930, c. 1932. Archives Olga Ruiz-Picasso. Courtesy Fundación Almine y Bernard Ruiz-Picasso para el Arte

working with a freedom that bespeaks months of immersion in its ways. For *Cock* he developed a dynamic, spiraling composition in which the rooster's head tilts gracefully to cast its gaze backward as its body turns forward. The open wings of the smaller bird and the two sweeping tail feathers in *Cock* add to the vivid sense of motion in both works. The French idiom "le coq du village," much like the British "cock of the walk," connotes a strutting, assertive type; *Cock*'s sense of proud animation would seem to give literal expression to the saying. Like many small works of this moment, *Bird* exists only in plaster, while *Cock* would be cast in bronze by Valsuani using the lost-wax method.[30]

MAY 6, 1932: Picasso visited the first monographic exhibition dedicated to the work of Alberto Giacometti, mounted at the Galerie Pierre Colle in Paris. In a letter to his family, Giacometti described the event: "Naturally, like most people, no Surrealists will come during the exhibition. Instead, the first to arrive was Picasso, who came at 12:30! He looks, he says, 'trés joli,' like a boy, and very much occupies himself with the material, but won't compromise himself by being recognized for it."[31]

JUNE 16–JULY 30, 1932: The first retrospective exhibition of Picasso's work was mounted at the Galeries Georges Petit, at 8, rue de Sèze, Paris (fig. 15). In the catalogue preface, gallery director Étienne Bignou underlined the exceptional commitment of the artist, who had himself selected and directed the hanging of the more than 230 works on display, which dated from 1901 to 1932. Picasso included only seven

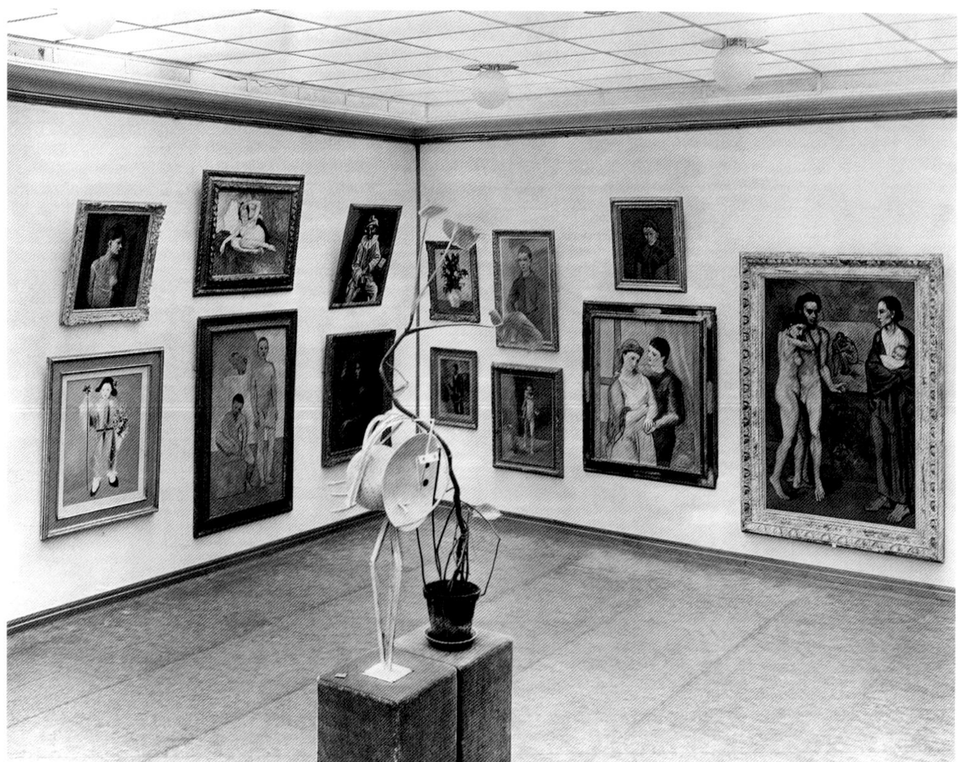

15. View of *Exposition Picasso* at the Galeries Georges Petit, Paris, 1932. *Head of a Woman* (1929–30) is at center. Kunsthaus Zürich

sculptures: four early works cast in bronze and three of his more recent creations. He decided that *Woman in the Garden* (pl. 41) would be presented in both of its versions (one of painted welded metal and the other a bronze cast), installed to face each other across the room (fig. 16; see also fig. 1 on p. 305). He chose to include none of the sculptures made in Boisgeloup, and thus the current chapter of his sculptural activity remained unknown. Moreover, sculpture was altogether absent from a special issue of *Cahiers d'Art* (nos. 3–5) devoted to Picasso on the occasion of the exhibition.

The show received a mixed response from the critics, but to Brassaï it was the true turning point in the artist's career. He would later write, "Picasso had just turned fifty. Of course, his reputation was already established. It was in that crucial year, however, that he would begin to achieve worldwide renown. The major retrospective of his work, inaugurated on 15 June in the gilded salons of the Georges Petit Gallery—the event was the culmination of the Paris season—was a turning point in his life. For the first time, a prestigious collection of 236 of his canvases was brought together, and in a single glance visitors could take in his blue, rose, cubist, and classical periods, the sum total of his existence."[32] French painter and writer Jacques-Émile Blanche would note in a review of the exhibition published in *L'Art vivant* that "no other than he would be able in the middle of summer to attract a wide audience weary of exhibits, art lovers and crowds."[33] Blanche wrote, "Having just barely entered, I bumped into Pablo Picasso, who was having his paintings hung, removed and reorganized by a team of exhausted men who had been trying, for the past week, to balance things according to his wishes. The foreman asked me if I was satisfied. 'Be patient!' I told him. 'I'm overwhelmed.'"[34] Picasso's close involvement in the exhibition paralleled his current commitment to actively reviewing his work for an encyclopedia-scaled catalogue raisonné of his work by Christian Zervos, founder of *Cahiers d'Art*. Comprehensive cataloguing was generally reserved for the work of an artist no longer living; Picasso's decision to pursue it underlines his and his collaborator's perception of his absolute singularity.[35] The first volume of Zervos, as it has come to be known, was published in 1932. The first volume of yet another catalogue raisonné, prepared by Bernard Geiser and recording the artist's engravings and lithographs, would be published in 1933.[36]

SEPTEMBER 11–NOVEMBER 13, 1932: A modified version of Picasso's retrospective exhibition at the Galeries Georges Petit was presented at the Kunsthaus Zürich. Of the seven sculptures seen in Paris, only the four early bronzes came to Zurich.

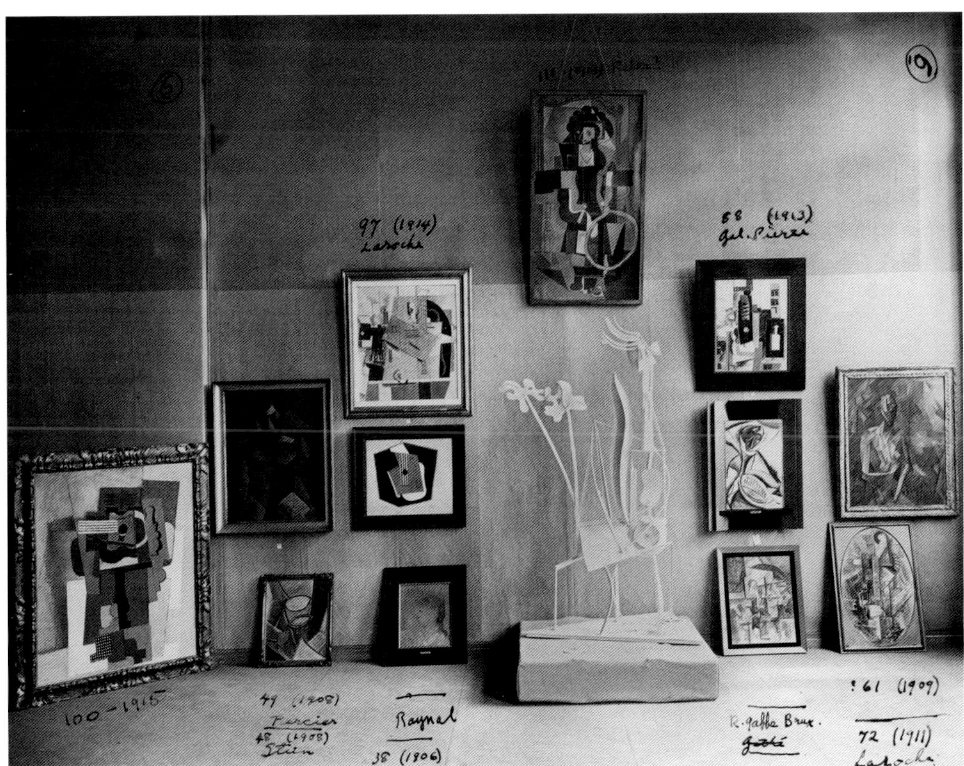

16. Photograph of *Exposition Picasso* at the Galeries Georges Petit annotated by Margaret Scolari Barr, with *Woman in the Garden* (spring 1929–30) at center, Paris, 1932. The Museum of Modern Art Archives, New York

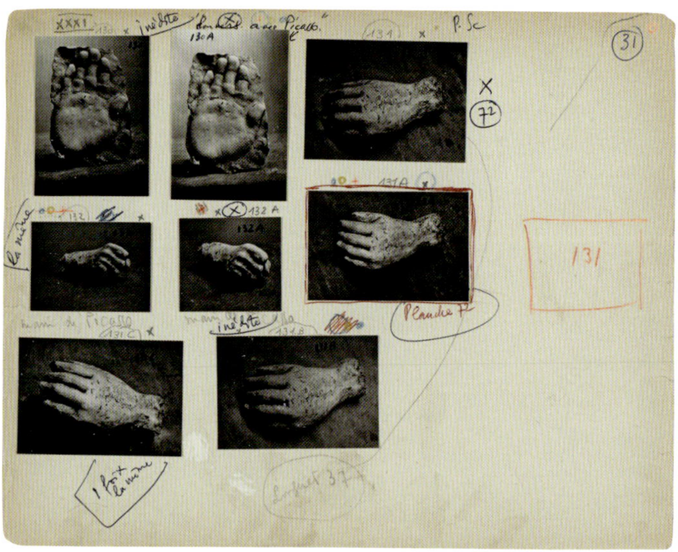

17. Brassaï. *Picasso's Sculptures: Contact Sheet 31*. Paris, [1946–late 1948]. Eight gelatin silver prints glued on cardboard, with annotations by the photographer, 9 7/16 × 12 5/8 in. (24 × 32 cm). Centre Georges Pompidou, Paris

Like many of the paintings, and as in Paris, these four sculptures were listed in the catalogue as being available for sale. Picasso came to Zurich with his wife, Olga Ruiz-Picasso, and son, Paulo, arriving on September 7 to check the installation. The artist's first museum exhibition achieved record-breaking attendance: thirty-four thousand visitors in nine weeks, with the original closing date of October 30 extended by two weeks.

HAND, [FALL 1932 OR EARLIER]

This sculpture (pl. 71) is the first in a series of hands that Picasso began to cast in plaster at Boisgeloup. Heretofore dated to 1933–34, *Hand* is visible in a number of photographs taken by Brassaï at Picasso's sculpture studio in December 1932, published in the June 1933 inaugural issue of *Minotaure*.[37]

The work is as much a paw as a hand, and its oversized proportion distinguishes it from the later renditions of hands Picasso made. Some areas of its surface are smooth, while others are rough in texture; a fragment of a Spanish newspaper is stuck in the plaster at the front of the work, on the underside of the fingers. Picasso used a knife and other cutting tools to carve out the contours of the elephantine fingers. In the mid-1940s Brassaï would photograph *Hand* for publication in *Les Sculptures de Picasso* (fig. 17).[38] The object would not be exhibited publicly until 1979–80, when it was presented in Paris as part of the selection of Picasso's work received by the French state in lieu of inheritance taxes.

EYE, _EYE_, _RELIEF_, AND _CRUMPLED PAPER_, 1931–34

At Boisgeloup Picasso used the ancient technique of sand casting, pressing forms (including everyday objects) into sand, and then pouring plaster into the resulting mold.[39] This technique not only allowed Picasso to cast all manner of objects, which he would later assemble in larger sculptures, but also provided the artist a chance to experiment with capturing textures, such as the folds of a cardboard box or creases of a crumpled piece of newspaper. The evocative results inspire various readings: Brassaï saw something "as monumental as the Great Wall of China" in *Relief* (pl. 72).[40]

A few *Eye* sculptures (including pls. 69 and 70), *Relief*, and *Crumpled Paper* (pl. 73) are among the numerous small plaster sand casts the artist made during this time. Some of them hung on the wall at Boisgeloup; they would be brought to rue des Grands-Augustins, in Paris, during World War II. That Picasso considered each one of them a significant sculpture is evidenced by the fact that a large number would be photographed by Brassaï in Paris and reproduced in *Les Sculptures de Picasso* in 1949. In 1944, concerned about the length of the book and the importance of the works therein, its publisher, Maurice Girodias, would urge Brassaï to ignore these small objects. But according to Brassaï, Picasso insisted: "Yes, yes, they are too very important! And I ab-so-lute-ly insist that they appear in your book."[41] In 1952, Picasso, then involved in making polychrome bronzes, would tell Kahnweiler that he had intended to paint the small sculptures.[42] However, like the other plasters from this period, they remained an untouched white.

DECEMBER 1932: Brassaï began to photograph Picasso's sculptures in Paris and Boisgeloup, commissioned for the first issue of the journal *Minotaure* by its directors, Tériade and Albert Skira. The journal's office was located at 25, rue La Boétie, next door to Picasso's home and studio.

JANUARY 28, 1933: A taxidermist sent a card to Picasso: "I am pleased to inform you that the roe antler and 4 feet you gave me to be taxidermied are ready and that I'm holding them here for you."[43] Along with the bat skeleton Brassaï had observed alongside Picasso's two casts of the Venus of Lespugue, the Boisgeloup studio was full of skeletons and bones of all kinds. Brassaï would later recall remarking to Picasso, "I knew you liked skeletons! I've studied them; I've had fun taking them apart and assembling them. To understand the genius of creation, there's no better way than to put a skeleton back together." The artist replied, "I have a real passion for bones. I have many others in Boisgeloup: skeletons of birds, dog's and sheep's heads. I even have a rhinoceros skull. Maybe you saw them in the barn? Have you noticed that bones are always modeled and not carved, that you always have the impression they come from a mold, that they were first modeled in clay?"[44]

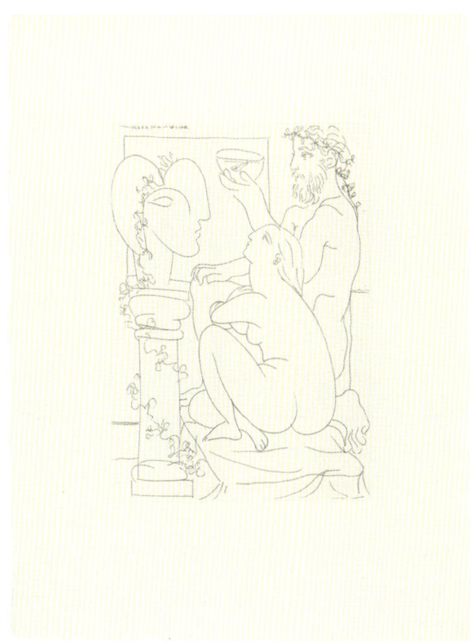

18. Pablo Picasso. *Sculptor and Model* from the *Vollard Suite*. March 21, 1933. Etching, plate: 10 ½ × 7 ⅝ in. (26.7 × 19.4 cm). The Museum of Modern Art, New York. Abby Aldrich Rockefeller Fund

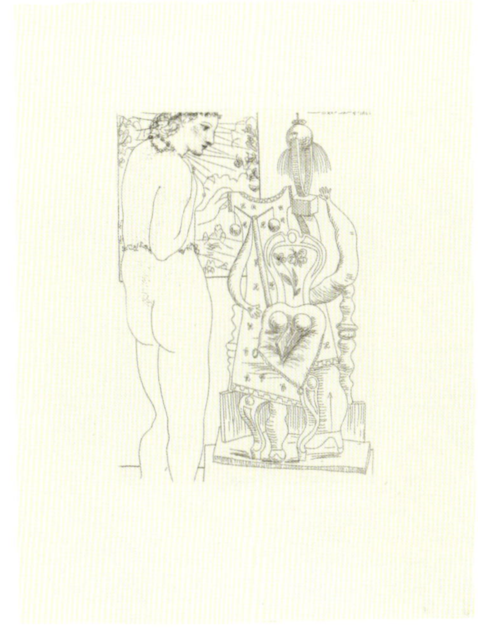

19. Pablo Picasso. *Marie-Thérèse Considering Her Sculpted Surrealist Effigy* from the *Vollard Suite*. May 4, 1933. Etching, plate: 10 ⁹⁄₁₆ × 7 ⅝ in. (26.8 × 19.3 cm). The Museum of Modern Art, New York. Abby Aldrich Rockefeller Fund

AN ANATOMY, 1933

Though Picasso was loosely involved with the Surrealist movement from its origin in the 1920s through the 1930s, his identification with its principles and visual imagery was particularly evident in his work of 1933. In February and March of that year he created *An Anatomy* (pls. 59–66), a group of graphite drawings of diverse forms and objects whimsically assembled as standing figures. Geometric shapes and inanimate objects such as chairs, cups, wheels, and cushions became the limbs, torsos, and heads of humanoid creatures. The sculptural logic of these figures would be increasingly borne out in Picasso's assemblages of the following decades. Already, in 1929–30, the artist had taken an early step in this direction with *Head of a Woman* (pl. 40), created in a variety of materials that included scavenged metal, springs, and two colanders. The *Anatomy* drawings remained with Picasso until his death.

MARCH 1933: Commissioned by the Parisian dealer Ambroise Vollard to create a set of one hundred etchings, Picasso commenced what would eventually be a group of forty-six images on the theme of the sculptor's studio. They compose one section of the *Vollard Suite*, published in 1939. Made over the course of several months, the etchings feature naturalistically detailed neoclassical figures of a male sculptor and his female models in the company of his works (fig. 18). In one of the suite's best known images, the model contemplates a fantastical Surrealist sculpture of a seated woman (fig. 19).

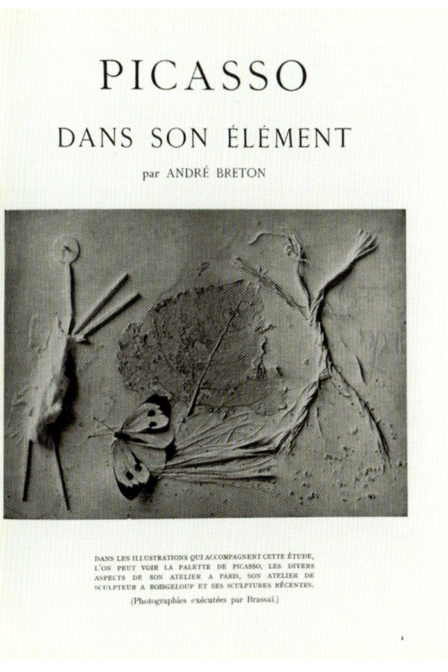

PICASSO

DANS SON ÉLÉMENT

par ANDRÉ BRETON

DANS LES ILLUSTRATIONS QUI ACCOMPAGNENT CETTE ÉTUDE, L'ON PEUT VOIR LA PALETTE DE PICASSO, LES DIVERS ASPECTS DE SON ATELIER A PARIS, SON ATELIER DE SCULPTEUR A BOISGELOUP ET SES SCULPTURES RÉCENTES.

(Photographies exécutées par Brassaï.)

20. First page of André Breton, "Picasso dans son élément" (Picasso in his element), *Minotaure* 1, no. 1 (June 1933)

JUNE 1933: The premier issue of the Surrealist journal *Minotaure*, with a cover by Picasso, was released. The issue featured André Breton's essay "Picasso dans son élément" (Picasso in his element), the first text devoted to the subject of Picasso's ateliers (fig. 20). The article accompanied a rich selection of photographs depicting Picasso's recent sculptures and his studios on rue La Boétie and in Boisgeloup, where Brassaï had spent many hours with his camera in December 1932

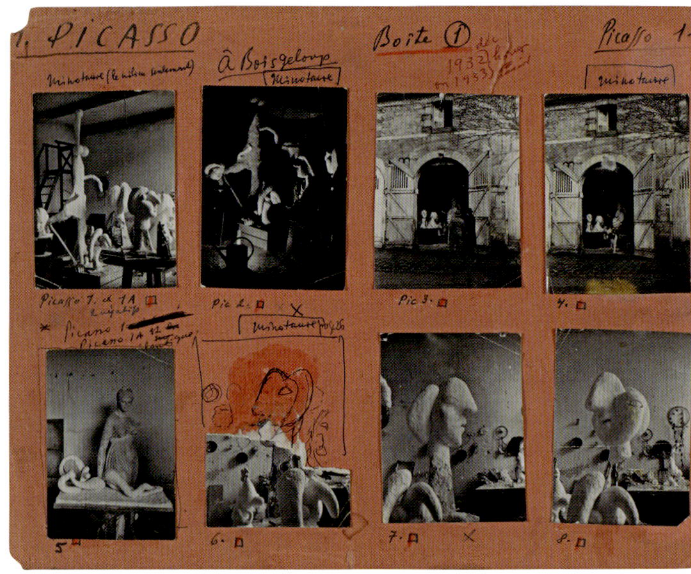

21. Brassaï. *Picasso 1: Contact Sheet 1*. Boisgeloup, [winter 1932–33]. Eight gelatin silver prints glued on cardboard, with annotations by the photographer, 9 7/16 × 12 5/8 in. (24 x 32 cm). Centre Georges Pompidou, Paris

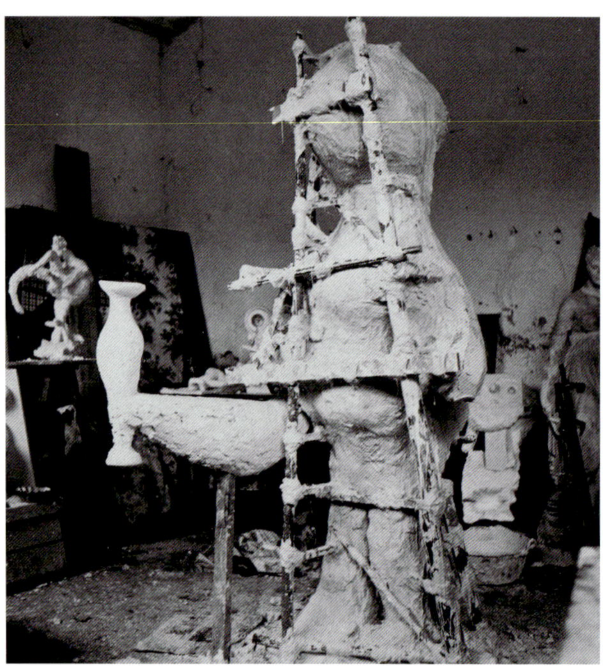

22. View of Picasso's studio at the Château de Boisgeloup, with *Woman with Vase* in progress, [1933 or 1936?]. Picasso Archives, Musée national Picasso–Paris

(fig. 21; see also figs. 10 and 11 on p. 19).[45] The issue also reproduced ten drawings from *An Anatomy* (including pls. 59–64 and 66) and a group of 1932 *Crucifixion* drawings that Picasso made after Matthias Grünewald's *Isenheim Altarpiece* (c. 1512–16).

In his essay, Breton praised Picasso's turn away from "the unconditional reproduction of the colored image (the painter at parrot school)" to the incorporation of nonart material and a drive toward the "reconstitution of the world."[46] He also defended the artist's use of the more traditional plaster, arguing that this "docile and immaculate substance" allowed the viewer to perceive clearly the play of shadow and light that define the sculpture's eccentric volumetric shifts and "the infinite possibility of their variation."[47]

WOMAN WITH VASE, SUMMER 1933

This monumental work (pl. 67), created in plaster in summer 1933 (fig. 22), stands more than seven feet tall and spans four feet at its widest point. The figure's overall form is one of exaggerated volume: her breasts and buttocks are buoyant, and a cartoonishly long arm grasps a large vase. The sculpture bears compelling similarities to ancient Iberian statues, which sometimes held offerings for the gods, as well as to prehistoric fertility figures.[48] Various commentators have interpreted the woman's vase as a torch, prefiguring the torch-bearing figures of the etching *Minotauromachie* (1935) and the painting *Guernica* (1937).[49]

The sculpture made its public debut, probably in a cement version, outside the Spanish Pavilion at the 1937 Paris World's Fair (fig. 23). Within the pavilion, *Guernica,* a hotly debated highlight of the fair, was displayed with Alexander Calder's *Mercury Fountain* (1937) in the entrance portico.

As Picasso neared the end of his life, he had two bronze casts of the work made at the Valsuani foundry. One would be placed over his grave at the Château de Vauvenargues after his death, in 1973 (see fig. 24 on p. 263). At Picasso's behest, the other cast was given to the Museo del Prado in Madrid, where it would later be joined by *Guernica*. Both works now reside at the Museo Nacional Centro de Arte Reina Sofía, Spain's national museum of twentieth-century art.

AUGUST 1933: Picasso's efforts to stop the publication of Fernande Olivier's memoirs of her years spent with the artist failed, and the book was published by Librairie Stock as *Picasso et ses amis* (*Picasso and His Friends*).[50] Excerpts had already appeared in *Le Soir,* in September 1930, and in *Mercure de France*, in May–July 1931. Olivier's memoirs provide an eyewitness account of Picasso's 1910 sale of a number of his early sculptures to Vollard, who thereafter cast them in bronze.

HEAD OF A WARRIOR, 1933

Sometime during the year, Picasso created the plaster *Head of a Warrior* (pl. 68), a sculpture that conveys the infinite variety of materials and creative processes he used in making his sculptures. For this work he used the so-called imprint technique, in which materials are pressed into fresh plaster to create indexical impressions, and objects are sometimes embedded in the work itself. Picasso also cast certain forms, such as the triangular base, for which he poured plaster inside

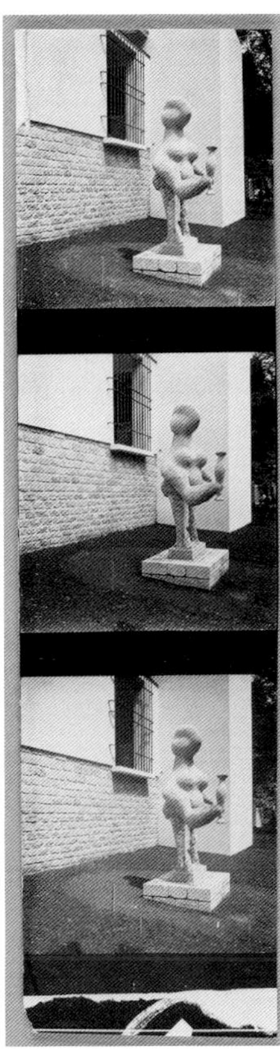

23. *Woman with Vase* installed in front of the Spanish Pavilion at the World's Fair, Paris, 1937. Photographs by Dora Maar. Picasso Archives, Musée national Picasso–Paris

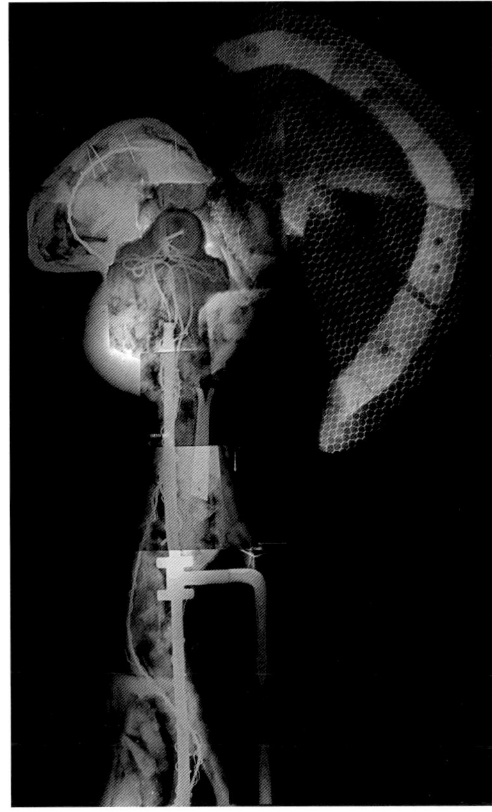

24. Composite x-radiograph of *Head of a Warrior*, in profile. X-radiograph by the Conservation Laboratory, The Museum of Modern Art, New York

a vessel made of corrugated cardboard—possibly a simple box he had cut into shape beforehand for use as a mold. The artist probably used keyed segments from a discarded plaster mold to indicate the plume of the Spartan-style helmet, while two tennis balls form the warrior's eyes. Other materials, such as a sculptor's stand, chicken wire, nails, wire, and a crowbar, are revealed in an x-radiograph taken of the original plaster in the Conservation Laboratory of The Museum of Modern Art (fig. 24).[51]

THE ORATOR, 1933–34

Like *Head of a Warrior*, *The Orator* (pl. 76) demonstrates Picasso's interest in the assemblage of cast forms, bringing together objects he had created through sand casting and by pouring wet plaster into vessels and other improvised molds. With its exaggerated facial features and roughly modeled outstretched hand, this work humorously reinterprets the standard classical subject of an orator gesturing to an unseen audience. To create the figure's distinctively textured toga, Picasso pressed chicken wire into wet plaster and made a cast of corrugated paper. The ready-made ridges and folds of this commercially manufactured material provided the artist with a wonderfully expedient means of "sculpting" classical drapery. In 1936–37 Picasso would include the figure in several overtly political drawings; in one, dated April 19, 1937, it brandishes a hammer and sickle. The sculpture's character translated well into the highly charged imagery of the *Guernica* moment. For that reason it was long considered to date from 1937, but photographs place it a few years earlier.[52]

THE REAPER, c. 1934

Probably begun sometime in 1934, *The Reaper* (pl. 74) was sculpted in plaster mounted on an iron framework.[53] According to Werner Spies, he filled a waffle iron with plaster to create the figure's head, then added a few additional pieces of material to suggest features in the negative imprint that formed a face.[54] On a visit to Jacqueline Picasso after the artist's death, André Malraux asked her whether the face of *The Reaper* had been created by the mold. She replied, "Oh, no! [Picasso] added it. He almost always changed everything once it was started. At first there wasn't any scythe there either. He used to say, 'It came to me just like that.'"[55] Indeed, a photograph believed to have been taken in winter 1934 by the Paris photography studio Bernès, Marouteau et Cie shows the small figure in progress, as yet without its scythe, while another early image shows him holding his tool (see fig. 22, background).[56] Picasso may have experimented with adding and removing the object that has long defined the reading of the sculpture before ultimately deciding to include it.

The Reaper is strongly associated with the World War II period, as the photographs showing the sculpture at Boisgeloup, before the war, were unknown for many years. Some commentators have inferred a funerary connotation: Malraux wrote, “The scythe obviously suggests death,” which to him made the work an ideal candidate for enlargement as a monument to the poet Charles Baudelaire, a plan that was never realized.[57] Others focused on the figure’s pastoral side: for Brassaï, it was a small character wearing “a large straw hat on his head, round and luminous as the Midi sun.”[58]

WOMAN WITH LEAVES, 1934, AND _WOMAN WITH ORANGE_ OR _WOMAN WITH APPLE_, c. 1934

Woman with Leaves (pl. 75) combines imprints of real leaves, cast plaster forms, and free modeling. Picasso built the sculpture in stages, beginning, according to Malraux, with “a rectangular head, to which [he] successively added a stem and a crinkled-paper body, before completing it with beech leaves and fluting.”[59] Always in search of new forms and texture and bemused by his own daring, Picasso is recalled by Malraux as having asked, “The leaves were mighty surprised to find themselves in my sculpture, right?”[60]

The six-foot *Woman with Orange* (pl. 77; also known as *Woman with Apple*) was created contemporaneously and with several of the same materials and found objects that Picasso used for *Woman with Leaves*. They share a face cast from a cigar box mold, and, like *The Orator*, clothing designed with wire mesh and corrugated cardboard.

By September 1943, *Woman with Orange* had been cast in bronze and was photographed by Brassaï at Picasso’s studio.[61] Titled *Standing Young Woman*, a bronze cast of *Woman with Orange* would first be shown publicly in 1949 at the Maison de la pensée française, the only sculpture in an exhibition of Picasso’s recent paintings.

LATE 1934: Zervos commissioned Bernès, Marouteau et Cie to document the works Picasso had produced at Boisgeloup since 1930. The eighteen photographs would be published a year later, in December 1935, in a special issue of *Cahiers d’Art* devoted to Picasso’s work from 1930 to 1935.[62] The issue included texts by Breton, Paul Eluard, and González, among others, along with an interview with Picasso by Zervos.

WOMAN CARRYING A VESSEL, 1935, AND _FIGURE_, SPRING 1938

Between 1935 and 1940 Picasso created very few sculptures; among those he made were a number of playful figures for his daughter Maya, born on September 5, 1935. Using a hammer and nails, Picasso assembled these wooden figurines from materials he found lying around his studio and home. *Woman Carrying a Vessel* (pl. 78) and *Figure* (pl. 79) stand sturdily affixed to small boxes. The colorful palette and decorative motifs are reminiscent of Hopi kachina figures and traditional simple wooden dolls.

NOVEMBER 3, 1935: Following his separation from Olga, Picasso, contemplating a divorce, drew up an inventory of his property, including paintings, drawings, sculptures, and graphic art, with the help of his friend and dealer Paul Rosenberg. Two lists were made of objects found at Boisgeloup, including a number of plasters and bronzes.[63] The divorce was never finalized.

MARCH 2–APRIL 19, 1936: The exhibition *Cubism and Abstract Art* at The Museum of Modern Art featured thirty-two works by Picasso, including two sculptures: *Head of a Woman* (pl. 11) and *Glass of Absinthe* (pl. 23).

MAY 22–29, 1936: Over the short span of eight days, the Galerie Charles Ratton at 14, rue de Marignan mounted *Exposition surréaliste d’objets* (Surrealist exhibition of objects) (fig. 25; see also fig. 9 on p. 78 and fig. 15 on p. 81). Conceived and organized by Breton, the show brought together a group of objects from diverse sources: natural and scientific, found and made, Western and non-Western. According to an undated handwritten checklist, Breton had at first thought to include from Picasso’s work only a cast of *Glass of Absinthe* (pl. 26). But as he later explained in a press announcement, a visit to Picasso’s studio had resulted in the addition of five other sculptures.[64]

JUNE 26–JULY 20, 1936: Galerie Cahiers d’Art, in Paris, presented an exhibition of recent sculptures by Picasso, including a number of bronze casts of the delicate statuettes he had carved in wood in the summer of 1930.[65] A text by González and photographs of the statuettes were published in *Cahiers d’Art* in tandem with the show. The article and exhibition also featured Picasso’s unique iron, brass, and bronze *Head of a Man* of 1930 (pl. 39). In his text, an homage to Picasso as sculptor, González described sculpture as the “mysterious side, the nerve center” of Picasso’s work.[66]

LATE SUMMER 1936: Picasso, in the company of Paul and Nusch Eluard and Dora Maar, first visited Vallauris, a town in southern France with a longstanding tradition in ceramic arts.[67]

FALL 1936: Picasso left the Château de Boisgeloup. He and Olga had agreed that she would keep the country home and he would retain the rue La Boétie apartment.

JANUARY 1937: Picasso rented a new studio space at 7, rue des Grands-Augustins in Paris, following a suggestion from Maar, who had moved into an apartment not far from there, at 6, rue de Savoie. The artist also maintained a studio at Vollard’s residence in Tremblay-sur-Mauldre, west of Paris, together with Walter and their daughter, Maya.

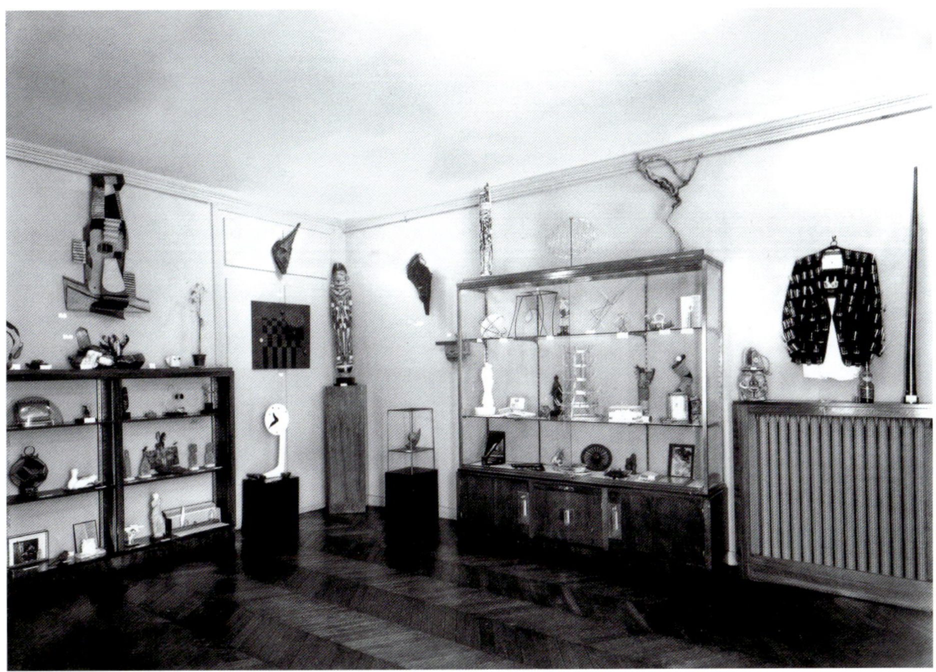

25. View of *Exposition surréaliste d'objets* (Surrealist exhibition of objects), Galerie Charles Ratton, Paris, May 22–29, 1936. Photograph by Man Ray. Guy Ladrière Archives, Paris

APRIL 30, 1937: An invoice of this date from the moldmaker M. Renucci indicates that Picasso had ordered several molds and plaster proofs of a number of his recent sculptures. The invoice outlines the terms: "Molding pieces and stamping plaster models at Boisgeloup, a two-meter face and three large busts. A plaster copy of each. Price agreed upon—10,000 francs" (fig. 26). The molds and plasters would be used to produce cement and bronze casts of the sculptures presented at the Paris World's Fair.

JULY 12–NOVEMBER 25, 1937: The Pavilion of the Spanish Republic, designed by the architects Luis Lacasa and Josep Lluís Sert, was inaugurated at the International Exhibition of Art and Technology in Modern Life, commonly known as the World's Fair, in Paris. The Spanish Pavilion opened several weeks after the fair itself, after a frantic effort on the part of its organizers to assemble a building and exhibits that would demonstrate the strength of the country's republican government, despite the fact that it was mired in a civil war. Along with *Guernica*, Picasso presented five of his most recent sculptures.

The exhibition marked the public premiere of works Picasso had made at the Boisgeloup sculpture studio. They had been published in *Minotaure* in June 1933, but visitors to the Spanish Pavilion had the first opportunity to see them in person. Cement casts of *Head of a Woman* and *Woman with Vase* were placed outdoors: the former near the stairway to the left of the building's main facade (see fig. 2 on p. 305), and the latter near the wall on the south side of the pavilion (see fig. 23).[68] *Montserrat*, an iron sculpture that González made for the occasion, joined Picasso's two works outdoors. The main hall on the third floor, devoted to the visual arts, featured three of Picasso's 1931 sculptures in the center of the room: *Head of a Woman* (pl. 49) and *Bust of a Woman* (pl. 50) in cement, and *Bather* (pl. 53) in bronze. Photographs of the two outdoor works, taken by Bernès, Marouteau et Cie, would be published later that year in an issue of *Cahiers d'Art* devoted to *Guernica*.[69]

MOULAGES - ARCHITECTURE

MOULAGES SUR NATURE
Bon Creux - Creux perdu
Gélatine -- Terre cuite
Stuc - Ciment

M. RENUCCI
7, Rue Fermat, 7 PARIS (XIVe)
R. C. Seine 88.514

SPÉCIALITÉ DE MAQUETTES
Médaillé à l'Exposition des Métiers - Paris 1924. -- Médaille d'Argent à l'Exposition des Arts Décoratifs 1925

Monsieur P. PICASSO

Doit

PARIS, le 30 Avril 1937

Moulage à pièces et estampage sur modèles plâtre à Boigeloup, une figure de 2 mètres et trois grands bustes.
Une épreuve plâtre de chaque. Prix convenu........ 10.000.Frs
Pour acquit.

26. Invoice sent by the moldmaker M. Renucci to Picasso, April 30, 1937. Picasso Archives, Musée national Picasso–Paris

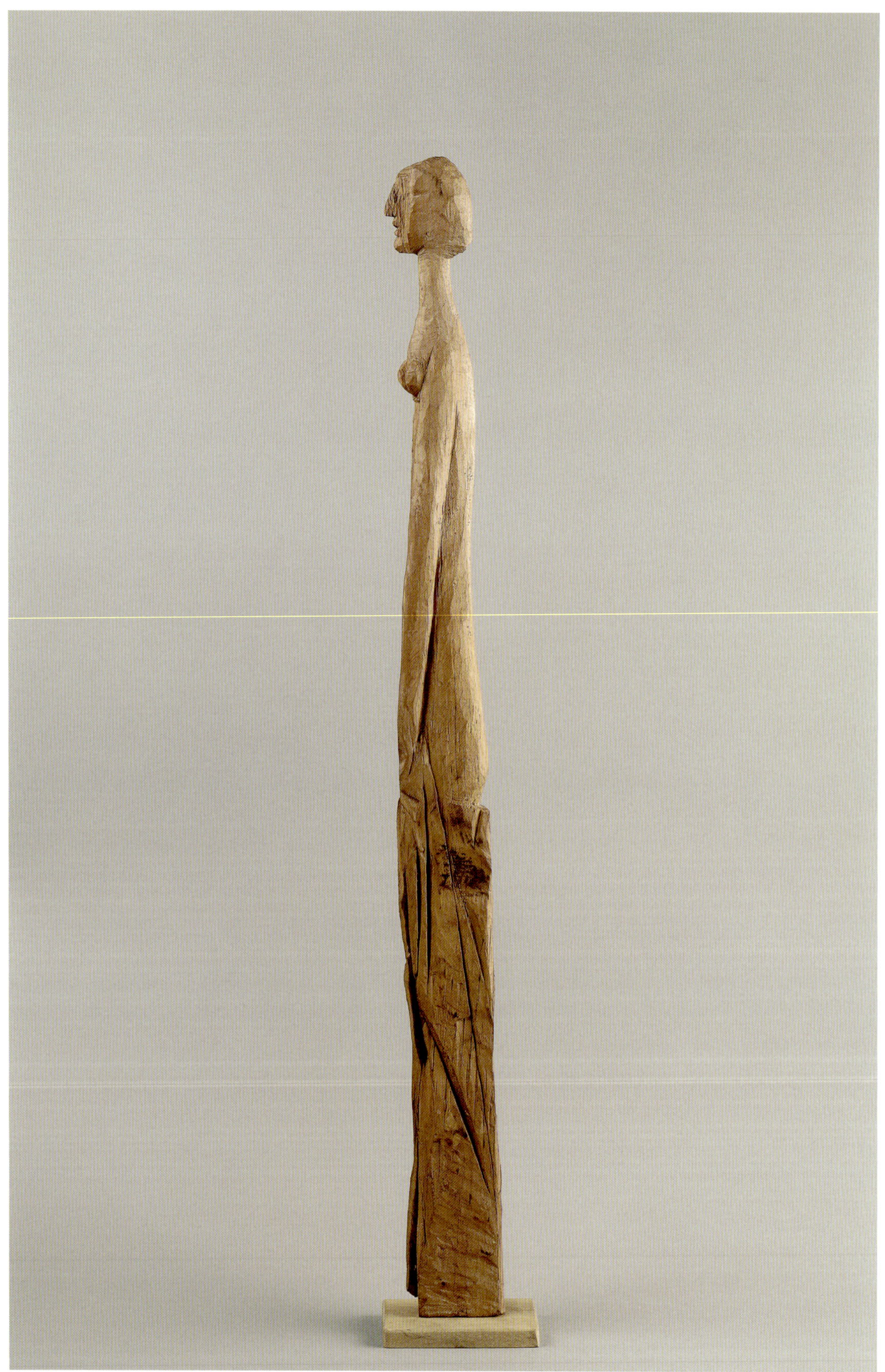

44. **SEATED WOMAN.** Boisgeloup, summer 1930
Fir
21 15⁄16 × 1 × 1 15⁄16 in. (55.8 × 2.5 × 5 cm)
Musée national Picasso–Paris. Dation Pablo Picasso

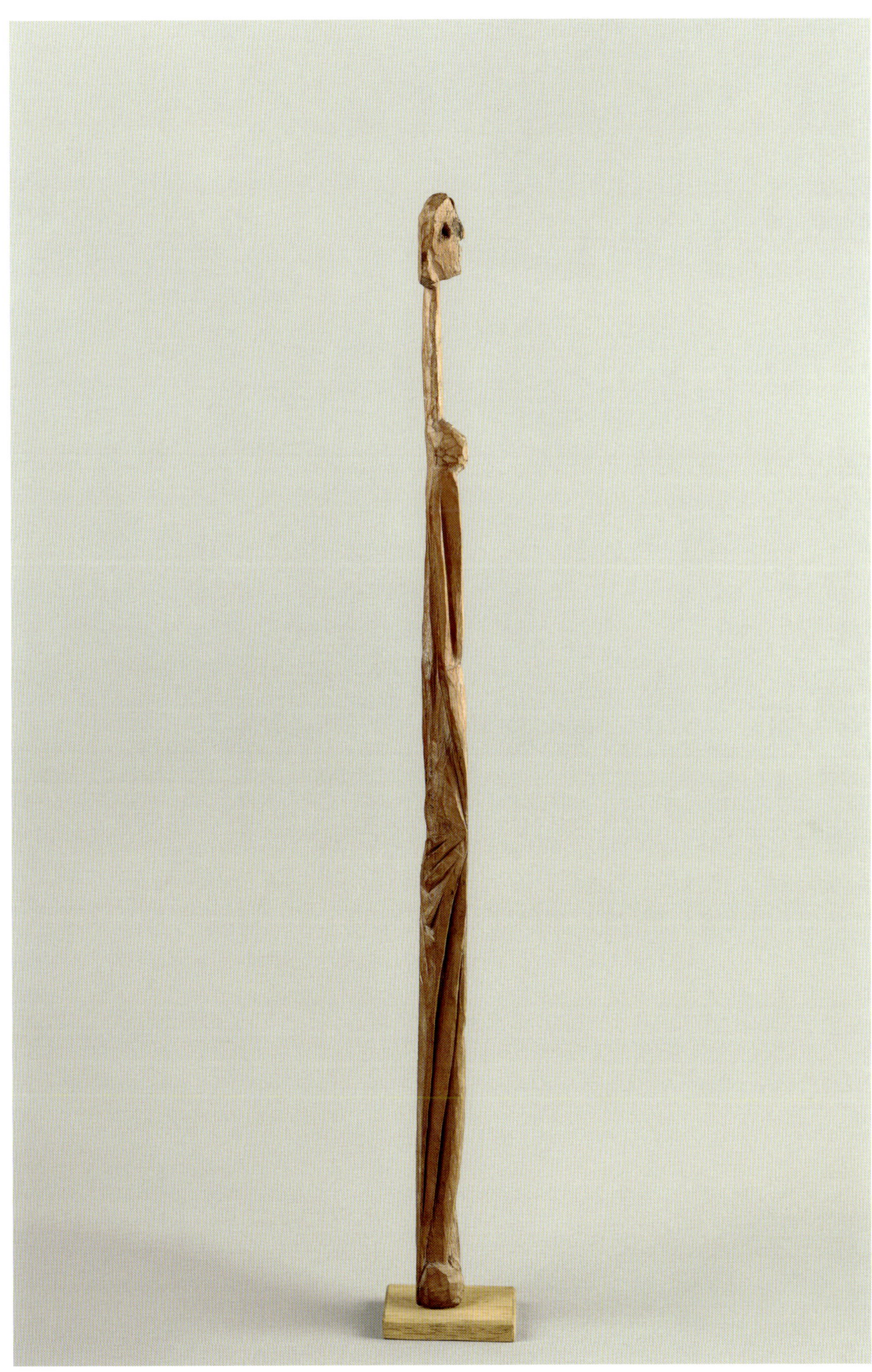

45. **STANDING WOMAN.** Boisgeloup, summer 1930
Fir
19 5⁄16 × 7⁄8 × 7⁄8 in. (49 × 2.3 × 2.2 cm)
Musée national Picasso–Paris. Dation Pablo Picasso

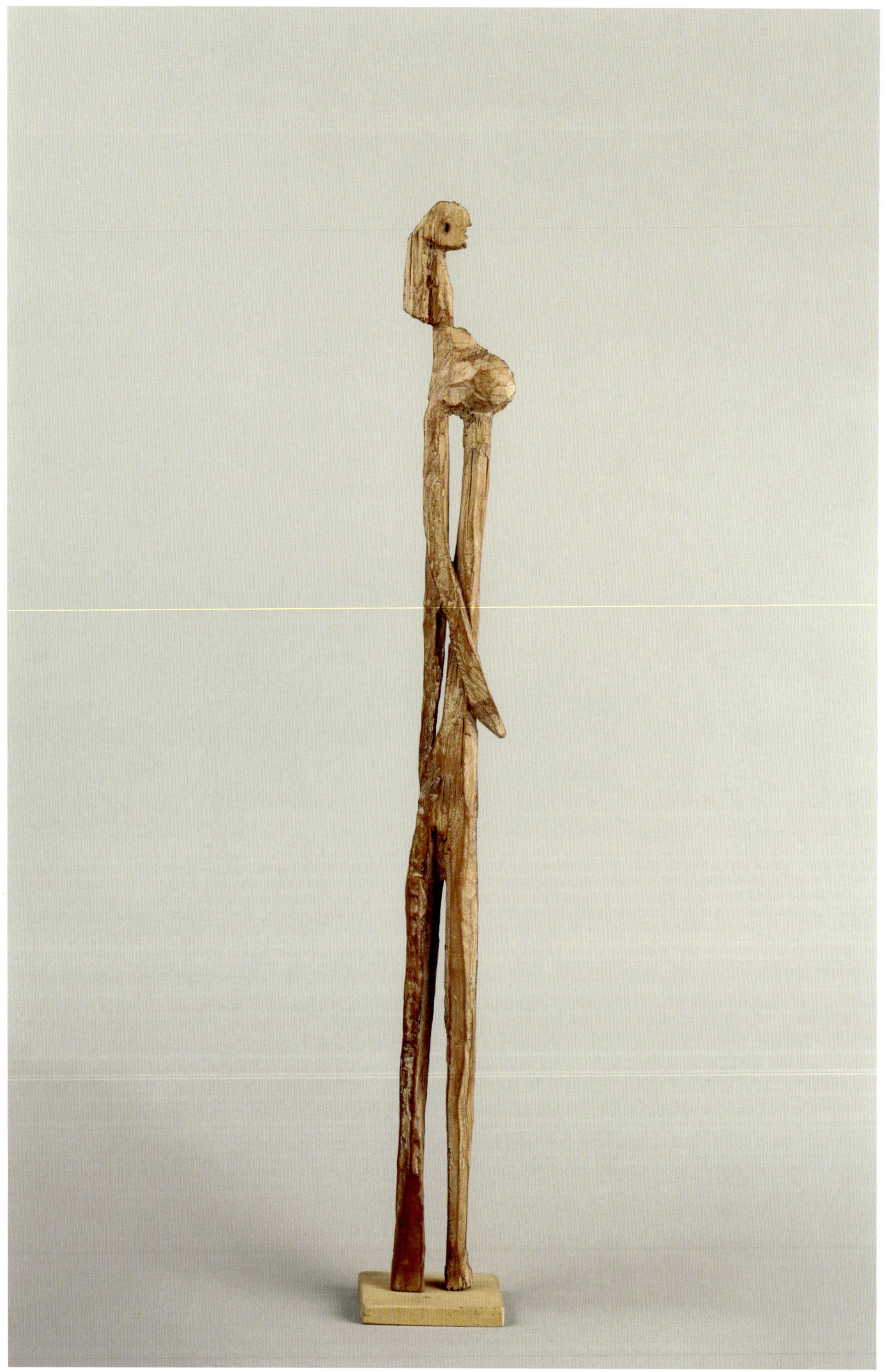

46. **STANDING WOMAN.** Boisgeloup, summer 1930
Fir
18 ¾ × 1 3/16 × 1 15/16 in. (47.6 × 3 × 5 cm)
Musée national Picasso–Paris. Dation Pablo Picasso

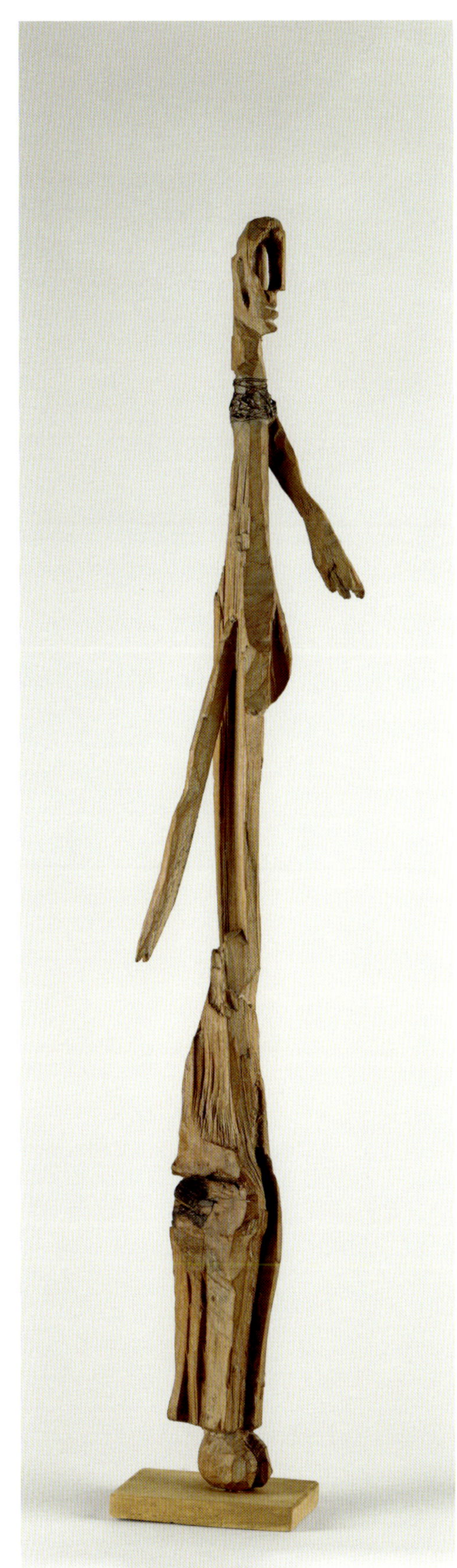

47. **STANDING WOMAN.** Boisgeloup, summer 1930
Fir and iron wire
18 9⁄16 × 1 3⁄8 × 3 1⁄8 in. (47.1 × 3.5 × 8 cm)
Musée national Picasso–Paris. Dation Pablo Picasso

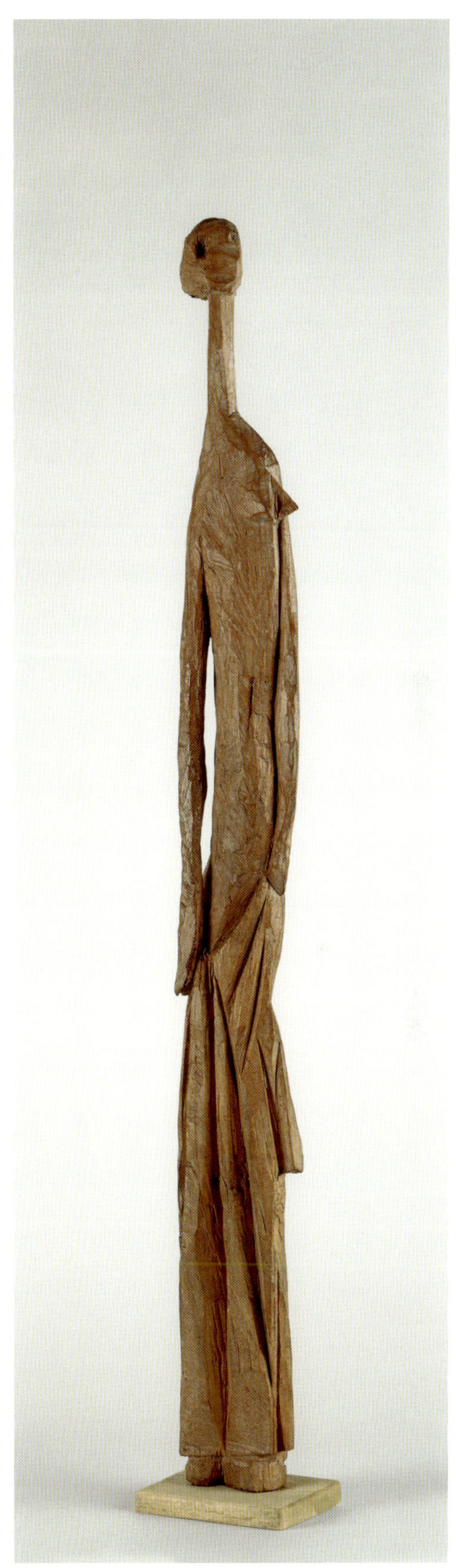

48. **STANDING WOMAN.** Boisgeloup, summer 1930
Fir
19 3⁄16 × 2 3⁄16 × 1 1⁄8 in. (48.8 × 5.5 × 2.8 cm)
Musée national Picasso–Paris. Dation Pablo Picasso

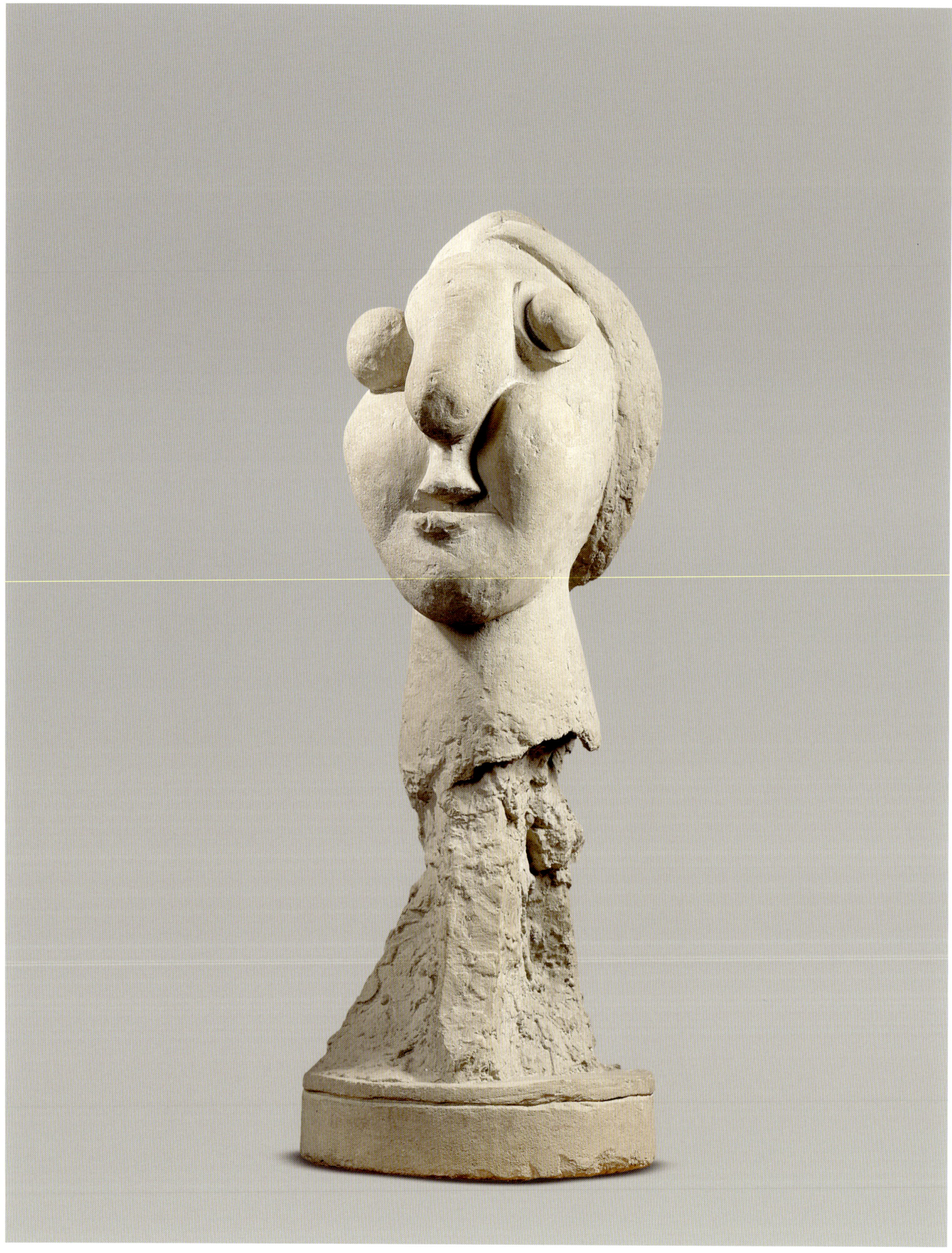

49. **HEAD OF A WOMAN.** Boisgeloup, 1931
Cement, unique, cast between April and July 1937
37 13/16 × 12 5/8 × 19 1/8 in. (96 × 32 × 48.5 cm)
Musée Picasso, Antibes. Gift of the artist

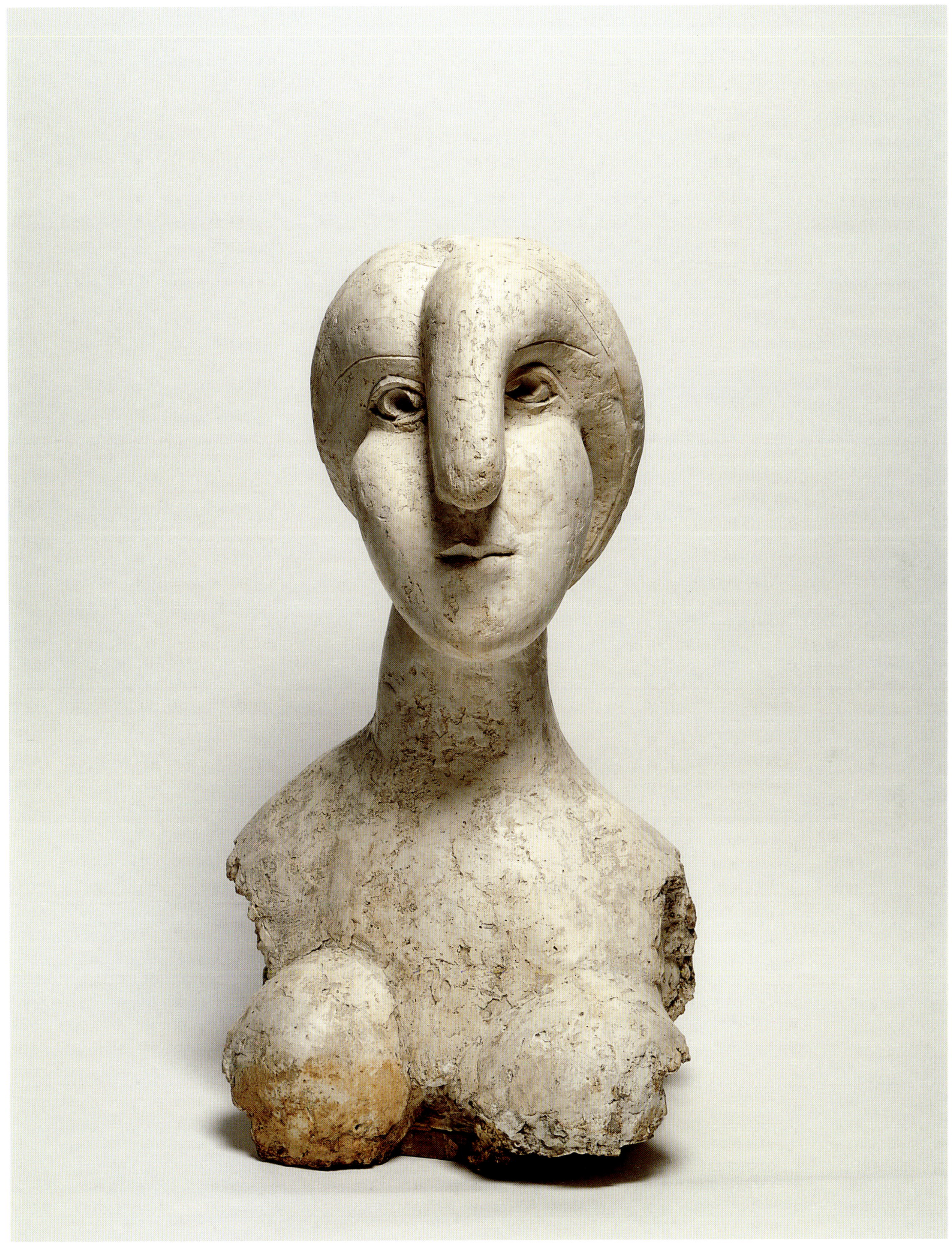

50. **BUST OF A WOMAN.** Boisgeloup, 1931
Plaster
29 15⁄16 × 18 1⁄8 × 18 7⁄8 in. (76 × 46 × 48 cm)
Private collection

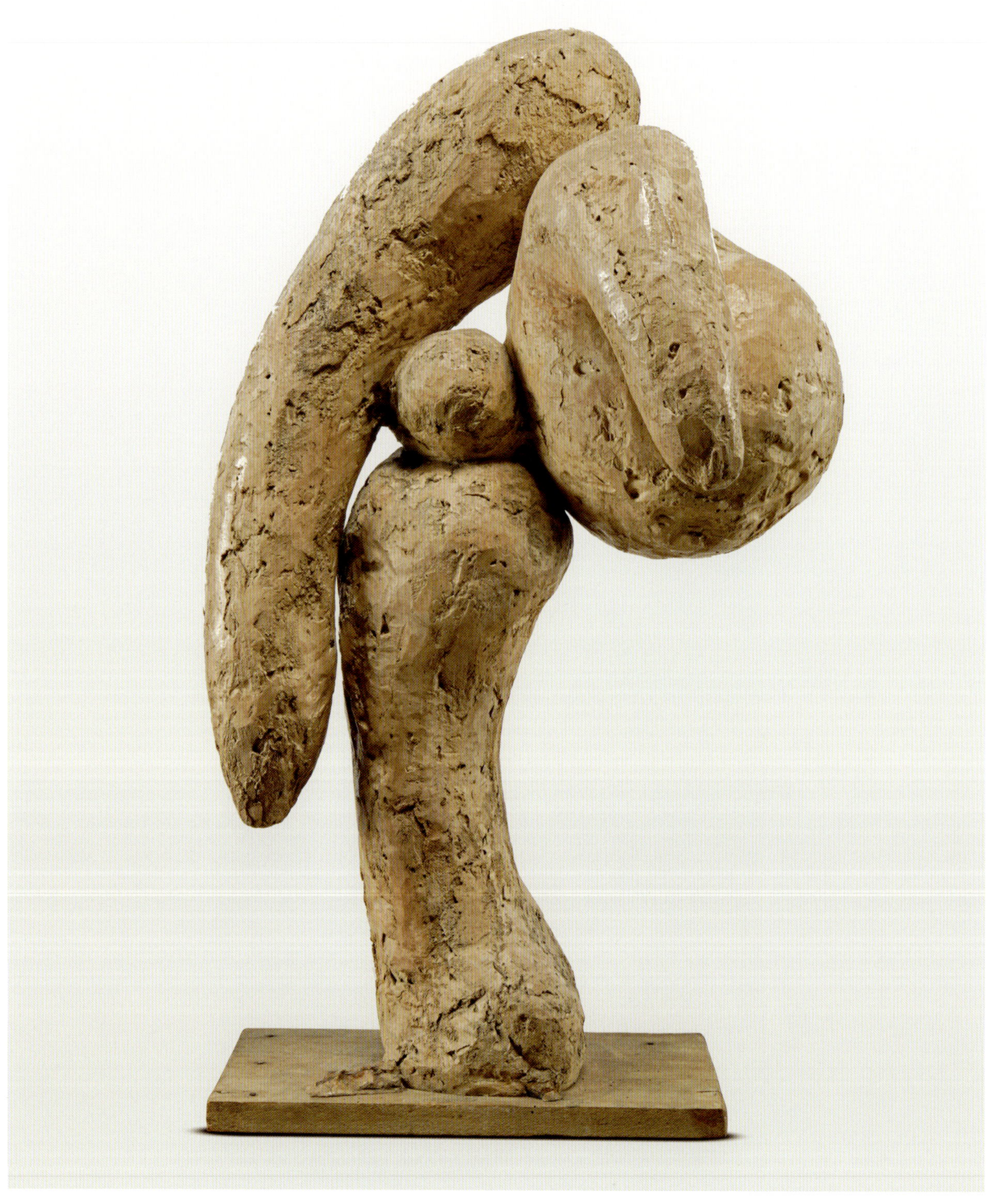

51. **HEAD OF A WOMAN.** Boisgeloup, 1931
Plaster
28 ⅛ × 16 ⅛ × 13 in. (71.5 × 41 × 33 cm)
Musée national Picasso–Paris. Dation Pablo Picasso

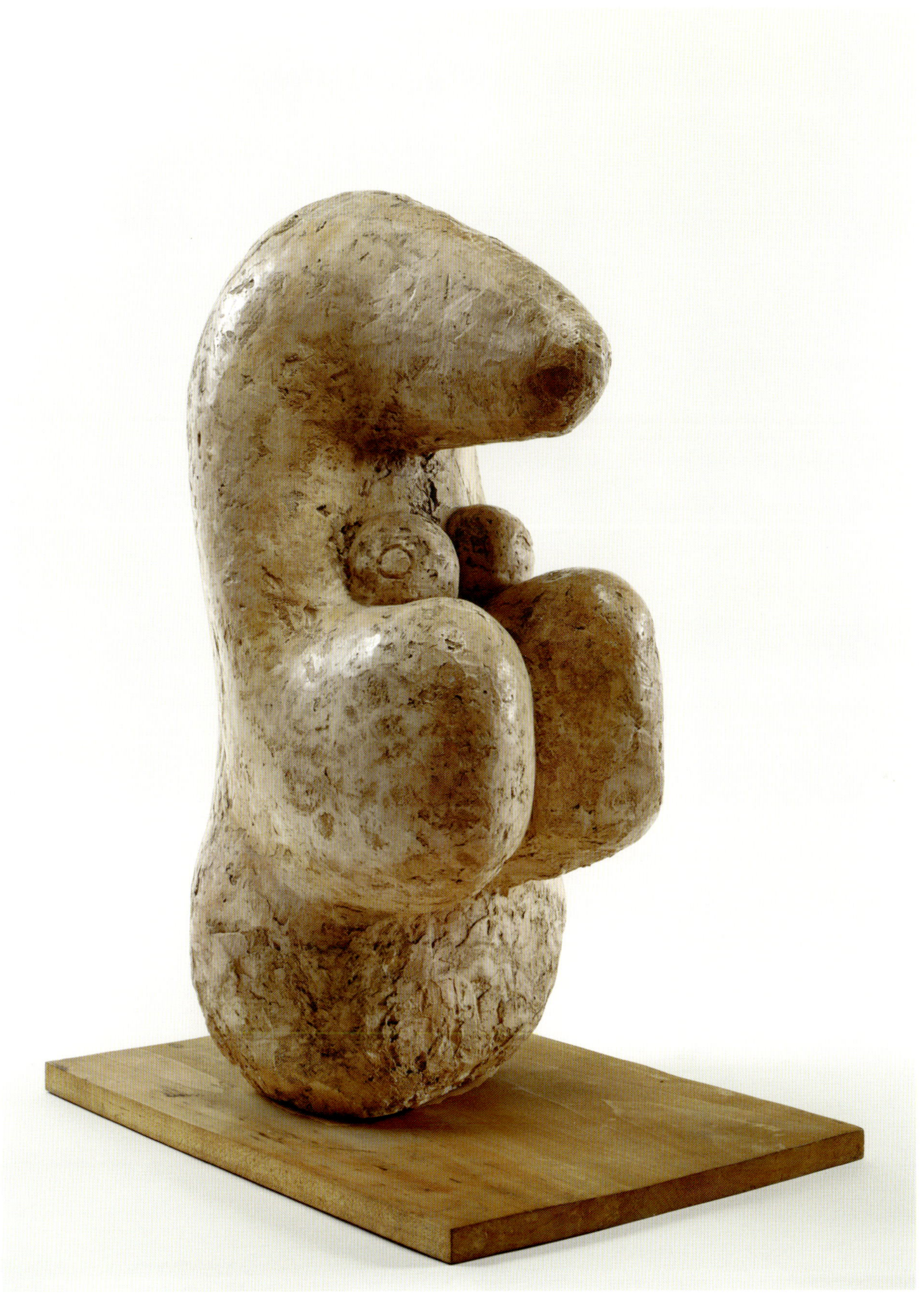

52. **BUST OF A WOMAN.** Boisgeloup, 1931
Plaster
28 3/16 × 16 1/8 × 13 in. (71.5 × 41 × 33 cm)
Musée national Picasso–Paris. Dation Pablo Picasso

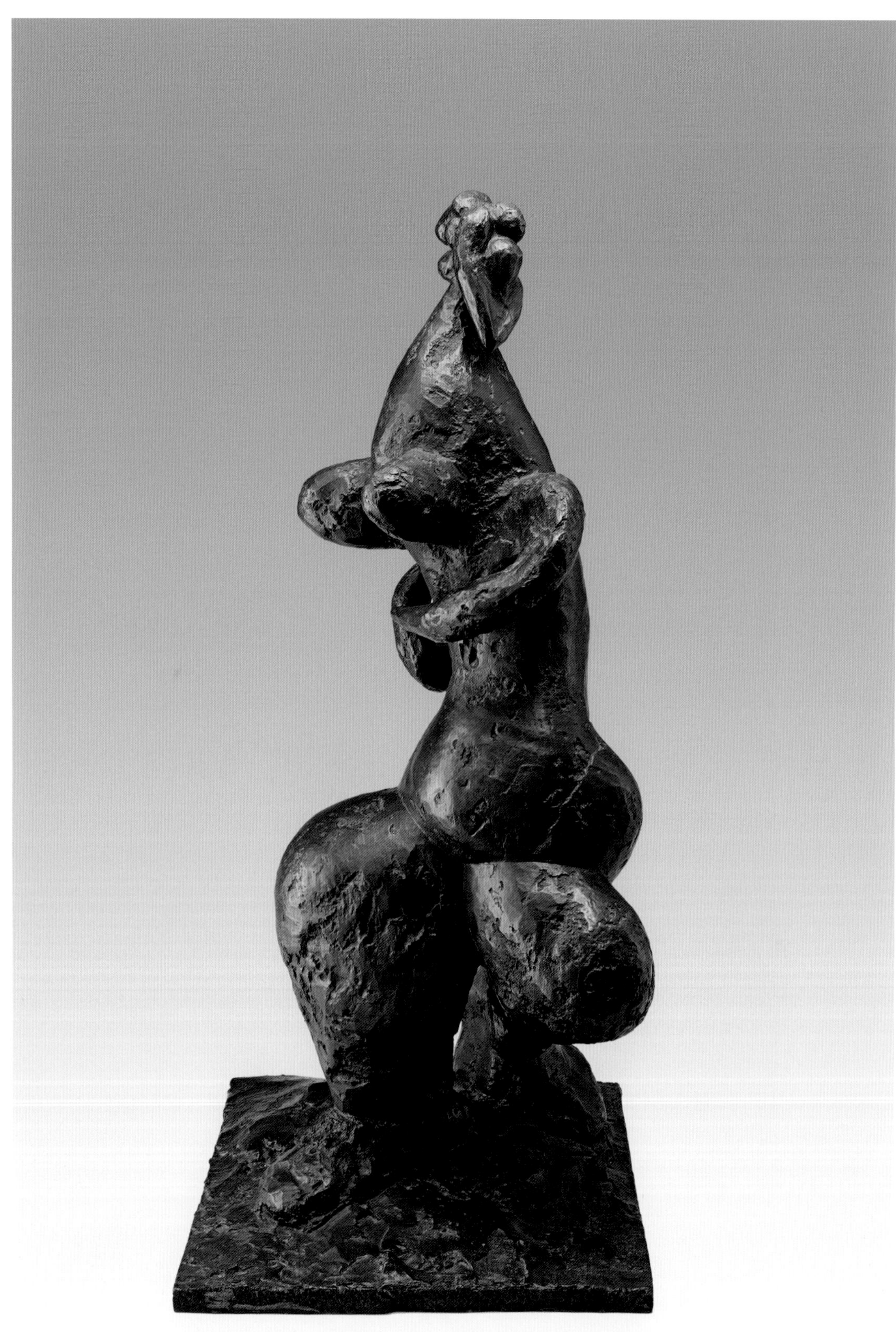

53. **BATHER.** Boisgeloup, 1931
Bronze, unique, cast by July 1937
27 9/16 × 15 13/16 × 12 3/8 in. (70 × 40.2 × 31.5 cm)
Musée national Picasso–Paris. Dation Pablo Picasso

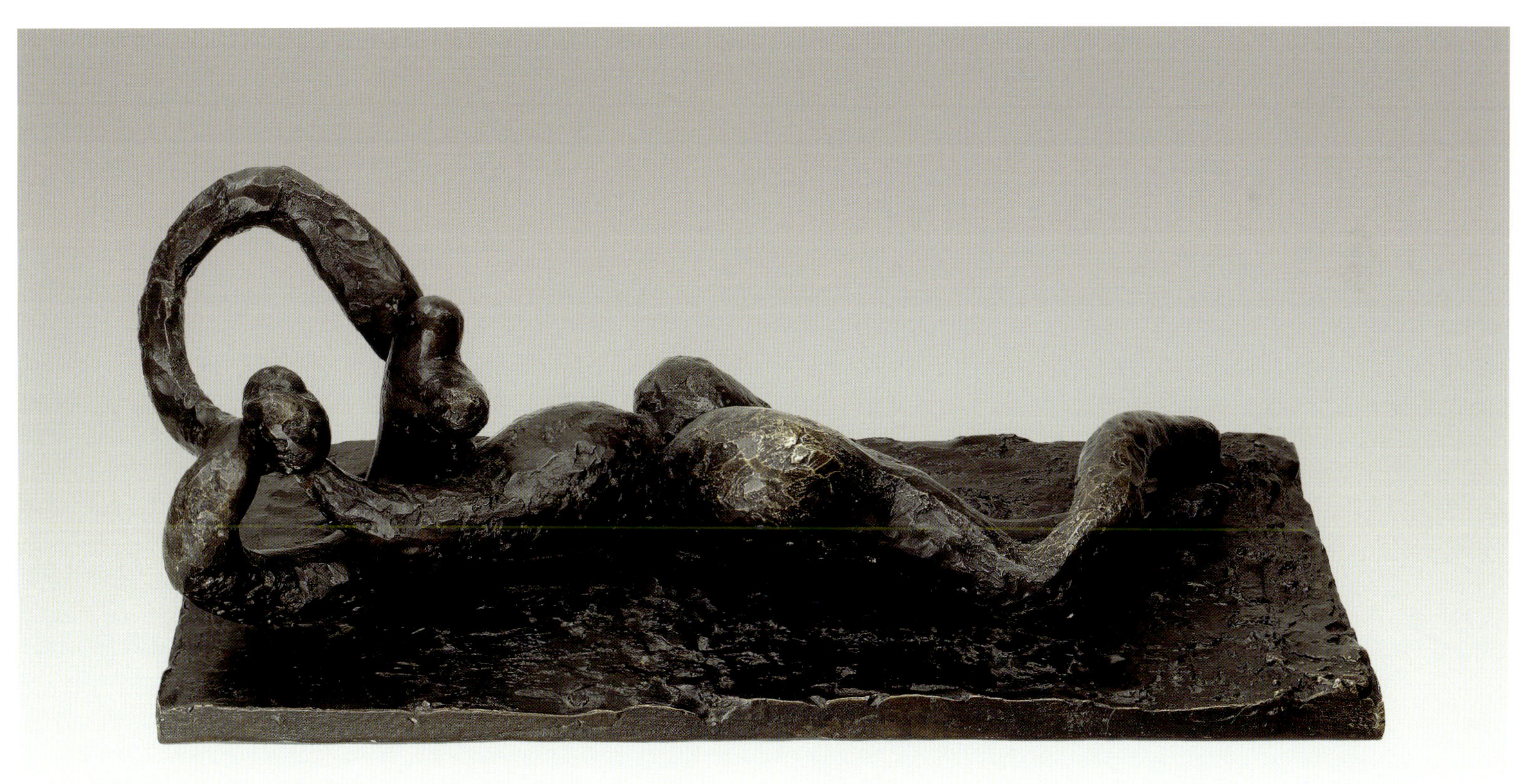

54. **RECLINING BATHER.** Boisgeloup, 1931
Bronze, unique, cast by 1943
9 ¹⁄₁₆ × 28 ³⁄₈ × 12 ³⁄₁₆ in. (23 × 72 × 31 cm)
Musée national Picasso–Paris. Dation Pablo Picasso

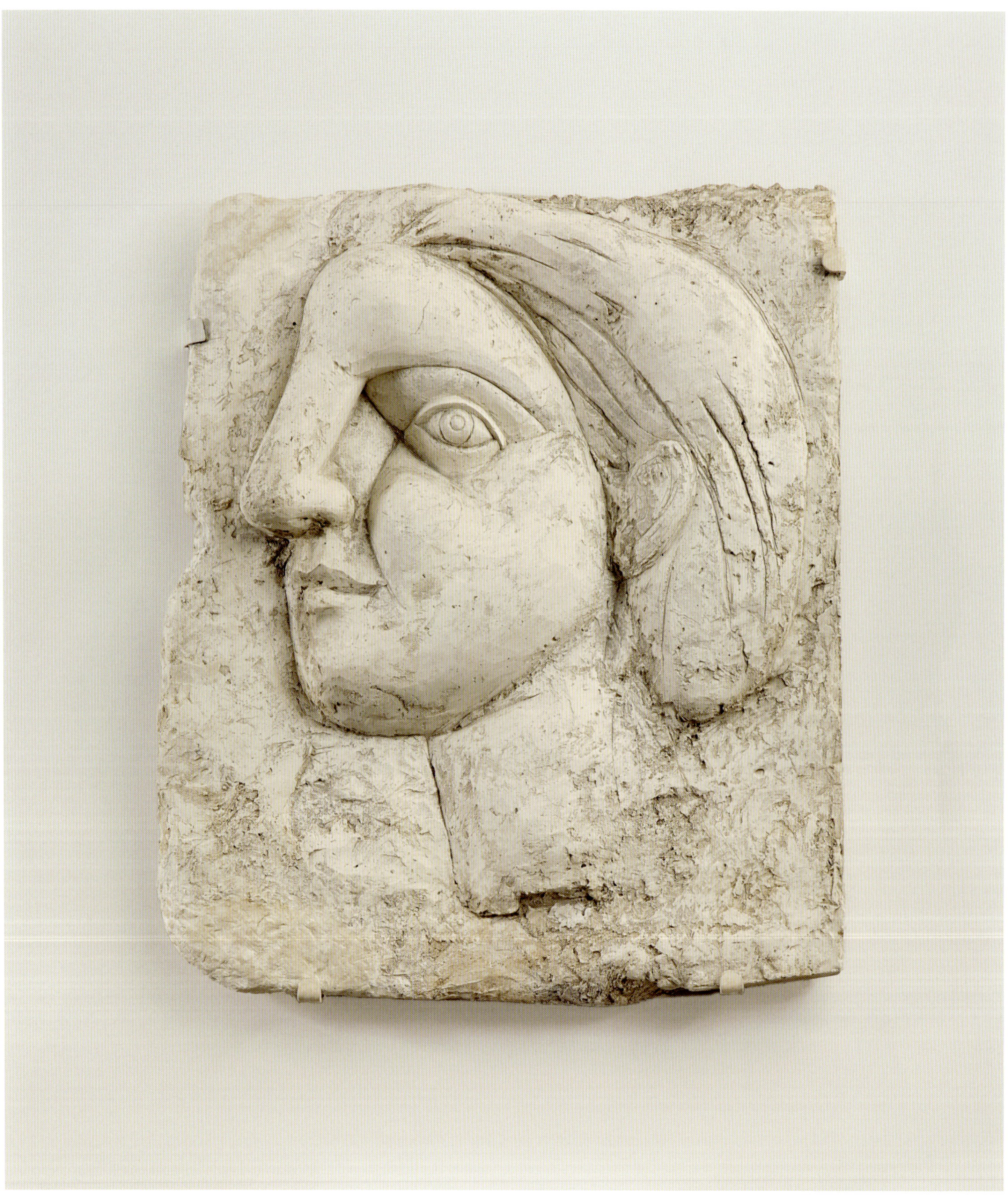

55. **HEAD OF A WOMAN.** Boisgeloup, 1931
Plaster
27 3/16 × 23 5/8 × 3 15/16 in. (69 × 60 × 10 cm)
Private collection

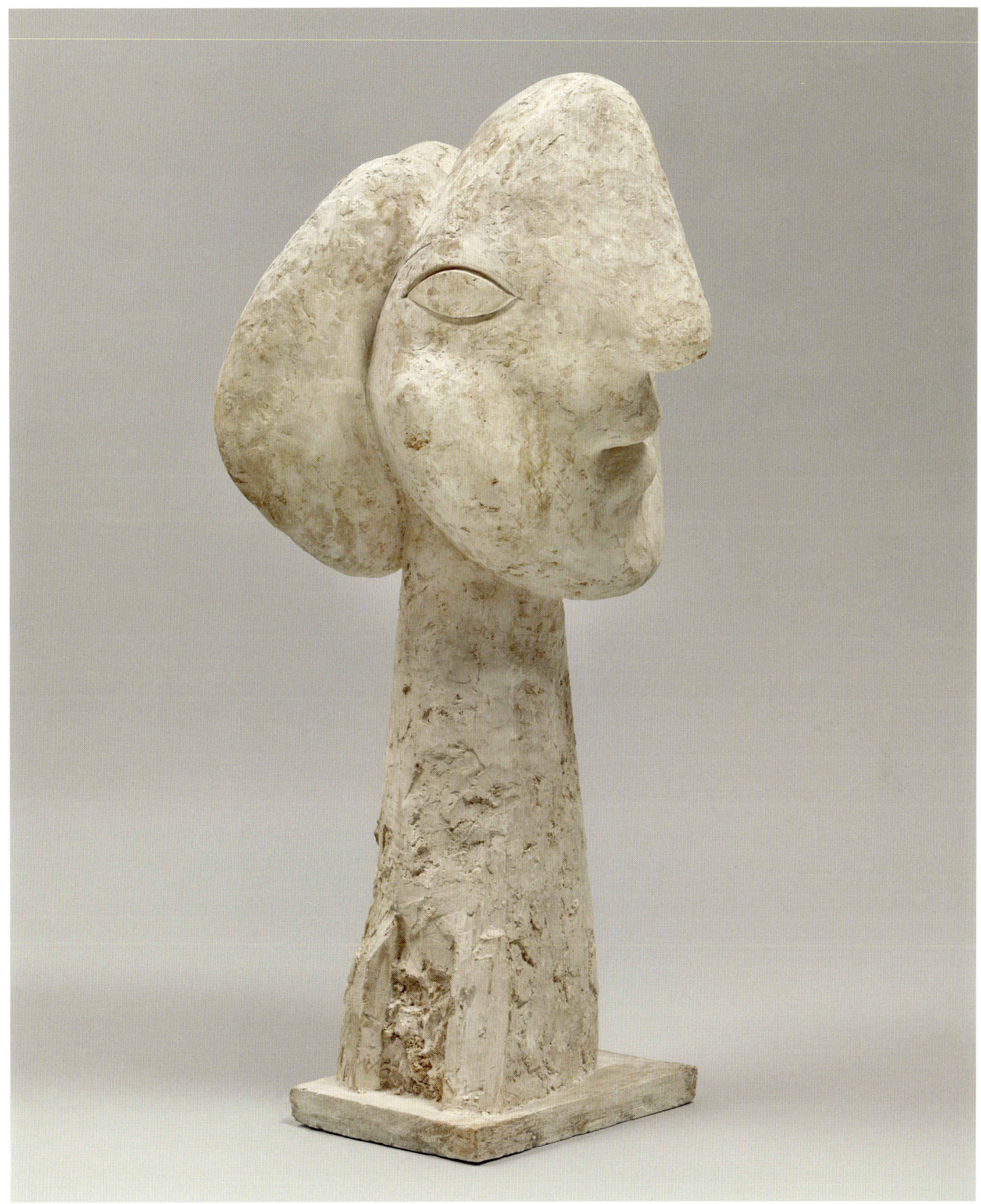

56. **HEAD OF A WOMAN.** Boisgeloup, 1931–32
Plaster, produced as plaster proof in April 1937
52½ × 25⅝ × 28 in. (133.4 × 65 × 71.1 cm)
The Museum of Modern Art, New York. Gift of Jacqueline Picasso in honor of the Museum's continuous commitment to Pablo Picasso's art

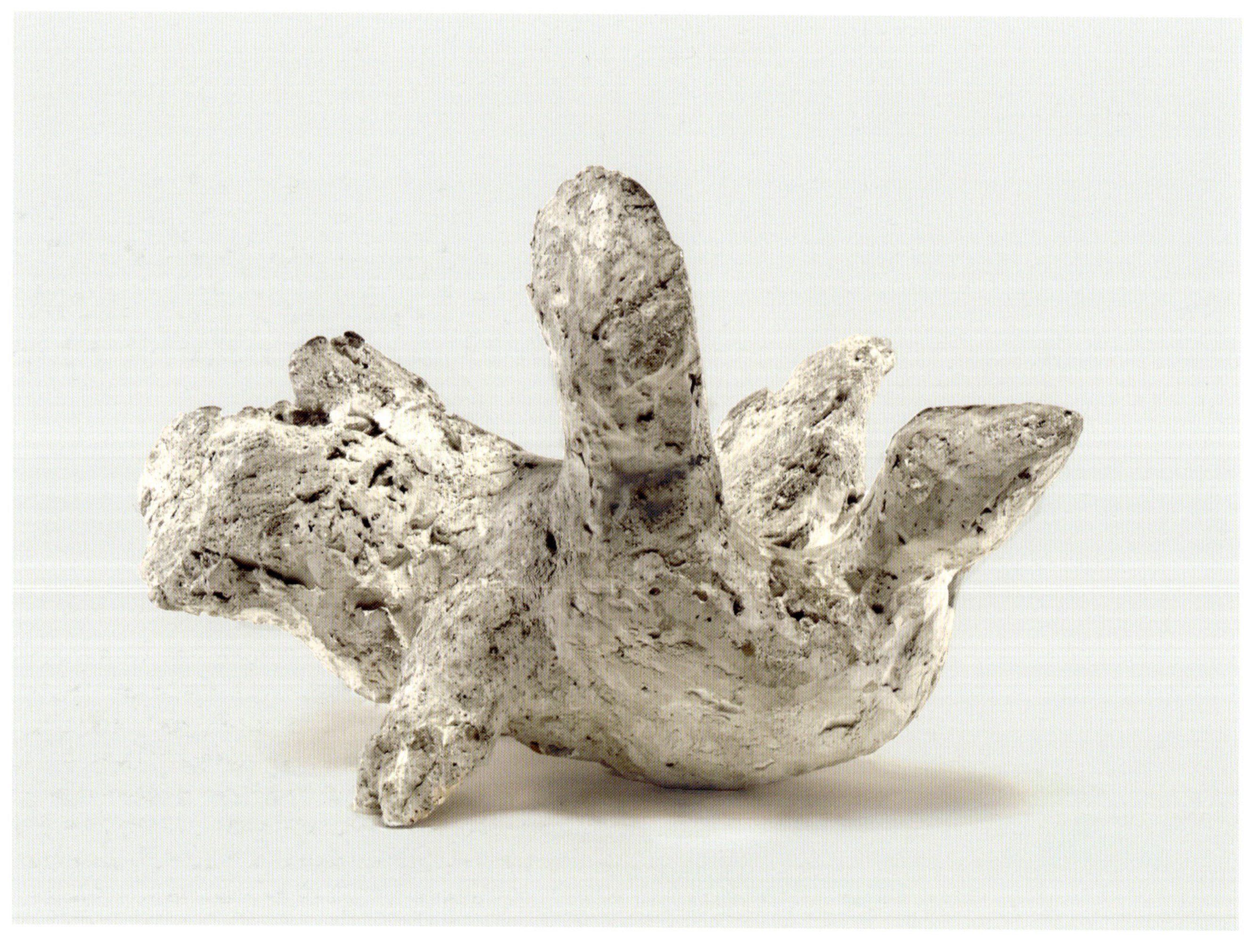

57. **BIRD.** Boisgeloup, 1931–32
Plaster
9 13/16 in. (25 cm) high
Private collection

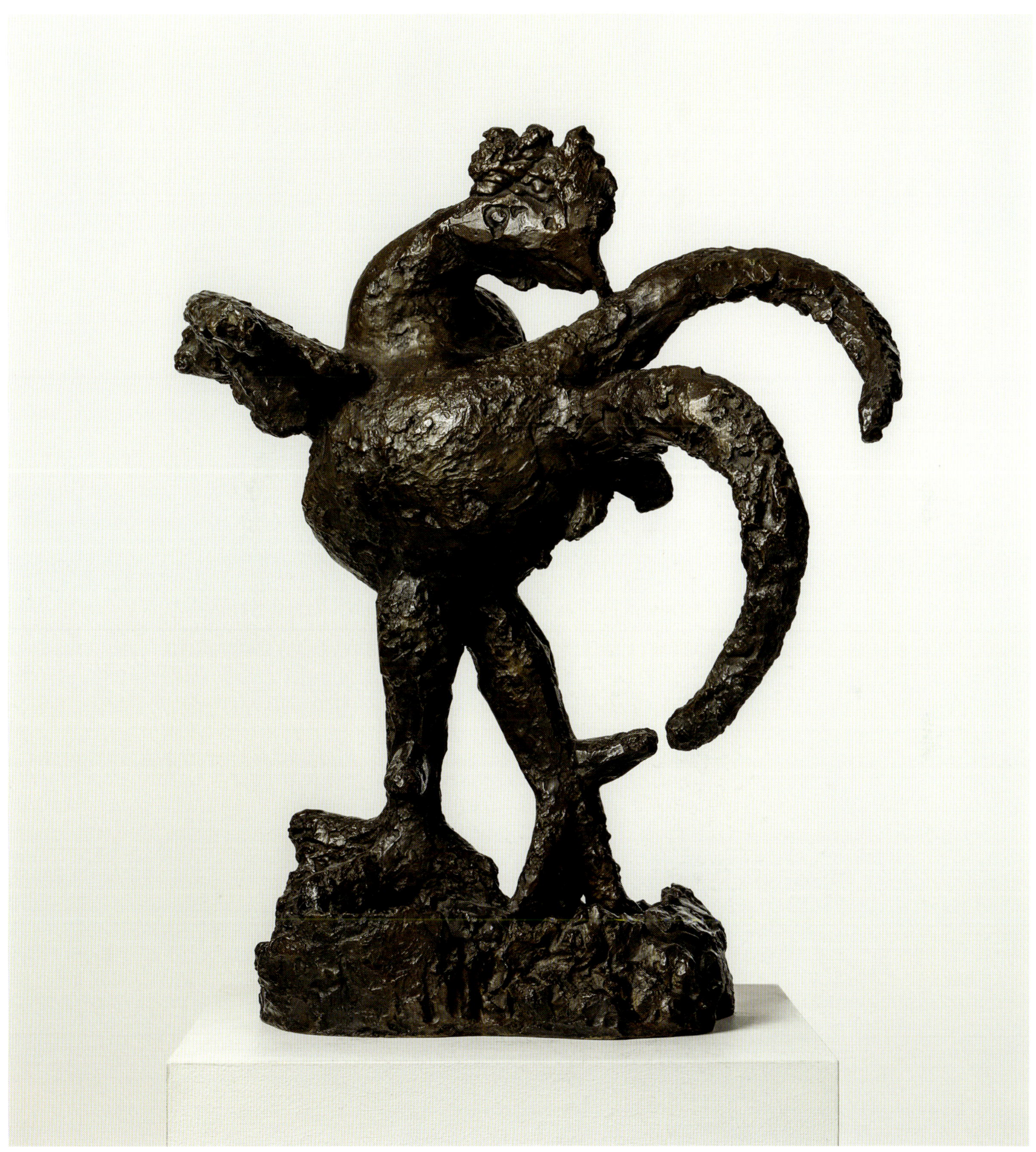

58. **COCK.** Boisgeloup, 1932
Bronze, cast 1952
25 13⁄16 × 22 15⁄16 × 15 9⁄16 in. (65.5 × 58.2 × 39.5 cm)
Tate. Purchase

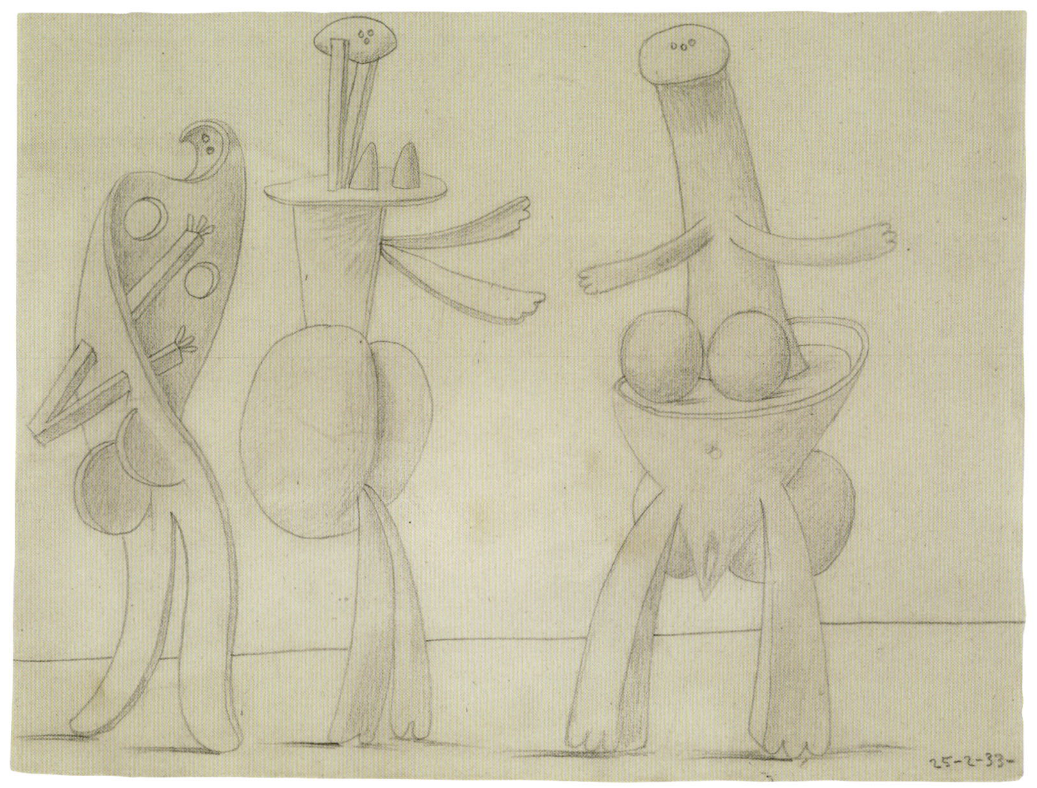

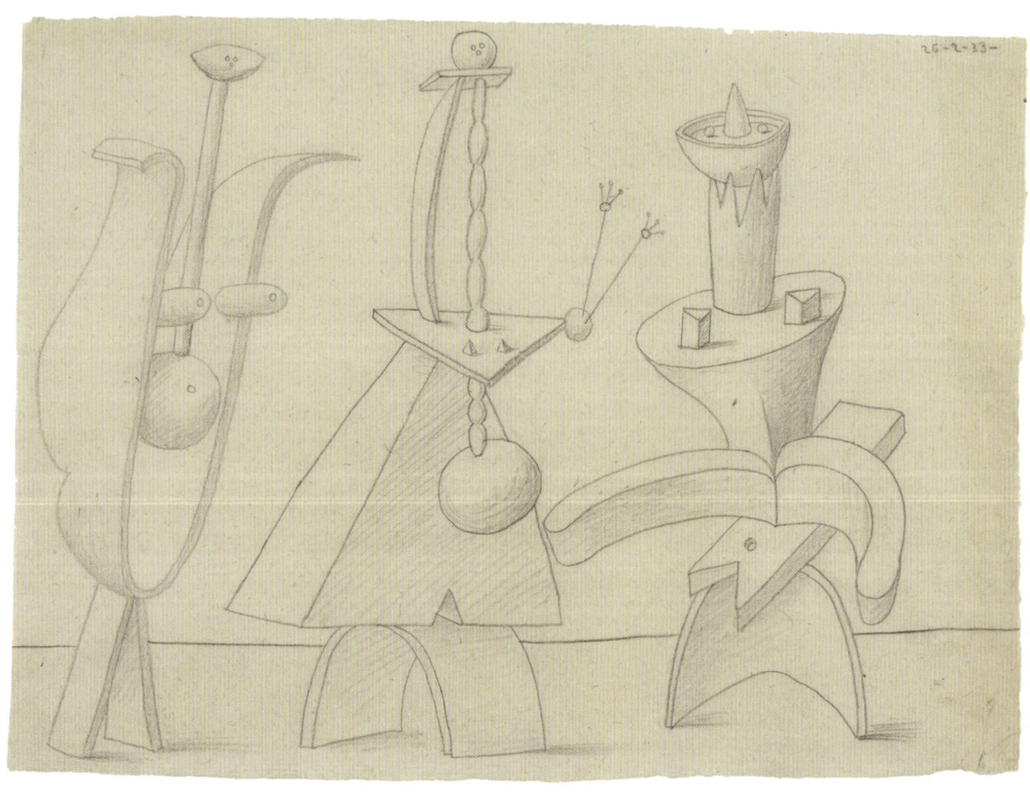

59. **AN ANATOMY: THREE WOMEN.** [Paris], February 25, 1933
Graphite on fine-textured wove paper
7 7⁄8 × 10 5⁄8 in. (20 × 27 cm)
Musée national Picasso–Paris. Dation Pablo Picasso

60. **AN ANATOMY: THREE WOMEN.** [Paris], February 26, 1933
Graphite on fine-textured wove paper
7 13⁄16 × 10 13⁄16 in. (19.9 × 27.5 cm)
Musée national Picasso–Paris. Dation Pablo Picasso

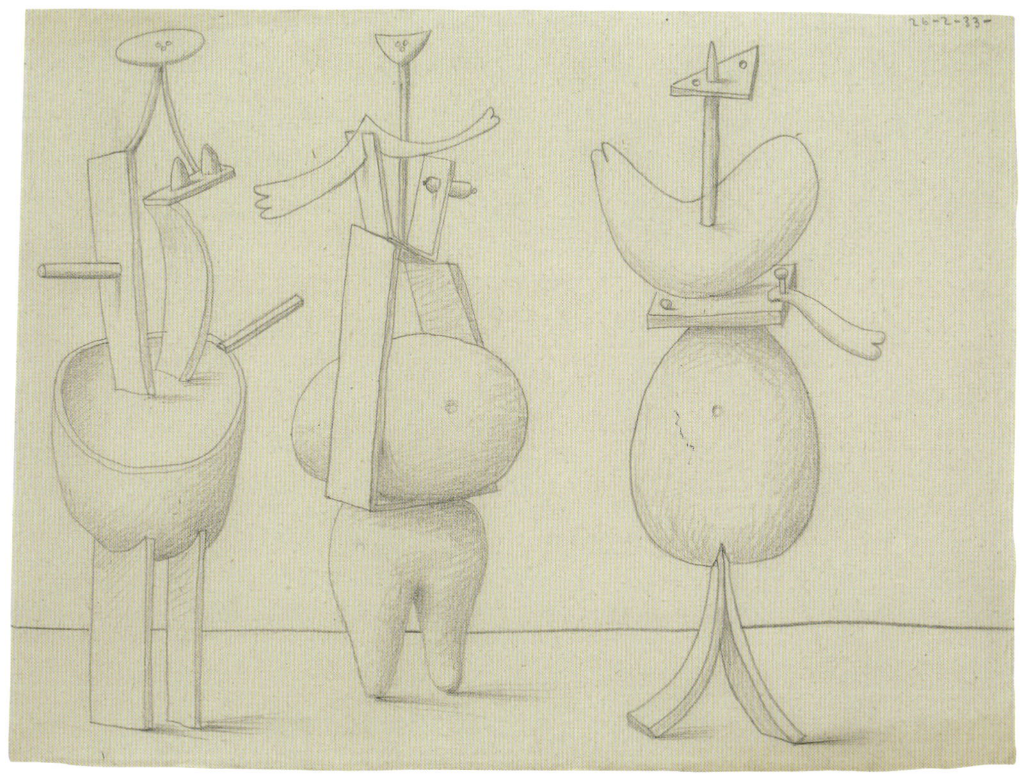

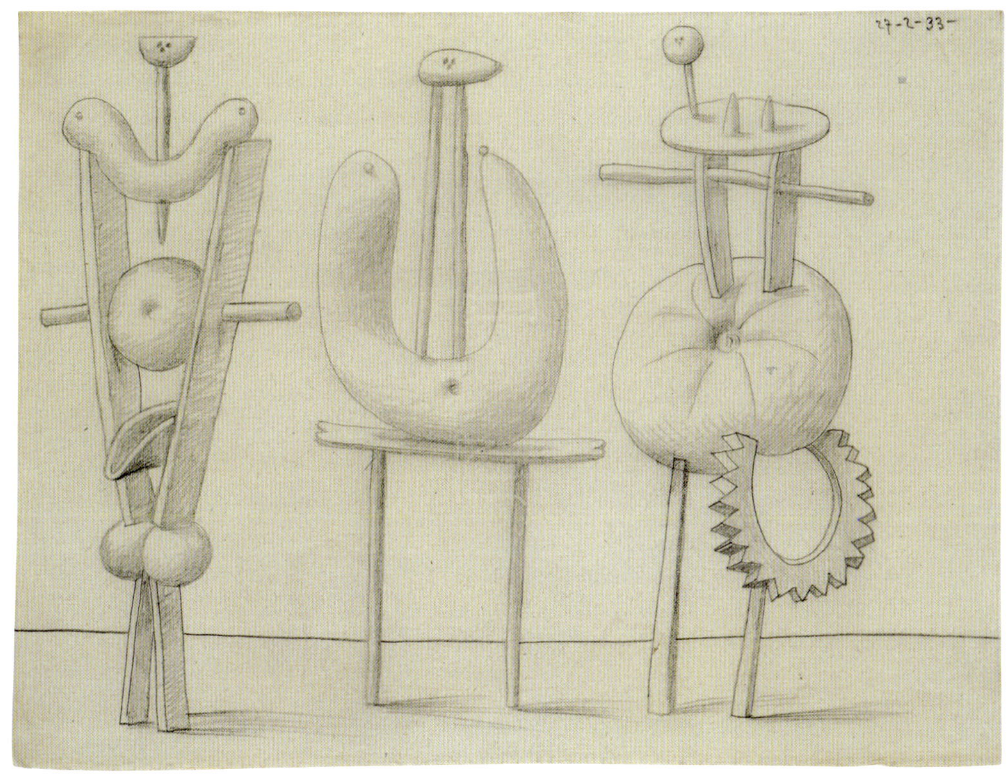

61. **AN ANATOMY: THREE WOMEN.** [Paris], February 26, 1933
Graphite on fine-textured wove paper
7 ⅞ × 10 ¾ in. (20 × 27.3 cm)
Musée national Picasso–Paris. Dation Pablo Picasso

62. **AN ANATOMY: THREE WOMEN.** [Paris], February 27, 1933
Graphite on fine-textured wove paper
7 ⅞ × 10 ⅝ in. (20 × 27 cm)
Musée national Picasso–Paris. Dation Pablo Picasso

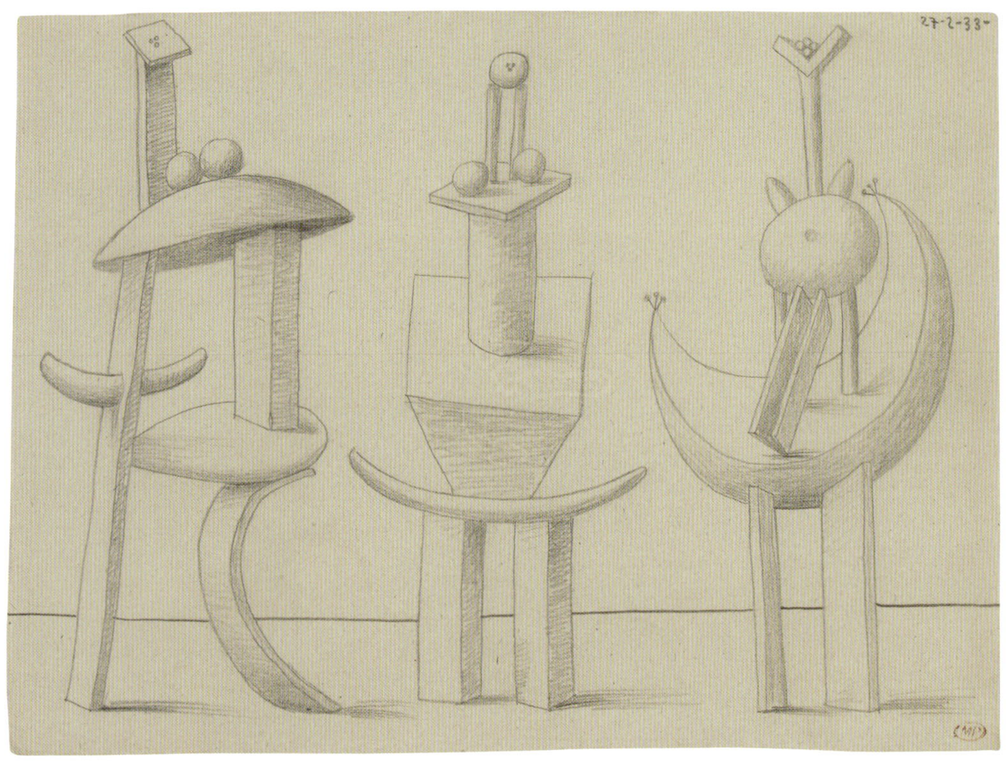

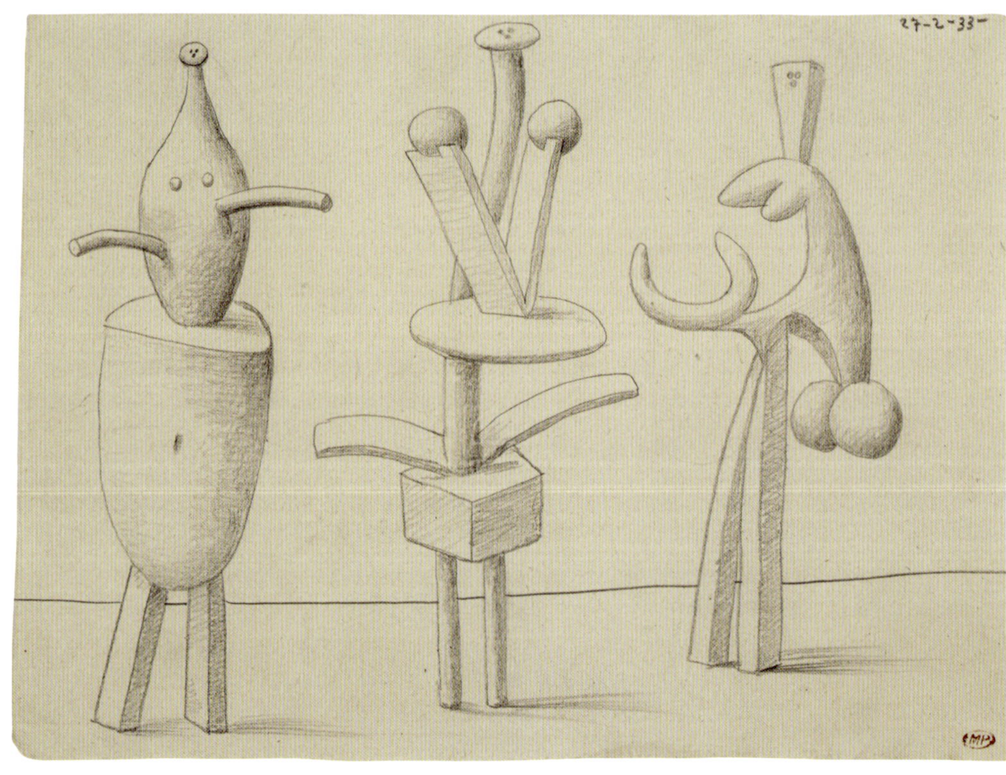

63. AN ANATOMY: THREE WOMEN. [Paris], February 27, 1933
Graphite on fine-textured wove paper
7 7/8 × 10 5/8 in. (20 × 27 cm)
Musée national Picasso–Paris. Dation Pablo Picasso

64. AN ANATOMY: THREE WOMEN. [Paris], February 27, 1933
Graphite on fine-textured wove paper
7 13/16 × 10 13/16 in. (19.8 × 27.4 cm)
Musée national Picasso–Paris. Dation Pablo Picasso

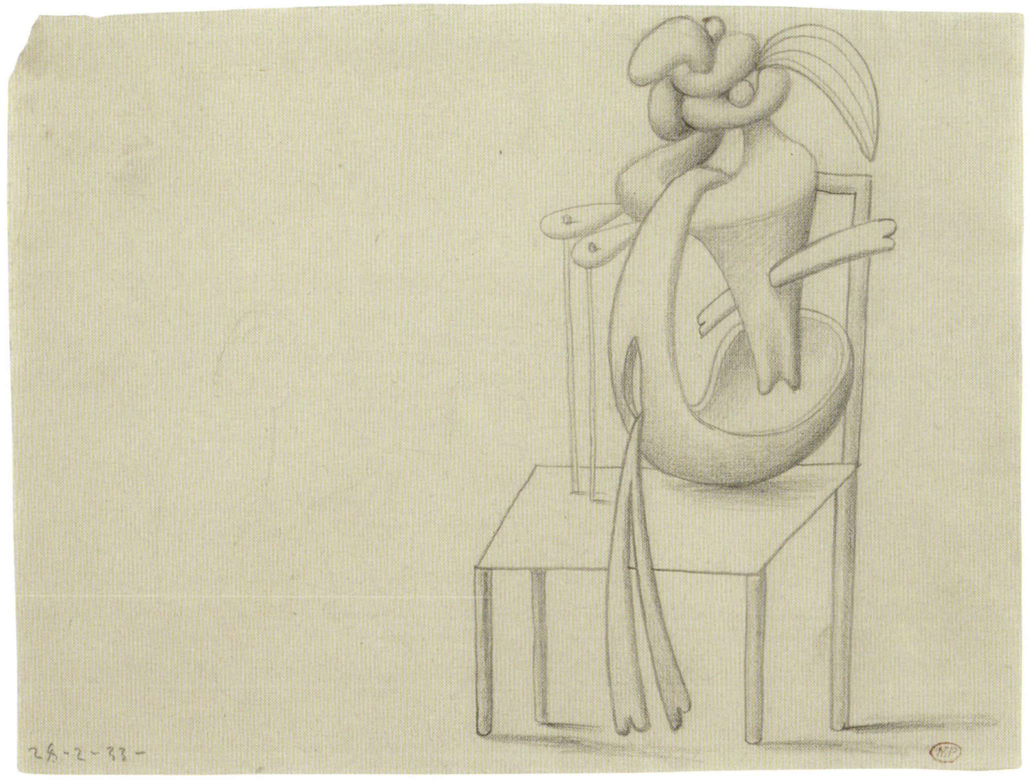

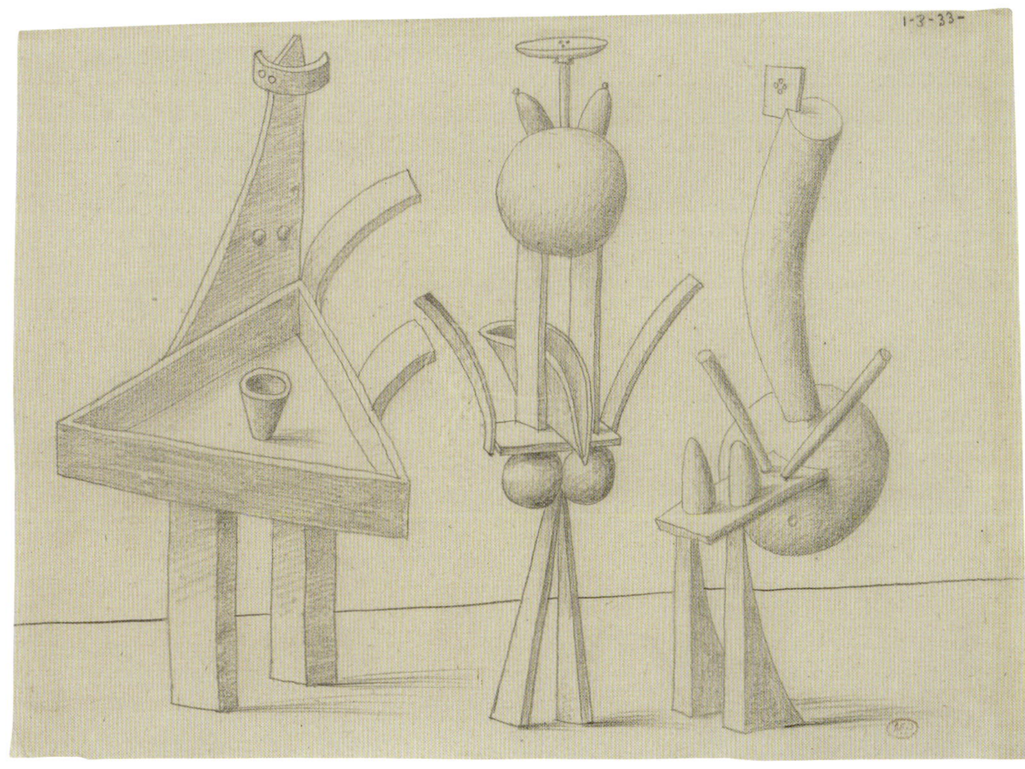

65. **AN ANATOMY: SEATED WOMAN.** [Paris], February 28, 1933
Graphite on fine-textured wove paper
7⅞ × 10⅝ in. (20 × 27 cm)
Musée national Picasso–Paris. Dation Pablo Picasso

66. **AN ANATOMY: THREE WOMEN.** [Paris], March 1, 1933
Graphite on fine-textured wove paper
7 11/16 × 10¾ in. (19.5 × 27.3 cm)
Musée national Picasso–Paris. Dation Pablo Picasso

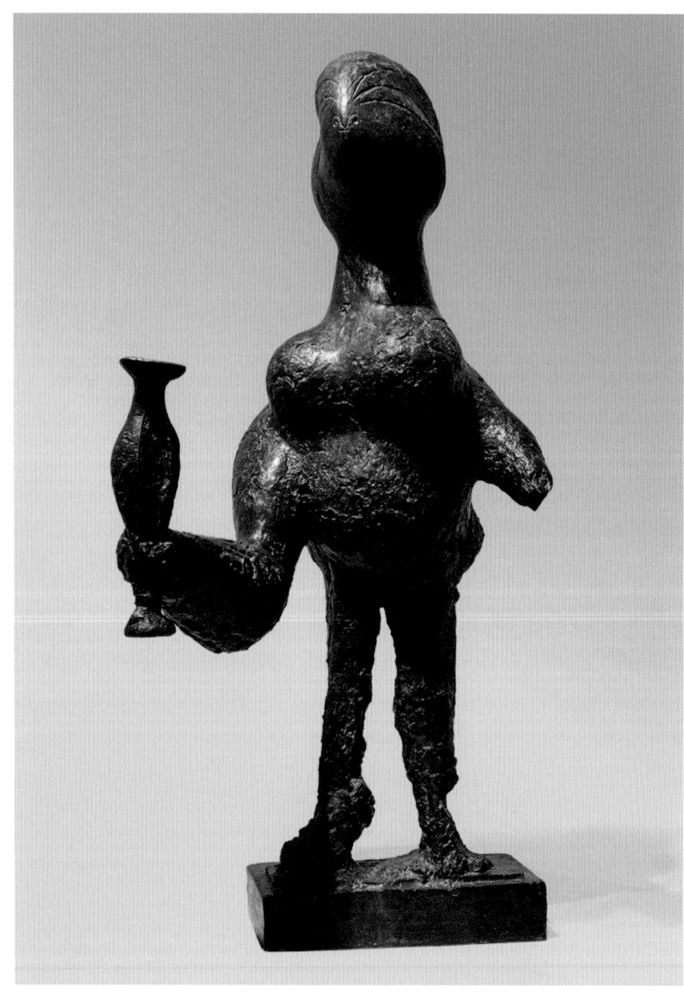

67. **WOMAN WITH VASE.** Boisgeloup, summer 1933
Bronze, cast 1972 or 1973
7 ft. 2 5/8 in. × 48 1/16 in. × 43 5/16 in. (220 × 122 × 110 cm)
Museo Nacional Centro de Arte Reina Sofía, Madrid. Picasso Bequest

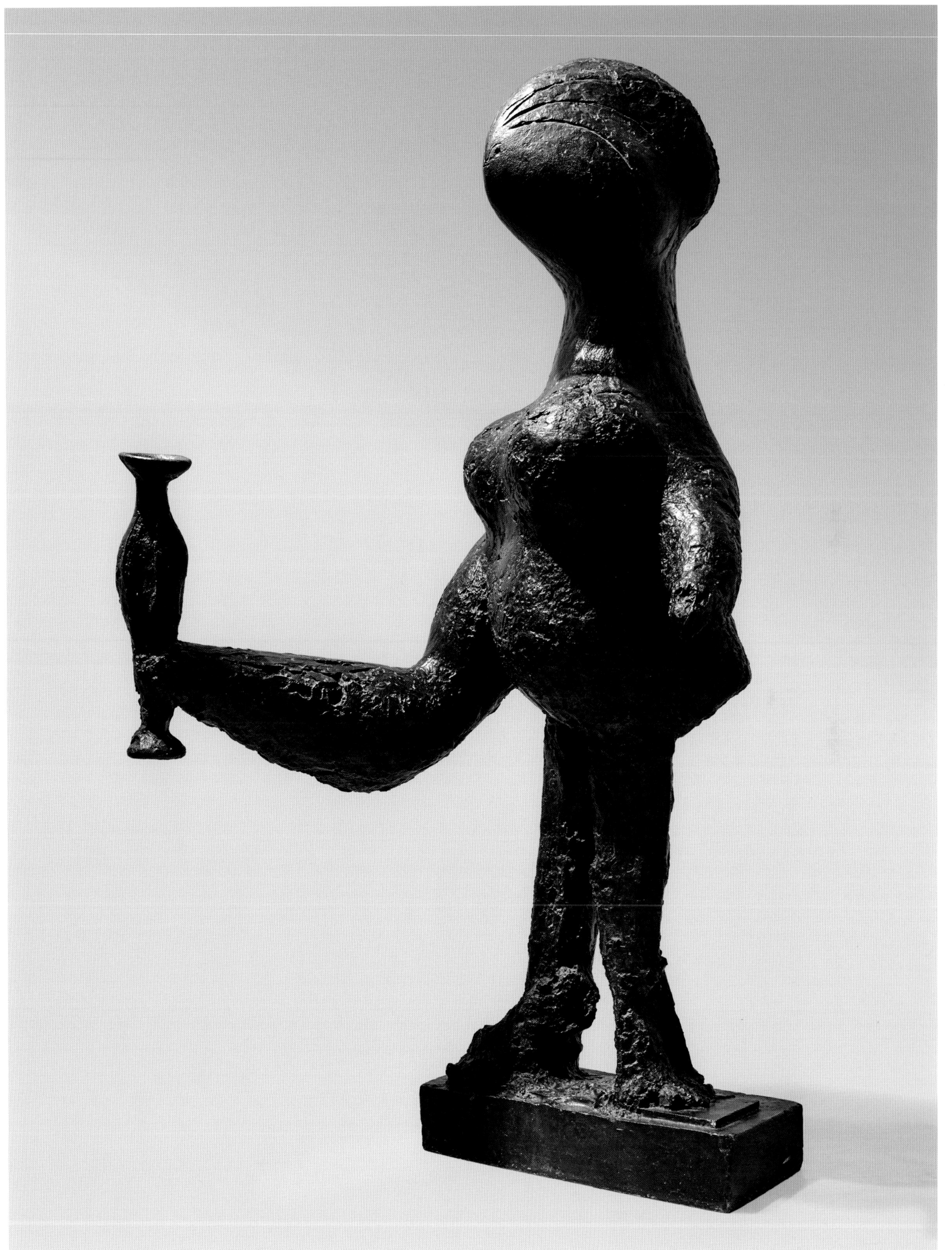

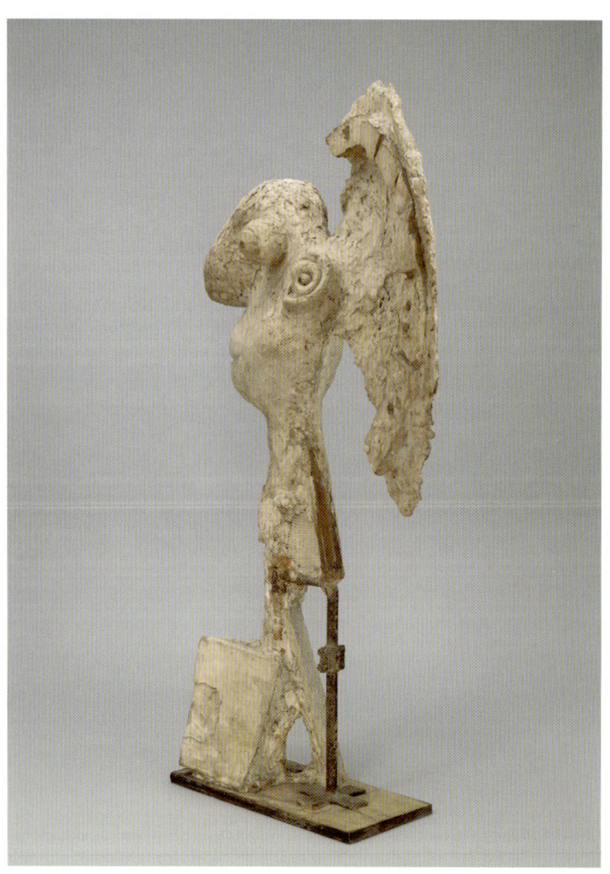

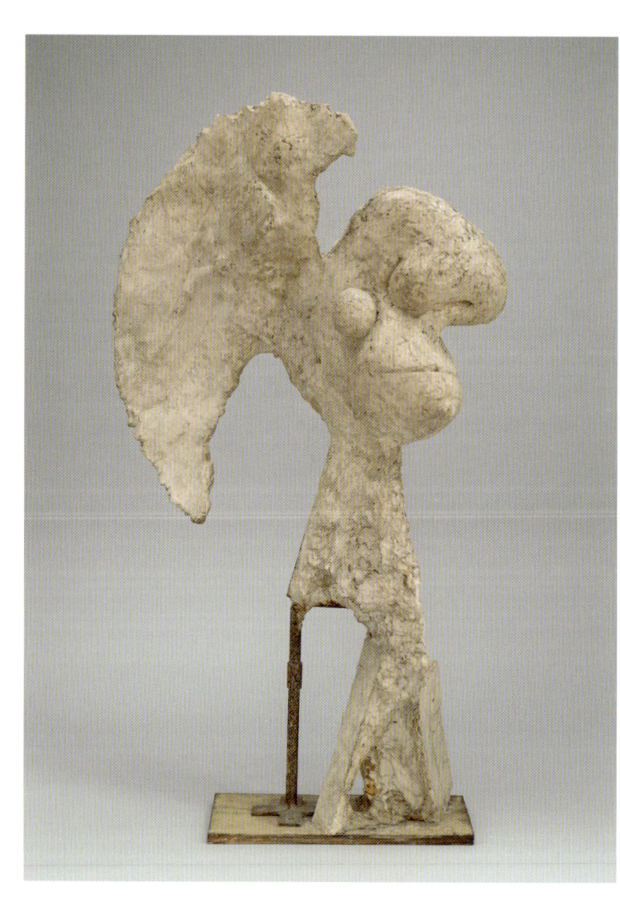

68. **HEAD OF A WARRIOR.** Boisgeloup, 1933
Plaster, metal, and wood
47½ × 9¾ × 27 in. (120.7 × 24.9 × 68.8 cm)
The Museum of Modern Art, New York. Gift of Jacqueline Picasso in honor of the Museum's continuous commitment to Pablo Picasso's art

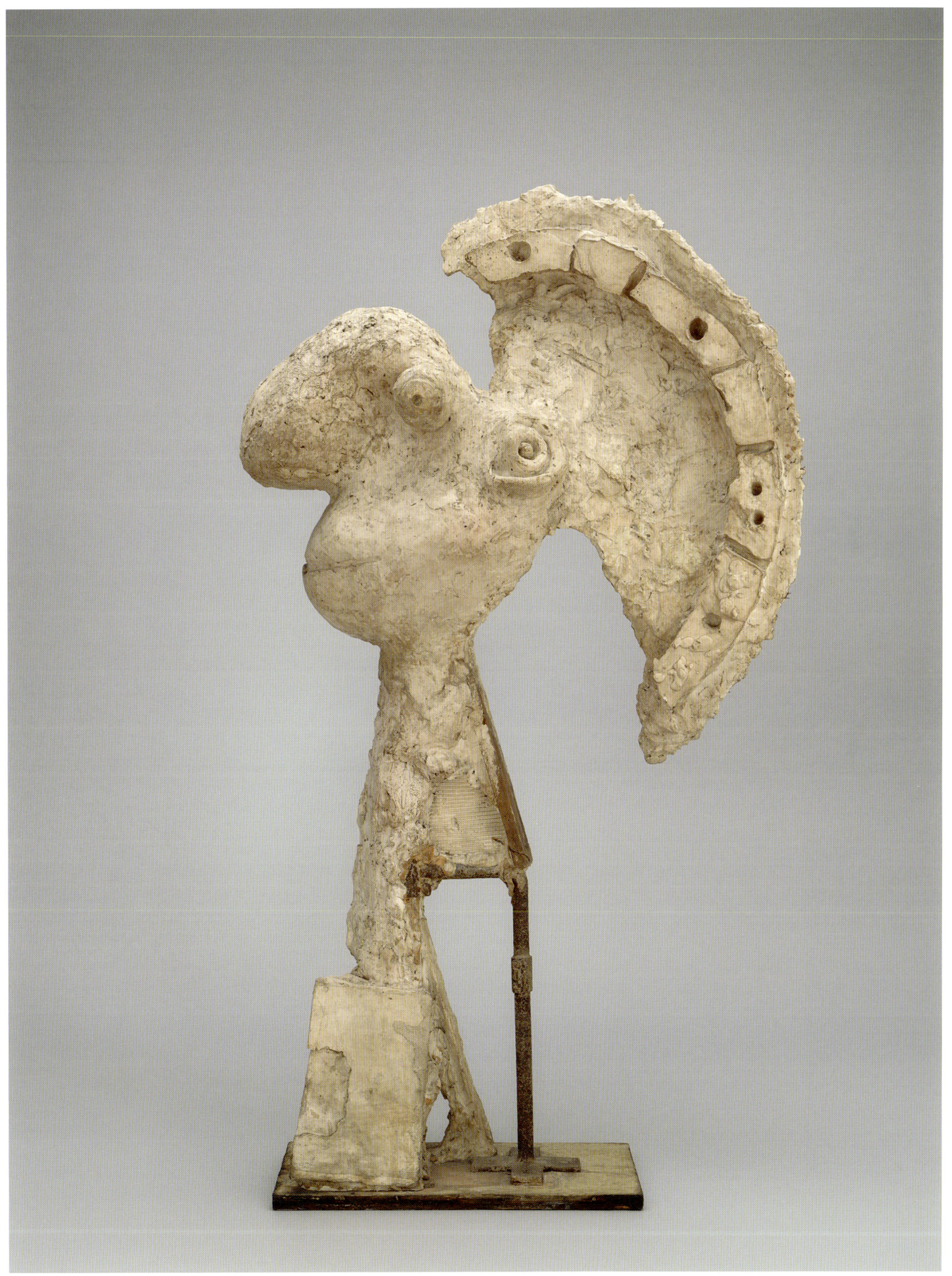

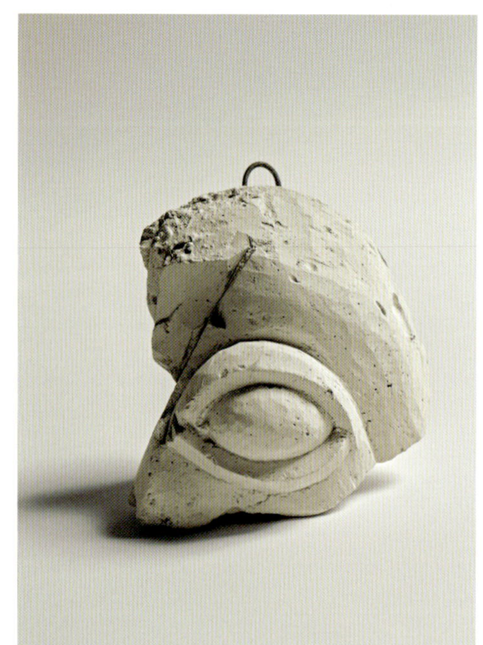

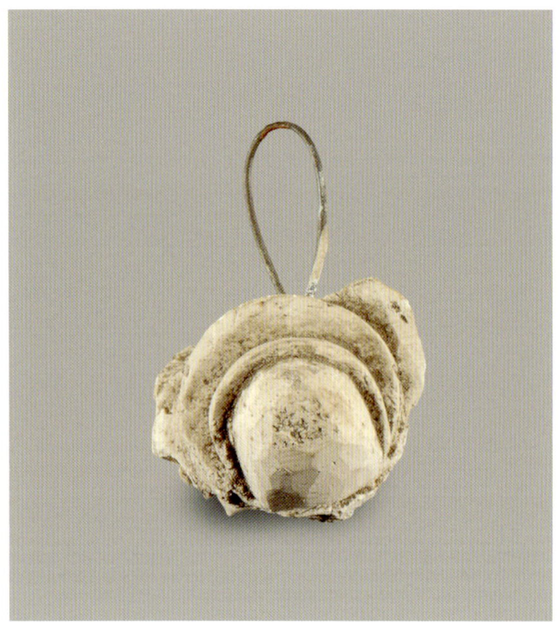

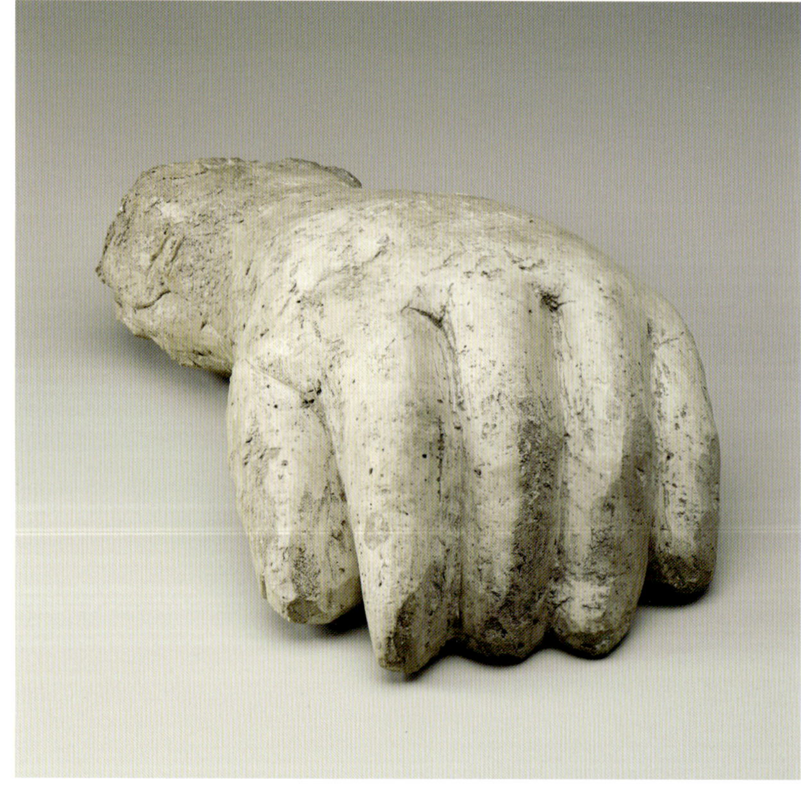

70. **EYE.** Boisgeloup, 1931
Plaster with iron-wire hook
2 3⁄16 × 5 1⁄8 × 4 1⁄2 in. (5.5 × 13 × 11.5 cm)
Private collection. Courtesy Fundación Almine y Bernard Ruiz-Picasso para el Arte

69. **EYE.** Boisgeloup, 1931–32
Plaster with iron-wire hook
3 3⁄8 × 2 3⁄8 × 1 9⁄16 in. (8.5 × 6 × 4 cm)
Kravis Collection

71. **HAND.** Boisgeloup, [fall 1932 or earlier]
Plaster with newspaper and wire hook
14 9⁄16 × 7 11⁄16 × 4 5⁄16 in. (37 × 19.5 × 11 cm)
Musée national Picasso–Paris. Dation Pablo Picasso

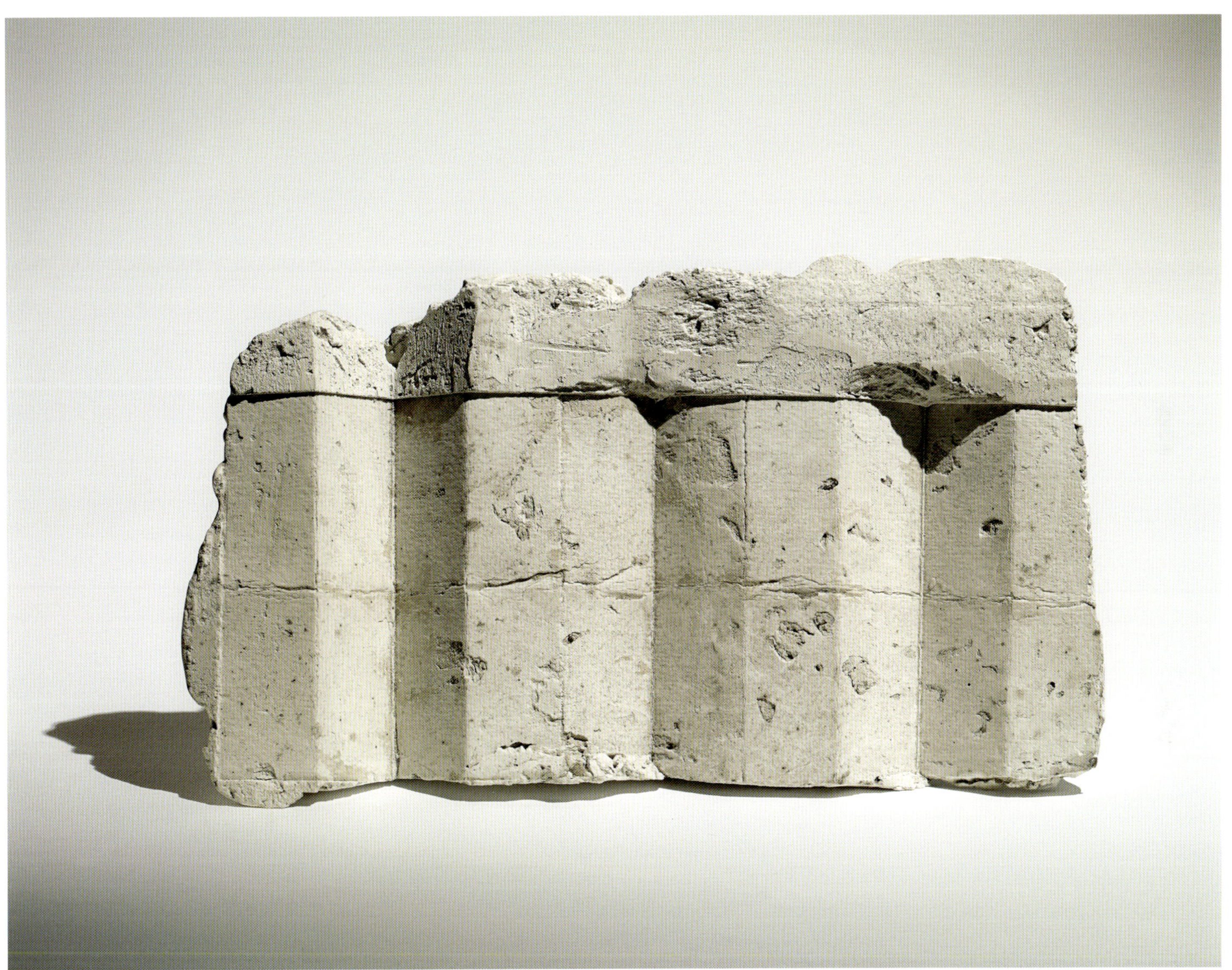

72. **RELIEF.** [Paris], 1934
Plaster, 5 ½ × 10 1/16 × 1 in. (14 × 25.5 × 2.5 cm)
Private collection. Courtesy Fundación Almine y Bernard Ruiz-Picasso para el Arte

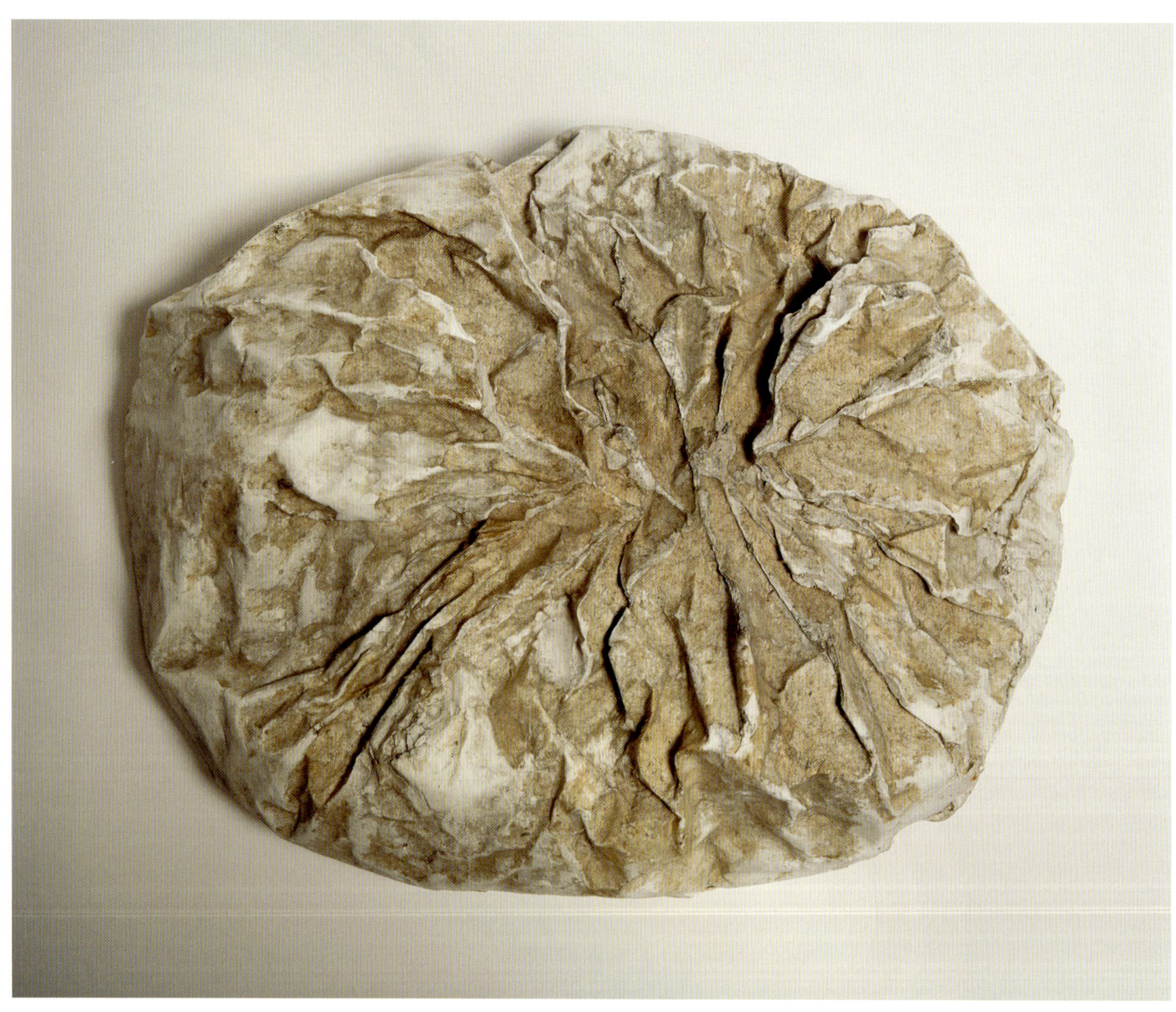

73. **CRUMPLED PAPER.** Boisgeloup, 1934
Plaster
4 5/16 × 12 3/8 × 9 7/16 in. (11 × 31.5 × 24 cm)
Musée national Picasso–Paris. Gift of Marina Ruiz-Picasso

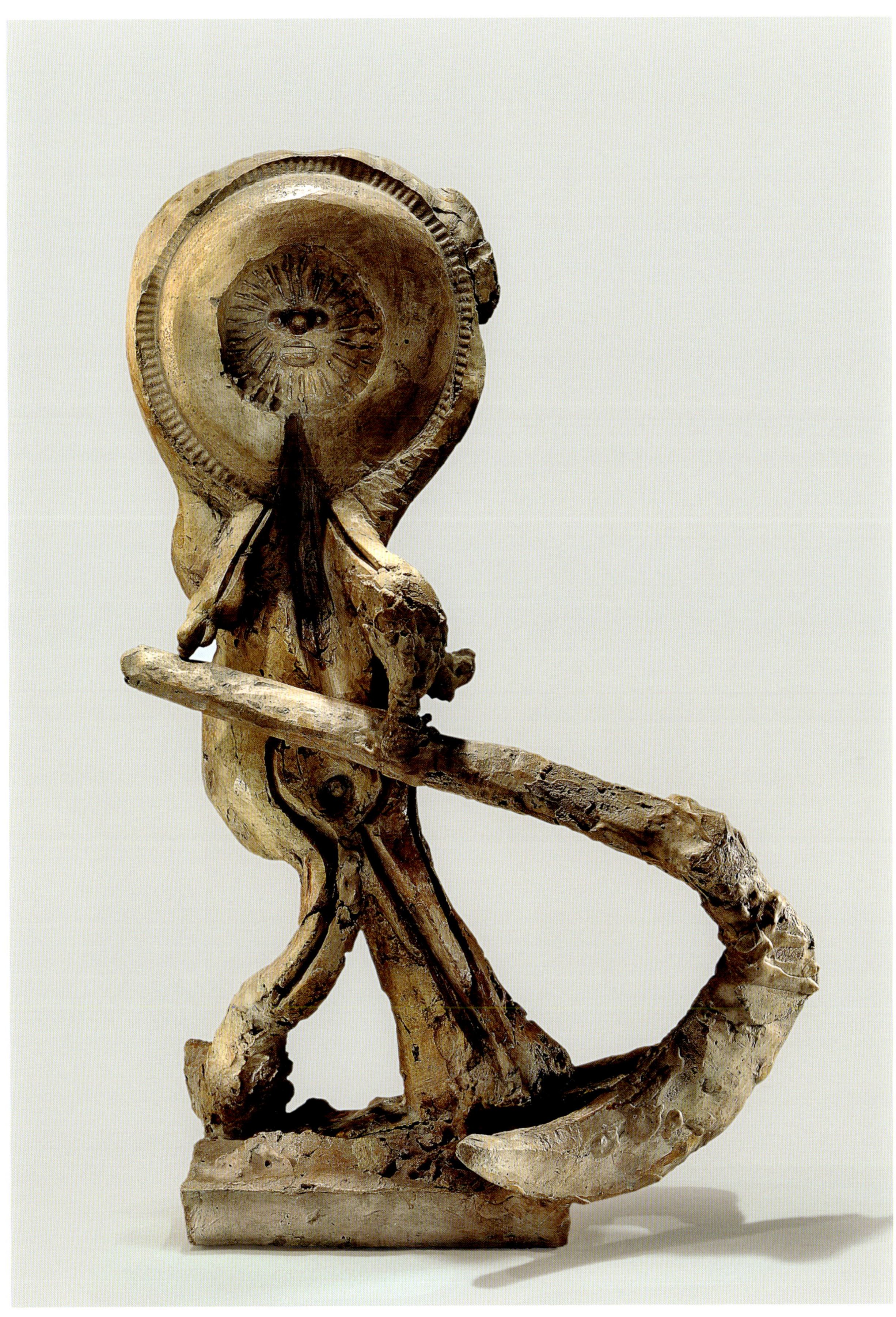

74. **THE REAPER.** Boisgeloup, c. 1934
Plaster and wood
20 ½ × 13 ⅜ × 8 ¼ in. (52 × 34 × 21 cm)
Private collection

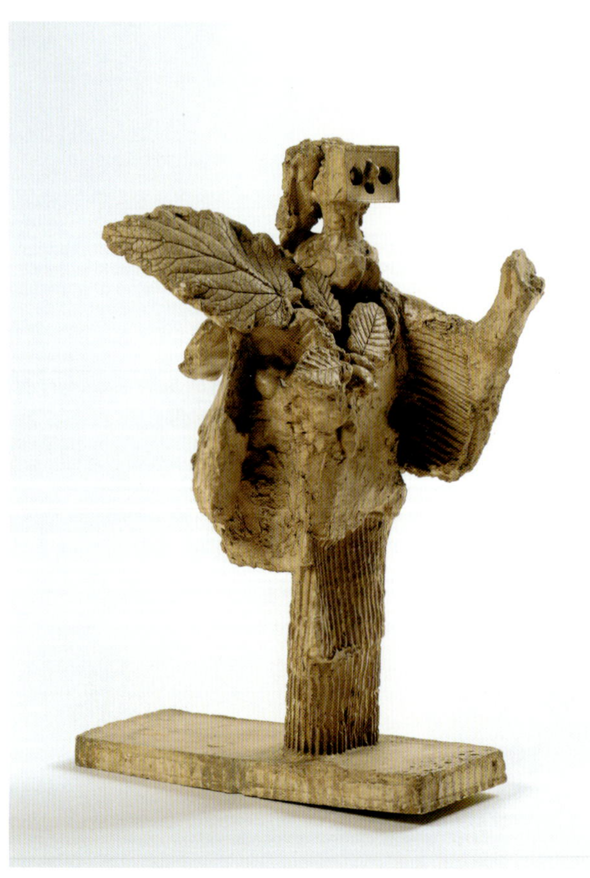

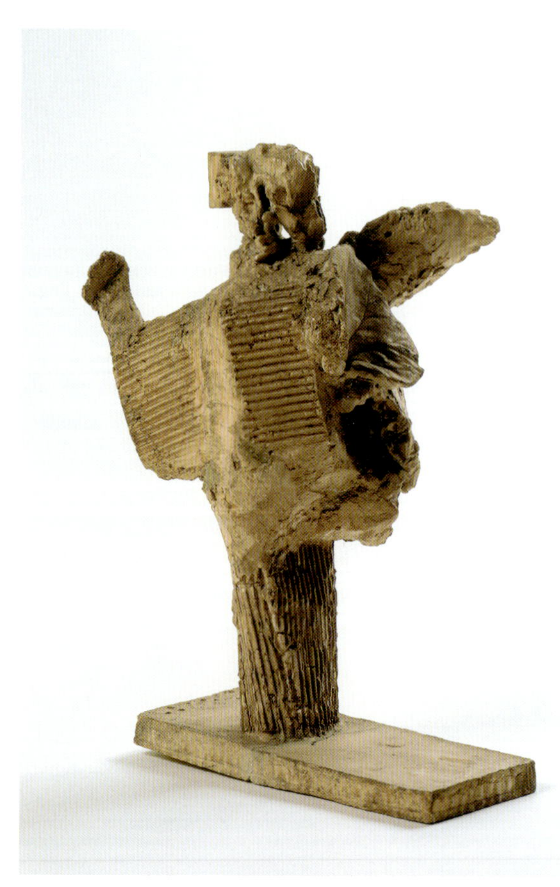

75. **WOMAN WITH LEAVES.** Boisgeloup, 1934
Plaster
15 3⁄16 × 10 13⁄16 × 8 1⁄4 in. (38.5 × 27.5 × 21 cm)
Private collection. Courtesy Fundación Almine y Bernard Ruiz-Picasso para el Arte

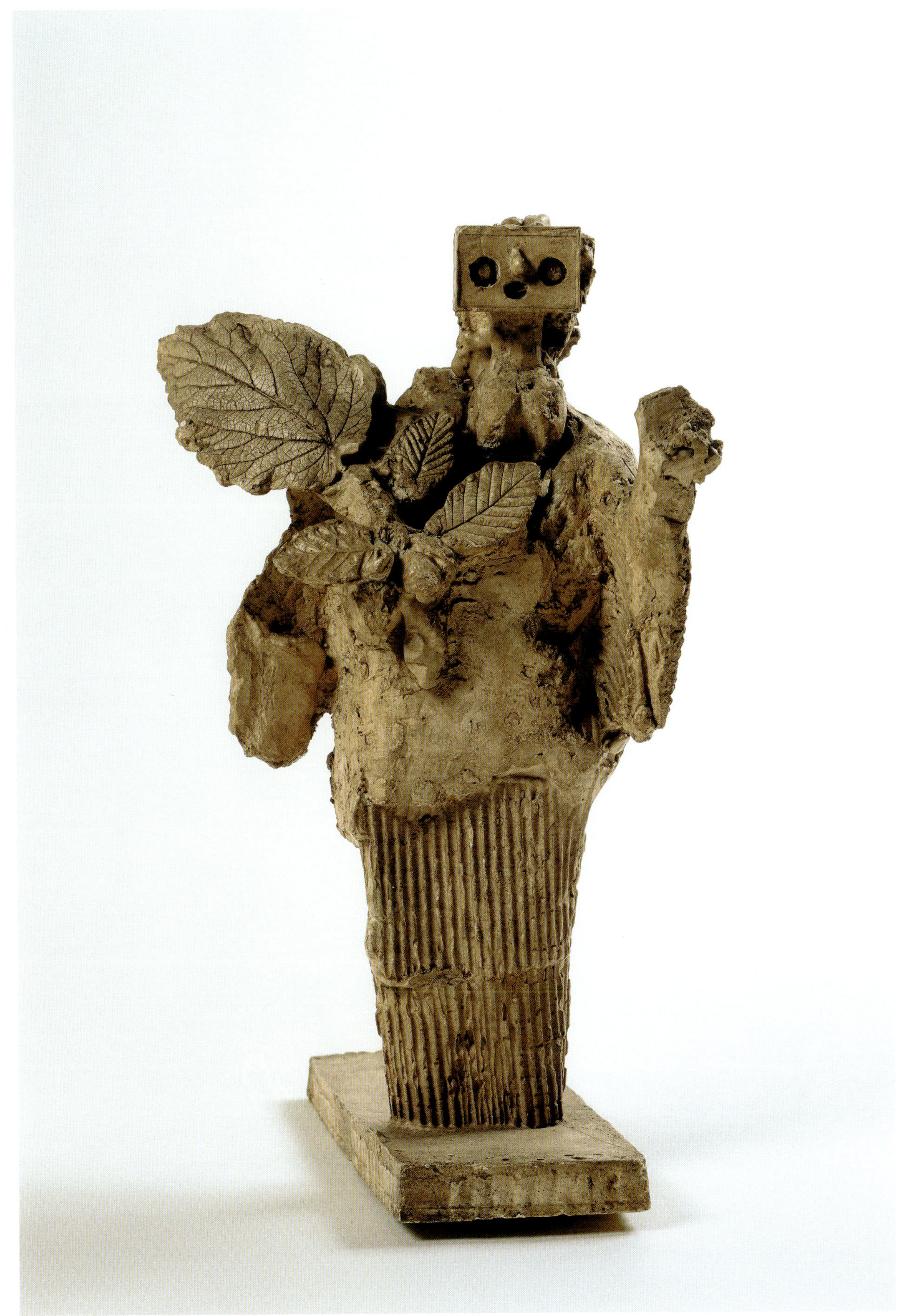

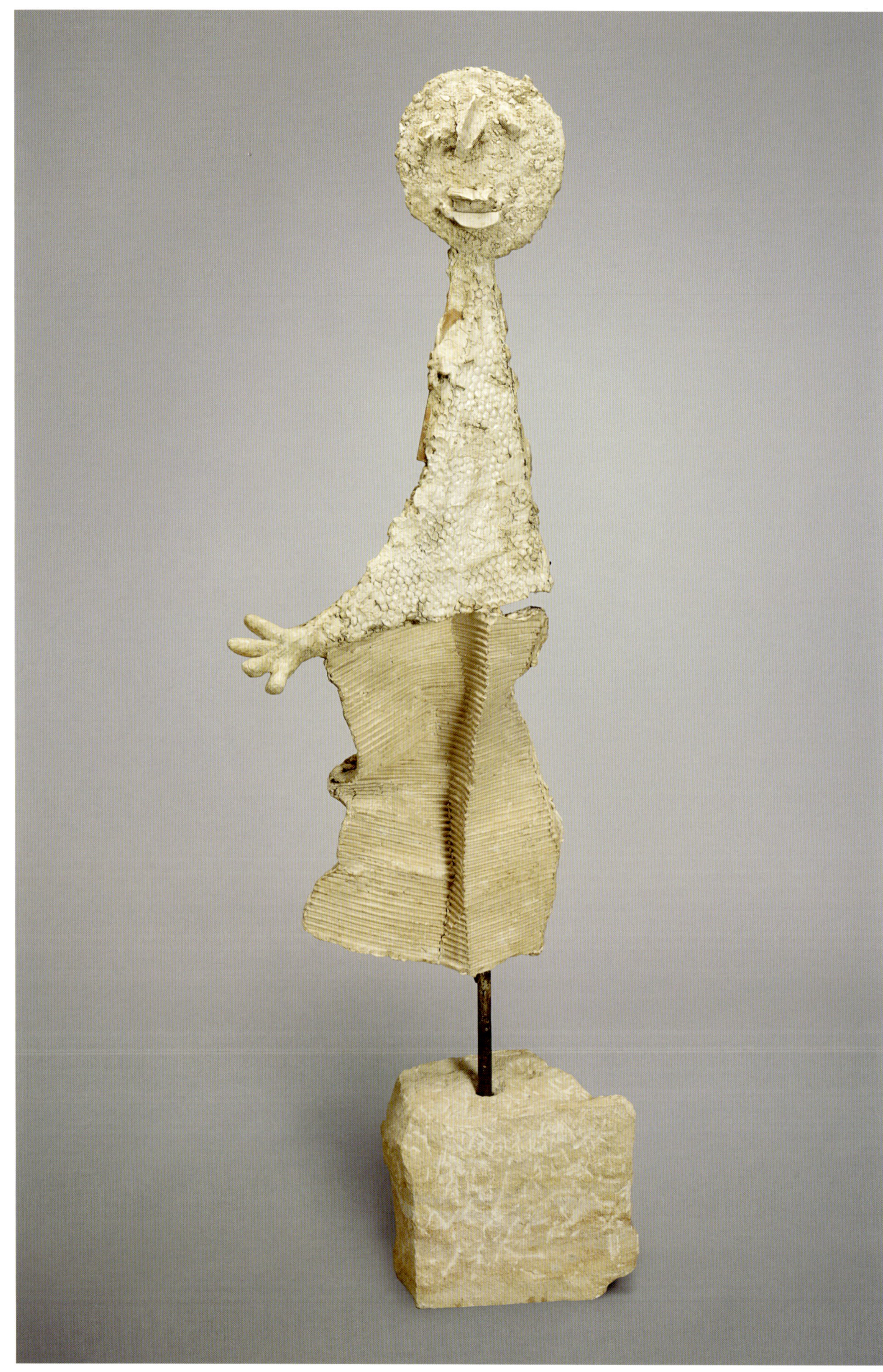

76. **THE ORATOR.** 1933–34
Plaster, stone, and metal dowel
72 × 26 × 10 ⅝ in. (182.9 × 66 × 27 cm)
Fine Arts Museums of San Francisco. Museum purchase,
Roscoe and Margaret Oakes Income Fund and Art Trust Fund

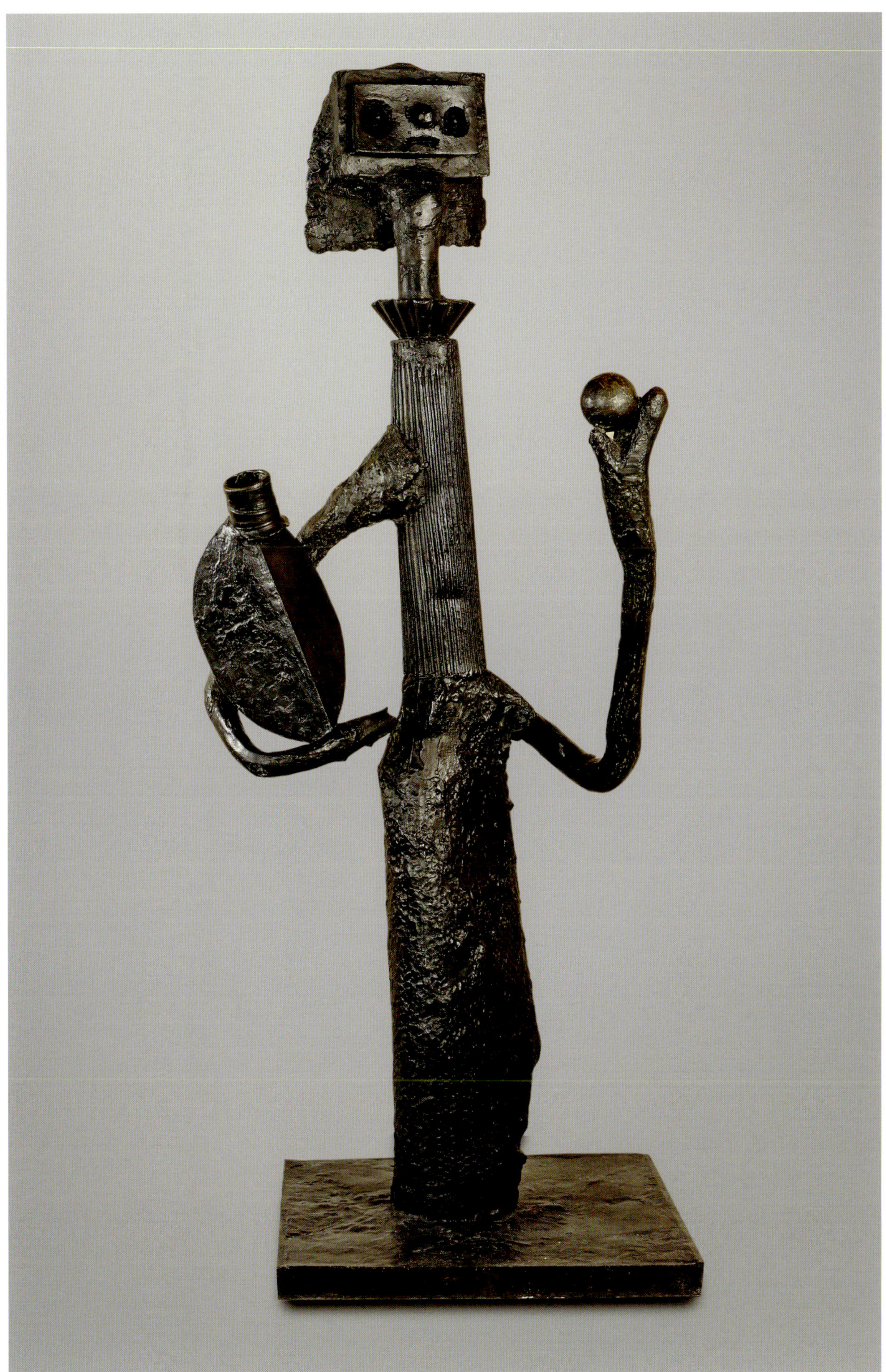

77. **WOMAN WITH ORANGE** or **WOMAN WITH APPLE.** Boisgeloup, c. 1934
Bronze, unique, cast by September 1943
71 1/16 × 29 1/2 × 26 9/16 in. (180.5 × 75 × 67.5 cm)
Musée national Picasso–Paris. Dation Pablo Picasso

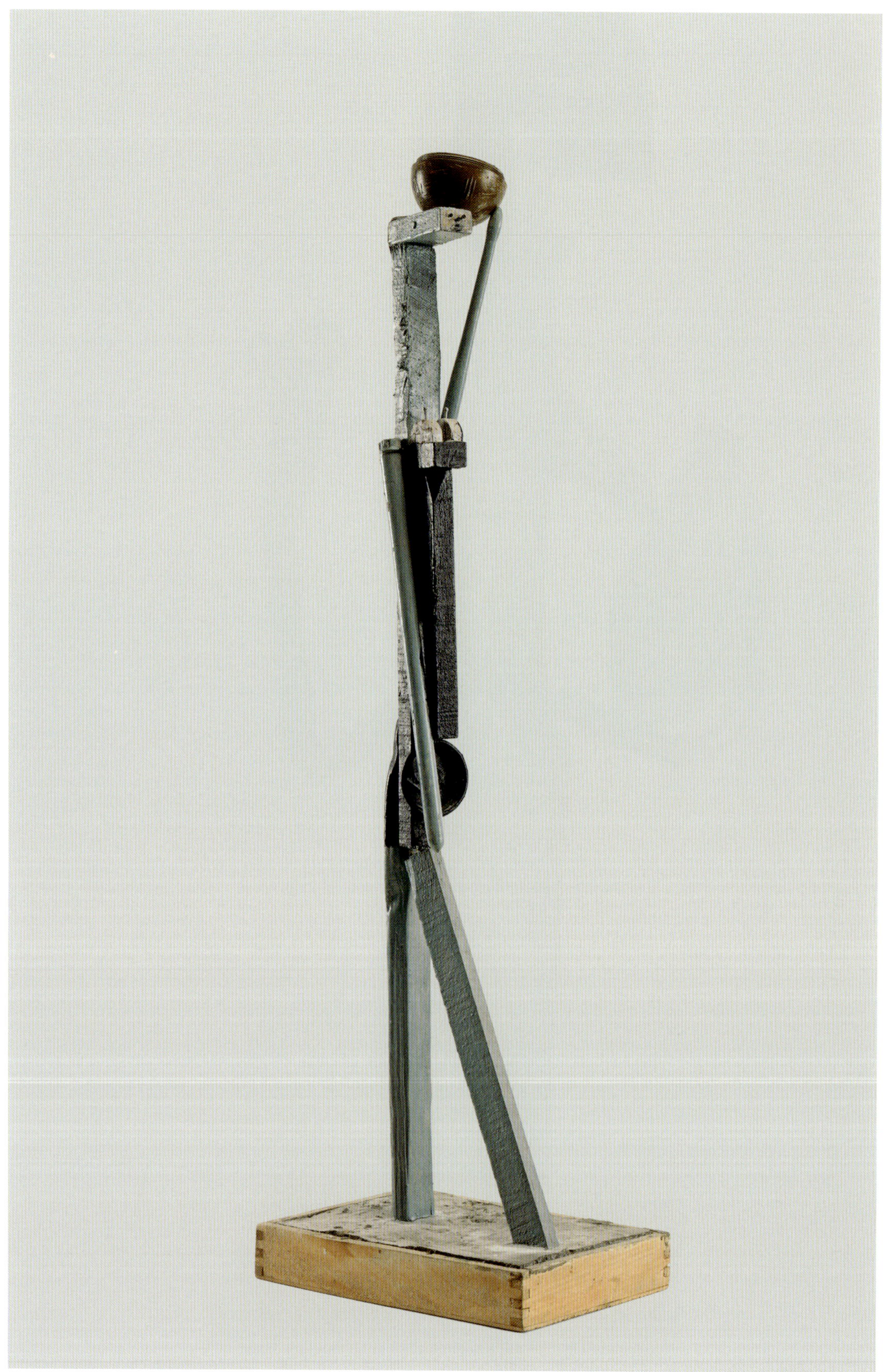

78. **WOMAN CARRYING A VESSEL.** [Paris or Boisgeloup], 1935
Painted pieces of wood, objects, and nails on a cement and wood base
23 5/8 × 5 1/2 × 7 1/4 in. (60 × 14 × 18.4 cm)
Musée national Picasso–Paris. Dation Pablo Picasso

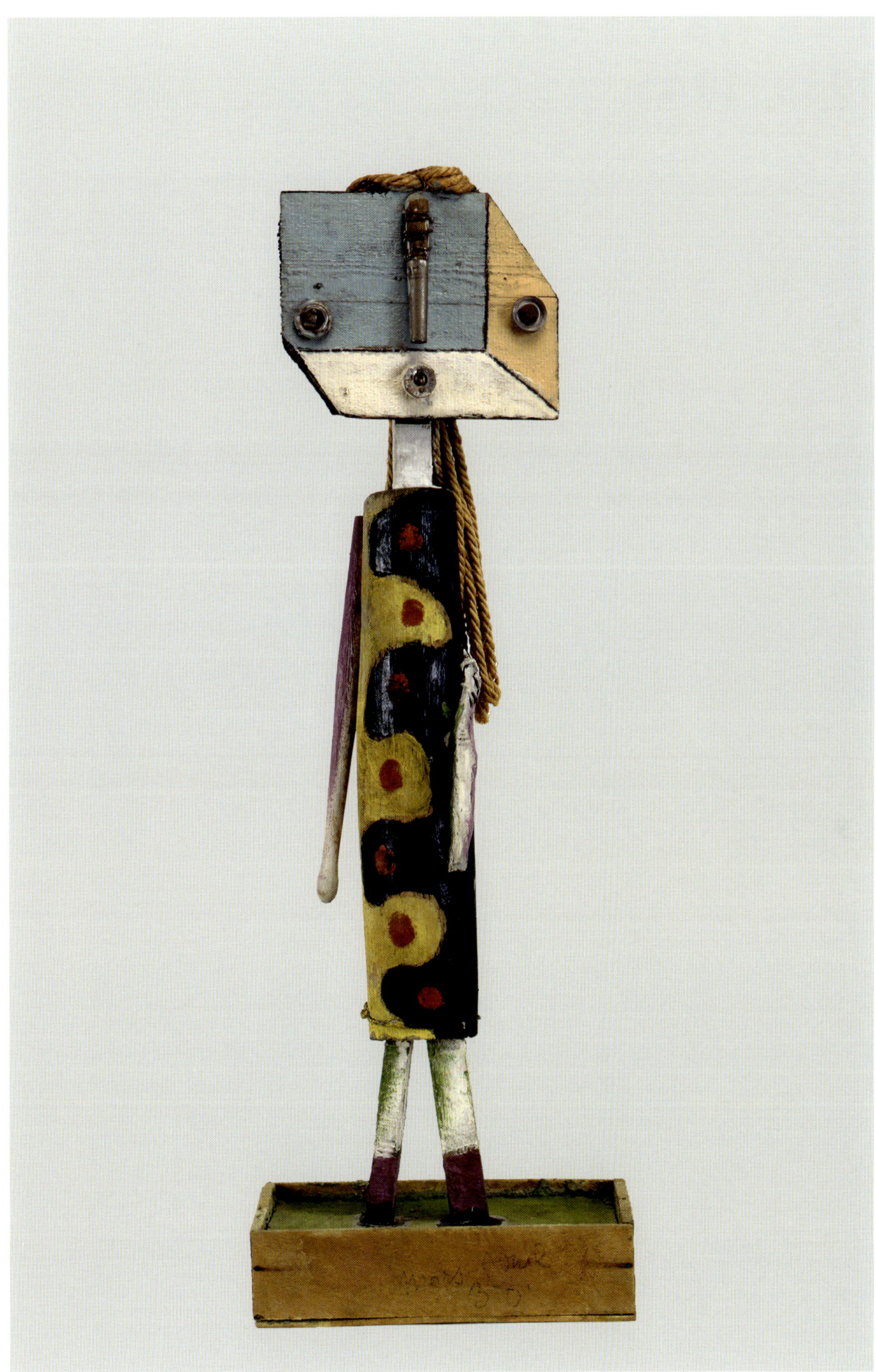

79. **FIGURE.** Mougins, spring 1938
Painted wood, nails, and screws with string, wire, paintbrush fragments, and push-bell hardware on an unfired clay and wood base
22 13/16 × 7 7/8 × 4 5/16 in. (58 × 20 × 11 cm)
Private collection

CHAPTER 6

THE WAR YEARS 1939–1945

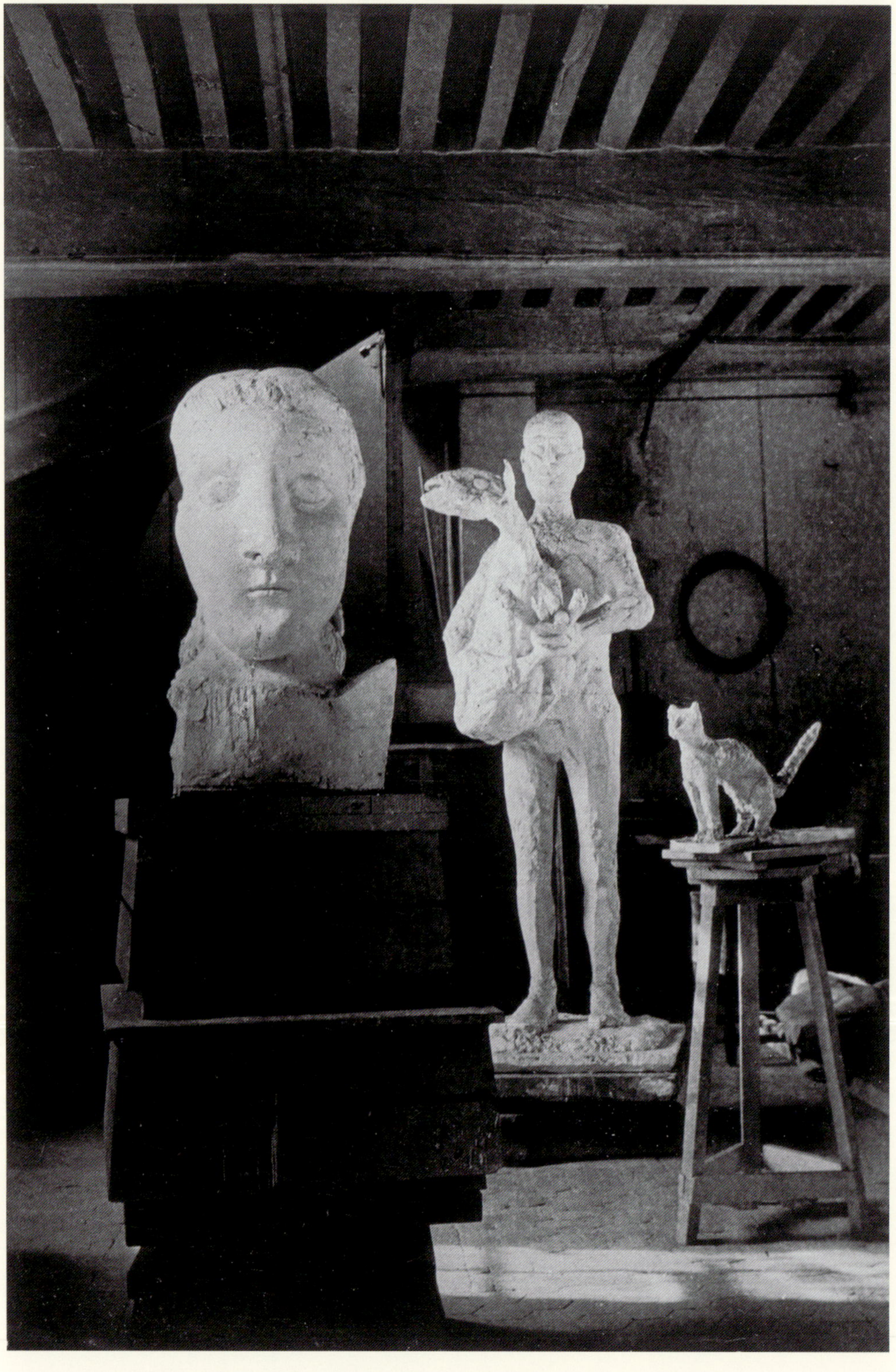

Picasso's studio at 7, rue des Grands-Augustins, with the artist's sculptures *Head of a Woman* (1941) at left, *Man with a Lamb* (1943) at center, and *Cat* (1941) at right, Paris, 1943. Photograph by Brassaï. Musée national Picasso–Paris

PICASSO WAS ONE of the few artists designated "degenerate" by the Germans to remain in occupied Paris during the war years. His home base was two floors at 7, rue des Grands-Augustins, on the Left Bank near the Seine, which he had rented as a studio space since 1937. This was a storied building, having served as a setting for Honoré de Balzac's 1831 novella *The Unknown Masterpiece*. But Paris itself was nearly unrecognizable. In the words of the photographer Brassaï, who also stayed during the Occupation, it was "a Paris without taxis, cigarettes, sugar, chocolate, fancy breads; a Paris of rhubarb, Jerusalem artichoke, rutabaga, saccharine; a Paris of lines and coupons, curfews and scrambled airwaves, propaganda newspapers and films; a Paris of German patrols, yellow stars, air raids, roadsteads, arrests, execution notices."[1]

Having declined many offers of emigration, Picasso chose an existence that was difficult and dangerous. He was forbidden to exhibit, and publication of his works was banned. The move into his studio from his grand apartment at 23, rue La Boétie in fall 1940 may have been prompted by lack of public transport but also by the advent of new neighbors: the Nazis had seized the gallery and home of Picasso's dealer Paul Rosenberg, at 21, rue La Boétie, and they soon installed there a bureau devoted to anti-Semitic propaganda. Picasso's defiance of rules during the Occupation ranged from eating meat on proscribed days of the week to secretly casting his plasters in bronze, transporting camouflaged sculptures to and from the foundry by night. Bronze casting was a measure taken in the interest of posterity that Picasso credited to the advice of his live-in amanuensis, Jaime Sabartés; it was applied to plasters brought from Boisgeloup as well as works newly made in Paris. The investment in bronze carried with it an irony that Picasso willfully ignored: the possibility of destruction—intentional or random—was an ongoing threat that no material could overcome.

Picasso had ceased making sculpture in the late 1930s, but the move to rue des Grands-Augustins brought with it an enthusiastic return to the enterprise. He converted the bathroom into a sculpture studio, explaining to visitors that it was the only room for which the city's restricted utilities provided adequate heat. Picasso returned to modeling, somehow managing to obtain enough clay and plaster to produce an imposing population of human and animal figures for his crowded spaces. As exemplified by the harrowing *Death's Head* (pl. 82), the spirit of these sculptures is understandably solemn, with none of the erotic pleasure or childlike whimsy of the works made in Boisgeloup. Unlike the fanciful creatures of the previous decade, the sculptures of the war years are generally quite lifelike in appearance; for equally naturalistic precedents one must go back almost forty years to figures such as *The Jester* (pl. 3) and *Head of a Woman (Fernande)* (pl. 4). But as was true even then, Picasso almost never worked from a model and instead relied on his memory and instincts to achieve verisimilitude.

The largest sculpture of this period, both physically and symbolically, is the seven-foot *Man with a Lamb* (pl. 87), modeled in clay in early 1943. Standing naked with his feet planted apart, gazing straight ahead, and firmly gripping a restless animal, the figure has a strikingly authoritative presence. This sculpture was made in a day, frantically assembled on an armature that was too weak for the quantities of clay Picasso piled upon it. Exceptionally among Picasso's sculptures, *Man with a Lamb* was the product of months of reflection. Numerous sketchbook drawings dating back to summer 1942 depict the anonymous hero, who began as a notably younger and frailer man. Haunting drawings of the finished figure suggest a rare instance in Picasso's career when the subject of a particular sculpture carried deep but unexplained meaning for him.

Picasso's penchant for witty assemblage did not altogether disappear during these somber times. *Bull's Head* (pl. 88) is simply a strategic pairing of a leather bicycle seat and a pair of metal handlebars, a relatively instantaneous sculpture later cast in bronze. Even more reductive is *The Venus of Gas* (pl. 89), which is nothing more than the iron burner of a gas stove that caught the artist's eye as a modern incarnation of an ancient fertility goddess. This work is the closest Picasso would come to making a Duchampian readymade, but its difference is key: whereas visual metaphor is secondary in Duchamp's reasoning, for Picasso the object holds interest on that basis only. Accordingly, *The Venus of Gas* is one of the few sculptures titled by Picasso himself, as his personal reading wholly defines its existence as a work of art.

SEPTEMBER 12, 1939: In preparation for the exhibition *Picasso: Forty Years of His Art*, Alfred H. Barr, Jr., director of The Museum of Modern Art, contacted Picasso to ask for his assistance in bringing "some representative pieces of your sculpture to America."[1] Less than two weeks before, on September 3, France had declared war on Germany, increasing the difficulty of securing loans of artworks from Europe. Barr had copies of his letter to Picasso sent to the dealers Daniel-Henry Kahnweiler and Paul Rosenberg and the artist and collector Mary (Meric) Callery, based in Paris, in the hope that they could help in procuring additional sculptures (fig. 1). In his letter Barr stated, "We do not need, however, any of the early bronzes, since some are already in this country—including the cubist head."[2] Kahnweiler forwarded his copy on to Picasso on September 20, adding, "I am sending you a letter from Barr who asks if you want to give him your sculptures, even if it's not a complete set. They don't need the older bronzes, nor the Cubist head. They have hired Lerondelle for the transport. He also says Dora [Maar] is supposed to send photographs of the sculptures.... It appears that your paintings have arrived safely, and that they are cleaning a few with great care, as you asked."[3]

Two years earlier, in June 1937, the Nazi party had begun a campaign to confiscate so-called degenerate modern art from German museums and art collections, and Picasso was among the artists whose works were seized. It was in this context that Barr began organizing Picasso's first monographic show at the Museum.[4]

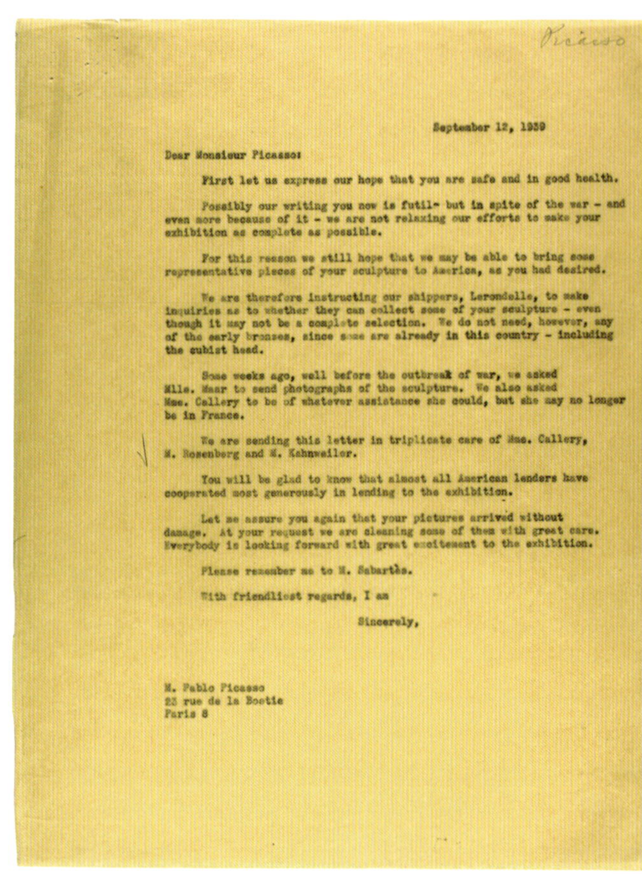

Picasso

September 12, 1939

Dear Monsieur Picasso:

First let us express our hope that you are safe and in good health.

Possibly our writing you now is futil- but in spite of the war - and even more because of it - we are not relaxing our efforts to make your exhibition as complete as possible.

For this reason we still hope that we may be able to bring some representative pieces of your sculpture to America, as you had desired.

We are therefore instructing our shippers, Lerondelle, to make inquiries as to whether they can collect some of your sculpture - even though it may not be a complete selection. We do not need, however, any of the early bronzes, since some are already in this country - including the cubist head.

Some weeks ago, well before the outbreak of war, we asked Mlle. Maar to send photographs of the sculpture. We also asked Mme. Callery to be of whatever assistance she could, but she may no longer be in France.

We are sending this letter in triplicate care of Mme. Callery, M. Rosenberg and M. Kahnweiler.

You will be glad to know that almost all American lenders have cooperated most generously in lending to the exhibition.

Let me assure you again that your pictures arrived without damage. At your request we are cleaning some of them with great care. Everybody is looking forward with great excitement to the exhibition.

Please remember me to M. Sabartès.

With friendliest regards, I am

Sincerely,

M. Pablo Picasso
23 rue de la Boetie
Paris 8

1. Carbon copy of a letter from Alfred H. Barr, Jr., to Picasso, care of Daniel-Henry Kahnweiler, September 12, 1939. The Museum of Modern Art Archives, New York

SEPTEMBER 18 OR 19, 1939: Brassaï, who had first photographed the sculptures at Boisgeloup in late 1932, visited Picasso in Paris. *Life* magazine had commissioned him to photograph Picasso and his work for an article to run that fall in conjunction with the exhibition at The Museum of Modern Art. Brassaï would become one of Picasso's closest associates during the war years in Paris. His memoir, *Conversations avec Picasso* (Conversations with Picasso), published in 1964, provides an unrivaled eyewitness account of the period.

NOVEMBER 15, 1939–JANUARY 7, 1940: *Picasso: Forty Years of His Art* was mounted at The Museum of Modern Art. Nine days before the exhibition opened, the Museum announced in a press release that the last of the European loans had passed through customs in New York, further explaining that despite "the war risk on the ocean, loans from abroad have been arriving at the Museum for the past two months."[5] Barr cabled the artist on December 15 to tell him that the show was a "colossal success" and, with more than sixty thousand visitors, had surpassed the attendance of a recent exhibition of work by Vincent van Gogh.[6] Barr not only asked for the prices of two objects illustrated in the catalogue but also inquired whether Picasso would agree to have his work go on a grand tour in the United States, since the war hindered its return to Paris. Between 1940 and 1943, four iterations of *Picasso: Forty Years of His Art* would travel the country, the most widely seen and circulated exhibition since the Museum's opening in 1929.

The exhibition included four early bronzes and a sand-covered relief construction of 1930. Barr had not succeeded in obtaining loans of many of the sculptures he had wished to include. In the catalogue he wrote, "The most serious disappointment caused by the war is the absence of a large and very important group of Picasso's recent sculpture some of which was being cast especially for the show."[7] The photographer Brassaï stated that new bronzes were cast specifically for the exhibition, but there is no evidence that this came to pass.[8] In the catalogue, Barr used photographs and paintings to illustrate the more recent sculptures. A photograph taken by A. E. Gallatin and titled "Sculpture in Picasso's studio at Gisors, 1933" was included with the caption, "Most of Picasso's recent sculpture has been done at his country estate, Boisgeloup, near Gisors on the border of Normandy. In Mr. Gallatin's photograph are two of a series of the large plaster heads."[9]

EARLY 1940: Picasso rented a studio at the villa Les Voiliers in Royan, a seaside resort in southwestern France. Between February and August 1940, he moved back and forth between Paris and this studio near the sea.

APRIL–MAY 1940: In a letter dated April 26, 1940, a "Mr. F. Guastini, Founder of Bronze Art Pieces" wrote to Picasso to make arrangements to retrieve several models from the artist's studio at 7, rue des Grands-Augustins, in Paris, which he had been renting since early 1937.[10] A second letter from Guastini, dated May 9, indicated that he had the models in his possession at his foundry on rue de Belleville, in Courbevoie, northeast of Paris, and casting work was about to begin: "In response to your letter, which I received today from the Galerie Simon, I am pleased to meet your needs concerning the models you gave me to be reproduced in bronze." Guastini named and provided pricing for three sculptures. "As soon as the wax models are ready, I will let you know a week beforehand, and I will ask you to be punctual about retouching them so that the wax models won't suffer from the heat, if it is hot out" (fig. 2).[11] The exchange between artist and founder indicates that Picasso was expected to retouch his wax models before they were transposed into bronze.

MAY 10, 1940: German forces invaded Belgium, successfully defeating French and British troops. They would cross the border into France two days later, on May 12, and eventually establish control over a large region of the country, including Paris. The German occupation, which lasted until 1944, imposed Nazi rule on much of the French populace as well as curfews, blackouts, and food shortages. Valsuani, the Paris foundry from which Picasso ordered most of his bronze casts, closed and would remain shuttered until 1947. Despite these hardships, of this period Picasso would later tell Brassaï, "Since Boisgeloup, I'd somewhat abandoned sculpture. Then suddenly, it got the better of me again."[12] Toward the end of May, he corresponded with Dante Canestri of Valsuani, which still held seven bronzes and several plasters by the artist.[13] Aware that the foundry could be bombed at any time, as Allied forces began a strategic campaign to destroy industrial facilities that could aid the German war effort, Picasso asked his close friend and secretary Jaime Sabartés to contact the foundry through Kahnweiler in order to bring the works to the safety of the rue des Grands-Augustins studio.

MAY 16, 1940: Picasso departed for Royan, and two weeks later Sabartés informed Guastini, through Kahnweiler, that the sculptor would be unable to retouch the wax models and so casting should proceed without him.[14]

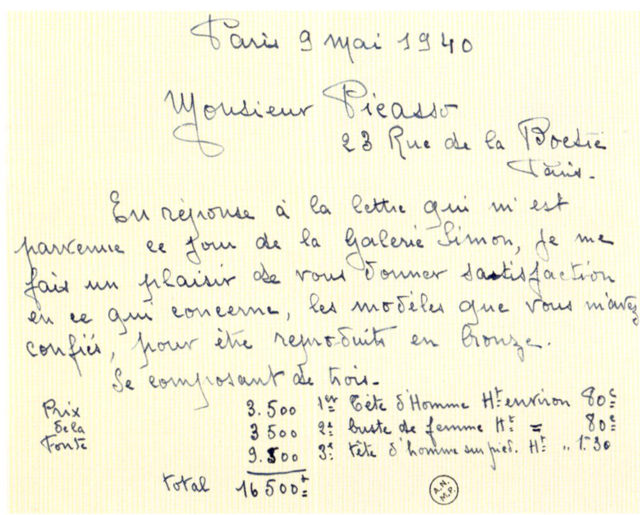

Paris 9 mai 1940

Monsieur Picasso
23 Rue de la Boetie
Paris.

En réponse à la lettre qui m'est parvenue ce jour de la Galerie Simon, je me fais un plaisir de vous donner satisfaction en ce qui concerne, les modèles que vous m'avez confiés, pour être reproduits en bronze.

Se composant de trois.

Prix de la Fonte
3.500 1re Tête d'Homme Ht environ 80c
3 500 2e buste de femme Ht = 80c
9.500 3e tête d'homme sur pied. Ht " 1m30

Total 16500f

2. Letter from F. Guastini to Picasso, May 9, 1940. Picasso Archives, Musée national Picasso–Paris

JUNE 10, 1940: In a letter dispatched from Paris to Royan, Christian Zervos, the artist's friend and publisher, informed Picasso, "A friend of mine coming from Gisors just told me that the Germans were there and that they were heading to Pontoise. You have told me, I believe, that all your works have been moved . . . to a secure place."[15] In a separate note enclosed in the envelope, Zervos added, "As I was about to mail this letter, I met a soldier coming from Gisors. He tells me that the Germans did not enter [the town], but what they did do is beyond imagination. It seems that nothing still stands and that the town is in complete ruins."[16] Picasso's country estate, Boisgeloup, was located near Gisors. German troops entered Paris on June 14.

JULY–AUGUST 1940: Zervos continued to write to Picasso in Royan to update him about mutual friends and the situation in Paris. On July 24, Zervos informed him that the Spanish ambassador had posted notices on the door at 23, rue La Boétie and 7, rue des Grands-Augustins, placing them under his protection.[17] Zervos assured the artist that everything was being done to keep his works, especially his sculpture, safe. He informed Picasso that a number of bronzes and plasters were being transported to his Paris studio with the help of Canestri from the Valsuani foundry; one bronze cast of the 1932 *Cock* (see pl. 58), however, had been left with Callery because it was too large and heavy to be carried on the Paris metro.[18] Zervos also entrusted Callery with part of the manuscript for the first book of the second volume of his catalogue raisonné of Picasso's work, which she took with her to New York. He told the artist that even if the manuscript remained unpublished, he hoped that at the very least it had been deposited safely at the library of The Museum of Modern Art.[19]

AUGUST 25, 1940: Picasso returned to Paris from Royan, which had been invaded by the Germans on June 23. For many years he had maintained a residence at 23, rue La Boétie, but by fall he would leave it, instead living and working in his studio on rue des Grands-Augustins for the remainder of the war. That same fall, the Nazis looted the home and gallery of Picasso's neighbor and dealer Paul Rosenberg, at 21, rue La Boétie. In its place, in May 1941, they would install the office of the Institut d'Étude des Questions Juives (Institute for the study of the Jewish question).

NOVEMBER 12, 1940: After finally casting the bronze pieces planned in May, Guastini organized their delivery to Picasso, who stored them at the rue des Grands-Augustins studio.[20] Transporting the plasters to Guastini had been a challenge for Picasso, who, having been declared a "degenerate" artist by the Nazis, was under regular surveillance and was forbidden from exhibiting his work. Returning the casts to the artist's studio was an equally difficult undertaking. Picasso would later tell Brassaï that friends had assisted him in conveying the bronzes in wheelbarrows from the foundry at night: "It was even riskier bringing them back here in bronze, under the noses of the German patrols," he explained to Brassaï. "The 'merchandise' had to be camouflaged."[21]

AUGUST 1941: The article "Picasseries et Picasso," by Pierre Malo, was published in the journal *Comœdia*. In it the writer recounted a visit to Picasso's studio, describing a number of plaster sculptures the artist was then working on.

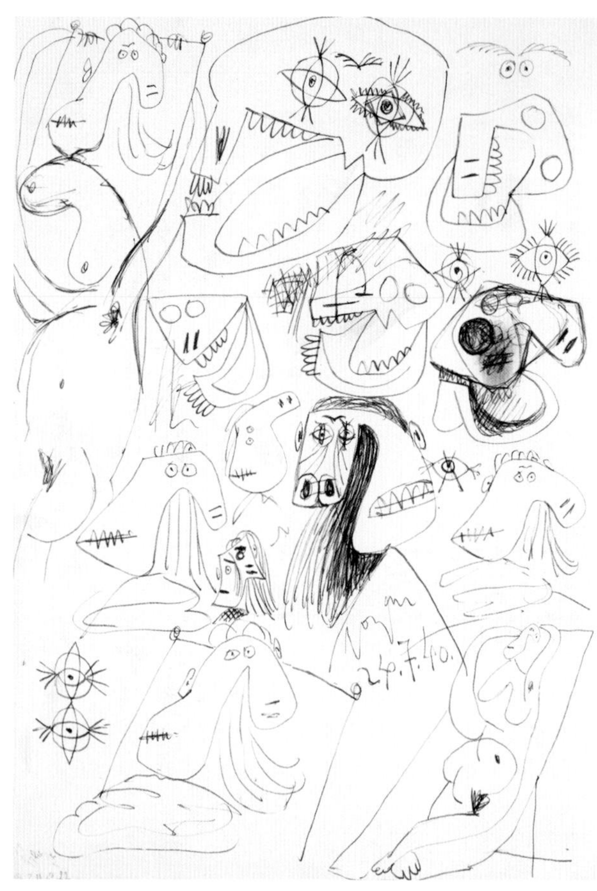

3. Pablo Picasso. Page from a sketchbook featuring death's heads. July 24, 1940. Pencil and ink on paper, 16 ¼ × 11 13/16 (41.3 × 30 cm). Musée national Picasso–Paris

***CAT*, 1941**

Picasso began modeling *Cat* (pl. 81) in plaster in the bathroom of the rue des Grands-Augustins studio, which was, with the severe fuel shortages during the war, "the only room you can heat in this big old barn," he told Brassaï.[22] In his article, Malo described seeing *Cat* "stretching at the bottom of the bath."[23] At least one of the two known bronze casts of the work would be made during the Occupation, as Brassaï recalled seeing the sculpture in bronze in September 1943.[24] *Cat* is characterized by a distinctive patina. The base of the sculpture is a brilliant gold, suggesting that it may have been cast in an alloy that incorporates a significant quantity of zinc; the dark patina above might have appeared naturally over time or it might have been applied by the artist.[25]

***DEATH'S HEAD*, [1941]**

During Malo's visit to Picasso's studio in 1941, he noticed, in addition to *Cat* in the bathtub, "a mocking death's head in the place of the sponge-bowl."[26] This reference strongly suggests that *Death's Head* (pl. 82)—which, like *Cat*, was modeled in plaster—was made in 1941.[27] The work has traditionally been dated to 1943, based on Françoise Gilot's description of its being cast in bronze in May of that year as well as its resemblance to other works of 1943, such as several paintings featuring animal skulls and a group of small terracotta death's heads.[28] But the motif of the death's head had been present in Picasso's imagination since at least 1940: a sketchbook page from July 24 of that year includes several, drawn in pencil and ink (fig. 3).

The asymmetry of *Death's Head* creates the impression of a grimace in contrapposto: viewed from the front, the right eye socket projects toward the viewer while the left recedes; the nasal cavity tilts to the left, while the mouth tilts upward to the right. Picasso used a variety of tools to mark the surface, leaving it rough and craggy, suggesting vestiges of flesh on the skull, or perhaps mummification.[29] Two bronze casts of *Death's Head* would be made during the Occupation, both of which appear on the floor of the rue des Grands-Augustins studio in a photograph by Brassaï taken in late September 1943 (fig. 4). Picasso admired Brassaï's ability to capture three-dimensional forms on film; he lamented of a previous

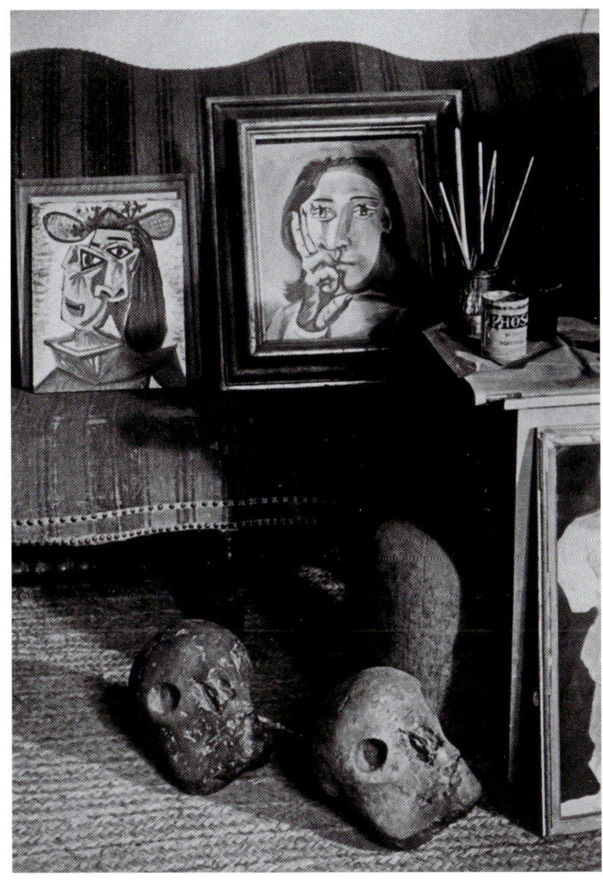

4. A corner of Picasso's studio at 7, rue des Grands-Augustins, with two casts of *Death's Head* on the floor, Paris, September 1943. Photograph by Brassaï. Musée national Picasso–Paris

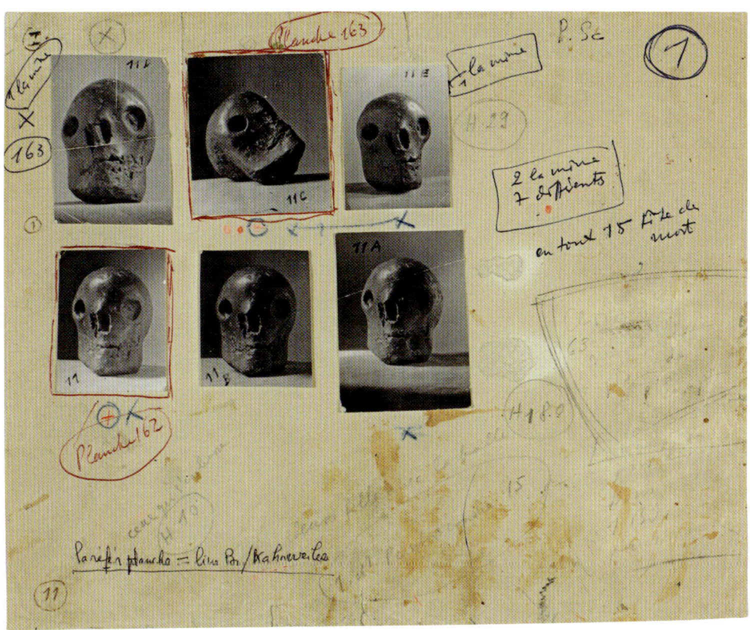

5. Brassaï. *Picasso's Sculptures: Contact Sheet 1*. Paris, [1946–late 1948]. Six gelatin silver prints glued on cardboard, with annotations by the photographer, 9 7/16 × 12 5/8 in. (24 × 32 cm). Centre Georges Pompidou, Paris

photographer's efforts, "My *Death's Head* has turned into a walnut."[30] Six work prints Brassaï pasted on a cardboard sheet reveal the various moods and faces of the sculpture and the careful attention with which he had recorded them (fig. 5).

HEAD OF A WOMAN, 1941

In the second half of 1941 Picasso sculpted a monumental head of his companion, the photographer and painter Dora Maar, in plaster (pl. 80). In addition to *Cat* and *Death's Head*, in his article Malo had mentioned "a goddess whose face Picasso has been tirelessly perfecting for months. Plaster runs in the sink, and a red feather duster springs from the drain hole. 'I brought all that back from the countryside,' my host informs me, his eyes sparkling with joy."[31] The "goddess," perched by the sink, was *Head of a Woman*; the work is visible in a photograph of the rue des Grands-Augustins bathroom taken around the same time.[32]

In 1959 a bronze cast of *Head of a Woman* would be placed in the square Laurent Prache in Paris, outside the church of Saint-Germain-des-Prés (fig. 6). Valsuani had created two

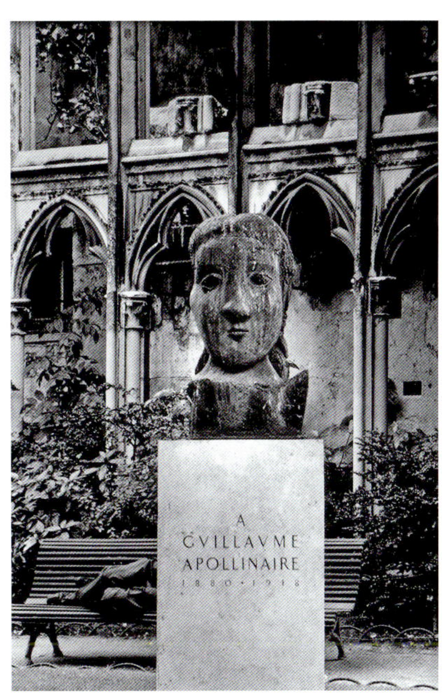

6. Bronze cast of *Head of a Woman* installed outside the church of Saint-Germain-des-Prés, Paris. Photograph by Gjon Mili. The Life Picture Collection/ Getty Images

casts of the sculpture sometime after the foundry reopened in 1947, and the Susse Frères foundry, also in Paris, created two more in 1958; it is a Valsuani cast that was installed at Saint-Germain-des-Prés. This event concluded a long saga that had begun in 1920, when a committee had first commissioned

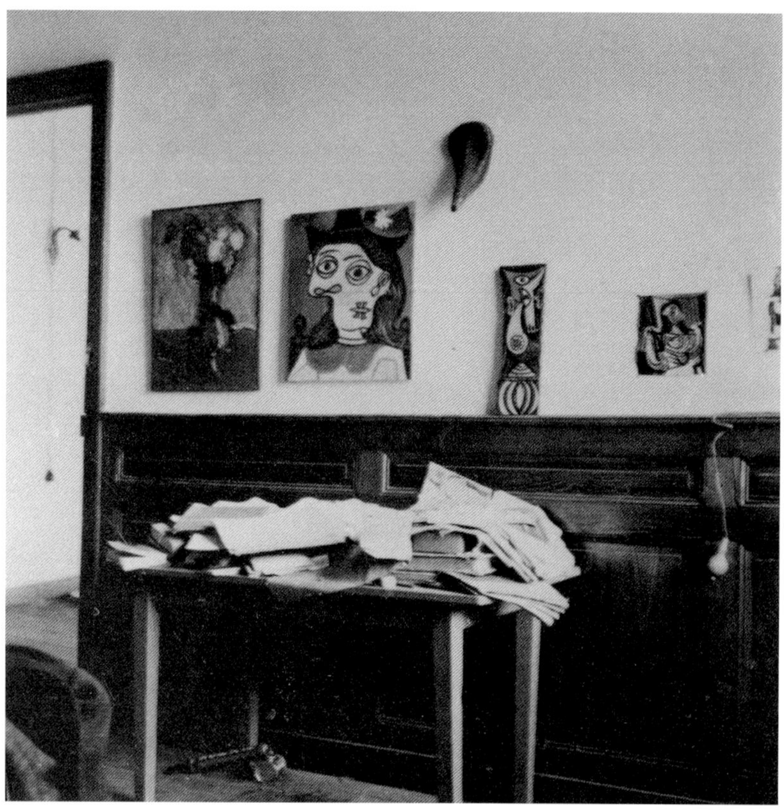

7. View of Picasso's studio, with a bicycle seat mounted on the wall, Royan, 1940. Picasso Archives, Musée national Picasso–Paris.

Picasso to create a memorial sculpture for the poet and critic Guillaume Apollinaire. The massive work bears no relation to Picasso's original designs for wire and welded metal sculptures (see Chapter 4), but its solemnity was well-suited to a commemorative task.

OCTOBER 11, 1941: After a voluntary collection program for metals proved unsuccessful, the French government, headquartered in Vichy during the Occupation, passed a law allowing public statuary to be salvaged for the war; numerous bronze statues were removed and melted down. Picasso nevertheless continued to find metal for his work, as his correspondence with foundries and the numerous bronze casts he had made in the period demonstrate. Brassaï would later marvel, "[By] what tour de force did he manage to procure so much metal at the very moment when the Occupier was unbolting from their bases all the bronze statues of Paris, France, and Navarre, and stripping bistros of their pretty 'zinc counters,' even when they were really copper, to make into cannons?"[33]

DECEMBER 31, 1941: Alberto Giacometti left Paris for Geneva, where he would spend the next three and a half years. With this departure, Picasso temporarily lost one of his closest friends and most forthright critics. The two had struck up a friendship on the occasion of a May 1932 exhibition of Giacometti's sculptures at the Galerie Pierre Colle.[34] Zervos had reviewed them in *Cahiers d'Art* with great enthusiasm, arguing, "Giacometti is at present the only young sculptor whose works confirm and expand new directions in sculpture."[35] The two had become close by the spring of 1937, and Giacometti made regular visits to rue des Grands-Augustins during the Occupation. According to James Lord, biographer and friend of the artists, "There was no other artist save Matisse whom [Picasso] sought out so readily or talked to so willingly about art. . . . He asked Giacometti to criticize whatever sculpture he happened to be doing at the moment, and when the criticism had been given he often altered his work in accord with it."[36] In her memoir, Françoise Gilot would affirm Giacometti's forthrightness, recounting an episode after the war during which the younger artist criticized *Woman in a Long Dress* (pl. 86), calling its assembled elements a "lucky accident" and counseling Picasso to eliminate them and "work up to the point where you can see that you've finished the thing in accordance with its generating force."[37] Picasso did not heed his friend's advice. Giacometti would return to Paris in September 1945, and the two artists would resume their visits to one another's studios.

MARCH 23, 1942: In his diary, Jean Cocteau recounted a visit to Picasso. He described a studio in disarray, "haunted by the monsters he invents and which make up his world. Giant bronze heads, canvases, wood and sheet metal objects."[38]

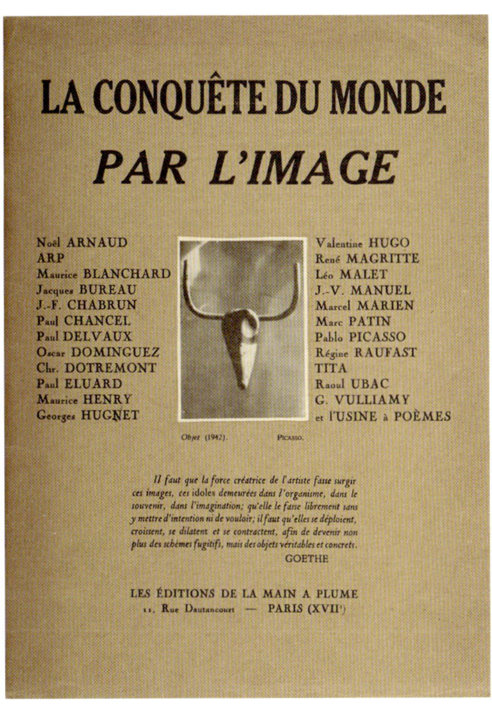

LA CONQUÊTE DU MONDE
PAR L'IMAGE

Noël ARNAUD
ARP
Maurice BLANCHARD
Jacques BUREAU
J.-F. CHABRUN
Paul CHANCEL
Paul DELVAUX
Oscar DOMINGUEZ
Chr. DOTREMONT
Paul ELUARD
Maurice HENRY
Georges HUGNET

Valentine HUGO
René MAGRITTE
Léo MALET
J.-V. MANUEL
Marcel MARIEN
Marc PATIN
Pablo PICASSO
Régine RAUFAST
TITA
Raoul UBAC
G. VULLIAMY
et l'USINE à POÈMES

Objet (1942). PICASSO.

Il faut que la force créatrice de l'artiste fasse surgir ces images, ces idoles demeurées dans l'organisme, dans le souvenir, dans l'imagination; qu'elle le fasse librement sans y mettre d'intention ni de vouloir; il faut qu'elles se déploient, croissent, se dilatent et se contractent, afin de devenir non plus des schèmes fugitifs, mais des objets véritables et concrets.
GOETHE

LES ÉDITIONS DE LA MAIN A PLUME
11, Rue Dautancourt — PARIS (XVIIe)

8. *Bull's Head* reproduced on the cover of *La Conquête du monde par l'image* (Conquest of the world by the image) (Paris: Éditions de la Main à plume, 1942)

MARCH 27, 1942: Picasso's longtime friend and collaborator Julio González died at his home in Arcueil, outside Paris. Due to the Occupation, González's family and friends were mostly in the South of France. Picasso and Zervos were among the very few in attendance at the funeral.

***BULL'S HEAD*, SPRING 1942**

Picasso made *Bull's Head* (pl. 88) by soldering together a bicycle seat and handlebars to create his most "astonishingly complete" transformation, as Roland Penrose observed.[39] Picasso would later tell Brassaï, "The idea of the *Bull's Head* came to me before I had a chance to think. All I did was weld them together."[40] Yet archival research seems to contradict the idea that this was a totally spontaneous act. Several photographs of Picasso's studio in Royan in 1940 show a bicycle seat mounted on the wall (fig. 7), indicating that Picasso not only possessed one of the components of his sculpture (or a very similar object) by then but was considering its potential as a work of art.[41]

In 1941 the writers Noël Arnaud and Jean-François Chabrun had brought together the group La Main à plume to maintain Surrealist activity in Paris while the movement's founder, André Breton, was in exile in the United States and the Caribbean. On April 24, 1942, they published *La Conquête du monde par l'image* (Conquest of the world by the image), the first issue of a new journal.[42] *Bull's Head* was reproduced on the cover in black and white with the caption "Objet (1942), Picasso," along with a quotation attributed to Johann Wolfgang von Goethe: "The artist's creative force must rouse the images, these idols that have remained in the organism, in the memory, in the imagination; it must do so freely without imparting any intention or will; they must unfurl, grow, dilate, and contract in order to become not simply fleeting frameworks, but real, concrete objects" (fig. 8).[43]

Bull's Head was cast in bronze soon after it was made. In a diary entry of June 3, Cocteau reported seeing a cast during a lunch at Picasso's rue des Grands-Augustins studio, and he noted on June 29 that Maar had confirmed to him that the assemblage had been cast in bronze.[44] Two casts are known—one assembled and the other in two pieces. At the time of the artist's death, the second cast had not been assembled. Claude Ruiz-Picasso, the artist's son, has averred that Picasso saw the bronze cast, not the original assemblage, as the true sculpture.[45] Of *Bull's Head*, Picasso would later tell Brassaï, "The marvelous thing about bronze is that it can give the most heterogeneous objects such unity that it's sometimes difficult to identify the elements that compose it. But," he noted, "that's also a danger: if you were to see only the bull's head and not the bicycle seat and handlebars that form it, the sculpture would lose some of its impact."[46]

APRIL 1942: A study on Picasso by the Catalan entrepreneur and writer Joan Merli, who was living in exile in Buenos Aires, was published. The book included reproductions of two of Picasso's early bronzes and an engraved pebble dating to 1937, as well as a photograph taken at the Boisgeloup sculpture studio showing three plasters.[47] In 1948, Poseidón, Merli's publishing house, would release a revised and much augmented second edition featuring thirty-nine reproductions of Picasso's sculptures and ceramics.[48]

JULY 2, 1942: In Vézelay, a town in Burgundy, southeast of Paris, Zervos completed the manuscript for the second book of the second volume of his catalogue raisonné of Picasso's work. Soon thereafter, seven hundred numbered copies were published. Dedicated to the years 1912 to 1917, the book contained the most complete selection of Picasso's Cubist constructions and sculpture published to that date. The first book in the two-part volume had been printed earlier in 1942, also in an edition of seven hundred; it had originally been planned to appear in June 1940. Zervos produced these two books despite continuous interruptions and delays due to the war.

***WOMAN IN A LONG DRESS*, 1943**

Picasso created the plaster head of *Woman in a Long Dress* (pl. 86) in 1942; its ruffled collar was made by pressing

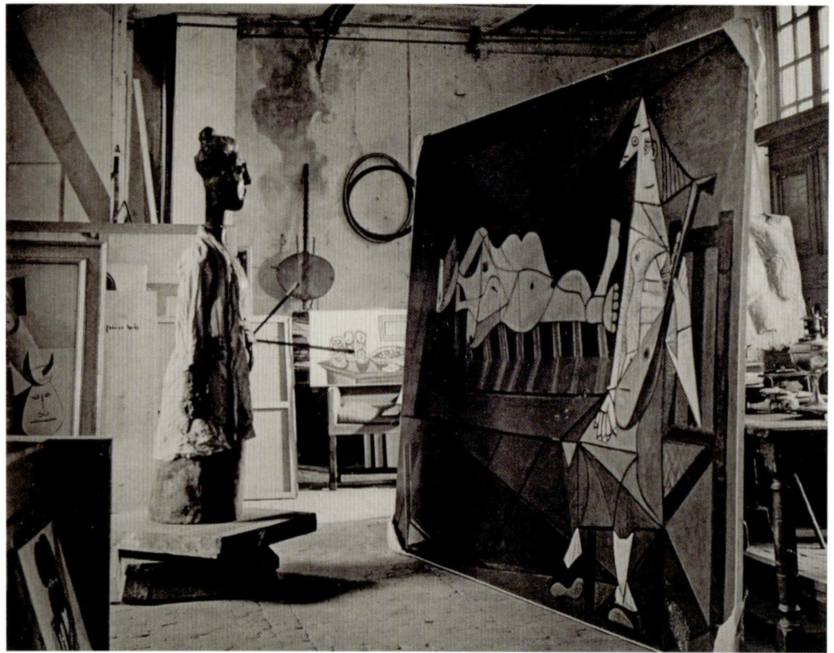

9. Picasso's studio at 7, rue des Grands-Augustins, Paris, 1946. Photograph by Brassaï. Musée national Picasso–Paris

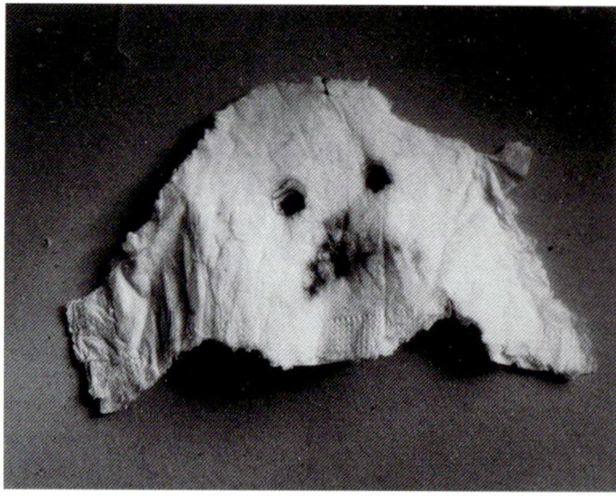

10. Picasso's torn-paper sculpture *Head of a Dog* in the artist's studio at 7, rue des Grands-Augustins, Paris, November 28, 1946. Photograph by Brassaï. Musée national Picasso–Paris

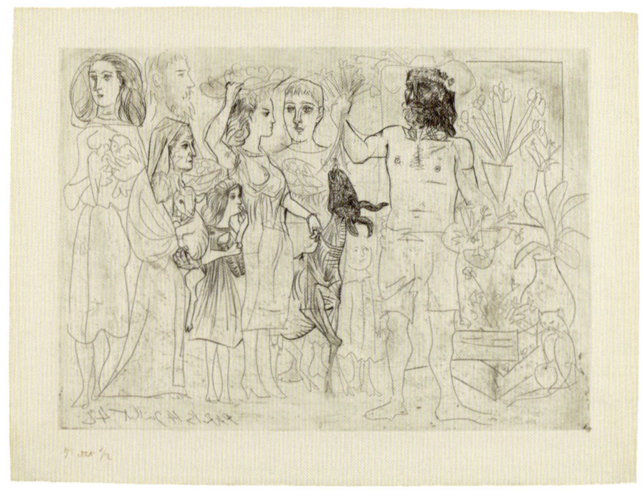

11. Pablo Picasso. *14 July 1942*. Etching, 17 13/16 × 25 1/4 in. (45.2 × 64.1 cm). Musée national Picasso–Paris

corrugated paper into wet plaster. The following year he joined the head and an arm, also sculpted of plaster, to a tailor's mannequin. A fragment from an Easter Island sculpture—a gift from art dealer Pierre Loeb—created the left hand and forearm, which the artist attached to the mannequin with additional plaster. A plan to add shoes was abandoned.[49]

Two bronze casts of the figure's body were made using the lost-wax method during the Occupation; Picasso had one of them assembled, while the other would still be in its various parts at the time of his death.[50] In 1946 he playfully dressed the assembled cast sculpture in a painter's smock, gave it a palette and brushes, and placed it in front of his large painting *L'Aubade* (1942; Centre Pompidou, Paris) (fig. 9). He set this scene to amuse Brassaï, crowing, "I wanted to give you a surprise! Strange fellow, huh?... The *artiste peintre* with his luminous, shimmering palette!"[51]

HEAD OF A DOG, *DEATH'S HEAD*, AND *GOAT*, 1943

Picasso made *Head of a Dog* (pl. 83) after the disappearance of Maar's beloved white lapdog, as a small consolation for her loss. He tore a white paper napkin into the shape of a dog's head and burned a design into it with his cigarette, creating holes for the eyes and nose and lines for the mouth and nostrils. According to Brassaï, Picasso continued to make a dog for Maar at every meal for several days after the disappearance.[52] He had been making modest yet ingenious sketchlike works in torn and cut paper since he was a child, when he created tiny animals to amuse his sisters; the Museo Picasso in Barcelona holds two of these, *Dove* and *Dog*, which he made in 1890 at the age of nine (see fig. 1 on p. 13). Picasso created many such objects to cheer Maar during the darkest days of the Occupation. *Death's Head* (pl. 84) and *Goat* (pl. 85), also made from paper, are torn not only along their outer contours but also within, creating the eye sockets and nasal cavity of *Death's Head* and in *Goat* a pattern that enlivens its character and suggests a face. Picasso asked Brassaï to include *Head of a Dog* and other torn-paper works as he photographed the artist's sculptures (fig. 10). He would revisit the technique of burning in April 1944, creating a design on a broomstick for the actor Jean Marais to use as a prop in a production of *Andromaque*, by Jean Racine, at the Théâtre Edouard-VII, Paris.

MAN WITH A LAMB, 1943

The larger than life-size *Man with a Lamb* (pl. 87) percolated in Picasso's imagination for around eight months before he began to sculpt. This is one of the few instances in which he made extensive drawings before finally realizing a motif in sculpture. On July 15, 1942, Picasso made the first studies, following the example of his print *14 July 1942* (fig. 11), in which a young man stands behind a sacrificial lamb. Sabartés would later confirm to Brassaï that this etching was the initial source of the sculpture, telling him that "the engraving preceded it, was its origin. . . . Afterward, Picasso, to get a clearer idea, did a very large number of drawings, about a hundred perhaps."[53]

The motif evolved over the following months, moving toward a dramatization of the theme in which the imploring lamb is bound while the bearded man holding it is depicted with chiaroscuro effects. Various studies—at least sixty-four, of which thirty-nine were produced before the final sculpture was created—lined the walls of Picasso's studio (fig. 12).[54] A small Rodinesque statuette from 1942 so strongly resembles the future sculpture that it could be a modello for it (fig. 13).

In March 1943, Picasso began to sculpt in clay over an armature. If planning the sculpture was an unusually protracted process, its execution was extremely swift. Picasso would later tell Brassaï that he completed the modeling in one session with the aid of the poet Paul Eluard and Marcel Boudin, his chauffeur and general assistant. Under the weight of the clay, the armature began to give way. They tied the sculpture to a ceiling beam, but "it threatened to collapse at any moment," Picasso reported. "I had to act fast. . . . I decided to cast it in plaster immediately. It was done the same afternoon. What a job!"[55]

Three years later, in the 1945–46 volume of *Cahiers d'Art*, Zervos would publish an illustrated article on the two-dimensional correlates of the sculpture, from July 1942 to October 1943.[56] The images reproduced in the article, including four photographs of the sculpture seen from different views (fig. 14), document the sculpture's unique conception on paper and emphasize its powerful presence as a work in three dimensions.[57]

Three bronze casts of the work would be made between 1948 and 1950 at the Valsuani foundry, which had reopened after the war. Picasso kept one (Musée national Picasso–Paris), sold one (see pl. 87), and donated the third to the city of Vallauris, where it was installed in the market square in 1950. Because it was so large, the plaster (Museo Nacional Centro de Reina Sofía, Madrid) was cut in two and cast in pieces. Valsuani sent Sabartés a quote, likely for the second casting, on November 26, 1949: "Attached, please find the inventory of Monsieur Picasso's models which are at the foundry. With a quote for *Man with a Lamb*: 450,000 francs."[58]

The donation to Vallauris was intended by the artist to "thank the population for the affectionate welcome it had given him," according to the phrase transcribed in the municipal council's deliberations.[59] For the residents of Vallauris, who inaugurated Picasso's sculpture in August 1950 (fig. 15), its symbolic valence was likely strong, given the Provençal

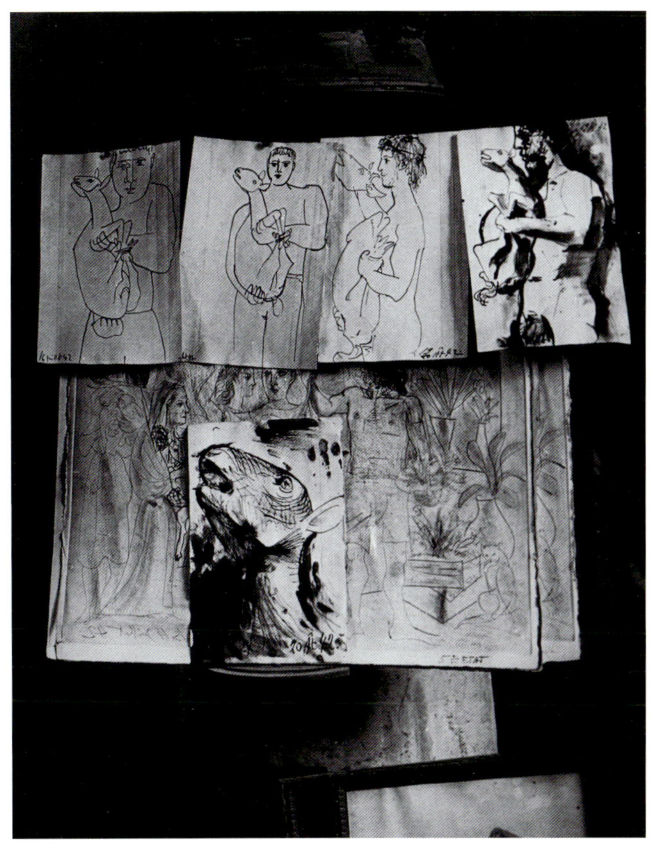

12. Picasso's studio at 7, rue des Grands-Augustins, with studies for *Man with a Lamb* on the wall, Paris, [December 1943]. Photograph by Brassaï. Musée national Picasso–Paris

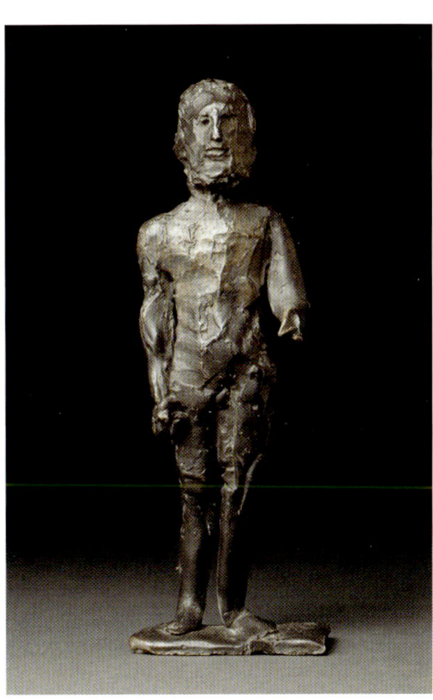

13. Pablo Picasso. *Standing Man*. 1942. Bronze, 7⅝ × 2¾ × 2 in. (19.3 × 7 × 5 cm). Musée national Picasso–Paris

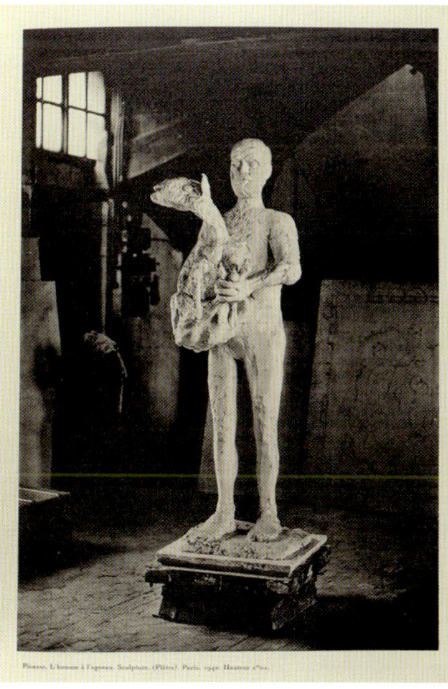

14. *Man with a Lamb* reproduced in Christian Zervos, "L'Homme à l'agneau de Picasso, juillet 1942–octobre 1943" (Picasso's *Man with a Lamb*, July 1942–October 1943), *Cahiers d'Art* (1945–46): 85

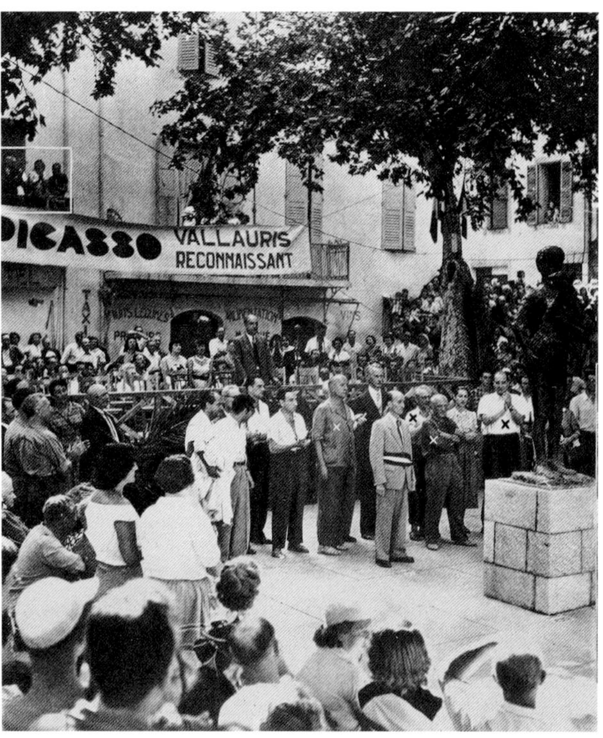

15. Inauguration of *Man with a Lamb* in the market square, Vallauris, August 1950. Photograph published in *Paris-Match*, September 9, 1950. Picasso Archives, Musée national Picasso–Paris

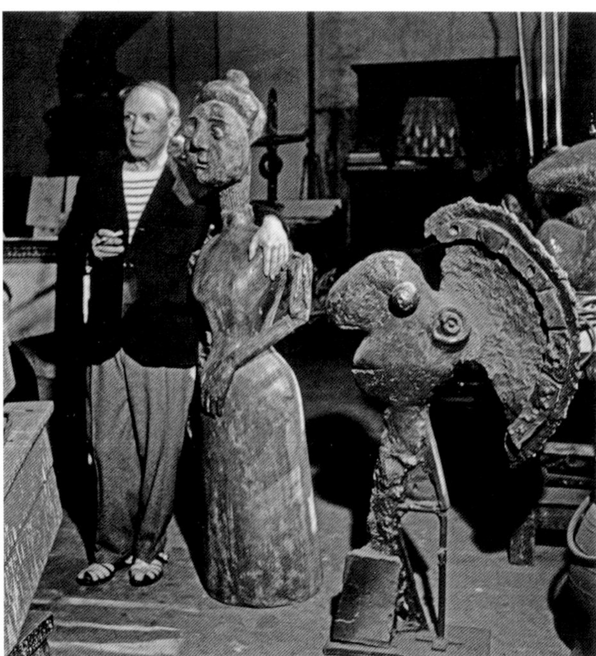

16. Picasso in his studio at 7, rue des Grands-Augustins, shortly after the liberation of Paris in 1944. Photograph by Robert Capa illustrating the article "New French Art: Picasso Fostered It Under Nazis," *Life* (November 13, 1944)

tradition of midnight mass on Christmas Eve, which has roots stretching back for centuries. The mass, even to this day, often includes the *pastrage*, or presentation of the lamb. During this ceremony, shepherds present a lamb to the priest in an offering of peace and religious devotion. Brassaï noted the religious associations of the sculpture, recalling that he discussed it with Sabartés: "appropriately, on Christmas Eve of this sinister year 1943."[60] To art historian J. P. Hodin, however, Picasso refuted the idea that there was symbolic content in the piece or similarities to religious or ancient images of the Good Shepherd or Hermes Kriophoros: "It is not at all religious. The man could be carrying a pig instead of a ram! There is no symbolism in it. It's simply beautiful. Symbolism is made by the public. It is the public that creates it. In *Man with a Lamb*, I expressed a human sentiment, a sentiment that exists today, just as it has always existed."[61]

SEPTEMBER 1943: Brassaï began making regular visits to Picasso's studio on rue des Grands-Augustins to photograph the artist's sculptures for a forthcoming monograph devoted to them. The publisher was the daring and resourceful Maurice Girodias of Les Éditions du Chêne, who was issuing books on modern art despite Nazi censorship and wartime paper shortages.

Girodias had endeavored to assign his own photographer, but Picasso insisted that Brassaï be hired for the job. He agreed to work on the project at great personal risk. Brassaï chose to photograph in secret rather than attempt to secure the necessary permits, and he personally obtained the supplies for the many photographs he took. His regular visits to the studio would continue through 1946 with two exceptions: in January–April 1944 when he went into hiding after being mobilized by the German army, and the busy weeks following the liberation of Paris in August 1944.

OCTOBER 20, 1943: A visit by Brassaï and Girodias to Picasso's studio turned contentious when the publisher counseled Brassaï not to photograph *Large Bird*, a cranelike figure assembled from the pieces of a scooter, a feather, and wood, because it was "more an object than a sculpture." Picasso later fumed, "An *object*! . . . Who does that man think he is, to tell me, Picasso, what is or is not a sculpture! . . . What is sculpture? What is painting? Everyone's still clinging to outdated ideas, obsolete definitions, as if the artist's role was not precisely to offer new ones."[62]

AUGUST 25, 1944: Defeated by the French Resistance and Allied forces, the Germans surrendered Paris, liberating the city. In the ensuing period, Picasso received countless visits from foreign journalists and photographers, among them Robert

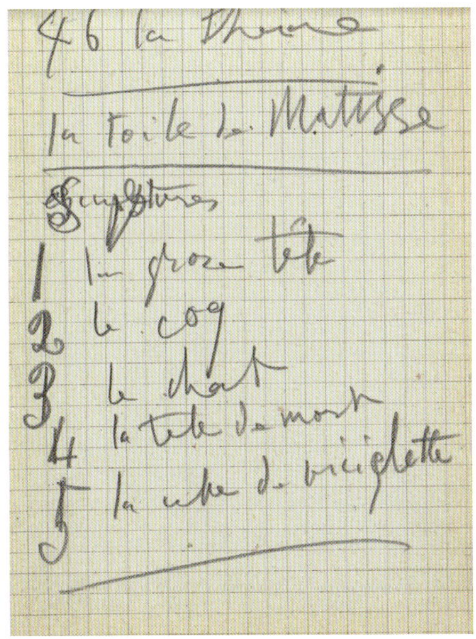
46 la [illegible]
la toile de Matisse
Sculptures
1 la grosse tête
2 le coq
3 le chat
4 la tête de mort
5 la selle de bicyclette

17. List by Picasso in his notebook of sculptures shown at the 1944 Salon d'Automne, Paris, summer 1944. Picasso Archives, Musée national Picasso–Paris

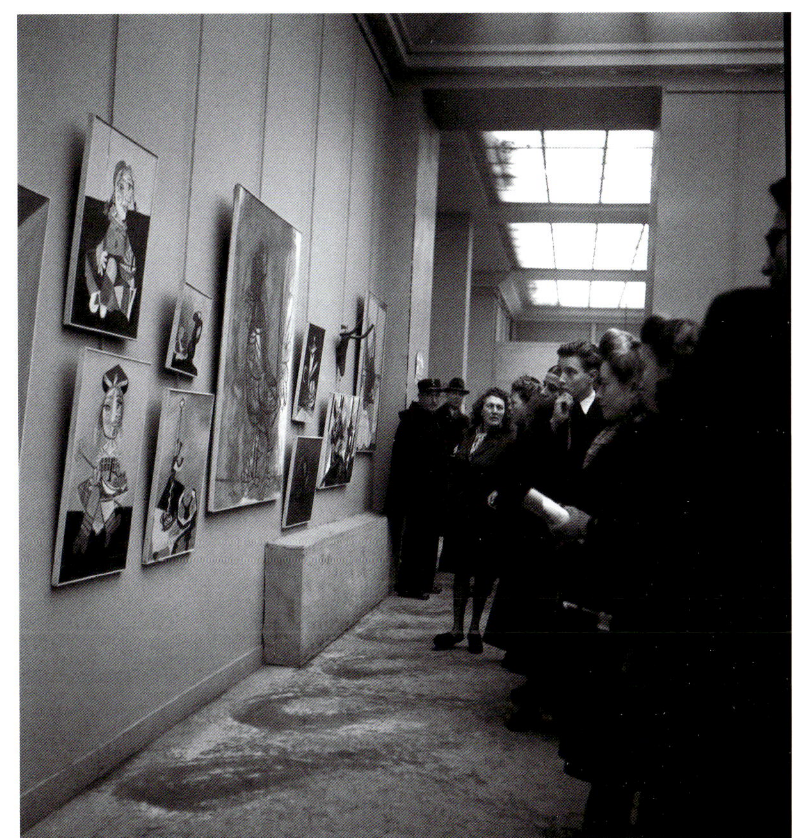

18. The Salon d'Automne with Picasso's sculpture *Bull's Head* mounted on the wall amid paintings, Paris, 1944. Photograph by Robert Doisneau. Gamma/Rapho

Capa, Henri Cartier-Bresson, and Lee Miller. Capa would later recall, "I climbed the turning stairs . . . banged on the door, and found Picasso—somewhat older but far livelier than anything else in Paris."[63] Photographs of the artist's rue des Grands-Augustins studio with *Man with a Lamb*, *Head of a Woman*, and the earlier *Head of a Warrior* prominently on display soon circulated around the world (see fig. 12 on p. 20). A photograph by Capa of Picasso embracing his *Woman in a Long Dress* was published in *Life* magazine on November 13, 1944 (fig. 16).[64]

OCTOBER 6–NOVEMBER 5, 1944: The Salon d'Automne was mounted at the Palais de Tokyo. Rechristened the Salon de la Libération to commemorate the liberation of Paris, the event was dedicated to the modern art the Nazi regime had suppressed during the Occupation. The catalogue states that the exhibition had been "prepared during enemy occupation, organized during the battle, and inaugurated in full independence."[65] The artist André Fougeron led a special effort to honor Picasso, organizing an exhibition of seventy-four paintings and five sculptures (see fig. 3 on p. 306); the artist's work had been virtually unseen in Paris for several years. In a small pocket notebook (fig. 17), Picasso listed the sculptures he showed at the Salon: three recent works—*Cat*, *Death's Head*, and *Bull's Head*—and bronze casts of two prewar sculptures, *Head of a Woman* (pl. 56) and *Cock* (pl. 58).[66] In his list of works, Picasso indicated *Bull's Head* as *La Selle de bicyclette* (The bicycle saddle), which the Salon committee adopted as the sculpture's official title in the catalogue (fig. 18).[67]

Picasso's exhibition provoked an uproar at the Salon's opening. His works startled visitors, who objected to their unfamiliar language and unorthodox workmanship. Also startling to many was the announcement, the day before, that Picasso had joined the French Communist Party.[68] *Bull's Head* was among the works deliberately jostled and removed from the wall by attendees, some of whom also burned effigies of Picasso's paintings outside the museum. Thereafter, the Picasso section of the exhibition was patrolled by uniformed policemen.

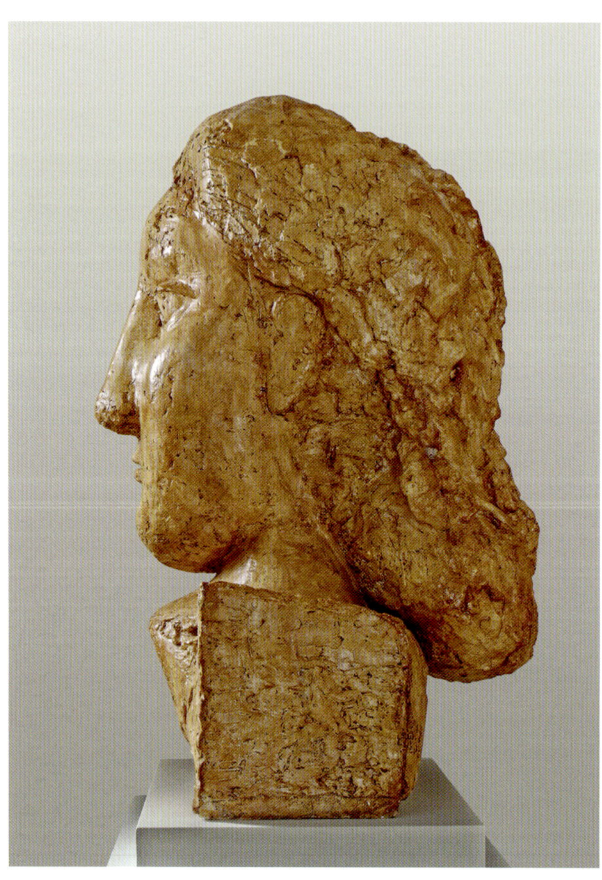

80. **HEAD OF A WOMAN.** Paris, 1941
Plaster
31½ in. (80 cm) high
Museum Ludwig, Cologne

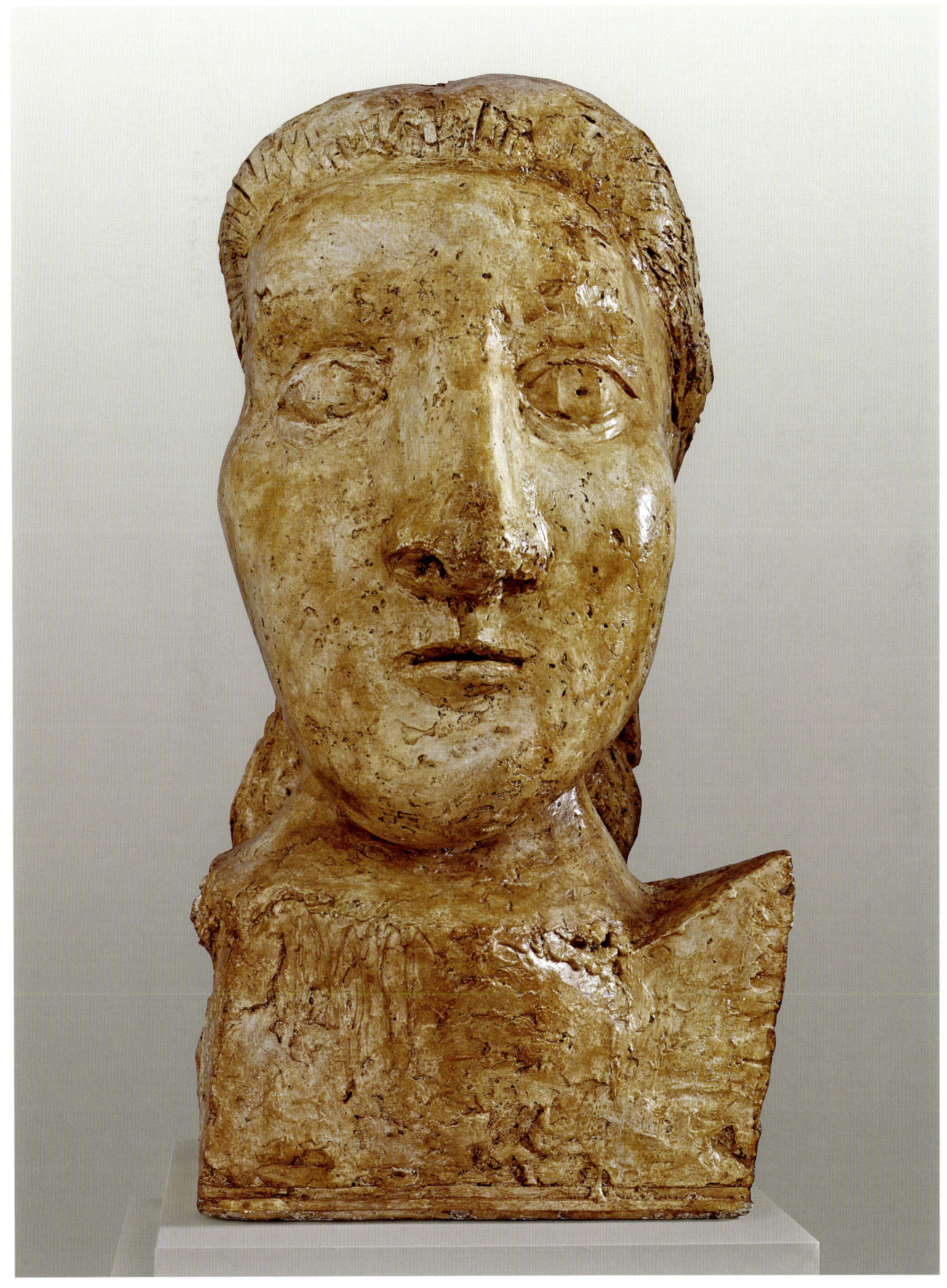

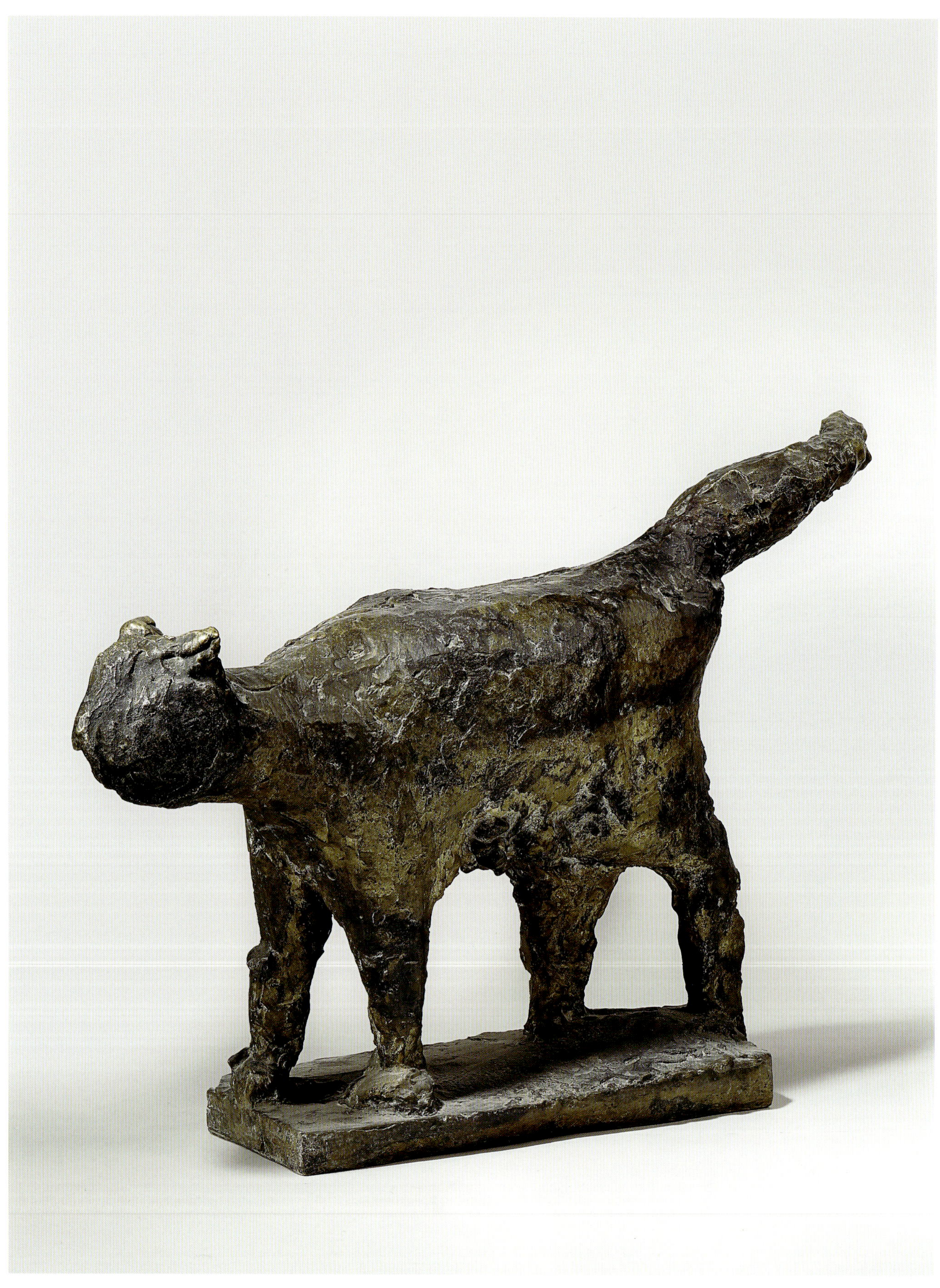

81. CAT. Paris, 1941
Bronze, cast by September 1943
18 × 28 ½ × 9 in. (46 × 72.5 × 23 cm)
Private collection

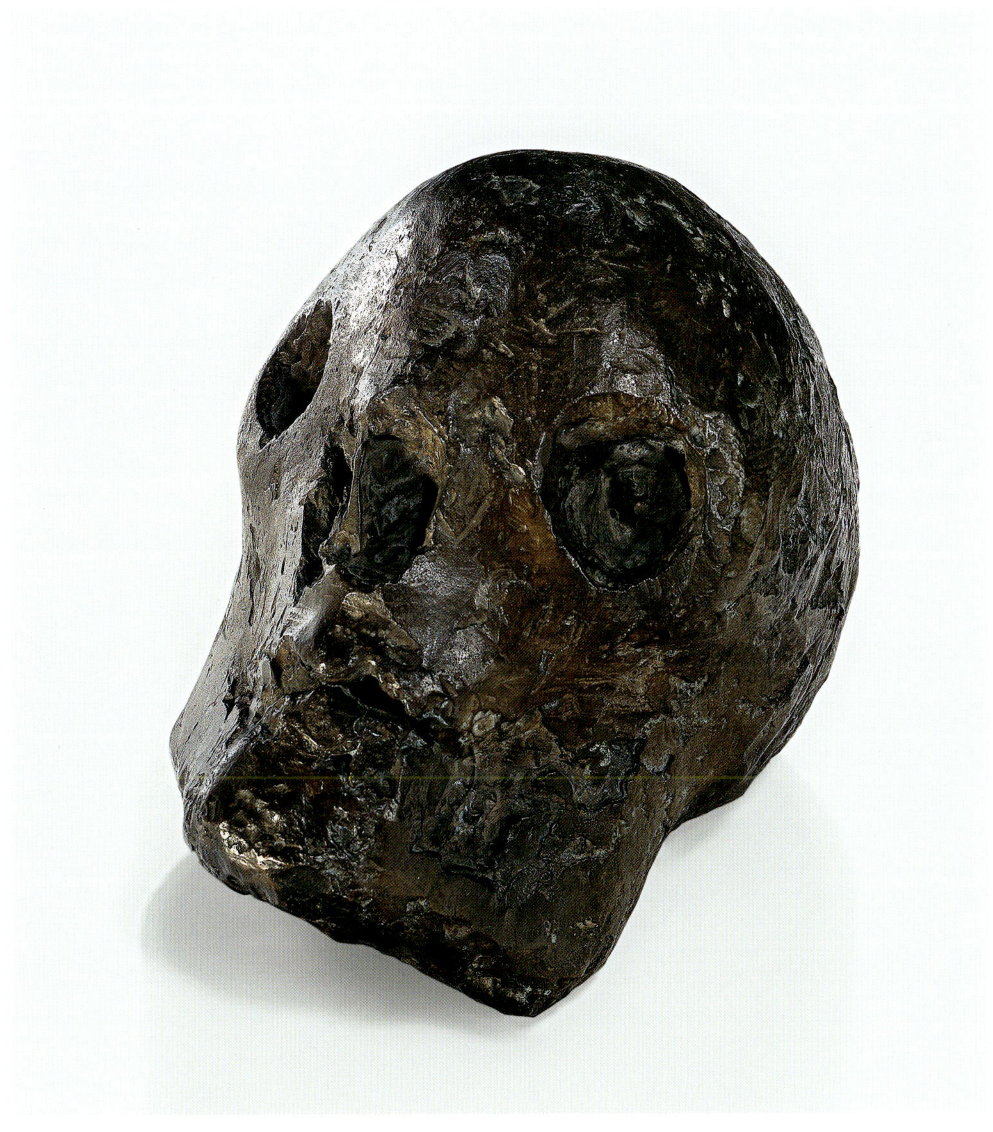

82. **DEATH'S HEAD.** Paris, [1941]
Bronze, cast by May 1943
9 ⅞ × 8 ¼ × 12 ⅝ in. (25 × 21 × 32 cm)
Private collection

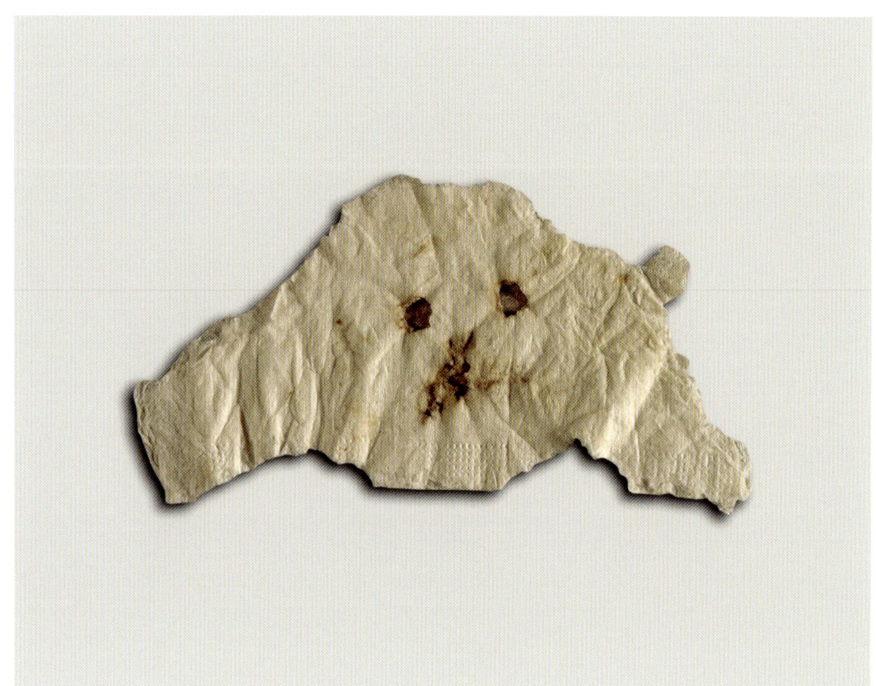

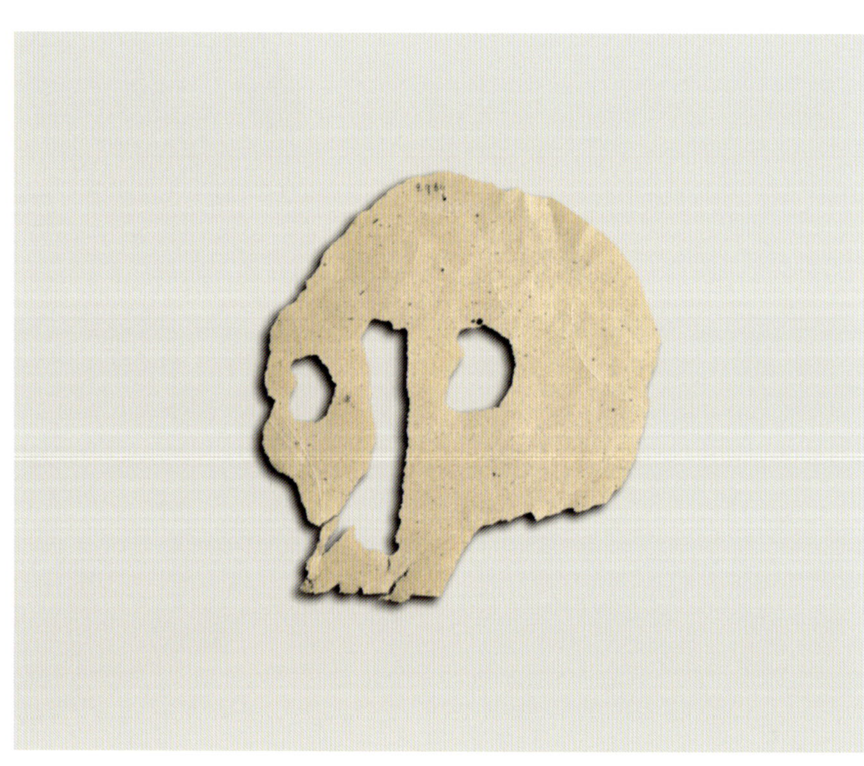

83. **HEAD OF A DOG.** Paris, 1943
Torn and burnt tissue paper (napkin)
3 15/16 × 10 5/8 in. (10 × 27 cm)
Musée national Picasso–Paris. Purchase

84. **DEATH'S HEAD.** Paris, 1943
Torn and scratched paper
6 7/16 × 5 15/16 in. (16.3 × 15.1 cm)
Musée national Picasso–Paris. Purchase

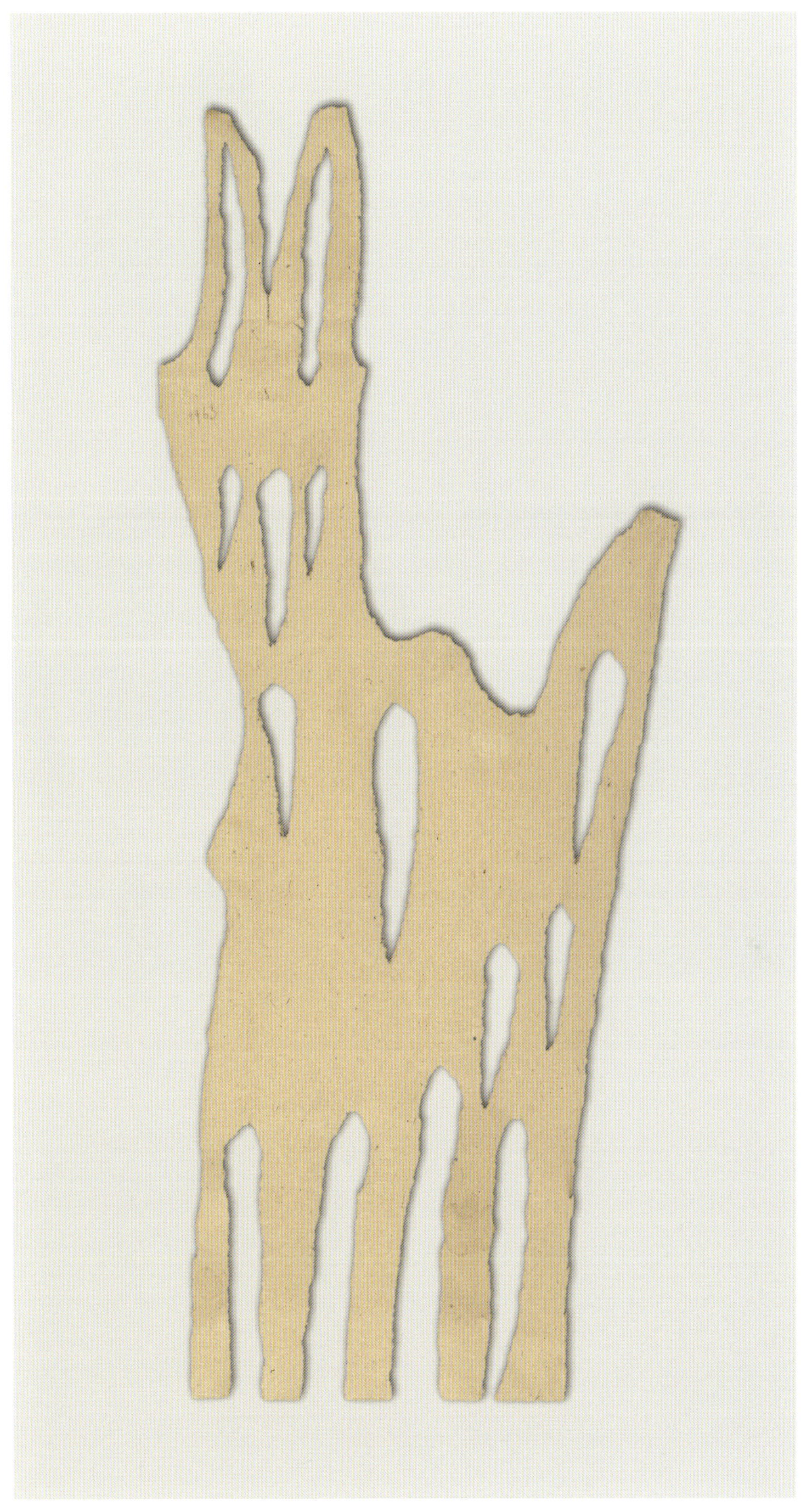

85. GOAT. Paris, 1943
Torn paper
14 15/16 × 6 5/16 in. (38 × 16.1 cm)
Musée national Picasso–Paris. Purchase

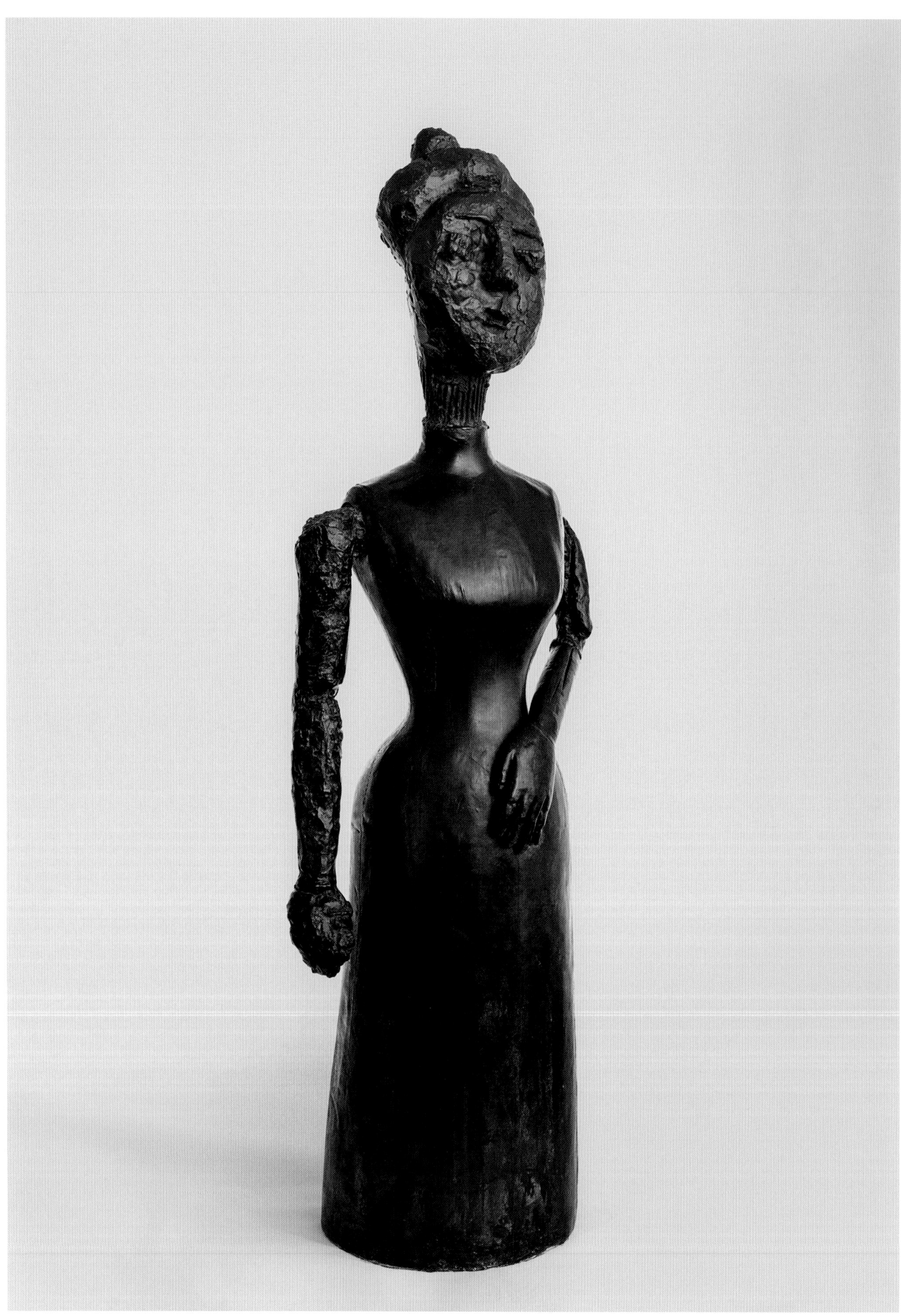

86. **WOMAN IN A LONG DRESS.** Paris, 1943
Bronze, cast by 1944
63 1/2 × 21 1/8 × 18 in. (161.3 × 53.7 × 45.7 cm)
Private collection

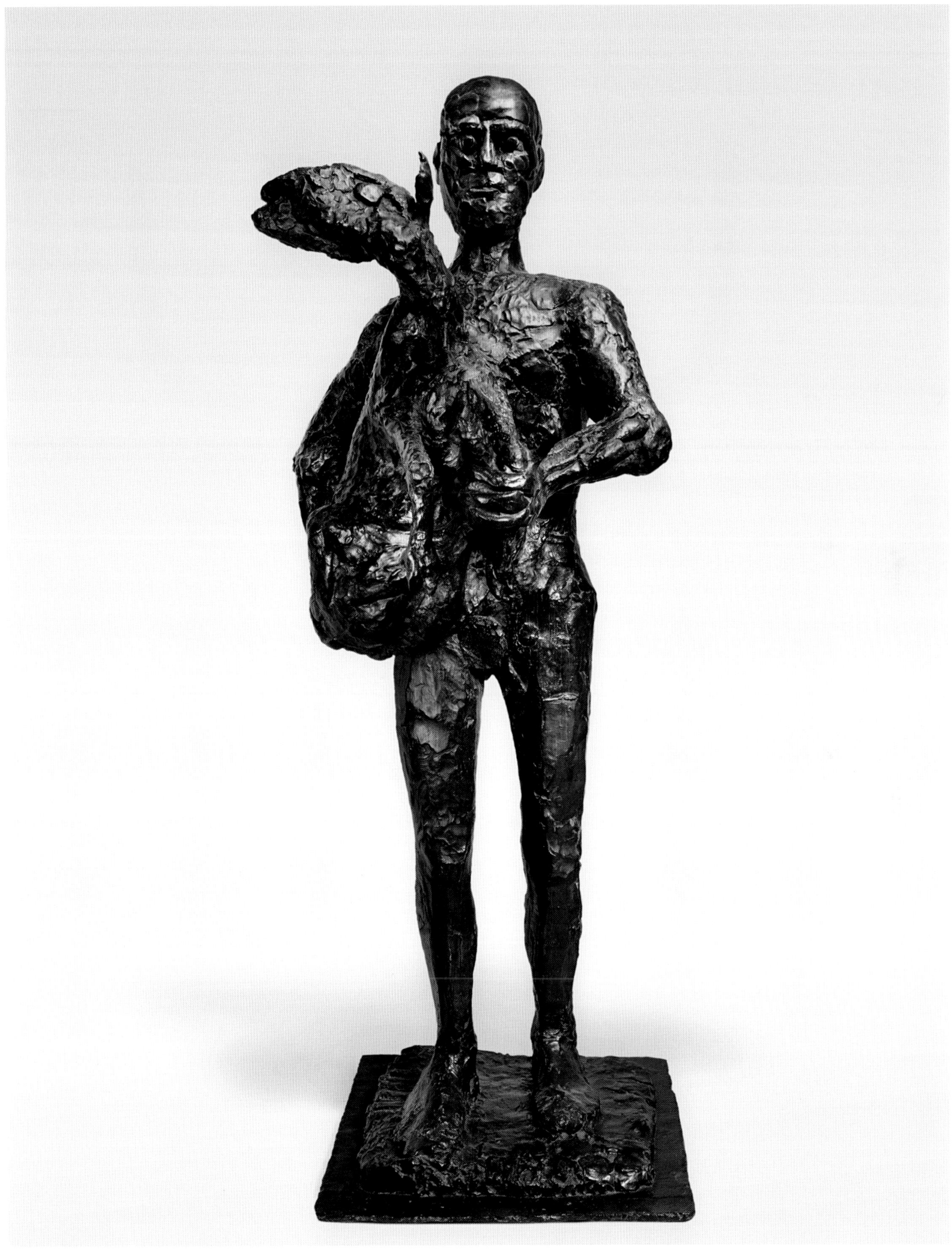

87. **MAN WITH A LAMB.** Paris, 1943
Bronze, cast between 1948 and 1950
6 ft. 7½ in. × 30 in. × 29½ in. (201.9 × 76.2 × 74.9 cm); base: 27 × 26 in. (68.6 × 66 cm)
Philadelphia Museum of Art. Gift of R. Sturgis and Marion B. F. Ingersoll

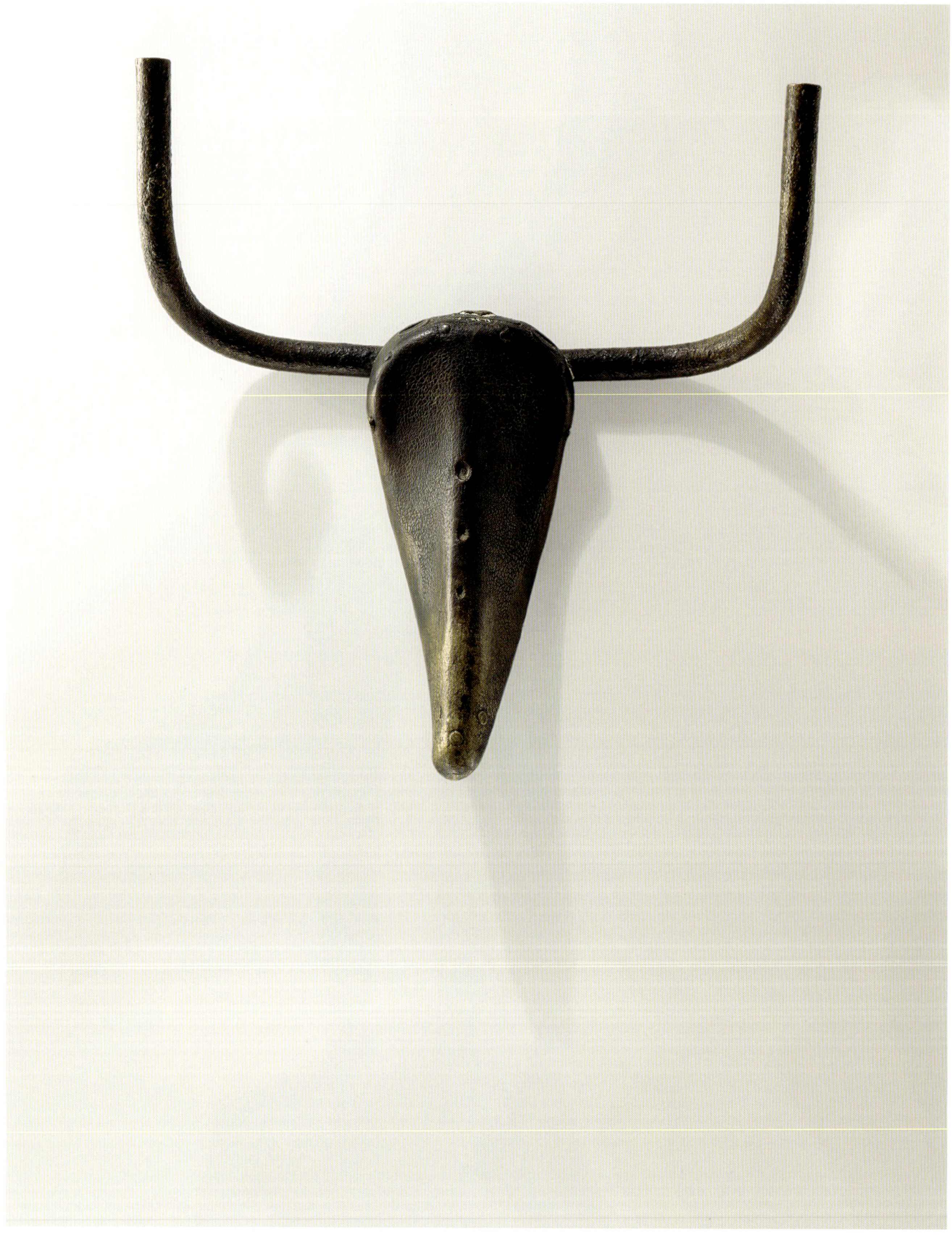

88. **BULL'S HEAD.** Paris, spring 1942
Bronze, cast 1943
16½ × 16⅛ × 5⅞ in. (42 × 41 × 15 cm)
Private collection

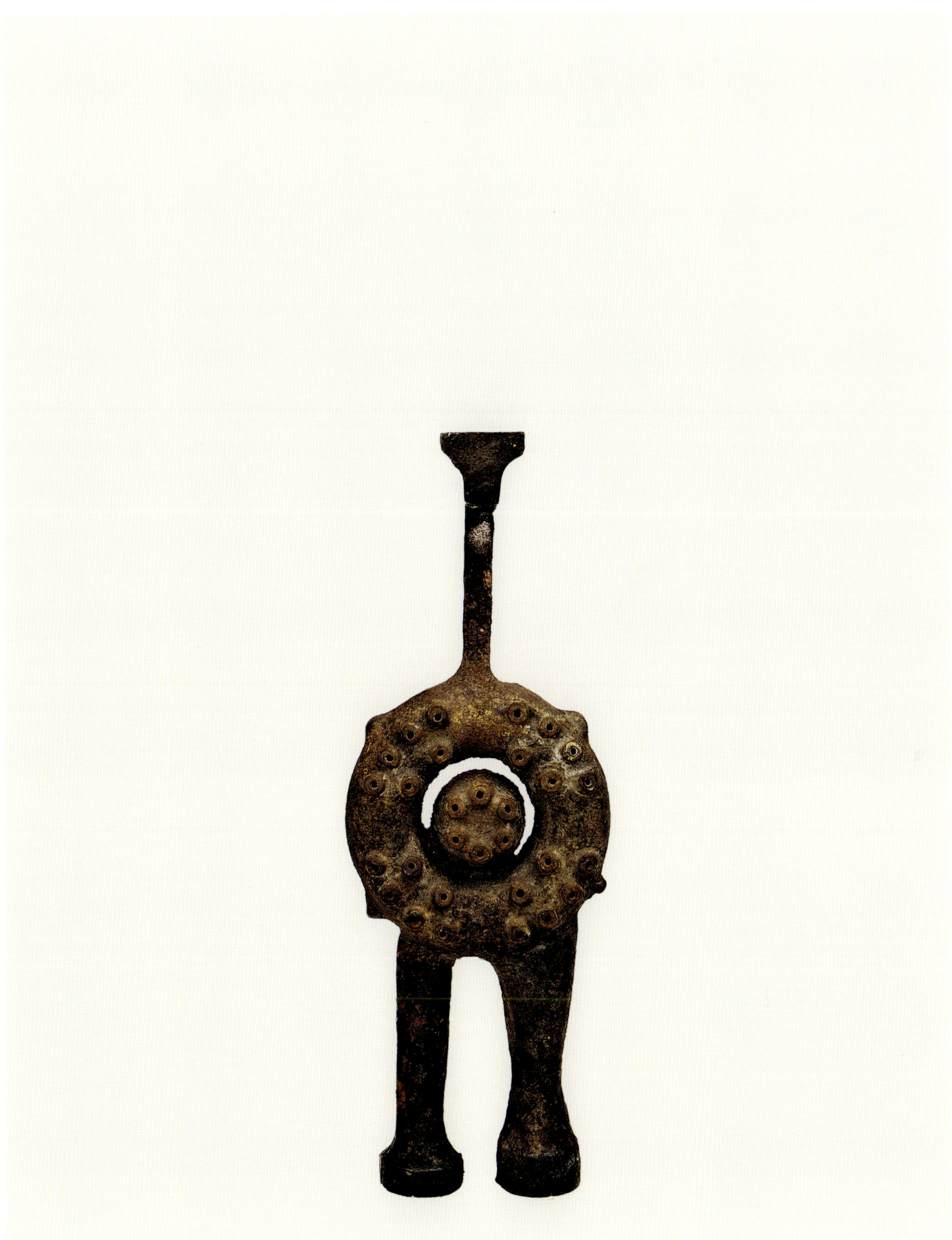

89. **THE VENUS OF GAS.** January 1945
Iron (burner and pipe from a gas stove)
$9\frac{13}{16} \times 3\frac{9}{16} \times 1\frac{9}{16}$ in. (25 × 9 × 4 cm)
Private collection

CHAPTER 7

VALLAURIS: CERAMICS AND ASSEMBLAGES 1945–1954

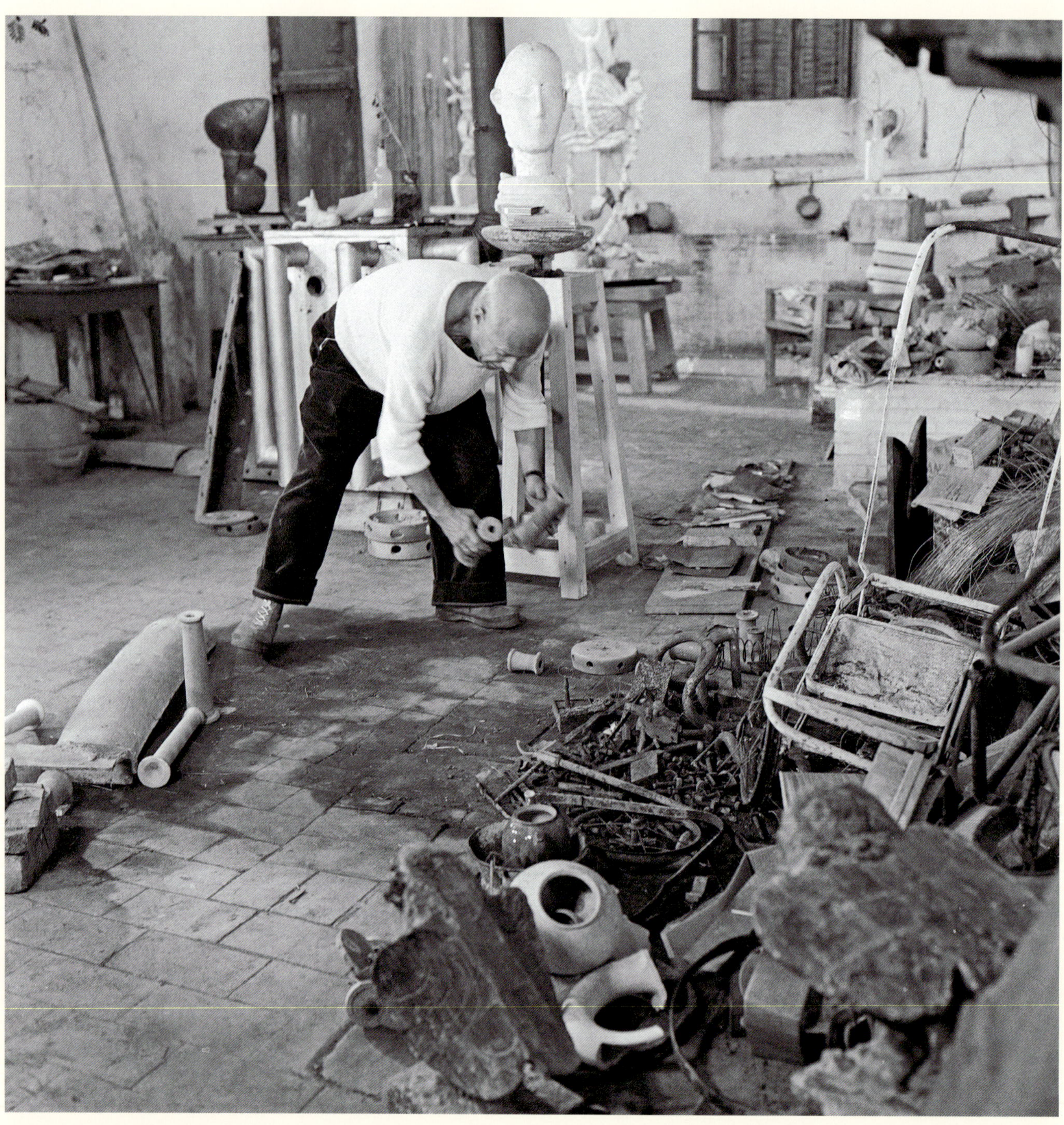

Picasso assembling *The Woman with a Key* (1953–54) on the floor of his rue du Fournas sculpture studio, Vallauris, October 1953. Photograph by Edward Quinn. Edward Quinn Archives

PARIS WAS LIBERATED on August 25, 1944, bringing the grim years of the German occupation to an end. The following summer Picasso returned to the Côte d'Azur for the first time since the war had begun. This renewed contact with the Mediterranean's sun, sand, and light, along with its deep connections to classical Greek and Roman culture and its primordial sense of time, ushered in a new phase in Picasso's sculpture. Among the earliest known works from this moment are a series of carved pebbles, bones, and shards of pottery picked up along the beach (see pls. 90–98). Into the smooth, water-eroded surfaces of these small objects Picasso, using a vocabulary with origins in archaic art as well as Cubism's schematic signs, incised dots and lines that doubled as facial features. Brassaï was among the first to see these talismanic carvings. He recalled Picasso speculating about what would happen were they to be thrown back into the sea for future generations to find, like artifacts from what he described as an "unknown Picassoan civilization."[1]

While in the South of France, Picasso was introduced to Suzanne and Georges Ramié, who were among a number of artisans trying to revive the ancient pottery industry of the town of Vallauris. The effort was one of many postwar projects aimed at restoring France's wounded sense of national pride. The Ramiés provided Picasso with space, supplies, and skilled ceramicists to work with. He learned and then pushed the limits of what could be done with the classic shapes of ceramic vessels, along with the range of surface effects obtainable using slips and glazes. Works like *Standing Bull (Vase)* (pl. 109) and *Owl (Vase)* (pl. 108) are among the most sculptural of Picasso's ceramics, with pottery-wheel-produced contours and traditional spouts and handles at once recognizable and transformed. The utilitarian associations of such elements invite thoughts of handling, which add to the tactile immediacy that characterizes all of Picasso's sculpture.

Picasso's magpie impulses had manifested themselves early on in his sculptural practice, from the single real-life spoon in *Glass of Absinthe* (pls. 21–26) to the riotous assembly of found metal pieces that compose *Woman in the Garden* (pl. 41) to the austere, iconic simplicity of the upended bicycle seat and handlebars that constitute *Bull's Head* (pl. 88). It was in Vallauris, however—in particular, in the old, junk-filled perfume factory on rue du Fournas that he converted into a studio—that Picasso's scavenger instincts found their most exuberant expression. They were perhaps honed by the deprivations of the war years—and perhaps, too, by Picasso's recent collaboration with Brassaï on the first book devoted to his sculpture, which surely encouraged him to revisit his most ephemeral material productions through the monumentalizing eye of Brassaï's camera lens. The result of this heightened attentiveness to the sculptural potential of detritus was a body of work that is one of Picasso's greatest postwar achievements: a series of assemblages created from an astounding array of found and scavenged objects held together by plaster and armatures of wood.

In many of these works, Picasso's proximity to the dump heaps of Vallauris's potteries is vividly apparent: the breasts and belly of *Pregnant Woman* (pl. 115), the udder of *She-Goat* (pl. 119), and the body of *Baboon and Young* (pl. 116) all began life as ceramic vessels. Picasso welcomed the metaphoric play between volumetric objects, designed to contain liquids, and body parts, whether human or beast. Other pilfered things were pressed into service, including a wicker basket that provided *She-Goat* with ribs and the toy cars of the artist's young son that produced the head of *Baboon*. In such works the sculptural act is redefined as one of prestidigitation. New meanings are conjured from objects that are transposed, and thereby transformed, but whose original meanings remain intact. Even things as humble as carpenters' nails, when put to work by Picasso, can function as goat bristles, a woman's manicured fingers, bird feathers, or, most improbably, materialized rays of radiant, immaterial light.

Picasso had most of his fragile 1950s assemblages cast in bronze, and for years the plaster-and-found-object originals were rarely seen outside his studio. This had an undeniable impact on perceptions of his 1950s sculptural oeuvre. As Picasso himself noted, the unity that bronze bestows on heterogeneous objects is both marvelous and dangerous, in the sense that the identity of individual components can sometimes be subsumed. The fame of the bronze versions makes it easy to forget how much Picasso's 1950s assemblages have in common with contemporaneous works by much younger artists. Yet, as the originals for the bronzes make clear, Picasso was once again, in his late sixties and early seventies, on the cutting edge of the latest trends in avant-garde art.

SUMMER 1945: Picasso spent his summer in Antibes and Golfe-Juan, along France's Côte d'Azur. He returned to Paris in August.

STANDING WOMAN, _STANDING WOMAN_, AND _STANDING WOMAN_, 1945

Picasso modeled a series of more than twenty small *Standing Woman* figures in clay, ranging from approximately five inches to just over ten inches in height (pls. 100–101).[1] To make these, he rolled, stretched, and pinched the pliant material in the free-spirited way a child might play with putty. The resulting figurines recall Venus fertility figures as well as the terracotta Tanagra statuettes created in Greece in the late fourth century BCE, renowned for their naturalism and refined execution. Picasso's group of sculptures would soon be cast in bronze at the Valsuani foundry in Paris in an edition of eleven, with one set remaining unnumbered.[2] *Standing Woman* (pl. 99) is one of the plaster casts produced in the course of that process.

From the late 1940s to the early 1960s, these bronzes would be among the artist's most widely exhibited sculptures in European and American galleries. Many of the more than two hundred casts found their ways into collectors' homes.

LATE SEPTEMBER 1945: Alberto Giacometti, who had left occupied Paris on December 31, 1941, when his residence permit expired, returned from Geneva.[3] Upon his arrival, he and Picasso "rediscover[ed] one another" and began again to visit each other's studios.[4] Picasso stopped by Giacometti's workspace on rue Hippolyte-Maindron only occasionally, but the Swiss artist's visits to the rue des Grands-Augustins studio were frequent.

NOVEMBER 1945: Artist Françoise Gilot, who had met Picasso in May 1943, visited him at the rue des Grands-Augustins studio. The ensuing partnership between Picasso and Gilot, forty years his junior, would last until 1953. To Picasso's chagrin, in 1964 she would publish an unvarnished account of their time together.[5] Her book is a key source in reconstructing the events of these years and also an eyewitness report on the making of some of Picasso's best-known sculptures.

MARCH–APRIL 1946: Around mid-March, Picasso joined Gilot in Golfe-Juan, where he had arranged for her to stay at the house of the master engraver and printer Louis Fort. The couple returned to Paris in late April, after which Gilot moved into the rue des Grands-Augustins studio.

SUMMER 1946: *Picasso: Fifty Years of His Art*, by Alfred H. Barr, Jr., a revised and expanded edition of his 1939 exhibition catalogue *Picasso: Forty Years of His Art*, was published by The Museum of Modern Art, New York. The monograph included a list headed, "Works by Picasso in American Museums."[6] This list records only three sculptures: a bronze cast of the 1909 Cubist *Head of a Woman* in the collection of The Museum of Modern Art; a *Glass of Absinthe* painted bronze (pl. 23), in the A. E. Gallatin Collection (housed at the Philadelphia Museum of Art); and a bronze cast of *The Jester* (1905) at the Phillips Memorial Gallery in Washington, D.C.

EARLY JULY 1946: Picasso and Gilot went back to the South of France, visiting Ménerbes, Antibes, and Golfe-Juan.

ENGRAVED PEBBLES AND BONE AND CERAMIC FRAGMENTS, 1945–47

When Brassaï visited Picasso's studio at 7, rue des Grands-Augustins on November 26, 1946, the artist presented him with many small things he had recently made. In Brassaï's account, Picasso had filled a box with "stones, bones, fragments of plates and crockery that have been ground by the sea, all engraved and sometimes carved slightly."[7] Captivated by their natural beauty, Picasso had engraved these on the beach in Golfe-Juan and elsewhere. The forms and personalities that the sea had bestowed on them conjured images that the artist had quickly translated into the head of a faun, a bird, or a human face (pls. 90–98). Picasso said, "the sea shapes them so nicely, gives them such pure, such complete, forms, that we have only to add a finishing touch to make them into works of art."[8]

Like the small objects Picasso had made during the war, Brassaï photographed the engraved pebbles for *Les Sculptures de Picasso*.[9] Curious about his method, the book's publisher, Maurice Girodias, asked Picasso about his tools. Picasso admitted that a little more than just "a finishing touch" was needed: "They are very hard. A dreadful amount of work. I start with anything, whatever's handy. And I continue with sharp scissors."[10] Girodias noticed a difference in style between these recent pebbles and the ones Picasso had made in 1937 and 1940.[11] Indeed, Picasso had treated the earlier pebbles and fragments more like grounds onto which he lightly engraved images, whereas the carving in 1945–47 further enhances the three-dimensional character of the individual stones and fragments. With a few exceptions, Picasso's later carving drove deeper into the material, creating shading and negative volume. Picasso recognized the distinction; as he told Girodias, "These are my different 'stone ages.'"[12]

JULY 21, 1946: While vacationing in Golfe-Juan, Picasso decided to visit nearby Vallauris to see its annual exhibition of work by local artisans, primarily ceramicists. Naturally rich in good clay, the town had been a thriving center for ceramics for centuries, but had languished since World War I. Taken by what he saw, Picasso accepted an invitation that day to visit the Madoura pottery workshop of Suzanne and Georges Ramié. With a bit of tutelage from the workshop's master potters, Picasso modeled three small works in clay: the head of a faun and two bulls.[13] After he departed, the Ramiés left the works to dry, unsure if the artist would return.

MAY 15, 1947: Claude Ruiz-Picasso, Picasso and Gilot's first child, was born.

AUGUST 1947: Picasso returned to the Ramiés' pottery and was pleased to find his small figures from the previous summer. According to Georges Ramié, the artist had continued to think about them and came bearing studies for new works.[14] Picasso would delve in deeply, working with the potters to produce nearly two thousand ceramics over the next year. Claude Ruiz-Picasso later described his father's relationship with the Ramiés as one of great nurturing and support.[15] Picasso's passionate involvement soon led to a revitalization of the town's ceramics industry; in Georges Ramié's recollection, it was not long before people began traveling to Vallauris to see what Picasso was creating with clay.[16]

The time lag and uncertainty inherent to the process of modeling or throwing clay, letting it dry, glazing it, and firing it presented a new set of challenges for Picasso. Gilot reported, "Pablo went to the L'Hospied chemical works in Golfe-Juan and talked with Mr. Cox, the head chemist, and found out all he needed to know about the properties of the enamels he was going to use. The next time he went to the Madoura pottery, he understood his work in the medium as an artistic experiment."[17] According to Gilot, Picasso was disappointed by the results of the first firings and struggled for at least six months to achieve the results he envisioned.

CERAMICS, 1947–51

Claude Ruiz-Picasso recalled that his father's work in ceramics at Vallauris began with "tiny figures."[18] The artist modeled these forms by hand rather than using the potter's wheel. They were mostly women, but also men, animals, and mythological figures; what Claude termed the "more ecstatic, bacchic, happy themes."[19] Works such as *Seated Woman* (pls. 102–103), *Seated Musician* (pl. 106), and *Seated Faun* (pl. 107) continued his experiments of the previous summer, while with medallions such as *Head of a Faun* (pls. 104–105) he investigated the use of tools to create designs in the clay.

Seeking his own path with the medium, Picasso also pioneered a hybrid breed of ceramic sculpture, building forms from combinations of turned and hand-modeled elements, and almost always redefining the sculptural forms with glazed and painted additions. *Owl (Vase)* (pl. 108) and *Standing Bull (Vase)* (pl. 109) are representative of Picasso's unique hybrids, combining elements made by hand with those turned on the potter's wheel. One of the potters at the Madoura workshop would later tell the poet Jean Cocteau, "M. Picasso knows the works as well as any of us now, but he dares what we would never dare imagine or try."[20] Picasso also experimented widely with traditional pottery forms such as tiles, plates, and vessels thrown on the wheel. Inspired by the sensual curves of these objects, he sought to breathe life into them by transforming them into zoomorphic creatures such as *Owl* (pl. 110) and female forms such as *Vase: Woman* (pl. 111) and *Bottle: Kneeling Woman* (pl. 112). Gilot offered a detailed perspective on his process:

> He decided first of all that the forms of the vessels needed renewing and he set about redesigning them. He tried to create form by taking the amphora as his point of departure. Whenever you turn a form in pottery, that form is cylindrical. It can be made into an amphora, with convex and concave forms, but it is always symmetrical and each cut is a circular one. If you want to come up with forms that are not circular... you have to make incisions on each side and afterwards fold them over.... After Pablo had had more experience, he decided to do the fold himself.... He would let the amphorae prepared for him by the potter dry overnight. The next morning the clay was still very plastic and could be twisted in every direction without being broken. With it Pablo began doing little statuettes of women as delicate as Tanagra. One didn't have the impression that these were water jars with arms added to make them look like women. He rekneaded the amphora completely and molded that hollow form, with its thickness of three millimeters, until it had been reinvented and emerged as one of his sculptures.[21]

In Claude's estimation, his mother was "a very straightforward, very ethically erect woman... [with] the profound certainty of the patrician Tanagras that unmistakably my father sculpted to represent her."[22]

For the white earthenware creature *Insect* (pl. 113), Picasso took as inspiration the *gus*, a Provençal vinegar or water vessel with six handles through which a rope can be threaded to hang the container on the wall. The six appendages reminded Picasso of the legs of an insect, and he therefore painted eyes on the vessel's lid and an additional set of little legs at its base.

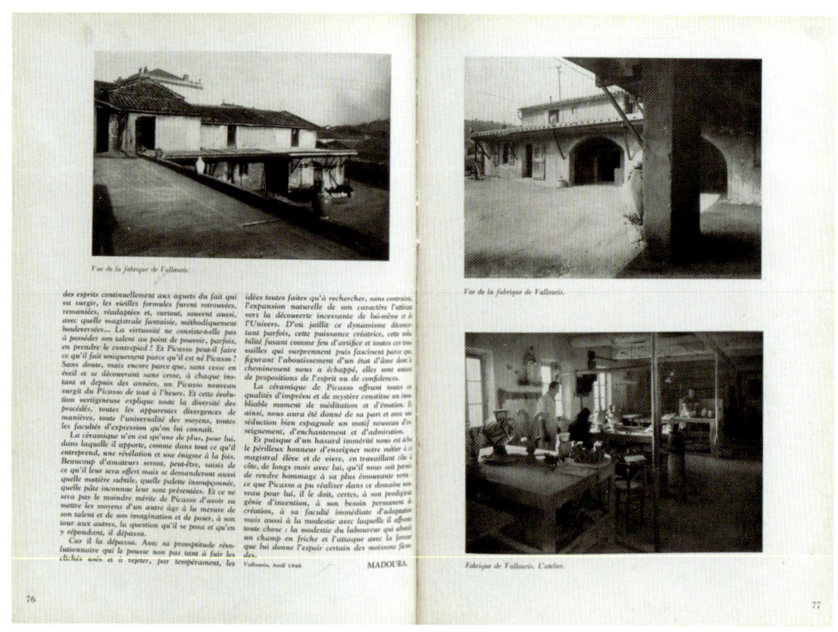

Vue de la fabrique de Vallauris.

des esprits continuellement aux aguets du fait qui va surgir, les vieilles formules furent retrouvées, remaniées, réadaptées et, surtout, souvent aussi, avec quelle magistrale fantaisie, méthodiquement bouleversées... La virtuosité ne consiste-t-elle pas à posséder son talent au point de pouvoir, parfois, en prendre le contrepied ? Et Picasso peut-il faire ce qu'il fait uniquement parce qu'il est né Picasso ? Sans doute, mais encore parce que, sans cesse en éveil et se découvrant sans cesse, à chaque instant et depuis des années, un Picasso nouveau surgit du Picasso de tout à l'heure. Et cette évolution vertigineuse explique toute la diversité des procédés, toutes les apparentes divergences de manières, toute l'universalité des moyens, toutes les facultés d'expression qu'on lui connaît.

La céramique n'en est qu'une de plus, pour lui, dans laquelle il apporte, comme dans tout ce qu'il entreprend, une révélation et une énigme à la fois. Beaucoup d'amateurs seront, peut-être, saisis de ce qu'il leur sera offert mais se demanderont aussi quelle matière subtile, quelle palette insoupçonnée, quelle pâte inconnue leur sont présentées. Et ce ne sera pas le moindre mérite de Picasso d'avoir su mettre les moyens d'un autre âge à la mesure de son talent et de son imagination et de poser, à son tour aux autres, la question qu'il se posa et qu'en y répondant, il dépassa.

Car il la dépassa. Avec sa promptitude révolutionnaire qui le pousse non pas tant à fuir les clichés usés et à rejeter, par tempérament, les idées toutes faites qu'à rechercher, sans contrainte, l'expansion naturelle de son caractère l'attirant vers la découverte incessante de lui-même et de l'Univers. D'où jaillit ce dynamisme déconcertant parfois, cette puissance créatrice, cette volubilité fusant comme feu d'artifice et toutes ces trouvailles qui surprennent puis fascinent parce que, figurant l'aboutissement d'un état d'âme dont le cheminement nous a échappé, elles sont autant de propositions de l'esprit ou de confidences.

La céramique de Picasso offrant toutes ces qualités d'imprévu et de mystère constitue un inoubliable moment de méditation et d'émotion. Et ainsi, nous aura été donné de sa part et avec une séduction bien espagnole un motif nouveau d'enseignement, d'enchantement et d'admiration.

Et puisque d'un hasard immérité nous est échu le périlleux honneur d'enseigner notre métier à ce magistral élève et de vivre, en travaillant côte à côte, de longs mois avec lui, qu'il nous soit permis de rendre hommage à sa plus émouvante vertu : ce que Picasso a pu réaliser dans ce domaine nouveau pour lui, il le doit, certes, à son prodigieux génie d'invention, à son besoin permanent de création, à sa faculté immédiate d'adaptation mais aussi à la modestie avec laquelle il affronte toute chose : la modestie du laboureur qui aborde un champ en friche et l'attaque avec la ferveur que lui donne l'espoir certain des moissons fécondes.

Vallauris, Avril 1948 MADOURA.

76

Vue de la fabrique de Vallauris.

Fabrique de Vallauris. L'atelier.

77

1. Pages from "Picasso céramiste," *Cahiers d'Art* 23, no. 1 (1948): 76–77. The photographs picture the Madoura pottery, Vallauris

MARCH 1948: Joan Miró visited Picasso in Vallauris. The two artists were old friends, having first met in Paris in 1920. Due to Miró's self-imposed exile in Spain during World War II, they had not seen each other for many years. Miró, too, would become deeply engaged with ceramics and sculpture during the postwar years.

APRIL 29, 1948: Henri Matisse wrote to his son Pierre: "Picasso has just purchased a house at Vallauris, on the high ground, with 10,000 [square] meters of garden, but no trees.... He's still carried away with his ceramics. He's been working on statues incorporating large, odd-shaped pots for a long while now. He sticks his hand inside where he wants the hollows. It's original, but I don't altogether go along with it. When you think of his panels at the museum with their very anemic and pale colors. They're very intriguing, but he's going through a sort of stage similar to the Blue or Rose periods. This time it's grey. With glazed colors, the designs come to life automatically [in the firing]. After molding his plates he always decorates them with kinds of pictures. Why use plates instead of panels?"[23]

MAY 1948: Picasso and Gilot relocated from Golfe-Juan to La Galloise, a villa in Vallauris. The move into their new home coincided with the publication of the first comprehensive documentation of Picasso's work in ceramic produced at the Madoura pottery, published in a special issue of the journal *Cahiers d'Art*.[24] Essays on this new aspect of his artistic practice—written by the journal's editor, Christian Zervos, and Jaime Sabartés, the artist's secretary and friend—were accompanied by scores of reproductions of individual works, including two glazed *Seated Woman* sculptures (pls. 102 and 103), *Owl (Vase)* (pl. 108), and *Standing Bull (Vase)* (pl. 109).[25] The text "Picasso céramiste" and Sabartés's essay "Picasso à Vallauris" were accompanied by descriptive photographs showing the Madoura workshop and facilities as well as Picasso's studio and the artist at work on his ceramics (fig. 1).

JULY 24–AUGUST 29, 1948: The potters collective of the Nérolium farming cooperative at Vallauris presented the first exhibition of Picasso's ceramic works, under the title *Poteries, fleurs, parfums* (Pottery, flowers, perfumes).[26]

NOVEMBER 26, 1948: The exhibition *Poterie et une sculpture de Picasso* (Pottery and a sculpture by Picasso) opened at the Maison de la pensée française in Paris, an art gallery run by the French Communist Party. It featured a single bronze, *Man with a Lamb*, together with 149 ceramics, including owls, human statuettes, doves, and decorated bowls, plates, tiles, and urns. Shortly before that exhibition's opening, Roland Penrose had written to Picasso to request the loan of a few ceramic works for a show he was organizing for the Institute of Contemporary Arts, London.[27] His exhibition, titled *40,000 Years of Modern Art*, would examine the ties between ancient and modern art. Due to the conflict in dates between the two exhibitions, Penrose was unable to secure the loans, but his request indicates the immediate response to Picasso's ceramics within the art world. The reaction from the general public was mixed, according to Gilot:

> Artistically [the Paris exhibition] made something of a sensation because it was the first time this new aspect of his creativity had been shown. That series was the finest—at least the most inventive—of all his pottery because that was the time of discovery, the period of the amphora in the form of a woman and the combined forms he put together in the first surge of his inspiration.... Those who understood to what degree Pablo had renewed the potter's art were very excited by what they saw but people in general took it rather mildly. It wasn't really what they expected of him.[28]

JANUARY 1949: Les Éditions du Chêne, the publishing house run by Girodias, published *Les Sculptures de Picasso*, the first comprehensive study solely devoted to this aspect of Picasso's practice (fig. 2).[29] The project had been initiated in September 1943, during the German occupation of Paris, on the suggestion of Girodias. A specialist in French art and design, he had published the wartime paintings of Picasso and Matisse despite Nazi censorship.[30] From its inception the book constituted a sort of collaboration between the artist, the publisher, and Brassaï, whom Picasso had personally requested to do the photography.[31] It would take three years to photograph all the sculptures produced between 1902 and 1946, and an additional three years before the book was published. In its final form, it included reproductions of more than two hundred sculptures, the great majority of which had been photographed by Brassaï (Dora Maar and the Galerie Louise Leiris in Paris also provided a few). Picasso had invited Brassaï to write the introduction, but he had declined.[32] Ultimately, Picasso's dealer, Daniel-Henry Kahnweiler, provided an impassioned short essay. Shortly after *Les Sculptures de Picasso* was released in France, Rodney Phillips in London published an English translation by the young art critic David Sylvester.

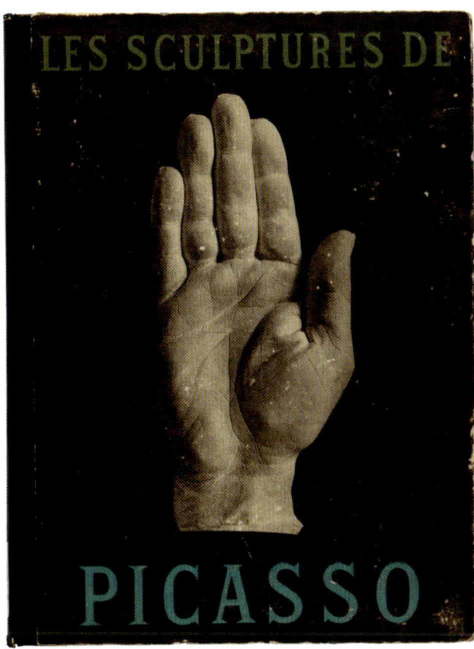

2. Brassaï and Daniel-Henry Kahnweiler, *Les Sculptures de Picasso* (Paris: Les Éditions du Chêne, 1949). The cover features a reproduction of the artist's plaster *Picasso's Right Hand* (1937). The Museum of Modern Art Library, New York

SPRING–SUMMER 1949: Picasso returned to La Galloise in Vallauris after a winter in Paris. His ceramic practice began to wane somewhat at this time. Gilot would recall, "Until the summer of 1949, Pablo had been satisfied to spend two or three afternoons a week doing pottery at the Ramiés', but now, suddenly, he had had enough of ceramics and had begun to look for a place where he could paint."[33] As the villa provided insufficient space for him to work on a large scale, he acquired an old perfume factory close by, on rue du Fournas.

During the summer he transformed the factory's ground floor into studios for painting and sculpture, and created storage areas for his ceramics on the second floor. The sculpture studio was situated in the right-hand wing of the perfume factory, "large and high-vaulted, about thirty-five feet by twenty-five."[34] Gilot recalled that it "took us about two months to put things in shape and in October Pablo began to work there."[35] Beginning that fall and continuing through the early 1950s, the period would see the creation of Picasso's most iconic assemblages and their iterations in bronze.

***PREGNANT WOMAN*, 1949**

Inspired by Gilot's pregnancy and the birth of their daughter, Paloma, on April 19, Picasso fashioned a totemic female form using plaster and what probably was "a palm frond stripped of its palm leaves" that he had collected in Vallauris.[36] Although the work is nearly life size, Picasso's execution is far from naturalistic: limbs, womb, and breasts are isolated from one another and suspended in space, connected only by a spiny central rod. Measuring nearly fifty-one inches in height, the slender and schematic *Pregnant Woman* (pl. 114) was preceded by a smaller, more compressed version of the same motif, made in 1948.[37] The larger *Pregnant Woman* was cast in an edition of two bronzes at the Valsuani foundry in Paris; both would remain with the artist until his death.

JANUARY 24–MARCH 19, 1950: The Museum of Modern Art presented *Picasso: The Sculptor's Studio*. The exhibition featured etchings comprising that section of the artist's *Vollard Suite* (see figs. 18 and 19 on p. 143).

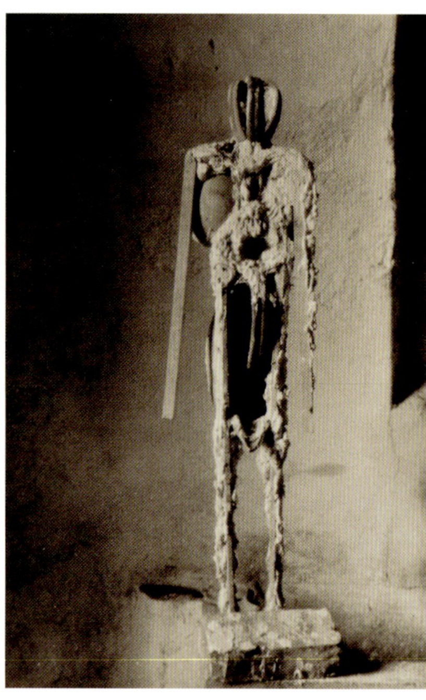

3. Early stage of *Pregnant Woman*, first state, at Picasso's rue du Fournas studio, Vallauris, May 1950. Photograph by Claire Batigne. Picasso Archives, Musée national Picasso–Paris

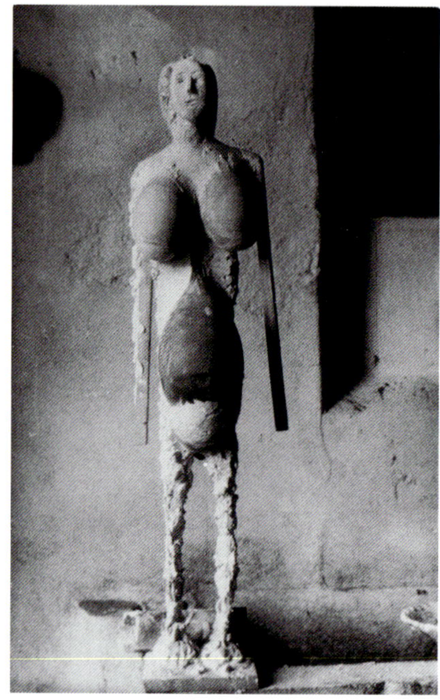

4. Subsequent stage of *Pregnant Woman*, first state, at Picasso's rue du Fournas studio, Vallauris, May 1950. Photograph by Claire Batigne. Picasso Archives, Musée national Picasso–Paris

PREGNANT WOMAN, FIRST STATE, 1950

Pregnant Woman (pl. 115) was among the first major works Picasso made at the rue du Fournas studio.[38] Claude was now three, and Paloma one; according to Gilot, Picasso wanted another child but she did not. Perhaps Picasso's desire found expression in this sculpture. By May 1950 he had begun to construct the plaster assemblage around a metal armature (fig. 3), to which he added a large ceramic vessel as a belly and two smaller ones as breasts (fig. 4).[39] Other ceramic fragments form the back of the neck and the woman's lower right arm, while nails and a plank of wood reinforce the left arm; nails and additional pieces of wood hold the composition together.

The sculpture depicts a small woman near the end of her term. Gilot described it as a "grotesque" version of herself and complained about the ill-defined proportions: "It always looked to me like a child-woman recently descended from the ape."[40] Between 1951 and 1953, three bronze casts of the sculpture would be made at the Valsuani foundry in Paris. Picasso made a second version of the sculpture in 1959, modifying the feet and adding naturalistic details such as nipples and a navel.[41]

WOMAN WITH A BABY CARRIAGE AND *LITTLE GIRL JUMPING ROPE*, 1950–[54]

Woman with a Baby Carriage (pl. 118) calls to mind a well-known photograph taken by Robert Capa in August 1948. It depicts the artist, accompanied by Gilot, pushing Claude along the beach in a stroller.[42] Such a vehicle served more than one purpose for Picasso's family, however. Gilot described their routine: "Often, on his way to work, Pablo would stop by the dump to see what might have been added since his last inspection.... He searched the dump daily and before he even got there, he rummaged around in any rubbish barrels we passed on our walk to the studio. I walked along with him, pushing an old baby carriage into which he threw whatever likely looking pieces of junk he found on the way. Or if it was something too big to fit into the carriage, he would send the car around for it afterward."[43] Scavenged objects that made their way into *Woman with a Baby Carriage* include a metal pushchair, a stove plate, a gas ring, cake tins, an old strainer, and pottery fragments. Although generally dated 1950, the making of it extended beyond that year. Penrose recalled from a visit to the rue du Fournas studio in June 1954 that "Picasso brought out large sculptures he was working on," and *Woman with a Baby Carriage* was among them.[44] Penrose, his wife Lee Miller, and Georges Braque, who was also at the studio, witnessed Picasso "playing with all manner of solutions, each position he tried brought a surprise" (see fig. 17 on p. 24).[45] In his biography of the artist, Penrose would note that "the alliance of the grotesque with Picasso's ability to metamorphose objects at will is a key to the power of these composite inventions."[46]

With *Little Girl Jumping Rope* (pl. 117), Picasso came close to accomplishing the impossible: a sculpture that defies gravity and does not "touch the ground."[47] Gilot recalled that the artist had asked the "ironmonger in Vallauris [to] make him a rectangular base from which rose, to a height of three or four feet, a curving iron tube in the shape the jump-rope would have as it reached the ground."[48] The work was equally

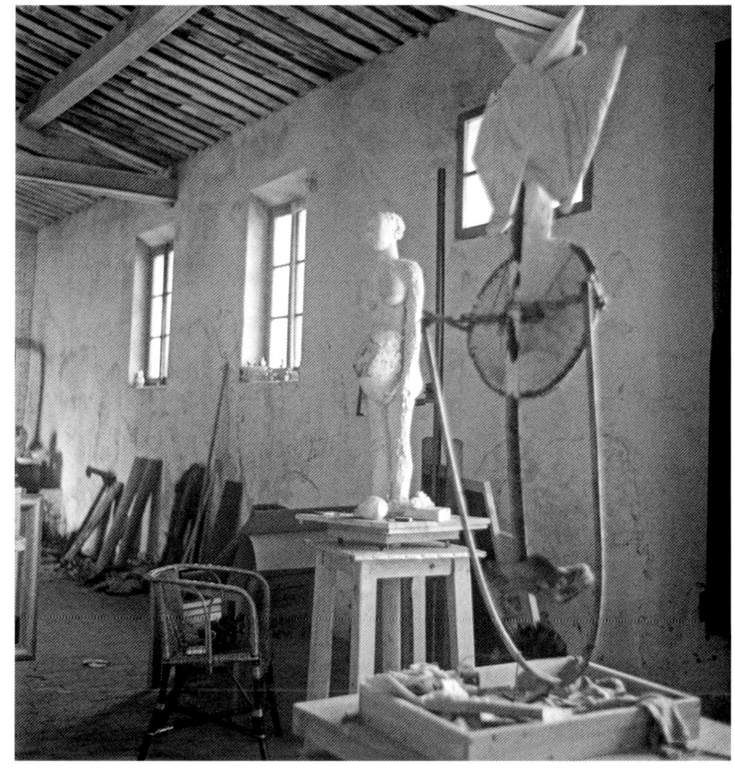

5. *Little Girl Jumping Rope* in progress at Picasso's rue du Fournas studio, Vallauris, 1950. The plaster assemblage *Pregnant Woman* is in the background. Photograph by Robert Picault. Picasso Archives, Musée national Picasso–Paris

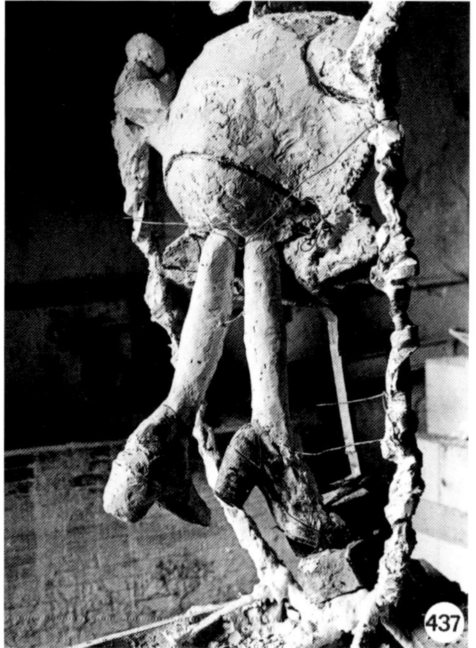

6. *Little Girl Jumping Rope* in progress at Picasso's rue du Fournas studio, Vallauris, 1951. Photograph by Robert Picault. Picasso Archives, Musée national Picasso–Paris

inventive in terms of its foraged ingredients: a basket served as the little girl's belly and torso, while the discarded lid of an oval chocolate box became her face. Photographs of Picasso's rue du Fournas studio show that work on the sculpture was underway by around mid-1950, when he had finished the plaster assemblage *Pregnant Woman* (figs. 5, 6). Studio photographs taken by Edward Quinn in October 1953 confirm that Picasso continued to work on the sculpture until at least that year; Quinn's pictures show *Little Girl Jumping Rope* still without its flower or the serpent on its base.[49]

Like other assemblages of this period, *Woman with a Baby Carriage* and *Little Girl Jumping Rope* would be cast in bronze at the Valsuani foundry in Paris. One of Miller's photographs of Picasso's home in Mougins proves that a bronze cast of *Woman with a Baby Carriage* existed by around 1963 (fig. 7). The image depicts the cast next to the original assemblage, which has been hoisted onto a sculptor's stand. *Little Girl Jumping Rope* was probably cast in 1956.[50] The bronze copies ensured the survival of these extremely fragile assemblages, and despite the unifying effect of casting on the sculpture's surface, the identity of the original found objects remains strong. Bronze casting also offered Picasso the possibility of creating unique copies; he had explored the practice of painting bronze casts as early as 1914 (see pls. 21–26). Werner Spies contends that Picasso had planned to paint his large-scale

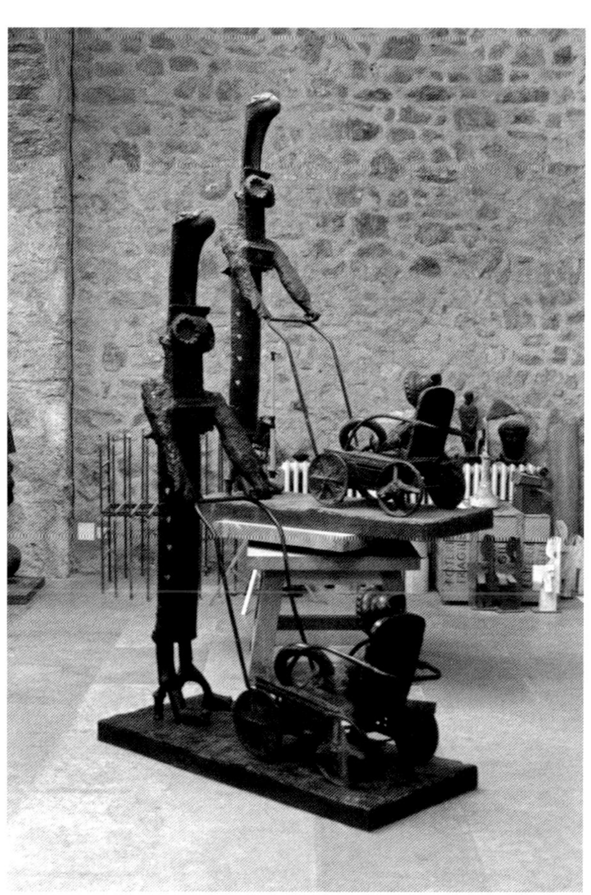

7. The original assemblage of *Woman with a Baby Carriage* and a bronze cast of the work (foreground) in Picasso's studio at Notre-Dame-de-Vie, Mougins, c. 1963. Photograph by Lee Miller or Roland Penrose. The Lee Miller Archives, London

assemblages.[51] In the end, however, neither the bronze casts of *Woman with a Baby Carriage* nor those of *Little Girl Jumping Rope* would be painted. Casts of the sculptures would be presented publicly for the first time in the 1966 exhibition *Hommage à Pablo Picasso*, at the Petit Palais in Paris.

SHE-GOAT, 1950

Perhaps the most lifelike sculpture Picasso made during the Vallauris period is a full-sized pregnant goat assembled from materials he had discovered on walks around town and scavenged from the dump near his studio. *She-Goat* (pl. 119) is, Penrose describes, "a composite construction pieced together from objects in which Picasso found new possibilities."[52] Picasso began work on *She-Goat* by selecting objects that specifically suited his vision of the finished sculpture.[53] In a palm frond Picasso saw the animal's spine and forehead, while a large woven basket was repurposed to become the goat's belly and two clay vessels her udders.[54] A piece of pipe and some folded cardboard were transfigured as the animal's anus and sex. These and other components, such as metal strips, wire, and wood, were then joined with plaster. During this process Picasso supported the animal's belly with bricks, so the sculpture wouldn't collapse (figs. 8, 9). In its final state, the work was for him "more like a goat than a goat," despite the fact that it never hides its "pure fabrication," as Elizabeth Cowling observes.[55]

The large and fragile plaster assemblage would be difficult to cast in bronze. Molds were made of its various parts, and by May 1952 at least one bronze had been produced at the Valsuani foundry: it was exhibited at the Salon de Mai in Paris. That same year, *She-Goat* was the subject of an illustrated book by André Verdet, titled *La Chèvre* (The goat).[56] In 1953 a bronze cast of the sculpture was shown in Rome in the Picasso retrospective at the Galleria nazionale d'arte moderna (fig. 10) and in Milan at the Palazzo Reale.

By 1957 one of the casts would be moved to Picasso's villa La Californie in Cannes, where it was displayed in the garden and sometimes used as tethering post for the artist's pet goat, Esmeralda (see fig. 18 on p. 25). In 1959 Barr would acquire a cast for The Museum of Modern Art, after a long pursuit. In summer 1952 he had described the work as "without question Picasso's most important sculpture since *Man with a Lamb* [pl. 87]," noting that, "I think Picasso is now the most important sculptor working in France."[57]

AUGUST 6, 1950: A bronze cast of Picasso's *Man with a Lamb* was erected in the market square of Vallauris under a banner that read "à Picasso Vallauris reconnaissant" (to Picasso, a grateful Vallauris) (see fig. 15 on p. 190). The artist had donated the sculpture to the people of the town in fall 1949. It was initially installed in the Cistercian chapel of the Château de Vallauris, but the chapel's poor lighting and the scale of the statue relative to the small space proved unsatisfactory, so the following summer the work was moved outside to the market square. Writers such as Paul Eluard and Tristan

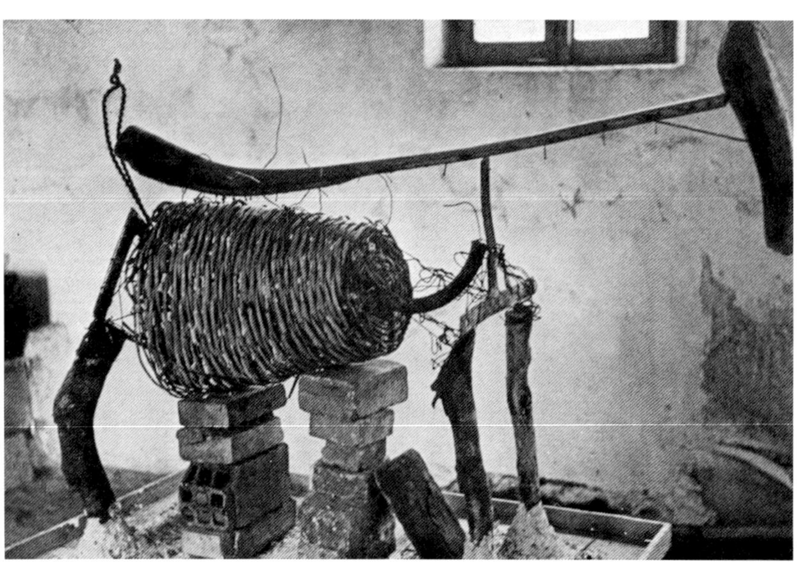

8. *She-Goat* in progress in Picasso's rue du Fournas studio, Vallauris, 1950. Picasso Archives, Musée national Picasso–Paris

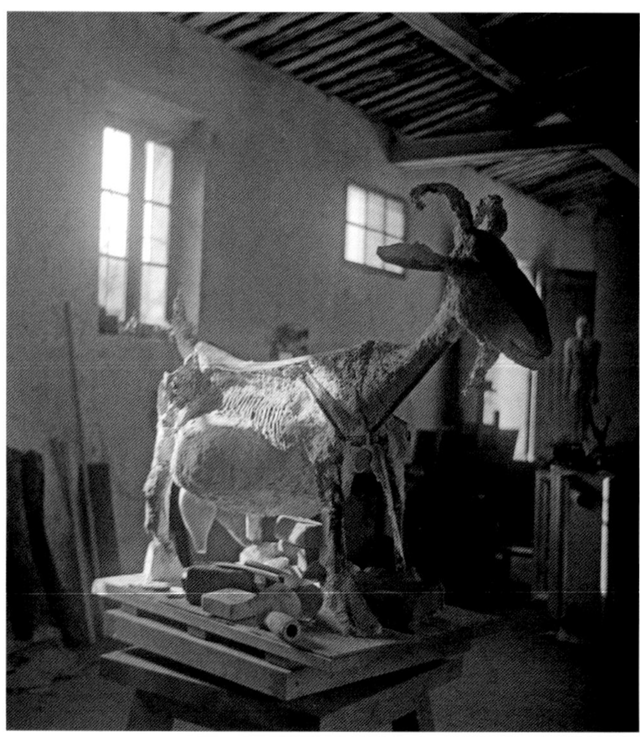

9. The plaster assemblage *She-Goat* at Picasso's rue du Fournas studio, Vallauris, 1950. Photograph by Robert Picault. Picasso Archives, Musée national Picasso–Paris

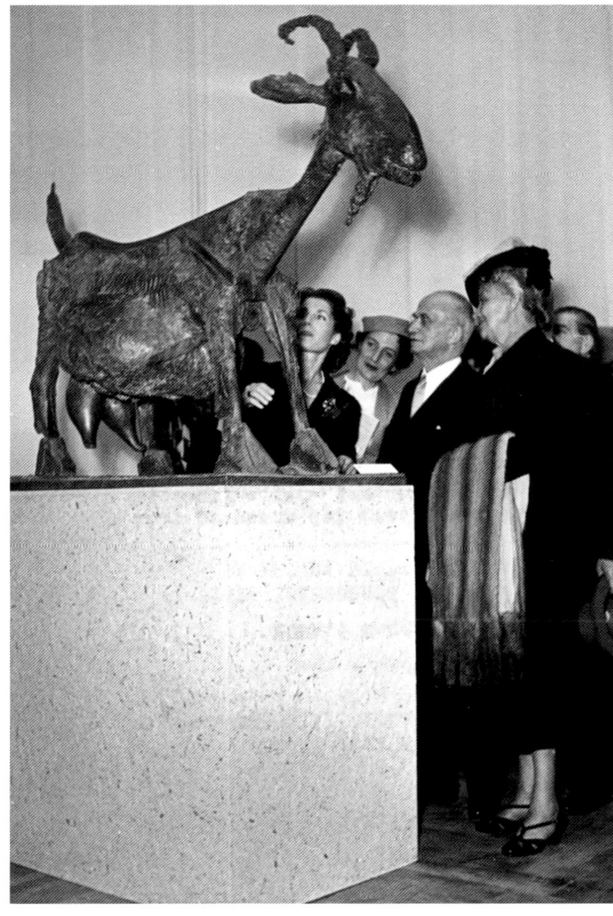

10. Luigi Einaudi, President of Italy, and others observing a bronze cast of *She-Goat* during a visit to the Picasso retrospective at the Galleria nazionale d'arte moderna, Rome, May 5, 1953. Picasso Archives, Musée national Picasso–Paris

Tzara gathered for the festive occasion, which included a speech by the Communist Party leader Laurent Casanova, remarks from Jean Cocteau, and a poem written for the occasion by André Verdet. Gilot described the well-attended dedication as having "the informal gayety of a village fête," celebrating an artist who that January had been named an honorary citizen.[58] Penrose reported that the local press was effusive: one writer covering the dedication averred, "Picasso is not only a great artist, he is also a man with heart."[59] Sometime that same year, Picasso presented the Musée Picasso in Antibes with two unique cement casts of sculptures that he had modeled in the 1930s at Boisgeloup: *Head of a Woman* (pl. 55) and *Head of a Woman* (1931–32). This followed an extensive gift of paintings and works on paper in 1946 and of seventy-five ceramics in 1947.

SEPTEMBER–OCTOBER 1950: Picasso and the filmmaker Frédéric Rossif designed stage sets featuring the artist's ceramic figures for a never-completed film. Robert Picault, a ceramicist and Picasso's neighbor in Vallauris, captured these scenes in his photographs; the little *Seated Faun* of 1950 (pl. 107) appeared as one of the main characters (figs. 11, 12).

NOVEMBER 1950–JANUARY 1951: The exhibition *Picasso: Sculptures, dessins* (Picasso: Sculptures, drawings) mounted at the Maison de la pensée française, Paris, juxtaposed forty-three of the artist's sculptures dating between 1914 and 1944 with forty-three of his ink drawings. The cover of the catalogue paired Brassaï's photograph of *Face* (pl. 97), one of the engraved pebbles from 1946, with a study for *Man with a Lamb* (see fig. 14 on p. 22). The book included a short introductory text titled "Picasso," by the poet Louis Aragon.[60]

***BABOON AND YOUNG*, OCTOBER 1951**

Baboon and Young (pl. 116) is a key work in the group of Vallauris sculptures that also includes *She-Goat* (pl. 119) and *Pregnant Woman* (pl. 115). This sculpture has traditionally been assumed to be a portrayal of a mother, beginning with the French title assigned to the work, *La Guenon et son petit*: "guenon" is a term for a female monkey as well as, colloquially, an ugly woman.[61] Yet the *Baboon*, unlike *She-Goat* and *Pregnant Woman*, bears no visible elements of female anatomy, and its demeanor is far more comical than is typical in Picasso's depictions of maternity. Photographs by Capa, Miller, and others capturing the family's life in Vallauris show Claude constantly in his father's arms.[62] Of course, at age seventy, Picasso was far closer in shape to the baboon than the trim Gilot. The animal is convincingly read as Picasso, the proud and exuberant father.[63]

Baboon and Young is best known for its inventive repurposing of two toy cars to form a distinctively simian face. Kahnweiler had visited Vallauris and given Claude toy versions of a Panhard and a Renault. Gilot would later explain that Claude, then about four years old, was fonder of breaking toys than playing with them, so Picasso, seeing new possibilities in them, claimed them for himself.[64] Joining the cars at their undercarriages, the artist utterly transformed their cutting-edge, sensual lines, revealing a delightfully silly-looking creature, its gentle expression created by the smilelike curve of the Panhard's grill.

The remainder of the baboon's form was likewise created with imaginative alchemy: the rotund body is a pot Picasso carved with a knife to indicate the animal's breasts, the shoulders are formed from the handles of a large bowl common to the area, the ears are cup handles, and the tail—in keeping with the automotive theme—is a type of suspension spring used in cars.[65] Picasso modeled a small baboon child of rudimentary plaster forms, and this figure clings to the larger rounded body.

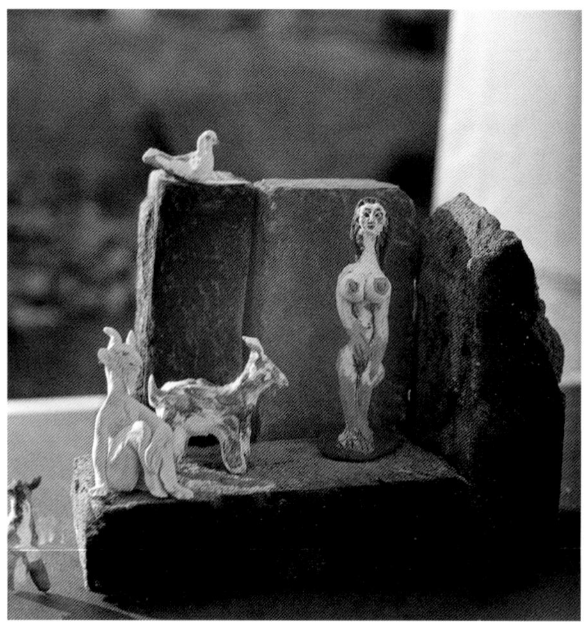

11. Staging of Picasso's earthenware figurines, including *Seated Faun* (second from left), for an unfinished film the artist made with Frédéric Rossif, Vallauris, 1950. Photograph by Robert Picault. Picasso Archives, Musée national Picasso–Paris

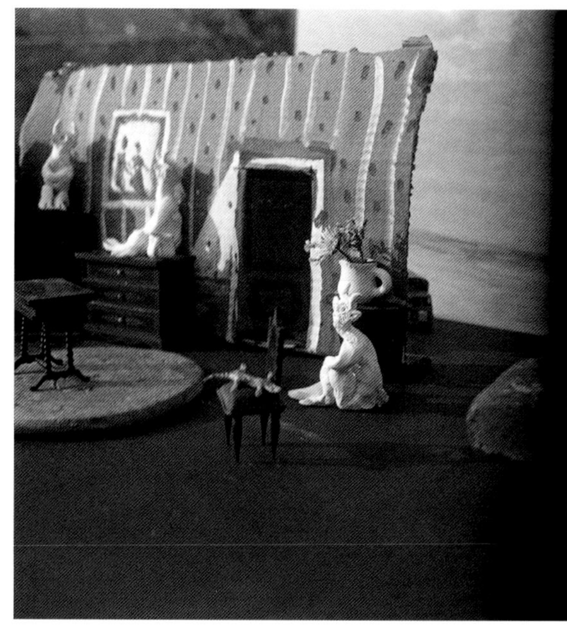

12. Staging of Picasso's earthenware figurines, including *Seated Faun* (center right), for an unfinished film the artist made with Frédéric Rossif, Vallauris, 1950. Photograph by Robert Picault. Picasso Archives, Musée national Picasso–Paris

The original plaster assemblage is dated October 1951 on the authority of an incised inscription on its base. It is seen in a photograph taken by Picault during his work on *Les Céramiques et les sculptures de Picasso*, a 1951 film about the artist (fig. 13). *Baboon and Young* would be cast in bronze in an edition of six at the Valsuani foundry starting in 1953, the year the sculpture was exhibited as part of the Picasso retrospective at the Galleria nazionale d'arte moderna in Rome and the Palazzo Reale in Milan.

FEBRUARY 1951: While Picasso was in Paris, Gilot supervised a photography shoot in Vallauris for an upcoming issue of *Verve* magazine devoted to his ceramics, recent paintings, and sculpture.[66] The issue, "Picasso à Vallauris, 1949–1951" would appear in the fall. It reproduced several dozen photographs of the artist's work in three dimensions, some of which were published in color.[67] Additional pictures showed the rue du Fournas studio with Picasso's most recent plaster assemblages on view—*She-Goat*, *Pregnant Woman*, and *Flowers in a Vase* (pl. 125) among them. This magazine also featured an extensive introduction by Kahnweiler, along with essays by Georges Ramié and the Greek poet Odysseus Elytis.

NOVEMBER 1951: A trip by Giacometti and his wife, Annette, to see Picasso at Vallauris erupted into a dispute when Picasso questioned Giacometti's respect for him. The argument resulted in the cooling of their friendship, and they ceased their practice of visiting one another's studios.[68] However, they would remain interested in each other's work throughout the years to come. Picasso was eager to hear the other's opinion, and though Giacometti kept a careful distance, they would see each other on occasion when Picasso was in Paris.

CRANE AND _LITTLE OWL_, 1951–52

The painted bronzes *Crane* (pl. 122) and *Little Owl* (pl. 120) illustrate Picasso's renewed exploration of polychrome sculpture. Within Western culture the application of paints to the surfaces of sculptures has origins in antiquity. One of its functions, particularly as seen in religious sculpture, was to make sacred figures appear as lifelike as possible. For Picasso, the painting of his sculptures made them more completely alive.

Picault documented the *Crane* assemblage in 1951 (fig. 14). Gilot described its creation:

> Finding the shovel which formed the tail-feathers . . . gave him the idea of making the sculpture of a crane. Then he found two roasting forks, a long one and another, much shorter and in bad condition, which he repaired by winding wire around it. These gave him the legs. The base he made, as he often did, by filling a candy box with plaster and when it had dried, tearing the box

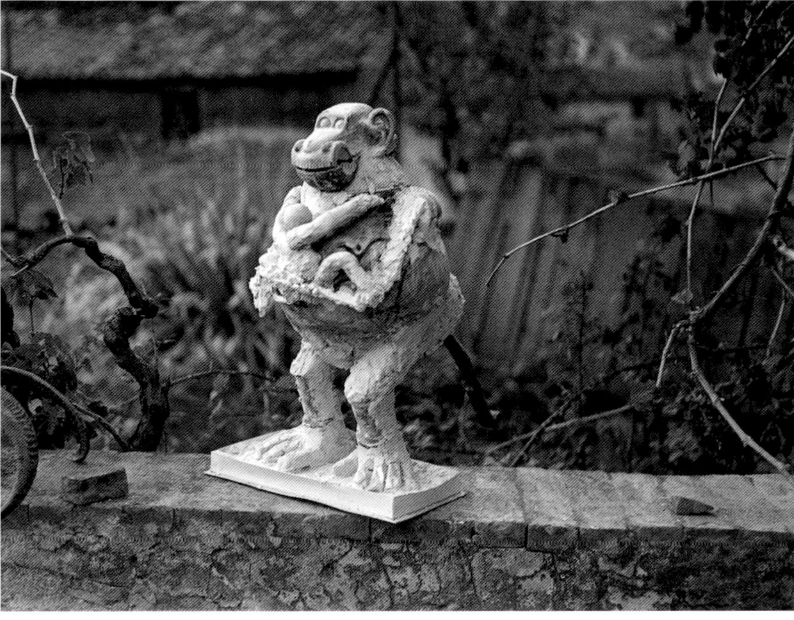

13. The original assemblage of *Baboon and Young* outside Picasso's rue du Fournas studio, Vallauris, 1951. Photograph by Robert Picault. Picasso Archives, Musée national Picasso–Paris

> away to leave the block of hardened plaster. For the head he used a brass faucet fitting into which he inserted a pointed metal wedge for a beak. Once it was cast in bronze, he painted it.[69]

Little Owl featured its own unconventional materials: the "iron blade of a hoe, a pair of pliers, nails, and screws."[70]

Two bronzes of *Crane* would be cast in 1952 at the Valsuani foundry in Paris. Back in his studio, Picasso painted the two casts black, decorating each with a unique pattern of white marks. In 1954 Picasso had two more bronzes of *Crane* cast, which he painted in a similar fashion. *Little Owl* exists in only two bronze casts, one painted and one not.

Like most of Picasso's bronze casts of assemblages, these two works immediately took on a public life. The two *Cranes* were presented for the first time in consecutive exhibitions held in Rome, Paris, Lyon, and Milan in 1953. That same year, the painted bronze *Little Owl* would join one of the painted bronzes of *Crane* in the exhibition of recent works by Picasso at the Galerie Louise Leiris.

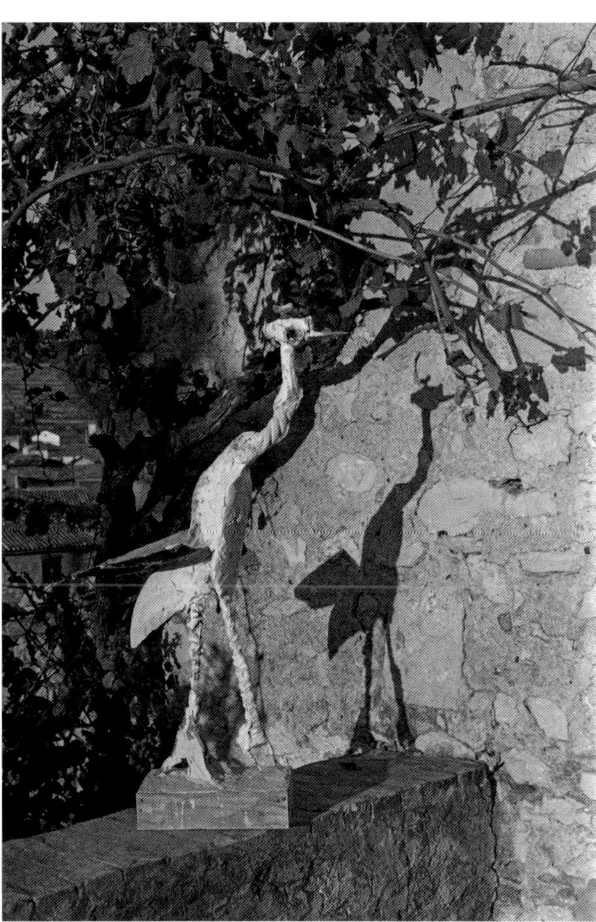

14. The original assemblage of *Crane* outside Picasso's rue du Fournas studio, Vallauris, 1951. Photograph by Robert Picault. Picasso Archives, Musée national Picasso–Paris

***FLOWERY WATERING CAN*, 1951–52, AND *FLOWERS IN A VASE*, 1951–53**

Flowery Watering Can (pl. 124) and *Flowers in a Vase* (pl. 125) are variations in a series of five flower still lifes Picasso began in 1951. Within this group, *Flowery Watering Can* is the most

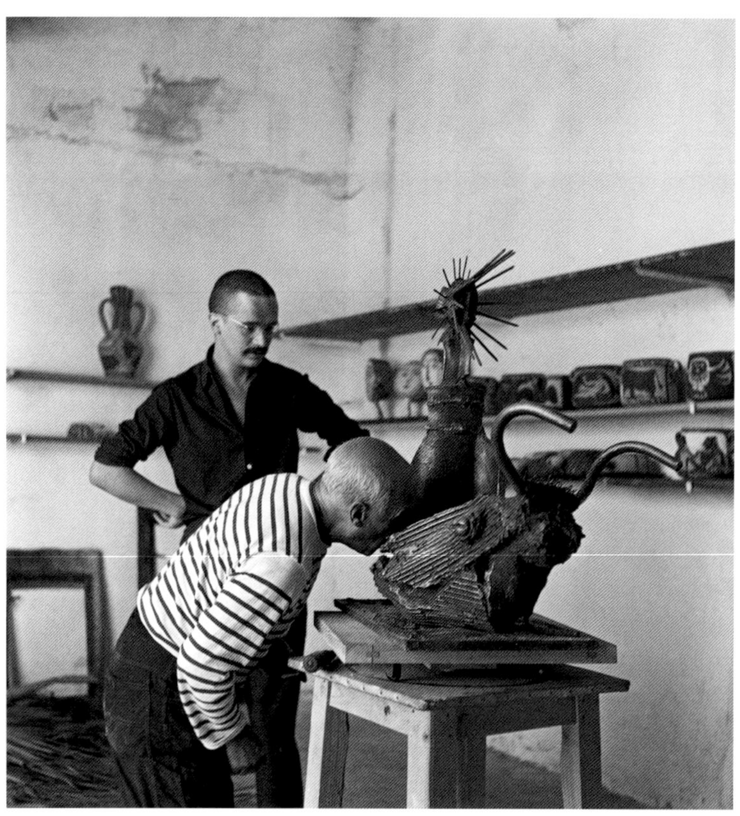

15. Picasso inspecting a bronze cast of *Goat Skull and Bottle* at his rue du Fournas studio with Marcel Valsuani, Vallauris, September 1952. Photograph by Robert Doisneau. Gamma/Rapho

fantastical, with its spiky, nail-decorated blossom reminiscent of a carnivorous plant. *Flowers in a Vase* illustrates the ease with which Picasso assigned various identities to the found objects he repurposed in his sculptures. The cake tins that appear here as flowers, for example, served as the woman's breasts in *Woman with a Baby Carriage* (pl. 118). A similar cake tin had already been turned into a small face during Picasso's plaster-casting experiments in Boisgeloup.[71] In fall 1951, an unfinished version of the original *Flowers in a Vase* plaster assemblage—one of the two flower heads had not yet been added—was reproduced in the special issue of *Verve* devoted to Picasso's recent work.[72] Both *Flowery Watering Can* and *Flowers in a Vase* would be cast in bronze at the Valsuani foundry in Paris.

WOMAN READING AND GOAT SKULL AND BOTTLE, 1951–53

Among the group of tabletop still life sculptures of the early 1950s, *Goat Skull and Bottle* (pl. 123) constitutes Picasso's most elaborate undertaking in terms of its painting technique, cutout forms, and use of overlapping planes. The original assemblage is larger in scale than other works made around the same time, and casting it in bronze was a difficult undertaking because of its fine detail. At least one of the two known bronzes had been cast by September 1952, when the photographer Robert Doisneau captured its arrival at Picasso's studio (fig. 15).[73] By May 1953 Picasso had painted each cast in a palette of black, gray, and white and sent them to simultaneous exhibitions in Paris (the Salon de Mai) and Rome, followed by a presentation in Milan (fig. 16).

Woman Reading (pl. 121) indicates Picasso's interest in enhancing "the textural elements of the sculpture" rather than the various viewpoints and spatial relations between objects he had explored in *Goat Skull and Bottle*.[74] The palette and motif of *Woman Reading* is related to contemporaneous paintings Picasso made of Gilot reading or resting in a recumbent position. Two of the three uniquely painted bronzes—one of which is painted white—were juxtaposed in an exhibition at the Galerie Louise Leiris in May 1953.[75] The exhibition included three more of the artist's most recent painted bronzes—*Crane, Still Life: Pitcher and Figs* (1951–53), and *Little Owl*, along with twenty-six of his ceramics.

SEPTEMBER 1, 1952: The Philadelphia collector R. Sturgis Ingersoll, president of the Philadelphia Museum of Art, acquired a bronze cast of *Man with a Lamb* (pl. 87) through the art dealers Curt Valentin and Kahnweiler.[76] Ingersoll and his wife, Marion, would give the sculpture to the Philadelphia Museum of Art in 1958.

***WOMAN CARRYING A CHILD*, 1953**

Picasso began a new phase of his sculpture practice in 1953, when he created seven painted wooden dolls for the four-year-old Paloma and three painted wooden figures of women. *Woman Carrying a Child* (pl. 127), the largest of these latter assemblages, features part of a palm frond coated with paint that suggests the hair of the standing woman; its inspiration is Gilot carrying Paloma in her arms.[77] These wooden figures (see fig. 13 on p. 256, foreground, for another) testify to Picasso's renewed attraction to the medium, with which he would work intensively for the remainder of the decade. They also echo earlier sculptural works, such as his Cubist constructions of 1912–15, and exemplify his rekindled interest in using planar elements to create the impression of volume.

***THE WOMAN WITH A KEY*, 1953–54**

The Woman with a Key (pl. 126) introduced a new approach to assemblage. The sculpture was constructed from found objects but without the use of modeling.[78] As documented in a series of photographs taken by Quinn in October 1953, Picasso assembled the sculpture on the floor of his rue du Fournas studio by abutting fired clay tiles, bricks, and drying stilts he had picked up at the nearby pottery dump, creating the form of a tall, slender female figure (see p. 202).

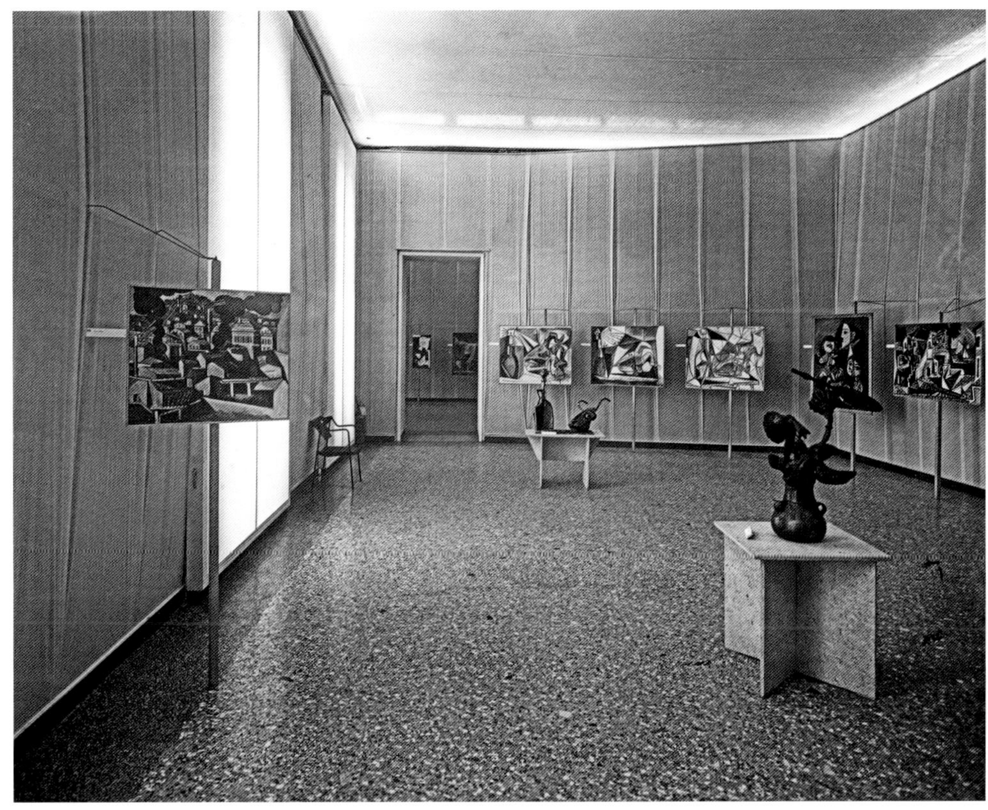

16. *Goat Skull and Bottle* (background) on view in the retrospective *Pablo Picasso* at the Palazzo Reale, Milan, 1953. A bronze cast of *Flowers in a Vase* is in the foreground. Photograph by Mario Perotti. Picasso Archives, Musée national Picasso-Paris

Some months after Picasso assembled *The Woman with a Key* he modified it under the influence of a new model: Sylvette David, who began posing for him in April 1954. According to Cowling, it was only after this that its various parts were cast in bronze and welded together so that it could stand upright.[79] The only real (uncast) object is the key, reminiscent of the absinthe spoon attached to the 1914 *Glass of Absinthe* casts, which Picasso added as he reworked *The Woman with a Key*. The right hand of the original assemblage had held a leafy branch, as seen in Quinn's photographs. The stone plinth would be added after the sculpture was brought to La Californie, Picasso's villa in Cannes, sometime before September 1958.

MAY–NOVEMBER 1953: Museum exhibitions during this period brought Picasso's sculptures to the public in the greatest quantities to date. A major retrospective of Picasso's work opened on May 19 at the Galleria nazionale d'arte moderna in Rome; in June, another retrospective exhibition opened at the Musée de Lyon. The Rome exhibition, which was organized by the Italian art historian and Cézanne catalogue raisonné author Lionello Venturi, included thirty-two sculptures and thirty-nine ceramics chosen from Picasso's collection. The sculpture selection placed emphasis on the last two decades and encompassed welded metal assemblages made in collaboration with González, modeled works from Boisgeloup, iconic war-years sculptures such as *Death's Head* and *Man with a Lamb*, and recent bronze casts of assemblages from Vallauris. A modified version of the Rome exhibition traveled in September to the Palazzo Reale in Milan. The Lyon retrospective, in contrast to the Italian exhibitions, was primarily drawn from private collections and dealers. Notably, it included two early Cubist assemblages—a *Glass of Absinthe* sculpture (pls. 21–26) and *Still Life* (pl. 15)—along with the 1950s polychrome bronzes *Woman Reading* and *Crane*. Together they highlighted Picasso's status both as a pioneer and contemporary practitioner of the freshly avant-garde 1950s art of assemblage.

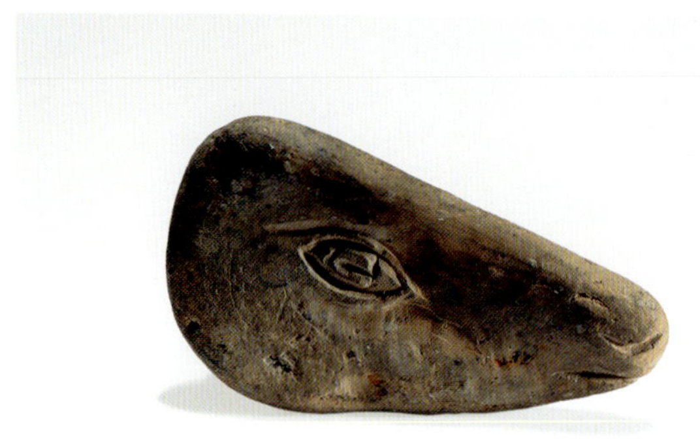

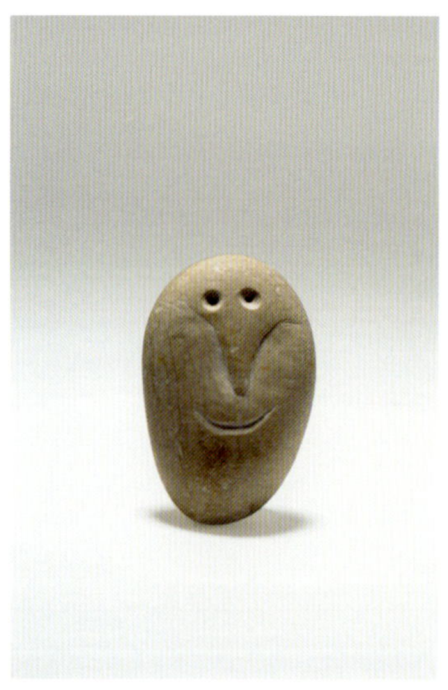

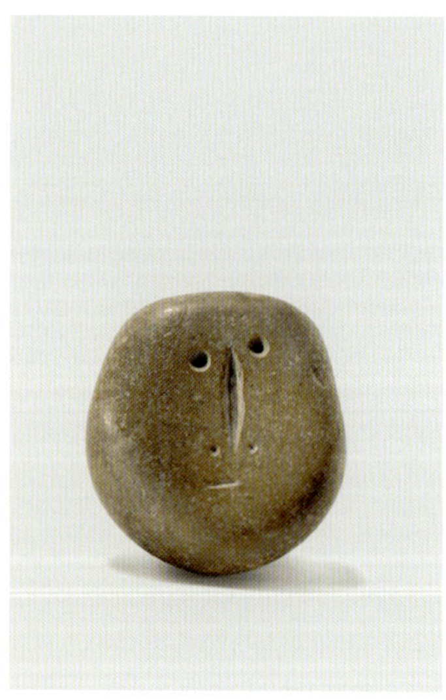

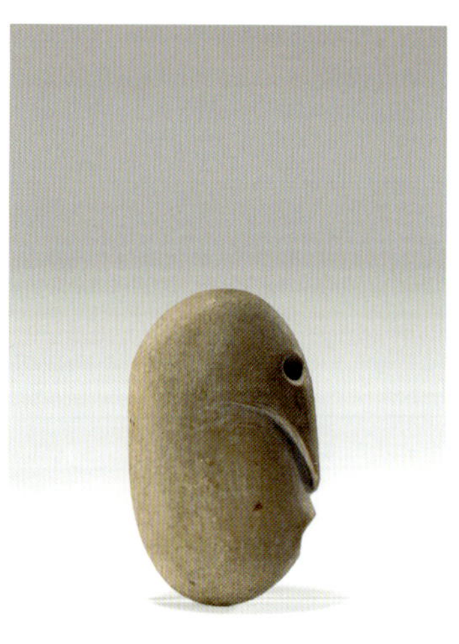

Clockwise from left:

90. FACE. Golfe-Juan, 1946
Engraved pebble
1 1/16 × 11/16 × 5/16 in. (2.7 × 1.7 × 0.8 cm)
Private collection

91. HEAD OF AN ANIMAL. 1945–46
Engraved pebble
1 1/4 × 2 3/8 × 5/16 in. (3.2 × 6 × 0.8 cm)
Private collection

92. HEAD. 1945
Engraved pebble
1 3/16 × 11/16 × 3/16 in. (3 × 1.8 × 0.5 cm)
Private collection

93. FACE. Golfe-Juan, 1946
Engraved pebble
1 1/4 × 1 1/8 × 1/2 in. (3.2 × 2.9 × 1.3 cm)
Private collection

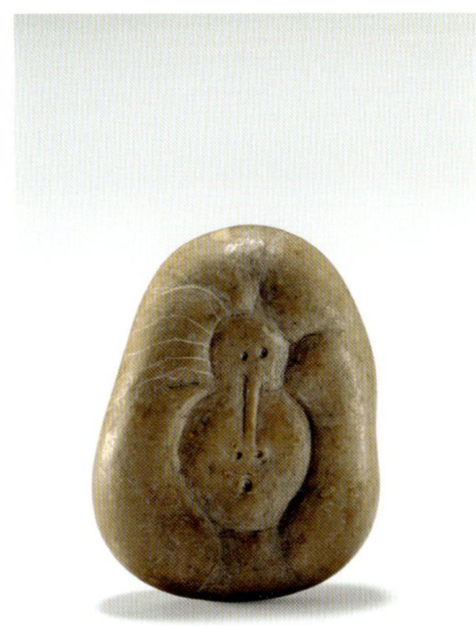

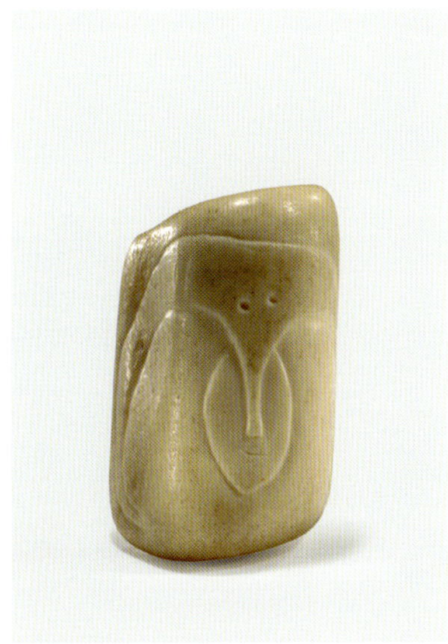

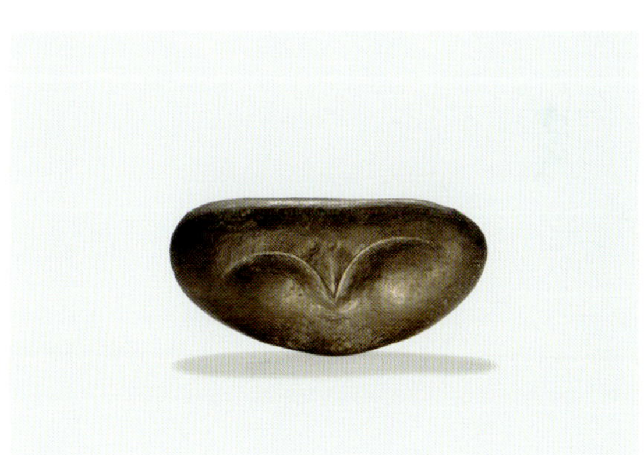

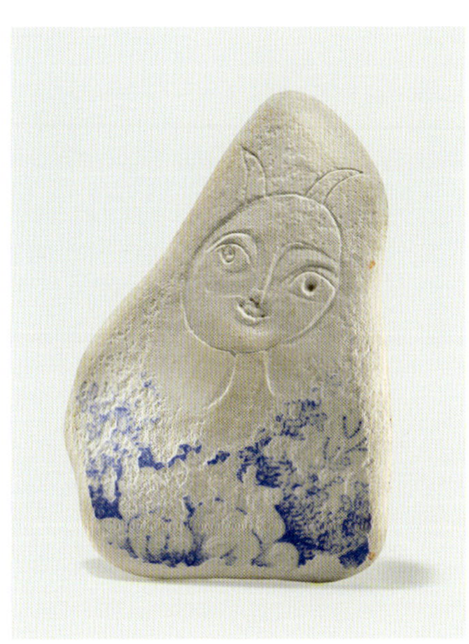

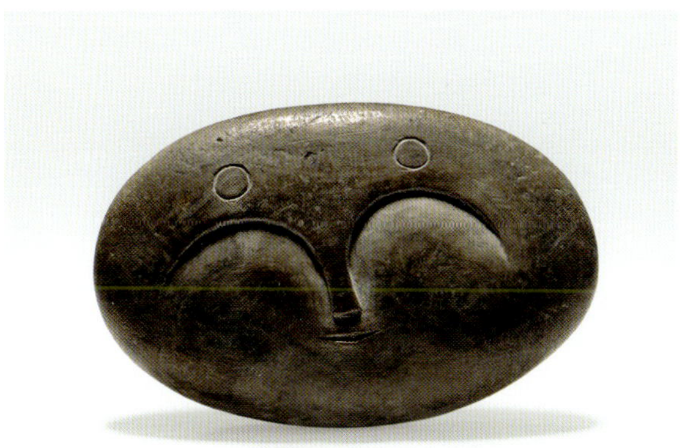

Clockwise from top left:

94. **PEAR-SHAPED FACE.** Golfe-Juan, c. 1946
Engraved pebble
1 9⁄16 × 1 1⁄4 × 1⁄2 in. (4 × 3.1 × 1.3 cm)
Private collection

95. **FACE.** Golfe-Juan, 1946–47
Engraved bone fragment
1 9⁄16 × 1 × 11⁄16 in. (4 × 2.6 × 2 cm)
Private collection

96. **FACE.** Golfe-Juan, 1946
Engraved pebble
11⁄16 × 1 9⁄16 × 5⁄16 in. (1.8 × 3.9 × 0.8 cm)
Private collection

97. **FACE.** Golfe-Juan, 1946
Engraved pebble
1 5⁄8 × 2 5⁄8 × 1⁄2 in. (4.2 × 6.7 × 1.2 cm)
Private collection

98. **HEAD OF A FAUN.** Golfe-Juan, 1946
Engraved ceramic fragment
2 13⁄16 × 2 3⁄16 × 1⁄4 in. (7.2 × 5.5 × 0.6 cm)
Private collection

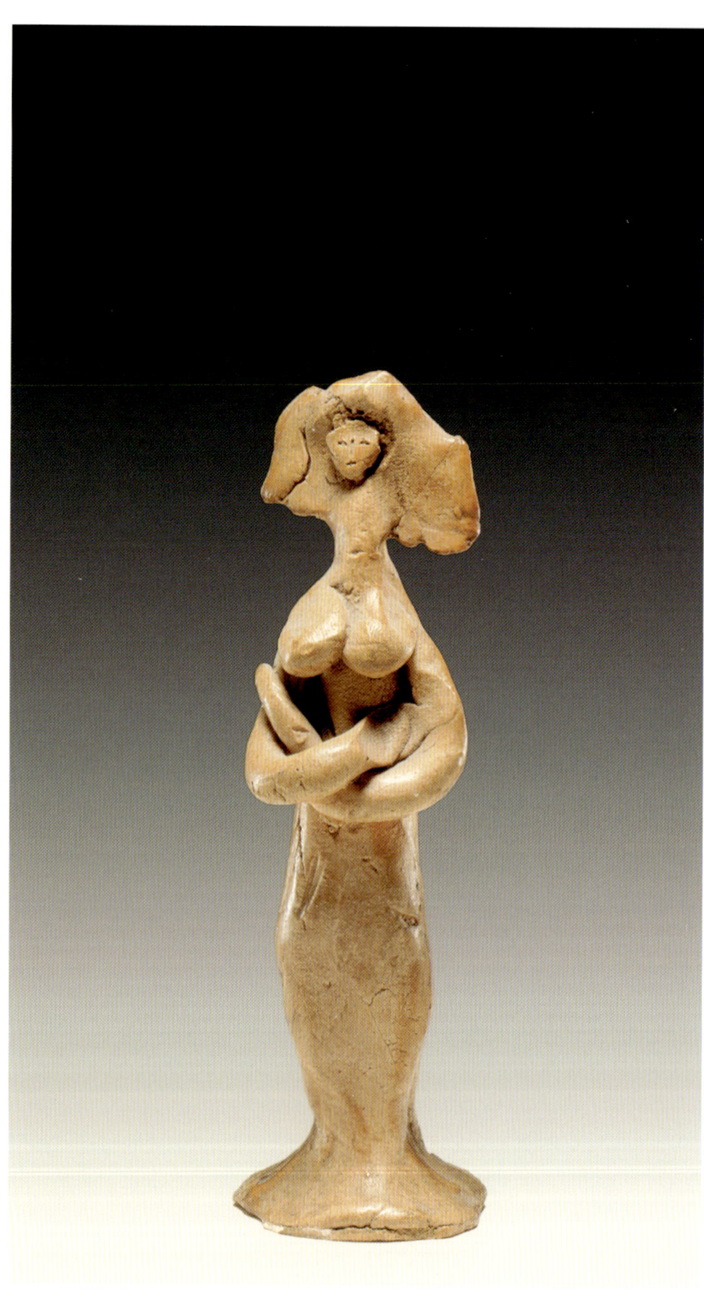

99. **STANDING WOMAN.** 1945
Foundry plaster
5½ × 1⅞ × 1¾ in. (14 × 4.8 × 4.5 cm)
Kravis Collection

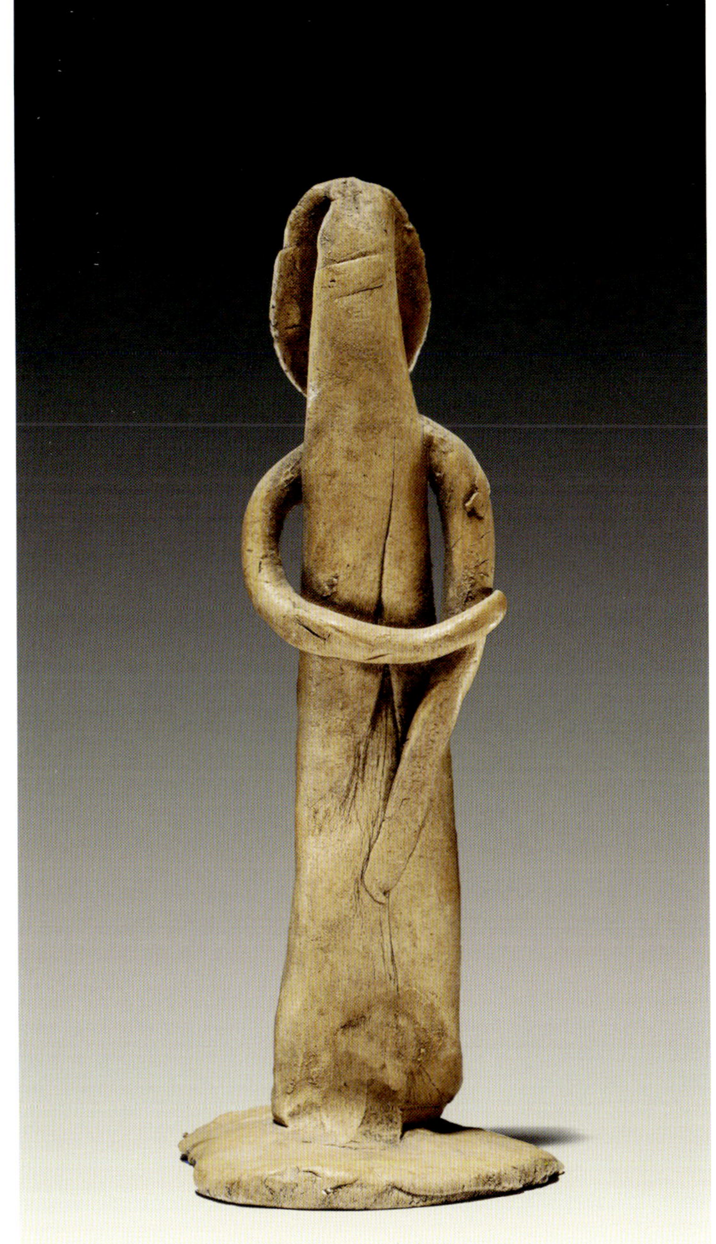

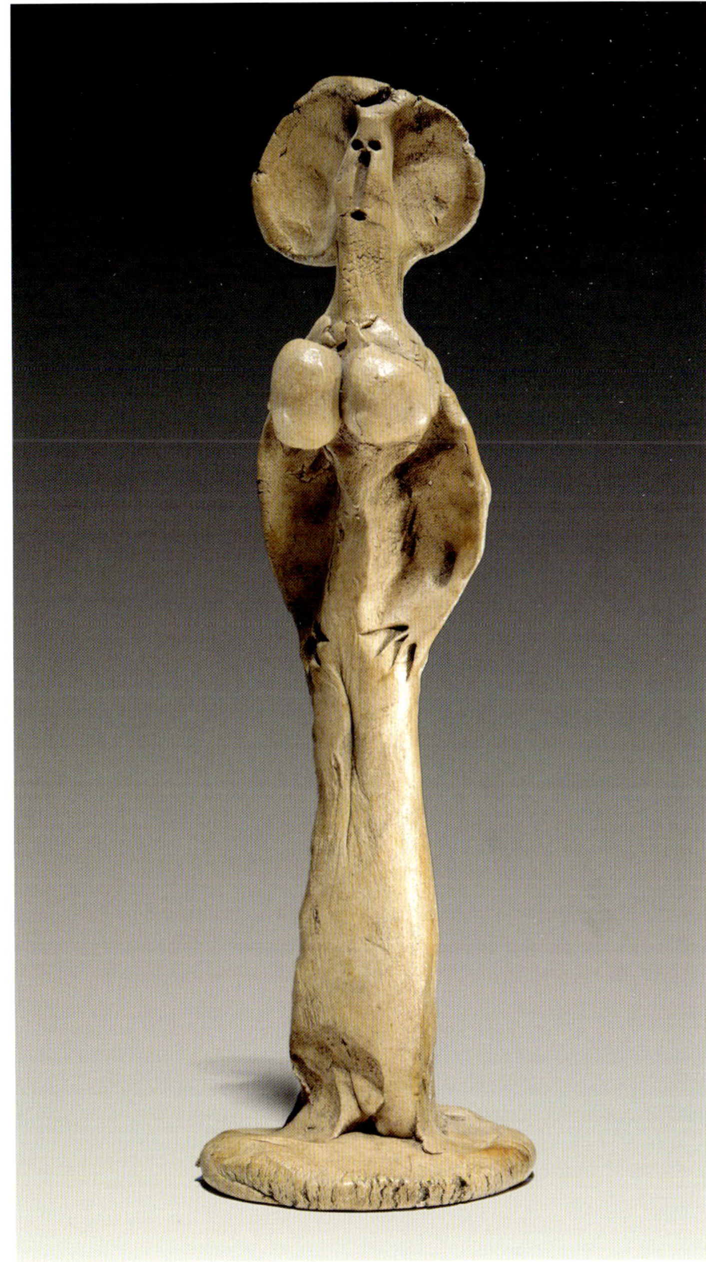

100. **STANDING WOMAN.** 1945
Terracotta
8 1/16 × 3 1/8 × 2 15/16 in. (20.5 × 8 × 7.5 cm)
Kravis Collection

101. **STANDING WOMAN.** 1945
Terracotta
10 7/16 × 3 1/8 × 2 11/16 in. (26.5 × 8 × 6.9 cm)
Kravis Collection

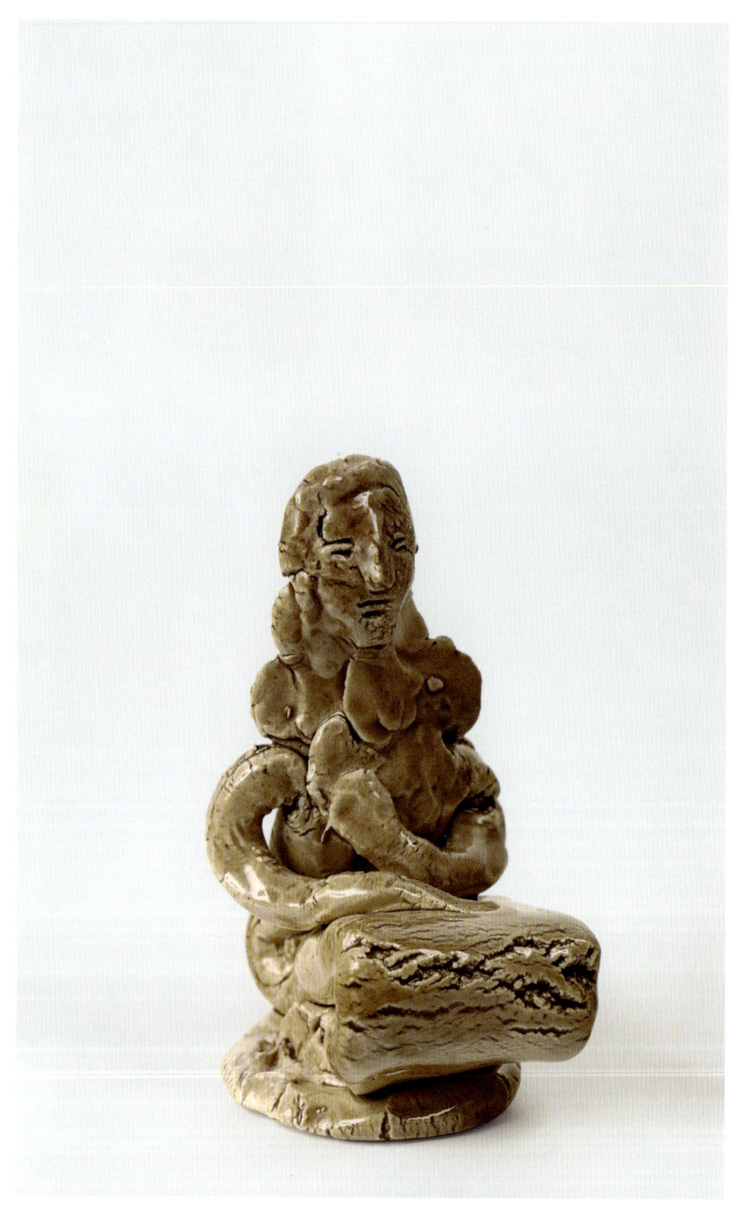

102. **SEATED WOMAN.** Vallauris, 1947
Glazed earthenware
4 3/4 × 2 3/4 × 2 15/16 in. (12 × 7 × 7.5 cm)
Private collection. Courtesy Fundación Almine y Bernard Ruiz-Picasso para el Arte

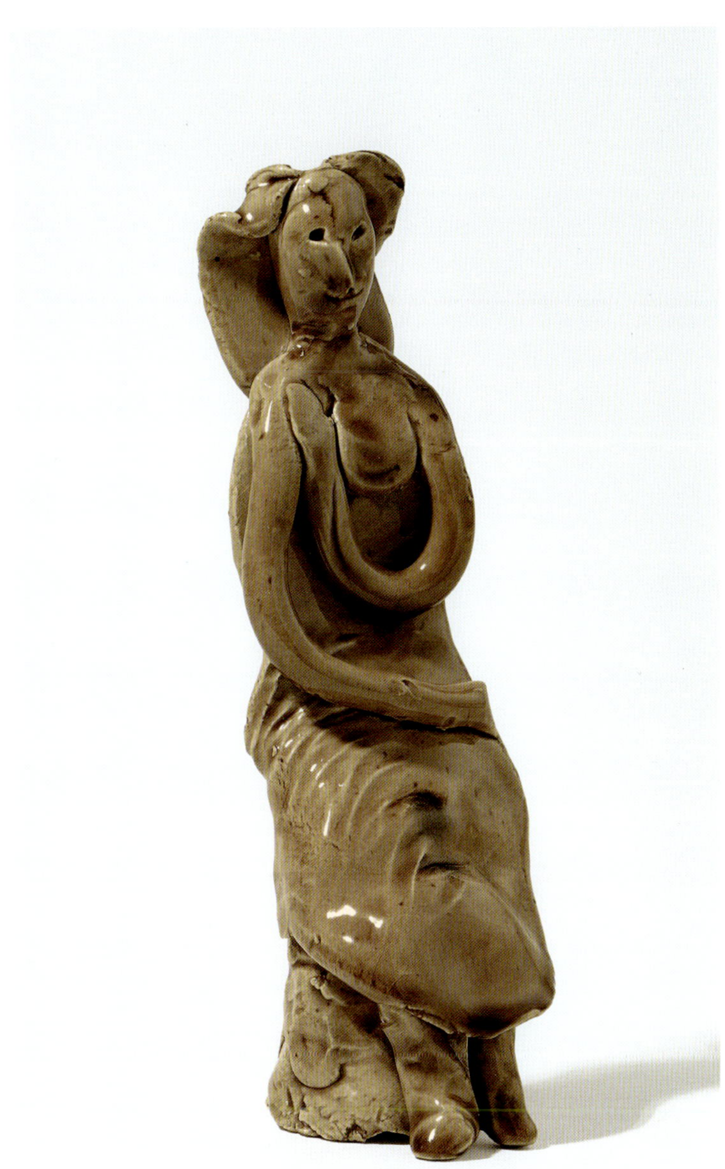

103. **SEATED WOMAN.** Vallauris, 1947
Glazed earthenware
7 ½ × 1 15⁄16 × 2 ¾ in. (19 × 5 × 7 cm)
Private collection. Courtesy Fundación Almine y Bernard Ruiz-Picasso para el Arte

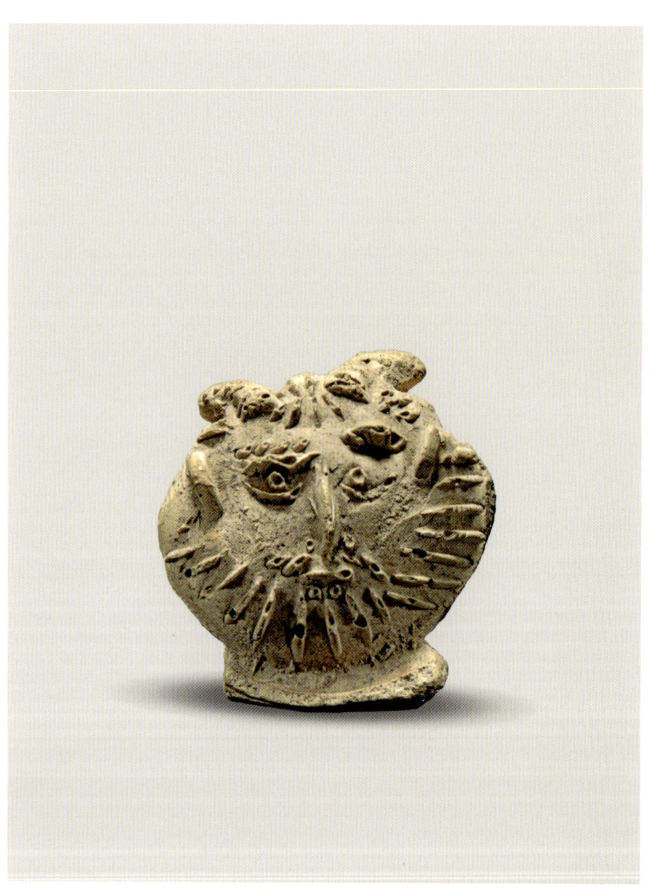

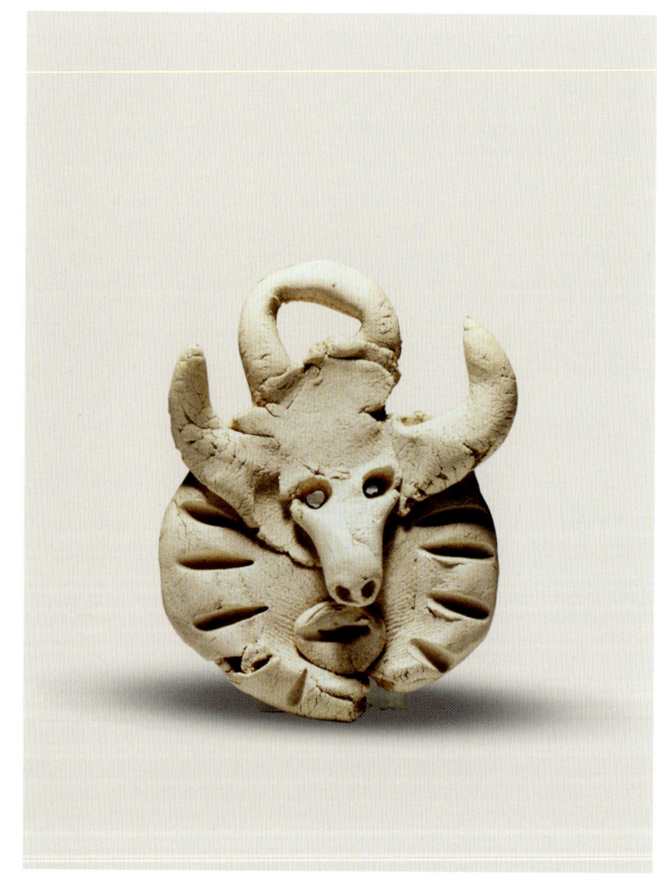

104. **HEAD OF A FAUN.** Vallauris, 1950
Fired white clay
3 × 2 ⅜ × ¹¹⁄₁₆ in. (7.6 × 6 × 1.7 cm)
Kravis Collection

105. **HEAD OF A FAUN.** Vallauris, 1950
Fired white clay
3 × 2 ⅜ × ¹¹⁄₁₆ in (7.6 × 6 × 1.7 cm)
Kravis Collection

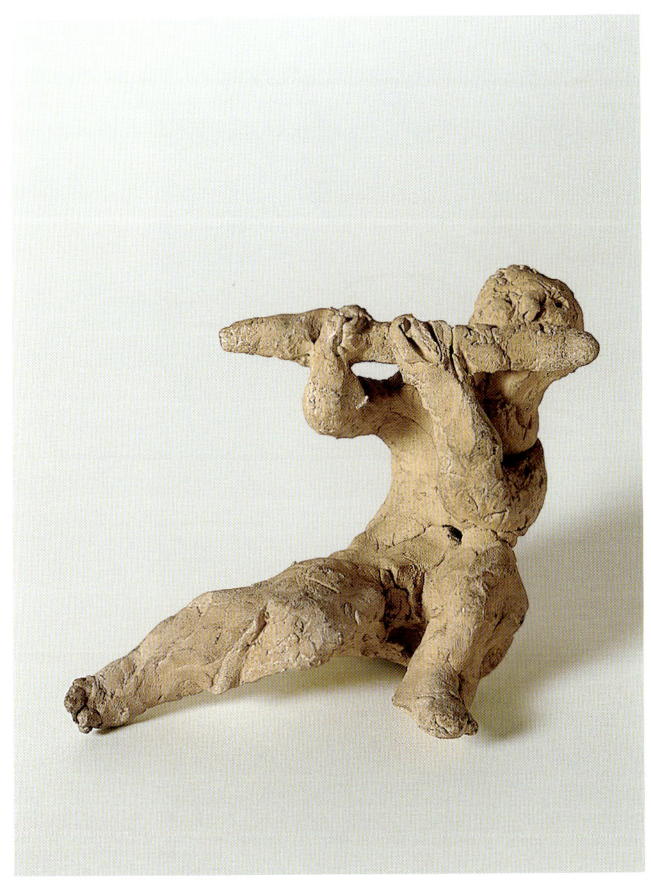

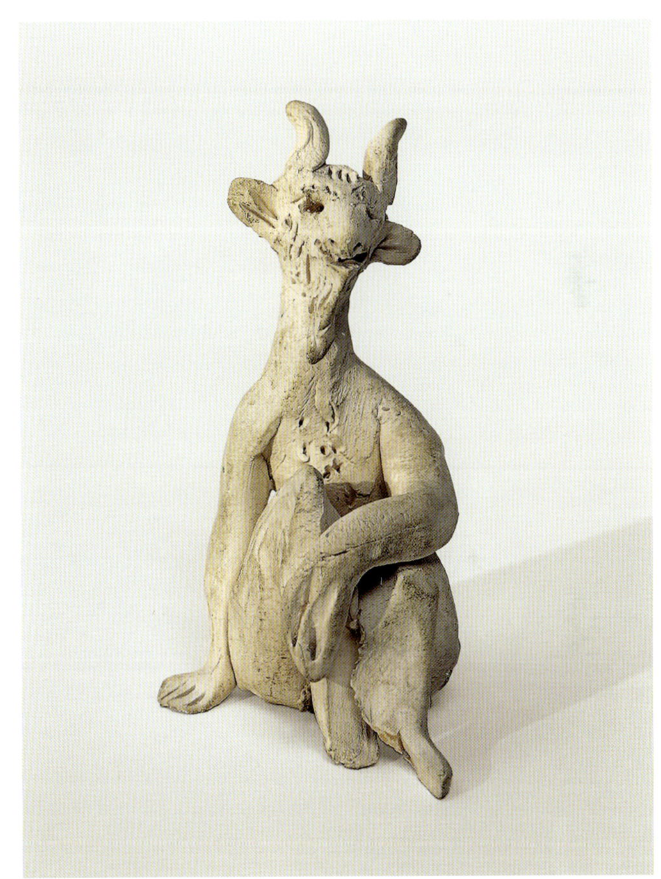

106. **SEATED MUSICIAN.** Vallauris, 1950
Fired red clay
3 ⅜ × 4 ¾ × 3 ⅛ in. (8.5 × 12 × 8 cm)
Museo Picasso Málaga. Gift of Christine Ruiz-Picasso

107. **SEATED FAUN.** Vallauris, 1950
White earthenware
3 ¾ × 1 $^{15}/_{16}$ × 2 ¾ in. (9.5 × 5 × 7 cm)
Museo Picasso Málaga. Gift of Bernard Ruiz-Picasso

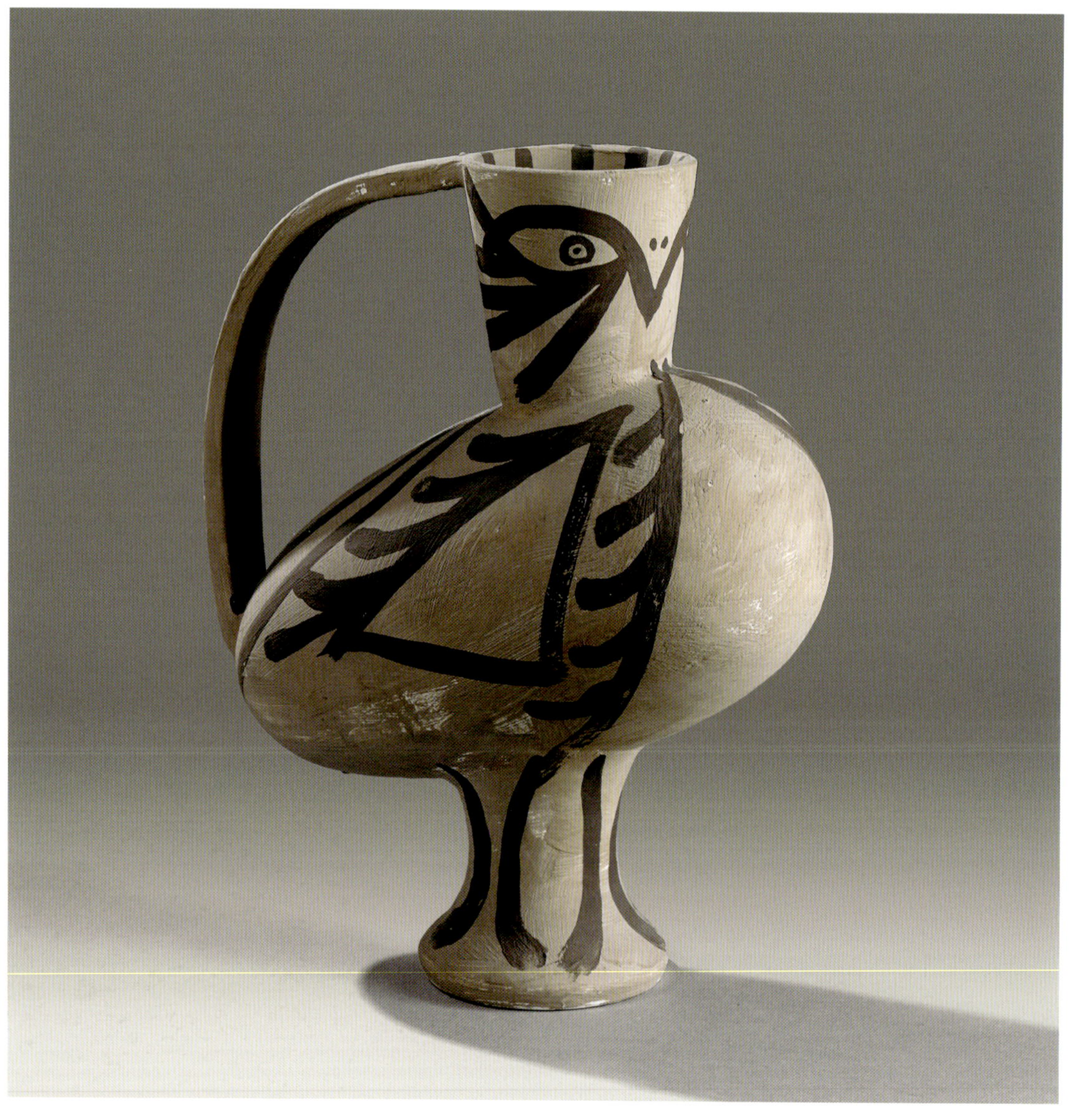

108. OWL (VASE). Vallauris, 1947 or 1948
White earthenware, painted with slips and oxides
14 15/16 × 13 × 4 3/4 in. (38 × 33 × 12 cm)
Musée Picasso, Antibes

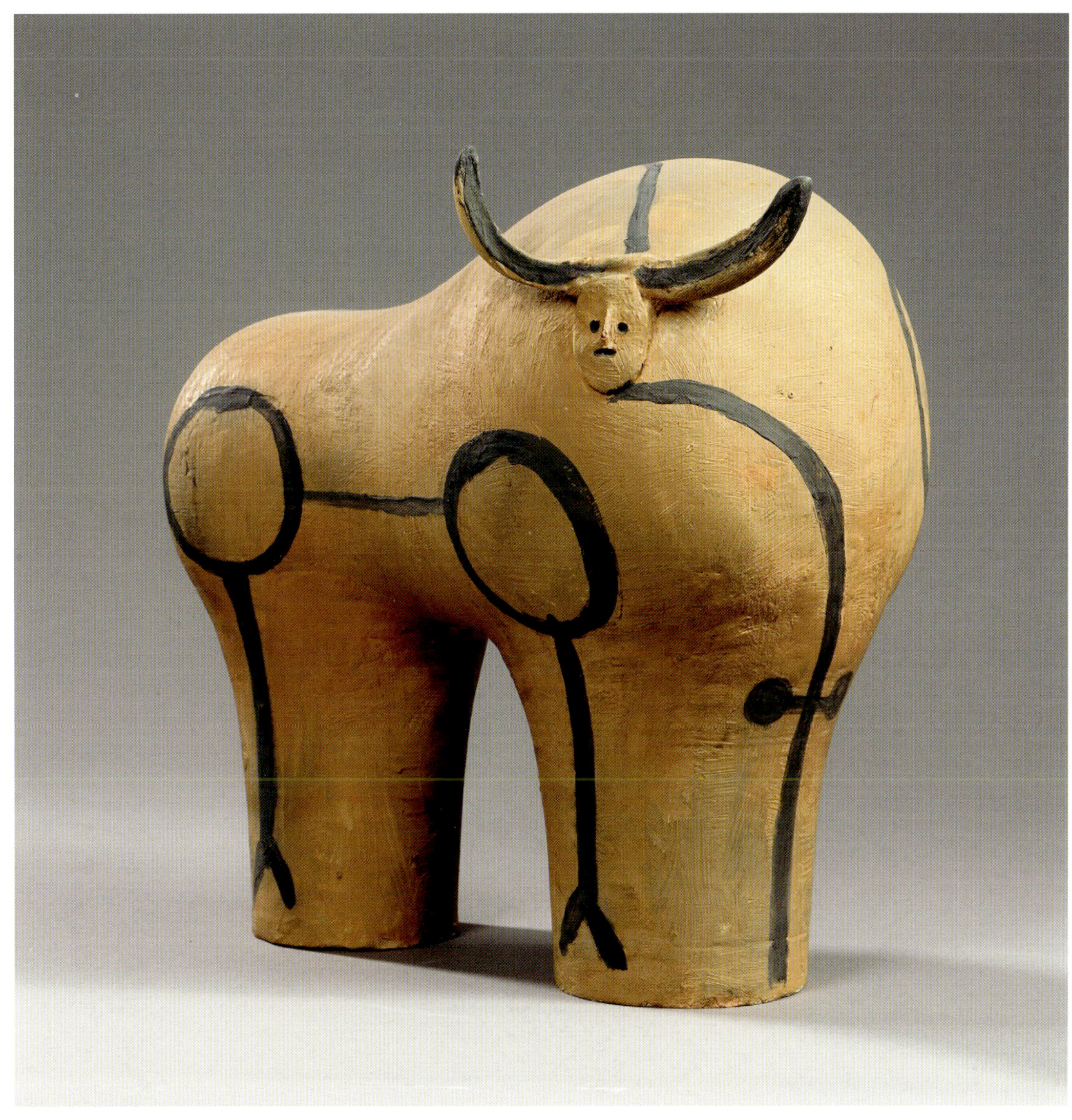

109. **STANDING BULL (VASE).** Vallauris, 1947 or 1948
White earthenware with applied elements, painted with slips and oxides
14 9/16 × 15 3/4 × 11 13/16 in. (37 × 40 × 30 cm)
Musée Picasso, Antibes

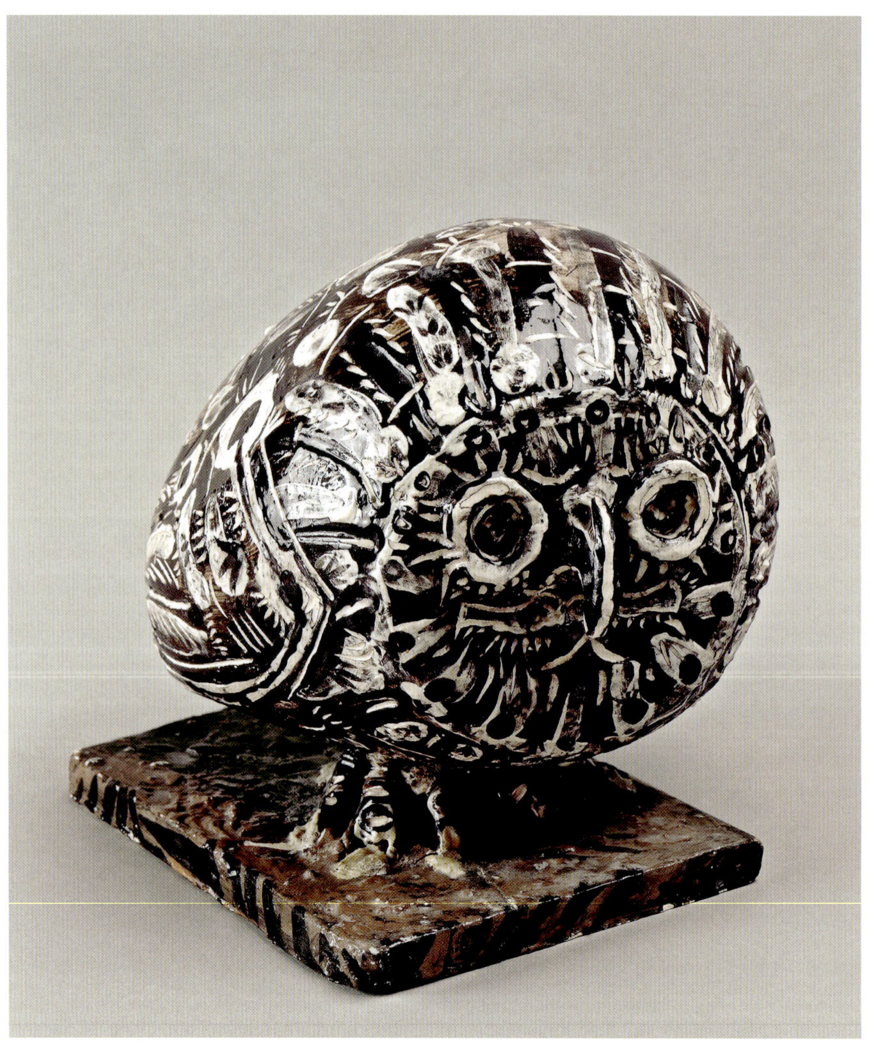

110. OWL. Vallauris, December 30, 1949
White earthenware, decorated with slips and white enamel, incisions, and brushwork
7 1/2 × 7 1/16 × 8 11/16 in. (19 × 18 × 22 cm)
Musée national Picasso–Paris. Dation Pablo Picasso

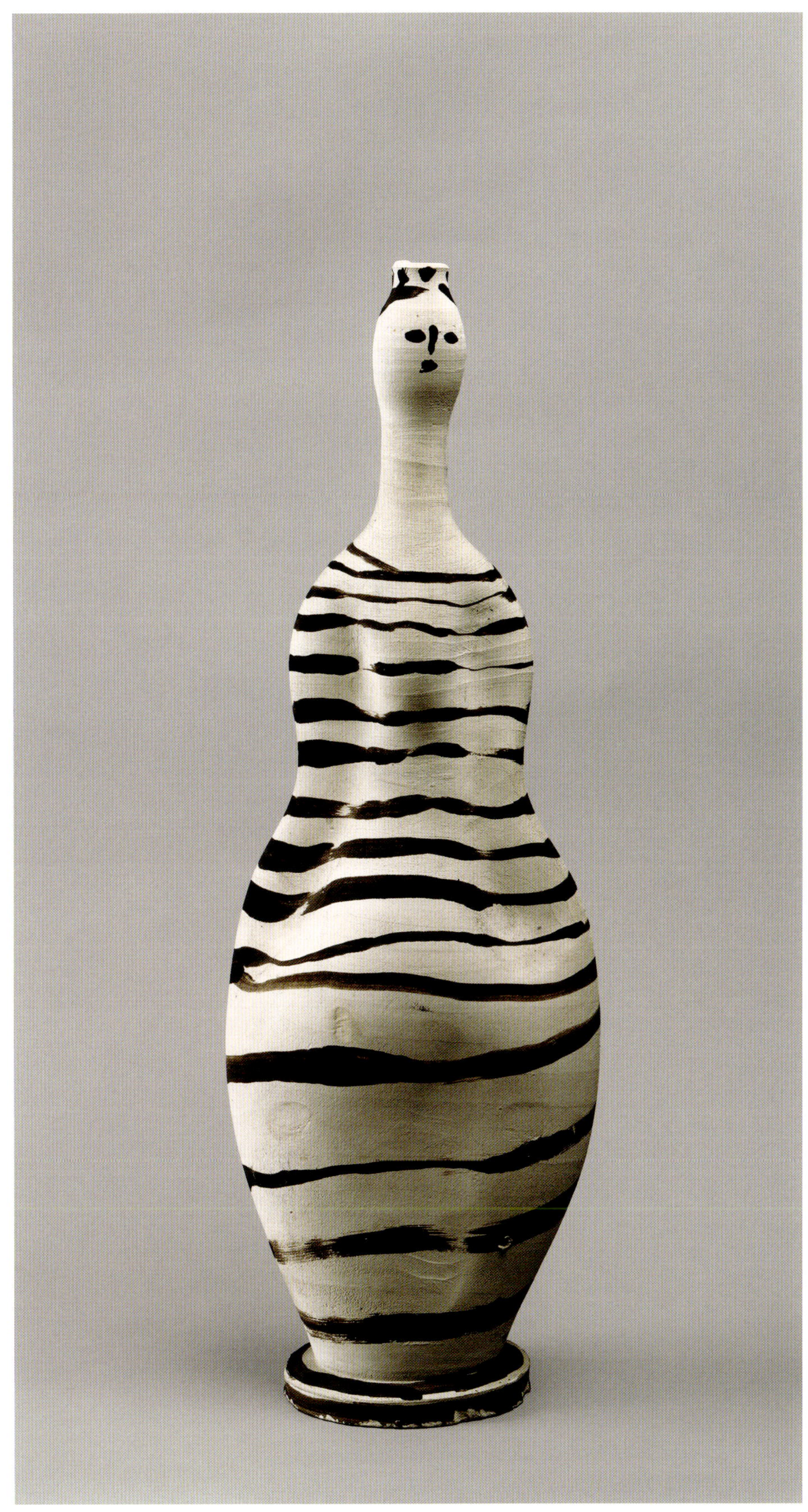

111. **VASE: WOMAN.** Vallauris, [1948]
White earthenware, painted with slips
18 11/16 × 6 1/2 × 4 5/16 in. (47.5 × 16.5 × 11 cm)
Musée national Picasso–Paris. Dation Pablo Picasso

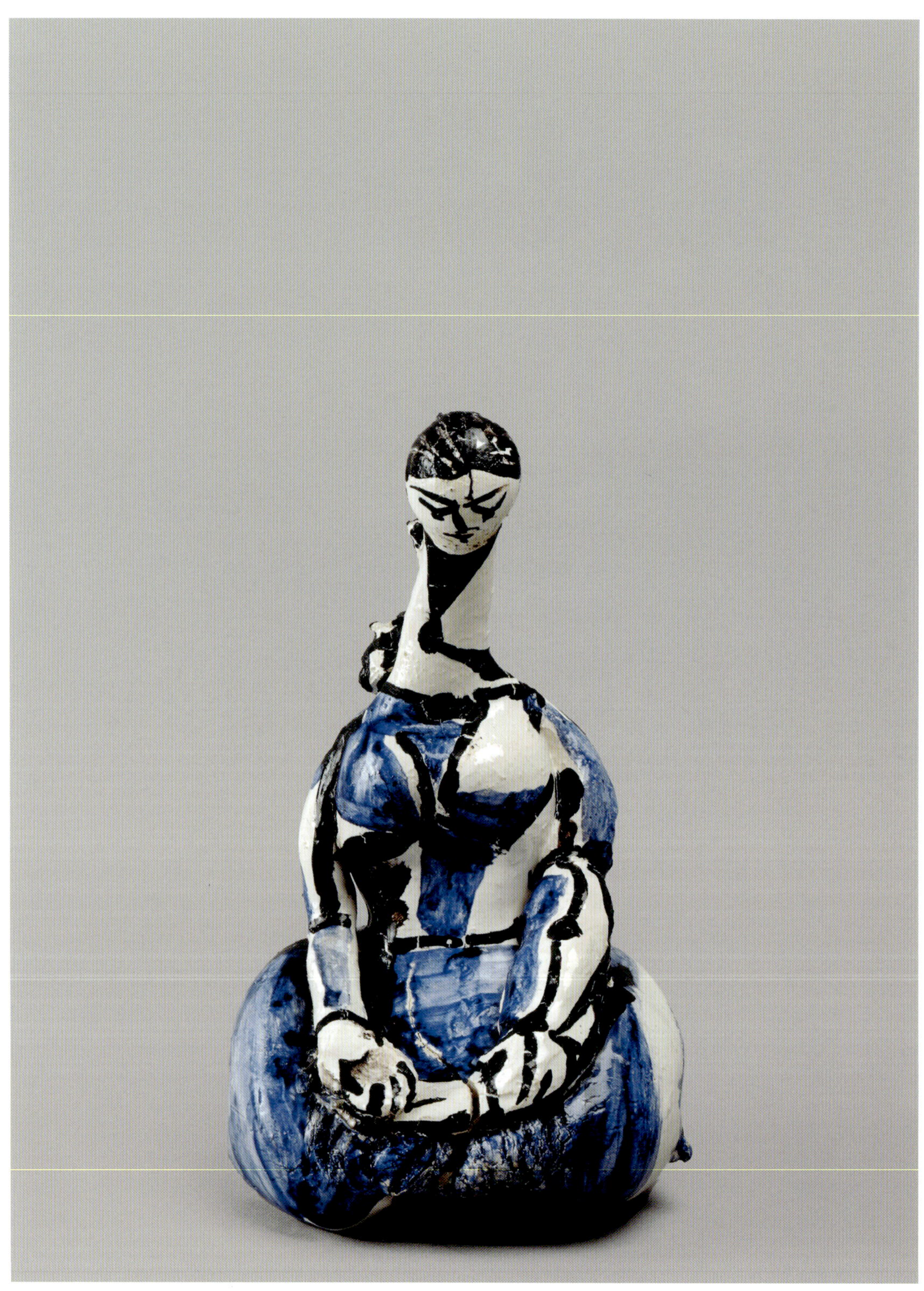

112. **BOTTLE: KNEELING WOMAN.** Vallauris, 1948–50
White earthenware, enameled and painted with oxides
11 7⁄16 × 6 11⁄16 × 6 11⁄16 in. (29 × 17 × 17 cm)
Musée national Picasso–Paris. Dation Pablo Picasso

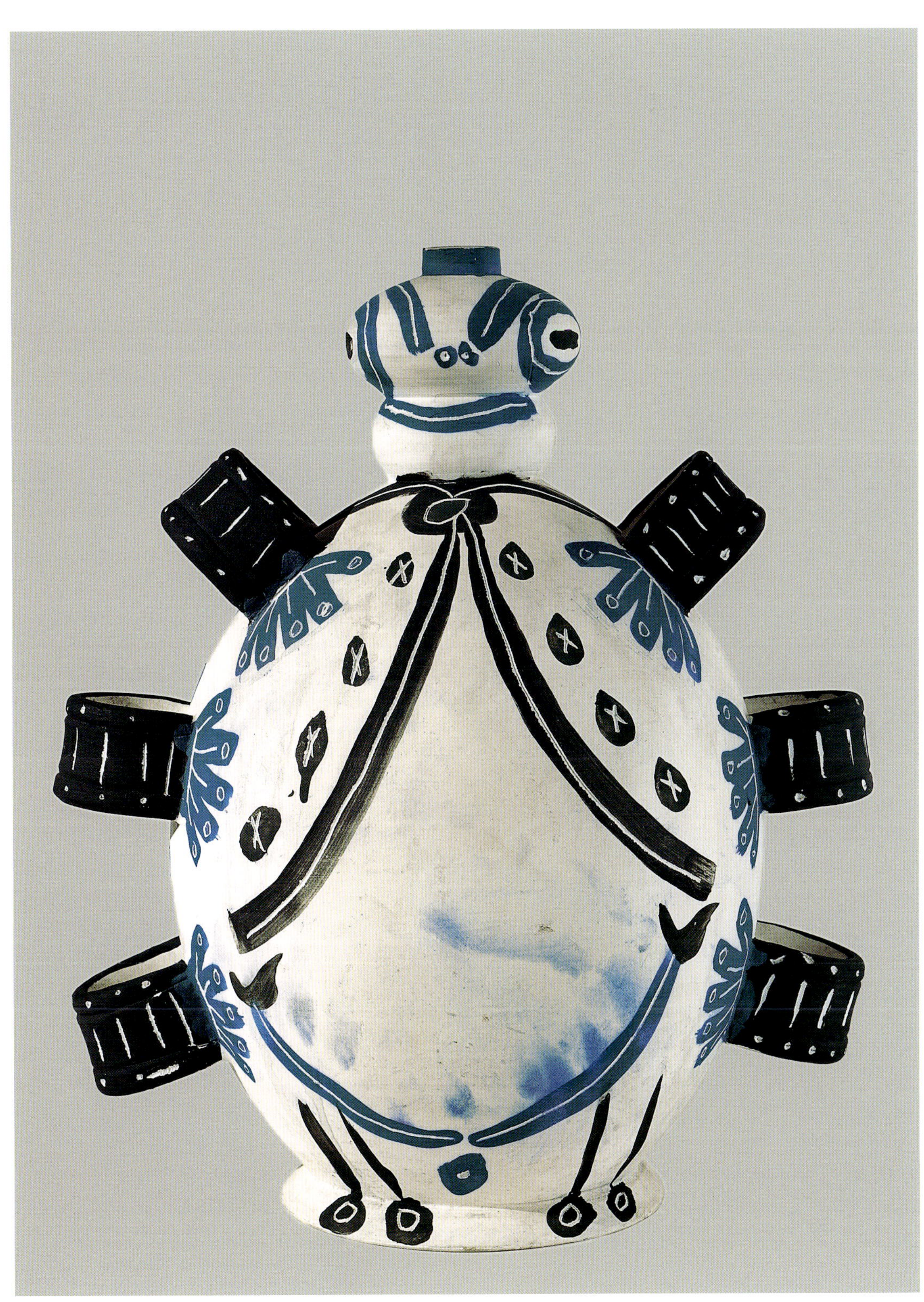

113. **INSECT.** Vallauris, 1951
Fired white clay with attached elements, incised and painted with slips
16 $\frac{9}{16}$ × 13 $\frac{3}{4}$ × 10 $\frac{1}{4}$ in. (42 × 35 × 26 cm)
Museo Picasso Málaga. Gift of Bernard Ruiz-Picasso

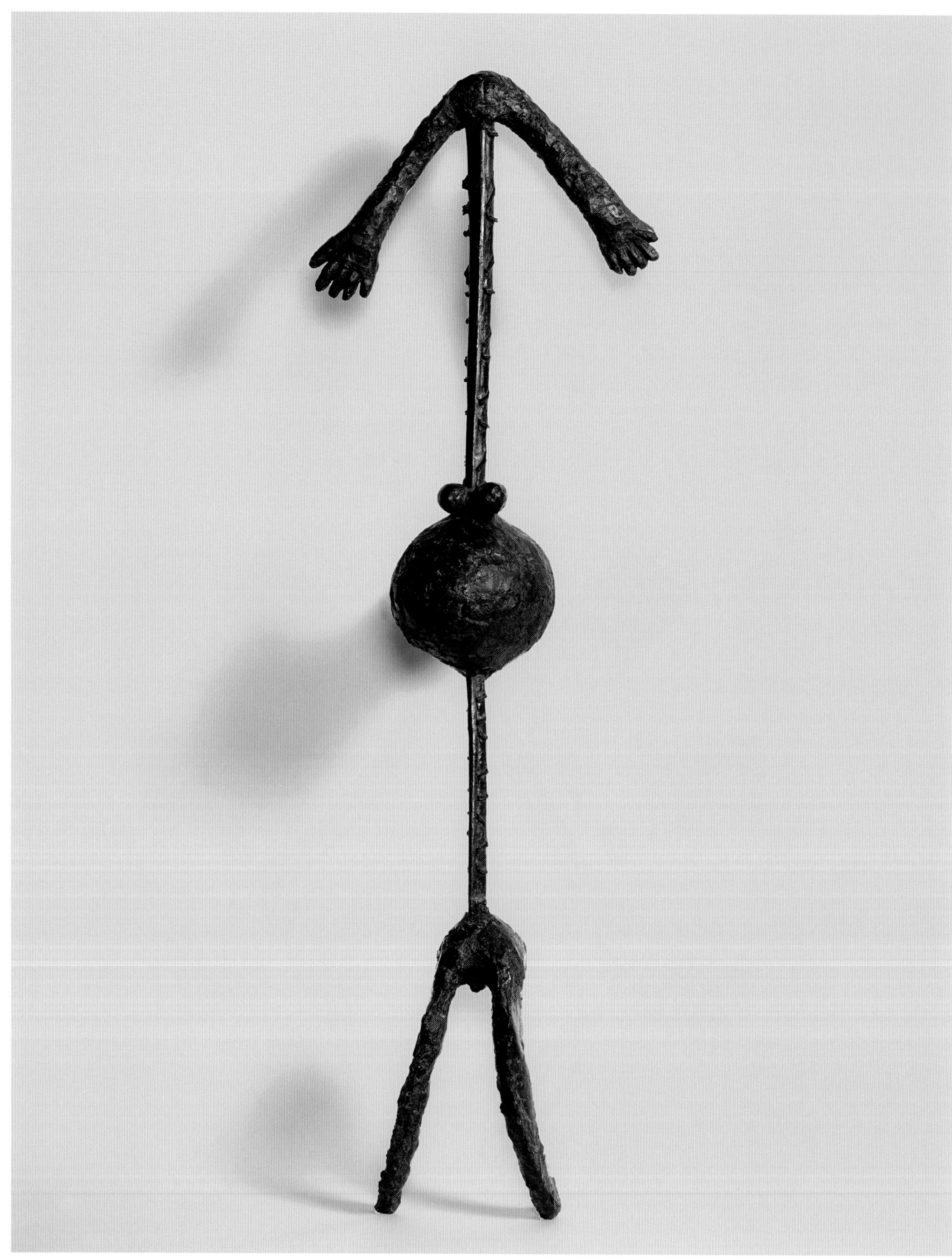

114. **PREGNANT WOMAN.** Vallauris, 1949
Bronze, casting date unknown
50 ⅜ × 14 $^{15}/_{16}$ × 4 ¾ in. (128 × 38 × 12 cm)
Private collection. Courtesy Fundación Almine y Bernard Ruiz-Picasso para el Arte

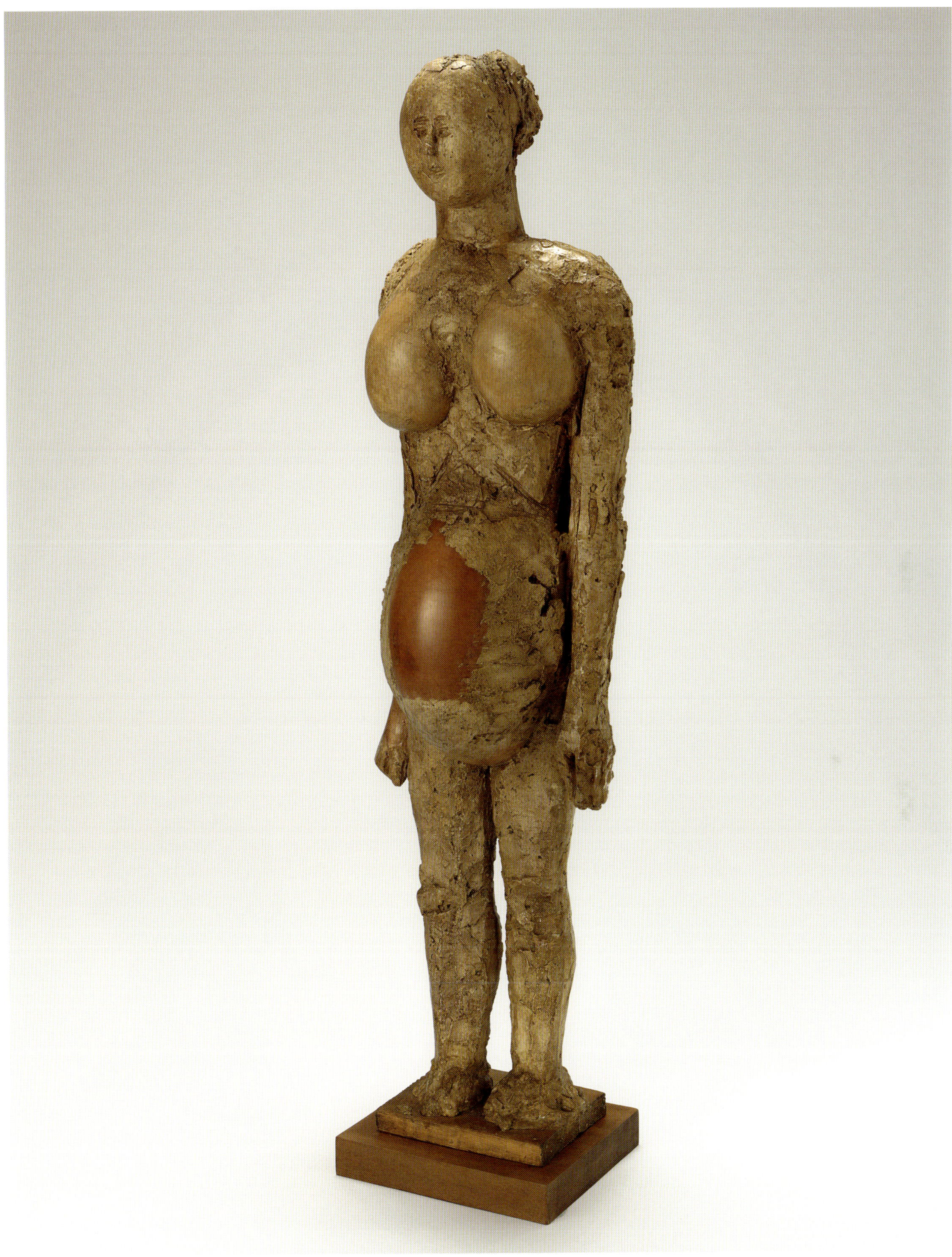

115. **PREGNANT WOMAN.** First state. Vallauris, 1950
Plaster with metal armature, wood, ceramic vessel, and pottery jars
43 ¼ × 8 ⅝ × 12 ½ in. (110 × 22 × 32 cm)
The Museum of Modern Art, New York. Gift of Louise Reinhardt Smith
and gift of Jacqueline Picasso (both by exchange)

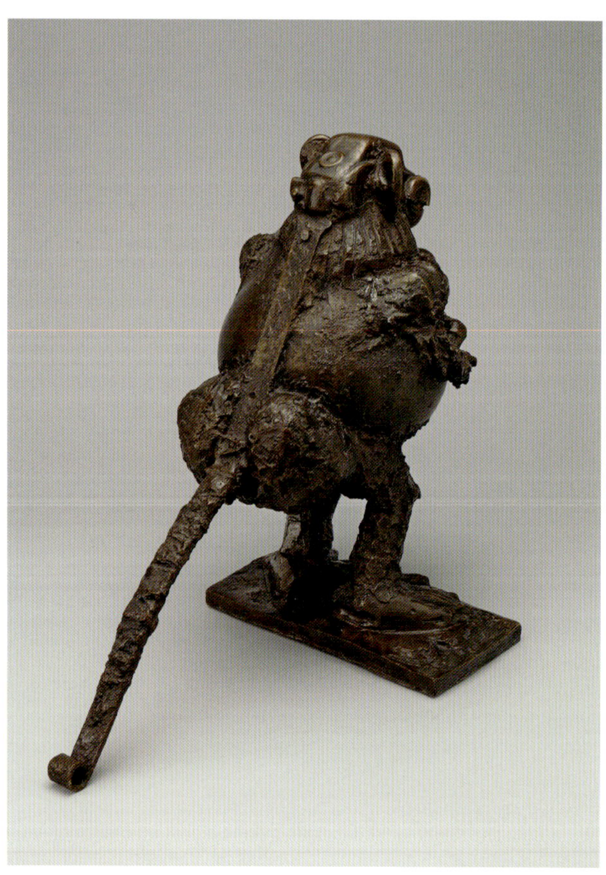

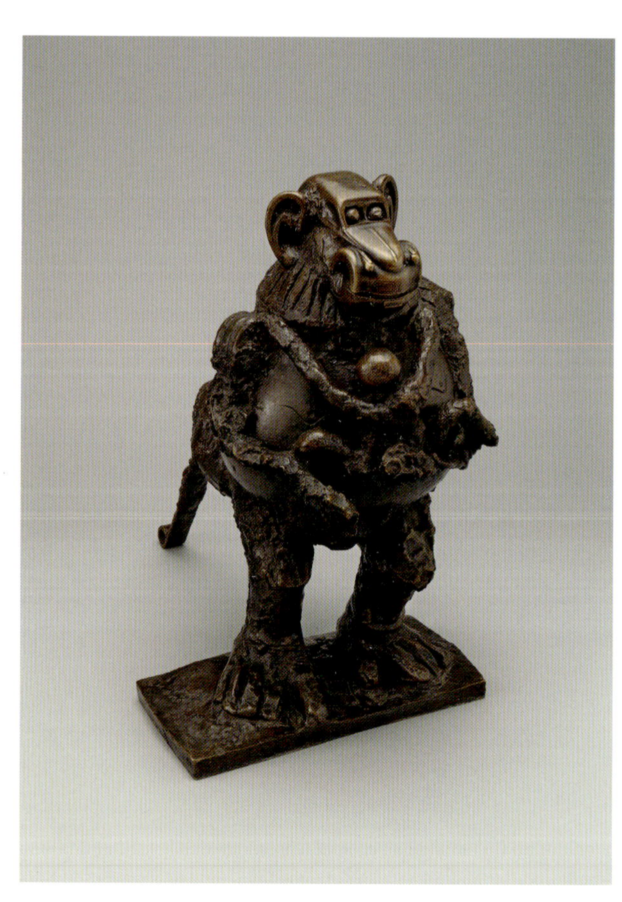

116. **BABOON AND YOUNG.** Vallauris, October 1951
Bronze, cast 1955
21 × 13 ¼ × 20 ¾ in. (53.3 × 33.3 × 52.7 cm)
The Museum of Modern Art, New York. Mrs. Simon Guggenheim Fund

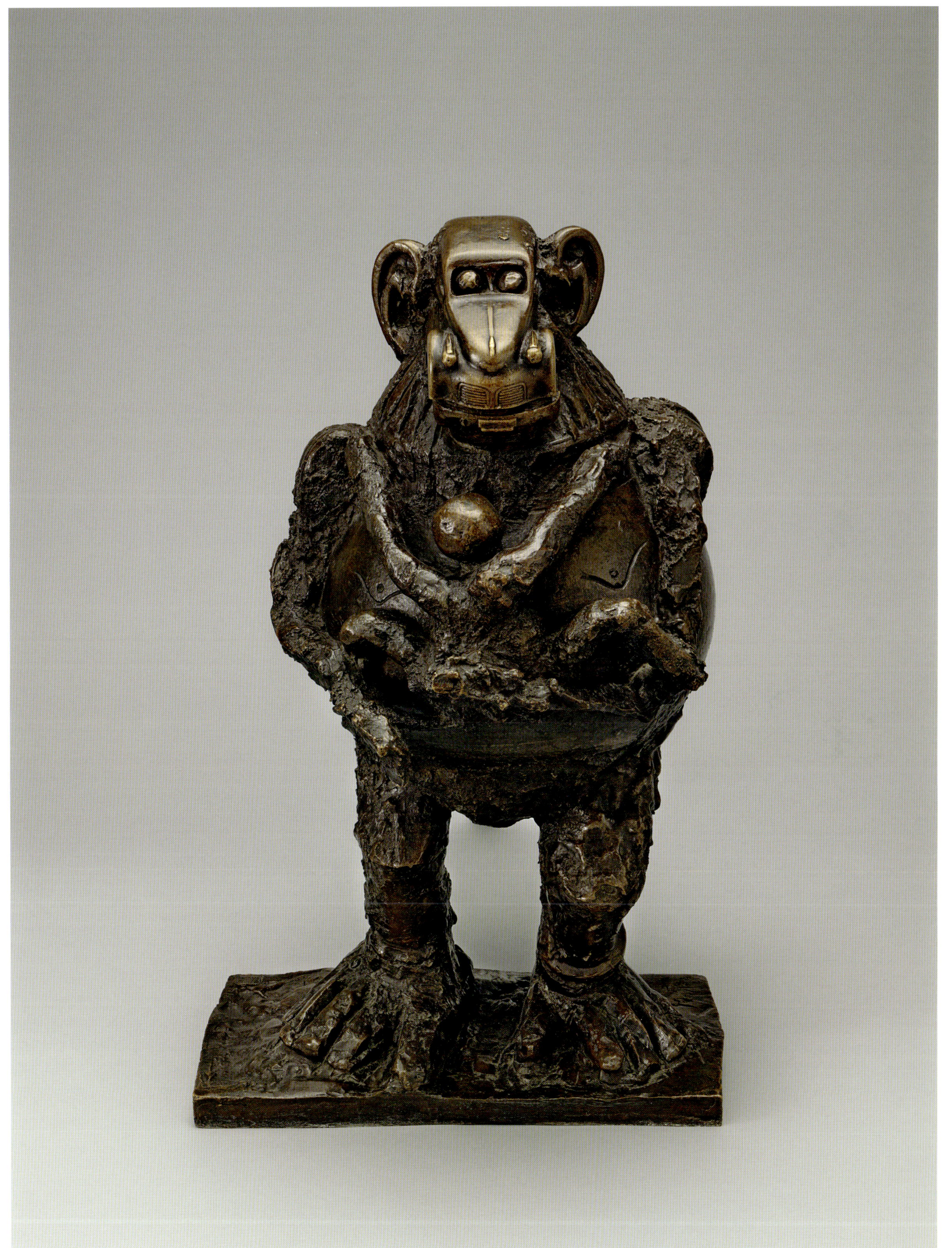

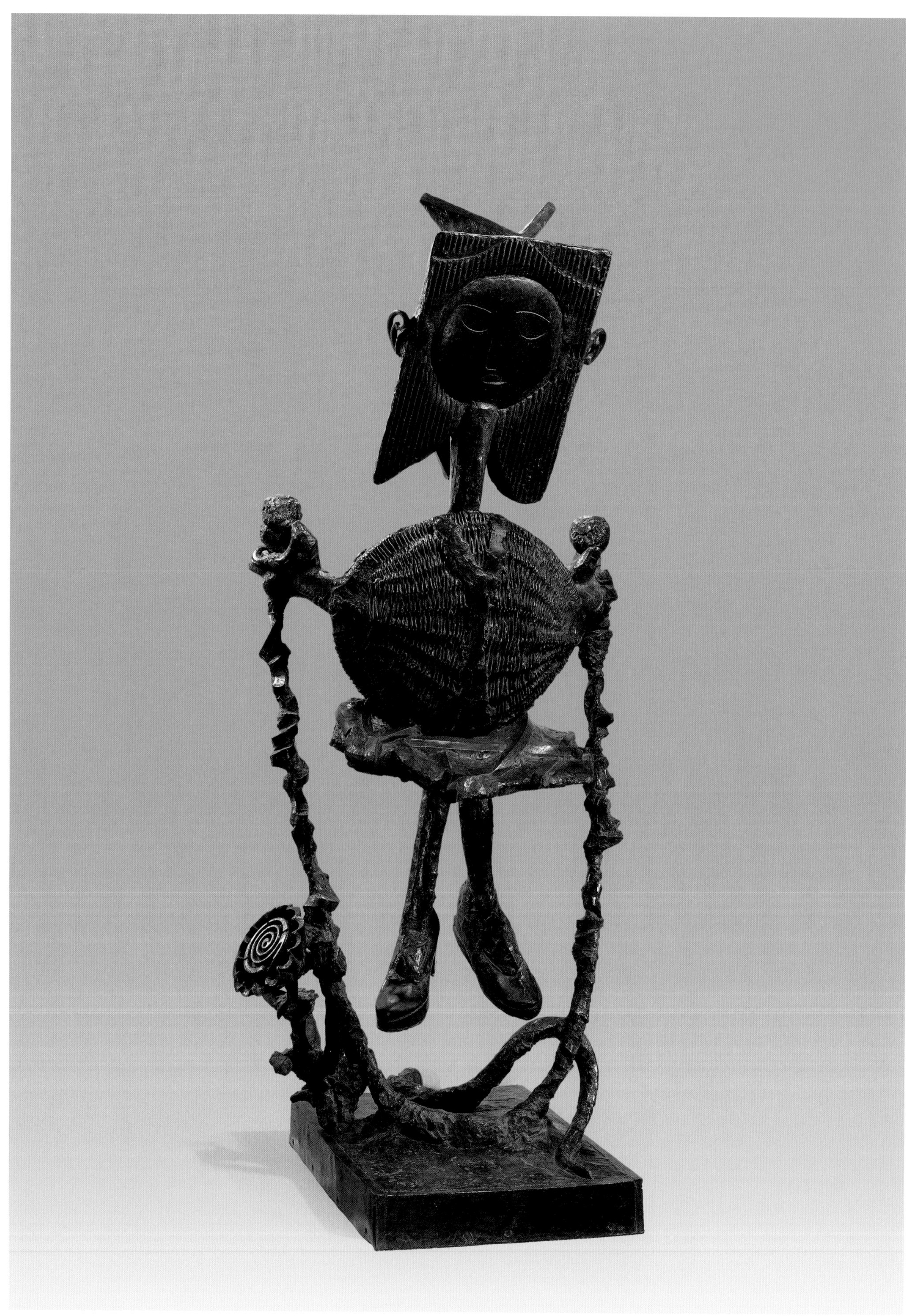

117. **LITTLE GIRL JUMPING ROPE.** Vallauris, 1950–[54]
Bronze, cast 1956 or later
60 ¼ × 24 $\frac{7}{16}$ × 25 ⅝ in. (153 × 62 × 65 cm)
Private collection

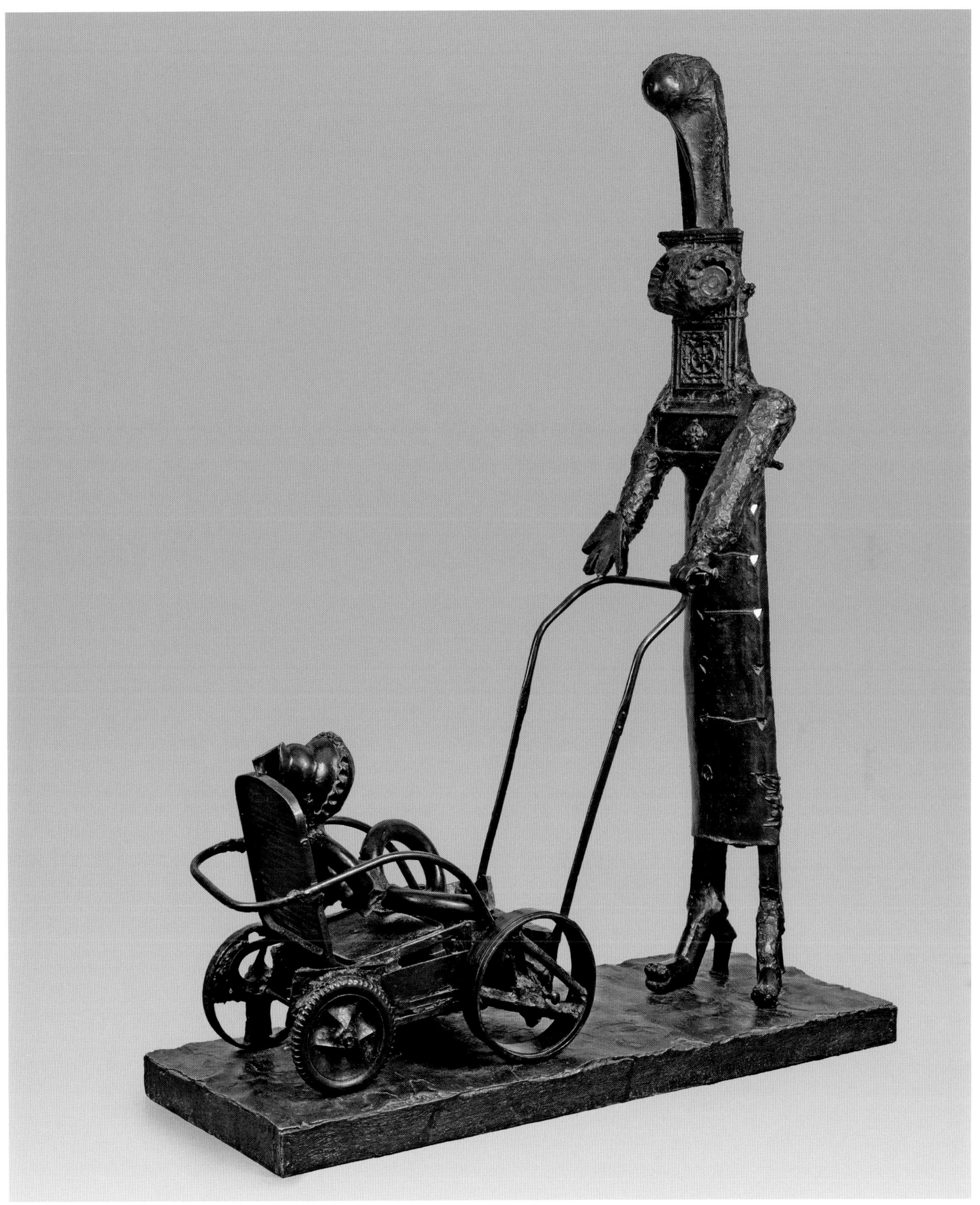

118. **WOMAN WITH A BABY CARRIAGE.** Vallauris, 1950–[54]
Bronze, cast 1962–[63]
6 ft. 7 15/16 in. × 57 7/16 in. × 24 in. (203 × 145 × 61 cm)
Musée national Picasso–Paris. Dation Pablo Picasso

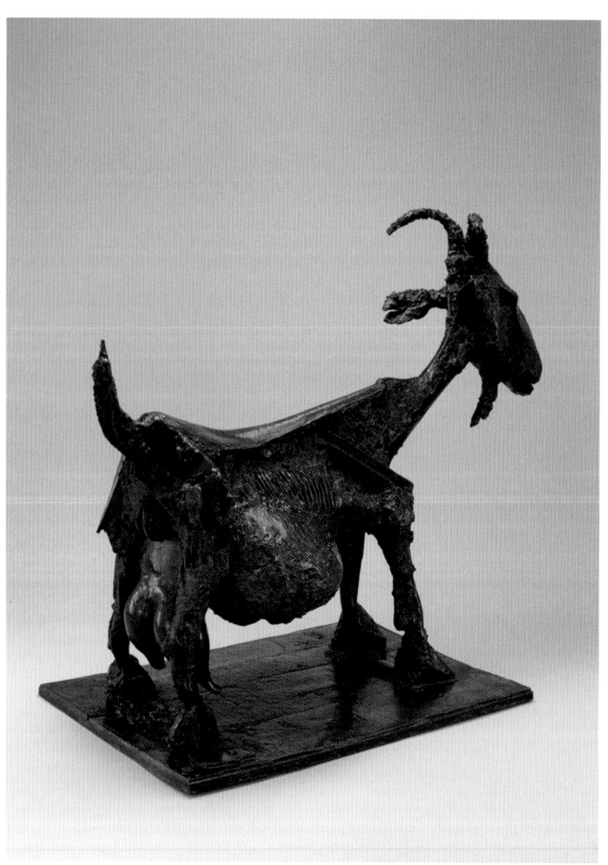

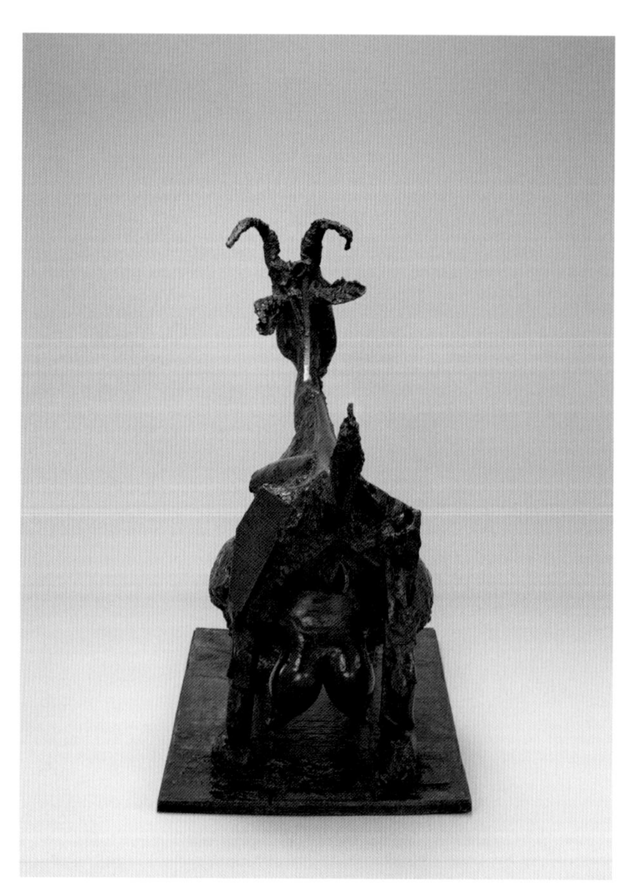

119. **SHE-GOAT.** Vallauris, 1950
Bronze, cast 1952
46 3/8 × 56 3/8 × 28 1/8 in. (117.7 × 143.1 × 71.4 cm)
The Museum of Modern Art, New York. Mrs. Simon Guggenheim Fund

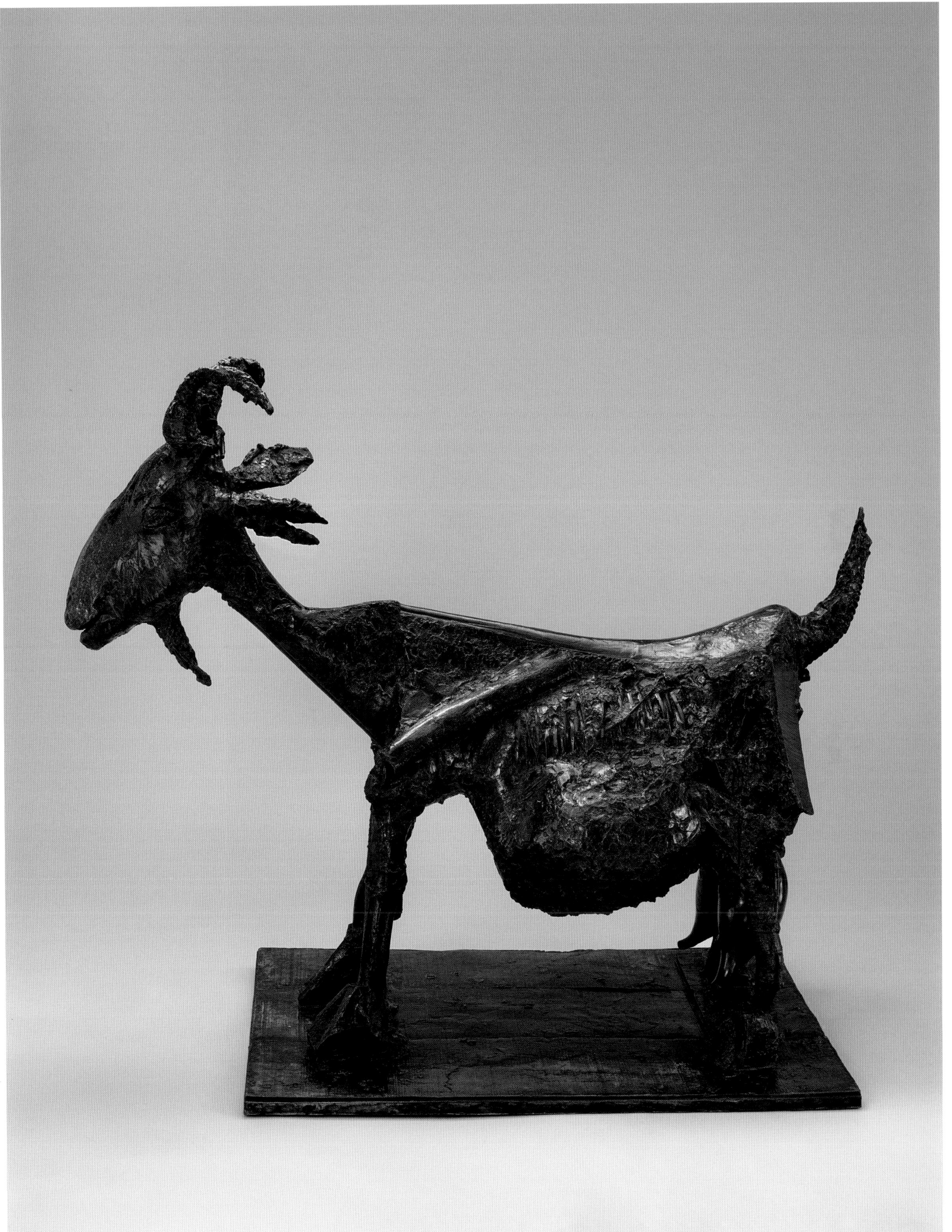

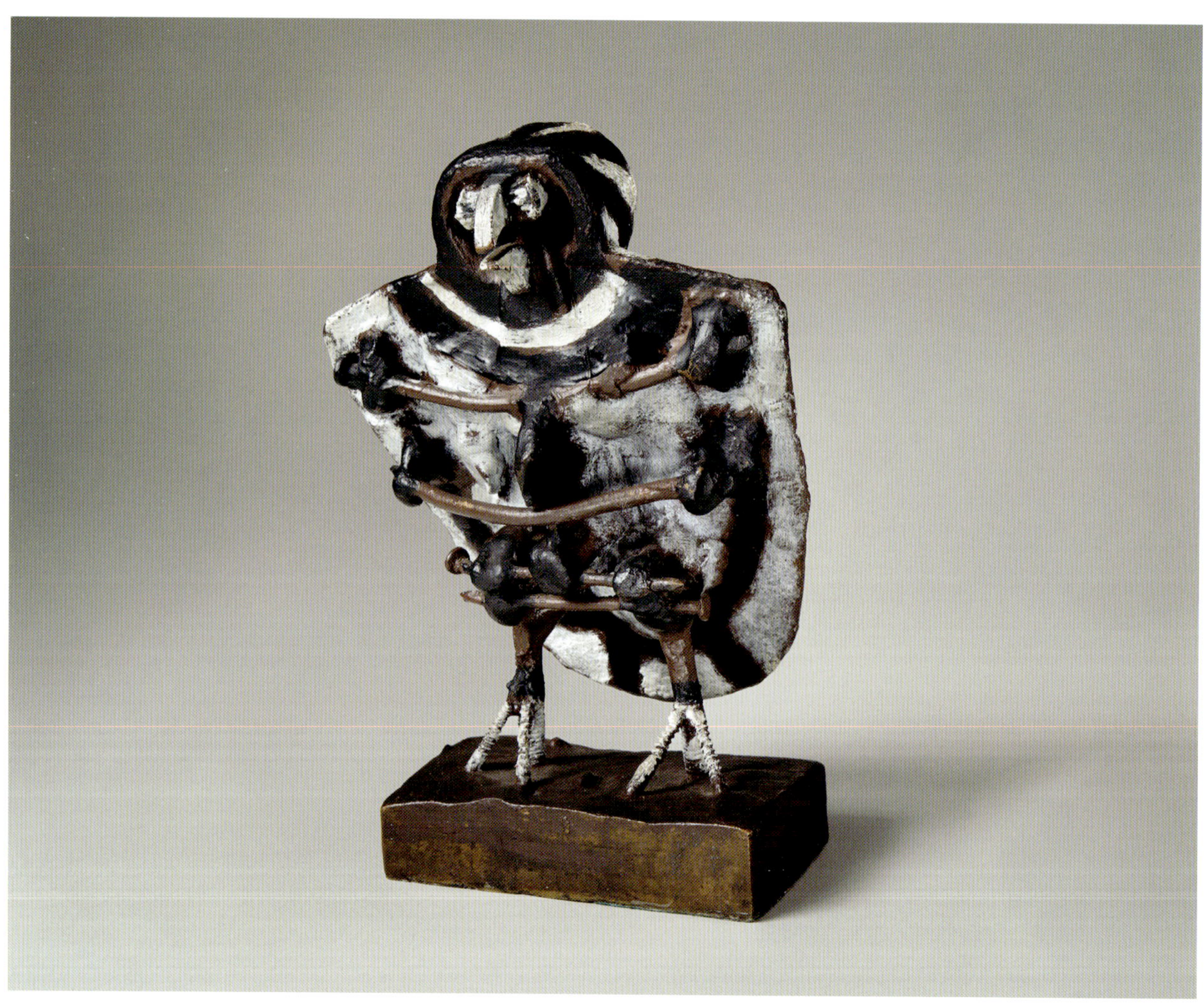

120. **LITTLE OWL.** Vallauris, 1951–52
Painted bronze, cast 1952
1 of an edition of 2 bronzes, one unpainted
10 ¼ × 7 ⅜ × 5 ¾ in. (26 × 18.7 × 14.6 cm)
Hirshhorn Museum and Sculpture Garden, Smithsonian Institution, Washington, D.C. Gift of Joseph H. Hirshhorn

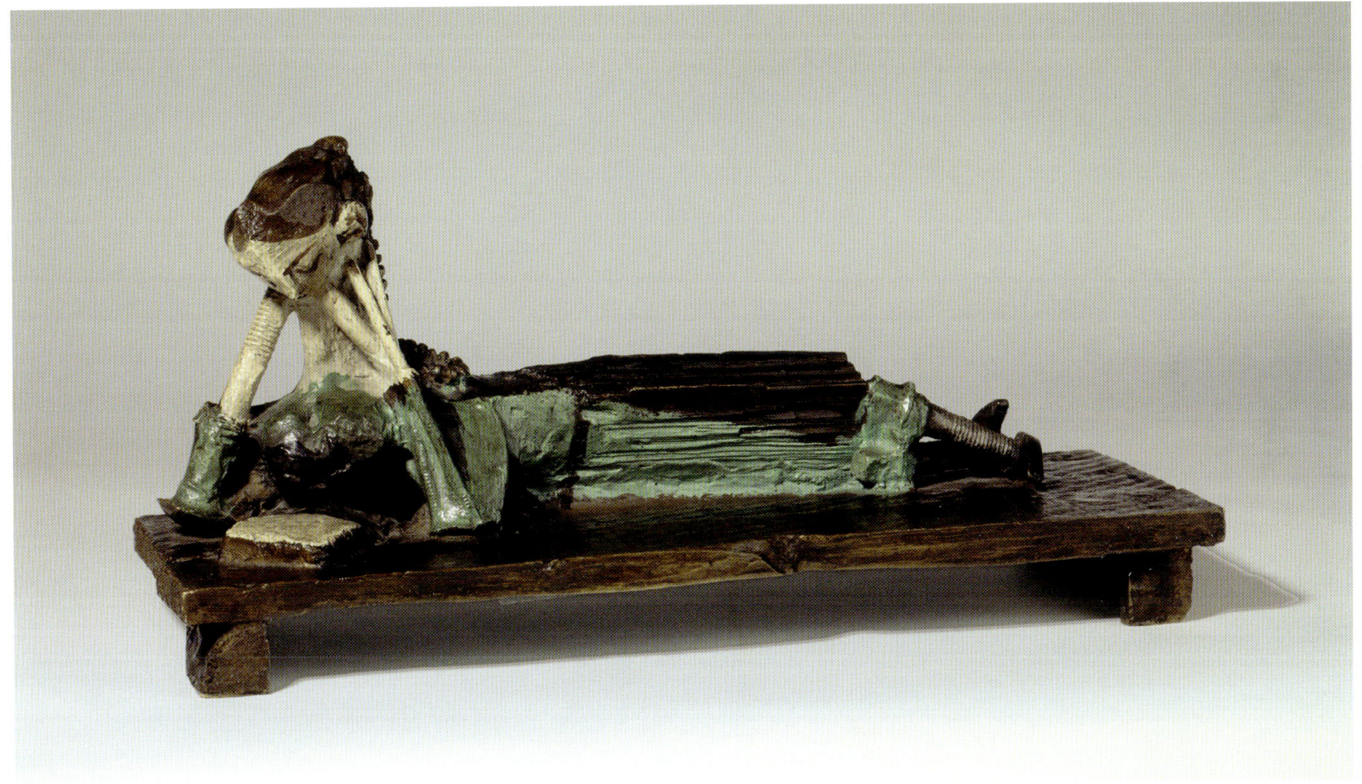

121. **WOMAN READING.** Vallauris, 1951–53
Painted bronze, cast May 1952
1 of an edition of 3 bronzes, each uniquely treated
6 ⅛ × 14 × 5 ⅛ in. (15.5 × 35.5 × 13 cm)
Centre national d'art et de culture Georges Pompidou, Paris.
Musée national d'art moderne/Centre de création industrielle

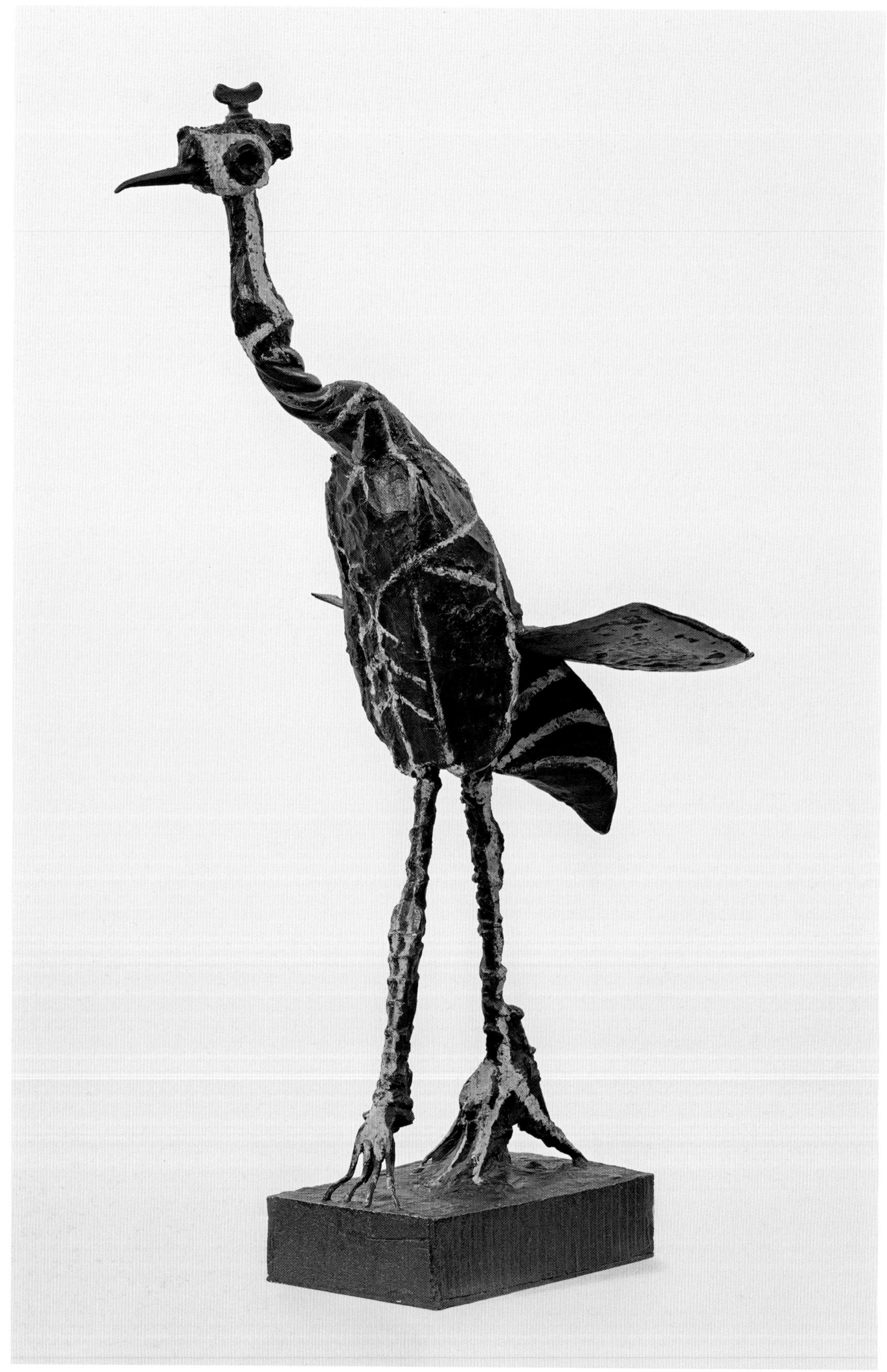

122. **CRANE.** Vallauris, 1951–52
Painted bronze, cast 1952
1 of an edition of 4 bronzes, each uniquely treated
29 ½ × 11 7/16 × 16 15/16 in. (75 × 29 × 43 cm)
Private collection. Courtesy Thomas Ammann Fine Art AG, Zurich

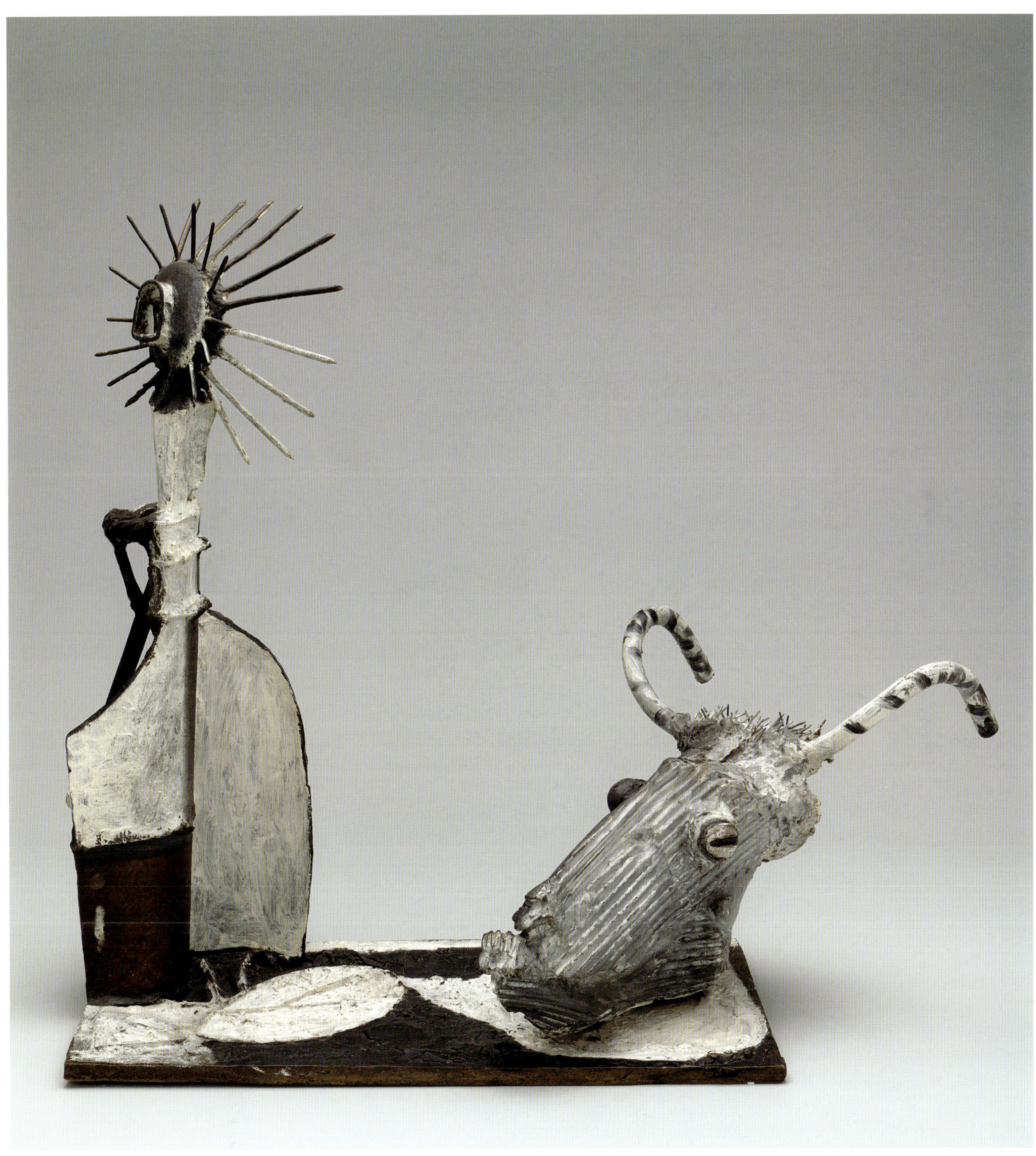

123. GOAT SKULL AND BOTTLE. Vallauris, 1951–53
Painted bronze, cast 1952
1 of an edition of 2 bronzes, each uniquely treated
31 × 37⅝ × 21½ in. (78.8 × 95.3 × 54.5 cm)
The Museum of Modern Art, New York. Mrs. Simon Guggenheim Fund

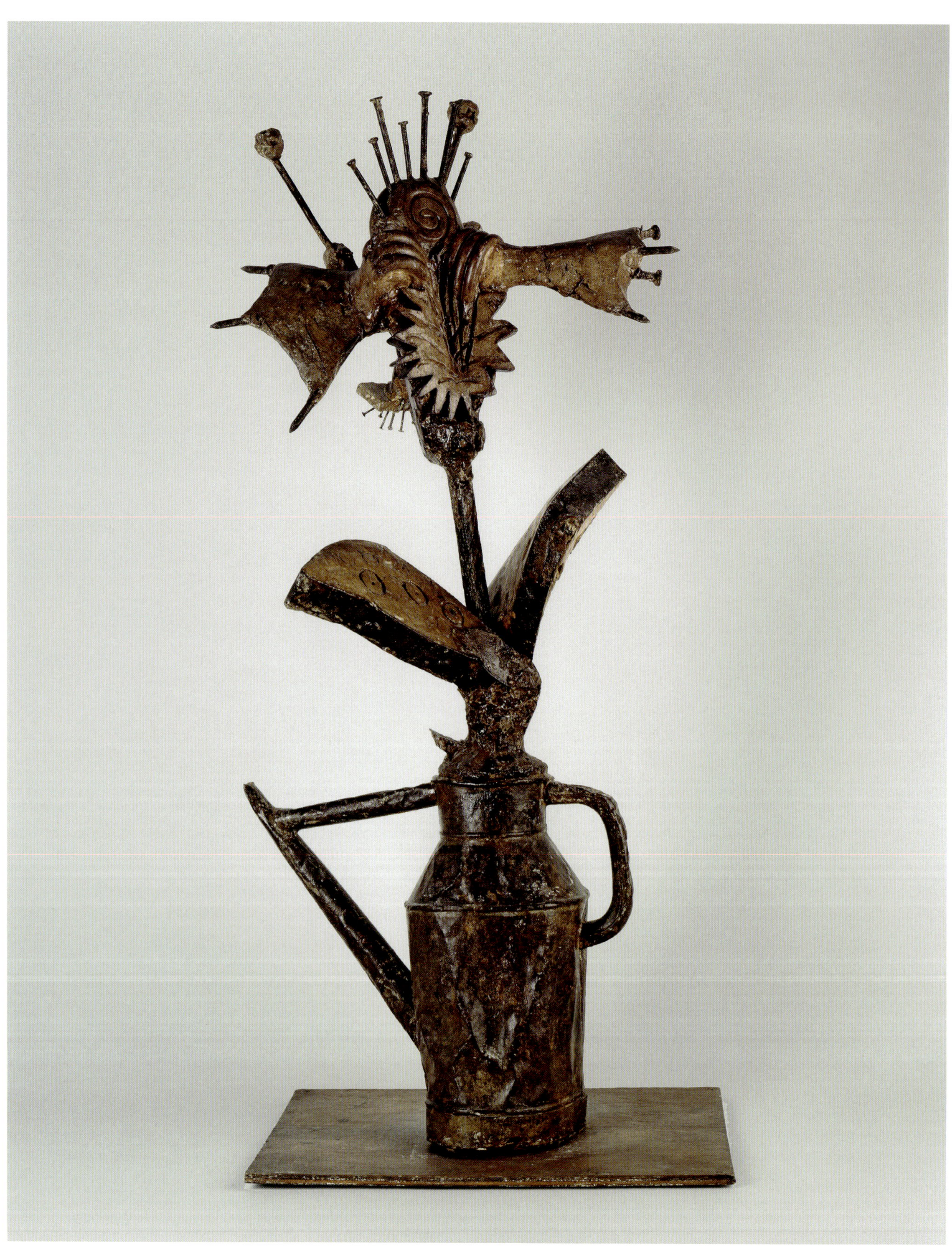

124. **FLOWERY WATERING CAN.** Paris, 1951–52
Plaster with watering can, metal parts, nails, and wood
33 11/16 × 16 9/16 × 14 15/16 in. (85.5 × 42 × 38 cm)
Musée national Picasso–Paris. Dation Pablo Picasso

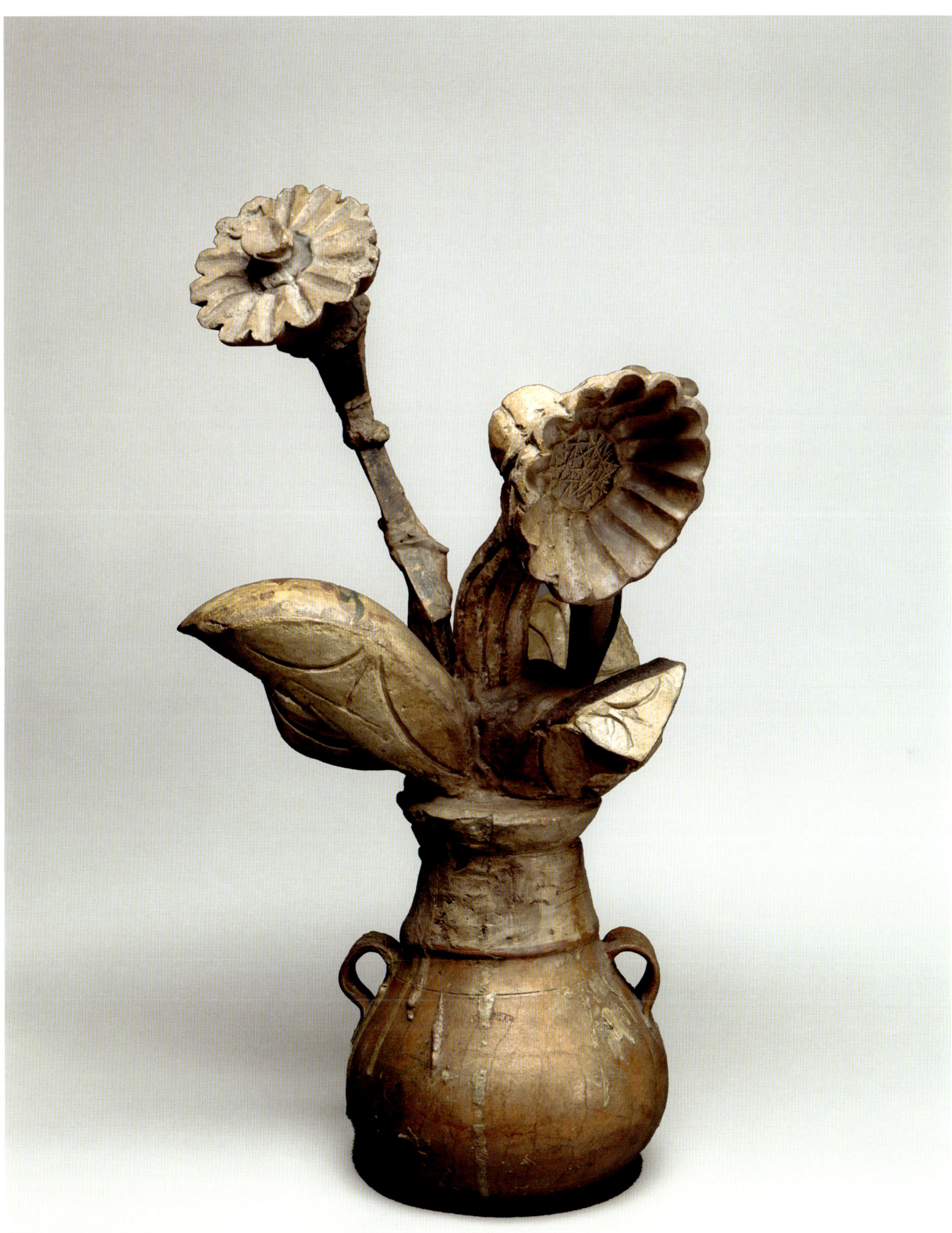

125. **FLOWERS IN A VASE.** Vallauris, 1951–53
Painted plaster, terracotta, and iron
30 ⅛ × 20 ¼ × 17 ¼ in. (76.5 × 51.4 × 43.8 cm)
Raymond and Patsy Nasher Collection, Nasher Sculpture Center, Dallas

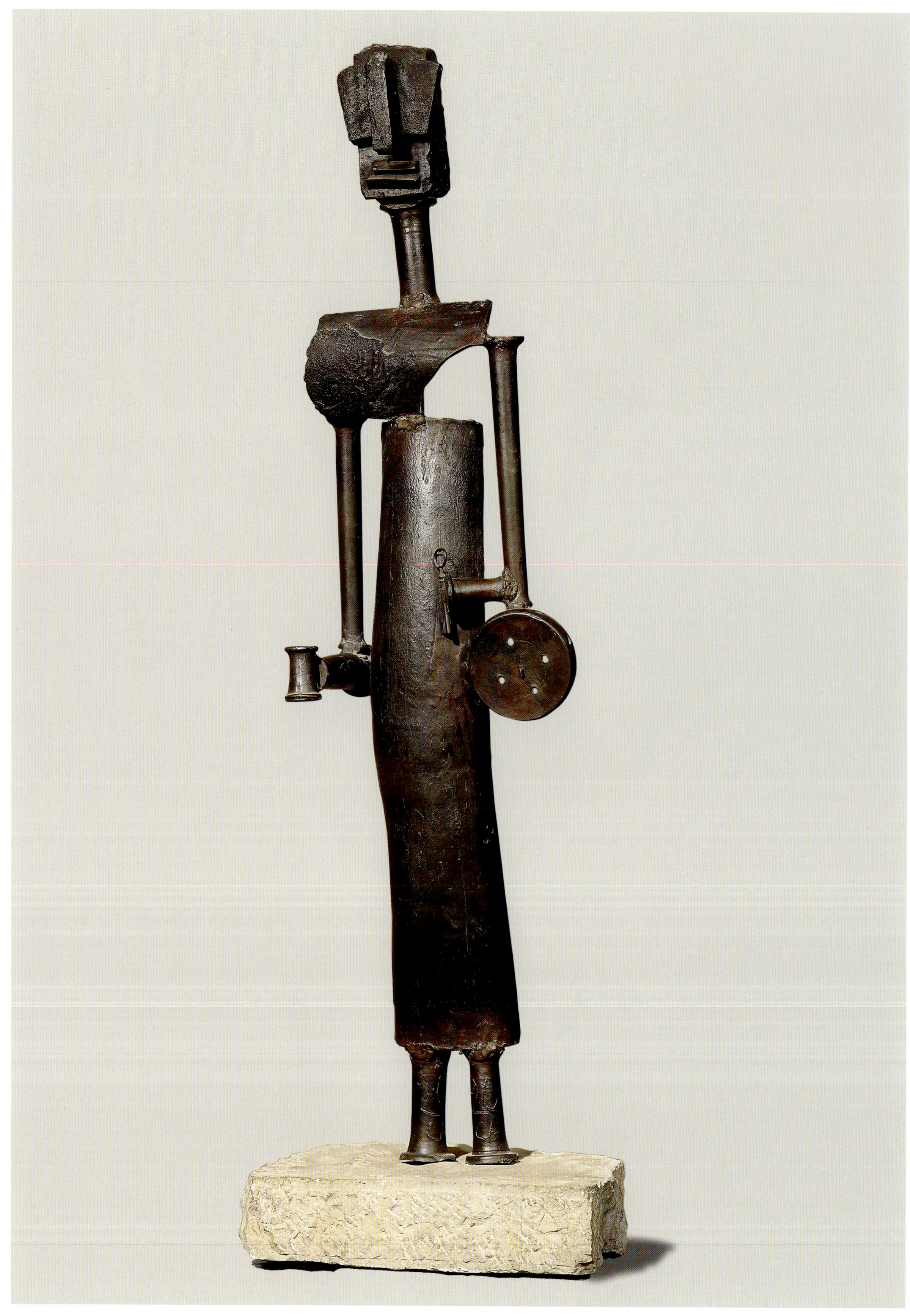

126. THE WOMAN WITH A KEY. Vallauris, October 1953–54;
stone base added in Cannes, by September 1958
Bronze with stone base, unique, cast 1954
67 11/16 × 16 15/16 × 11 13/16 in. (172 × 43 × 30 cm)
Private collection

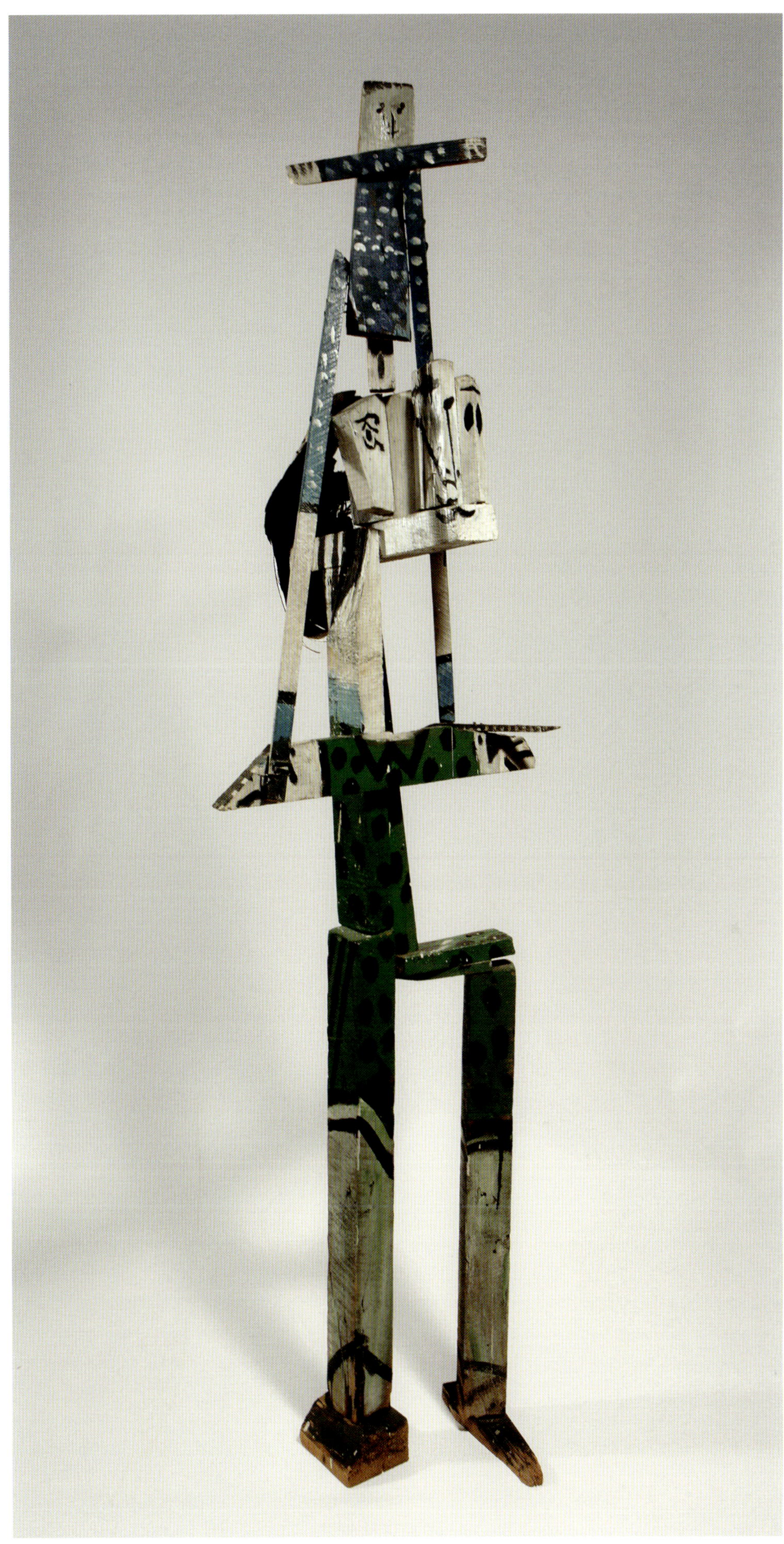

127. **WOMAN CARRYING A CHILD.** Vallauris, 1953
Painted wood and section of palm frond
68 ⅛ × 21 ¼ × 13 ¾ in. (173 × 54 × 35 cm)
Private collection

CHAPTER 8

WOOD ASSEMBLAGES, SHEET METAL SCULPTURES, AND PUBLIC MONUMENTS 1954–1973

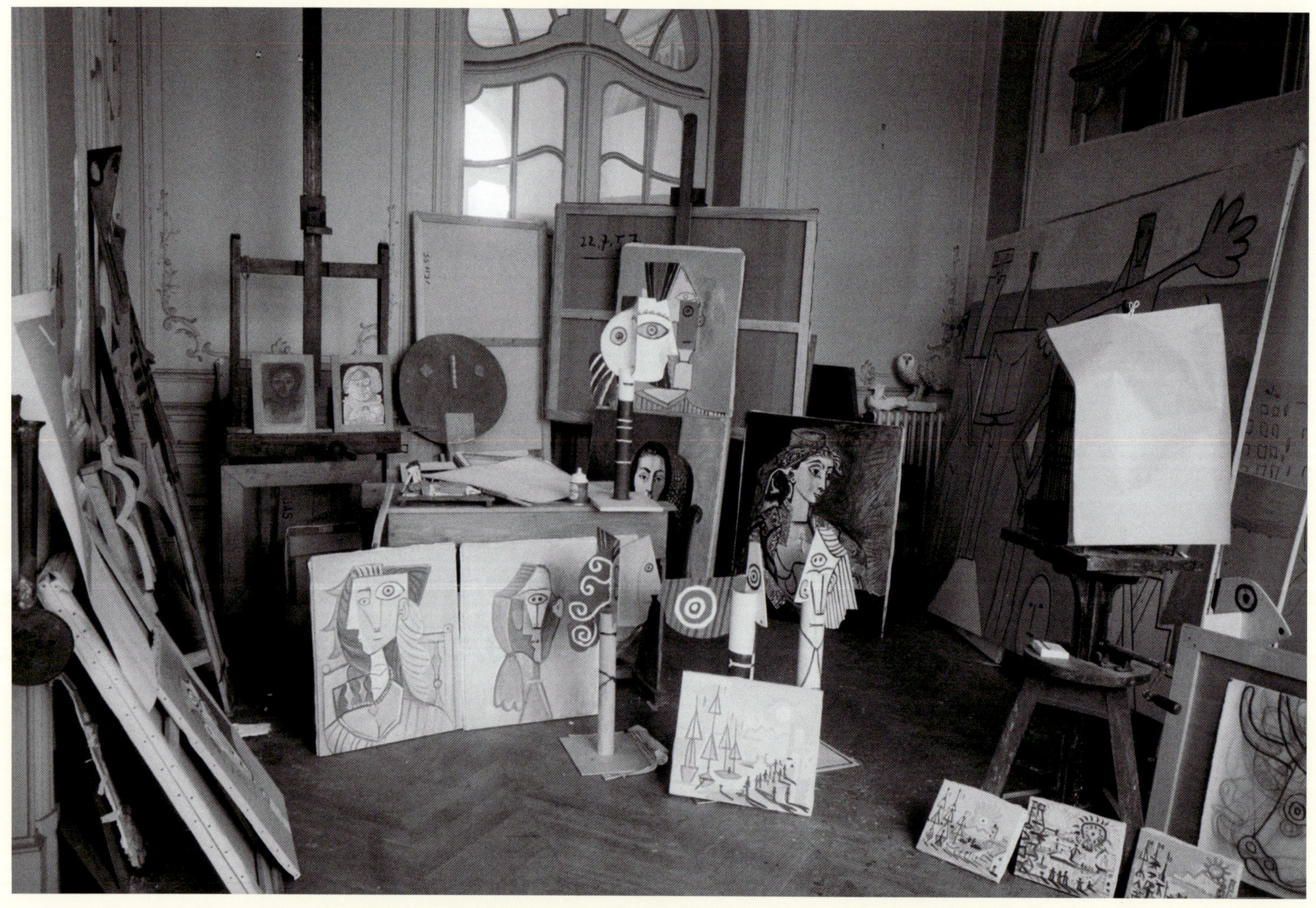

Picasso's studio at La Californie, Cannes, 1959.
Photograph by Edward Quinn. Edward Quinn Archives

THE FINAL DECADE of Picasso's sculpture took an unpredictable turn away from the robustly modeled forms of the ceramics and assemblages made in Vallauris toward constructions that were decidedly planar and frontal in nature. Two materials would govern his new sculptural explorations: wood, in works constructed from lumber scraps and other salvage; and sheet metal, in works fabricated at Société Tritub, a small metal-tubing factory in Vallauris. The sheet metal objects, in turn, prompted the final manifestation of Picasso's sculptural impulses: the creation of monumental outdoor works that he authorized but would never see, as they rose in far-flung sites across Europe and North America.

The wood constructions took center stage in the years 1956–58. In 1955 Picasso had moved with Jacqueline Roque to the villa La Californie, just above Cannes. In this elegant residential neighborhood the artist no longer had a junkyard right at hand, as in Vallauris, but his passion for ragpicking did not abate. Bits of old furniture, crates, picture frames, and sticks now formed the basis for his transformations. Picasso's choice of wood brings to mind the Cubist constructions and *tableaux-reliefs* of 1912–14, in which wood scraps served as glasses, newspapers, and dice. More recent precedents were the jaunty wooden dolls he had made in the 1930s for a young Maya, and then again in 1953 for four-year-old Paloma. At La Californie those impulses gave form to works of larger scale and more complex structure, albeit with the playfulness of the dolls fully retained. A commanding troupe of six life-size *Bathers* (pls. 128–33) materializes from a variety of wooden planks and found objects, including two picture frames that remind us of the figures' dual existence on the beach and in the studio.

Sheet metal was the next, and final, material with which Picasso reinvented himself as a sculptor. As was often true in his sculpture career, the new direction can be attributed in part to skillful and inspiring collaborators. Picasso's first endeavors date from 1954, in Vallauris, where the model Sylvette David inspired not only paintings but several cut and folded sheet metal sculptures. These were designed in paper or cardboard by Picasso and fabricated at the Tritub workshop by David's fiancé, Tobias Jellinek, a designer and sculptor. Picasso briefly returned to sheet metal in 1957, working directly with Tritub's founder, a craftsman named Joseph-Marius Tiola. Then, in late 1960, an art-loving entrepreneur named Lionel Prejger acquired Tritub and invited Picasso to resume his work with Tiola. Thus began a phase of nonstop creativity that produced more than 120 sheet metal sculptures by fall 1961.

Picasso's approach to the sheet metal maquettes centered on cutting, the technique governing the colored paper cutouts that formed Henri Matisse's triumphant final phase of work. But in Picasso's case the result encompassed three dimensions, involving Cubist-inspired folds and bends and a virtuosic choreography of positive and negative space that evokes the sheet metal *Guitar* of 1914 (pl. 14). Sculpture acquired a daily rhythm: Picasso gave a paper or cardboard maquette to Prejger, who would return the next day with Tiola's 1:1 scale copy in sheet metal coated white. Soldered lines echoed Picasso's drawing, but the surface was ready for any painting the artist might wish to add. Many of the sheet metal works portray the striking profile of Roque, continually transformed as a viewer circles the sculpture. Bathers, mothers, and other friendly characters share a lightness of spirit that belies their complex conception and intricate execution.

The sheet metal creations were natural candidates for enlargement. Picasso's fantasies of "monuments," first evident in his sketchbooks of the late 1920s, were now realizable, facilitated by new technologies as well as a hearty international appetite for works of art at an architectural scale. Once again, Picasso's new venture began at another's invitation. In 1957 a young Norwegian artist named Carl Nesjar introduced Picasso to a process for concrete engraving that employed high-intensity sandblasting. This allowed for Picasso's sheet metal personages to be interpreted as giant concrete figures with corresponding contours and surface details. Picasso's delight in seeing his work at a large scale also led him to accept a commission from the architecture firm Skidmore, Owings & Merrill to design a work for the plaza of the new Chicago Civic Center. His iron and sheet metal maquette of 1964 was translated into a fifty-foot sculpture of Cor-Ten steel, unveiled to great acclaim in 1967. Picasso's own sculpture making came to a close nearly a decade before his death, at age ninety-one in 1973. But his ongoing engagement with the construction of nearly twenty large-scale outdoor works ensured a final act as a sculptor of the sixties.

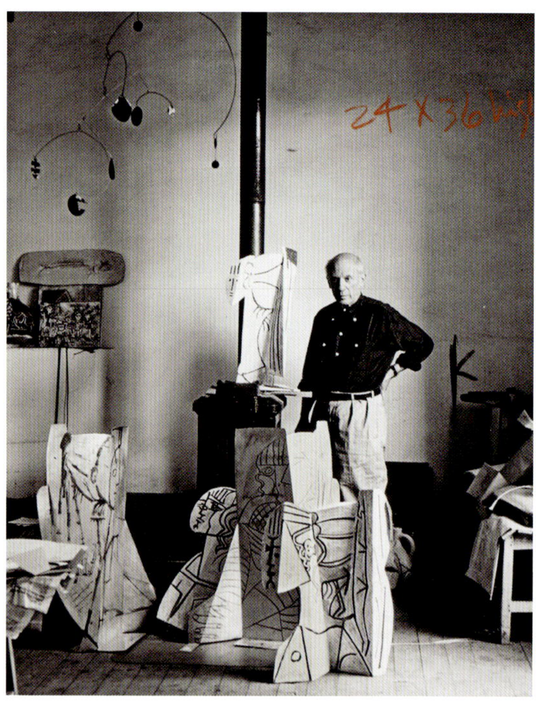

1. Picasso with sculptures from his series of portrayals of Sylvette David, c. 1960. Photograph by Alexander Liberman. The Alexander Liberman Photography Archive, The Getty Research Institute

EARLY 1954: Picasso met Sylvette David in Vallauris together with her fiancé, Tobias Jellinek, a young British artist and furniture designer. The couple visited Picasso at his villa La Galloise in Vallauris to deliver several chairs that Jellinek had designed.[1] Several weeks later, Picasso asked Sylvette to model for him.

***SYLVETTE*, 1954**

Between April and June, Picasso created dozens of portraits of David in two dimensions, capturing her distinctive blonde high ponytail and wavy bangs. At the same time, he began to experiment with a new sculpture technique, folding and painting forms cut from sheet metal (fig. 1). Picasso ultimately forged a new nexus between painting and sculpture, constructing works by juxtaposing planar surfaces, as in earlier Cubist compositions such as the 1914 *Guitar* (pl. 14); he painted these surfaces with distinct, visible brushwork in a stark palette of white and intermediate grays and added animated lines in black enamel.

Sylvette (pl. 139) is one of a number of sheet metal sculptures created with Jellinek and the local craftsman Joseph-Marius Tiola, who was trained as a locksmith and ironworker and ran a company that made metal furniture and other household items. Using folded cardboard maquettes created by Picasso, Jellinek cut matching pieces of sheet metal; Tiola then used a machine to fold the sheets according to the artist's example.[2] With *Sylvette*, the planes of this bent metal created contrasting areas of light and dark, which Picasso enhanced with white and black paint. Both sides of the sculpture show Sylvette's face, one side in a more naturalistic style and the other in a more schematic linear arrangement; her ponytail provides a faceted anchor that is convex on one side and concave on the other.

LATE JUNE 1954: Picasso left Vallauris for Perpignan, bringing an end to this brief burst of collaborative energy. Jellinek would later estimate that he collaborated with Picasso on ten to fifteen sheet metal sculptures.[3]

AUGUST 1954: Curt Valentin, Daniel-Henry Kahnweiler's agent in New York and a dealer of Picasso's sculptures, died of a heart attack while visiting the Italian sculptor Marino Marini in Italy. The following year Valentin's gallery was liquidated; his assistant, Jane Wade, and several of the artists he had represented joined Fine Arts Associates, a New York gallery owned by Otto M. Gerson, who became an important distributor of Picasso's sculptural work.

SEPTEMBER 8, 1954: André Derain, an artist who had been key to Picasso's development as a sculptor during the first decade of the century, died in a car accident.

NOVEMBER 3, 1954: Henri Matisse died in Nice. His death affected Picasso deeply. During the past decade he had maintained a respectful friendship with the bedridden Matisse and their work had continued to be of profound mutual interest.

JUNE–SEPTEMBER 1955: Henri-Georges Clouzot began work on his film *Le Mystère Picasso* (The mystery of Picasso) at La Victorine studios in Nice. The film is best known for the sequence in which Picasso draws with white paint on transparent glass. But it also showed Picasso making the large wooden construction *Centaur* (summer 1955; Los Angeles County Museum of Art), composed of several wooden planks coated in black on which Picasso then painted the mythological figure in white.[4] Picasso, dressed in a painted board and mask, appeared on camera alongside *Centaur* together with a smaller birdlike sculpture. The trio portrayed on film anticipates the artist's sculptural ensemble *The Bathers* of 1956. Clouzot's film would premiere at the Cannes Film Festival in 1956.

FALL 1955: Picasso purchased La Californie, a grand villa near Cannes; he was unperturbed by its ostentatious style, which the biographer Patrick O'Brian likened to "a vast wedding-cake . . . wealth as expressed in the uninhibited days of 1900."[5] Picasso moved there with Jacqueline Roque, a former employee at the Madoura pottery showroom, who had become his partner a year earlier. The artist was drawn to La Californie

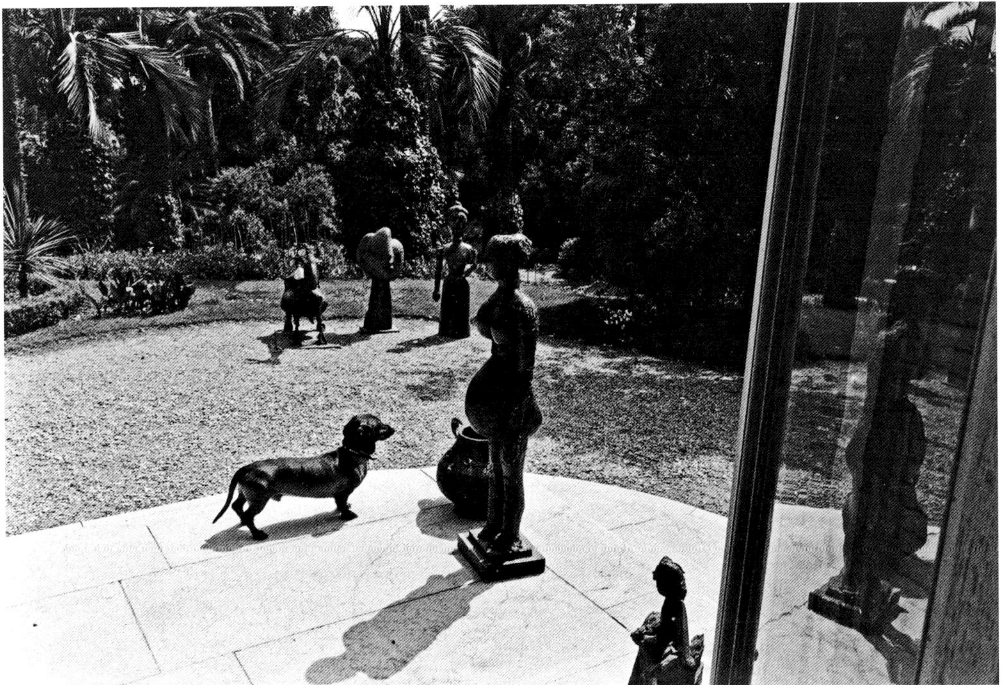

2. The garden at La Californie, with Picasso's dachshund, Lump, and sculptures by the artist, Cannes, 1957. Photograph by Edward Quinn. Edward Quinn Archives

for its abundant light, the privacy afforded by its extensive garden, and its view of the Mediterranean Sea. Picasso quickly "Picassoized" the residence, transforming it into a chaotic, overflowing jumble of art and belongings.[6] He placed many bronze sculptures outdoors, including recent works such as *She-Goat* and *Man with a Lamb* (fig. 2), meanwhile converting the majority of the ground floor into studios where he could paint and sculpt.

OCTOBER 25–DECEMBER 18, 1955: Munich's Haus der Kunst mounted *Picasso 1900–1955*. This exhibition added thirty-five sculptures and thirteen ceramics to the approximately two hundred paintings and works on paper in *Picasso: Peintures 1900–1955*, which had been presented at the Musée des arts décoratifs in Paris that summer. The sculptures all dated from 1944 to 1953, thus providing a rich window onto Picasso's productivity in Vallauris. Among these works were bronze casts of *Pregnant Woman* (pl. 114) and *Flowers in a Vase* (pl. 125). The exhibition would travel to the Rheinisches Museum Köln-Deutz and then to the Kunstverein Hamburg.

MARCH 31, 1956: In a letter to Picasso about an exhibition of his work planned for the next year at The Museum of Modern Art, New York, Alfred H. Barr, Jr., stressed his desire to give the artist's sculpture pride of place in order to better acquaint American visitors with it. "Besides paintings, we want to show your sculpture at full length, using the Museum sculpture garden and the galleries adjacent to it on the ground floor to give the sculpture a special and conspicuous attention," he wrote. "We are particularly interested in a comprehensive review of your sculpture which is too little known here. We also hope to include a fine representation of your original ceramics if this can be done safely."[7]

MAY 12, 1956: Barr wrote to Picasso once again (fig. 3):

> Probably Mr. Kahnweiler has told you that our Museum has bought four of your recent sculptures:
>
> Crâne de Chèvre et Bouteille
> Tête de Femme
> Femme Enceinte
> Guenon avec son petit
>
> Only the *Guenon* has arrived. We look forward to receiving the others with great excitement.[8]

Barr would send a follow-up message on January 30, 1957, enclosing three photographs of these recent acquisitions on display in the galleries and noting that they had been met with "great admiration."[9]

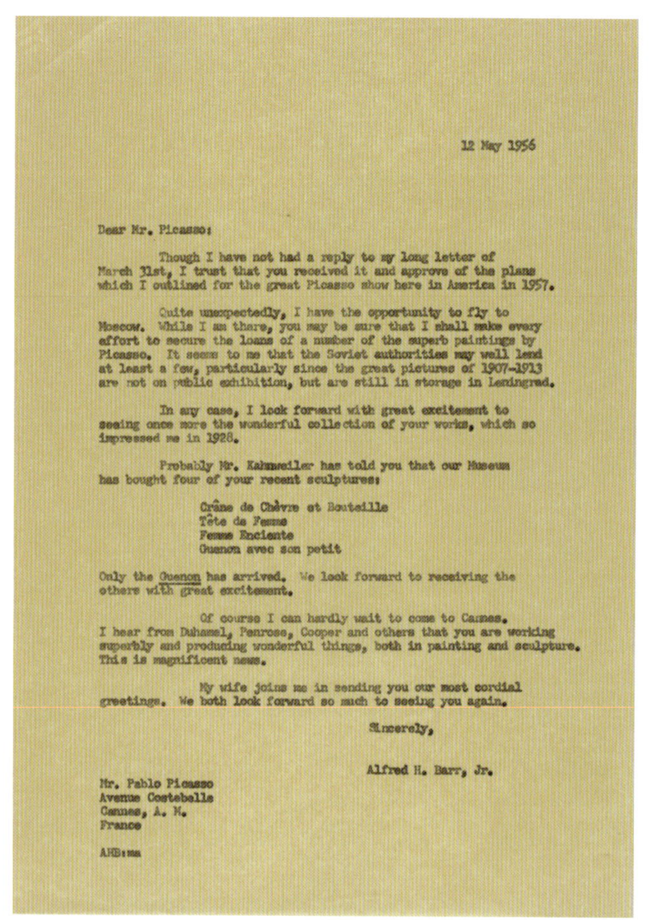

12 May 1956

Dear Mr. Picasso:

Though I have not had a reply to my long letter of March 31st, I trust that you received it and approve of the plans which I outlined for the great Picasso show here in America in 1957.

Quite unexpectedly, I have the opportunity to fly to Moscow. While I am there, you may be sure that I shall make every effort to secure the loans of a number of the superb paintings by Picasso. It seems to me that the Soviet authorities may well lend at least a few, particularly since the great pictures of 1907-1913 are not on public exhibition, but are still in storage in Leningrad.

In any case, I look forward with great excitement to seeing once more the wonderful collection of your works, which so impressed me in 1928.

Probably Mr. Kahnweiler has told you that our Museum has bought four of your recent sculptures:

Crâne de Chèvre et Bouteille
Tête de Femme
Femme Enciente
Guenon avec son petit

Only the Guenon has arrived. We look forward to receiving the others with great excitement.

Of course I can hardly wait to come to Cannes. I hear from Duhamel, Penrose, Cooper and others that you are working superbly and producing wonderful things, both in painting and sculpture. This is magnificent news.

My wife joins me in sending you our most cordial greetings. We both look forward so much to seeing you again.

Sincerely,

Alfred H. Barr, Jr.

Mr. Pablo Picasso
Avenue Costebelle
Cannes, A. M.
France

AHB:mm

3. Carbon copy of a letter from Alfred H. Barr, Jr., to Picasso, May 12, 1956. The Museum of Modern Art Archives, New York

***THE BATHERS*, 1956**

The Bathers (pls. 128–33) is Picasso's first sculptural ensemble. The elongated, geometrical bodies of this sextet of bathers are composed of pieces of salvaged wood such as footboards, broomsticks, and painting stretchers; Picasso used only a hammer and nails to assemble them. He inscribed anatomical details such as eyes, ribcages, chests, genitalia, and kneecaps through carving and painting. In the case of the first four bathers—*Woman Diver* (pl. 128), *Man with Folded Hands* (pl. 129), *Fountain Man* (pl. 130), and *Woman with Outstretched Arms* (pl. 132)—these markings are particularly elaborate and can also be found on their backs. The results are strikingly spare compared with his recent assemblages, such as *Baboon and Young* (pl. 116) and *She-Goat* (pl. 119). In a 1958 essay on *The Bathers*, Georges A. Salles would write that Picasso "creates simple but extraordinarily meaningful forms.... from the very poverty of these resources has sprung an artistic miracle."[10]

A group of various ages and sexes, the bathers are each involved in a different seaside activity. *Woman Diver* prepares herself to jump into the water, while *Man with Folded Hands* appears to serenely contemplate the maritime scene. The round-headed *Child* (pl. 131) swims, while *Fountain Man* earns his name by pissing in the water. *Woman with Outstretched Arms* and *Young Man* (pl. 133) each stretch out their arms, as if to enjoy the breeze or wave to friends on the sand.

All six bathers had been completed and their sequence finalized by September 16, 1956, as indicated by a sketch of that date (fig. 4). Picasso had conceived of the scene as a theatrical tableau, with each figure facing the viewer: the sequence was important to him, and the bathers remained in the order he imagined in this sketch. The arrangement shows one pair, *Woman Diver* and *Man with Folded Arms*, to the left, on a pier; two swimmers, *Fountain Man* and *Child*, in the center, standing in the water; and another pair, *Woman with Outstretched Arms* and *Young Man*, standing on top of a diving board, a female bather in front, observed from behind by the youth.

Picasso's dialogue between painting and sculpture continued with the slow gestation of the large-scale oil painting *Bathers on the Beach at La Garoupe* (Musée d'art et d'histoire, Geneva; see p. 246, visible at right), which he began before the sculptures but did not finish until July 1957.[11] Here the six bathers appear against a blue backdrop that evokes the Mediterranean, the composition of the figures echoing that of the sculptures in Picasso's sketches. The detailed rendering of the figures in this painting and related drawings reflects the fact that the artist made them after he completed the sculptures.[12]

Shortly after creating the original wood figures, Picasso had them cast in bronze at the Valsuani foundry in Paris, using the lost-wax technique. He indicated to Kahnweiler, who oversaw the production, that he meant to install pipes in *Fountain Man* to allow water to circulate through it, and a drawing he made on September 14 shows the figure urinating (fig. 5). On November 12, Kahnweiler wrote:

> [We] arranged for water pipes to be installed in the bronze.... It's an adult Manneken-Pis. We absolutely want to install it in the garden at Saint-Hilaire, and we have already found the place for it. I would simply like to know if it will always be pissing? If so, obviously, we would have to make a small basin for it with a drain. If, on the other hand, it will only "function" from time to time, it can urinate without a problem on the lawn it will be placed on.[13]

Soon after they were cast, the group of bronze sculptures embarked on a robust touring schedule that would take them to venues in Europe and the United States.

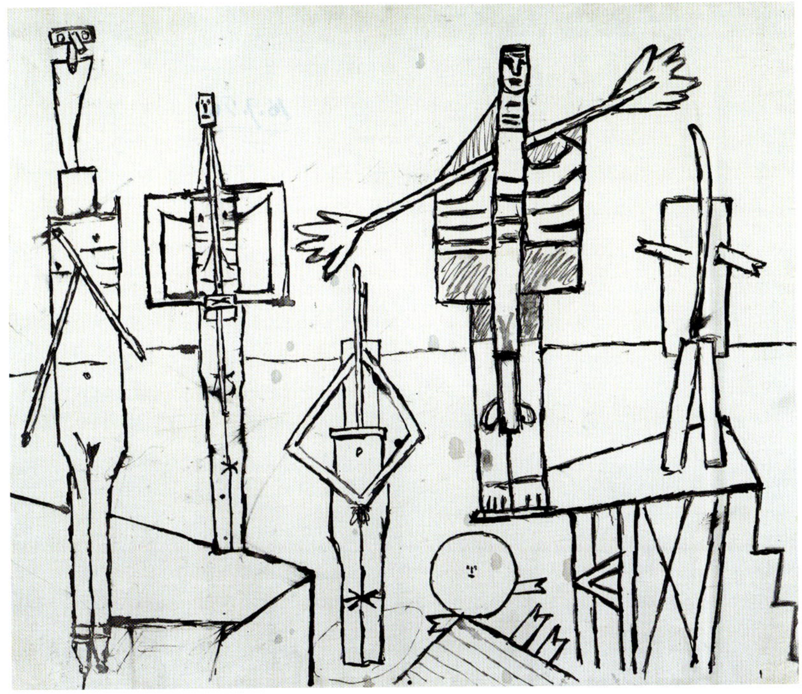

4. Pablo Picasso. Study for *The Bathers at La Garoupe*. Cannes, September 16, 1956. India ink on canvas, 21¼ × 25⅝ in. (54 × 65 cm). Private collection. Courtesy Fundación Almine y Bernard Ruiz-Picasso para el Arte

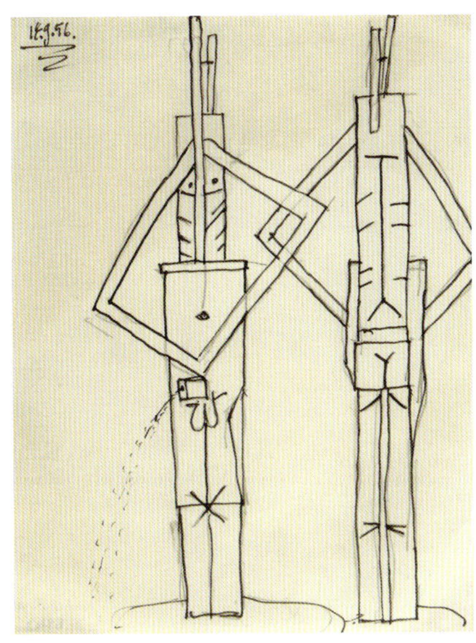

5. Pablo Picasso. Study for *The Bathers: Fountain Man*. Cannes, September 14, 1956. India ink and pencil on paper, 10⅝ × 8¼ in. (27 × 21 cm). Private collection

JANUARY 15–FEBRUARY 9, 1957: On January 15 the exhibition *Picasso, Sculpture (Part I)* opened at New York's Fine Arts Associates. It featured twenty-three bronzes and three ceramics. An accompanying brochure included a translated excerpt of Kahnweiler's essay "Les Sculptures de Picasso" along with sixteen black-and-white photographs of the works on view. The exhibition presented early sculptures such as *Kneeling Woman Combing Her Hair* and *Head of a Woman*, as well as more recent works such as *Little Owl*. But work of the 1910s, 1920s, and 1930s was virtually absent: *Cock* was the only sculpture on display that had been made between 1909 and 1945.

JANUARY 1957: The Norwegian sculptor, photographer, and printmaker Carl Nesjar visited Picasso to propose that he create an edition of 250 lithographs for a fine art magazine published by the Norwegian art club Aktuell Kunst. Picasso agreed to the commission immediately.[14] On that first visit, Nesjar also brought with him several photographs of an experimental new sculpture technique he had been working with, called betograve. This method involves pouring gravel into a model, filling it with concrete, and, once the material has dried, using precision sandblasting to engrave the concrete surface with a given design. The underlying dark gravel revealed by this process articulates the image. Picasso was immediately intrigued, telling his new friend, "You should have been here last week. I have been waiting for you."[15]

Over the course of the next seventeen years, Nesjar and Picasso would collaborate on more than thirty works in concrete, including monumental enlargements of many of the artist's sculptures, as well as murals that translated Picasso's drawings into etched concrete.[16] Nesjar created these murals on-site; he executed the first one in 1957 for a government building complex in Oslo. The first sculpture in the round that Nesjar enlarged was Picasso's *Head of a Woman* (1957), which in 1958 was transformed into a ten-foot concrete totem and installed at a private residence outside of Larvik, Norway.[17] The Larvik work was conceived as an experiment to test whether the betograve method could be used to create free-standing sculpture; Picasso was delighted when Nesjar brought him photographs of the finished work.[18] In 1962 Nesjar executed a set of five murals for the Château de Castille in Argilliers, France, the home of Douglas Cooper, an art historian and collector of Cubism. Although the Argilliers murals were the only examples of Nesjar's projects that Picasso ever saw in person, the artist was highly involved in each of them: he created preparatory studies and maquettes and supervised Nesjar's progress via photographs and letters.

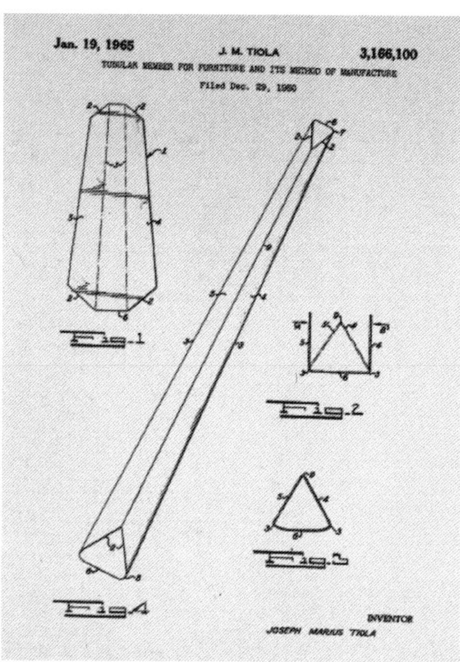

6. "Tubular Member for Furniture and Its Method of Manufacture." Patent filing by Joseph-Marius Tiola, December 29, 1960. DWP Editions

EARLY 1957: Picasso returned to his work in metal. Experiments with the bent metal tubes used by Tiola in his furniture allowed him to explore the formal possibilities of the medium and the combinatory shapes that could be created through welding (fig. 6). These metal works developed from a series of wooden sculptures, made in collaboration with a carpenter in Vallauris, that were characterized by intersecting planar profiles of Roque, inserted at the top of narrow poles.[19]

***HEAD OF A WOMAN*, 1957**

For *Head of a Woman* (pl. 141), Picasso designed a two-part head slotted into the top of one of Tiola's metal tubes. The woman's head is composed of a rectangular plane that makes up the lower half of her face, on which the artist painted an ear and a mouth in black enamel; above this form, inserted at a perpendicular angle, is the top of her head, defined on each side by a painted eye, nostril, and strip of hair. A triangular element shaped like a dorsal fin juts out behind her, perhaps hair or a dress blowing in the wind. All white, with schematic black details, this early example of Picasso's sheet metal sculptures is among his most reductive and austere. *Head of a Woman* made its public debut in fall 1966 at the Petit Palais in Paris in the exhibition *Hommage à Pablo Picasso* (fig. 7).

SUMMER 1957: Bronze casts of *The Bathers* went on view at the Galerie Louise Leiris one by one, as each was cast. The bronze *Man with Folded Hands*, as well as a bronze titled *Bouquet*, traveled to the Triennale di Milano at the Palazzo dell'arte for its opening at the end of July. In September, Pierre Matisse, Henri's son and a friend of Picasso, would write to report of the exhibition, "Your bronzes did very well."[20]

MAY 22–SEPTEMBER 8, 1957: To honor Picasso's seventy-fifth birthday, The Museum of Modern Art, New York, presented *Picasso: 75th Anniversary Exhibition,* a joint project with the Art Institute of Chicago and the Philadelphia Museum of Art (fig. 8). The exhibition of some 250 objects included forty-three sculptures and three ceramics. The selection of sculptures

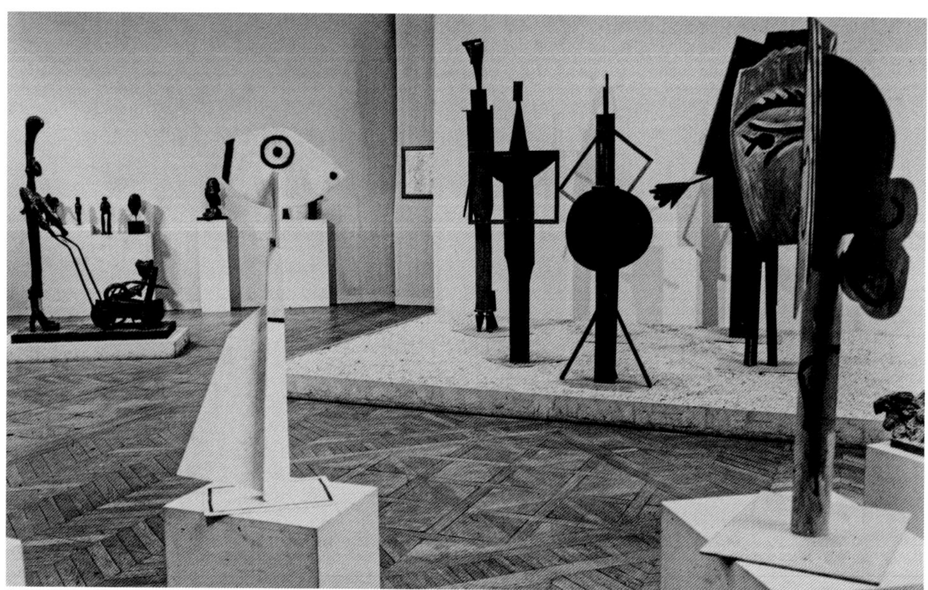

7. View of the 1966 exhibition *Hommage à Pablo Picasso* at the Petit Palais in Paris, with *Head of a Woman* at front left, installed among Picasso's sculptures from the 1950s, c. November 1966. Archives Petit Palais. Musée des Beaux-Arts de la Ville de Paris

ranged from Picasso's early works, such as *Head of a Picador with a Broken Nose* (pl. 2), to more contemporary works that had recently been acquired by the Museum, such as *Baboon and Young* (pl. 116) and *Goat Skull and Bottle* (pl. 123). However, the Museum was only able to borrow three sculptures from the 1930s: the bas-relief *Composition with Glove* (pl. 43), *Seated Woman* (1930),[21] and *Cock* (pl. 58). Kahnweiler had written to Picasso on March 12 to discuss the recent bronze sculptures that Barr sought to include, but despite his and Barr's efforts the selection of sculptures was not as extensive as they had hoped. Barr stated in the catalogue, "Had the many major pieces still in Picasso's possession been available (as we expected), the artist would, I believe, have been revealed as one of the great sculptors of our time."[22]

During the exhibition, the Museum implemented longer hours to accommodate record-breaking crowds. The show next traveled to Chicago, where it opened on October 29 and ran through December 8, 1957, with equal success.

OCTOBER 14, 1957: *Life* magazine published "Picasso, the Sculptor: Colossus of Painting Reveals His Prowess in Another Art." This seven-page article, illustrated with many color photographs by Gordon Parks, showed a wide range of the artist's bronzes and ceramics juxtaposed with relevant paintings in pairings composed by Parks himself. In an introduction to these images, *Life* staff writers identified the impetus for the article as the "variety and inventiveness" of Picasso's sculpture as revealed by the *75th Anniversary Exhibition*.[23] They included photographs presenting a bronze *Head of a Picador with a Broken Nose* (pl. 2) in front of *Yo, Picasso* (1901; private collection),[24] a bronze *Cock* (pl. 58) in front of *Large Still Life with a Pedestal Table* (1931; Musée national Picasso–Paris), and *Man with a Lamb* (pl. 87) in front of *Guernica* (1937; Museo Nacional Centro de Arte Reina Sofía, Madrid). Captions—such as "Bronze mask made by Picasso in 1904 wears same intent stare as Picasso's 1901 self-portrait in background"—further invited comparisons between his paintings and sculptures.

DECEMBER 17, 1957: Following the considerable impact that Picasso's sculptures made during The Museum of Modern Art's summer exhibition, Barr wrote to Picasso about the need for a retrospective of his work in sculpture (fig. 9). "May I say that in my thirty years of Museum work I have never put on an exhibition with greater interest or excitement. My one great regret is that we were not able to present your sculpture adequately. Perhaps in the future our Museum may have the privilege of putting on a really comprehensive exhibition of your work as a sculptor."[25]

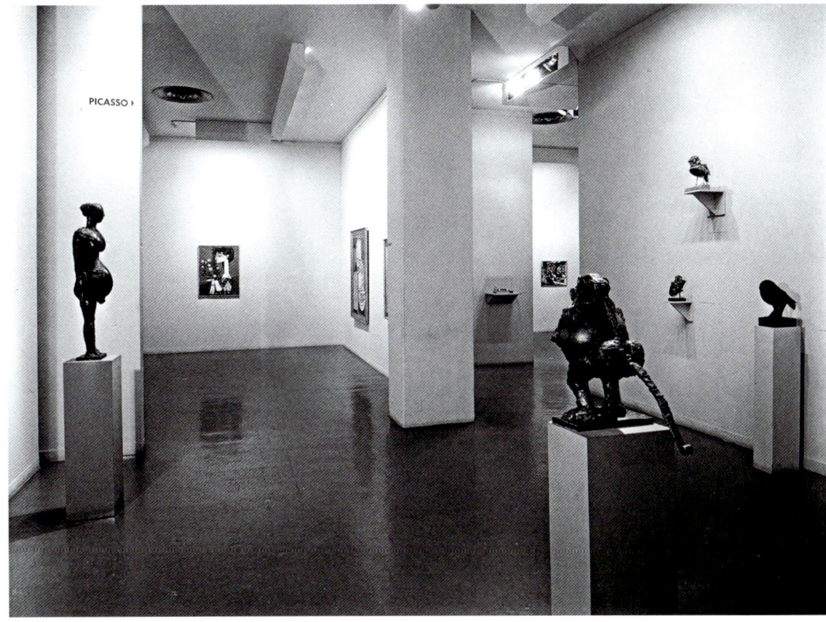

8. View of *Picasso: 75th Anniversary Exhibition* at The Museum of Modern Art, New York, 1957. The Museum of Modern Art Archives, New York

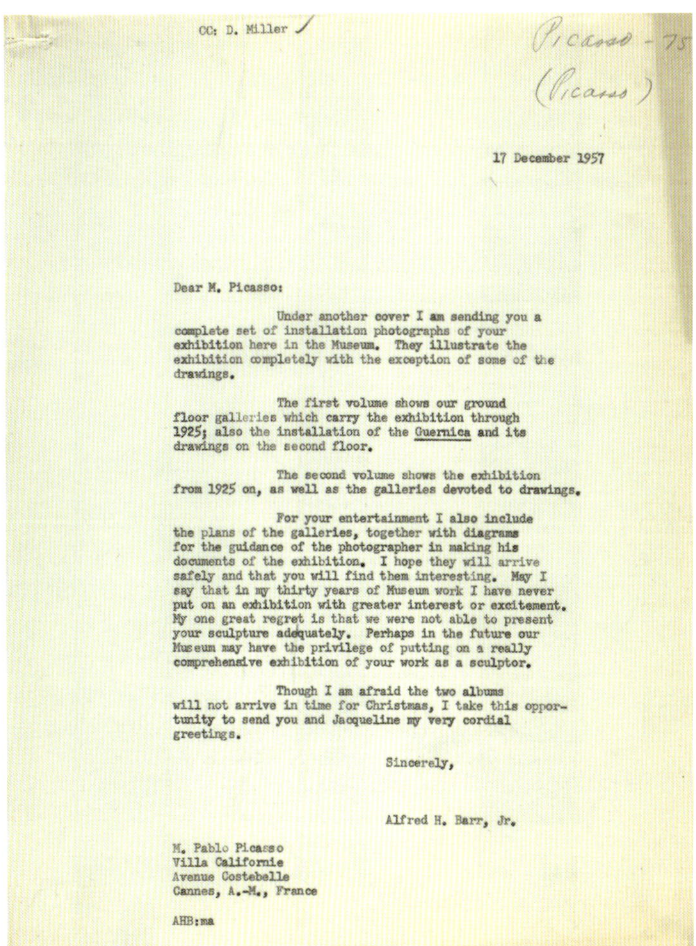

CC: D. Miller

Picasso - 75
(Picasso)

17 December 1957

Dear M. Picasso:

Under another cover I am sending you a complete set of installation photographs of your exhibition here in the Museum. They illustrate the exhibition completely with the exception of some of the drawings.

The first volume shows our ground floor galleries which carry the exhibition through 1925; also the installation of the Guernica and its drawings on the second floor.

The second volume shows the exhibition from 1925 on, as well as the galleries devoted to drawings.

For your entertainment I also include the plans of the galleries, together with diagrams for the guidance of the photographer in making his documents of the exhibition. I hope they will arrive safely and that you will find them interesting. May I say that in my thirty years of Museum work I have never put on an exhibition with greater interest or excitement. My one great regret is that we were not able to present your sculpture adequately. Perhaps in the future our Museum may have the privilege of putting on a really comprehensive exhibition of your work as a sculptor.

Though I am afraid the two albums will not arrive in time for Christmas, I take this opportunity to send you and Jacqueline my very cordial greetings.

Sincerely,

Alfred H. Barr, Jr.

M. Pablo Picasso
Villa Californie
Avenue Costebelle
Cannes, A.-M., France

AHB:ma

9. Carbon copy of a letter from Alfred H. Barr, Jr., to Picasso, December 17, 1957. The Museum of Modern Art Archives, New York

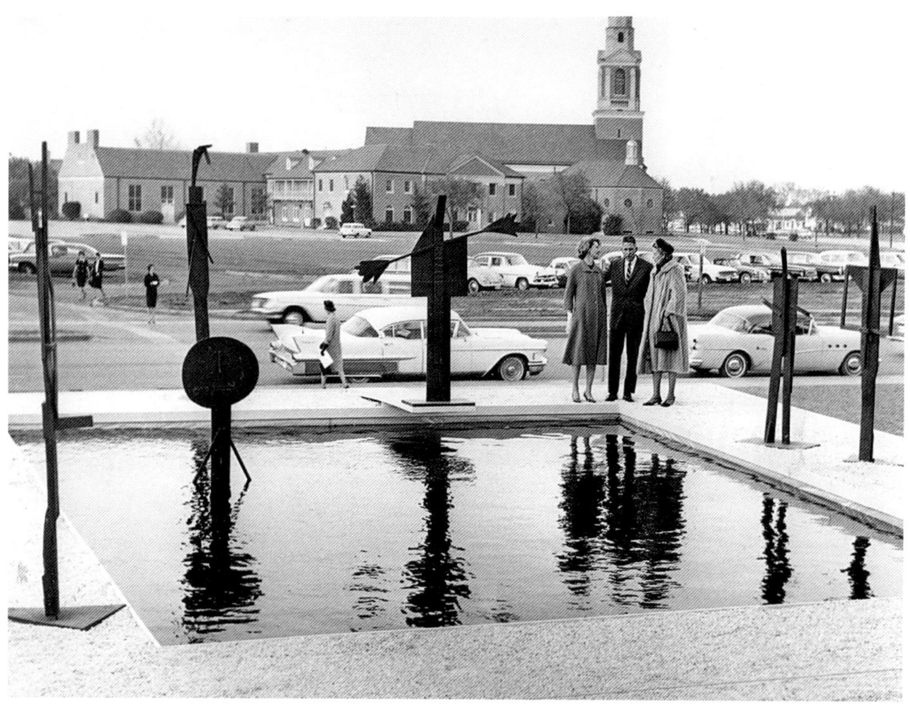

10. Photograph published with the article "Traffic stopping 'Bathers' have own pool and beach in front of Cullinan Hall," *Houston Chronicle*, February 6, 1962. Photograph by Al Startzman

JANUARY 8–FEBRUARY 28, 1958: The Philadelphia Museum of Art mounted *Picasso: A Loan Exhibition of His Paintings, Drawings, Sculpture, Ceramics, Prints and Illustrated Books*, an adaptation of the *Picasso: 75th Anniversary Exhibition* presented in New York and Chicago in 1957. The show in Philadelphia placed greater emphasis on the ceramics, of which seventy-five were on view. A room dedicated to Picasso's most recent sculptures featured a bronze cast of *Man with a Lamb* (pl. 87), which would enter the museum's collection as a gift from R. Sturgis and Marion B. F. Ingersoll that same year.

APRIL 24, 1958: Kahnweiler wrote to Picasso to report that James Johnson Sweeney, director of the Solomon R. Guggenheim Museum in New York, wanted to purchase all six of the bronze *Bathers* and situate the group around a pool with a diving board.[26] Although correspondence on the subject continued through at least the end of July, no acquisition was made. In 1962 Sweeney would place *The Bathers* on temporary display at the Museum of Fine Arts, Houston, where he was then director. *The Bathers* were arranged around a pool installed for this purpose in front of the museum (fig. 10).

***BULL*, APRIL 1958**

Picasso began work on this wood figure (pl. 136) with several preparatory studies exploring how to combine plywood surfaces to create the animal's form. Six study sheets dated April 27, 1958, develop the planar structure of *Bull*; Roman numerals identify the different wood segments and how Picasso planned to assemble them (fig. 11).[27] A cardboard model of the head of *Bull* is visible in a photograph taken by Edward Quinn at La Californie (fig. 12); Picasso also made a model of the head in painted wood.[28] For the final version, Picasso used nails and screws to affix palm fronds and tree branches from La Californie's grounds to the plywood body. The branches act as stabilizing agents but also reinforce the contours of the animal's form, such as the position of its legs in the front and the curve of its spine in the rear. The smattering of nails on either side of the sculpture suggests the mottled pattern of the bull's bristly fur.

In 1983, during one of William Rubin's frequent visits to Jacqueline Picasso in Mougins, he spotted *Bull* among the sculptures that she had inherited. *Bull* had never been exhibited or published; it was not included in Werner Spies's 1971 catalogue raisonné of the artist's sculpture. Soon thereafter, Mme. Picasso presented it as a gift to The Museum of Museum of Art, following her 1982 donation of the 1931–32 plaster *Head of a Woman* (pl. 56).

***BIRD*, MAY 22, 1958**

Birds were a recurring subject in the work of Picasso, who kept pigeons and doves at home. *Bird* (pl. 138), made in May 1958, combines wood, forks, plaster, nails, screws, and eyebolts into a distinctive avian form. Picasso added paint to create colorful plumage and a face that at once resembles a bird's visage and the nib of a fountain pen.

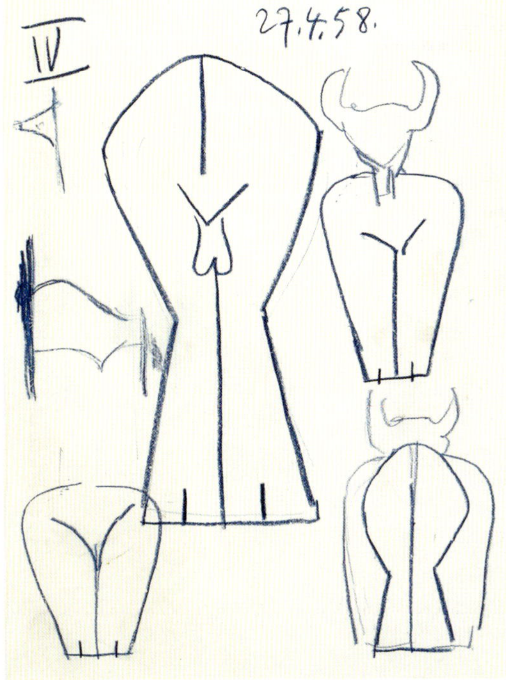

11. Pablo Picasso. Study for *Bull*. Cannes, April 27, 1958. Blue pencil, 10 ⅝ × 8 ¼ in. (27 × 21 cm). Private collection

FEMALE BATHER PLAYING, HEAD, AND MAN, 1958

In June 1958 Picasso deepened his engagement with found wooden objects. *Head* (pl. 137) consists of a painted wooden box, buttons, nails, plaster, and synthetic resin, all mounted on a ceramic dish. He carved abstracted ears onto either side of the sculpture, creating an anthropomorphic effect that can be glimpsed in a sketch of June 9–10, 1958.[29] *Man* (pl. 134) is composed of a handmade, open form that resembles a canvas stretcher, bisected by a baton that provides a spinelike support and a head. White-painted wood pieces suggest arms, rectangular scraps of wood define a pelvis. The two small furniture legs at bottom are mates to those supporting *Woman Diver*, of *The Bathers* (pl. 128). A thicker vertical plank at center forms the genitals, with an erect penis further articulated by a small hole drilled at its tip.

These two sculptures exemplify Picasso's ability to sustain the contradiction between the original characteristics of his materials and the images he created by combining them. Both works remained with the artist until his death. In 1984 Jacqueline Picasso donated *Head* to The Museum of Modern Art, together with *Head of a Warrior* (pl. 68).

The everyday components of these final assemblages stay clearly legible even when cast in bronze. Picasso built *Female Bather Playing* from wood, iron, and plaster and had it cast at the Valsuani foundry in Paris (pl. 135). The original assemblage and its bronze iteration vividly conjure the image of a woman about to splash water while playing with her child. Marilyn McCully suggests that Picasso may have had in mind a new series of bathers, following *The Bathers* of 1956.[30] His interest in the theme continued to extend across mediums: *Female Bather Playing* closely resembles a character in the large-scale mural *The Fall of Icarus,* painted for the Palais de l'Unesco in Paris in 1958.

SEPTEMBER 1958: During a dinner following a bullfight in Arles, Douglas Cooper informed Picasso that the Château de Vauvenargues, just outside Aix-en-Provence, was for sale. The château is situated to the north of Sainte-Victoire, the mountain that inspired dozens of paintings by Paul Cézanne, whom Picasso had famously called his "one and only master."[31] Picasso soon purchased Vauvenargues and had his art collection in Paris and many of his sculptures at La Californie transferred there; he arranged several bronzes on the terrace and in the foyer. Picasso would set up his studios on the first floor but would only live intermittently at the château, still spending a great deal of time in Cannes and continuing to work at La Californie.

FEBRUARY 15, 1959: The dealer Heinz Berggruen was introduced to Picasso in 1950 by the poet Tristan Tzara. In February 1959 he traveled to Cannes to ask for the artist's authorization to issue a new edition of bronze casts of Picasso's 1906 *Head of a Woman (Fernande)* (pl. 4).[32] Picasso agreed, and proposed the edition be limited to nine, with three of the bronzes going to him as author's rights. The original of the work had been purchased from Ambroise Vollard's estate by the Paris businessman and collector Jacques Ulmann. According to Berggruen,

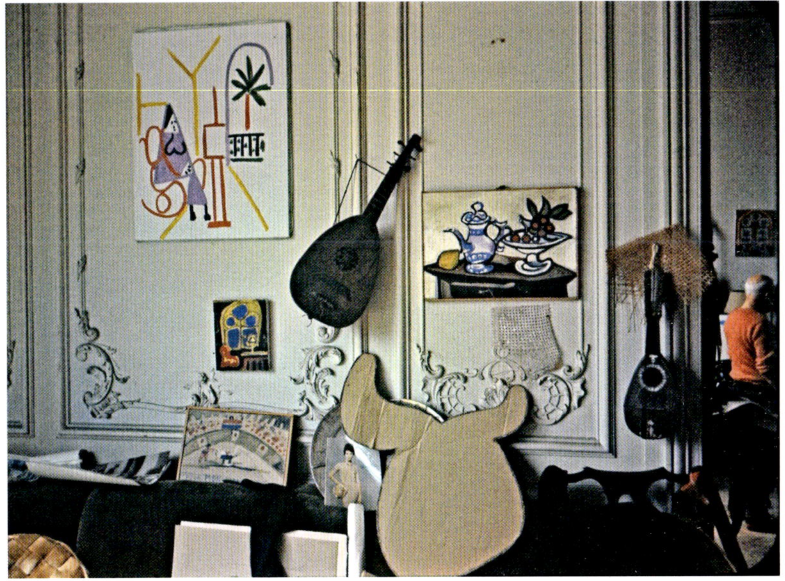

12. View of Picasso's studio at La Californie, with a cardboard maquette the artist probably used for his wood sculpture *Bull*, Cannes, n.d. Photograph by Edward Quinn. Edward Quinn Archives

"Ulmann was prepared to assign the reproduction rights to me for a certain sum of money."[33] Picasso signed a brief agreement drafted by Berggruen authorizing the new edition of nine bronzes on February 15, 1959.[34]

SPRING 1959: In New York, Fine Arts Associates organized *Picasso: The Bathers,* featuring one of two sets of bronze casts of the 1956 wooden sculptures. The exhibition traveled to Boston's Museum of Fine Arts. The second set of bronze casts of *The Bathers* would be shown that summer at Documenta, in Kassel, Germany, where *Fountain Man* was apparently activated for the first time. Of the event, Kahnweiler would write, "That is where the Baigneurs will be presented for the first time outdoors (don't worry, protected from the wind) around a pool, with the Manneken-Pis working."[35]

JUNE 5, 1959: Picasso's bronze cast of *Head of a Woman* (pl. 80) was inaugurated as a monument to Apollinaire at the Laurent Prache square outside the church of Saint-Germain-des-Prés, near the late poet's home (see fig. 6 on p. 185). Picasso did not come to Paris for the event. Philippe Devraigne, president of the Paris City Council, Jean Cocteau, and André Salmon presented remarks. Although this resolution to the Apollinaire commission elicited a mixed response within Parisian artistic circles, the many artists and writers in attendance included Tzara, Gino Severini, and Sonia Delaunay.[36]

JANUARY 31, 1960: Berggruen returned to Cannes seeking Picasso's authorization to make new bronze casts of three additional works from Vollard's estate in Ulmann's possession; among them was Picasso's *Head of a Woman*, the Cubist sculpture modeled in clay in 1909 and first cast in bronze in 1910–12 by Vollard (pl. 11). As he had done before, Picasso permitted Berggruen to make nine bronze casts, stipulating that three casts from the new edition be given to him.[37] Berggruen's casts of *Head of a Woman* would be completed by the Valsuani foundry in February.[38] A picture taken by Quinn at La Californie shows three bronze casts of *Head of a Woman*—likely the ones given to the artist by Berggruen—lined up on the parquet floor and surrounded by Picasso's canvases and other sculptures (fig. 13).[39]

NOVEMBER 1960: Lionel Prejger, who owned a demolition business and a scrap-metal yard in Cannes-La Bocca, purchased the Société Tritub factory, which Tiola had founded to manufacture his bent metal tubing. Prejger and Picasso were already acquaintances: they had first met in 1946 at a restaurant in Golfe-Juan, where their conversation had led the young Prejger to take over the care of an injured owl that the artist had been nursing.[40] The two remained friends, and, as Prejger described it, "One day I showed him the kinds of tubes we made [at the Société Tritub]. And suddenly he said: 'Listen, perhaps we could work together.'"[41] The ensuing collaboration, which would continue until October 1961, formed a unique and intense episode in Picasso's sculptural career. Prejger soon made Tiola his foreman, and the artisan continued to translate Picasso's paper and cardboard maquettes into sheet metal, as he had begun to do in the 1950s. According to a list that Prejger sent to Picasso on March 8, 1961, the factory had already made fifty-two sculptures for Picasso, including "1 eagle, 2 owls, . . . 1 chair, . . . 1 cock, 3 large projects, . . . 1 woman."[42] A second list, sent on May 23, mentioned an additional forty-seven works.[43] According to Diana Widmaier Picasso, Picasso and Tiola together produced at least 126 sheet metal sculptures, the great majority of which were made during the period of Prejger's involvement.[44] Prejger acted as an energetic envoy, bringing Picasso's maquettes to Tiola and the finished products back to Picasso. In most cases the artist was satisfied with Tiola's work, Prejger said; if not, they would "have to begin all over again."[45]

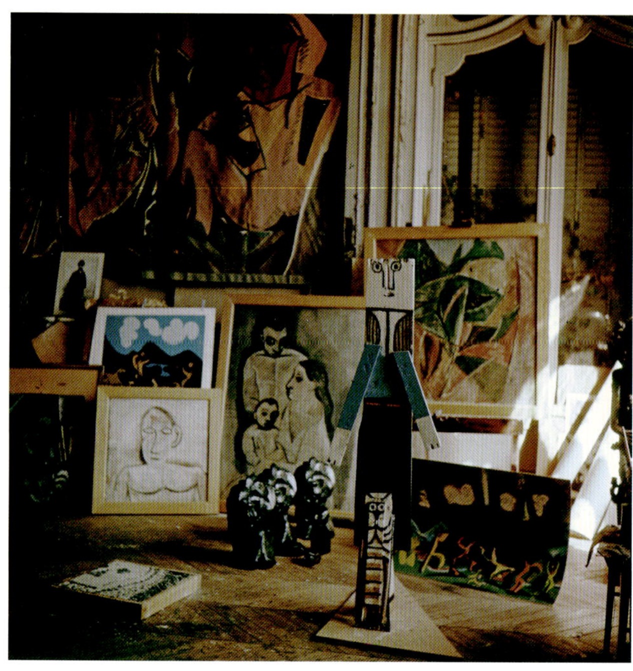

13. Picasso's studio at La Californie, with three bronze casts of *Head of a Woman* at center, Cannes, September 8, 1960. Photograph by Edward Quinn. Edward Quinn Archives

***CHAIR*, 1961**

Chair (pl. 142) was one of the most complex sheet metal works executed in 1961. Picasso had initially drawn *Chair* on brown wrapping paper: it was rendered completely flat, according to Prejger, and "spread out like an octopus."[46] Picasso compared the drawing to a chair flattened by a steamroller.[47] The artist cut along his charcoal lines and folded the paper in an intricate pattern of solids and voids, giving one leg a distinctive accordion fold. As with all his sheet metal sculptures, the workers at Tritub coated the final version in white paint.[48] Usually Picasso would add painted details to the surface. In the case of *Chair*, however, the sculpture remained a pure white, allowing light and shadow free play across the folded planes. Prejger would come to see this work as a landmark in Picasso's sculptural oeuvre. He wrote about *Chair* and Picasso's other sheet metal works in the article "Picasso découpe le fer" (Picasso cuts iron), published in the October 1961 issue of *L'Œil* magazine (fig. 14).

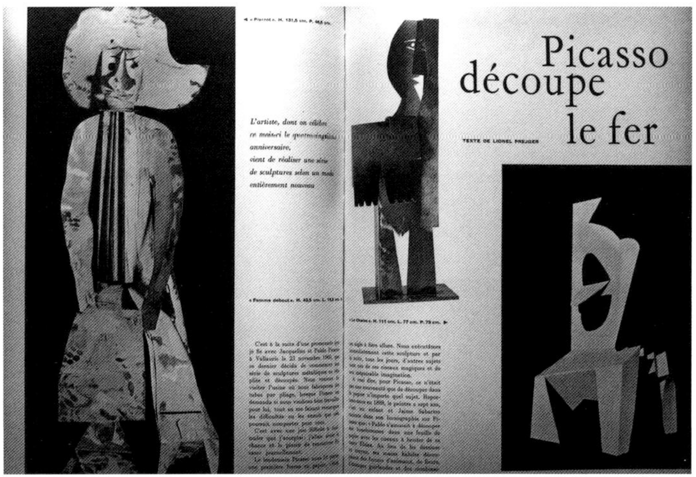

Picasso
découpe
le fer

14. Lionel Prejger, "Picasso découpe le fer" (Picasso cuts iron), *L'Œil*, no. 82 (October 1961): 28–29

LITTLE HORSE, 1961

Picasso composed this small steed from six pieces of metal tubing. He added wheels to its legs so that two-year-old Bernard—whose father was Paulo, Picasso's son with his first wife, Olga—could ride around on it. Prejger recalled Picasso telling him, at the advent of their collaboration in late 1960, "We'll begin by making a toy for my grandson, Bernard" (fig. 15).[49] However, the production lists that Prejger compiled for Picasso indicate that *Little Horse* (pl. 140) was made between March 8 and May 23, 1961.[50]

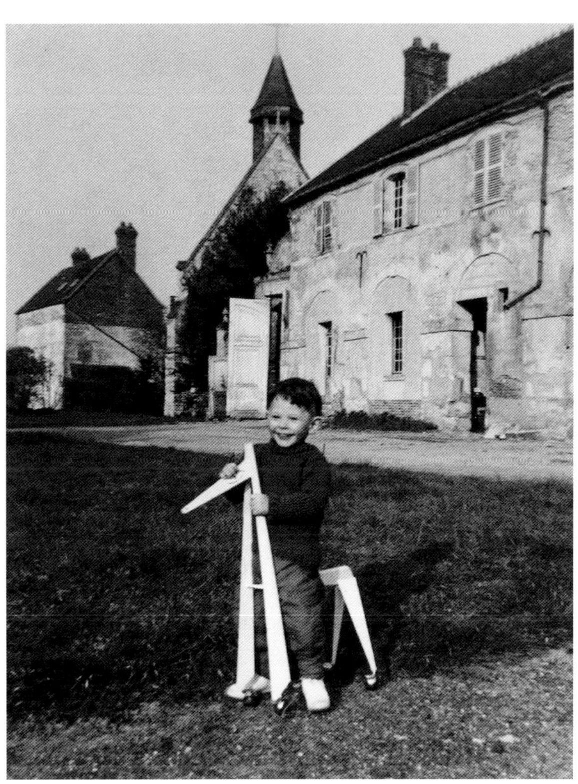

15. Bernard Ruiz-Picasso on *Little Horse*, a toy made for him by Picasso, Château de Boisgeloup, c. 1961. Private collection. Courtesy Fundación Almine y Bernard Ruiz-Picasso para el Arte

WOMAN AND CHILD AND *WOMAN WITH CHILD*, 1961

Woman and Child (pl. 143) and *Woman with Child* (pl. 144) are among Picasso's few sheet metal sculptures that take on the subject of motherhood. To create *Woman and Child*, the artist combined a paper maquette that he had used for an earlier work entitled *Standing Woman* with a new maquette for the figure of a child.[51] Metalworkers at Tritub translated the maquettes into sheet metal and welded the two figures together, bending the mother's arms around her child.

Standing more than four feet tall, *Woman with Child* is one of Picasso's largest sheet metal works. In this case, the mother lifts her child high above her head. The vertical form of the mother's head merges with the horizontal form of the raised child in a complex play of positive and negative space. This upper region of the sculpture retains the feathery lightness of the paper cutouts on which it was based, while the mother's torso and legs provide a sturdy foundation for the happy outburst above. Picasso added a touch of black enamel to delineate the mother's face, pubic hair, and navel, but used incisions in the metal to signify her breasts. The work was finished by the time André Gomès photographed it at La Californie around early April 1961 (fig. 16).

JUNE 1961: Picasso and Jacqueline, who had married in March, moved into an expansive Provençal villa called Notre-Dame-de-Vie. It was located in Mougins, a village perched above Cannes. At La Californie, a series of large new apartment buildings had cut off the view to the sea and spoiled its seclusion. Life at Vauvenargues was also troublesome: Picasso told Brassaï that a curious public had far too much access to him there and that "droves" of people came to observe him through binoculars and telescopes.[52] His new wife was not at all fond of Vauvenargues: Kahnweiler told Brassaï that she was "truly

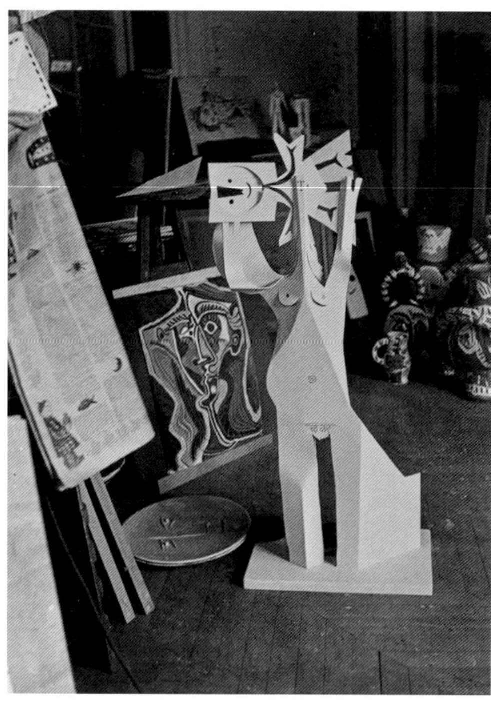

16. View of Picasso's studio at La Californie, with *Woman with Child*, Cannes, 1961. Photograph by André Gomès. Picasso Archives, Musée national Picasso–Paris

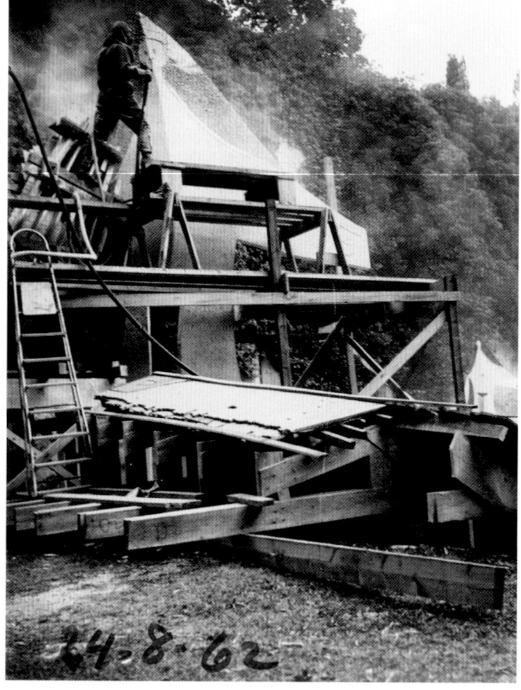

17. Carl Nesjar working on the 1962 enlargement in concrete of *Woman with Outstretched Arms*, August 24, 1962. Photograph by Cameron. Picasso Archives, Musée national Picasso–Paris

frightened in that isolated, haunted, almost lugubrious castle."[53] Notre-Dame-de-Vie offered a modern and comfortable alternative. Picasso ordered that everything he had stored and created at Vauvenargues be sent to Mougins. The sculptures—from his early Cubist works to his Boisgeloup heads to his most recent assemblages and their bronze iterations—haphazardly filled a large hall on the ground floor.

***WOMAN WITH OUTSTRETCHED ARMS*, 1961**

Rendered in thick steel, *Woman with Outstretched Arms* (pl. 145) is among Picasso's larger sheet metal works. Tiola first made three small metal versions, all approximately 14 by 14 inches—the size of the artist's paper maquette. Picasso painted each one in black and white to represent a nude woman. He then selected one of the three versions for translation to a grander scale.[54] For the two resulting large-scale sculptures, Tiola's workers used found fragments of black metal grillwork to define the figure's head, right arm and leg, and pubic hair. These dark, textured areas of grillwork, neatly finished with soldered wire, provide a stark contrast to the white sheet metal. The other relief details—the facial features, navel, fingernails, and toenails—were fashioned from sheet metal scraps.

In late spring 1962, *Woman with Outstretched Arms* would travel to the United States, making its public debut in June at the Otto Gerson Gallery, New York, in an exhibition titled *Monumental Sculpture*. The sculpture would go on view the following year in the exhibition *Sculptors of Our Time* at the Washington Gallery of Modern Art, in Washington, D.C.; it featured on the cover of the accompanying catalogue. In 1966 the work entered the collection of the Museum of Fine Arts, Houston. James Johnson Sweeney's efforts to acquire a large-scale sculpture by Picasso, which began with the plan to acquire *The Bathers* for the Guggenheim in 1958, finally met with success.

The second enlargement of *Woman with Outstretched Arms* (Musée national Picasso–Paris) served as a model for a monumental sculpture that Kahnweiler had requested for his garden at Saint-Hilaire, in Essonne, southwest of Paris. On June 21, 1961, the dealer wrote to Picasso specifying that the sculpture would be realized by Nesjar in betograve.[55] A year later, in July 1962, the sheet metal sculpture arrived at Kahnweiler's residence for Nesjar to use as a template, and by October he had completed a freestanding concrete sculpture nearly twenty feet tall (figs. 17, 18).[56] This iteration of *Woman with Outstretched Arms* now stands in the sculpture garden of the Lille métropole musée d'art moderne, d'art contemporain et d'art brut in Villeneuve d'Ascq.

***WOMAN WITH HAT*, 1961/1963**

Picasso began to explore the theme of *Woman with Hat* in drawings and paintings in January 1961.[57] The sheet metal sculpture parallels the artist's many painted portrayals of Jacqueline Picasso, whose features also often informed the

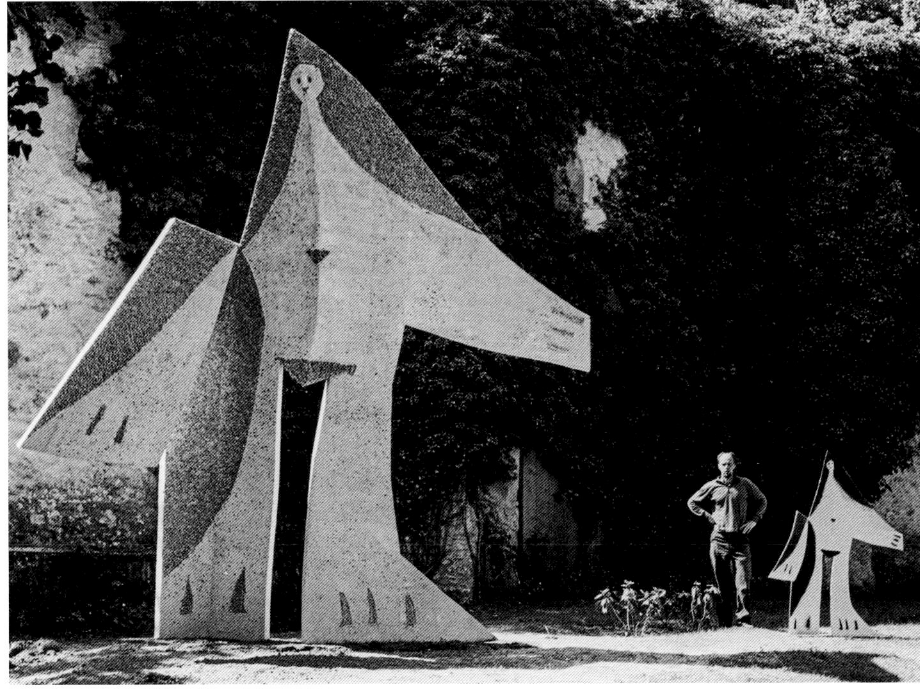

18. Nesjar standing between the sheet metal sculpture *Woman with Outstretched Arms* and its finished 1962 enlargement in concrete in the garden of Daniel-Henry Kahnweiler's house in Saint-Hilaire, around October 1962. Picasso Archives, Musée national Picasso–Paris

figures in his adaptions of Old Master paintings. This complex sculpture (pl. 146) comprises five separate planar forms, a base, and an additional support.[58] It is the only polychromatic version within a group of four identical sheet metal works made from the artist's paper maquette.[59] Picasso painted it in Mougins in 1963, a period in which he was increasingly focused on images of his wife.

HEAD OF A WOMAN, 1961, AND HEAD OF A WOMAN, LATE 1962

Head of a Woman exists in two versions, one colorfully painted (pl. 147), the other white with engraved drawing. The painted version is one of several sheet metal heads distinguished by a boldly striped design of red, white, yellow, and turquoise verticals. These verticals, applied like face paint, invoke the naturalistic volume of her head: its left and right sides, center, and hair.

In fall 1961, Prejger sold his businesses in Cannes and Vallauris and decamped for Paris, where he became director of Galerie Knoedler. His departure would soon bring an end to Picasso's sheet metal activity; the artist did, however, produce one last group of sheet metal heads, to which *Head of a Woman* (pl. 148) belongs. As on many other occasions, Tiola used solder to delineate details such as eyes, nostrils, and hair. Picasso added painted accents that complete a vivid image of Jacqueline. A cutout at the sculpture's center forms a negative space that accentuates Picasso's juxtaposition of multiple perspectives; Tiola's expertise is especially evidenced by the curving bend along the center of her face.

APRIL 25–MAY 12, 1962: *Picasso: An American Tribute* was presented at nine art galleries in New York, with a joint catalogue by John Richardson. The Otto Gerson Gallery organized an exhibition of the sculptures, featuring thirty-five objects. In the catalogue Richardson declared that "Picasso's achievements as a painter overshadow the fact that he is also the most inventive sculptor of the twentieth century."[60]

MAY 20, 1963: Roland Penrose visited Picasso at Notre-Dame-de-Vie to raise the question of a large outdoor sculpture for the city of Chicago. Earlier that spring, William Hartmann, a partner at the Chicago-based architecture firm Skidmore, Owings & Merrill (SOM), had contacted Penrose with the idea of constructing a monumental sculpture for the plaza of the new Chicago Civic Center (now known as the Richard J. Daley Center), a thirty-one-story skyscraper whose construction was already underway. The architects were keen to have Picasso design an original piece especially for the project, which they considered to be an opportunity to create "the most important public sculpture in America."[61] Picasso agreed to meet the architects the following day. Hartmann and two associates arrived at the studio with a model of the plaza, and Picasso was impressed. According to Penrose, the discussion

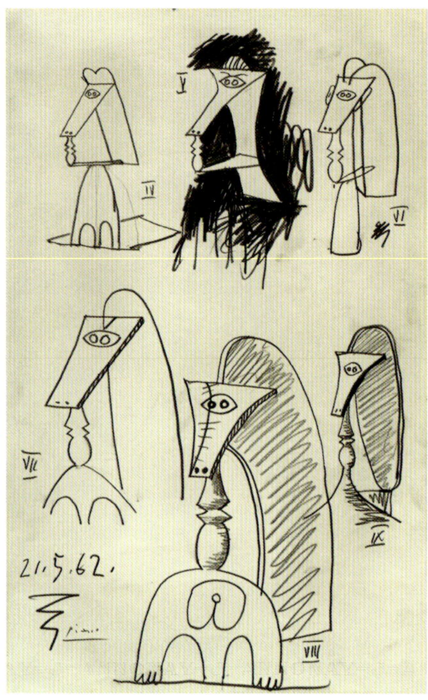

19. Pablo Picasso. *Six Busts of Women*. May 21, 1962. Graphite on ivory wove paper, 16 ½ × 10 ⅝ in. (41.9 × 27 cm). Restricted gift of William E. Hartmann, The Art Institute of Chicago

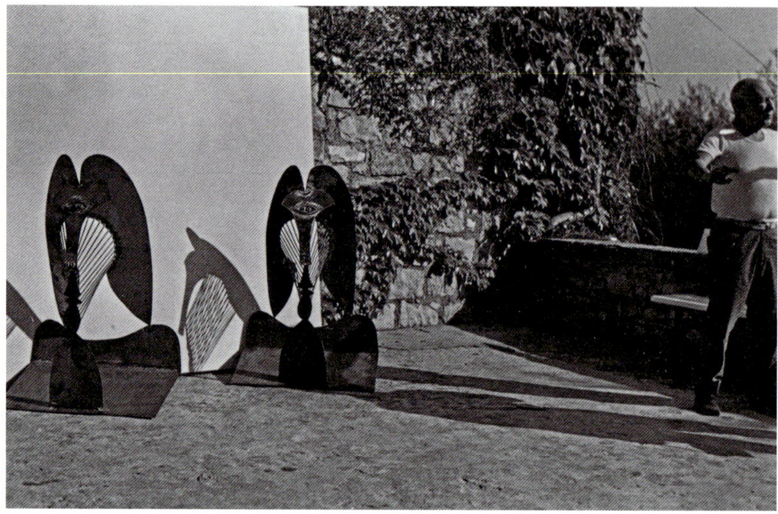

20. Picasso at Notre-Dame-de-Vie with the two maquettes for the *Richard J. Daley Center Sculpture*, Mougins, 1964. Picasso Archives, Musée national Picasso–Paris

centered on a variety of existing sculptures, including the 1928 *Figures* Picasso had originally conceived for his monument to Apollinaire (pls. 34–36). The May 21 meeting ended with Picasso's support of the project.[62]

JUNE 17–18, 1964: Penrose and Hartmann paid Picasso an unannounced visit, after a long period during which Picasso's interest in the Chicago project seemed to have stagnated. Picasso presented Hartmann with a new model for a sculpture depicting a tall head, which he had first shown to Penrose in March.[63] Studies for this head (fig. 19) date back to May 1962.[64] Hartmann reacted with enthusiasm.

***MAQUETTE FOR RICHARD J. DALEY CENTER SCULPTURE*, 1964**

This sculpture (pl. 149, fig. 20) is one of two steel maquettes built by Joseph-Marius Tiola based on Picasso's design for the Chicago monument. The sculpture conflates portrayals of Picasso's wife, Jacqueline, and their pet Afghan hound, Kabul.[65] The angled plane representing the upper part of the face closely resembles the artist's paintings of Kabul, while the vertical section below suggests a woman's mouth, chin, and shoulders. Two winglike panels of flowing hair can also read as the dog's long ears. While this maquette echoes Picasso's recent sheet metal sculptures, it also possesses the qualities that he had sought to develop at a large scale with the monument to Apollinaire: openness, transparency, and stark planar and linear articulation. Long metal rods connect the hair to the face and neck, such that the heart of the sculpture is an area of open rather than solid form.

A visit by Hartmann to Notre-Dame-de-Vie on April 30, 1965, resulted in final agreement on the project;[66] Picasso then sent this maquette to Chicago. When it arrived, on May 25, 1965, Hartmann telegrammed Penrose: "Mougins dame has arrived. Champagne for all!"[67] The construction of the fifty-foot monument began immediately in Gary, Indiana, at the American Bridge Company, a division of US Steel. The 162-ton work was realized in Cor-Ten steel, a relatively new material also used in the Civic Center skyscraper (fig. 21). Picasso donated the monument to the city of Chicago and made a gift of the maquette to the Art Institute of Chicago.

SPRING 1964: Pontus Hultén, the director of the Moderna Museet in Stockholm, approached Nesjar about creating a concrete enlargement of one of Picasso's sculptures for the museum's sculpture park.[68] Nesjar soon went to visit Picasso in Mougins; the artist revealed a large group of cardboard maquettes of nude bathers, created nearly two years prior as part of his ongoing dialogue with Édouard Manet's painting *Le Déjeuner sur l'herbe* (1863).[69] Ultimately, four were selected for enlargement as works ranging from ten to thirteen feet high, and the ensemble was installed on the museum's grounds in 1966. Over the next few years, Nesjar would construct other concrete versions of Picasso's works for commissions in Jerusalem, Rotterdam, and other cities.

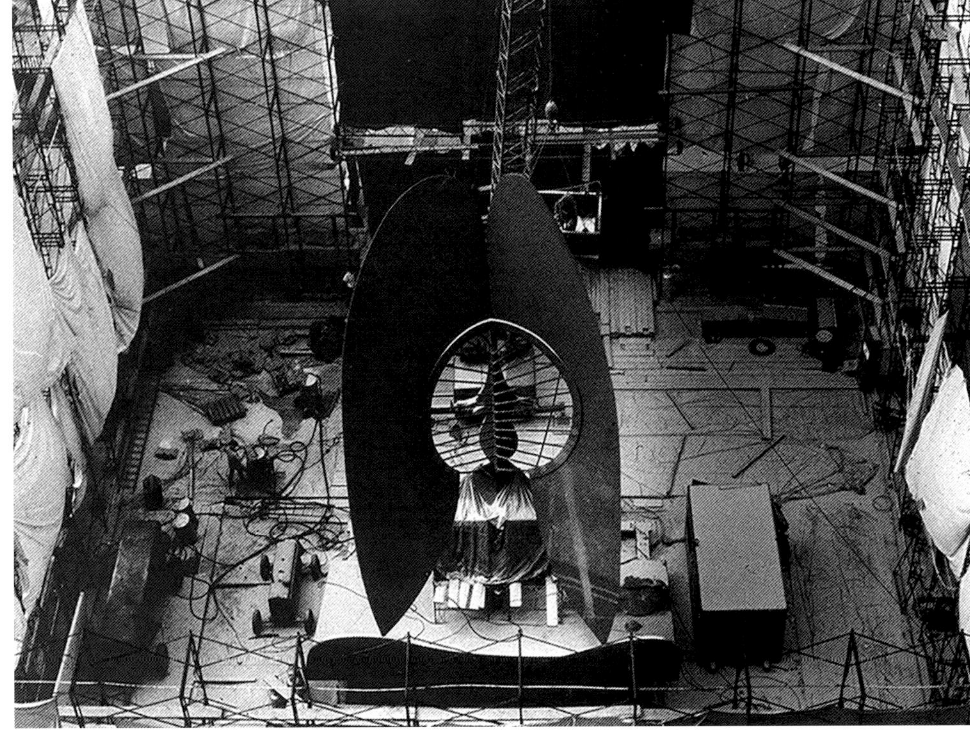

21. The erection of Picasso's *Richard J. Daley Center Sculpture* at the Chicago Civic Center plaza, 1967. Archives, Skidmore, Owings & Merrill

NOVEMBER 18, 1966–FEBRUARY 12, 1967: More than seven hundred works by Picasso, including 187 sculptures and 116 ceramics, went on view in Paris in the exhibition *Hommage à Pablo Picasso*, a retrospective celebrating the artist's eighty-fifth birthday. Overseen by Jean Leymarie, the show was divided into two parts: Picasso's paintings were exhibited at the Grand Palais and his drawings, sculptures, and ceramics at the Petit Palais. A separately organized show of his graphic works was on view at the Bibliothèque nationale. Most of the sculptures came from Picasso's personal collection and had never before been exhibited. Leymarie wrote, "As for the sculptures, which until now we had only a partial knowledge of and are now finally shown, like the paintings, in all their breadth and their variety of style, technique, and materials, they constitute a true revelation."[70] The exhibition was heralded by the press as the "Biggest One-Man Show on Earth" and seen by thousands.[71]

APRIL 27–OCTOBER 29, 1967: One of the two bronze versions of *The Bathers* was presented at Expo 67 in Montreal. Nelson Rockefeller would acquire this version later that year and install it at Kykuit, his Hudson Valley estate.

JUNE 9–AUGUST 13, 1967: After the closing of *Hommage à Pablo Picasso*, the artist's sculptures traveled to London for the exhibition *Picasso: Sculpture, Ceramics, Graphic Work*, organized by the Arts Council of Great Britain and presented at the Tate Gallery. Penrose and Barr had begun joint preparations for this exhibition in 1965. Penrose was responsible for the selection, the catalogue essay, and the London installation. The exhibition included about two hundred sculptures, thirty ceramics, and forty works on paper; it generated spirited debate as to the merit of the sculptures and their significance in Picasso's work.[72]

AUGUST 15, 1967: *Head of a Woman* was inaugurated in front of an enormous crowd at the Chicago Civic Center (fig. 23 on p. 29). The sculpture aroused immediate controversy: many of the city's residents were baffled by its radical composition and dismayed that it did not pay homage to a historical figure. Nevertheless, the work quickly became a city landmark, fulfilling Mayor Daley's prediction that "what is strange to us today will be familiar tomorrow."[73]

OCTOBER 11, 1967: The exhibition *The Sculpture of Picasso* opened to wide acclaim at The Museum of Modern Art. The selection of works, primarily the same as that in London, was made by Penrose; the installation was that of René d'Harnoncourt, the Museum's director (see fig. 21 on p. 27). The presentation also included a group of etchings from the Sculptor's Studio section of the *Vollard Suite* and a selection of Brassaï's photographs of Picasso's sculptures.[74] Despite Barr's hope that some of the works might be added to the Museum's collection after the closing of the exhibition on January 1, 1968, all of Picasso's loans were shipped back to Notre-Dame-de-Vie (fig. 22).

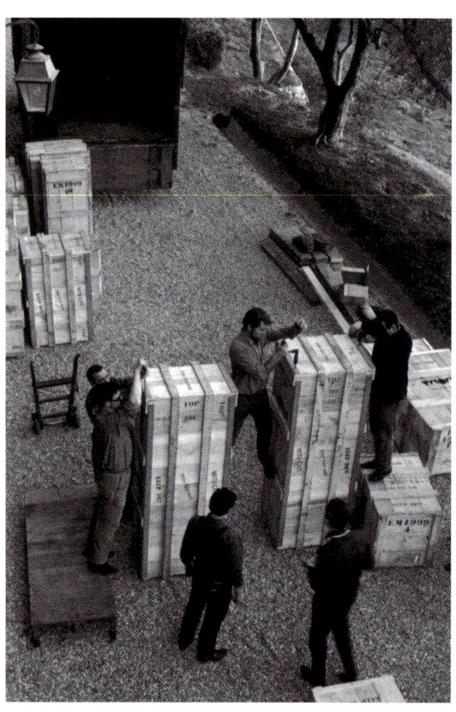

22. Crates of works by Picasso returning to Notre-Dame-de-Vie, Mougins, from the 1966–67 exhibition tour, c. January 1968. Photograph by Lee Miller. Lee Miller Archives, London

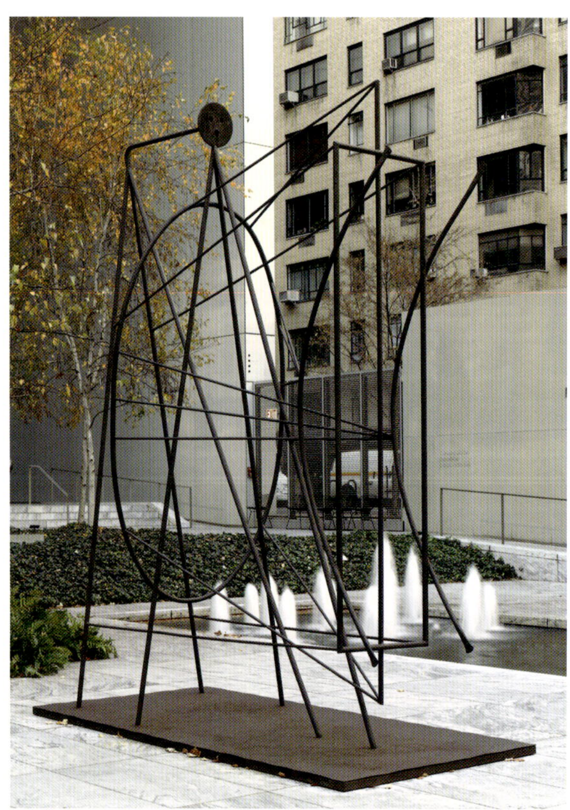

23. Pablo Picasso. *Monument*. New York, 1972. Cor-Ten steel, 12 ft. 11 ⅝ in. × 58 ¾ in. × 10 ft. 5 ¾ in. (395.3 × 149.2 × 319.3 cm) including base. The Museum of Modern Art, New York. Gift of the artist

DECEMBER 9, 1968: A thirty-six-foot-tall concrete sculpture, *Bust of Sylvette*, was officially dedicated at New York University (NYU) (see fig. 22 on p. 28). In 1967 the architect I. M. Pei had asked Nesjar to propose a large-scale sculpture by Picasso for the outdoor plaza of a new housing complex he was designing for the university. It was not the first time Pei had proposed a monumental Picasso for Manhattan: in 1957 he had envisioned a large sculpture by the artist for the park at the residential Kips Bay Towers, but financial considerations thwarted that plan.[75] Picasso had immediately agreed to Pei's new proposal, suggesting one of the busts of Sylvette David; Pei selected *Sylvette* (pl. 139). NYU had formally announced the plan in November 1967, while the work was still on view in the sculpture exhibition at The Museum of Modern Art.

FEBRUARY 8, 1971: Picasso made an unexpected gift of the 1914 sheet metal *Guitar* (pl. 14) to The Museum of Modern Art. The acquisition of this work had been a long-standing goal for the Museum's curators; while the 1967 exhibition was on view, Barr had placed *Guitar* first on a list of sculptures he considered essential for the collection.[76] The donation received an extraordinary amount of coverage in the media (see fig. 6 on p. 77).

1971: The first catalogue raisonné of Picasso's sculpture was published: *Pablo Picasso. Das plastische Werk (Sculpture by Picasso)*, by Werner Spies. With the encouragement of Kahnweiler and publisher Gerd Hatje, Spies had embarked on the documentary project in the late 1960s. He worked in close collaboration with the artist, whom he interviewed at length at Notre-Dame-de-Vie.

EARLY MARCH 1973: A monumental sculpture based on Picasso's 1928 wire construction *Figure* (pl. 35) was installed in the Abby Aldrich Rockefeller Sculpture Garden at The Museum of Modern Art. Around 1962, Picasso had instructed Tiola to make two steel enlargements of the original sculpture, increasing its height to six-and-a-half feet. In 1972 the artist sent one of them to New York, where it served as a model for a sculpture twice as large. This outdoor version was fabricated for the Museum by artist Maurice Brouha using Cor-Ten steel (fig. 23). The intermediary enlargement remained in the collection of The Museum of Modern Art.

APRIL 8, 1973: Picasso died at Mougins. He was buried outside the Château de Vauvenargues. His widow and his son Paulo decided to place a bronze cast of *Woman with Vase* (pl. 67) over his grave (fig. 24).

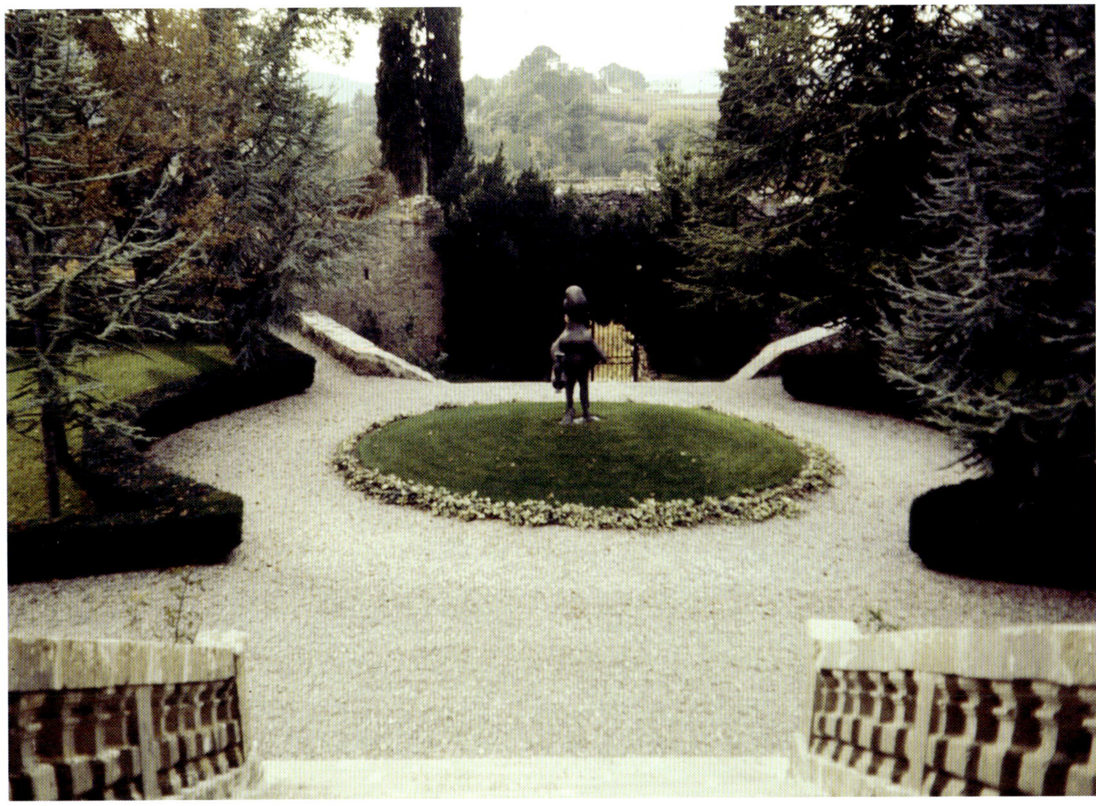

24. Picasso's burial site at the Château de Vauvenargues, with a bronze cast of *Woman with a Vase* (1933), n.d. Photograph by Edward Quinn. Edward Quinn Archives

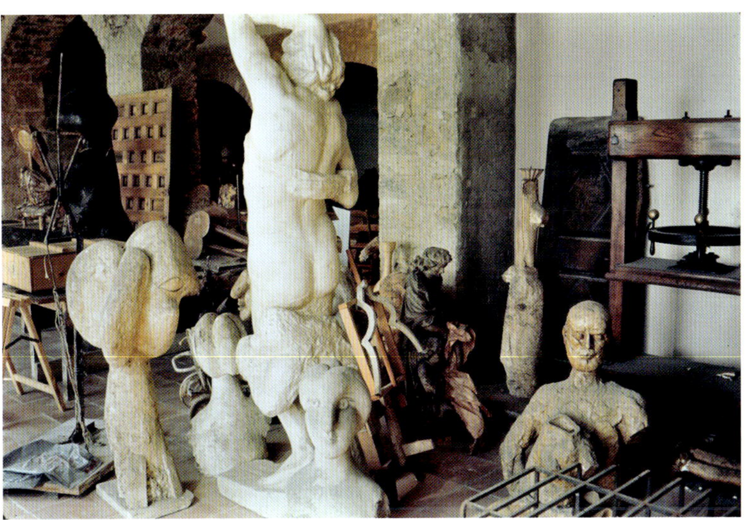

25. Sculptures by Picasso with a plaster cast of Michelangelo's *Dying Slave* (1514–16; Musée du Louvre) at Notre-Dame-de-Vie, Mougins, July 1974. Photograph by Edward Quinn. Edward Quinn Archives

EPILOGUE: Picasso did not leave a will. The multitude of paintings, sculptures, ceramics, and works on paper at his several residences, particularly La Californie and Notre-Dame-de-Vie, took several years to inventory after his death (fig. 25). A law initiated by André Malraux, Minister of Cultural Affairs, and passed on December 31, 1968, authorized the French state to accept artworks in lieu of inheritance taxes, in an effort to preserve France's artistic and cultural heritage. In Picasso's case, a committee chaired by Leymarie made a selection prior to the division of the artist's estate among his heirs. The so-called Dation Picasso, finalized in March 1979, included 149 sculptures and eighty-five ceramics as well as hundreds of paintings and works on paper.[77] These works of art would compose the core collection of the future Musée national Picasso. In March 1975 the Paris City Council had announced that the museum would be housed in the Hotel Salé, a grand seventeenth-century mansion at 5, rue de Thorigny in the Marais district of Paris. Originally a private residence, the building provided an appropriate setting for the works of art with which Picasso had lived at home. After a decade of planning and renovation, the Musée national Picasso was officially inaugurated in October 1985.

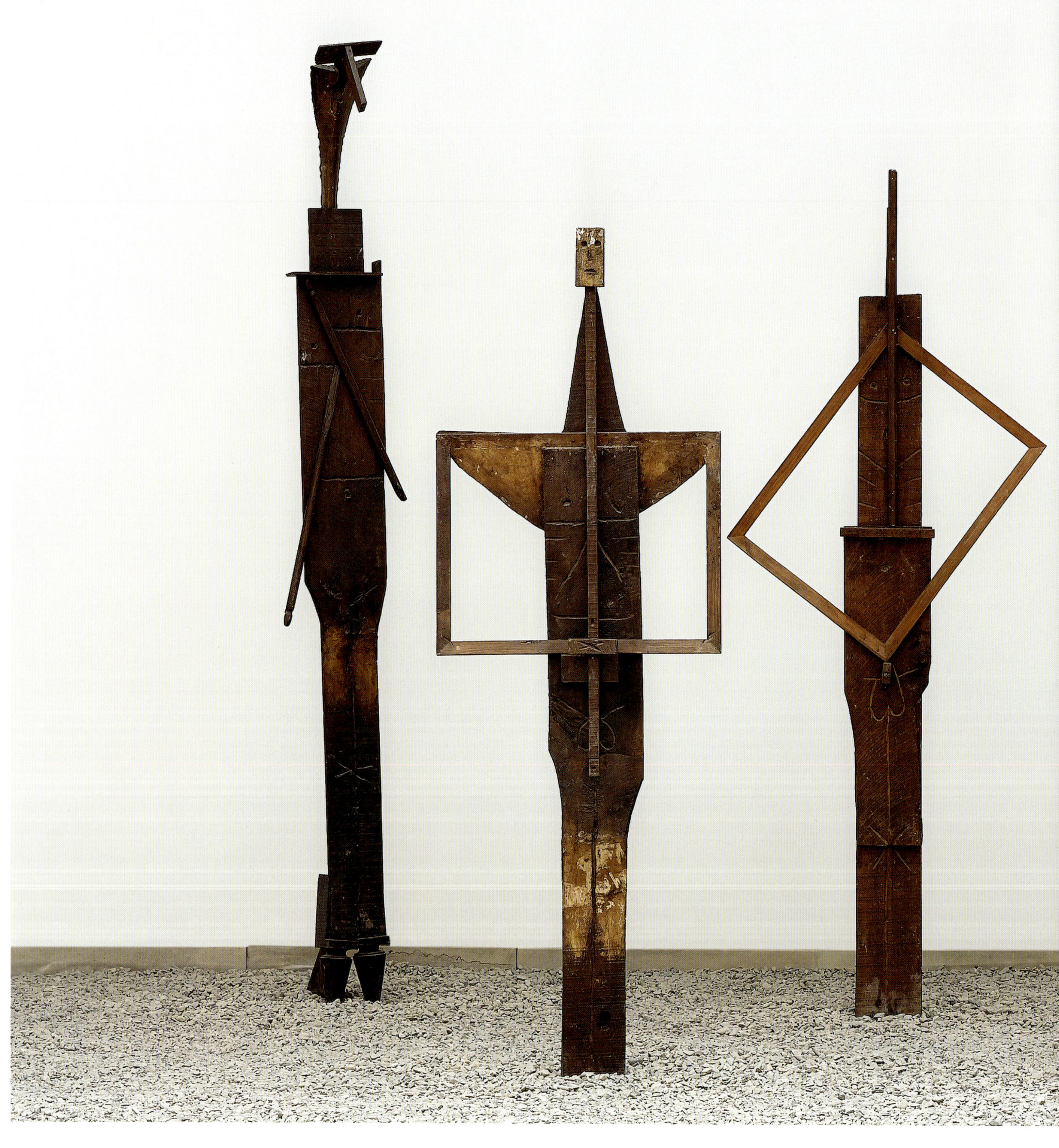

Left to right:

128. **THE BATHERS: WOMAN DIVER.** Cannes, 1956
Wood, filler (possibly gesso), and palm frond
8 ft. 8 5⁄16 in. (264 cm) high
Staatsgalerie Stuttgart

129. **THE BATHERS: MAN WITH FOLDED HANDS.** Cannes, 1956
Wood and filler (possibly gesso)
7 ft. ¼ in. (214 cm) high
Staatsgalerie Stuttgart

130. **THE BATHERS: FOUNTAIN MAN.** Cannes, 1956
Wood
7 ft. 5 ⅜ in. (227 cm) high
Staatsgalerie Stuttgart

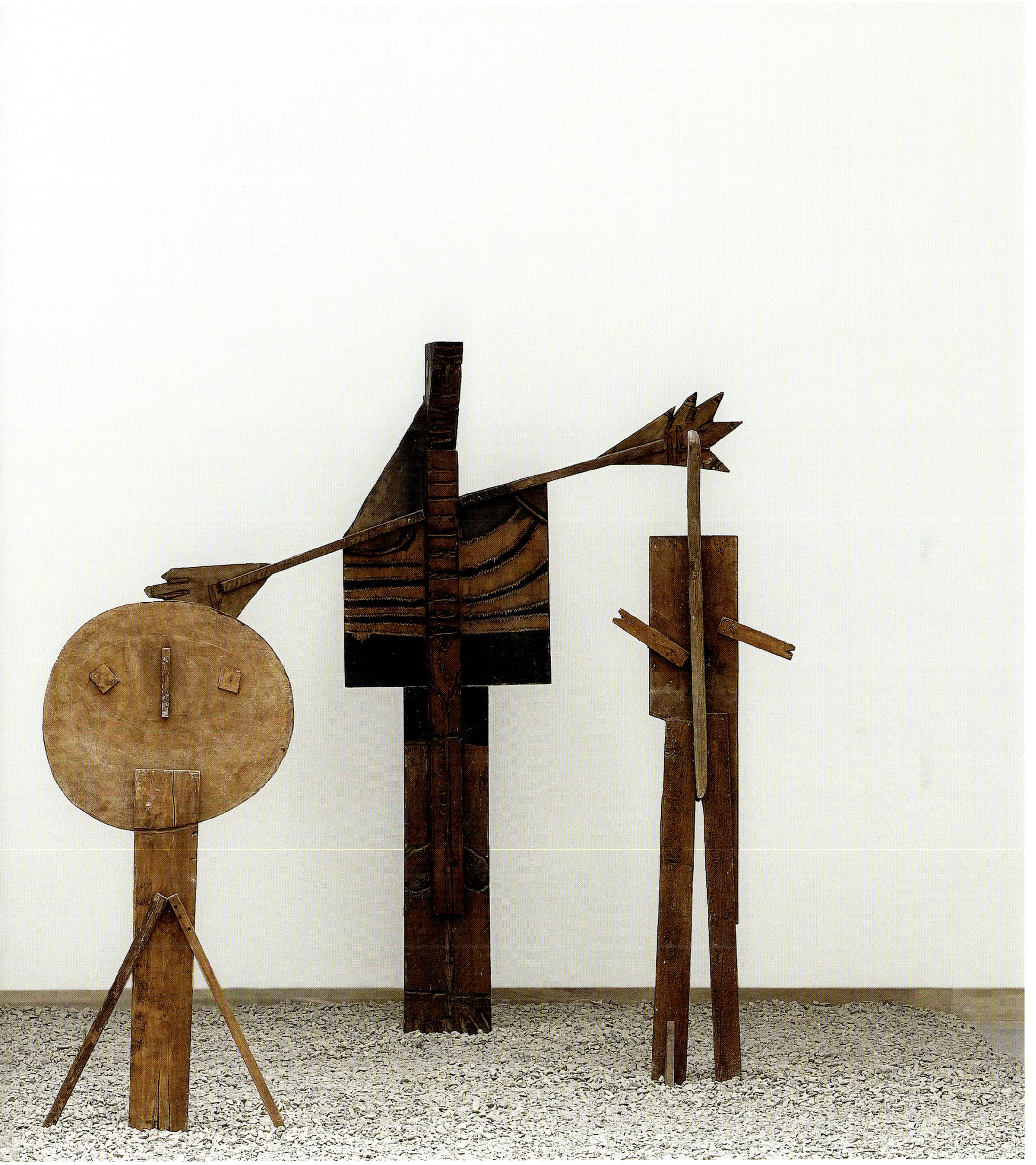

131. **THE BATHERS: CHILD.**
Cannes, 1956
Wood
53 9⁄16 in. (136 cm) high
Staatsgalerie Stuttgart

132. **THE BATHERS: WOMAN WITH OUTSTRETCHED ARMS.** Cannes, 1956
Painted wood
6 ft. 5 15⁄16 in. (198 cm) high
Staatsgalerie Stuttgart

133. **THE BATHERS: YOUNG MAN.**
Cannes, 1956
Wood
69 5⁄16 in. (176 cm) high
Staatsgalerie Stuttgart

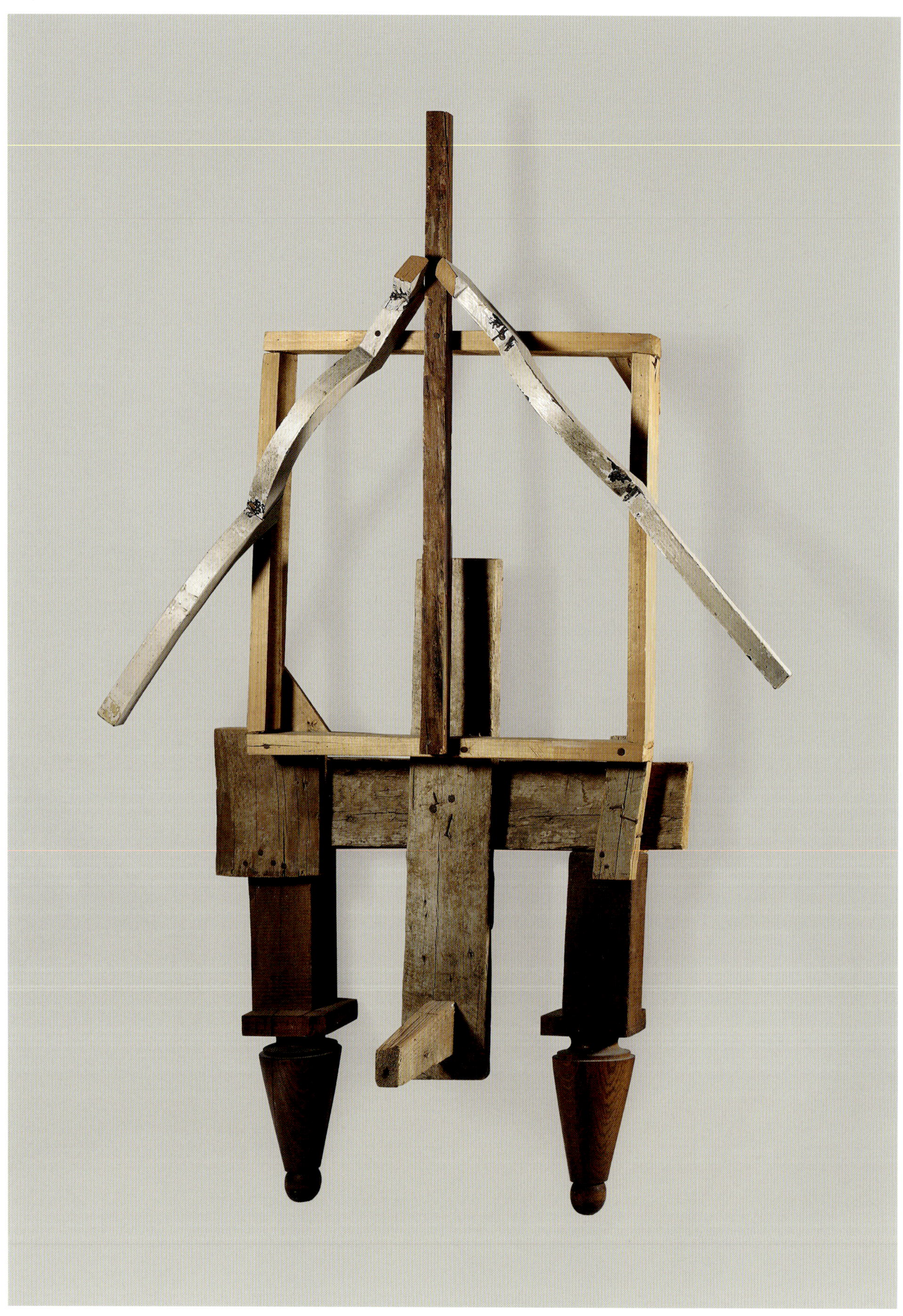

134. MAN. Cannes, 1958
Wood and nails
46 ⅛ × 29 ⅞ × 9 ⅞ in. (117 × 76 × 25 cm)
Private collection

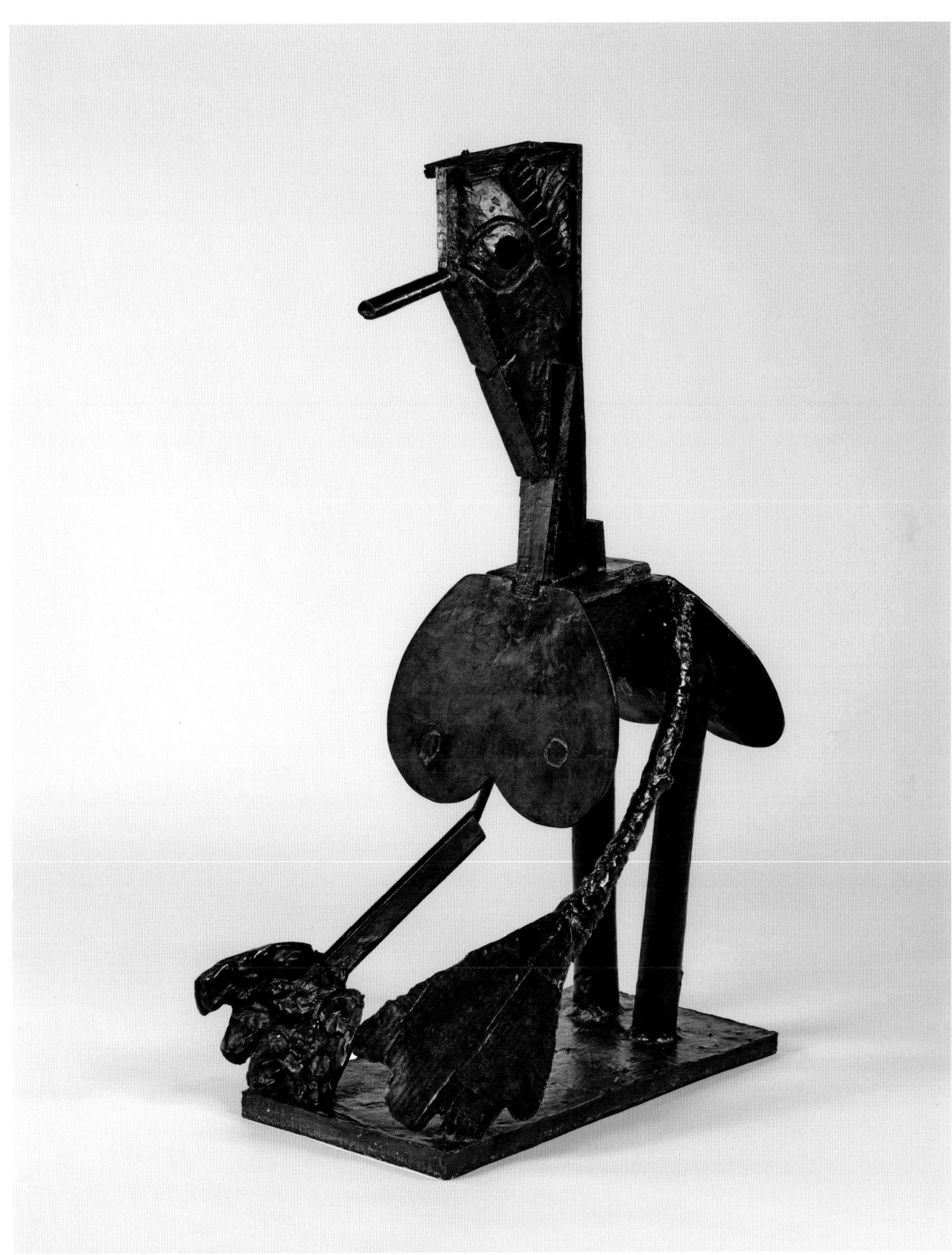

135. FEMALE BATHER PLAYING. Cannes, 1958
Bronze, casting date unknown
44½ × 15½ × 25½ in. (113 × 39.4 × 64.8 cm)
Albright-Knox Art Gallery, Buffalo, New York. Gift of The Seymour H. Knox Foundation, Inc.

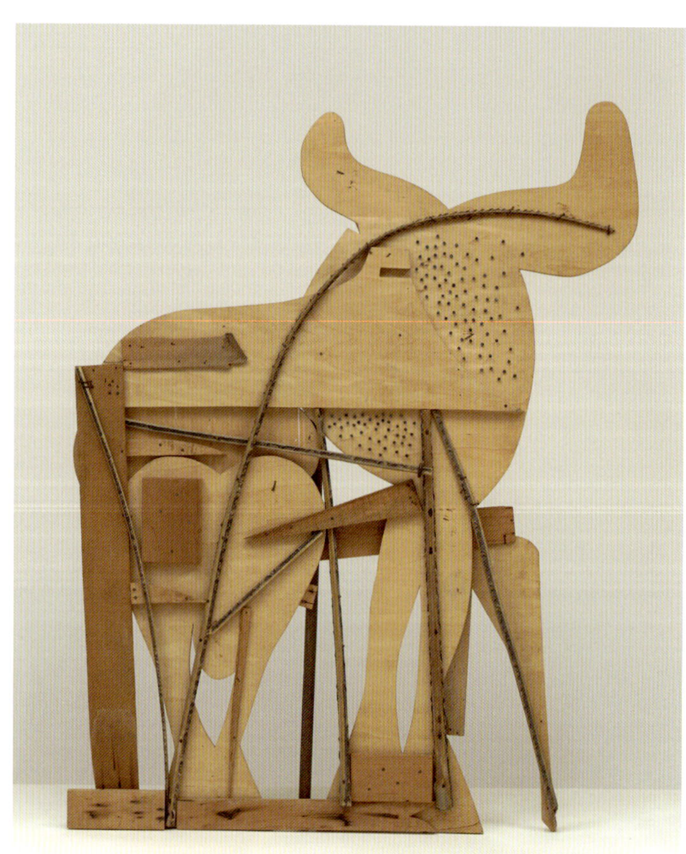

136. BULL. Cannes, April 1958
Blockboard (wood base panel), palm frond and various other tree branches, eyebolt, nails, and screws, with drips of alkyd and pencil markings
56 ¾ × 46 ⅛ × 4 ⅛ in. (144.1 × 117.2 × 10.5 cm)
The Museum of Modern Art, New York. Gift of Jacqueline Picasso in honor of the Museum's continuous commitment to Pablo Picasso's art

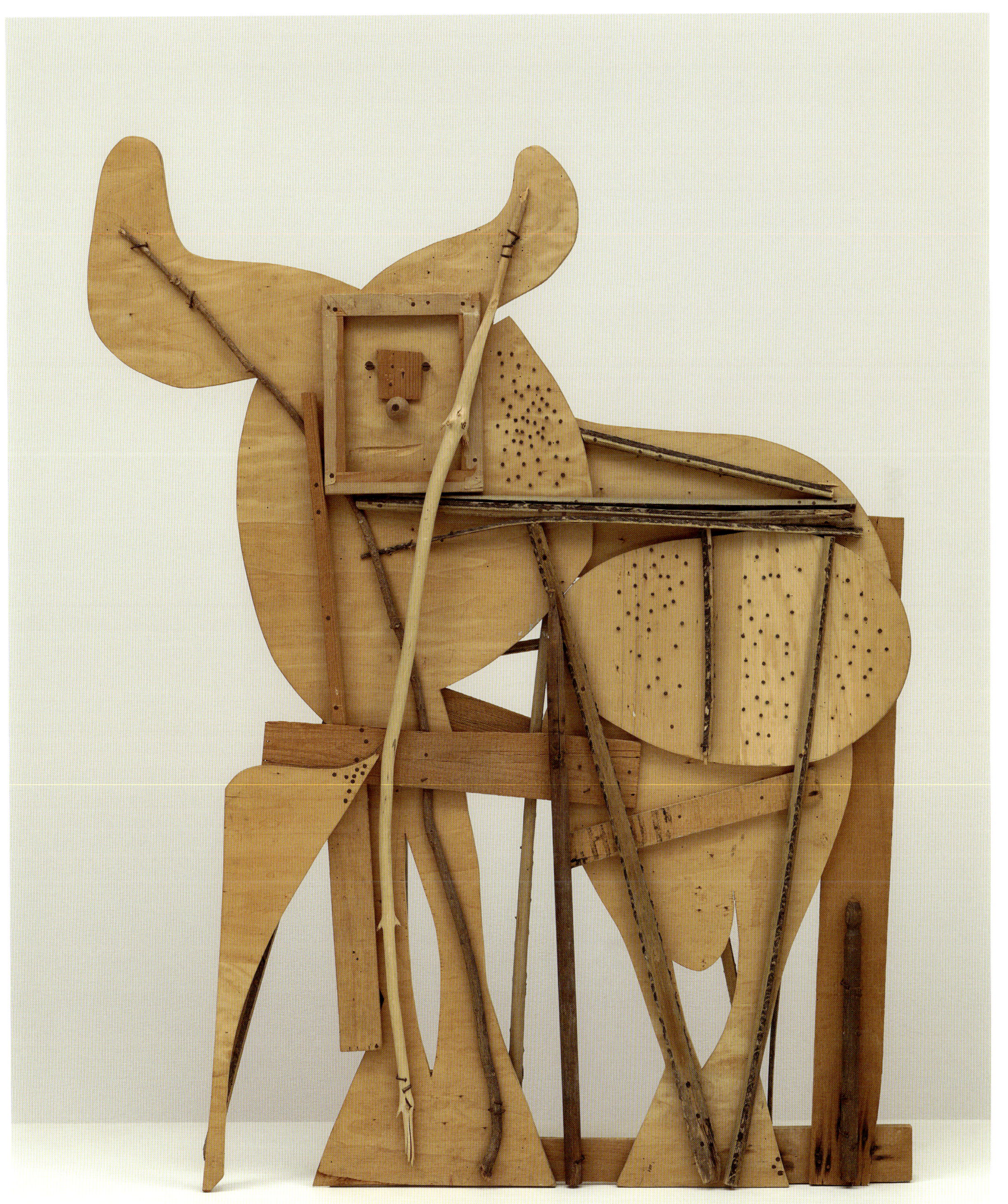

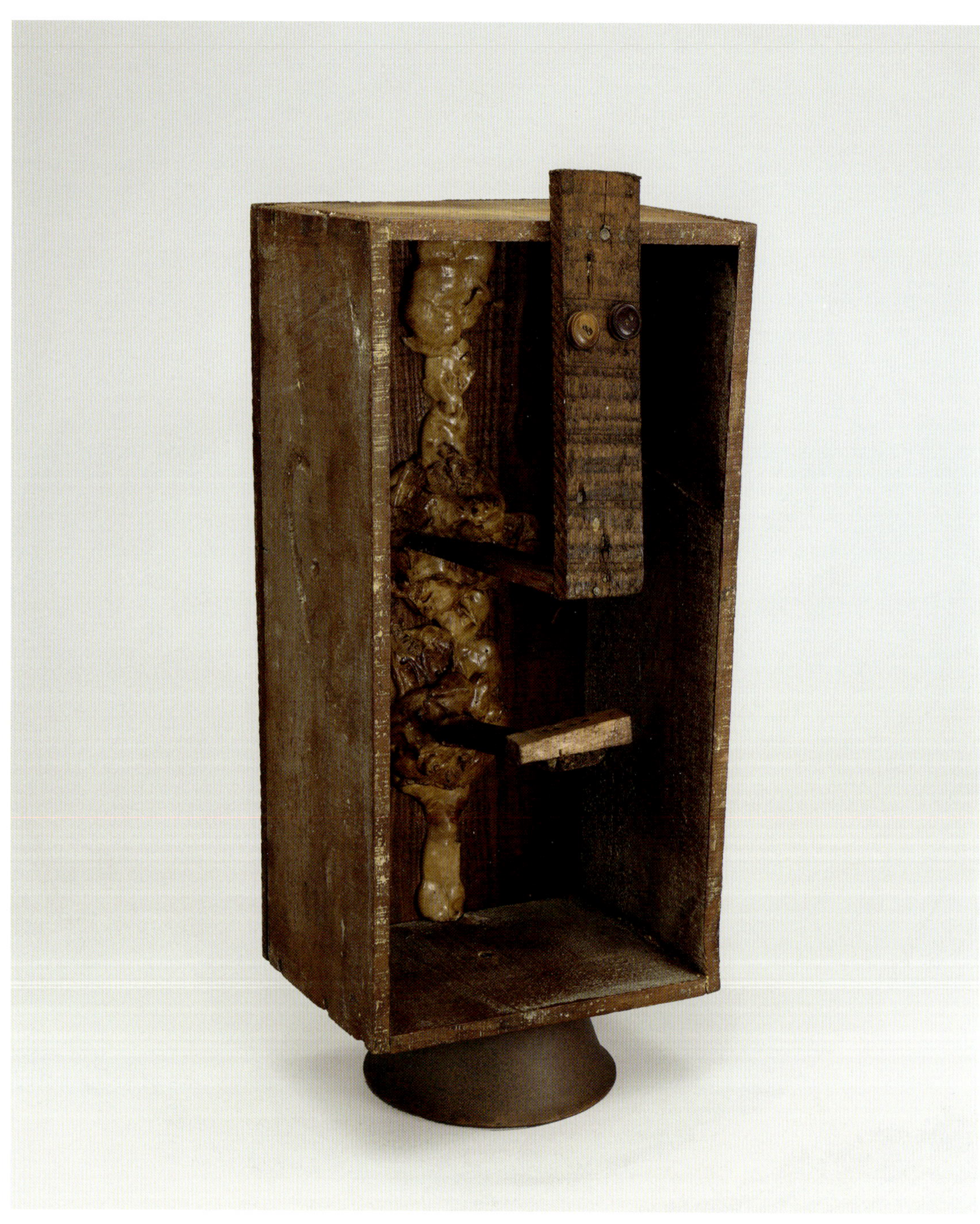

137. HEAD. Cannes, 1958
Wood box, nails, buttons, painted plaster, and painted synthetic resin mounted on ceramic dish
19 ⅞ × 8 ¾ × 8 in. (50.5 × 22.2 × 20.3 cm)
The Museum of Modern Art, New York. Gift of Jacqueline Picasso in honor of the Museum's continuous commitment to Pablo Picasso's art

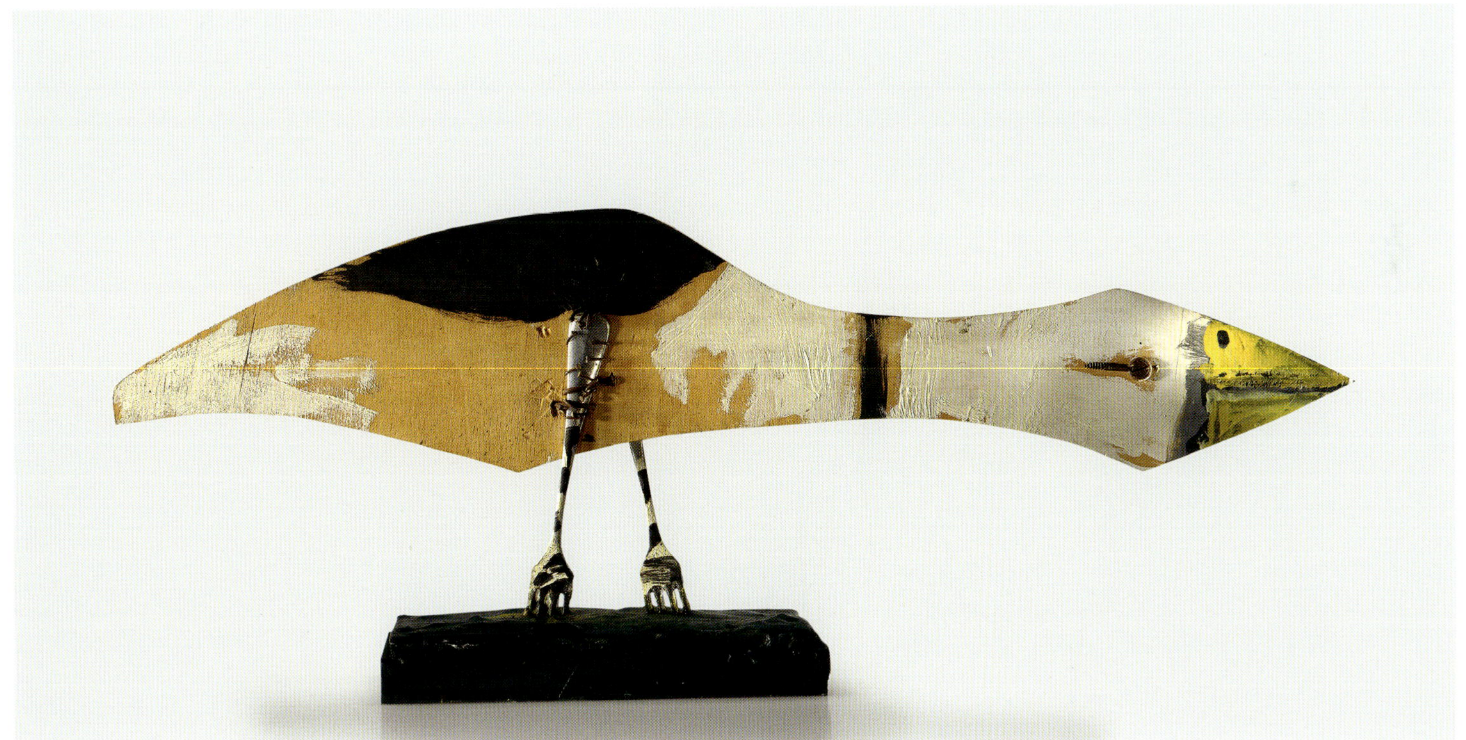

138. **BIRD.** Cannes, May 22, 1958
Painted wood and forks, plaster, nails, screws, and eyebolts
10 ¼ × 26 9/16 × 4 15/16 in. (26 × 67.5 × 12.5 cm)
Private collection

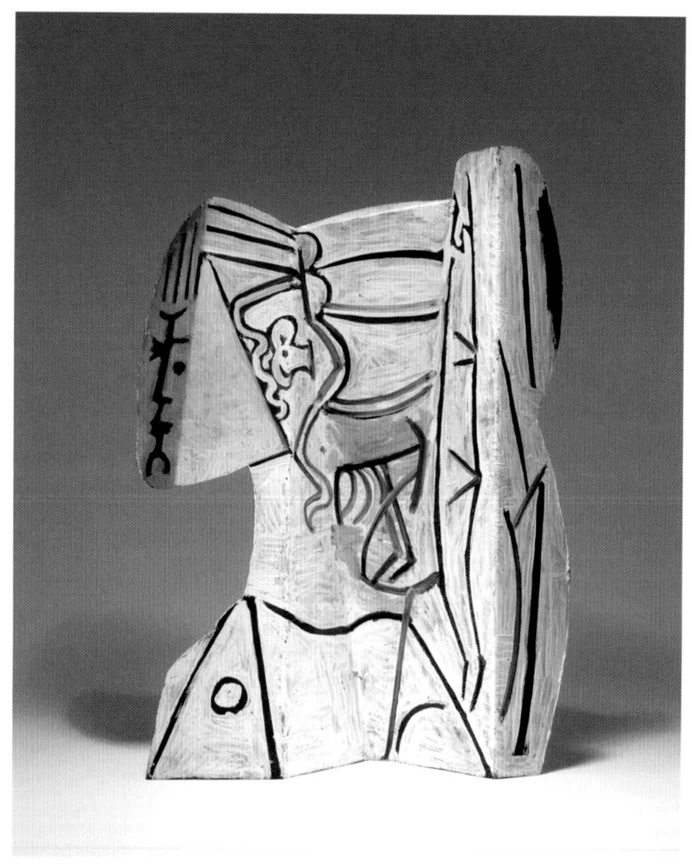

139. **SYLVETTE.** Vallauris, 1954
Painted sheet metal
26 ⅜ × 19 ¹¹⁄₁₆ × 4 ⁵⁄₁₆ in. (67 × 50 × 11 cm)
Private collection

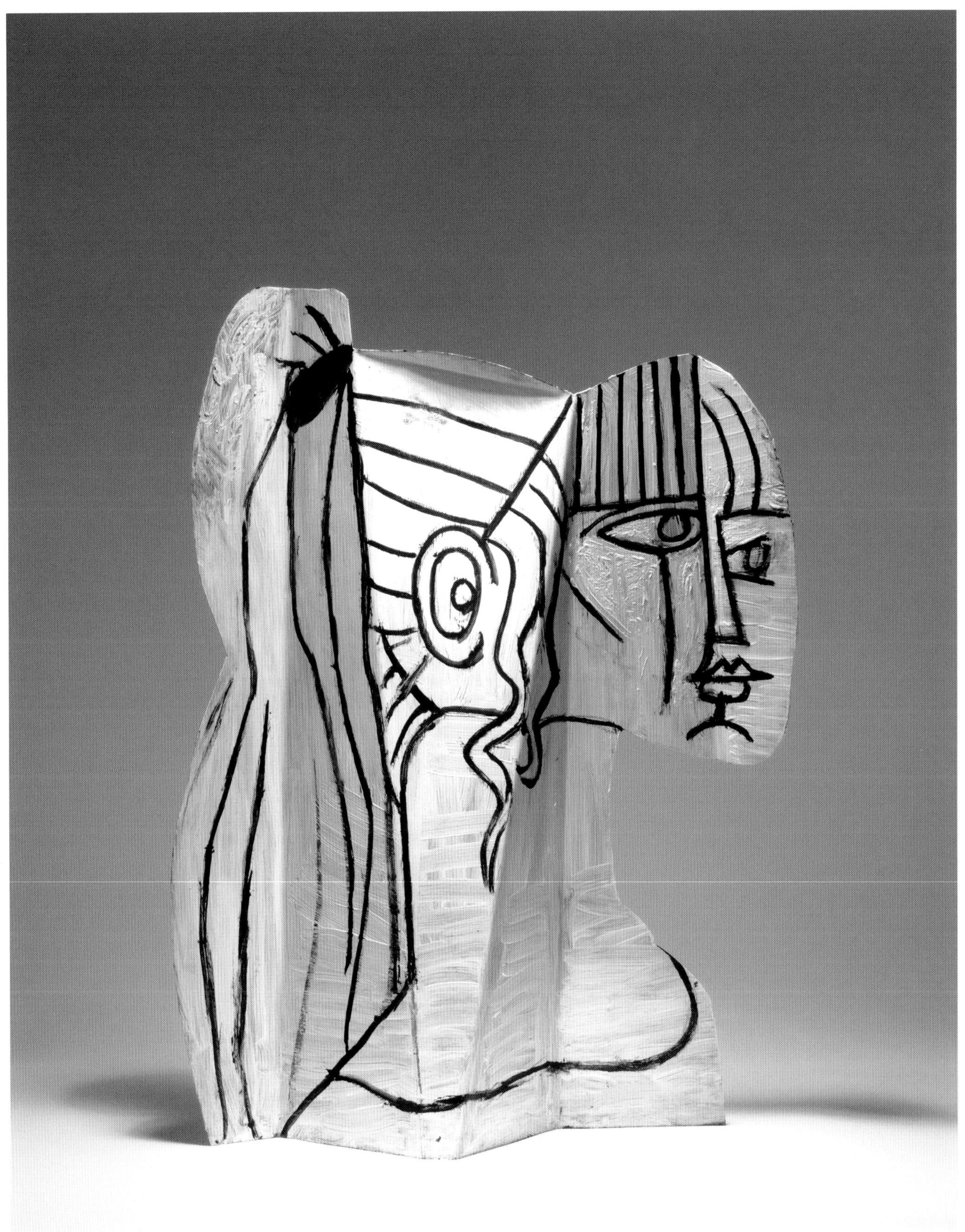

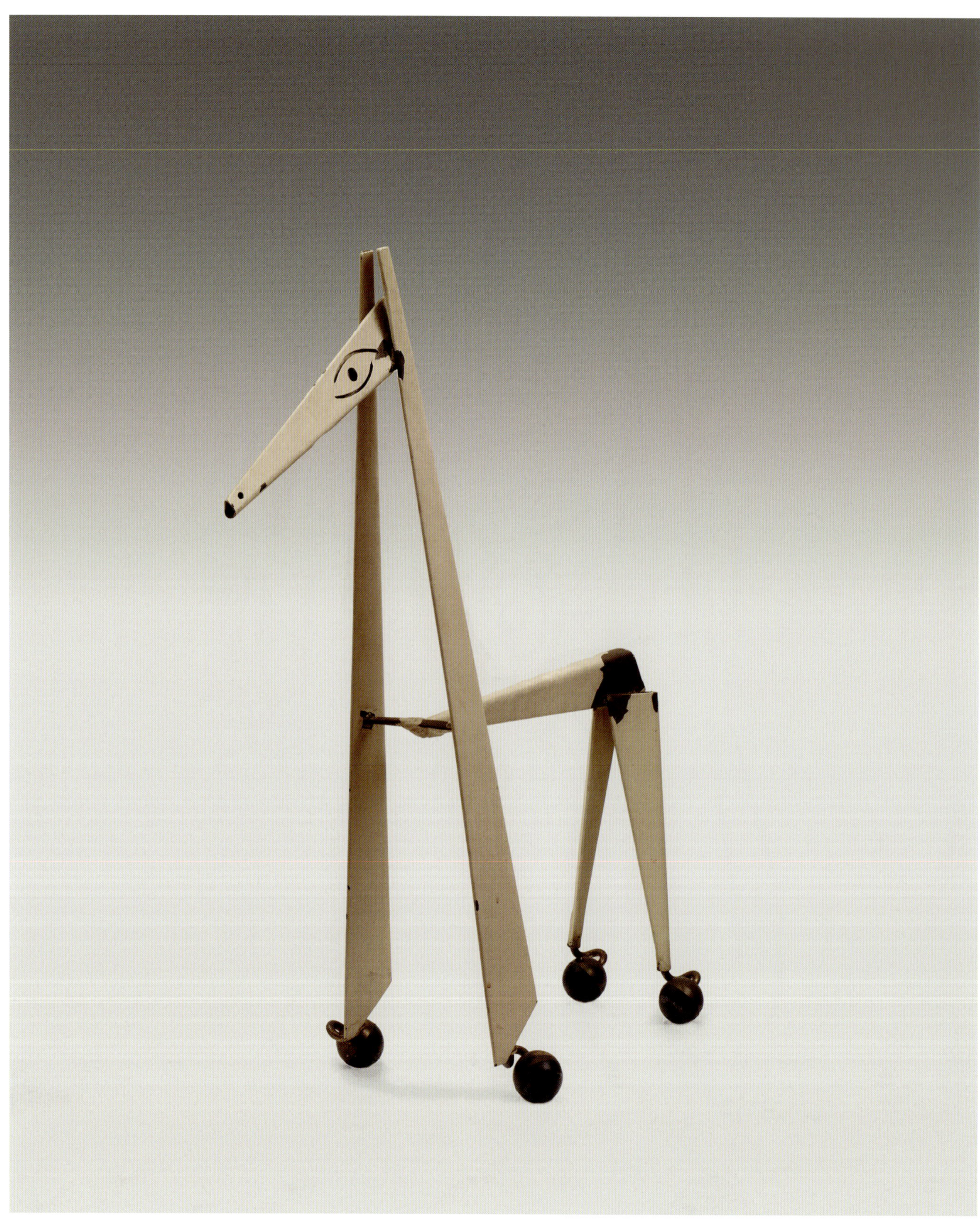

140. LITTLE HORSE. Vallauris, 1961
Painted metal with wheels
26 3⁄16 × 7 1⁄16 × 23 13⁄16 in. (66.5 × 18 × 60.5 cm)
Private collection. Courtesy Fundación Almine y Bernard Ruiz-Picasso para el Arte

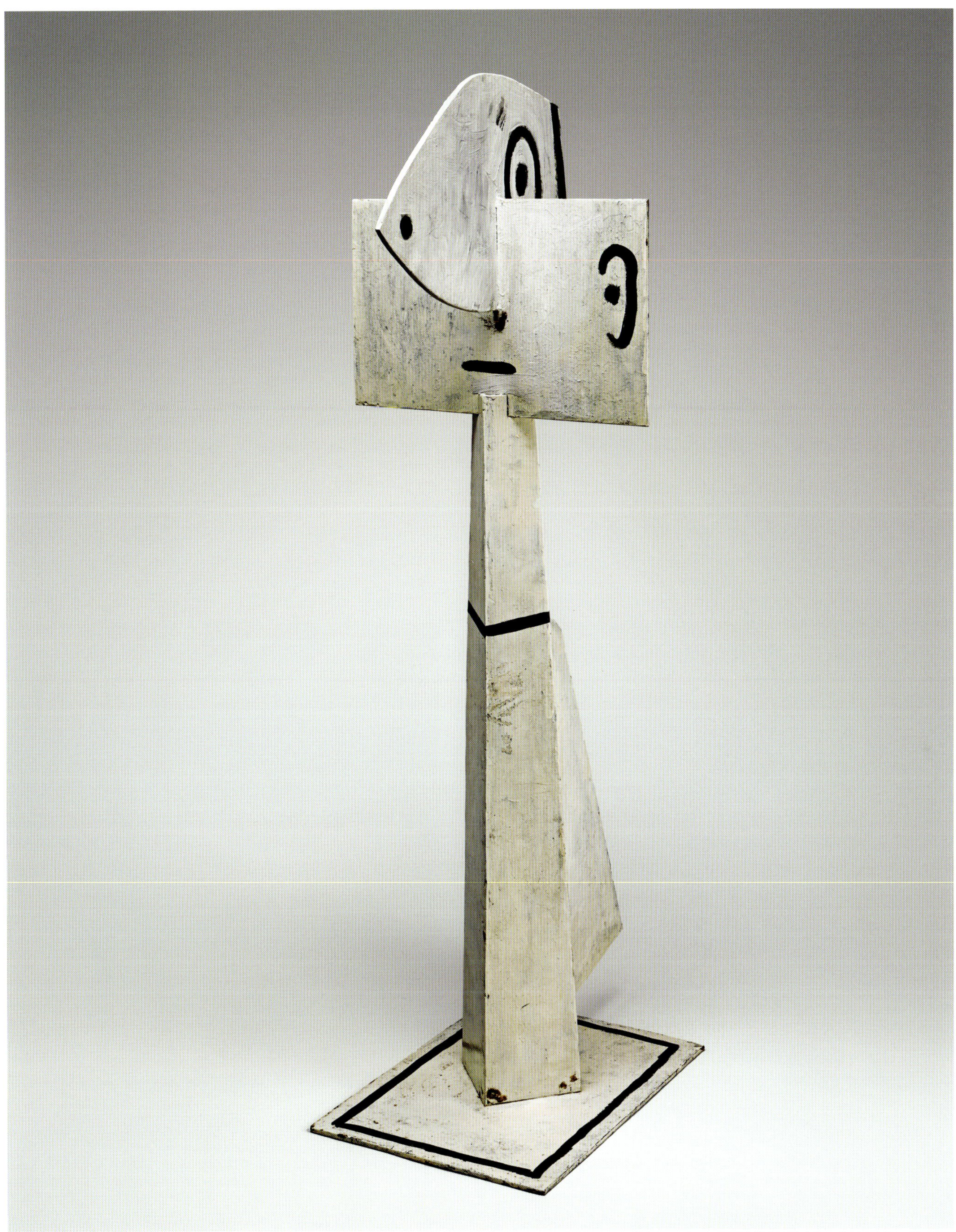

141. **HEAD OF A WOMAN.** Cannes, 1957
Painted sheet metal
34 ¼ × 11 × 16 $\frac{9}{16}$ in. (87 × 28 × 42 cm)
Musée national Picasso–Paris. Dation Pablo Picasso

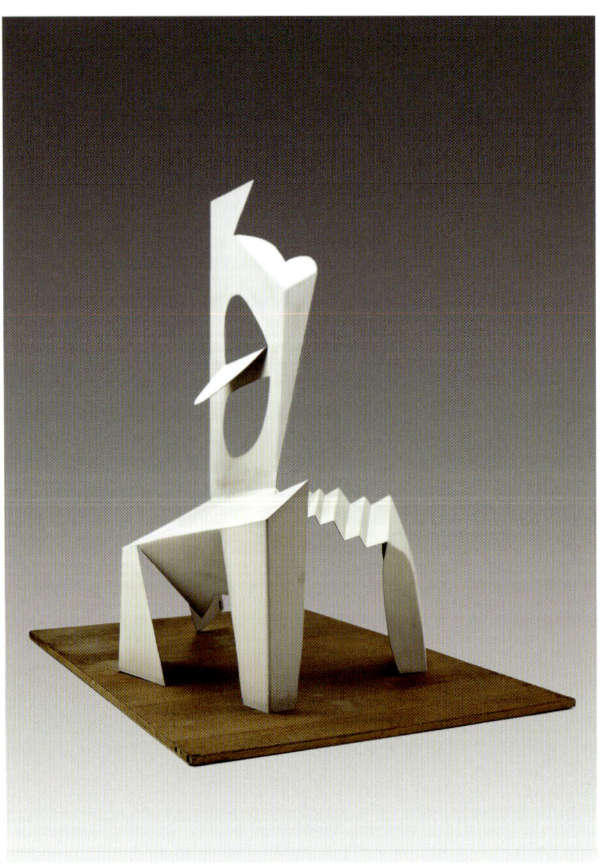
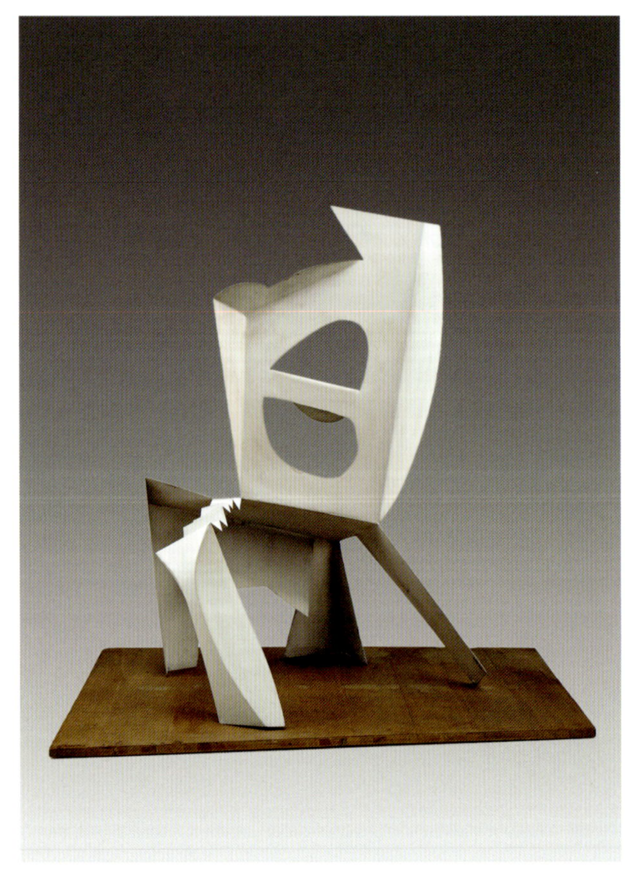

142. **CHAIR.** Cannes, 1961
Painted sheet metal
45 ½ × 45 1/16 × 35 1/16 in. (115.5 × 114.5 × 89 cm)
Musée national Picasso–Paris. Dation Pablo Picasso

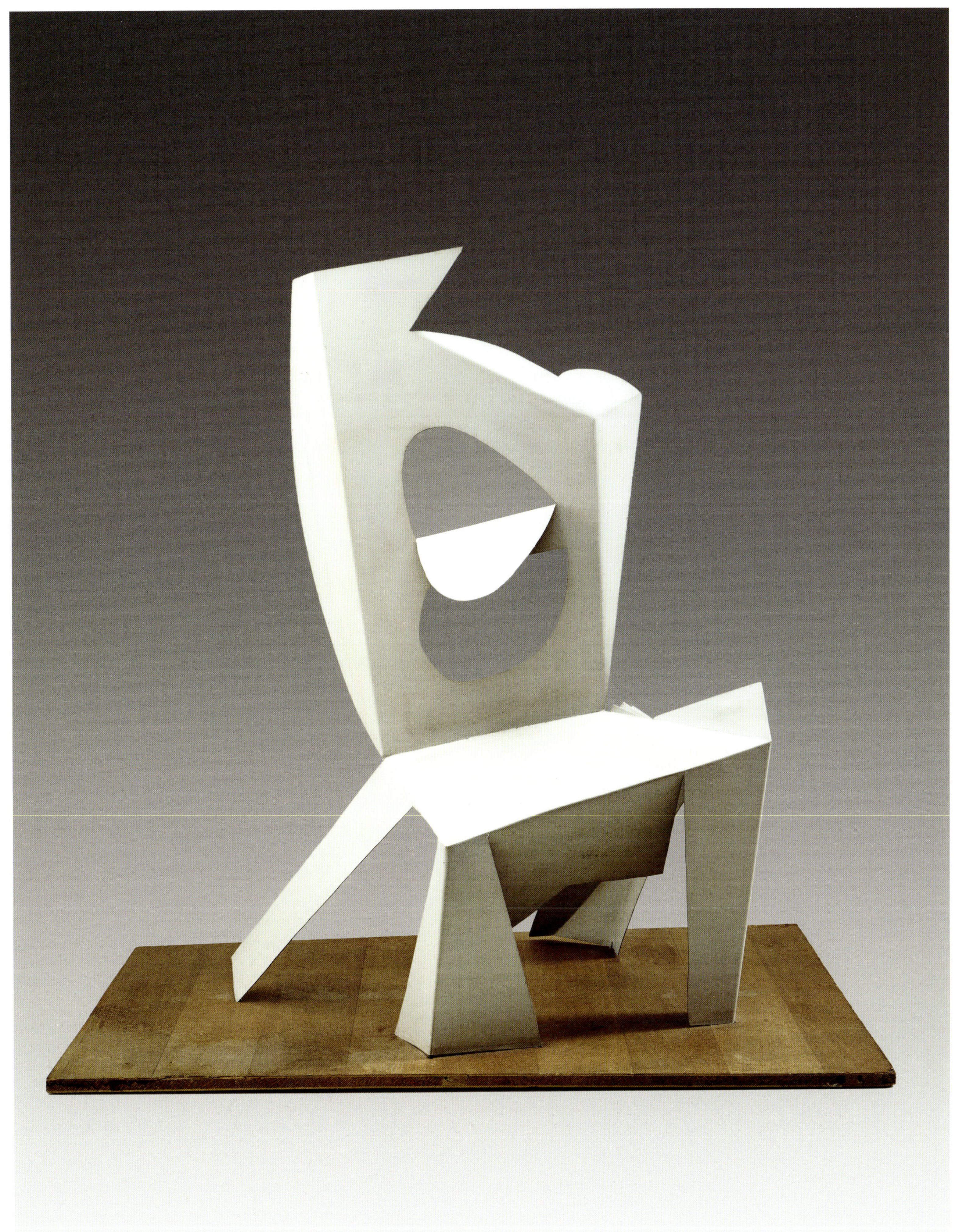

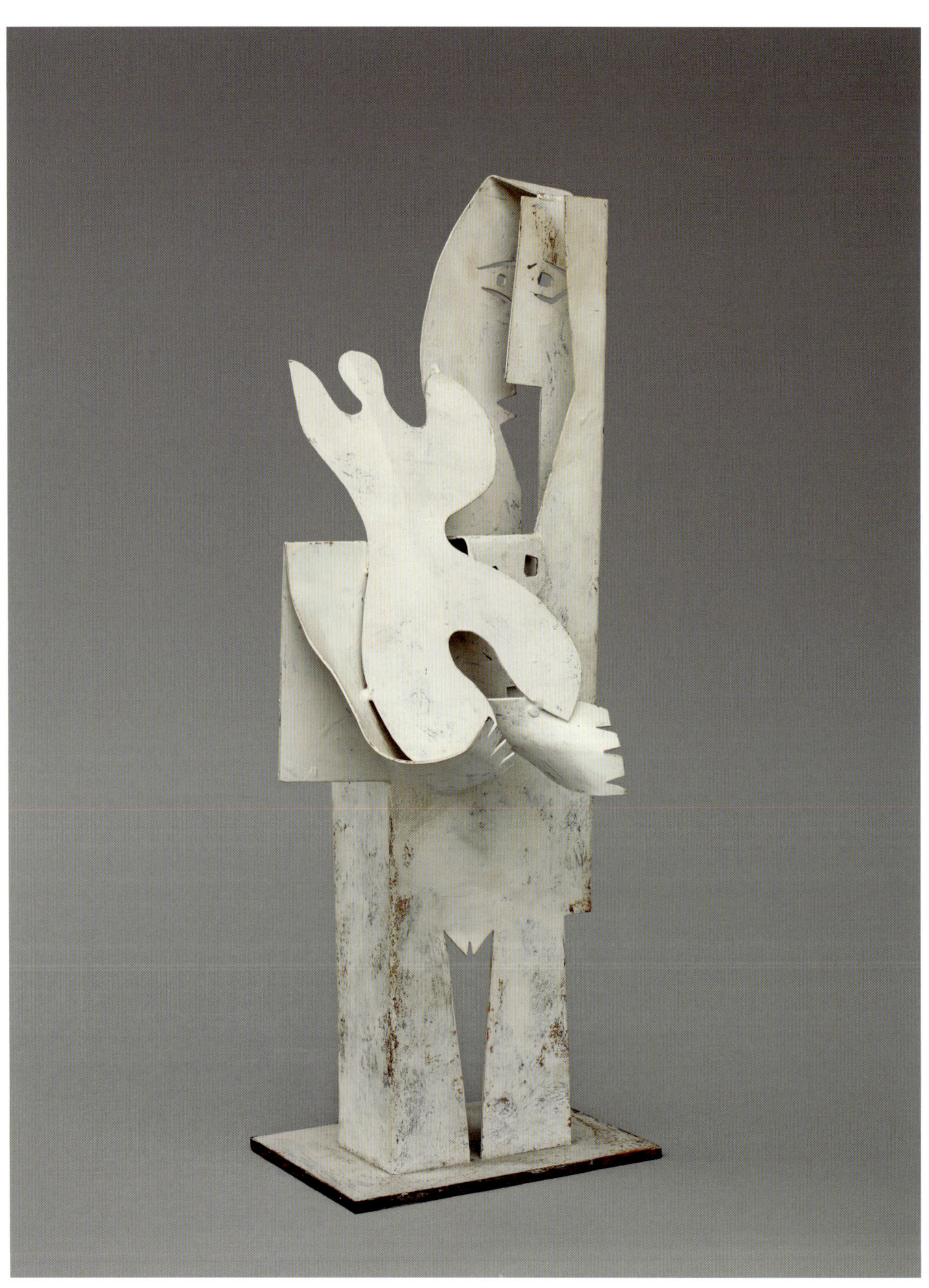

143. **WOMAN AND CHILD.** Cannes, 1961
Painted sheet metal
17 3/8 × 7 3/16 × 6 5/16 in. (44.2 × 18.2 × 16 cm)
Private collection

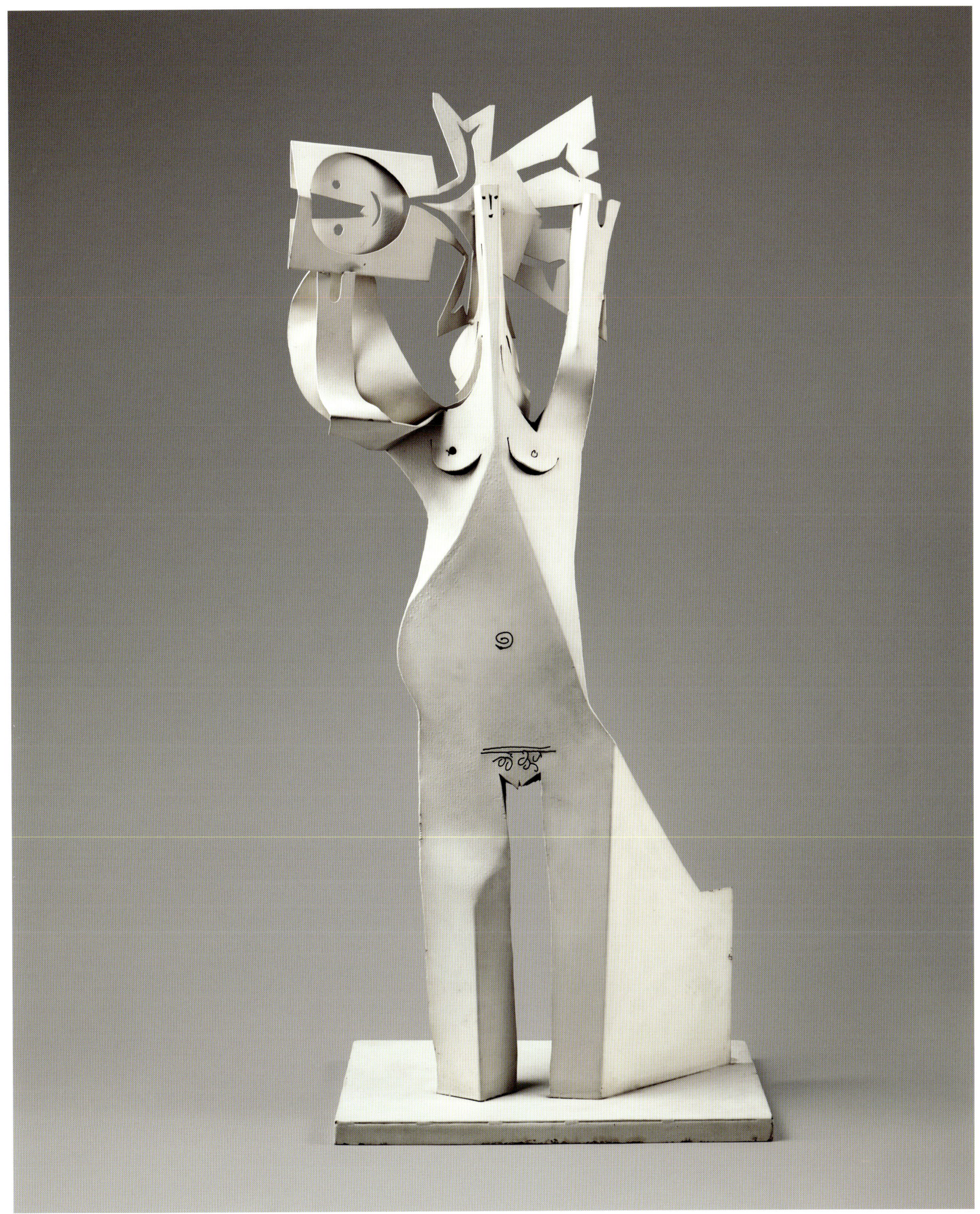

144. **WOMAN WITH CHILD.** Cannes, early 1961
Painted sheet metal
50 ⅜ × 23 ⅝ × 13 ¾ in. (128 × 60 × 35 cm)
Musée national Picasso–Paris. Dation Pablo Picasso

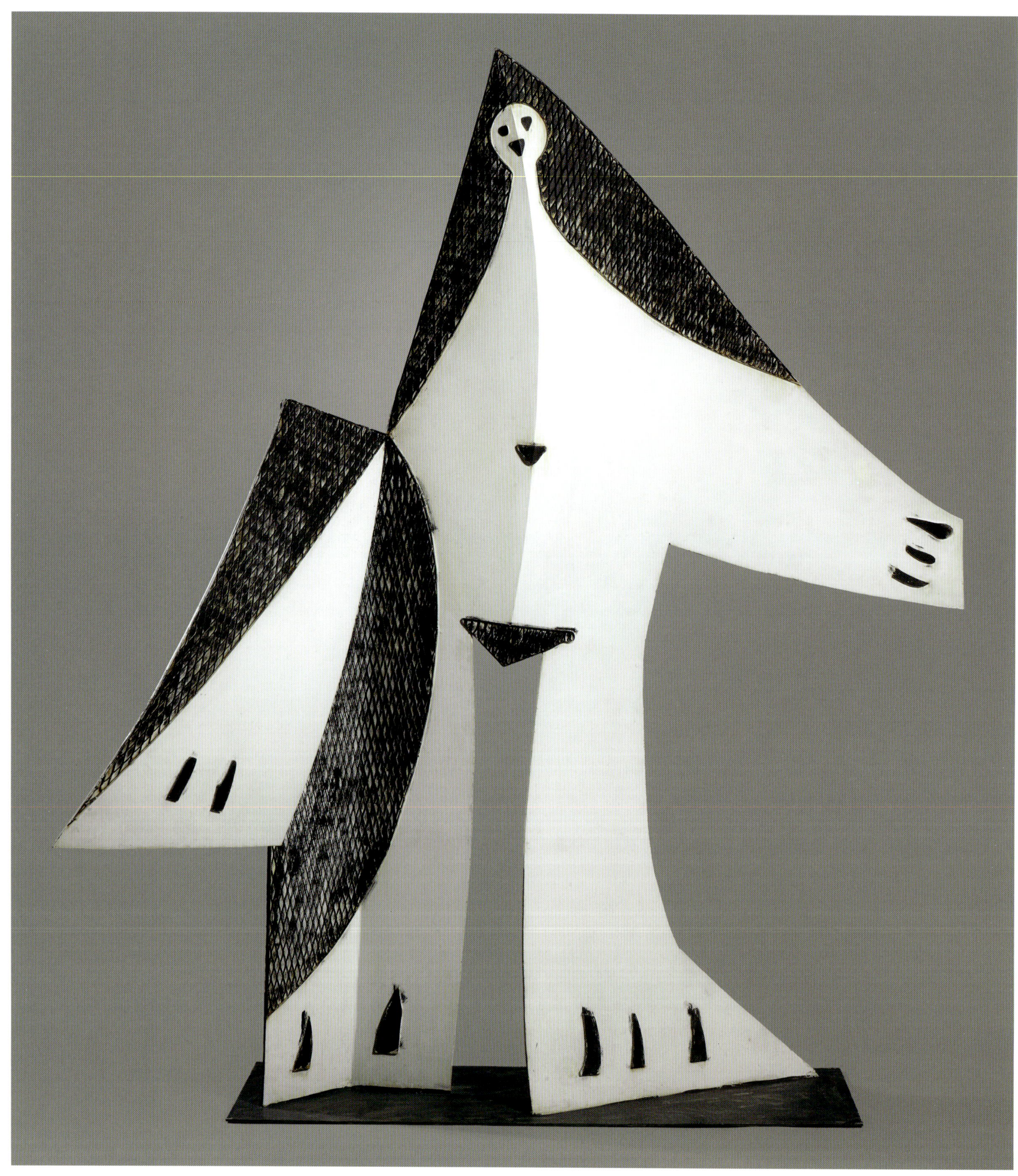

145. **WOMAN WITH OUTSTRETCHED ARMS.** Cannes, 1961
Painted iron and sheet metal
70 5⁄16 × 61 9⁄16 × 28 9⁄16 in. (178.6 × 156.4 × 72.5 cm)
The Museum of Fine Arts, Houston. Gift of the Esther Florence Whinery Goodrich Foundation

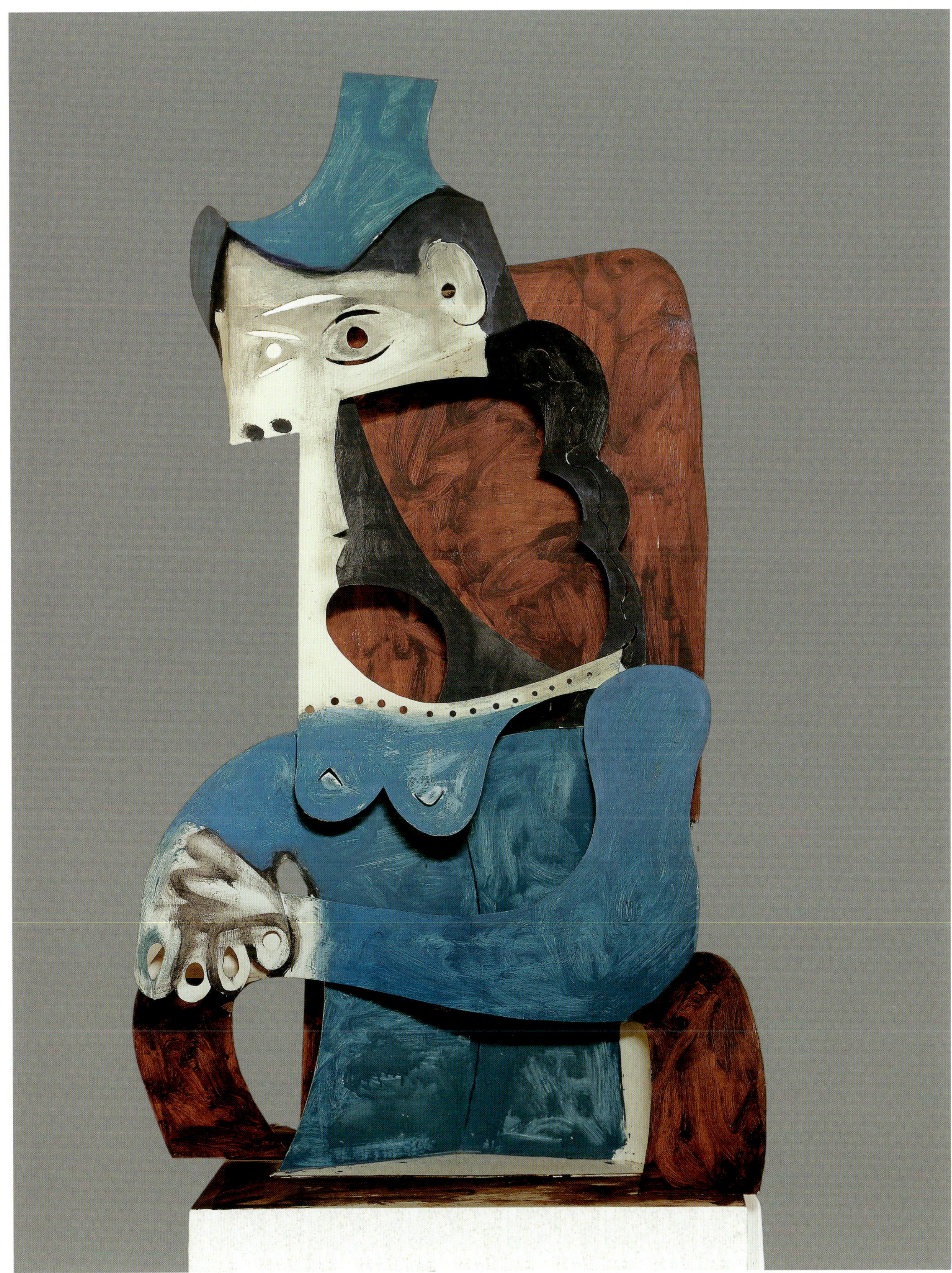

146. **WOMAN WITH HAT.** Cannes, 1961/Mougins, 1963
Sheet metal, painted 1963
49 ⅝ × 28 ¾ × 16 ⅛ in. (126 × 73 × 41 cm)
Fondation Beyeler, Riehen/Basel, Beyeler Collection

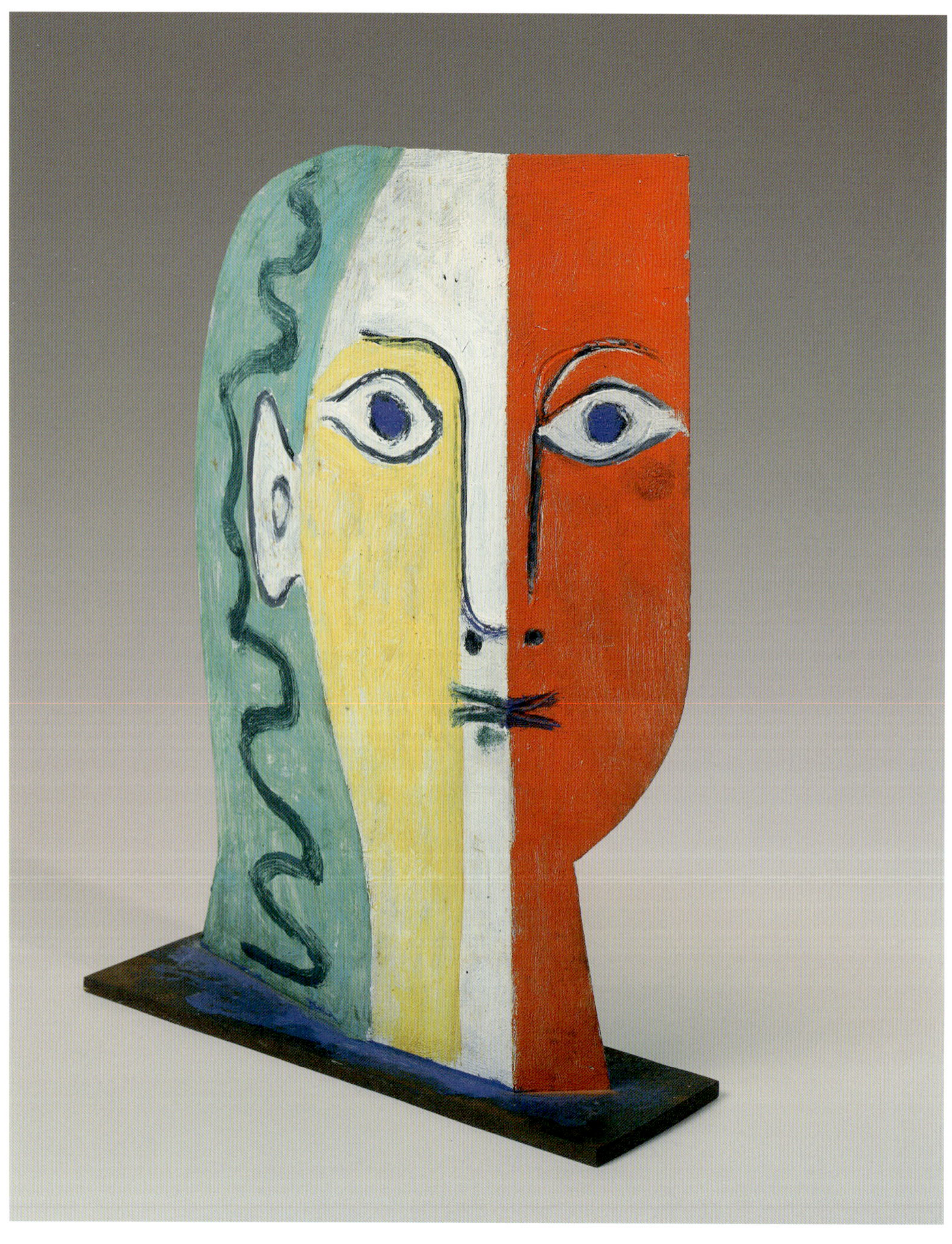

147. **HEAD OF A WOMAN.** Cannes, 1961
Painted sheet metal
11 7/16 × 8 7/16 × 2 3/4 in. (29 × 21.5 × 7 cm)
Private collection. Courtesy Fundación Almine y Bernard Ruiz-Picasso para el Arte

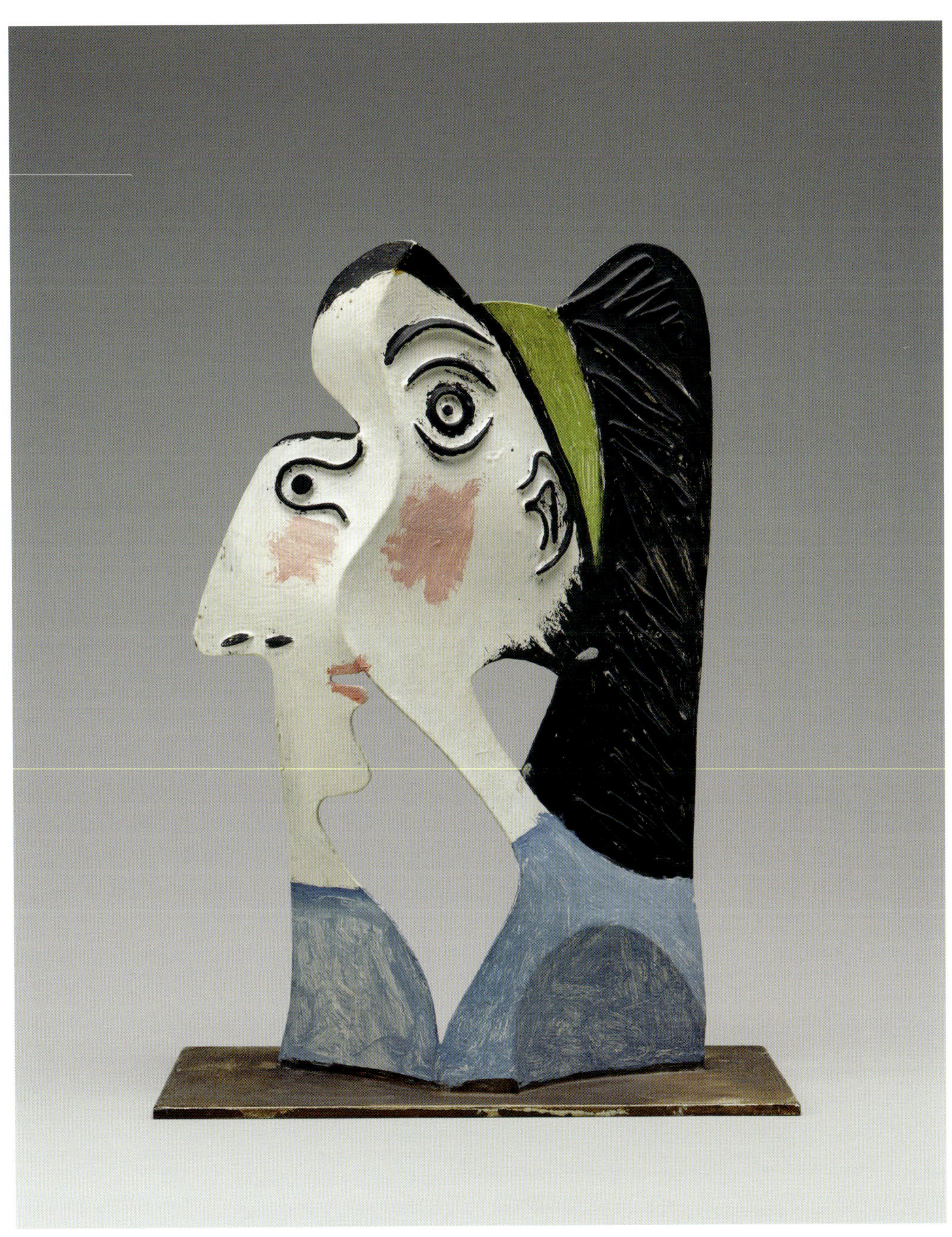

148. **HEAD OF A WOMAN.** Mougins, late 1962
Painted sheet metal and iron wire
12 ⅝ × 9 7/16 × 6 5/16 in. (32 × 24 × 16 cm)
Musée national Picasso–Paris. Dation Pablo Picasso

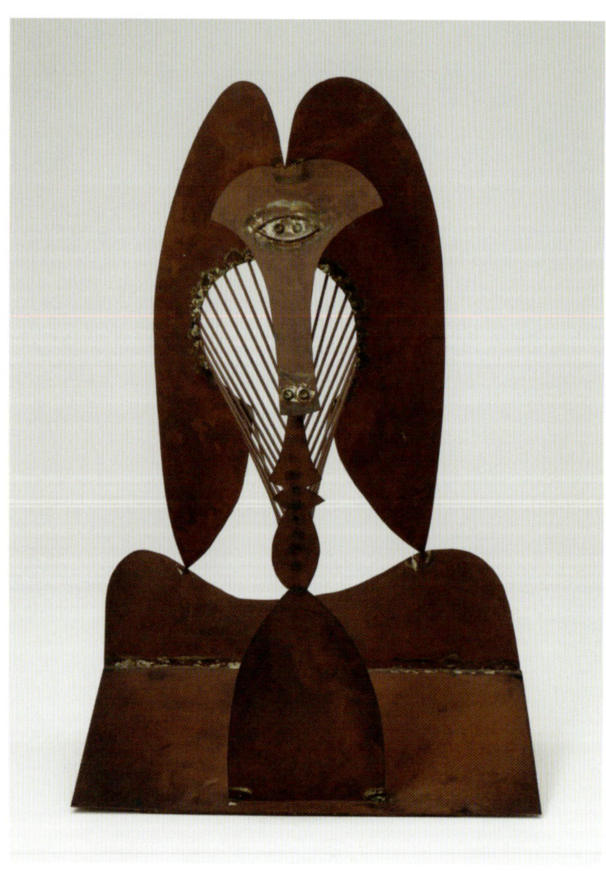

149. **MAQUETTE FOR RICHARD J. DALEY CENTER SCULPTURE.** Mougins, 1964
Simulated and oxidized welded steel
41¼ × 27½ × 19 in. (104.8 × 69.9 × 48.3 cm)
The Art Institute of Chicago. Gift of Pablo Picasso

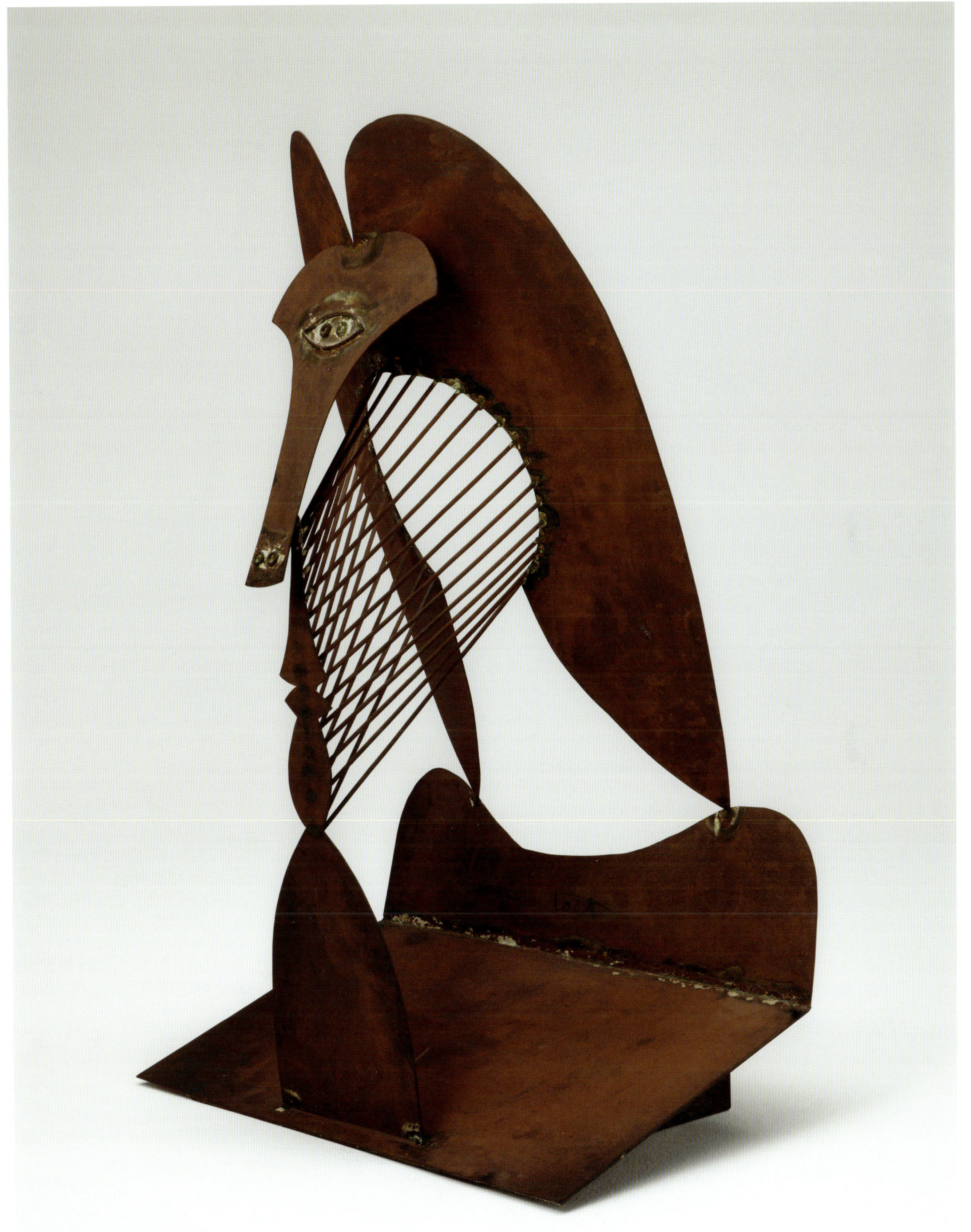

NOTES

The historical chronicle of Picasso's sculptures presented in the Documentary Chronology is a selective synthesis of existing literature and new research on the subject. The authors are greatly indebted to the work of previous scholars, as acknowledged in the Notes that follow. A key to the abbreviations used may be found in the References, p. 312.

Works catalogued in key references are identified by an abbreviation for the source and the number assigned to the work in that publication. These references are Z I–V (Zervos 1932–52), BK (Brassai and Kahnweiler 1949), DR (Daix and Rosselet 1979), S (Spies 1971), and SP (Spies and Piot 2000).

Unless otherwise indicated, translations are by the authors.

PICASSO SCULPTURE AN INTRODUCTION

1 Brassaï and Kahnweiler 1949, n.p.
2 Spies and Piot 2000, p. 8.
3 Ibid., p. 16.
4 See Cowling 2011.
5 Apollinaire 1913. Trans. in Hartzell 2011, p. 98.
6 *Soirées de Paris* 1913, pp. 13, 27, 39, and 45.
7 Rauschenberg's oft-quoted remark appears in his statement for the exhibition catalogue *Sixteen Americans* (New York: The Museum of Modern Art, 1959), p. 58: "Painting relates to both art and life. Neither can be made. (I try to act in the gap between the two.)"
8 Aragon and Breton 1924. Quoted in Cowling 1985, p. 86. Trans. by Rachel Silveri.
9 Breton 1925, p. 30. Trans. in Baldassari 2005, p. 30.
10 Brassaï and Kahnweiler 1949, n.p.
11 Leiris 1929, p. 210. Trans. in Clifford 1986, p. 39.
12 The phrase "convulsive beauty" appears in André Breton's novels *Nadja* (1928) and *L'Amour fou* (Mad love, 1937).
13 Clark 2013, p. 237.
14 Brassaï, quoted in Sayag and Lionel-Marie 2000, p. 14.
15 Gilot and Lake 1964, p. 318.
16 "Primitive," Merriam-Webster.com.
17 Greenberg 1986, p. 318.
18 Dubuffet 1951. Quoted in Rowell 1973, p. 18.
19 Alfred H. Barr, Jr., letter to Picasso, March 31, 1956. Alfred H. Barr, Jr. Papers, The Museum of Modern Art Archives, New York.
20 Daniel-Henry Kahnweiler, letter to Barr, April 13, 1956. Alfred H. Barr, Jr. Papers, The Museum of Modern Art Archives, New York.
21 Barr, letter to Kahnweiler, April 9, 1956. Alfred H. Barr, Jr. Papers, The Museum of Modern Art Archives, New York.
22 Seitz 1961, p. 25.
23 Roland Penrose, letter to Monroe Wheeler, September 28, 1966. Exhibition Files, The Museum of Modern Art Archives, New York.
24 Kramer 1967, p. 55.

CHAPTER 1 BEGINNINGS 1902–1906

Chronology:
1 For Picasso's academic training, see Staller 1997, pp. 67–85, and Cowling 2002, esp. pp. 35–36.
2 For an account of Picasso's introduction to modern art and to the work of Edgar Degas in particular, see Torras 2010.
3 The Exposition was open April 15–November 12, 1900.
4 Picasso and Carles Casagemas, letter to Ramon Reventós, October 25, 1900. Trans. in McCully 1982, p. 28.
5 *Exposition Rodin*, Pavilion de place de l'Alma, Paris, June 1–November 27, 1900. The exhibition included 150 sculptures, figurines, sketches, and studies.
6 Cabot i Rovira 1901. The article's illustrations included a photograph of *The Thinker* inscribed with a dedication to the painter Ramón Casas y Carbó. The authors thank Violette Andrès of the Musée national Picasso–Paris for her inspection of a print of the studio photograph.
7 Claris 1902 and 1901. The text in *La lectura* includes numerous images of works by Medardo Rosso and Auguste Rodin. No reproductions accompanied the 1901 French version.
8 Rosso 1902, p. 55.
9 In addition to Picasso and Emili Fontbona, the gatherings at Le Zut included Jaime Sabartés (a.k.a. Jaume Sabartés y Gual), Mateu de Soto, Manolo, and Paco Durrio. See Sabartés 1948, pp. 73–74.
10 Spies and Piot 2000, pp. 17–18.
11 The research of Diana Widmaier Picasso confirms this exhibition as the sculpture's first.
12 Brassaï and Kahnweiler 1949, pl. 1.
13 Richardson 1962, no. 2.
14 Spies 1971, p. 301.
15 Titled *Exposición de arte antiguo*, the show attempted to survey the artistic heritage of Catalonia. See Bofarull i Sans 1902.
16 Richardson 1991, p. 246.
17 For an earlier dating of *Head of a Picador with a Broken Nose* to 1901, see Riedl 1962. *Mask of a Blind Singer* is SP 2.
18 For the creation of *Head of a Picador*, see McCully 2011, p. 126. It is likely that *Mask of a Blind Singer* was also modeled in clay and made at Fontbona's studio.
19 Ambroise Vollard wrote to Paul Gauguin on May 18, 1902, to express his newfound interest in his sculpture and the mask in particular. See Druick 2006, p. 372.
20 Picasso's exhibition at Galerie Vollard was open June 24–July 14, 1901.
21 A letter from Henri-Pierre Roché to Picasso most likely dated May 8, 1905, speaks to their meeting the next day. Picasso Archives, Musée national Picasso–Paris. Cited in Baldassari et al. 2002, p. 362.
22 See "Dr. Claribel Cone Ledger, 1925," Dr. Claribel and Miss Etta Cone Papers, Archives and Manuscripts Collections, Baltimore Museum of Art. Cited in Richardson 1985, p. 175.
23 The authors thank Ann Boulton and Oliver Shell for sharing their expertise in analyzing this cast.
24 Level 1928, p. 29 n. 1.
25 Olivier 1965, p. 51. Fernande Olivier's memoirs were first published in excerpts in the Paris newspapers *Le Soir* and *Mercure de France* in 1930 and 1931, respectively. They appeared in book format in French in 1933.
26 *Cone Collection of Modern Paintings and Sculptures*, May–October 1930.
27 Daniel-Henry Kahnweiler, letter to Peter Anselm Riedl, December 12, 1961. Quoted in Riedl 1962, p. 83 n. 1. The authors thank Anna Heinze for drawing this to her attention.
28 Widmaier Picasso, unpublished transcriptions of records in the Valsuani Archives.
29 Riedl 1962, p. 83 n. 1. Additional provenance information provided by Ute Haug of the Hamburger Kunsthalle.
30 The dealer Otto Gerson purchased a cast of *Head of a Picador with a Broken Nose*, marked "3/6" and titled *Masque*, from Kahnweiler in March 1961 and sold it to Mr. and Mrs. M. J. Lebworth of Greenwich, Conn., a little over two years later. Otto and Ilse Gerson Papers, 1933–1980, Archives of American Art, Smithsonian Institution, Washington, D.C.
31 The review, "La pintura y la escultura allende los pirineos," by Carles Junyer Vidal, discussed

the book *La pintura en la Exposición Universal de París de 1900*, by Rodriguez Codolá. See Richardson 1991, pp. 241 and 501 n. 15.
32 Doñate 2001, p. 247.
33 Rodin's bust of Jules Dalou is listed in the official catalogue of the 1900 Exposition (titled *Dalou*) and in the catalogue of the place de l'Alma retrospective. See *Exposition internationale universelle* 1900, no. 1794, and Alexandre 1900, no. 77.
34 Carles Junyer Vidal, "Picasso y su obra," *El Liberal*, March 24, 1901. The notice of April 11–12 is quoted and trans. in McCully 1997, p. 41.
35 Durrio, quoted in McCully 2011, p. 133.
36 It has been generally believed that these sculptures were first exhibited in Paris in 1905–06. However, they were excavated in Spain between 1902 and 1904, and, as Maria Luisa Catoni argues, it is likely that they arrived soon thereafter in Paris. See Catoni 1990, esp. pp. 123–25.
37 See Salon d'Automne 1904, nos. 1762–63.
38 The exhibition also presented works by the Swiss painter and architect Albert Trachsel and the French artist Auguste Gérardin.
39 Guillaume Apollinaire, "Picasso, peintre et dessinateur," *La Revue immoraliste* (April 1905). This review was Apollinaire's first article on Picasso's work. For the text in English, see Apollinaire 2001.
40 Brassaï and Kahnweiler 1949, n.p. Richardson states that the head was likely modeled at Durrio's studio. Richardson 1991, p. 349. For the circumstances of the making of the sculpture, see also Penrose 1981, p. 116.
41 Spies and Piot 2000, pp. 23 and 334 n. 65.
42 Richardson 1991, esp. pp. 343–49.
43 *Bust of a Man* is SP 9.
44 Johnson 1977, p. 42. Cited in Widmaier Picasso 2006, p. 182.
45 Widmaier Picasso writes, "The fact that technique and quality of execution vary significantly from one sculpture to the next is a clear indication that Vollard used several different foundries to cast Picasso's bronzes." Widmaier Picasso 2006, p. 182.
46 Vincenc Kramář, cited in Sadílková and Hubatová-Vacková 2002, p. 217. A letter from Picasso to Gertrude Stein dated April 30, 1912, confirms Kramář's visit. The letter is cited in Cousins 1989, p. 389, and Monod-Fontaine 1984a, p. 166.
47 Widmaier Picasso's research confirms this exhibition as the sculpture's first.
48 The photograph appeared in *feuilles volantes* 1927, p. 3. Widmaier Picasso shared her information on this publication.
49 See Ritchie 1952, p. 61, and Galerie Charpentier 1954, lot 69 ("Terre cuite originale, enduite de vernis-cire"). More recently, Werner Spies stated that the sculpture was modeled in wax. See Spies and Piot 2000, p. 23. The 1954 auction is cited in Widmaier Picasso 2006, p. 188. Widmaier Picasso shared her information on this sculpture.
50 Jacques Dubourg, a Parisian dealer active during the interwar and postwar years, assisted the auctioneers at the 1954 sale. See also Kahnweiler, letters to Picasso, March 27 and 30, 1954. Picasso Archives, Musée national Picasso–Paris.
51 Kahnweiler, letter to Picasso, March 30, 1954. Picasso Archives, Musée national Picasso–Paris. The hammer price of 410,000 French francs is listed in an annotated copy of the auction catalogue preserved in the library of the Getty Research Institute, Los Angeles. See Galerie Charpentier 1954, lot 69.
52 For a detailed account of the artists' first meeting, see Baldassari et al. 2002, p. 362.
53 Cowling 2010, p. 167. Cowling cites Spies and Piot 2000, p. 28.
54 Marilyn McCully posits that this drawing, executed in Gósol in summer 1906, "served as a template for the sculpture," which would date the creation of *Head of a Woman (Fernande)* not to spring 1906, as is traditional, but to after Picasso's return to Paris in August 1906. McCully 2011, p. 203. For the dating of the work to spring 1906, see Spies and Piot 2000, p. 31, and Cowling 2010, p. 167.
55 For Degas's influence on Picasso's sculpture, see Cowling 2010, esp. pp. 167–68.
56 For the title "La Coiffure," see Z I 329.
57 Cowling 2010, pp. 181–82.
58 Richardson 1991, p. 461. The original terracotta was at one time in the collection of Georges Pellequer of Paris and is today housed in a different private collection.
59 Cowling 2010, pp. 181–82.
60 For Durrio's connection to Gauguin, see Richardson 1991, pp. 456–61.
61 See Baldassari 1997, pp. 62–65, figs. 73 and 74.
62 Level 1928, pl. 55, and Zervos 1928, p. 285. Widmaier Picasso's research confirms these publications as the sculpture's first.

CHAPTER 2
WOOD CARVING AND THE FIRST CUBIST SCULPTURES
1907–1909

Introduction:
1 Penrose 1981, p. 138.
2 Brassaï 1999, p. xvii.
Chronology:
1 Jacob 1927, p. 202.
2 Matisse 1941, p. 31.
3 Ibid.
4 In a postcard Leo Stein sent to Picasso on April 12, 1906, Stein proposes to postpone their visit to Gustave Fayet to the first Monday after the Easter holidays that year. Picasso Archives, Musée national Picasso–Paris.
5 Fayet would lend two wooden sculptures and seven ceramics by Paul Gauguin to the 1906 Salon d'Automne. See n. 10.
6 Richardson 2007, p. 552 n. 25.
7 Picasso, letter to Enric Casanovas, June 27, 1906. Quoted in Richardson 1991, pp. 442 and 444.
8 Picasso, letter to Casanovas, July 1906. Quoted in Richardson 1991, p. 444.
9 Ibid., pp. 451–52.
10 The retrospective was mounted at the Grand Palais, Paris, October 6–November 15, 1906. For detailed information about the objects on view, see Salon d'Automne 1906, p. 193.
11 Cahn 2003, p. 291.
12 Géry Pieret was also known as Honoré-Joseph Géry Pieret. For detailed accounts of Picasso's purchase and the events following the theft, see Read 2008, pp. 59–67, and Richardson 1996, esp. pp. 21–24 and 200–205. The statues involved in the scandal are now in the collection of the Musée d'Archéologie nationale, Saint-Germain-en-Laye.
13 Read 2008, p. 60.
14 Olivier 1965, p. 147.
15 *Head* (SP 14) is now in a private collection. Cowling 2002, p. 654 n. 163.
16 Ibid.
17 For a full transcription of the annotations, see Léal 1996, vol. 1, p. 138.
18 For a full transcription of the annotations, see ibid.
19 André Derain's studio was located in the complex Les Fusains, at 22, rue de Tourlaque, in Montmartre. Pieyre de Mandiargues and Monod-Fontaine 2007, p. 244.
20 For Derain's trips to London, see ibid., pp. 243–44. Concerning his purchase, see Cousins 1989, p. 342.
21 Picasso 1937, p. 33.
22 McCully 2007, p. 30.
23 For a discussion of these and a number of the other woodcarvings Picasso executed around this time, see ibid., pp. 16–41.
24 Ibid., p. 30.
25 McCully later noticed that the nail holes made to fix the leg to the chair's seat are still visible on the back of the object. McCully 2011, p. 208.
26 For a detailed account of Picasso's friendship with Antoinette and Germaine "Mémène" Fornerod, see McCully 2007, esp. pp. 36–39.
27 See Cowling, Golding, and Ruiz-Picasso 1994, pp. 255–56, and Cowling 2002, esp. pp. 191–92.
28 Cowling 2002, esp. pp. 191–92.
29 Cowling 2002, p. 192. Spies 1971, p. 23.
30 Cowling and Pullen 1994.
31 The label and the possibility that Picasso started work while vacationing were first noted by Alexandra Parigoris in her review of the 1983 exhibition of Picasso's sculpture organized by Spies at the Nationalgalerie, Berlin, and the Kunsthalle Düsseldorf. Parigoris 1984. For Picasso's stay at La Rue-des-Bois, see Cousins 1989, p. 354.
32 The two paintings, *Head and Shoulders of the Farmer's Wife* and *The Farmer's Wife*, are now in the collection of the State Hermitage Museum, St. Petersburg. For the drawings, see Z VI 1002–1006, 1008–1009. The information on Madame Putnam is recorded in Richardson 1996, pp. 94–95.
33 Cowling 2002, p. 192.
34 For a portrait by Gelett Burgess of Derain next to his sculpture, see Cousins 1989, p. 366.
35 The authors thank Diana Widmaier Picasso for sharing information on the exhibition history of these two sculptures.
36 Inez Haynes Irwin's diary entry is published in Cousins and Seckel 1988, p. 560.
37 Ibid. For "The Wild Men of Paris," see Burgess 1910.
38 A detail of fig. 13, showing Picasso seated below two New Caledonian ridgepole figures, accompanied the 1910 article. Burgess does not mention Picasso's recent sculptures but reproduces a number of the artist's paintings, including the 1907 *Les Demoiselles d'Avignon*. For the portrait of Picasso, see Burgess 1910, p. 407. For a discussion of the individual sculptures visible in the 1908 photograph and Picasso's collection of non-Western art in general, see Stepan 2006, esp. pp. 94 and 116–46.

39 For a detailed analysis of the making of *Head of a Woman*, see Fletcher 2003. For Picasso's work in clay at Manolo's studio, see ibid., esp. pp. 166–68, and Spies and Piot 2000, p. 57. Una Johnson contends that the sculpture was produced in Julio González's studio. See Johnson 1977, p. 41.
40 González 1936, p. 189.
41 For a discussion of the formal relationship between the *écorché* and Picasso's paintings and sculpture of Fernande Olivier in this period, see Weiss 2003, esp. pp. 40–41. For the metaphor of the *écorché*, see Tuma 2003, esp. pp. 146–55.
42 Picasso, quoted in Penrose 1967, p. 19. Cited in Cowling 2002, p. 213.
43 Fletcher 2003, p. 172.
44 Fletcher cites an exchange between Cowling and John Richardson, who recalled a conversation between Picasso, the Cubist collector Douglas Cooper, and himself of around 1955 in which the artist conveyed that he had visited the foundry and reworked the master plaster cast. Ibid., p. 175. Cited in Cowling, Golding, and Ruiz-Picasso 1994, p. 256.
45 Cowling and Pullen 1994.
46 Sadílková and Hubatová-Vacková 2002, p. 208. This bronze is now in the collection of the Národní Galerie, Prague.
47 Vollard's January 15, 1912, agenda book entry recording Edward Steichen's purchase is cited in Fletcher 2003, p. 183 n. 35.
48 The cast is dated 1911. See Galerie Flechtheim 1913, p. 135.
49 For the sculpture on display in Ambroise Vollard's gallery, see Johnson 1977, p. 42. For Vollard's success in selling this and other sculptures by Picasso, see Widmaier Picasso 2006, esp. pp. 185–86.
50 This letter is quoted in Fletcher 2003, p. 181 n. 33.
51 Guillaume Apollinaire, "Première Exposition de sculpture futuriste du peintre et sculpteur futuriste Boccioni," *L'Intransigeant* (June 21, 1913): 2. Trans. in Apollinaire 2001, p. 320. Cited in Weiss 2003, p. 25. The show was mounted at Galerie La Boétie, June 20–July 16, 1913.
52 The sculpture is not reproduced. Aksenov 1917, pp. 54 and 62. Trans. in McCully 1982, p. 113. Cited in Weiss 2003, p. 25. Referred to as "Polemical Supplement" and widely known as having been written in 1915, the text is in fact dated "June 1914." Aksenov visited Paris in spring 1914, during which time he visited Picasso's studio and frequented the artist's circles. For Aksenov's sojourn in the French capital, see Adaskina 2012, pp. 15–19.
53 For the receipt, see Sadílková and Hubatová-Vacková 2002, p. 208, ill. 25. Vollard used the generic description "un buste de Picasso" in a May 26, 1911, entry for Vincenc Kramář's purchase in his agenda book. Fonds Ambroise Vollard, Bibliothèque des musées nationaux, Musée d'Orsay, Paris. For the dealer's use of the title *Tête* or *Tête de femme*, see Fletcher 2003 and Widmaier Picasso 2006.
54 *International Exhibition* 1913, no. 598, p. 45; Skupina Výtvarných Umělců 1913, no. 25; and Galerie Flechtheim 1913, p. 135.
55 The sculpture is erroneously dated to 1900 in the Paris catalogue and to around 1908 in the German edition published by Kunsthaus Zürich. See Galeries Georges Petit 1932, p. 71, no. 226, and Kunsthaus Zürich 1932, p. 16, no. 230.
56 Weiss 2003, esp. pp. 4–12.
57 Aksenov 1917, p. 54. Trans. in McCully 1982, p. 113. Cited in Weiss 2003, p. 25. For Aksenov's trip to Paris that year, see n. 52.
58 The sculpture was first titled *Head of a Woman (Fernande)* in Spies and Piot 1983 rev, p. 373, no. 24.
59 *Head* is SP 25. For a formal analysis and discussion of *Apple*, see Tuma 2003, esp. pp. 158–63.
60 For *Head*, see Spies and Piot 2000, p. 395. A conservation report by Laurence Labbe (May 2014) in the object files for *Apple* in the Musée national Picasso–Paris suggests that Picasso first modeled the sculpture in clay or a malleable earthlike medium, from which he made a plaster cast that he worked using a sharp tool while the plaster was still wet.
61 See Z II (2) 717–19. Widmaier Picasso's research confirms these reproductions as the sculptures' first.
62 In 1967 Roland Penrose adopted Christian Zervos's date, followed by William Rubin, who, in 1972, dated *Apple* to early 1910. A revision of the date to the end of 1909 was first suggested by Spies and Christine Piot in 1983. See Penrose 1967, p. 19; Rubin 1972, p. 203; and Spies and Piot 1983 rev, p. 53.
63 Titled *Picasso: Œuvres reçues en paiement des droits de succession* but more commonly known as *Dation Picasso*, the exhibition ran from October 11, 1979, to January 7, 1980. See RMN 1979, p. 70, no. 42.

CHAPTER 3
REINVENTING SCULPTURE: THE CUBIST YEARS 1912–1915

Introduction:
1 Picasso, letter to Georges Braque, October 9, 1912. Reproduced in Monod-Fontaine and Carmean 1982, figs. 39–40. Quoted in Cousins 1989, p. 407.
2 Daniel-Henry Kahnweiler, letter to Vincenc Kramář, cited in Sadílková and Hubatová-Vacková 2002, p. 235. Quoted in Sawicki 2015, p. 26 n. 56.
3 Brassaï and Kahnweiler 1949, n.p.
Chronology:
1 Quoted in Cousins 1989, p. 403. For a full transcription of Braque's letter, see Monod-Fontaine 1984b, pp. 26–27.
2 *Head of a Woman* of 1909 was the only sculpture reproduced among a number of Picasso's other works. Cousins 1989, pp. 403, 407, and 443 n. 159. For the entire article about Picasso, see *Camera Work* 1912, pp. 29–44.
3 *Camera Work* 1912, p. 29.
4 Quoted in Cousins 1989, p. 403.
5 Rainey, Poggi, and Wittman 2009, p. 537.
6 Boccioni 2009, p. 118.
7 Quoted in Cousins 1989, p. 407.
8 For a study of *Guitar* and a summary of past scholars who have placed the making of the work in the fall of 1912, see Hartzell 2014a, esp. p. 3.2 n. 1.
9 On dating these photographs, see ibid., pp. 3.4–3.5.
10 The slanted tabletop, which had been added to an earlier version of *Guitar* some time before November 1913, was cut from a cardboard box. See Scott Gerson's technical analysis of *Guitar* in Gerson 2014a, pp. 3.23–3.27.
11 For the arrangement's components, see Umland 2011, p. 18. Christine Poggi suggests that this wooden molding might have been corrugated cardboard. See Poggi 2012, p. 283.
12 For an account of the acquisition of the cardboard *Guitar*, see Hartzell 2014a, pp. 3.28–3.31 nn. 1–2.
13 For a facsimile of the letter formalizing the agreement between Picasso and Kahnweiler, see Daix and Rosselet 1979, p. 359. For a full transcription in the original French, see Geelhaar 1993, p. 27.
14 Isabelle Monod-Fontaine first remarked on the emphasis given to sculpture in Picasso's contract with Kahnweiler and the lack of this category in the dealer's November 30, [1912], contract with Braque, even though the latter was experimenting with paper sculpture. Monod-Fontaine 1982, p. 42.
15 Apollinaire 1913, p. 272. Trans. in Hartzell 2011, p. 98.
16 The catalogue checklist, which lists Umberto Boccioni's sculptures only by title, is headed "ensembles plastiques." As in his 1912 manifesto, Boccioni signed the catalogue preface "Umberto Boccioni, peintre et sculpteur futuriste." Boccioni 1913, pp. 27, 9.
17 Boccioni may have seen Picasso's sculpture at Ambroise Vollard's gallery during visits to Paris in 1911 and 1912.
18 Only three of Boccioni's eleven sculptures shown in Paris in 1913 still exist today. *Fusion of a Head and a Window* and *Head + House + Light* were probably destroyed in 1916, after a posthumous exhibition held in honor of the artist in Milan that winter. The description of the materials used is based on photographs of the installation in Paris taken by Lucette Korsoff and on notes later inscribed by the artist on some of Korsoff's images. For reproductions of these photographs, see Ginex 2004, esp. pp. 74–76.
19 For Apollinaire's review, see n. 51 in chap. 2.
20 Cited in Coen 1988, p. 255.
21 In 1942, Christian Zervos titled this work *Mandolin*. The sculpture appeared as *Musical Instrument* in the 1966 *Hommage à Pablo Picasso* exhibition catalogue, a title that Werner Spies adopted in his 1971 catalogue raisonné. The current title may originate from Pierre Daix and Jean Rosselet's 1979 catalogue raisonné of Picasso's Cubist work. See Z II (2) 853; Petit Palais 1966, no. 223; Spies 1971, p. 302; and Daix and Rosselet 1979, p. 311. Lewis Kachur established that the "clarinet" is, in fact, a Catalan woodwind called a *tenora*. Kachur 1993, pp. 252–60.
22 Monod-Fontaine 1984a, p. 119.
23 The construction has been dated to 1914 by Zervos and tentatively to the fall of 1913 by Daix and Rosselet, and Spies. Pepe Karmel places the sculpture in spring 1914. Elizabeth Cowling dates *Mandolin and Clarinet* to 1913–14 but speculates that Picasso could have produced it as late as 1915, when he made other Cubist wood and sheet metal constructions depicting musical instruments. See Z II (2) 853; Daix and Rosselet 1979, p. 311; Spies and Piot 1983 rev, p. 374; Karmel 1993, pp. 431–32; and Cowling 2002, pp. 261 and 657 n. 125. In her technical study of the 1914 *Still Life* construction (pl. 15), Jackie Heuman has established that various materials found in *Mandolin and Clarinet* and the [fall] 1915 *Violin and Bottle on a Table* construction (pl. 27) correspond to elements incorporated in the spring 1914 *Still Life* and thus

might have originated from the same pieces of wood. She concludes, "Picasso either retained these pieces of wood from one year to the next or . . . he worked on several constructions at the same time." See Heuman 2008, esp. p. 753.

24 One example is a photograph of an early variant of *Guitar and Bottle of Bass* of 1913 (SP 33a) taken at Picasso's studio by Émile Delétang for Kahnweiler (The Metropolitan Museum of Art, New York). See Hartzell 2014a, p. 3.6, fig. 12.

25 Salto 1917, n.p. Trans. in McCully 1982, p. 126.

26 SP 56 (DR 631).

27 The four Cubist constructions were SP 33a (DR 630), SP 34 (DR 629a), SP 48 (DR 633), and SP 56 (DR 631). The painting was DR 457.

28 Hartzell 2014a, esp. p. 3.19 n. 34.

29 Ibid., pp. 3.18–3.19 n. 32.

30 Kahnweiler, letter to Kramář, cited in Sadílková and Hubatová-Vacková 2002, p. 235. Quoted in Sawicki 2015, p. 26 n. 56.

31 Breton 1961, p. 155. Trans. and quoted in McCully 1982, p. 243.

32 The exhibition catalogue *Ostern 1919* (Easter 1919) states that Alfred Flechtheim's Düsseldorf gallery opened on Christmas 1913. Galerie Flechtheim 1919.

33 Galerie Flechtheim 1913, p. 135.

34 For the dating of this sculpture, see Hartzell 2014b, esp. pp. 15.3–15.4.

35 For the making of *Guitar* and a review of the literature on the object to date, see ibid., pp. 15.2–15.5; Gerson 2014b, pp. 15.10–15.11; and Poggi 2012, pp. 281–82.

36 Oxidation has darkened the ferrous sheet metal over time. Gerson 2014b, p. 15.10.

37 For the dating of André Salmon's manuscript of this chapter, see Hartzell 2014b, pp. 15.7–15.8 n. 9.

38 Salmon 1919, pp. 102–104. Trans. and quoted in Hartzell 2014b, p. 15.13. For an annotated translation of Salmon's book, see Gersh-Nešic 2005, pp. 93–152.

39 Kramer 1971, p. 1. More than one hundred related press clippings from February–June 1971 are preserved in The Museum of Modern Art Archives, New York. Hartzell 2014b, p. 15.15.

40 For William Rubin's personal account of the gift, see Rubin 2012, pp. 90–95. For archival materials relevant to the events that took place between 1967 and 1971, see Umland 2011, pp. 29–30, and Hartzell 2014b, pp. 15.13–15.15.

41 Kurchanova 2013, p. 299. As Natasha Kurchanova points out, the variation in dates may be due to the two-week difference between the Julian and the Gregorian calendars. (Russia adopted the Gregorian calendar in February 1918.) Scholars differ on the dates of Tatlin's visit but agree that it must have occured sometime between March and mid-April 1914. See Strigalev and Harten 1993, p. 386; Gough 1999, p. 43; Dorontchenkov 2009, p. 316; and Hartzell 2011, p. 99.

42 Komardenkov 1973, p. 56. Cited in Bowlt 1988, p. 36.

43 Gough 1999, esp. pp. 43–45.

44 From December 6, 1914, to 1915, *Painterly Relief ("Bottle")* was presented as part of the charity exhibition *The Painters of Moscow to the Victims of War*, organized by the Moscow Province District Council Committee for Assistance to the Wounded and the Central Bureau at the Municipal Administration and held at Lianozov's House at Kamergerskii Lane, 3. See index of exhibitions in Strigalev and Harten 1993, p. 400. The authors thank Maria Marchenkova for translating this information from the Russian.

45 For an analysis of the techniques and materials Picasso used to make this sculpture, see Heuman 2008, pp. 749–54; later published online in *Tate Papers*, no. 11 (April 1, 2009), http://www.tate.org.uk/download/file/fid/7282.

46 Heuman 2008, p. 752.

47 *Glass, Newspaper, and Bottle* shows a lot of underpainting, which implies that Picasso reworked it a number of times. It is not known whether this canvas preceded the sculpture, but *Still Life* shows a similar degree of reworking, which might suggest that he considered the two works alongside each other. For the painting's formal relationship to *Still Life*, see Heuman 2008, esp. pp. 753–54; Daix and Rosselet 1979, p. 341; and Cowling, Golding, and Ruiz-Picasso 1994, p. 261.

48 The authors thank Elizabeth Cowling for drawing their attention to this correlation.

49 Probably in the spring of 1913 he had given Gertrude Stein his *Guitarist with Sheet Music* (present location unknown; SP 31, DR 582). Another small work, titled *Dice to Play*, c. 1917–21 (formerly in the collection of Jean Cocteau but not documented in the catalogue raisonné of Picasso's sculptures), also left his studio early on. The authors thank Widmaier Picasso for sharing information on these constructions that left Picasso's studio.

50 Monroe Wheeler was Director of Exhibitions and Publications at The Museum of Modern Art. Penrose, letter to Wheeler, September 28, 1966, Registrar Files, Exhibition 841, The Museum of Modern Art Archives, New York.

51 London Gallery 1947, no. 31, p. 27.

52 Cowling and Pullen 1994.

53 Z II (2) 848, 849, and 852.

54 Spies and Piot 2000, p. 88.

55 MoMA conservator Lynda Zycherman presented a historical and technical analysis of Picasso's *Glass of Absinthe* casts during the first study session of the Museum Research Consortium at The Museum of Modern Art, February 6, 2015.

56 In conversation, Kahnweiler told Spies that the bronzes had been produced by Godard using a sand-casting process. Spies and Piot 1983 rev, p. 71. The authors thank Widmaier Picasso for sharing information on this series of sculptures.

57 The "H" stands for Henry, which Kahnweiler commonly used to sign his correspondence. The numbers I–V are cast in bronze relief, but the "0" is incised, and may have been added at a later date.

58 The alloy composition of the "0" cast slightly varies from that of the three other casts that have been examined to date at The Museum of Modern Art by Zycherman and conservation scientists Ana Martins and Chris McGlinchey, using X-ray fluorescence (XRF) spectrometry.

59 Kahnweiler, cited in Sadílková and Hubatová-Vacková 2002, pp. 236–37. This and another letter, dated July 18, 1914, believed to have included images of the *Glass of Absinthe* casts, are preserved in the archives of the Národní Galerie in Prague.

60 Kahnweiler, quoted in Sadílková and Hubatová-Vacková 2002, p. 237.

61 According to annotations on one of the photographs, Kramář was especially interested in the cast now in the Leonard A. Lauder Cubist Trust (pl. 24). Kahnweiler, cited in ibid.

62 It illustrated the cast that now belongs to the Museum Berggruen, Berlin (pl. 26).

63 Zervos 1928.

64 The exhibition ran from November 23 to around December 24, 1929. Galerie Flechtheim 1929, p. 22. The authors thank Widmaier Picasso for sharing information on this exhibition.

65 Daix and Rosselet 1979, p. 333.

66 For the date of the Kahnweiler sequestration, see Jozefacka and Mahler 2014.

67 That was the only sale to include sculpture. Kahnweiler was not ordinarily a sculpture dealer, and aside from *Glass of Absinthe* he had editioned only the work of the Spanish sculptor Manolo. For Kahnweiler's pricing of the painted bronzes, see Kahnweiler, cited in Sadílková and Hubatová-Vacková 2002, p. 237. In the auction catalogue, the *Glass of Absinthe* casts are listed as lot 139, a group of five bronzes; each was sold individually for 55 to 100 French francs, according to an annotated copy. Hôtel Drouot 1921, p. 27.

68 Cowling and Pullen 1994.

69 Level 1928, p. 57.

70 Widmaier Picasso's research confirms this exhibition as the sculpture's first.

71 André Breton's press release was published in *La Semaine de Paris*, May 22–28, 1936. Quoted in Beaumelle, Monod-Fontaine, and Schweisguth 1991, p. 229.

CHAPTER 4
AROUND "THE MONUMENT TO APOLLINAIRE"
1927–1931

Introduction:

1 Brassaï and Kahnweiler 1949, n.p.

Chronology:

1 Sketchbook no. 011, September 11–24, 1927, sheet 4 recto. Musée national Picasso–Paris. Léal 1996, vol. 2, p. 93.

2 Cited and trans. in Read 2008, p. 140. The two authoritative sources on this subject are ibid. and FitzGerald 1987.

3 Read 2008, p. 141.

4 Cited and trans. in Read 2008, p. 151.

5 Ibid. The letter was signed by Serge Férat and André Salmon, members of the Apollinaire monument committee.

6 For the article in *Cahiers d'Art*, see Zervos 1927. See also Stepan 2006, pp. 43 and 118.

7 Paul Léautaud in *Journal littéraire,* December 14, 1927. Cited and trans. in Read 2008, p. 160.

8 For example, Level 1928, pls. 58–59. For *Les Sculptures de Picasso,* see Brassaï and Kahnweiler 1949, n.p.

9 Léal 1996, vol. 2, pp. 96–105.

10 Julio González, letter to Picasso, May 13, 1928. Cited and trans. in McCully 1994, p. 215.

11 See Spies 1995. Paris sketchbook, p. 37 ff.

12 Zervos 1928, p. 280.

13 SP 56 (DR 631).

14 Cowling 2002, p. 510.

15 Spies and Piot 2000, p. 133.

16 Widmaier Picasso 2003, pp. 15 and 17. It was long thought that three variants existed, but Diana Widmaier Picasso posits that the confusion arose because at some point after the work was reproduced in *Cahiers d'Art* in 1929, the artist repainted the version he retained, making the back leg and half of the ring white.
17 The fourth work is now in a private collection.
18 Brassaï and Kahnweiler 1949, n.p.
19 Ibid.
20 Werner Spies states that, in conversation, Picasso invoked *Le Poète assassiné* as a source for his proposals. Spies and Piot 2000, p. 117. For an English edition, see Apollinaire 2000.
21 Apollinaire 2000, p. 151.
22 Ibid.
23 Ibid., p. 152.
24 Spies 1995. Dinard sketchbook 54.
25 Tériade 1928, p. 6. Cited and trans. in Read 2008, p. 176.
26 Zervos 1929a, pp. 6 and 11.
27 Ibid., p. 11.
28 Zervos 1929b, p. 342.
29 Ibid.
30 Ibid.
31 Bach, Rowell, and Temkin 1995, p. 383.
32 Picasso, quoted in Brassaï 1999, p. 95.
33 Mme González recalled this fact in a 1967 interview with Josephine Withers. Withers 1978, p. 25.
34 Zervos 1932c, pp. 2–3. Cited and trans. in Read 2008, p. 191.
35 Rubin 1984, p. 322.
36 See for example *The Studio*, winter 1927–28, in the collection of The Museum of Modern Art, New York.
37 Brassaï 1999, p. 17.
38 Salmon, letter to Picasso, November 15, 1930. Quoted in Read 1994, p. 206.
39 See Ors 1930. Goeppert, Goeppert-Frank, and Cramer 1983, p. 52.
40 Ors 1930, pl. 48.
41 Zervos 1929a, pp. 5–6. Trans. by Marion Tande. Elizabeth Cowling cites this remark to argue for an earlier date for this group of figures in Cowling, Golding, and Ruiz-Picasso 1994, p. 262.
42 González, letter to Picasso, April 2, 1931. Quoted and trans. in McCully 1994, p. 217.
43 Breton 1933, p. 16.
44 González 1931–32, p. 135; original French on p. 142. The manuscript for "Picasso et les cathédrales" is in the Valencia/Julio González Archives, Paris. Although the essay was not published in full during González's lifetime, it was modified and excerpted as "Picasso sculpteur" in González 1936.
45 Ibid.
46 See Read 2008, pp. 201–2.

CHAPTER 5 THE BOISGELOUP SCULPTURE STUDIO 1930–1937

Chronology:
1 Richardson 2007, esp. pp. 414–15.
2 Brassaï 1999, p. 16.
3 Zervos 1930, p. 275. Quoted in Baldassari et al. 2002, p. 375.
4 See esp. Bois 1998, p. 67, and Baldassari et al. 2002, pp. 265–71.
5 These works are SP 86–95 and SP 98–103. In Spies and Piot 2000, it states in the main text that the works were produced late in summer 1930, but they are given the date of fall 1930 in the catalogue section of the book (pp. 157 and 398). The "summer" date adopted here corresponds to Cowling 2002, p. 514.
6 Cowling 2002, pp. 514–15.
7 The reproductions of Etruscan bronzes in *Documents* 2, no. 4 (1930) are suggested in Spies and Piot 2000, p. 157.
8 González 2007, pp. 129–30. For the original publication, see González 1936.
9 The work is SP 107. According to John Richardson the first preparatory drawings for the sculpture date to November 8, 1930. Richardson 2007, p. 552 n. 32.
10 The fragility of the sculpture's structure required it to be supported in many places in order not to teeter under its own weight. The plaster broke at some point and, unlike other sculptures Picasso made at Boisgeloup, it was never cast in bronze or restored by the artist. Picasso apparently did want to restore the statue; he said to Werner Spies, "When I am gone, no one will be able to put it back together." Spies and Piot 2000, p. 167. The authors thank Diana Widmaier Picasso, who confirmed that the sculpture is today in a private collection in a broken state.
11 These two and subsequent letters are transcribed and trans. in McCully 1994, p. 216.
12 Ibid., p. 216.
13 These casts are SP 86-II and SP 97-II.
14 See Brassaï and Kahnweiler 1949.
15 Brassaï 1999, p. 99.
16 Richardson 2014, pp. 161–69.
17 Sketchbook 068, sheet 81, 1931. Private collection.
18 Cowling 2008, p. 33.
19 Cowling and Pullen 1994.
20 Richardson 2007, pp. 452, 553 n. 56.
21 Doña Maria, letter to Picasso, June 7, 1931. Picasso Archives, Musée national Picasso–Paris. Quoted in Widmaier Picasso 2004, p. 30.
22 The other is SP 129-I.
23 Cowling and Pullen 1994.
24 The bronzes editioned by Hébrard became state property in 1931, when they were acquired through the generosity of the artist's heirs and Hébrard. The authors thank Daranyi Sylphide of the Musée de l'Orangerie for sharing this information. For Picasso's visit to the exhibition, see Kendall 2010, esp. pp. 151–53.
25 See MP1051–1059 in Besnard-Bernadac, Richet, and Seckel 1987, pp. 301–03.
26 Picasso, quoted in Spies and Piot 2000, p. 174.
27 Ibid.
28 Brassaï remarked on the importance of plaster to the effect of the Boisgeloup heads. See Brassaï 1999, p. 59.
29 Brassaï remarked, "In addition to the large heads, there were a thousand other things, in particular, a magnificent rooster, its head cocked toward the bristling plume of its tail." Brassaï 1999, p. 17.
30 See Cowling, Golding, and Ruiz-Picasso 1994, p. 271, and Spies and Piot 2000, p. 400.
31 Letter, Alberto Giacometti to his family, May 6, 1932. Trans. Talia Kwartler. Alberto Giacometti-Siftung, Zurich. The authors thank Serena Bucalo of the Fondation Giacometti in Paris for this information.
32 Brassaï 1999, pp. 3–4.
33 Blanche 1932, p. 333.
34 Ibid., p. 334.
35 Weiss 2008, pp. 118–33.
36 See Geiser 1933.
37 Breton 1933, p. 17.
38 Brassaï and Kahnweiler 1949, no. 72.
39 Picasso described his technique to his dealer Daniel-Henry Kahnweiler in a conversation of October 2, 1933. A transcript of the conversation, as reported by Kahnweiler, is published in Kahnweiler 1952. Quoted in Ashton 1972, p. 115.
40 Brassaï 1999, p. 185.
41 Picasso, quoted in ibid., p. 187.
42 Kahnweiler 1952, p. 22. Quoted in Ashton 1972, p. 115.
43 Lyon, taxidermist, card to Picasso, January 28, 1933. Trans. by Sharon Bowman. Picasso Archives, Musée national Picasso–Paris.
44 Brassaï 1999, p. 100.
45 Breton 1933.
46 Ibid., p. 10. Trans. in Breton 1999, p. 112.
47 Breton 1933, p. 20. Trans. in Breton 1999, p. 120.
48 Giménez Martín 2012, p. 33.
49 For example, see Blanton Freedberg 1986, p. 331.
50 See Olivier 1965.
51 The authors thank Lynda Zycherman, Sculpture Conservator, and Sam Sackeroff, Museum Research Consortium Fellow, The Museum of Modern Art, New York, for a discussion of Picasso's use and casting of found materials during an examination of the plaster in MoMA's Conservation Laboratory, November 24, 2014.
52 Nash 1995, p. 30. See also Cowling, Golding, and Ruiz-Picasso 1994, pp. 273–74.
53 Although *The Reaper* has traditionally been dated to 1943, Widmaier Picasso has shown that Picasso created the sculpture at Boisgeloup. Widmaier Picasso 2004, p. 31. She also pointed out that the sculpture is dated 1934 in the catalogue of the 1953 exhibition *Picasso: Exposition organisée sous l'égide du Syndicat d'Initiative de Lyon*, in which it is no. 155.
54 Spies and Piot 2000, p. 207.
55 Jacqueline Picasso, quoted in Malraux 1976, p. 36.
56 The image of the sculpture without the scythe appears in Derouet 2011, p. 156. Derouet was the first to notice that it depicted an early version of *The Reaper*. Unlike many other photographs taken by Bernès, Marouteau et Cie in the winter of 1934, this image was not published in the 1935 issue of *Cahiers d'Art* devoted to Picasso. For the second photograph, see Widmaier Picasso 2004, p. 31, where it is dated to 1936.
57 Malraux 1976, p. 36.
58 Brassaï 1999, p. 106.
59 Malraux 1976, p. 45.
60 Ibid., p. 128
61 Brassai 1999, p. 61. In Brassai and Kahnweiler 1949, no. 168, the bronze is dated 1943.
62 *Cahiers d'Art* 10, nos. 7–10 (1935). Among the more than twenty-five sculptures reproduced in the photographs taken by Bernès, Marouteau et Cie were SP 75, *Composition with Glove* (1930; pl. 42); SP 78, *Object with Palm Leaf* (1930; pl. 43); SP 105, *Seated Woman* (1931); SP 114, *Bather with Outstretched Arms* (1931); SP 130, *Head of a Woman* (1931; pl. 54); SP 131, *Bust of a Woman* (1931; pl. 53); SP 132, *Head of a Woman* (1931); SP 134, *Cock* (1932);

SP 135, *Woman with Vase* (1933); SP 136, *Head of a Warrior* (1933–34; pl. 68); SP 152, *Bust of a Bearded Man* (1933); SP 153, *Woman Leaning on Her Elbow* (1933); and SP 157, *Woman with Leaves* (1934; pl. 74).
63 The inventory lists are preserved in Listes d'œuvres, Picasso Archives, Musée national Picasso–Paris.
64 For a reproduction of Breton's initial list, and the press announcement published in *La Semaine de Paris*, May 22–28, 1936, see Beaumelle, Monod-Fontaine, and Schweisguth 1991, pp. 229–31.
65 Reproductions in *Cahiers d'Art* confirm that SP 86-II, SP 94-II, SP 95-II, and SP 97 were present.
66 González 1936, p. 189. Trans. in González 2007, p. 130.
67 According to Brassaï, Picasso and Dora Maar met in fall 1935. Other accounts place their first meeting in 1936. Brassaï 1999, p. 51.
68 Blanton Freedberg 1986, pp. 316–17.
69 Bergamin 1937.

CHAPTER 6 THE WAR YEARS 1939–1945

Introduction:
1 Brassaï 1999, pp. 56–57.
Chronology:
1 Alfred H. Barr, Jr., letter to Picasso, September 12, 1939. Exhibition Files, The Museum of Modern Art Archives, New York.
2 Ibid. The "cubist head" is *Head of a Woman* (1909).
3 Daniel-Henry Kahnweiler, letter to Picasso, September 20, 1939. Trans. Sharon Bowman. Correspondence Kahnweiler, Picasso Archives, Musée national Picasso–Paris.
4 On July 25, 1937, shortly after the July 19 opening of the Nazis' *Entartete Kunst* (Degenerate art) exhibition in Munich, the *New York Times* reported on the event. See Nyson 1937. The article illustrates that Americans paid close attention to these developments, and there can be no question that Barr was aware of them.
5 "Final Paintings Arrive from Europe in Time for Big Picasso Exhibition at Museum of Modern Art," November 6, 1939. Press Release Archives, The Museum of Modern Art Archives, New York.
6 Barr, telegram to Picasso, December 15, 1939. Musées États-Unis 1925–1970, Pochette MoMA, Picasso Archives, Musée national Picasso–Paris.
7 Barr 1939, p. 6.
8 Brassaï 1999, p. 58.
9 Barr 1939, pp. 160–61.
10 F. Guastini, letter to Picasso, April 26, 1940. Trans. Sharon Bowman. Picasso Archives, Musée national Picasso–Paris. Very little information is known about Guastini's foundry. Elisabeth Lebon indicates that the founder "worked for Picasso, at least from March to November 1940. He seems to have picked up the sculptor's business, normally entrusted to Claude Valsuani, who had closed for the duration of the war." Lebon 2003, p. 179.
11 Guastini, letter to Picasso, May 9, 1940. Picasso Archives, Musée national Picasso–Paris. The works Guastini describes have yet to be identified.
12 Brassaï 1999, p. 60.
13 Dante Canestri, letter to Picasso, June 1, 1940. Listes d'œuvres, Fondeurs, Picasso Archives, Musée national Picasso–Paris. The letter refers to correspondence between the two in the preceding weeks.
14 Jaime Sabartés, letter to Kahnweiler, May 31, 1940. Trans. Sharon Bowman. Picasso Archives, Musée national Picasso–Paris.
15 Christian Zervos, letter to Picasso, June 10, 1940. Correspondence Christian Zervos, Picasso Archives, Musée national Picasso–Paris. See Derouet 2011, p. 161.
16 Ibid.
17 Zervos, letter to Picasso, July 24, 1940. Correspondence Christian Zervos, Picasso Archives, Musée national Picasso–Paris. See Derouet 2011, pp. 162–63.
18 Ibid.
19 Ibid.
20 Letter from Guastini, 41, rue Brancion, Paris, November 12, 1940, in an envelope addressed to Picasso, 23, rue La Boétie. Trans. Sharon Bowman. Listes d'œuvres, Fondeurs, Picasso Archives, Musée national Picasso–Paris.
21 Picasso, quoted in Brassaï 1999, p. 59.
22 Ibid., p. 60.
23 Malo 1941.
24 "On another small turntable is an all-white cat, its tail standing straight up in an exclamation point. Another bronze cat . . . has a swollen belly." Brassaï 1999, p. 60.
25 Cowling and Pullen 1994.
26 Malo 1941.
27 In the 1948 revised edition of Juan Merli's monograph on Picasso, *Death's Head* is also dated to 1941. See Merli 1948, p. 606, no. 689. The authors thank Diana Widmaier Picasso for pointing out this reference. The sculpture is not discussed or reproduced in the first edition of Merli's book, published in Buenos Aires in April 1942.
28 Gilot and Lake 1964, p. 17. The latter sculptures are SP 212–15.
29 Cowling and Pullen 1994.
30 Picasso, quoted in Brassaï 1999, p. 59.
31 Malo 1941.
32 Ibid. For the photograph, see Spies and Piot 2000, p. 232.
33 Brassaï 1999, p. 58.
34 Lord 1983, p. 16.
35 Zervos 1932b, p. 342. Quoted and trans. in Lord 1983, p. 16.
36 Lord 1983, p. 18.
37 Gilot and Lake 1964, p. 206.
38 Cocteau 1989, p. 53.
39 Penrose 1981, p. 345.
40 Picasso, quoted in Brassaï 1999, p. 61.
41 The authors thank Widmaier Picasso for discussing this subject.
42 See *Conquête* 1942. In an attempt to avoid Nazi censorship, subsequent issues of the journal were each given a different name.
43 Ibid.
44 Cocteau 1989, pp. 142 and 171. The authors thank Clare Finn for this source.
45 Cowling, Golding, and Ruiz-Picasso 1994, p. 274.
46 Picasso, quoted in Brassaï, 1999, p. 61.
47 See Merli 1942, n.p.
48 See Merli 1948, pp. 606–607, nos. 665–704. Nos. 691–704 are ceramics.
49 Cowling, Golding, and Ruiz-Picasso 1994, p. 274–75.
50 See SP 238-II. It is not known where the two casts were made. The head was cast once in 1943 and then three more times at the Godard foundry in Paris in 1950–51. Picasso painted one of these heads and mounted it on a wooden base (Musée national Picasso–Paris).
51 Brassaï 1999, p. 286.
52 Ibid., p. 276.
53 Ibid., p. 150.
54 Sixty-four are reproduced in Zervos's catalogue raisonné: Z XII 87–96, 115–41, 152, 220, 238–41, 291, 297–302, and 304–306. Dominique Forest notes two periods of intensity in the creation of these studies: Picasso made a first series of ten in July 1942 (Z XII 87–96) and another twenty-five in August 1942 (Z XII 115–37 and 140–41). Forest 1999, p. 22.
55 Picasso, quoted in Brassaï 1999, pp. 220–21.
56 Zervos 1945–46. The article included reproductions of fifty-two studies as well as four photographs of *Man with a Lamb* installed at Picasso's rue des Grands-Augustins studio in Paris.
57 See also Aragon 1950, p. 8, for a discussion of the sculpture and its related drawings.
58 Valsuani foundry, quote addressed to Jaime Sabartés for Picasso, November 26, 1949. A few days earlier, the Valsuani foundry had contacted the crate maker Maurice Desvaux regarding the production of a slatted crate measuring 100 × 95 × 220 cm ($39\frac{3}{8}$ in. × $37\frac{7}{16}$ in. × 7 ft. $2\frac{5}{8}$ in.) to transport the sculpture. Desvaux, quote for M. Valsuani, November 22, 1949. On November 3, 1950, Picasso received a quote from the Susse Frères foundry, stating a price of 600,000 French francs with the offer to reduce it to 500,000. See Listes d'œuvres, Fondeurs, Picasso Archives, Musée national Picasso–Paris.
59 "Délibération du conseil municipal," October 21 1949. Archives Municipales, Vallauris.
60 Brassaï 1999, p. 150.
61 See Hodin 1964, pp. 18–19.
62 Picasso, quoted in Brassaï 1999, p. 69. This work is SP 201 (probably destroyed).
63 Capa 1974, p. 95.
64 *Life* 1944, p. 73.
65 Salon d'Automne 1944, p. 6. Quoted in Utley 2000, p. 50.
66 *Head of a Woman* was cast by 1943; *Cock* was cast in 1937 or 1939. The notebook is preserved in the Picasso Archives, Musée national Picasso–Paris.
67 Salon d'Automne 1944, p. 61. In a review in the newspaper *Libération*, Arthur Merlin discussed the sculptures, and *Bull's Head* in particular. Merlin 1944. The article is preserved in Lit Tout, Picasso Archives, Musée national Picasso–Paris.
68 Utley 2000, pp. 49–51.

CHAPTER 7 VALLAURIS: CERAMICS AND ASSEMBLAGES 1945–1954

Introduction:
1 Brassaï 1999, p. 264.
Chronology:
1 See SP 303–16, SP 322–24, and SP 326–29. Two additional sculptures belonging in this series—SP 325 and 331—depict seated female figures.
2 Brassaï photographed bronze casts of SP 304 and 314 for the 1949 monograph *Les Sculptures de Picasso*.
3 Alberto Giacometti left Geneva for Paris on September 17, 1945. Lord 1985, pp. 217, 244, and 247.
4 Lord 1985, p. 251.

5 See Gilot and Lake 1964.
6 Barr 1946, pp. 280–84.
7 Brassaï 1999, p. 264.
8 Picasso, quoted in ibid.
9 Brassaï and Kahnweiler 1949, nos. 197–210, n.p.
10 Picasso, quoted in Brassaï 1999, p. 264.
11 For the 1937 engraved stones and fragments, see SP 171–77 and 180.
12 Picasso, quoted in Brassaï 1999, p. 265.
13 Ramié 1976, p. 12.
14 Ibid., p. 14.
15 Ruiz-Picasso 1994, p. 224.
16 Ramié 1976, pp. 100 and 118.
17 Gilot and Lake 1964, p. 184.
18 Ruiz-Picasso 1994, p. 224.
19 Ibid.
20 Jean Cocteau recorded this remark in his diary on February 25, 1953. Cocteau, quoted in Richardson 2010, p. 328.
21 Gilot and Lake 1964, p. 184.
22 Ruiz-Picasso 1994, p. 224.
23 Henri Matisse, letter to Pierre Matisse, April 29, 1948. Quoted in Baldassari et al. 2002, p. 386.
24 *Cahiers d'Art* 1948.
25 Ibid., pp. 74–85.
26 Richardson 2010, p. 352.
27 Roland Penrose, letter to Picasso, October 11, 1948. Transcribed in Cowling 2006, p. 58.
28 Gilot and Lake 1964, p. 218.
29 See Brassaï and Kahnweiler 1949. In the Picasso literature, the book is generally dated 1948, as stated on the title page. But the copyright page opposite specifies a publication date of January 1949.
30 In 1943, Les Éditions du Chêne published *Matisse: Seize peintures 1939–1943* and *Picasso: Seize peintures 1939–1943*.
31 For the most detailed account of the making of the book to date, see Brassaï 1999. Brassaï does not mention Maurice Girodias's name and hints that there had been difficulties along the way.
32 Brassaï 1999, p. 279.
33 Gilot and Lake 1964, p. 253.
34 Ibid., p. 254.
35 Ibid.
36 The authors thank Elizabeth Cowling for sharing information regarding Picasso's use of a palm frond. The material is described as plaster and wood in Spies and Piot 2000, p. 409.
37 This earlier work is SP 335.
38 Gilot and Lake 1964, p. 320.
39 A series of photographs taken by Claire Batigne indicates that Picasso's work on this sculpture had begun by May 1950. Cowling, Golding, and Ruiz-Picasso 1994, p. 276.
40 Gilot and Lake 1964, p. 320.
41 SP 350.
42 For a reproduction of Capa's photograph, see Müller 2002, p. 58
43 Gilot and Lake 1964, pp. 317–18.
44 Penrose, quoted in Cowling 2006, p. 78. For Lee Miller's photographs documenting the visit, see Cowling 2006, pp. 80–81.
45 Ibid.
46 Penrose 1981, p. 383.
47 Gilot and Lake 1964, p. 318.
48 Ibid., pp. 318–19.
49 For a reproduction of one of Quinn's photographs of the unfinished plaster assemblage of *Little Girl Jumping Rope*, see Spies and Piot 2000, p. 276.
50 For the dating of the casts of *Little Girl Jumping Rope*, see Cowling, Golding, and Ruiz-Picasso 1994, p. 279.
51 Spies and Piot 2000, pp. 266 and 277–78.
52 Penrose 1981, p. 382.
53 Gilot and Lake 1964, p. 318.
54 Ibid., pp. 317–18.
55 Picasso made this comment to his neighbor Robert Picault. Quoted in Cowling 1994, p. 236.
56 Verdet 1952.
57 Alfred H. Barr, Jr., note to The Museum of Modern Art, New York, sent from Venice probably in the summer of 1952. Exhibition Files, The Museum of Modern Art Archives, New York.
58 Gilot and Lake 1964, p. 313.
59 Penrose 1981, p. 372.
60 See Aragon 1950–51, pp. 5–10.
61 In the exhibition catalogue for the sculpture's first public presentation, for example, the sculpture was titled *Scimmia col piccolo (Guenon avec son petit)*. See Venturi 1953, pl. 160, n.p.
62 Gilot and Lake 1964, p. 171.
63 This idea was proposed by Rebecca Lowery during the second study session of the Museum Research Consortium at The Museum of Modern Art, May 14–15, 2015.
64 Gilot and Lake 1964, p. 319.
65 The cup and its handle, which Picasso repurposed for the animal's ears, are illustrated in a preparatory study for the sculpture reproduced in Spies and Piot 1983 rev, p. 250.
66 Gilot and Lake 1964, p. 338.
67 *Verve* 7, nos. 25–26 (Fall 1951).
68 Lord 1985, pp. 323–26.
69 Gilot and Lake 1964, p. 320.
70 Cowling, Golding, and Ruiz-Picasso 1994, p. 280.
71 See SP 211.
72 *Verve* 7, nos. 25–26 (Fall 1951), p. 34.
73 Robert Doisneau was reporting for *Le Point*. "Picasso," *Le Point* 42, special issue (October 1952). The review included texts by Maurice Raynal, Daniel-Henry Kahnweiler, Pierre Reverdy, and Tristan Tzara, among others.
74 Spies and Piot 2000, p. 266.
75 The white version of *Woman Reading* is SP 462-IIb and today belongs in a private collection. The authors thank Diana Widmaier Picasso for sharing her research on this particular cast.
76 R. Sturgis Ingersoll, letter to Anne d'Harnoncourt, September 3, 1968. Curatorial Files, Philadelphia Museum of Art Archives.
77 Cowling, Golding, and Ruiz-Picasso 1994, p. 282.
78 For an in-depth study of *The Woman with a Key*, see Cowling 2014, pp. 210–17.
79 Cowling posits that the cast was likely produced between mid-May and late June 1954. Cowling 2014, p. 212.

CHAPTER 8 WOOD ASSEMBLAGES, SHEET METAL SCULPTURES, AND PUBLIC MONUMENTS 1954–1973

Chronology:

1 Detlef Stein, "'Picasso Must Be Rejoicing Up in Heaven!' Interview with Sylvette David," in Grunenberg and Becker 2014, pp. 118–19.
2 See Widmaier Picasso 2014, pp. 160–75. This account is based on interviews with Tobias Jellinek.
3 Ibid., p. 173 n. 28. Only four such sculptures are catalogued in Spies and Piot 2000 (SP 488–91).
4 *Centaur* is SP 500–501.
5 O'Brian 1976, p. 428.
6 Daix 1993, p. 327.
7 Alfred H. Barr, Jr., letter to Picasso, March 31, 1956. Alfred H. Barr, Jr. Papers, The Museum of Modern Art Archives, New York.
8 These are *Goat Skull and Bottle* (pl. 123), *Head of a Woman* (SP 411-II), *Pregnant Woman* (SP 349-II), and *Baboon and Young* (pl. 116).
9 Barr, carbon copy of a letter to Picasso, January 30, 1957. Alfred H. Barr, Jr. Papers, The Museum of Modern Art Archives, New York.
10 Salles 1958, pp. 4–10. Cited and trans. in Leymarie 1971, p. 147.
11 See Conzen 2005, pp. 149–50.
12 Ibid., p. 147.
13 Daniel-Henry Kahnweiler, letter to Picasso on Saint-Hilaire letterhead, November 12, 1956. Daniel-Henry Kahnweiler Photographs, Picasso Archives, Musée national Picasso–Paris.
14 The issue was released in a run of 250, each including a lithograph by Picasso, distributed by lottery to the club's members. See Antoniou-Nesjar 2013 and Antoniou-Nesjar 2014, pp. 198–203.
15 Antoniou-Nesjar 2013.
16 For a list of these works, see Antoniou-Nesjar 2014, p. 203.
17 *Head of a Woman* of 1957 is SP 493.
18 See Fairweather 1982, pp. 37–39.
19 Widmaier Picasso 2014, p. 167. See, for example, *Head of a Woman* (SP 493; Musée national Picasso–Paris).
20 Pierre Matisse, letter to Picasso, September 30, 1957. Picasso Archives, Musée national Picasso–Paris. This letter was accompanied by two photographs of *Man with Folded Hands* in the park area of the Triennale.
21 This is SP 86-II. The sculpture was identified as *Standing Woman* and dated 1931 in the exhibition catalogue.
22 Barr 1957, p. 3.
23 *Life* 1957, p. 77.
24 *Yo, Picasso* is Z XXI 192.
25 Barr, carbon copy of letter to Picasso, December 17, 1957. Exhibition Files, The Museum of Modern Art Archives, New York.
26 James Johnson Sweeney's correspondence with Kahnweiler is preserved in the Picasso Archives, Musée national Picasso–Paris.
27 Along with two additional studies, four of these six study sheets are illustrated in Zervos 1967, nos. 84, 85, and 87–90.
28 SP 545.
29 The sketch, dated June 9–10, 1958, shows both *Head* and another sculpture, entitled *Man* (SP 544). It is described as a study for two wood sculptures in Zervos 1967, no. 252.
30 Godefroy and McCully 2010, p. 208.
31 Brassaï 1999, p. 107.
32 Berggruen 1998, pp. 93–95.
33 Ibid, p. 93.
34 For a reproduction of the original agreement, see ibid., p. 94.
35 Kahnweiler, letter to Picasso, July 8, 1959. Picasso Archives, Musée national Picasso–Paris.
36 Read 2008, pp. 231–43

37 For a transcription of Berggruen's second agreement with Picasso, dated January 31, 1960, see Berggruen 1998, p. 95.
38 The authors thank Diana Widmaier Picasso for sharing her research in the archives of the Valsuani foundry.
39 The authors thank Wolfgang Frei, Edward Quinn's nephew, for his expert assistance with Quinn's photographs of Picasso's sculptures.
40 Prejger 1994, p. 241.
41 Ibid., p. 242.
42 Lionel Prejger, letter to Picasso, March 8, 1961. Correspondance Lionel Prejger, Picasso Archives, Musée national Picasso–Paris. The "eagle" is *Sparrow Hawk* (SP 564), which he considered "the first piece that one can really call a sculpture that we made for Picasso." See Prejger 1994, p. 242.
43 Prejger, list sent to Picasso, May 23, 1961. Picasso Archives, Musée national Picasso–Paris.
44 Widmaier Picasso 2014, p. 169.
45 Prejger 1994, p. 243.
46 Prejger 1961, p. 32.
47 Ibid.
48 Prejger 1994, p. 243
49 Ibid., p. 242.
50 Prejger's list of May 23, 1961, is the only one to list a horse. Picasso Archives, Musée national Picasso–Paris.
51 For *Standing Woman*, see SP 580.
52 Brassaï 1999, p. 319.
53 Ibid., p. 354.
54 The small version of *Woman with Outstretched Arms* that Picasso selected for enlargement is SP 594.2a. The two metal enlargements are SP 596 and SP 597 (pl. 145).
55 Kahnweiler, letter to Picasso, June 21, 1961. Picasso Archives, Musée national Picasso–Paris.
56 According to a letter from Nesjar to Picasso, July 12, 1962, the sculpture arrived at Kahnweiler's the day before and work on the concrete enlargement would begin shortly. Picasso Archives, Musée national Picasso–Paris. The authors thank Althea Ruoppo for sharing information about the sculpture's exhibition history.
57 These are Z XIV 410, 411, 414–18, 420, and 422–31.
58 The authors thank Elizabeth Cowling for sharing her observations on this sculpture.
59 SP 626.
60 Richardson 1962, n.p.
61 William E. Hartmann, letter to Roland Penrose, April 2, 1963. Sir Roland Penrose Archives, National Galleries of Scotland.
62 Cowling 2006, pp. 250–55.
63 Ibid., pp. 258–67.
64 For more studies, see Rubin 1996, p. 474.
65 Rubin 1996, p. 475.
66 Cowling 2006, pp. 285–87.
67 Hartmann, telegram to Penrose, May 25, 1965. Sir Roland Penrose Archives, National Galleries of Scotland.
68 Fairweather 1982, p. 90.
69 SP 652.
70 Leymarie 1966, n.p.
71 For the news headline, see Canaday 1966.
72 For a roundtable discussion between Anthony Caro, Robert Rosenblum, and David Sylvester in a 1967 radio BBC broadcast, see *Modern Painters* 7, no. 1 (Spring 1994): 35–39.
73 For the remarks made by Richard J. Daley at the unveiling, see *Chicago Tribune* 1967.
74 Press release, October 11, 1967. Alfred H. Barr, Jr. Papers, The Museum of Modern Art Archives, New York.
75 Cleeman 2012.
76 Barr, letter to Kahnweiler, November 8, 1967. Department of Painting and Sculpture Curatorial Files, The Museum of Modern Art, New York.
77 A group of them would be shown, some for the first time, in an exhibition at the Grand Palais in fall 1979 entitled *Picasso: Œuvres reçues en paiement des droits de succession*. It was organized by Dominique Bozo, founding director of the Musée national Picasso–Paris.

PHOTOGRAPHS BY BRASSAÏ

COMPILED BY LUISE MAHLER

The following checklist documents the photographs by the Hungarian photographer Brassaï (born Gyula Halász, Transylvania, 1899; died France, 1984) included in the present exhibition. These images, made between 1932 and 1946, are presented in the order in which they were taken. Places and dates are based on information published along with Brassaï's work in *Minotaure* magazine in June 1933 and on his autobiographical account *Conversations avec Picasso* (*Conversations with Picasso*), which first appeared in 1964. Photographs that could not be dated to a specific day or month are listed last under a given year. The order of photographs taken on or around the same date is based on curatorial choice. Places and dates are enclosed in square brackets when they are not founded on primary documentation or where no consensus has been reached among scholars.

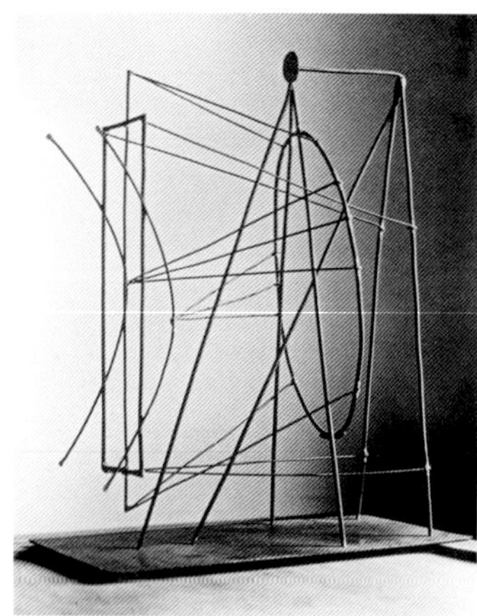

Figure (fall 1928). Paris, rue La Boétie, December 1932. Gelatin silver print, 11 3/8 × 9 in. (29 × 22.8 cm). Musée national Picasso–Paris. Purchase, 1996

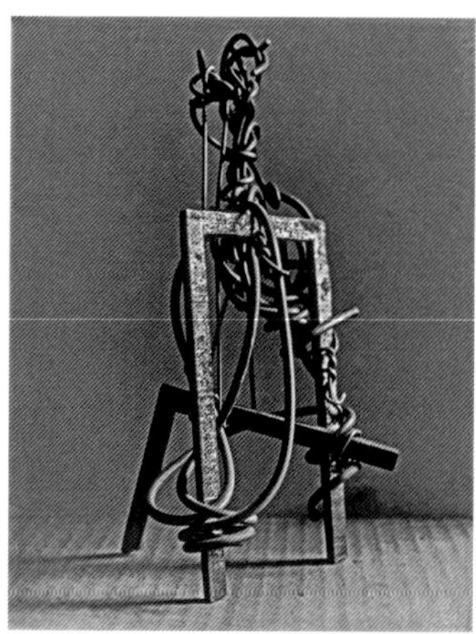

Figure ([1931]). Paris, rue La Boétie, December 1932. Gelatin silver print, 12 × 9 1/4 in. (30.5 × 23.5 cm). Musée national Picasso–Paris. Purchase, 1996

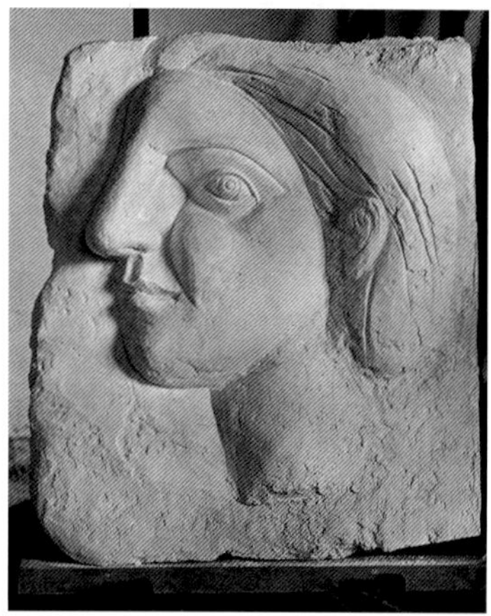

Head of a Woman (1931), plaster. Boisgeloup, December 1932. Gelatin silver print, 8 3/8 × 6 7/8 in. (21.3 × 17.5 cm). Musée national Picasso–Paris. Purchase, 1996

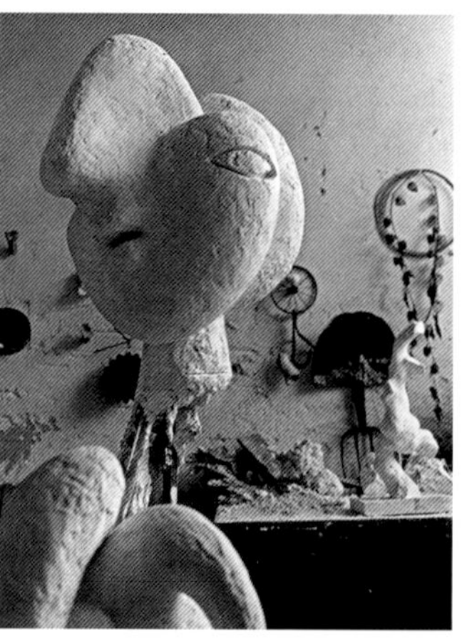

Head of a Woman (1931–32), plaster (unfinished). Boisgeloup, December 1932. Gelatin silver print, 9 5/16 × 7 1/16 in. (23.7 × 17.9 cm). Musée national Picasso–Paris. Purchase, 1996

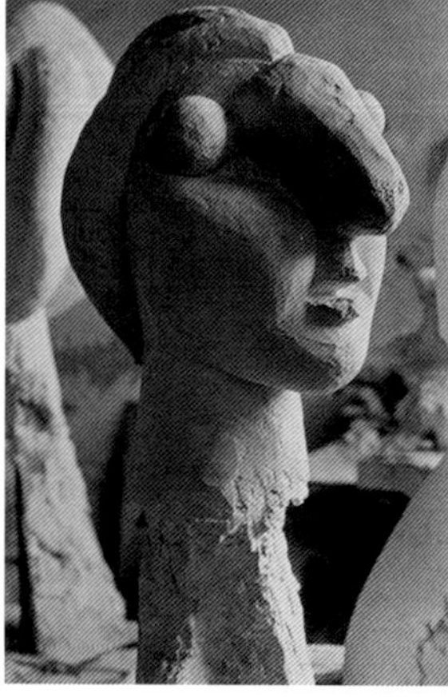

Head of a Woman (1931), plaster. Boisgeloup, December 1932. Gelatin silver print, 9 1/16 × 6 1/8 in. (23 × 15.5 cm). Musée national Picasso–Paris. Purchase, 1996

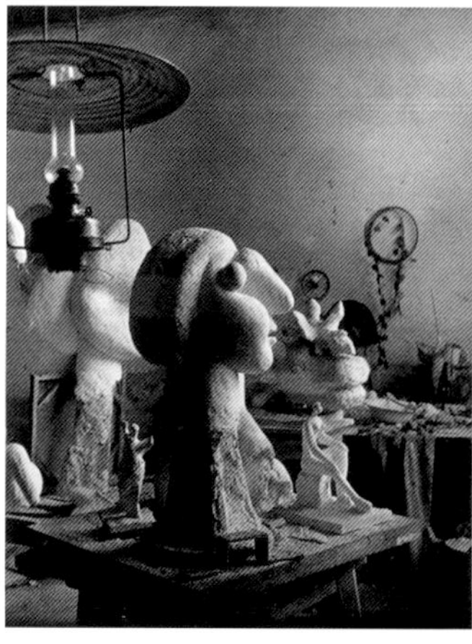

Head of a Woman (1931) and other plaster sculptures. Boisgeloup, December 1932. Gelatin silver print, 11 5/8 × 9 in. (29.5 × 22.8 cm). Musée national Picasso–Paris. Purchase, 1986

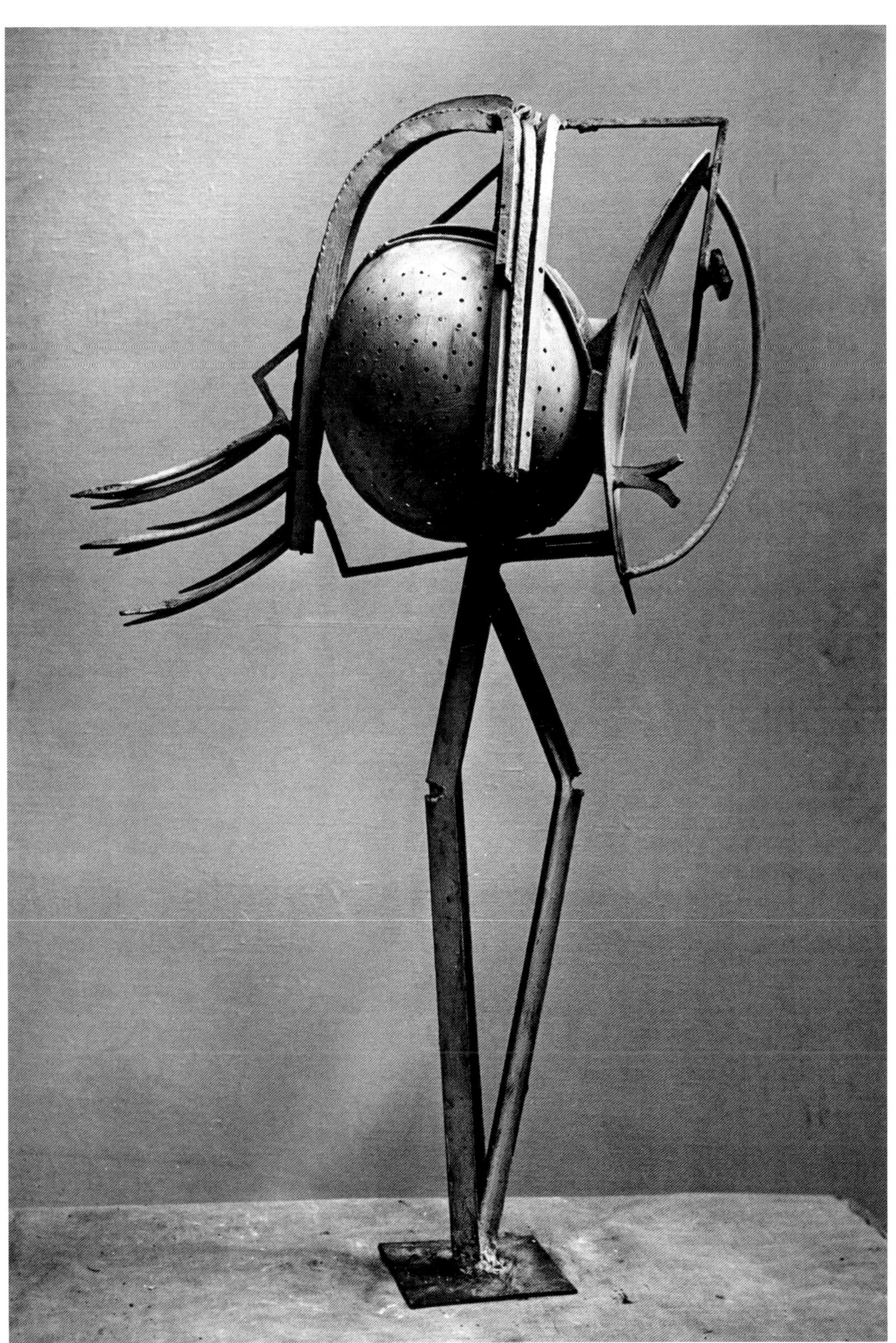

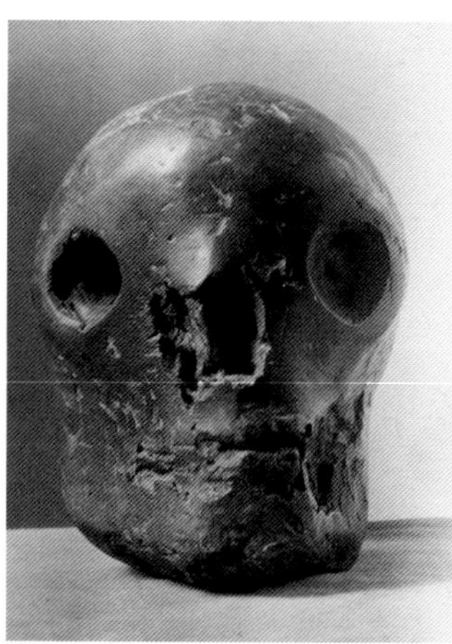

Death's Head ([1941]), bronze cast. Paris, rue des Grands-Augustins, late September 1943. Gelatin silver print, 11 3⁄16 × 8 3⁄4 in. (28.4 × 22.3 cm). Musée national Picasso–Paris. Purchase, 1996

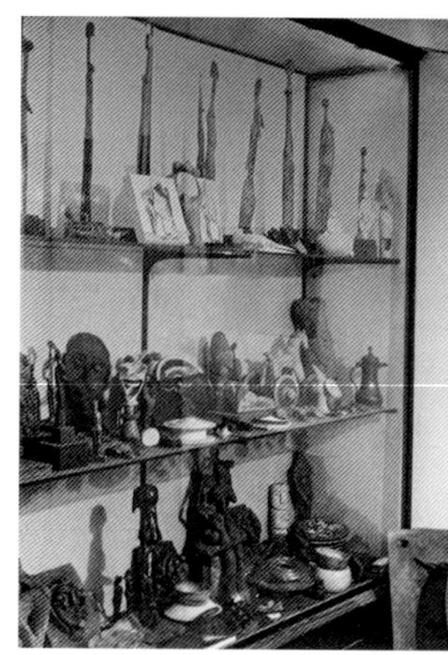

The vitrine in the artist's studio. Paris, rue des Grands-Augustins, on or after October 25, 1943. Gelatin silver print, 9 1⁄4 × 6 7⁄8 in. (23.5 × 17.5 cm). Musée national Picasso–Paris. Purchase, 1996

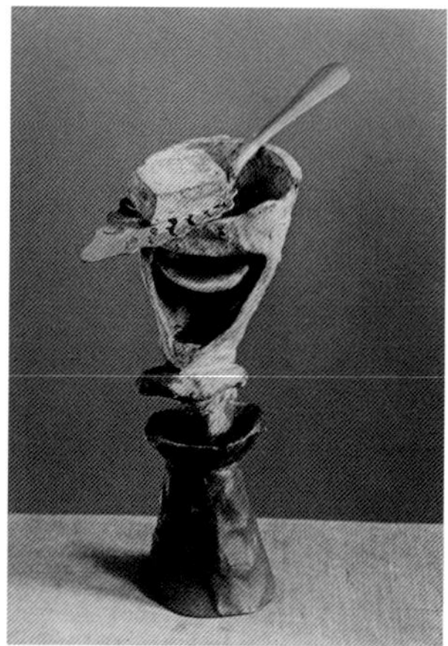

Glass of Absinthe (spring 1914). Paris, rue des Grands-Augustins, on or after October 25, 1943. Gelatin silver print, 9 5⁄16 × 6 1⁄2 in. (23.6 × 16.5 cm). Musée national Picasso–Paris. Purchase, 1996

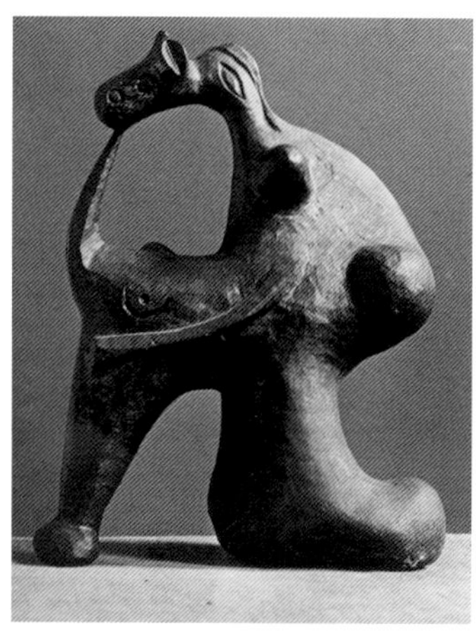

Metamorphosis II (1928), bronze cast. Paris, rue des Grands-Augustins, on or after October 25, 1943. Gelatin silver print, 11 5⁄8 × 9 in. (29.5 × 22.8 cm). Musée national Picasso–Paris. Purchase, 1996

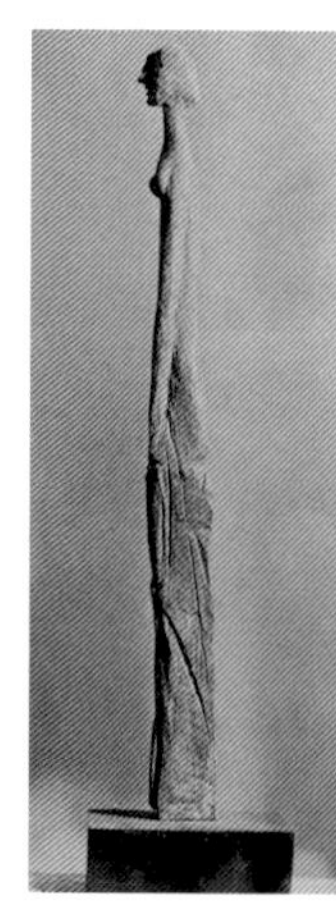

Seated Woman (summer 1930), bronze cast. Paris, rue des Grands-Augustins, on or after October 25, 1943. Gelatin silver print, 11 3⁄4 × 4 1⁄2 in. (29.8 × 11.5 cm). Musée national Picasso–Paris. Purchase, 1996

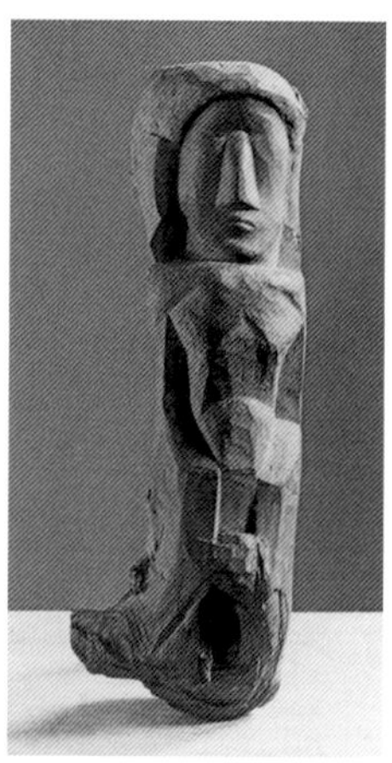

Figure (1907). Paris, rue des Grands-Augustins, during or after December 1943. Gelatin silver print, 11 13⁄16 × 6 3⁄16 in. (30 × 15.7 cm). Musée national Picasso–Paris. Purchase, 1996

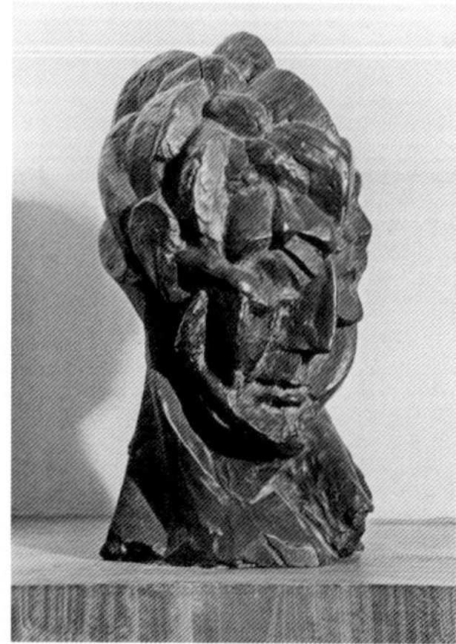

Head of a Woman (fall 1909), bronze cast. Paris, rue des Grands-Augustins, [1943]. Gelatin silver print, 11 1⁄8 × 8 in. (28.3 × 20.3 cm). Musée national Picasso–Paris. Purchase, 1996

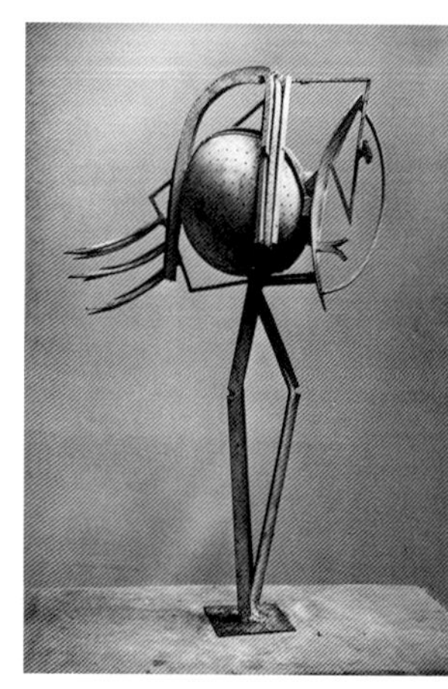

Head of a Woman (1929–30). Paris, [1943]. Gelatin silver print, 11 3⁄4 × 8 1⁄16 in. (29.8 × 20.5 cm). Musée national Picasso–Paris. Purchase, 1996

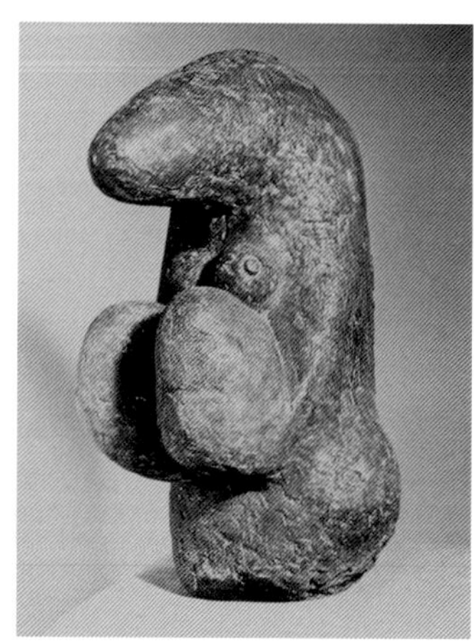

Bust of a Woman (1931), bronze cast. Paris, rue des Grands-Augustins, 1943. Gelatin silver print, 9 3⁄16 × 6 13⁄16 in. (23.3 × 17.3 cm). Musée national Picasso–Paris. Purchase, 1996

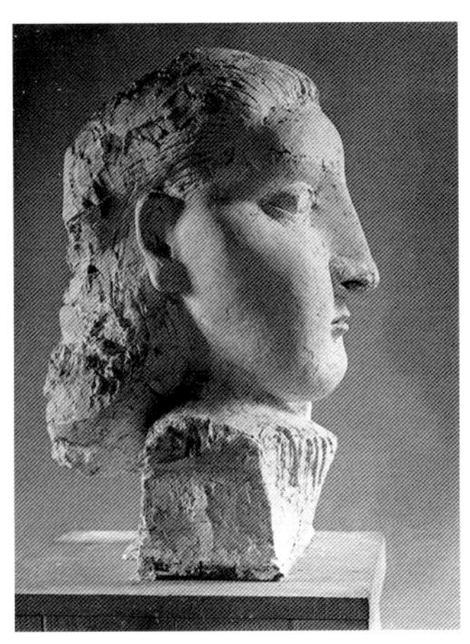

Head of a Woman (1941), plaster. Paris, rue des Grands-Augustins, 1943. Gelatin silver print, 11 ¾ × 8 ⅞ in. (29.8 × 22.5 cm). Musée national Picasso–Paris. Purchase, 1996

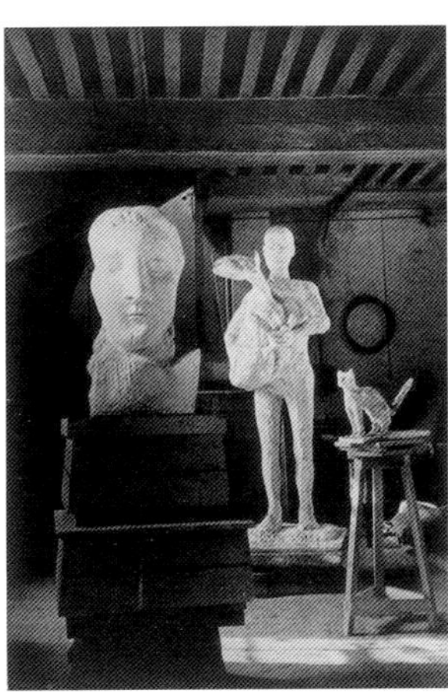

Head of a Woman (1941), *Man with a Lamb* (1943), and *Crouching Cat* (1943), plasters. Paris, rue des Grands-Augustins, 1943. Gelatin silver print, 11 ¹³⁄₁₆ × 8 ¹⁄₁₆ in. (30 × 20.5 cm). Musée national Picasso–Paris. Purchase, 1986

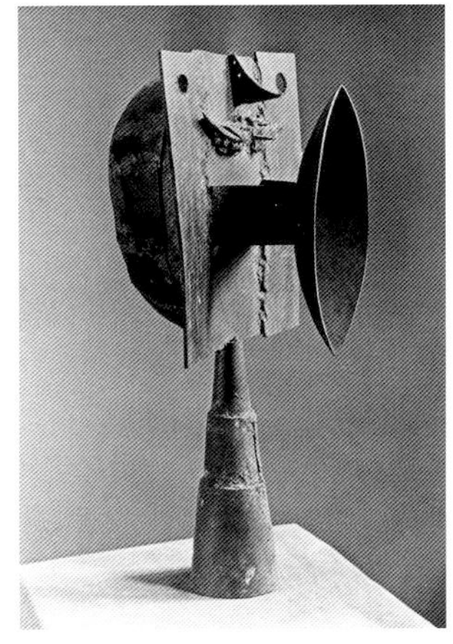

Head of a Man (1930). Paris, rue des Grands-Augustins studio annex, [on or after May 5, 1944]. Gelatin silver print, 11 ⅝ × 8 ¼ in. (29.6 × 21 cm). Musée national Picasso–Paris. Purchase, 1996

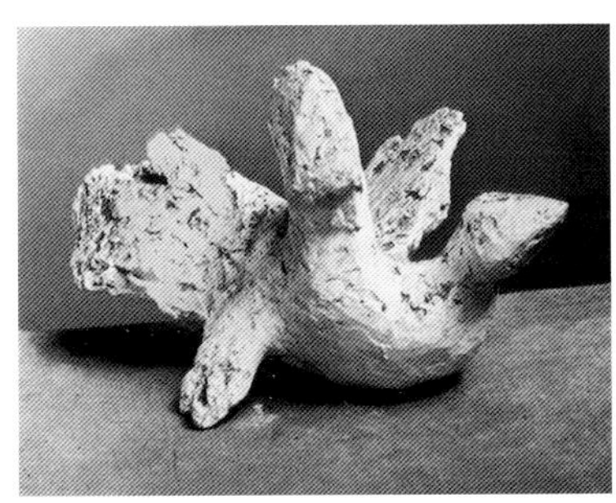

Bird (1931–32), plaster. [Paris, rue des Grands-Augustins studio annex, on or after May 5, 1944]. Gelatin silver print, 6 ¹⁵⁄₁₆ × 9 ⅛ in. (17.6 × 23.1 cm). Musée national Picasso–Paris. Purchase, 1996

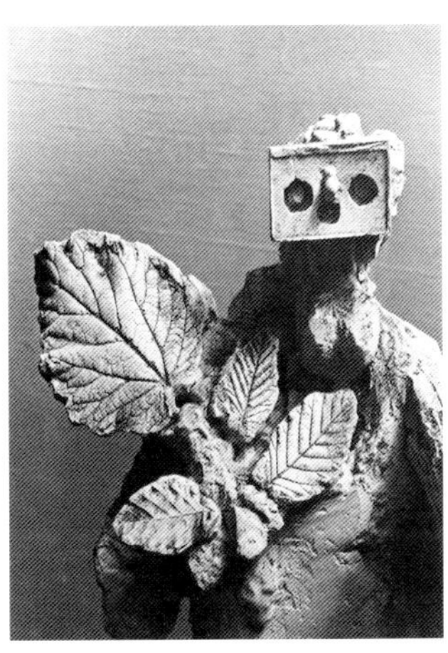

Woman with Leaves (1934), plaster (detail). [Paris, rue des Grands-Augustins studio annex, on or after May 5], 1944. Gelatin silver print, 10 ¹¹⁄₁₆ × 8 ¾ in. (27.2 × 22.2 cm). Musée national Picasso–Paris. Purchase, 1996

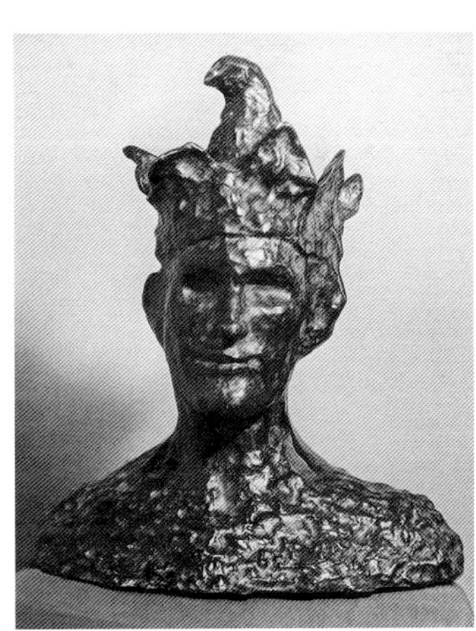

The Jester (1905), bronze cast. Paris, photographed at an unknown private collection, before May 12, 1945. Gelatin silver print, 11 ⅝ × 9 ³⁄₁₆ in. (29.5 × 23.3 cm). Musée national Picasso–Paris. Purchase, 1996

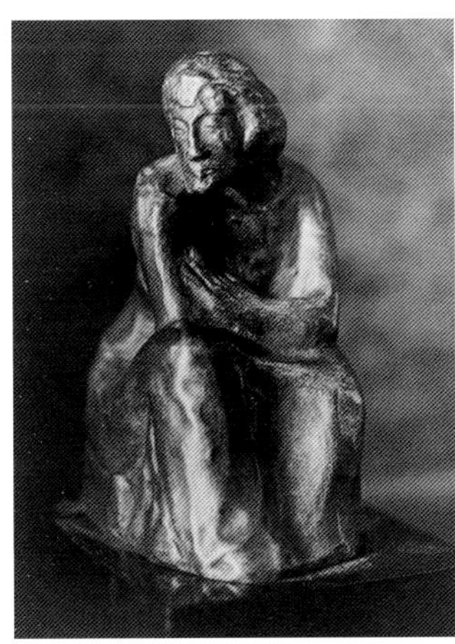

Seated Woman (1902), bronze cast. Paris, rue des Grands-Augustins, on or after May 12, 1945. Gelatin silver print, 11 ¹⁵⁄₁₆ × 8 ¹¹⁄₁₆ in. (30.3 × 22 cm). Musée national Picasso–Paris. Purchase, 1996

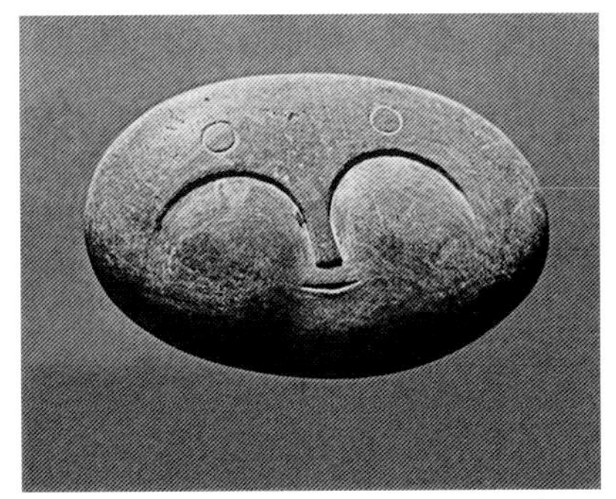

Face (1946). Paris, rue des Grands-Augustins, November 27, 1946. Gelatin silver print, 9 ⅛ × 11 ⁷⁄₁₆ in. (23.2 × 29 cm). Musée national Picasso–Paris. Purchase, 1996

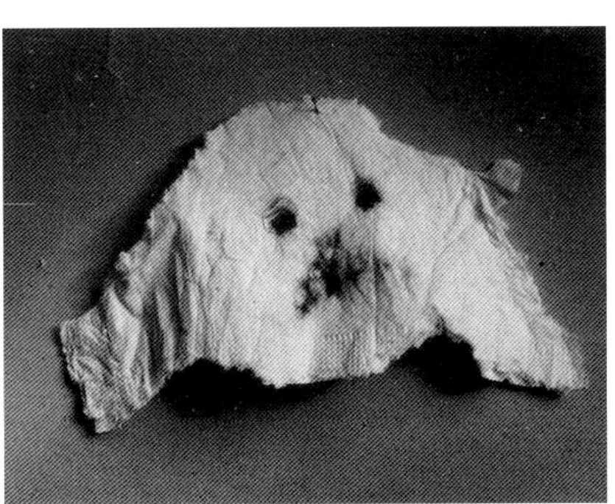

Head of a Dog (1943). Paris, rue de Savoie (studio of Dora Maar), November 28, 1946. Gelatin silver print, 7 ¹⁄₁₆ × 9 ¼ in. (18 × 23.5 cm). Musée national Picasso–Paris. Purchase, 1996

CHECKLIST OF THE EXHIBITION

COMPILED BY NANCY LIM AND LUISE MAHLER

The following checklist records the sculptures and works on paper shown in the exhibition *Picasso Sculpture*, held at The Museum of Modern Art, New York, September 14, 2015–February 7, 2016. The checklist's eight sections correspond to the chapters in this catalogue. The works in each section are organized chronologically by date of execution; the order of works made on or around the same date is based on curatorial choice. Titles are those provided by the current owners of the works. Where they differ from those documented in the first catalogue raisonné of Picasso's sculpture, compiled by Werner Spies and published during the artist's lifetime (Spies 1971), the catalogue raisonné titles are given in brackets.

Places and dates of execution are based on information from the lenders, the key references listed below, and primary documentation. Dates of execution are additionally based on Picasso's inscriptions on the works. Places and dates are enclosed in square brackets where no consensus has been reached among scholars. Materials, dimensions, and markings have been provided by the owners of the works, in some cases augmented by firsthand examination by curators and conservators. In dimensions, height precedes width precedes depth, unless otherwise noted.

Works catalogued in key references are identified by an abbreviation for the source and the number assigned to the work in that publication. These references are Z I–V (Zervos 1932–1952), BK (Brassaï and Kahnweiler 1949), DR (Daix and Rosselet 1979), S (Spies 1971), and SP (Spies and Piot 2000). The latter represents the most exhaustive list of Picasso's sculpture published to date. See References, p. 312, for full citations.

CHAPTER 1
BEGINNINGS
1902–1906

Seated Woman. Barcelona, 1902. Unfired clay, 5 11/16 × 3 3/8 × 4 1/2 in. (14.5 × 8.5 × 11.5 cm). Musée national Picasso–Paris. Dation Pablo Picasso, 1979. BK 1, S 1, SP 1-I. Plate 1

Head of a Picador with a Broken Nose. Barcelona, 1903. Bronze, cast by July 1925, approx. 7 11/16 × 5 11/16 × 4 1/2 in. (19.6 × 14.5 × 11.4 cm). Signed and dated in bronze at lower left: *Picasso / 04*. Marked in a different hand below: *1905*. Baltimore Museum of Art. The Cone Collection, formed by Dr. Claribel Cone and Miss Etta Cone of Baltimore, Maryland, 1950. S 3, SP 3-II. Plate 2

The Jester. Paris, 1905. Bronze, cast between 1910 and 1937 for Ambroise Vollard, 16 5/16 × 14 9/16 × 9 in. (41.5 × 37 × 22.8 cm). Incised on back at center of lower edge: *PICASSO*. Musée d'art moderne de la Ville de Paris. Gift of Ambroise Vollard, 1937. Z I 322, BK 2, S 4, SP 4. Plate 3

Head of a Woman (Fernande). Paris, 1906. Bronze, cast between 1910 and 1937 for Ambroise Vollard, 13 3/4 × 9 7/16 × 9 13/16 in. (35 × 24 × 25 cm). Incised on back at center of lower edge: *PICASSO*. Musée d'art moderne de la Ville de Paris. Gift of Ambroise Vollard, 1937. Z I 323, S 6, SP 6-II. Plate 4

Kneeling Woman Combing Her Hair [Woman Arranging Her Hair]. Paris, 1906. Bronze, cast between 1910 and 1939 for Ambroise Vollard, 16 5/8 × 10 3/16 × 12 1/2 in. (42.2 × 25.9 × 31.8 cm). Incised at bottom, center left: *Picasso*. Hirshhorn Museum and Sculpture Garden, Smithsonian Institution, Washington, D.C. Gift of Joseph H. Hirshhorn, 1972. Z I 329, S 7, SP 7-II. Plate 5

CHAPTER 2
WOOD CARVING AND THE FIRST CUBIST SCULPTURES
1907–1909

Doll. Paris, 1907. Wood, brass pins, and traces of oil paint and gesso, 9 1/4 × 2 3/16 × 2 3/16 in. (23.5 × 5.5 × 5.5 cm). Art Gallery of Ontario, Toronto. Purchase, 1980. S 21, SP 21-I. Plate 6

Figure. Paris, 1907. Boxwood with pencil and traces of paint on top of the head, 13 7/8 × 4 13/16 × 4 3/4 in. (35.2 × 12.2 × 12 cm). Musée national Picasso–Paris. Dation Pablo Picasso, 1979. Z II (2) 668, BK 4, S 15, SP 15. Plate 7

Head [Head of a Woman]. 1907. Beech, partially painted, 14 9/16 × 7 7/8 × 4 3/4 in. (37 × 20 × 12 cm). Musée national Picasso–Paris. Dation Jacqueline Picasso, 1990. Z II (2) 611, S 11, SP 11. Plate 9

Figure. Paris, 1908. Oak with painted accents, 31 11/16 × 9 7/16 × 8 3/16 in. (80.5 × 24 × 20.8 cm). Musée national Picasso–Paris. Dation Pablo Picasso, 1979. Z II (2) 608, BK 6, S 19, SP 19. Plate 8

Head of a Woman. Paris, fall 1909. Bronze, cast between 1910 and 1912 for Ambroise Vollard, 16 1/4 × 9 3/4 × 10 1/2 in. (41.3 × 24.7 × 26.6 cm). Signed at back of neck near bottom: *Picasso*. The Art Institute of Chicago. Alfred Stieglitz Collection, 1949. Z II (2) 573, BK 8, S 24, SP 24-II. Plate 11

Apple. Paris, fall–winter 1909. Plaster, 4 1/8 × 3 15/16 × 2 15/16 in. (10.5 × 10 × 7.5 cm). Musée national Picasso–Paris. Dation Pablo Picasso, 1979. Z II (2) 718–19, S 26, SP 26. Plate 10

CHAPTER 3
REINVENTING SCULPTURE: THE CUBIST YEARS
1912–1915

Still life with *Guitar*. Variant state. Paris, assembled before November 15, 1913. Subsequently preserved by the artist. Paperboard, paper, thread, string, twine, and coated wire installed with cut cardboard box, overall 30 × 20 1/2 × 7 3/4 in. (76.2 × 52.1 × 19.7 cm). The Museum of Modern Art, New York. Gift of the artist, 1973. Z II (2) 577, DR 633, SP 27A. Plate 13

Mandolin and Clarinet [Musical Instrument]. Paris, [fall 1913]. Painted fir with pencil, 22 13/16 × 14 3/16 × 9 1/16 in. (58 × 36 × 23 cm). Musée national Picasso–Paris. Dation Pablo Picasso, 1979. Z II (2) 853, DR 632, S 54, SP 54. Plate 12

Guitar. Paris, January–February 1914. Ferrous sheet metal and wire, 30 1/2 × 13 3/4 × 7 5/8 in. (77.5 × 35 × 19.3 cm). The Museum of Modern Art, New York. Gift of the artist, 1971. Z II (2) 773, DR 471, S 27, SP 27. Plate 14

Still Life. Paris, spring 1914. Painted pine and poplar, nails, and upholstery fringe, 10 × 18 × 3 5/8 in. (25.4 × 45.7 × 9.2 cm). Tate. Purchase, 1969. DR 746, S 47, SP 47. Plate 15

Bottle of Bass, Glass, and Newspaper. Paris, spring 1914. Painted tin plate, sand, iron wire, and paper, 7 7/8 × 5 1/2 × 3 3/8 in. (20 × 14 × 8.5 cm). Musée national Picasso–Paris. Dation Pablo Picasso, 1979. Z II (2) 849, DR 751, S 53, SP 53. Plate 16

Glass. Paris, spring 1914. Painted tin plate, nails, and wood, 5 1/2 × 7 7/8 × 3 15/16 in. (14 × 20 × 10 cm). Musée national Picasso–Paris. Dation Pablo Picasso, 1979. Z II (2) 848, DR 752, S 52, SP 52. Plate 17

Glass and Dice. Variant state. Paris, spring 1914. Painted wood, 9 1/4 × 8 5/8 × 1 7/8 in. (23.5 × 22 × 4.8 cm). Private collection. Z II (2) 840, DR 748, S 43, SP 43. Plate 18

Glass, Newspaper, and Dice. Paris, spring 1914. Painted fir and tin plate, iron wire, and oil on wood panel, 6 7/8 × 5 5/16 × 1 3/16 in. (17.4 × 13.5 × 3 cm). Musée national Picasso–Paris. Dation Pablo Picasso, 1979. Z II (2) 838, DR 749, S 42, SP 42. Plate 19

Glass of Absinthe. Paris, spring 1914. Bronze, painted in oil, and perforated white metal absinthe spoon, 1 of an edition of 6 bronzes cast 1914 for Daniel-Henry Kahnweiler, each uniquely treated, 8 1/4 × 5 1/2 × 2 3/4 in. (21 × 14 × 7 cm). Signed in raised bronze near the base: *P.* Incised inside the bottom cone: *0*. Private collection. Courtesy Fundación Almine y Bernard Ruiz-Picasso para el Arte. DR 754, BK 12, S 36, SP 36-b. Plate 21

Glass of Absinthe. Paris, spring 1914. Bronze, painted in oil, and perforated white metal absinthe spoon, 1 of an edition of 6 bronzes cast 1914 for Daniel-Henry Kahnweiler, each uniquely treated, 8 7/16 × 6 1/2 × 2 9/16 in. (21.5 × 16.5 × 6.5 cm). Signed in raised bronze near the base: *P.* Marked in raised bronze inside the bottom cone: *I HK* [last letter facing backward]. Centre national d'art et de culture Georges Pompidou, Paris. Musée national d'art moderne/Centre de création industrielle. Donation Louise et Michel Leiris, 1984. Z II (2) 579, DR 753, S 36, SP 36-a. Plate 22

Glass of Absinthe. Paris, spring 1914. Bronze, painted in oil, and perforated white metal absinthe spoon, 1 of an edition of 6 bronzes cast 1914 for Daniel-Henry Kahnweiler, each uniquely treated, 8 7/8 × 4 3/4 × 3 3/8 in. (22.5 × 12.1 × 8.6 cm). Signed in raised bronze near the base: *P.* Marked in raised bronze inside the bottom cone: *II HK* [last letter facing backward]. Philadelphia Museum of Art. A. E. Gallatin Collection, 1952. Z II (2) 582, DR 757, S 36, SP 36-e. Plate 23

Glass of Absinthe. Paris, spring 1914. Bronze, painted in oil, and perforated white metal absinthe spoon, 1 of an edition of 6 bronzes cast 1914 for Daniel-Henry Kahnweiler, each uniquely treated, 8 7/8 × 5 × 2 1/2 in. (22.5 × 12.7 × 6.4 cm). Signed in raised bronze near the base: *P.* Marked in raised bronze inside the bottom cone: *III HK* [last letter facing backward]. Leonard A. Lauder Cubist Trust. Z II (2) 583, DR 758, S 36, SP 36-f. Plate 24

Glass of Absinthe. Paris, spring 1914. Bronze, painted in oil, and perforated white metal absinthe spoon, 1 of an edition of 6 bronzes cast 1914 for Daniel-Henry Kahnweiler, each uniquely treated, 8 1/2 × 6 1/2 × 3 3/8 in. (21.6 × 16.4 × 8.5 cm). Signed in raised bronze near the base: *P.* Marked in raised bronze inside the bottom cone: *IIII HK* [last letter facing backward]. The Museum of Modern Art, New York. Gift of Louise Reinhardt Smith, 1956. Z II (2) 584, DR 756, S 36, SP 36-d. Plate 25

Glass of Absinthe. Paris, spring 1914. Bronze, painted in oil, and perforated white metal absinthe spoon, 1 of an edition of 6 bronzes cast 1914 for Daniel-Henry Kahnweiler, each uniquely treated, 8 11/16 × 5 7/8 × 2 15/16 in. (22 × 15 × 7.5 cm). Signed in raised bronze near the base: *P.* Marked in raised bronze inside the bottom cone: *V HK*. Staatliche Museen zu Berlin, Nationalgalerie, Museum Berggruen. Z II (2) 581, DR 755, S 36, SP 36-c. Plate 26

Glass and Newspaper. Avignon, summer 1914. Painted wood, pencil, and oil on wood panel, 6 1/16 × 6 7/8 × 1 3/16 in. (15.4 × 17.5 × 3 cm). Inscribed and dated on verso at right: *A AVIGNON / 1914*. Musée national Picasso–Paris. Dation Pablo Picasso, 1979. Z II (2) 846, DR 789, S 49, SP 49. Plate 20

Violin and Bottle on a Table. Paris, [fall] 1915. Painted fir, string, nails, and charcoal, 17 11/16 × 15 3/4 × 9 1/16 in. (45 × 40 × 23 cm). Musée national Picasso–Paris. Dation Pablo Picasso, 1979. Z II (2) 826, DR 833, S 57, SP 57. Plate 27

Violin [Musical Instrument]. Paris, [1915]. Painted sheet metal and iron wire, 39 3/8 × 25 1/16 × 7 1/16 in. (100 × 63.7 × 18 cm). Musée national Picasso–Paris. Dation Pablo Picasso, 1979. Z II (2) 580, DR 835, S 55, SP 55. Plate 28

Guitar. Paris, 1924. Painted sheet metal, painted tin box, and iron wire, 43 11/16 × 25 × 10 1/2 in. (111 × 63.5 × 26.6 cm). Musée national Picasso–Paris. Dation Pablo Picasso, 1979. Z V 217, S 63, SP 63. Plate 29

CHAPTER 4
AROUND "THE MONUMENT TO APOLLINAIRE"
1927–1931

Metamorphosis I [Figure of a Woman]. Paris, 1928. Bronze, unique, cast by October 1943, 9 × 7 1/16 × 4 5/16 in. (22.8 × 18 × 11 cm). Musée national Picasso–Paris. Dation Pablo Picasso, 1979. S 67, SP 67-II. Plate 30

Metamorphosis II. Paris, 1928. Bronze, unique, cast by October 1943, 9 × 7 3/16 × 4 5/16 in. (22.8 × 18.3 × 11 cm). Private collection. Courtesy Fundación Almine y Bernard Ruiz-Picasso para el Arte. BK 13-14, SP 67A-II. Plate 31

Head. Paris, October 1928. Painted brass and iron, 7 1/16 × 4 5/16 × 3 3/4 in. (18 × 11 × 9.5 cm). Musée national Picasso–Paris. Dation Pablo Picasso, 1979. S 66, SP 66-A. Plate 32

Figure [Wire Construction]. Paris, October 1928. Iron wire and sheet metal, 14 3/4 × 3 15/16 × 7 11/16 in. (37.5 × 10 × 19.6 cm). Musée national Picasso–Paris. Dation Pablo Picasso, 1979; on long-term loan to the Centre national d'art et de culture Georges Pompidou, Paris. Musée national d'art moderne/Centre de création industrielle. S 71, SP 71. Plate 34

Figure [Wire Construction]. Paris, fall 1928. Iron wire and sheet metal, 19 7/8 × 7 5/16 × 16 1/16 in. (50.5 × 18.5 × 40.8 cm). Musée national Picasso–Paris. Dation Pablo Picasso, 1979. BK 21, S 68, SP 68. Plate 35

Figure [Wire Construction]. Paris, fall 1928. Iron wire and sheet metal, 23 7/16 × 5 1/8 × 12 5/8 in. (59.5 × 13 × 32 cm). Musée national Picasso–Paris. Dation Pablo Picasso, 1979. BK 20, S 69, SP 69. Plate 36

Seated Woman. Paris, spring 1929. Bronze, unique, cast by 1943, 16 3/4 × 6 1/2 × 9 13/16 in. (42.5 × 16.5 × 25 cm). Signed at back of base: Picasso. Musée national Picasso–Paris. Dation Pablo Picasso, 1979. BK 48, S 106, SP 106-II. Plate 37

Seated Woman. Paris, spring 1929. Bronze, unique, cast by 1943, 31 11/16 × 7 7/8 × 8 11/16 in. (80.5 × 20 × 22 cm). Signed at back of base on right along edge: Picasso. Musée national Picasso–Paris. Dation Pablo Picasso, 1979. BK 25, S 104, SP 104-II. Plate 38

Head of a Man [Head]. Paris, 1930. Iron, brass, and bronze, 32 7/8 × 15 3/4 × 14 3/16 in. (83.5 × 40 × 36 cm). Musée national Picasso–Paris. Dation Pablo Picasso, 1979. BK 27–28, S 80, SP 80. Plate 39

Head of a Woman. Paris, 1929–30. Iron, sheet metal, springs, and metal colanders; all painted, 39 ⅜ × 14 $^{9}/_{16}$ × 23 ¼ in. (100 × 37 × 59 cm). Musée national Picasso–Paris. Dation Pablo Picasso, 1979. BK 29–30, S 81, SP 81. Plate 40

Woman in the Garden. Paris, spring 1929–30. Welded and painted iron, 6 ft. 9 ⅛ in. × 46 $^{1}/_{16}$ in. × 33 $^{7}/_{16}$ in. (206 × 117 × 85 cm). Musée national Picasso–Paris. Dation Pablo Picasso, 1979. BK 15, S 72, SP 72-I. Plate 41

Object with Palm Leaf. Juan-les-Pins, August 27, 1930. Cardboard, plants, nails, and objects sewn and glued to back of canvas and stretcher and coated with sand; sand partially painted, 9 $^{13}/_{16}$ × 13 × 1 ¾ in. (25 × 33 × 4.5 cm). Dated on verso at center: *Juan / le 27 Août 1930*. Musée national Picasso–Paris. Dation Pablo Picasso, 1979. S 78, SP 78. Plate 42

Composition with Glove [*Construction with Glove*]. Juan-les-Pins, August 22, 1930. Glove, cardboard, and plants sewn and glued to back of canvas and stretcher and coated with sand; sand partially painted, 10 $^{13}/_{16}$ × 14 × 3 ⅛ in. (27.5 × 35.5 × 8 cm). Dated on verso at center: *le 22 Août 1930*. Musée national Picasso–Paris. Dation Pablo Picasso, 1979. BK 83, S 75, SP 75. Plate 43

Figure [*Figurine*]. [1931]. Iron and iron wire, 10 ¼ × 4 $^{15}/_{16}$ × 4 ⅜ in. (26 × 12.5 × 11.1 cm). Musée national Picasso–Paris. Dation Pablo Picasso, 1979. BK 17, S 84, SP 84. Plate 33

CHAPTER 5 THE BOISGELOUP SCULPTURE STUDIO 1930–1937

Seated Woman [*Woman*]. Boisgeloup, summer 1930. Fir, 21 $^{15}/_{16}$ × 1 × 1 $^{15}/_{16}$ in. (55.8 × 2.5 × 5 cm). Musée national Picasso–Paris. Dation Pablo Picasso, 1979. S 86, SP 86-I. Plate 44

Standing Woman [*Woman*]. Boisgeloup, summer 1930. Fir, 19 $^{5}/_{16}$ × ⅞ × ⅞ in. (49 × 2.3 × 2.2 cm). Musée national Picasso–Paris. Dation Pablo Picasso, 1979. S 93, SP 93-I. Plate 45

Standing Woman [*Woman*]. Boisgeloup, summer 1930. Fir, 18 ¾ × 1 $^{3}/_{16}$ × 1 $^{15}/_{16}$ in. (47.6 × 3 × 5 cm). Musée national Picasso–Paris. Dation Pablo Picasso, 1979. S 90, SP 90-I. Plate 46

Standing Woman [*Woman*]. Boisgeloup, summer 1930. Fir and iron wire, 18 $^{9}/_{16}$ × 1 ⅜ × 3 ⅛ in. (47.1 × 3.5 × 8 cm). Musée national Picasso–Paris. Dation Pablo Picasso, 1979. S 94, SP 94-I. Plate 47

Standing Woman [*Woman*]. Boisgeloup, summer 1930. Fir, 19 $^{3}/_{16}$ × 2 $^{3}/_{16}$ × 1 ⅛ in. (48.8 × 5.5 × 2.8 cm). Musée national Picasso–Paris. Dation Pablo Picasso, 1979. S 95, SP 95-I. Plate 48

Head of a Woman. Boisgeloup, 1931. Cement, unique, cast between April and July 1937, 37 $^{13}/_{16}$ × 12 ⅝ × 19 ⅛ in. (96 × 32 × 48.5 cm). Musée Picasso, Antibes. Gift of the artist, 1950. S 132, SP 132-III. Plate 49

Bust of a Woman. Boisgeloup, 1931. Plaster, 29 $^{15}/_{16}$ × 18 ⅛ × 18 ⅞ in. (76 × 46 × 48 cm). Private collection. S 131, SP 131-Ia. Plate 50

Head of a Woman. Boisgeloup, 1931. Plaster, 28 ⅛ × 16 ⅛ × 13 in. (71.5 × 41 × 33 cm). Musée national Picasso–Paris. Dation Pablo Picasso, 1979. S 110, SP 110-I. Plate 51

Bust of a Woman. Boisgeloup, 1931. Plaster, 28 $^{3}/_{16}$ × 16 ⅛ × 13 in. (71.5 × 41 × 33 cm). Musée national Picasso–Paris. Dation Pablo Picasso, 1979. S 111, SP 111-I. Plate 52

Head of a Woman. Boisgeloup, 1931. Plaster, 27 $^{3}/_{16}$ × 23 ⅝ × 3 $^{15}/_{16}$ in. (69 × 60 × 10 cm). Private collection. S 130, SP 130-I. Plate 55

Bather [*Woman*]. Boisgeloup, 1931. Bronze, unique, cast by July 1937, 27 $^{9}/_{16}$ × 15 $^{13}/_{16}$ × 12 ⅜ in. (70 × 40.2 × 31.5 cm). Stamped with foundry mark on base: *CIRE / C. VALSUANI / PERDUE*. Musée national Picasso–Paris. Dation Pablo Picasso, 1979. BK 47, S 108, SP 108-II. Plate 53

Reclining Bather [*Reclining Woman*]. Boisgeloup, 1931. Bronze, unique, cast by 1943, 9 $^{1}/_{16}$ × 28 ⅜ × 12 $^{3}/_{16}$ in. (23 × 72 × 31 cm). Musée national Picasso–Paris. Dation Pablo Picasso, 1979. BK 65, S 109, SP 109-II. Plate 54

Eye. Boisgeloup, 1931. Plaster with iron-wire hook, 2 $^{3}/_{16}$ × 5 ⅛ × 4 ½ in. (5.5 × 13 × 11.5 cm). Private collection. Courtesy Fundación Almine y Bernard Ruiz-Picasso para el Arte. BK 56, S 124, SP 124. Plate 70

Eye. Boisgeloup, 1931–32. Plaster with iron-wire hook, 3 ⅜ × 2 ⅜ × 1 $^{9}/_{16}$ in. (8.5 × 6 × 4 cm). Kravis Collection. BK 55, S 123, SP 123. Plate 69

Bird. Boisgeloup, 1931–32. Plaster, 9 $^{13}/_{16}$ in. (25 cm) high. Private collection. BK 70, S 125, SP 125. Plate 57

Hand [*Picasso's Hand*]. Boisgeloup, [fall 1932 or earlier]. Plaster with newspaper and wire hook, 14 $^{9}/_{16}$ × 7 $^{11}/_{16}$ × 4 $^{5}/_{16}$ in. (37 × 19.5 × 11 cm). Musée national Picasso–Paris. Dation Pablo Picasso, 1979. BK 72, S 222, SP 222. Plate 71

Head of a Woman. Boisgeloup, 1931–32. Plaster, produced as plaster proof in April 1937 by M. Renucci, 52 ½ × 25 ⅝ × 28 in. (133.4 × 65 × 71.1 cm). The Museum of Modern Art, New York. Gift of Jacqueline Picasso in honor of the Museum's continuous commitment to Pablo Picasso's art, 1982. S 133, SP 133-Ib. Plate 56

Cock. Boisgeloup, 1932. Bronze, cast 1952, 25 $^{13}/_{16}$ × 22 $^{15}/_{16}$ × 15 $^{9}/_{16}$ in. (65.5 × 58.2 × 39.5 cm). Stamped with foundry mark at bottom of base underneath tail feathers: *CIRE / C. VALSUANI / PERDUE*. Incised on side of base: *1/6*. Tate. Purchase, 1953. BK 57, S 134, SP 134-II. Plate 58

An Anatomy: Three Women. [Paris], February 25, 1933. Graphite on fine-textured wove paper, 7 ⅞ × 10 ⅝ in. (20 × 27 cm). Inscribed in graphite on recto at lower right corner: *25-2-33-*. Inscribed in graphite on verso at top left corner, probably at a later date: *II*. Musée national Picasso–Paris. Dation Pablo Picasso, 1979. Plate 59

An Anatomy: Three Women. [Paris], February 26, 1933. Graphite on fine-textured wove paper, 7 $^{13}/_{16}$ × 10 $^{13}/_{16}$ in. (19.9 × 27.5 cm). Inscribed in graphite on recto near upper right corner: *26-2-33-*. Inscribed in graphite on verso at top left corner, probably at a later date: *III*. Musée national Picasso–Paris. Dation Pablo Picasso, 1979. Plate 60

An Anatomy: Three Women. [Paris], February 26, 1933. Graphite on fine-textured wove paper, 7 ⅞ × 10 ¾ in. (20 × 27.3 cm). Inscribed in graphite on recto near upper right corner: *26-2-33-*. Inscribed in graphite on verso at top left corner, probably at a later date: *IV*. Musée national Picasso–Paris. Dation Pablo Picasso, 1979. Plate 61

An Anatomy: Three Women. [Paris], February 27, 1933. Graphite on fine-textured wove paper, 7 ⅞ × 10 ⅝ in. (20 × 27 cm). Inscribed in graphite on recto near upper right corner, probably at a later date: *27-2-33-*. Musée national Picasso–Paris. Dation Pablo Picasso, 1979. Plate 62

An Anatomy: Three Women. [Paris], February 27, 1933. Graphite on fine-textured wove paper, 7 ⅞ × 10 ⅝ in. (20 × 27 cm). Inscribed in graphite on recto at upper right corner: *27-2-33-*. Inscribed in graphite on verso at top left corner, probably at a later date: *VI*. Musée national Picasso–Paris. Dation Pablo Picasso, 1979. Plate 63

An Anatomy: Three Women. [Paris], February 27, 1933. Graphite on fine-textured wove paper, 7 $^{13}/_{16}$ × 10 $^{13}/_{16}$ in. (19.8 × 27.4 cm). Inscribed in graphite on recto near upper right corner: *27-2-33-*. Inscribed in graphite on verso at top left corner, probably at a later date: *VII*. Musée national Picasso–Paris. Dation Pablo Picasso, 1979. Plate 64

An Anatomy: Seated Woman. [Paris], February 28, 1933. Graphite on fine-textured wove paper, 7 7/8 × 10 5/8 in. (20 × 27 cm). Inscribed in graphite on recto at lower left corner: *28-2-33-.* Inscribed in graphite on verso at top left corner, probably at a later date: *I.* Musée national Picasso–Paris. Dation Pablo Picasso, 1979. Plate 65

An Anatomy: Three Women. [Paris], March 1, 1933. Graphite on fine-textured wove paper, 7 11/16 × 10 3/4 in. (19.5 × 27.3 cm). Inscribed in graphite on recto near upper right corner: *1-3-33-.* Inscribed in graphite on verso at top left corner, probably at a later date: *IX.* Musée national Picasso–Paris. Dation Pablo Picasso, 1979. Plate 66

Woman with Vase. Boisgeloup, summer 1933. Bronze, cast 1972 or 1973, 7 ft. 2 5/8 in. × 48 1/16 in. × 43 5/16 in. (220 × 122 × 110 cm). Stamped with foundry mark on back of base at upper left: *CIRE / C. VALSUANI / PERDUE.* Museo Nacional Centro de Arte Reina Sofía, Madrid. Picasso Bequest, 1986. S 135, SP 135-II. Plate 67

Head of a Warrior [*Helmeted Head (Head of a Warrior)*]. Boisgeloup, 1933. Plaster, metal, and wood, 47 1/2 × 9 3/4 × 27 in. (120.7 × 24.9 × 68.8 cm). The Museum of Modern Art, New York. Gift of Jacqueline Picasso in honor of the Museum's continuous commitment to Pablo Picasso's art, 1984. S 136, SP 136-I. Plate 68

Relief [*Composition*]. [Paris], 1934. Plaster, 5 1/2 × 10 1/16 × 1 in. (14 × 25.5 × 2.5 cm). Private collection. Courtesy Fundación Almine y Bernard Ruiz-Picasso para el Arte. BK 179, S 243, SP 243. Plate 72

Crumpled Paper [*Fragment*]. Boisgeloup, 1934. Plaster, 4 5/16 × 12 3/8 × 9 7/16 in. (11 × 31.5 × 24 cm). Musée national Picasso–Paris. Gift of Marina Ruiz-Picasso, 1983. BK 176, S 246, SP 246. Plate 73

The Orator [*Standing Figure*]. 1933–34. Plaster, stone, and metal dowel, 72 × 26 × 10 5/8 in. (182.9 × 66 × 27 cm). Fine Arts Museums of San Francisco. Museum purchase, Roscoe and Margaret Oakes Income Fund and Art Trust Fund, 1994. BK 213, S 181, SP 181-I. Plate 76

The Reaper. Boisgeloup, c. 1934. Plaster and wood, 20 1/2 × 13 3/8 × 8 1/4 in. (52 × 34 × 21 cm). Private collection. S 234, SP 234-I. Plate 74

Woman with Leaves. Boisgeloup, 1934. Plaster, 15 3/16 × 10 13/16 × 8 1/4 in. (38.5 × 27.5 × 21 cm). Private collection. Courtesy Fundación Almine y Bernard Ruiz-Picasso para el Arte. BK 170–71, S 157, SP 157-I. Plate 75

Woman with Orange or Woman with Apple [*Woman with Apple*]. Boisgeloup, c. 1934. Bronze, unique, cast by September 1943, 71 1/16 × 29 1/2 × 26 9/16 in. (180.5 × 75 × 67.5 cm). Musée national Picasso–Paris. Dation Pablo Picasso, 1979. BK 168, S 236, SP 236-II. Plate 77

Woman Carrying a Vessel [*Woman Carrying a Pot*]. [Paris or Boisgeloup], 1935. Painted pieces of wood, objects, and nails on a cement and wood base, 23 5/8 × 5 1/2 × 7 1/4 in. (60 × 14 × 18.4 cm). Musée national Picasso–Paris. Dation Pablo Picasso, 1979. S 162, SP 162. Plate 78

Figure. Mougins, spring 1938. Painted wood, nails, and screws with string, wire, paintbrush fragments, and push-bell hardware on an unfired clay and wood base, 22 13/16 × 7 7/8 × 4 5/16 in. (58 × 20 × 11 cm). Inscribed in pencil at front of base: *Mars–Avril / 38.* Private collection. S 164, SP 164. Plate 79

CHAPTER 6
THE WAR YEARS
1939–1945

Head of a Woman. Paris, 1941. Plaster, 31 1/2 in. (80 cm) high. Museum Ludwig, Cologne. BK 116, S 197, SP 197-I. Plate 80

Cat. Paris, 1941. Bronze, cast by September 1943, 18 × 28 1/2 × 9 in. (46 × 72.5 × 23 cm). Private collection. BK 113, S 195, SP 195-II. Plate 81

Death's Head. Paris, [1941]. Bronze, cast by May 1943, 9 7/8 × 8 1/4 × 12 5/8 in. (25 × 21 × 32 cm). Private collection. BK 162-163, S 219, SP 219-II. Plate 82

Bull's Head. Paris, spring 1942. Bronze, cast 1943, 16 1/2 × 16 1/8 × 5 7/8 in. (42 × 41 × 15 cm). Private collection. BK 187, S 240, SP 240-II. Plate 88

Head of a Dog. Paris, 1943. Torn and burnt tissue paper (napkin), 3 15/16 × 10 5/8 in. (10 × 27 cm). Musée national Picasso–Paris. Purchase, 1998. BK 135, S 252, SP 252. Plate 83

Death's Head. Paris, 1943. Torn and scratched paper, 6 7/16 × 5 15/16 in. (16.3 × 15.1 cm). Musée national Picasso–Paris. Purchase, 1998. BK 139, S 257, SP 257. Plate 84

Goat. Paris, 1943. Torn paper, 14 15/16 × 6 5/16 in. (38 × 16.1 cm). Musée national Picasso–Paris. Purchase, 1998. BK 145, S 260, SP 260. Plate 85

Woman in a Long Dress. Paris, 1943. Bronze, cast by 1944, 63 1/2 × 21 1/8 × 18 in. (161.3 × 53.7 × 45.7 cm). Private collection. BK 192, S 238, SP 238-II. Plate 86

Man with a Lamb [*Man with Sheep*]. Paris, 1943. Bronze, cast between 1948 and 1950, 6 ft. 7 1/2 in. × 30 in. × 29 1/2 in. (201.9 × 76.2 × 74.9 cm); base: 27 × 26 in. (68.6 × 66 cm). Stamped with foundry mark on back of base near left corner: *CIRE / C. VALSUANI / PERDUE.* Incised on top of base at left corner: *No. 1.* Philadelphia Museum of Art. Gift of R. Sturgis and Marion B. F. Ingersoll, 1958. S 280, SP 280-II. Plate 87

The Venus of Gas. January 1945. Iron (burner and pipe from a gas stove), 9 13/16 × 3 9/16 × 1 9/16 in. (25 × 9 × 4 cm). Private collection. SP 302A. Plate 89

CHAPTER 7
VALLAURIS: CERAMICS AND ASSEMBLAGES
1945–1954

Standing Woman. 1945. Foundry plaster, 5 1/2 × 1 7/8 × 1 3/4 in. (14 × 4.8 × 4.5 cm). Kravis Collection. S 329, SP 329-Ib. Plate 99

Standing Woman. 1945. Terracotta, 8 1/16 × 3 1/8 × 2 15/16 in. (20.5 × 8 × 7.5 cm). Kravis Collection. S 322, SP 322-Ia. Plate 100

Standing Woman. 1945. Terracotta, 10 7/16 × 3 1/8 × 2 11/16 in. (26.5 × 8 × 6.9 cm). Kravis Collection. S 314, SP 314-Ia. Plate 101

Head. 1945. Engraved pebble, 1 3/16 × 11/16 × 3/16 in. (3 × 1.8 × 0.5 cm). Private collection. SP 291A. Plate 92

Head of an Animal. 1945–46. Engraved pebble, 1 1/4 × 2 3/8 × 5/16 in. (3.2 × 6 × 0.8 cm). Private collection. BK 202, S 289, SP 289. Plate 91

Face. Golfe-Juan, 1946. Engraved pebble, 1 1/16 × 11/16 × 5/16 in. (2.7 × 1.7 × 0.8 cm). Private collection. BK 199, S 285, SP 285. Plate 90

Face. Golfe-Juan, 1946. Engraved pebble, 1 1/4 × 1 1/8 × 1/2 in. (3.2 × 2.9 × 1.3 cm). Private collection. BK 199, S 284, SP 284. Plate 93

Pear-shaped Face [*Figure*]. Golfe-Juan, c. 1946. Engraved pebble, 1 9/16 × 1 1/4 × 1/2 in. (4 × 3.1 × 1.3 cm). Private collection. BK 205, S 298, SP 298. Plate 94

Face. Golfe-Juan, 1946. Engraved pebble, 11/16 × 1 9/16 × 5/16 in. (1.8 × 3.9 × 0.8 cm). Private collection. BK 201, S 288, SP 288. Plate 96

Face. Golfe-Juan, 1946. Engraved pebble, 1 5/8 × 2 5/8 × 1/2 in. (4.2 × 6.7 × 1.2 cm). Private collection. BK 204, S 291, SP 291. Plate 97

Head of a Faun. Golfe-Juan, 1946. Engraved ceramic fragment, 2 13/16 × 2 3/16 × 1/4 in. (7.2 × 5.5 × 0.6 cm). Private collection. BK 198, S 283, SP 283. Plate 98

Face. Golfe-Juan, 1946–47. Engraved bone fragment, 1 9/16 × 1 × 11/16 in. (4 × 2.6 × 2 cm). Private collection. SP 291C. Plate 95

Seated Woman. Vallauris, 1947. Glazed earthenware, 4 3/4 × 2 3/4 × 2 15/16 in. (12 × 7 × 7.5 cm). Private collection. Courtesy Fundación Almine y Bernard Ruiz-Picasso para el Arte. Plate 102

Seated Woman. Vallauris, 1947. Glazed earthenware, 7 1/2 × 1 15/16 × 2 3/4 in. (19 × 5 × 7 cm). Private collection. Courtesy Fundación Almine y Bernard Ruiz-Picasso para el Arte. Plate 103

Owl (Vase). Vallauris, 1947 or 1948. White earthenware, painted with slips and oxides, 14 15/16 × 13 × 4 3/4 in. (38 × 33 × 12 cm). Musée Picasso, Antibes. Plate 108

Standing Bull (Vase). Vallauris, 1947 or 1948. White earthenware with applied elements, painted with slips and oxides, 14 9/16 × 15 3/4 × 11 13/16 in. (37 × 40 × 30 cm). Musée Picasso, Antibes. Plate 109

Vase: Woman [*Woman with Hands Hidden*]. Vallauris, [1948]. White earthenware, painted with slips, 18 11/16 × 6 1/2 × 4 5/16 in. (47.5 × 16.5 × 11 cm). Musée national Picasso–Paris. Dation Pablo Picasso, 1979. S C1, SP C1. Plate 111

Owl. Vallauris, December 30, 1949. White earthenware, decorated with slips and white enamel, incisions, and brushwork, 7 1/2 × 7 1/16 × 8 11/16 in. (19 × 18 × 22 cm). Incised under the base on the right: *30.12.49*. Musée national Picasso–Paris. Dation Pablo Picasso, 1979. Plate 110

Bottle: Kneeling Woman. Vallauris, 1948–50. White earthenware, enameled and painted with oxides, 11 7/16 × 6 11/16 × 6 11/16 in. (29 × 17 × 17 cm). Musée national Picasso–Paris. Dation Pablo Picasso, 1979. Plate 112

Pregnant Woman [*Female Form*]. Vallauris, 1949. Bronze, casting date unknown, 50 3/8 × 14 15/16 × 4 3/4 in. (128 × 38 × 12 cm). Stamped with foundry mark at lower center of back of figure: *CIRE / C. VALSUANI / PERDUE*. Private collection. Courtesy Fundación Almine y Bernard Ruiz-Picasso para el Arte. S 347, SP 347-II. Plate 114

Pregnant Woman. First state. Vallauris, 1950. Plaster with metal armature, wood, ceramic vessel, and pottery jars, 43 1/4 × 8 5/8 × 12 1/2 in. (110 × 22 × 32 cm). The Museum of Modern Art, New York. Gift of Louise Reinhardt Smith and gift of Jacqueline Picasso (both by exchange), 2003. S 349, SP 349-I. Plate 115

She-Goat [*Goat*]. Vallauris, 1950. Bronze, cast 1952 at the Valsuani foundry, 46 3/8 × 56 3/8 × 28 1/8 in. (117.7 × 143.1 × 71.4 cm). The Museum of Modern Art, New York. Mrs. Simon Guggenheim Fund, 1959. S 409, SP 409-II. Plate 119

Head of a Faun. Vallauris, 1950. Fired white clay, 3 × 2 3/8 × 11/16 in. (7.6 × 6 × 1.7 cm). Kravis Collection. S 378, SP 378-I. Plate 104

Head of a Faun. Vallauris, 1950. Fired white clay, 3 × 2 3/8 × 11/16 in. (7.6 × 6 × 1.7 cm). Kravis Collection. S 377, SP 377-I. Plate 105

Seated Musician. Vallauris, 1950. Fired red clay, 3 3/8 × 4 3/4 × 3 1/8 in. (8.5 × 12 × 8 cm). Museo Picasso Málaga. Gift of Christine Ruiz-Picasso. S 426, SP 426-I. Plate 106

Seated Faun [*Seated Satyr*]. Vallauris, 1950. White earthenware, 3 3/4 × 1 15/16 × 2 3/4 in. (9.5 × 5 × 7 cm). Museo Picasso Málaga. Gift of Bernard Ruiz-Picasso. S 419, SP 419-I. Plate 107

Insect. Vallauris, 1951. Fired white clay with attached elements, incised and painted with slips, 16 9/16 × 13 3/4 × 10 1/4 in. (42 × 35 × 26 cm). Museo Picasso Málaga. Gift of Bernard Ruiz-Picasso. Plate 113

Baboon and Young. Vallauris, October 1951. Bronze, cast 1955, 21 × 13 1/4 × 20 3/4 in. (53.3 × 33.3 × 52.7 cm). Incised near right rear corner on top of base: *10.51*. Stamped with foundry mark at left rear corner on top of base: *CIRE / C. VALSUANI / PERDUE*. Incised near left rear corner on top of base: 5/6. The Museum of Modern Art, New York. Mrs. Simon Guggenheim Fund, 1956. S 463, SP 463-II. Plate 116

Flowery Watering Can [*The Flowering Watering-can*]. Paris, 1951–52. Plaster with watering can, metal parts, nails, and wood, 33 11/16 × 16 9/16 × 14 15/16 in. (85.5 × 42 × 38 cm). Musée national Picasso–Paris. Dation Pablo Picasso, 1979. S 239, SP 239-I. Plate 124

Crane. Vallauris, 1951–52. Painted bronze, cast 1952, 1 of an edition of 4 bronzes, each uniquely treated, 29 1/2 × 11 7/16 × 16 15/16 in. (75 × 29 × 43 cm). Stamped with foundry mark on top of base at right rear corner: *CIRE / C. VALSUANI / PERDUE*. Private collection. Courtesy Thomas Ammann Fine Art AG, Zurich. S 461, SP 461-IIc. Plate 122

Little Owl. Vallauris, 1951–52. Painted bronze, cast 1952, 1 of an edition of 2 bronzes, one unpainted, 10 1/4 × 7 3/8 × 5 3/4 in. (26 × 18.7 × 14.6 cm). Stamped with foundry mark at upper left of back of base: *CIRE / C. VALSUANI / PERDUE*. Stamped at upper right corner on back of base: *BRONZE*. Hirshhorn Museum and Sculpture Garden, Smithsonian Institution, Washington, D.C. Gift of Joseph H. Hirshhorn, 1966. S 475, SP 475-II. Plate 120

Woman Reading. Vallauris, 1951–53. Painted bronze, cast May 1952, 1 of an edition of 3 bronzes, each uniquely treated, 6 1/8 × 14 × 5 1/8 in. (15.5 × 35.5 × 13 cm). Stamped with foundry mark at upper right corner of base: *CIRE / C. VALSUANI / PERDUE*. Centre national d'art et de culture Georges Pompidou, Paris. Musée national d'art moderne/Centre de création industrielle. Donation Louise et Michel Leiris, 1984. S 462, SP 462-IIa. Plate 121

Goat Skull and Bottle. Vallauris, 1951–53. Painted bronze, cast 1952, 1 of an edition of 2 bronzes, each uniquely treated, 31 × 37 5/8 × 21 1/2 in. (78.8 × 95.3 × 54.5 cm). Stamped with foundry mark at front right corner of base: *CIRE / C. VALSUANI / PERDUE*. The Museum of Modern Art, New York. Mrs. Simon Guggenheim Fund, 1956. S 410, SP 410-IIb. Plate 123

Flowers in a Vase. Vallauris, 1951–53. Painted plaster, terracotta, and iron, 30 1/8 × 20 1/4 × 17 1/4 in. (76.5 × 51.4 × 43.8 cm). Raymond and Patsy Nasher Collection, Nasher Sculpture Center, Dallas, 1987. S 413, SP 413-I. Plate 125

Woman Carrying a Child. Vallauris, 1953. Painted wood and section of palm frond, 68 1/8 × 21 1/4 × 13 3/4 in. (173 × 54 × 35 cm). Private collection. S 478, SP 478. Plate 127

The Woman with a Key [*The Madame*]. Vallauris, October 1953–54; stone base added in Cannes, by September 1958. Bronze with stone base, unique, cast 1954, 67 11/16 × 16 15/16 × 11 13/16 in. (172 × 43 × 30 cm). Private collection. S 237, SP 237-II. Plate 126

Little Girl Jumping Rope [*Little Girl Skipping*]. Vallauris, 1950–[54]. Bronze, cast 1956 or later, 60 1/4 × 24 7/16 × 25 5/8 in. (153 × 62 × 65 cm). Stamped with foundry mark at back of base: *CIRE / C. VALSUANI / PERDUE*. Private collection. S 408, SP 408-II. Plate 117

Woman with a Baby Carriage. Vallauris, 1950–[54]. Bronze, cast 1962–[63] at the Valsuani foundry, 6 ft. 7 15/16 in. × 57 1/16 in. × 24 in. (203 × 145 × 61 cm). Musée national Picasso–Paris. Dation Pablo Picasso, 1979. S 407, SP 407-II. Plate 118

CHAPTER 8
WOOD ASSEMBLAGES, SHEET METAL SCULPTURES, AND PUBLIC MONUMENTS
1954–1973

Sylvette. Vallauris, 1954. Painted sheet metal, 26 3/8 × 19 11/16 × 4 5/16 in. (67 × 50 × 11 cm). Private collection. S 491, SP 491. Plate 139

The Bathers: Woman Diver. Cannes, 1956. Wood, filler (possibly gesso), and palm frond, 8 ft. 8 5/16 in. (264 cm) high. Staatsgalerie Stuttgart. S 503, SP 503-I. Plate 128

The Bathers: Man with Folded Hands. Cannes, 1956. Wood and filler (possibly gesso), 7 ft. 1/4 in. (214 cm) high. Staatsgalerie Stuttgart. S 504, SP 504-I. Plate 129

The Bathers: Fountain Man. Cannes, 1956. Wood, 7 ft. 5 3/8 in. (227 cm) high. Staatsgalerie Stuttgart. S 505, SP 505-I. Plate 130

The Bathers: Child. Cannes, 1956. Wood, 53 9/16 in. (136 cm) high. Staatsgalerie Stuttgart. S 506, SP 506-I. Plate 131

The Bathers: Woman with Outstretched Arms. Cannes, 1956. Painted wood, 6 ft. 5 15/16 in. (198 cm) high. Staatsgalerie Stuttgart. S 507, SP 507-I. Plate 132

The Bathers: Young Man. Cannes, 1956. Wood, 69 5/16 in. (176 cm) high. Staatsgalerie Stuttgart. S 508, SP 508-I. Plate 133

Head of a Woman. Cannes, 1957. Painted sheet metal, 34 1/4 × 11 × 16 9/16 in. (87 × 28 × 42 cm). Musée national Picasso–Paris. Dation Pablo Picasso, 1979. S 495, SP 495-2. Plate 141

Bull. Cannes, April 1958. Blockboard (wood base panel), palm frond and various other tree branches, eyebolt, nails, and screws, with drips of alkyd and pencil markings, 56 3/4 × 46 1/8 × 4 1/8 in. (144.1 × 117.2 × 10.5 cm). The Museum of Modern Art, New York. Gift of Jacqueline Picasso in honor of the Museum's continuous commitment to Pablo Picasso's art, 1983. SP 545A. Plate 136

Bird. Cannes, May 22, 1958. Painted wood and forks, plaster, nails, screws, and eyebolts, 10 1/4 × 26 9/16 × 4 15/16 in. (26 × 67.5 × 12.5 cm). Private collection. SP 547A. Plate 138

Man. Cannes, 1958. Wood and nails, 46 1/8 × 29 7/8 × 9 7/8 in. (117 × 76 × 25 cm). Private collection. S 538, SP 538. Plate 134

Female Bather Playing [*Bather Playing*]. Cannes, 1958. Bronze, casting date unknown, 44 1/2 × 15 1/2 × 25 1/2 in. (113 × 39.4 × 64.8 cm). Stamped with foundry mark at rear right of base: *CIRE / C. VALSUANI / PERDUE*. Incised: *2/2*. Albright-Knox Art Gallery, Buffalo, New York. Gift of The Seymour H. Knox Foundation, Inc., 1965. S 537, SP 537-II. Plate 135

Head. Cannes, 1958. Wood box, nails, buttons, painted plaster, and painted synthetic resin mounted on ceramic dish, 19 7/8 × 8 3/4 × 8 in. (50.5 × 22.2 × 20.3 cm). The Museum of Modern Art, New York. Gift of Jacqueline Picasso in honor of the Museum's continuous commitment to Pablo Picasso's art, 1984. S 539, SP 539-I. Plate 137

Chair. Cannes, 1961. Painted sheet metal, 45 1/2 × 45 1/16 × 35 1/16 in. (115.5 × 114.5 × 89 cm). Musée national Picasso–Paris. Dation Pablo Picasso, 1979. S 592, SP 592-2. Plate 142

Little Horse. Vallauris, 1961. Painted metal with wheels, 26 3/16 × 7 1/16 × 23 13/16 in. (66.5 × 18 × 60.5 cm). Private collection. Courtesy Fundación Almine y Bernard Ruiz-Picasso para el Arte. Plate 140

Woman and Child. Cannes, 1961. Painted sheet metal, 17 3/8 × 7 3/16 × 6 5/16 in. (44.2 × 18.2 × 16 cm). Private collection. S 600, SP 600-2. Plate 143

Woman with Child. Cannes, early 1961. Painted sheet metal, 50 3/8 × 23 5/8 × 13 3/4 in. (128 × 60 × 35 cm). Musée national Picasso–Paris. Dation Pablo Picasso, 1979. S 599, SP 599-2. Plate 144

Woman with Outstretched Arms. Cannes, 1961. Painted iron and sheet metal, 70 5/16 × 61 9/16 × 28 9/16 in. (178.6 × 156.4 × 72.5 cm). The Museum of Fine Arts, Houston. Gift of the Esther Florence Whinery Goodrich Foundation, 1966. S 597, SP 597. Plate 145

Head of a Woman. Cannes, 1961. Painted sheet metal, 11 7/16 × 8 7/16 × 2 3/4 in. (29 × 21.5 × 7 cm). Private collection. Courtesy Fundación Almine y Bernard Ruiz-Picasso para el Arte. S 613, SP 613-2. Plate 147

Head of a Woman. Mougins, late 1962. Painted sheet metal and iron wire, 12 5/8 × 9 7/16 × 6 5/16 in. (32 × 24 × 16 cm). Musée national Picasso–Paris. Dation Pablo Picasso, 1979. S 631, SP 631-2. Plate 148

Woman with Hat. Cannes, 1961/Mougins, 1963. Sheet metal, painted 1963, 49 5/8 × 28 3/4 × 16 1/8 in. (126 × 73 × 41 cm). Signed on back at center right: Picasso. Fondation Beyeler, Riehen/Basel, Beyeler Collection. S 626, SP 626-2a. Plate 146

Maquette for Richard J. Daley Center Sculpture [*Maquette for Chicago Civic Center*]. Mougins, 1964. Simulated and oxidized welded steel, 41 1/4 × 27 1/2 × 19 in. (104.8 × 69.9 × 48.3 cm). Inscribed by the artist at center of rear vertical plane: *souder tout*. The Art Institute of Chicago. Gift of Pablo Picasso, 1966. S 643, SP 643-2b. Plate 149

SELECTED EXHIBITIONS, 1910–1967

COMPILED BY LUISE MAHLER

This list of more than one hundred exhibitions traces the public presentation of Picasso's sculptures through 1966–67, when retrospectives of his three-dimensional work were mounted for the first time in Paris, London, and New York. The list is not exhaustive; it gives preference to monographic exhibitions and those that featured the sculptures discussed in this catalogue. The exhibitions are organized in chronological order by opening date. For shows that included twenty-five or fewer sculptures, the individual artworks are listed by title and date. Works are further identified by their plate number in this catalogue; those not included in the present exhibition are identified by their number in the most recent edition of the catalogue raisonné compiled by Werner Spies with Christine Piot (SP; see References, p. 312). An asterisk accompanies a plate number when the specific object featured in the historical exhibition also appears in the present exhibition. Information is enclosed in square brackets where no consensus has been reached among scholars. If a publication accompanied the exhibition, this is noted; the abbreviation "ill." specifies that the object listed was illustrated therein.

This list is greatly indebted to previous publications on Picasso's sculptures and to the research of Diana Widmaier Picasso.

1910

Paris, Galerie Ambroise Vollard. *Pablo Picasso.* December 1910–late February 1911
On view: possibly a bronze cast of *Head of a Woman* (1909; plate 11)

1913

New York, Armory of the Sixty-ninth Regiment. *International Exhibition of Modern Art* (The Armory Show). February 17–March 15. Catalogue
On view: a bronze cast of *Head of a Woman* (1909; plate 11*) (New York venue only)

Prague, Obecní Dům Města. *Third Exhibition of the Skupina Výtvarných Umělců.* May–June. Catalogue
On view: a bronze cast of *Head of a Woman* (1909; plate 11)

Düsseldorf, Galerie Alfred Flechtheim. *Beiträge zur Kunst des 19. Jahrhunderts und unserer Zeit.* Opened on Christmas. Catalogue
On view: bronze casts of *The Jester* (1905; plate 3), *Head of a Woman (Fernande)* (1906; plate 4), and *Head of a Woman* (1909; plate 11)

1915

New York, Modern Gallery. *Picasso Exhibition.* December 13, 1915–January 3, 1916
On view: Glass, Pipe, and Playing Card (1914; SP 45)

1927

Berlin, Galerien Thannhauser. *Erste Sonderausstellung in Berlin.* January 9–mid-February. Catalogue
On view: bronze casts of *The Jester* (1905; plate 3), *Head of a Woman (Fernande)* (1906; plate 4), and an unidentified work titled *Head* in the catalogue

Berlin, Galerie Alfred Flechtheim. *Picasso: Pastelle, Aquarelle, Zeichnungen, Bronzen, usw., 1902–1927.* October 16–November 10. Catalogue
On view: bronze casts of *The Jester* (1905; plate 3), a work titled *Head* in the catalogue (possibly *Head of a Woman [Fernande]* of 1906; plate 4), a work titled *Head of a Woman* in the catalogue (possibly SP 12), and *Head of a Woman* (1909; plate 11)

1929

Berlin, Galerie Alfred Flechtheim. *Seit Cézanne in Paris.* November 23–Christmas. Catalogue
On view: bronze casts of *The Jester* (1905; plate 3), *Head of a Woman (Fernande)* (1906; plate 4), and *Head of a Woman* (1909; plate 11); and one painted bronze from the Glass of Absinthe series (1914; plates 21–26)

1930

Düsseldorf, Galerie Alfred Flechtheim. *Kleinplastik.* March 22–April 20. Catalogue
On view: a bronze cast of *Head of a Woman (Fernande)* (1906; plate 4); and one painted bronze from the Glass of Absinthe series (1914; plates 21–26)

Baltimore, Baltimore Museum of Art. *Cone Collection of Modern Paintings and Sculptures.* April. Catalogue
On view: a bronze cast of *Head of a Picador with a Broken Nose* (1903; plate 2*)

Tokyo, Tokyo Metropolitan Art Museum. *17th Nikakai (Second Session Association and Exhibition).* Fall
On view: a bronze cast of *The Jester* (1905; plate 3).

1932

Paris, Galeries Georges Petit. *Exposition Picasso.* June 16–July 30. Catalogue (fig. 1)
On view: bronze casts of *The Jester* (1905; plate 3), *Head of a Woman (Fernande)* (1906; plate 4), *Kneeling Woman Combing Her Hair* (1906; plate 5), and *Head of a Woman* (1909; plate 11); *Head of a Woman* (1929–30; plate 40*); *Woman in the Garden* (1929–30; plate 41*); and *Woman in the Garden* (1929–30; SP 72-II)

Zurich, Kunsthaus Zürich. *Picasso.* September 11–November 13 (extended closing date). Catalogue
On view: bronze casts of *The Jester* (1905; plate 3), *Head of a Woman (Fernande)* (1906; plate 4), *Kneeling Woman Combing Her Hair* (1906; plate 5), and *Head of a Woman* (1909; plate 11)

1936

New York, The Museum of Modern Art. *Cubism and Abstract Art: Painting, Sculpture, Constructions, Photography, Architecture, Industrial Art, Theatre, Films, Posters, Typography.* March 2–April 19. Catalogue
On view: a bronze cast of *Head of a Woman* (1909; plate 11); and *Glass of Absinthe* (1914; plate 23*), ill.

Paris, Galerie Charles Ratton. *Exposition surréaliste d'objets.* May 22–29. Catalogue
On view: Still Life (1914; plate 15*); *Glass, Pipe, and Playing Card* (1914; SP 45); *Glass of Absinthe* (1914; plate 26*); *Violin* ([1915]; plate 28*); *Guitar* (1924; plate 29*); and possibly *Figure* ([1931]; plate 33*)

Paris, Galerie Cahiers d'Art. *Exposition de sculptures récentes de Picasso, peintures et sculptures J. González, sculptures Joan Miró, peintures et objets Louis Fernandez, peintures.* June 26–July 20
On view: Head of a Man (1930; plate 39*); bronze casts of *Seated Woman* (1930; SP 86-II), *Standing Woman* (1930; SP 93-II), *Standing Woman* (1930; SP 94-II), and *Standing Woman* (1930; SP 95-II); and other unidentified sculptures

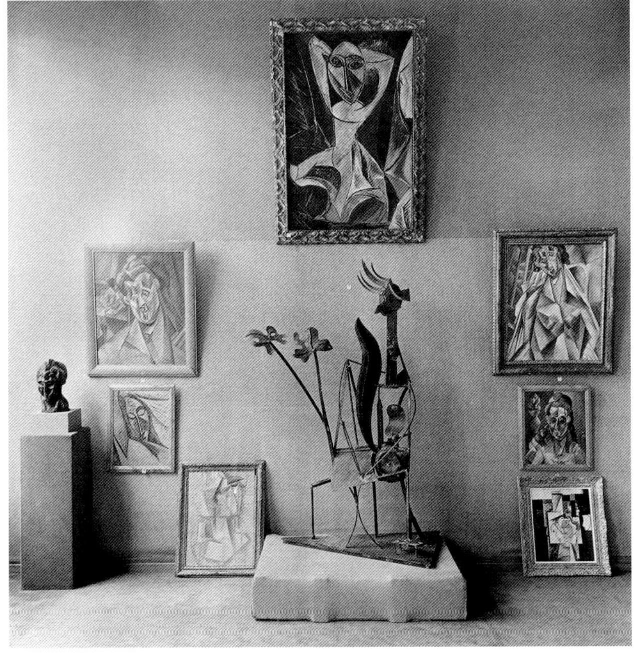

1. View of *Exposition Picasso* at the Galeries Georges Petit, Paris, 1932, with a bronze cast of *Head of a Woman* (1909) at far left and *Woman in the Garden* (1929–30) at center. Kunsthaus Zürich

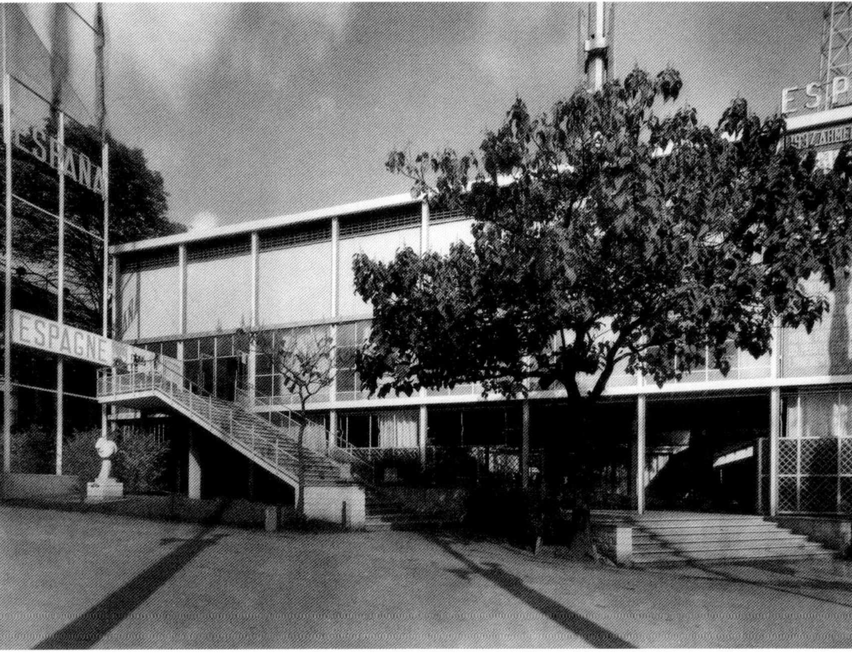

2. The Spanish Pavilion at the Paris World's Fair, held at the Esplanade du Trocadéro, 1937, with a cement cast of *Head of a Woman* (1931–32) at left. Photograph by François Kollar. Ministère de la Culture, La Médiathèque de l'Architecture et du Patrimoine, France

1937

Paris, Petit Palais. *Les Maîtres de l'art indépendant 1895–1937*. June 17–October 10. Catalogue
On view: bronze casts of *The Jester* (1905; plate 3) and *Head of a Young Woman* (possibly *Head of a Woman [Fernande]* of 1906; plate 4)

Paris. Esplanade du Trocadéro. Spanish Pavilion at the Paris World's Fair. July 12–November 25 (fig. 2)
On view: a bronze cast of *Bather* (1931; plate 53*); and cement casts of *Head of a Woman* (1931; SP 131-III), *Head of a Woman* (1931; plate 49*), *Head of a Woman* (1931–32; SP 133-III), and *Woman with Vase* (1933; SP 135)

Paris, Jeu de Paume. *Origines et développement de l'art international indépendant*. July 30–October 31. Catalogue
On view: a cement cast of a work titled *Head of a Woman* in the catalogue

1939

New York, Westermann Gallery. *Picasso: Etchings, Lithographs, Reproductions*. January 28–February 28. Catalogue
On view: a bronze cast of *The Jester* (1905; plate 3)

New York, Buchholz Gallery. *Sculpture by Painters*. October 31–November 25. Catalogue
On view: a bronze cast of *The Jester* (1905; plate 3)

New York, The Museum of Modern Art. *Picasso: Forty Years of His Art*. November 15, 1939–January 7, 1940. Catalogue. The exhibition traveled extensively in varying editions to venues across the United States in 1940–43, including the Art Institute of Chicago, February 1–March 3, 1940; City Art Museum of Saint Louis, March 16–April 14, 1940; Museum of Fine Arts, Boston, April 26–May 25, 1940; San Francisco Museum of Art, June 25–July 22, 1940; Cincinnati Art Museum, September 28–October 27, 1940; Cleveland Museum of Art, November 7–December 8, 1940; Isaac Delgado Museum, New Orleans, December 20, 1940–January 17, 1941; Minneapolis Institute of Arts, February 1–March 2, 1941; and Carnegie Institute, Pittsburgh, March 15–April 13, 1941
On view in New York: bronze casts of *The Jester* (1905; plate 3), ill., *Head of a Woman (Fernande)* (1906; plate 4) and *Head of a Woman* (1909; plate 11), ill.; *Glass of Absinthe* (1914; plate 23*), ill; and *Composition with Glove* (1930; plate 43*), ill.

1940

New York, Buchholz Gallery. *Pablo Picasso: Drawings and Watercolors*. March 5–30. Catalogue
On view: bronze casts of *The Jester* (1905; plate 3) and *Kneeling Woman Combing Her Hair* (1906; plate 5)

1941

Richmond, Virginia Museum of Fine Arts. *Collection of Walter P. Chrysler, Jr.* January 16–March 4. Catalogue. The exhibition traveled to the Philadelphia Museum of Art, March 29–May 11
On view: bronze casts of *The Jester* (1905; plate 3), *Kneeling Woman Combing Her Hair* (1906; plate 5), and *Head of a Woman* (1909; plate 11), all ill.

New York, Buchholz Gallery. *From Rodin to Brancusi: European Sculpture of the Twentieth Century*. February 11–March 8. Catalogue
On view: a bronze cast of *Seated Woman* (1930; SP 86-II), ill.

1942

New York, Buchholz Gallery. *Homage to Rodin: European Sculpture of Our Time*. November 10–December 5. Catalogue
On view: bronze casts of *Seated Woman* (1902; plate 1) and *The Jester* (1905; plate 3)

1944

Paris, Palais des Beaux-Arts de la Ville de Paris. Salon d'Automne (also known as the Salon de la Libération). October 6–November 5. Catalogue (fig. 3)
On view: bronze casts of *Head of a Woman* (1931–32; SP 133-II), *Cock* (1932; plate 58), *Cat* (1941; plate 81*), *Death's Head* ([1941]; plate 82), and *Bull's Head* (1942; plate 88*)

1945

Philadelphia, Philadelphia Museum of Art. *The Callery Collection: Picasso—Léger*. January–February. Catalogue published in *Philadelphia Museum Bulletin*
On view: a bronze cast of *Seated Woman* (1930; SP 86-II), ill.

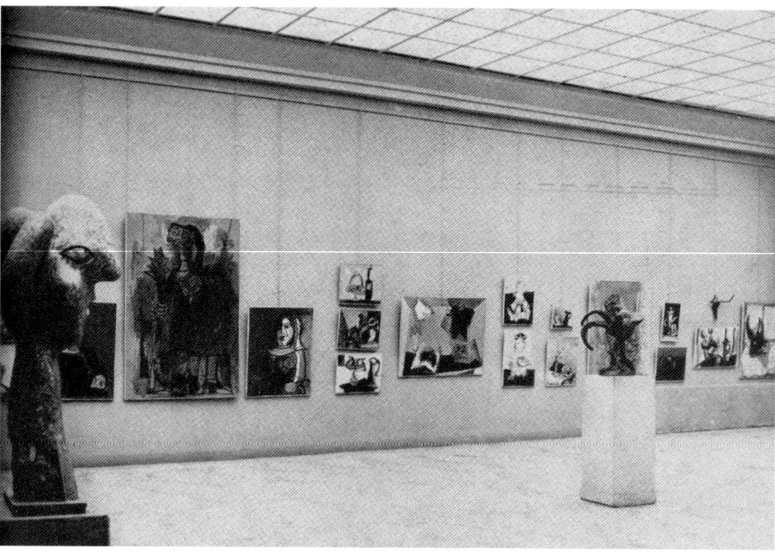

3. View of the Picasso exhibition at the 1944 Salon d'Automne (Salon de la Libération), held at the Palais des Beaux-Arts de la Ville de Paris, with bronze casts of *Head of a Woman* (1931–32) at far left, *Cock* (1932) on the plinth at right, and *Bull's Head* (1942) on the wall at far right. Photograph by Marc Vaux

Denver, Denver Art Museum. *A Retrospective Exhibition of Paintings, Drawings, Sculpture, and Prints by Picasso.* April 12–May 12. Exhibition checklist
On view: a bronze cast of *Head of a Woman* (1909; plate 11)

1946
Paris, Musée du Petit Palais. *Présentation des collections du Petit Palais: I Art moderne.* Catalogue
On view: bronze casts of *The Jester* (1905; plate 3*), ill., and a work titled *Head of a Woman* in the catalogue (probably *Head of a Woman [Fernande]* of 1906; plate 4*)

1947
London, London Gallery, Ltd. *The Cubist Spirit in Its Time.* March 18–May 3. Catalogue
On view: Still Life (1914; plate 15*), ill.

Bern, Kunstmuseum. *Quelques œuvres des collections de la ville de Paris: Art moderne.* March 29–April 14. Catalogue. The exhibition traveled to the Musée des beaux-arts in La Chaux-de-Fonds, April 16–24; the Musée Rath in Geneva, April 26–May 4; and the Kunsthalle Basel, May 6–28
On view: bronze casts of *The Jester* (1905; plate 3*), ill., and a work titled *Head of a Woman* in the catalogue (probably *Head of Woman [Fernande]* of 1906; plate 4*)

Zurich, Kunsthaus Zürich. *Petit Palais: Musée de la ville de Paris.* June 9–August 31. Catalogue
On view: bronze casts of *The Jester* (1905; plate 3*), ill., and a work titled *Head of a Woman* in the catalogue (probably *Head of a Woman [Fernande]* of 1906; plate 4*)

1948
New York, Buchholz Gallery. *Sculpture.* September 28–October 16. Catalogue
On view: a bronze cast of *The Jester* (1905; plate 3), ill

Paris, Galerie Louise Leiris. *Picasso: Œuvres de Provence 1945–1948.* October 5–20. Catalogue
On view: ten unidentified bronzes dated 1945 in the catalogue; and fourteen unidentified bronzes dated 1947–48 in the catalogue

Paris, Maison de la pensée française. *Picasso: Poterie et une sculpture.* November 26, 1948–January 5, 1949
On view: possibly a bronze cast of *Man with a Lamb* (1943; plate 87)

London, Institute of Contemporary Arts (ICA). *40,000 Years of Modern Art: A Comparison of Primitive and Modern.* December 20, 1948–January 29, 1949. Catalogue
On view: Still Life (1914; plate 15*)

1949
New York, Buchholz Gallery. *Pablo Picasso: Recent Work.* March 8–April 2. Catalogue
On view: nineteen bronze casts titled *Standing Woman* (1945; SP 303-II to 316-II, 322-II, 326-II, 327-II, 329-II, 331) and *Hand with Sleeve* (1947; SP 338-II), all ill.; and four additional sculptures (possibly SP 323-II, SP 324-II, SP 325-II, and SP 328-II)

New York, Buchholz Gallery. *Cubism: Braque, Gris, Laurens, Léger, Lipchitz, Picasso.* April 5–30. Catalogue
On view: a bronze cast of *Head of a Woman* (1909; plate 11), ill.

Toronto, Art Gallery of Toronto. *Picasso.* April. Brochure
On view: a bronze cast of *Head of a Woman* (1909; plate 11), ill.

Paris, Maison de la pensée française. *Œuvres récentes de Picasso.* July–c. November. Exhibition pamphlet (fig. 4)
On view: a bronze cast of *Woman with Orange* (c. 1934; plate 76*)

New York, Buchholz Gallery. *Sculpture* September 26–October 14. Catalogue
On view: bronze casts of *Head of a Woman* (1909; plate 11) and *Hand with Sleeve* (1947; SP 338-II), ill.; and two bronze casts titled *Seated Woman* and *Standing Woman* dated 1947 in the catalogue

1950
Venice, XXV Biennale Internazionale d'Arte (room V). June 8–October 15. Catalogue
On view: Still Life (1914; plate 15*)

Brussels, Knokke, Le Zoute, Albert Plage, Grande salle des expositions de "La reserve." *Picasso.* July 15–August 27. Catalogue
On view: a bronze cast of *The Jester* (1905; plate 3)

London, Arts Council of Great Britain. *Picasso in Provence.* November–December. Catalogue
On view: bronze casts of *Standing Woman* (1945; SP 327-II) and *Seated Woman* (1945; SP 331), ill.; twenty-two unidentified bronze casts dated 1945 and 1947 in the catalogue; and eleven ceramics dated 1948 in the catalogue, two ill.

Paris, Maison de la pensée française. *Picasso: Sculptures, dessins.* November 1950–January 1951. Catalogue
On view: bronze casts of *Cock* (1932; plate 58), *Head of a Warrior* (1933; SP 136-II), *Head of a Woman* (1941; SP 197-II), *Man with a Lamb* (1943; plate 87), *Death's Head* ([1941]; plate 82), *Woman with Leaves* (1934; SP 157-II), and *Hand with Sleeve* (1947; SP 338-II), all ill.; one painted bronze from the Glass of Absinthe series (1914; plates 21–26); and thirty-five unidentified sculptures dated between 1929 and 1944 in the catalogue. *Face* (1946; plate 97*), ill. on the cover, is not listed in the catalogue checklist

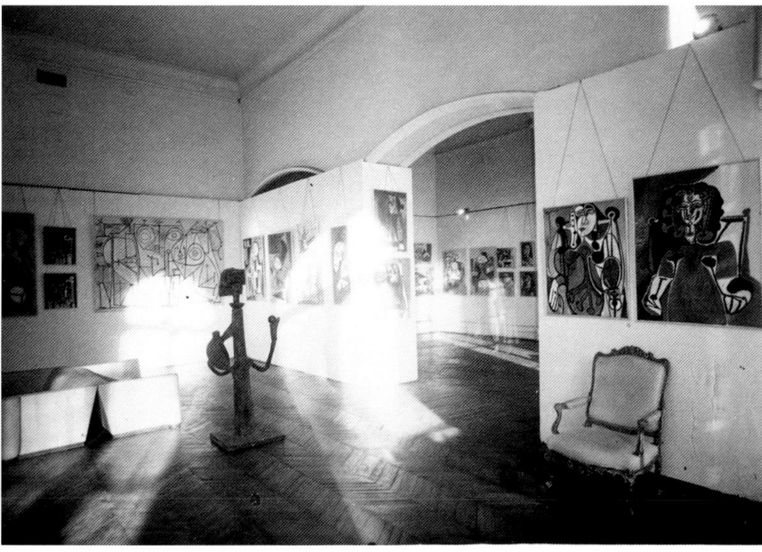

4. View of the exhibition *Œuvres récentes de Picasso* at the Maison de la pensée française, Paris, 1949, with the unique bronze cast of *Woman with Orange* (c. 1934) standing at center left. The Morgan Library & Museum, New York. Gift of the Pierre Matisse Foundation.

1951
New York, Curt Valentin Gallery. *Sculpture by Painters*. November 20–December 15. Catalogue
On view: bronze casts of *The Jester* (1905; plate 3), *Head of a Woman (Fernande)* (1906; plate 4), ill., *Standing Woman* (1945; SP 327-II and SP 329-II), ill., *Hand* (1947; SP 338), ill., and *Owl* ([1950–51]; SP 403-II), ill.; and one bronze cast titled *Nude* and dated 1947 in the catalogue

New York, Curt Valentin Gallery. *Contemporary Paintings and Sculpture*. December 18, 1951–January 12, 1952. Catalogue
On view: bronze cast of *Owl* ([1950–51]; SP 403-II)

1952
New York, Curt Valentin Gallery. *Pablo Picasso: Paintings, Sculpture, Drawings*. February 19–March 15. Catalogue
On view: bronze casts of *The Jester* (1905; plate 3), ill., *Head of a Woman (Fernande)* (1906; plate 4), *Standing Woman* (1945; SP 313-II, SP 322-II, SP 329-II), ill., *Owl* ([1950–51]; SP 403-II), ill., and *Man with a Lamb* (1943; plate 87*); three bronze casts titled *Seated Nude, Nude*, and *Owl II* in the catalogue; and six ceramics, two ill.

Paris, Musée d'art moderne de la Ville de Paris. VIIIe Salon de Mai. May 9–29. Catalogue
On view: a bronze cast of *She-Goat* (1950; plate 119)

Philadelphia, Philadelphia Museum of Art. *Sculpture of the Twentieth Century*. October 11–December 7. Catalogue. The exhibition traveled to the Art Institute of Chicago, January 22–March 8, 1953; and The Museum of Modern Art, New York, April 29–September 7, 1953
On view: bronze casts of *Head of a Woman* (1909; plate 11), *Seated Woman* (1930; SP 86-II), *Man with a Lamb* (1943; plate 87*), ill., and *Owl* ([1950–51]; SP 403-II)

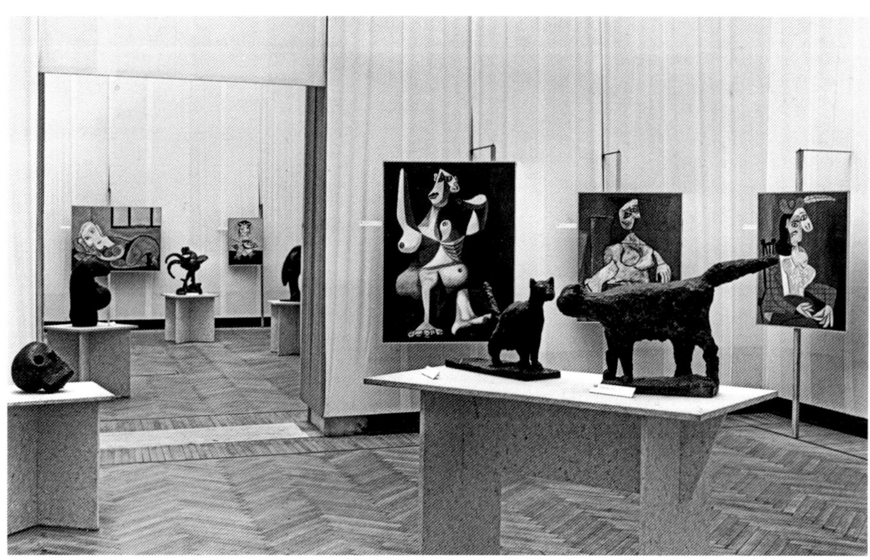

5. View of the exhibition *Picasso, 200 opere dal 1920 al 1953* at the Galleria nazionale d'arte moderna, Rome, 1953, with bronze casts of *Death's Head* ([1941]), *Crouching Cat* (1943), and *Cat* (1941) in the foreground from left to right. Photograph by Mathieu Rabeau. Picasso Archives, Musée national Picasso-Paris

1953
Paris, Musée national d'art moderne. *Le Cubisme*. January 30–April 9. Catalogue
On view: Glass of Absinthe (1914; plate 22*), ill.; and *Still Life* (spring 1914; plate 15*)

London, Lefevre Gallery. *Picasso (1898–1936)*. May–June. Catalogue
On view: a bronze cast of *The Jester* (1905; plate 3)

Rome, Galleria nazionale d'arte moderna. *Picasso, 200 opere dal 1920 al 1953*. May 5–July 5. Catalogue (fig. 5)
This exhibition included thirty-two sculptures, all ill.; and thirty-nine ceramics.

Paris, Palais de New York. IXe Salon de Mai. May 7–31. Catalogue
On view: Goat Skull and Bottle (1951–53; plate 123*)

Paris, Galerie Louise Leiris. *Picasso*. May 19–June 13. Catalogue and Supplement to the Catalogue
On view: bronze casts of *Owl* ([1950–51]; SP 403-II), *Owl with Raised Wings* (1951–53; SP 404-II), and *Head of a Woman* (1951; possibly SP 411-II or SP 412-II); a painted bronze of *Crane* (1951–52; SP 461-IIa–d); a bronze cast of *Baboon and Young* (October 1951; plate 116); a painted bronze of *Still Life: Pitcher and Figs* (1951–53; SP 460-IIa–b); *Little Owl* (1951–52; plate 120); a painted bronze of *Woman Reading* (1951–53; SP 462-IIb–c); *Woman Reading* (1951–53; plate 121*); *Small Owl* (1951–53; SP 476-II); and twenty-six ceramics

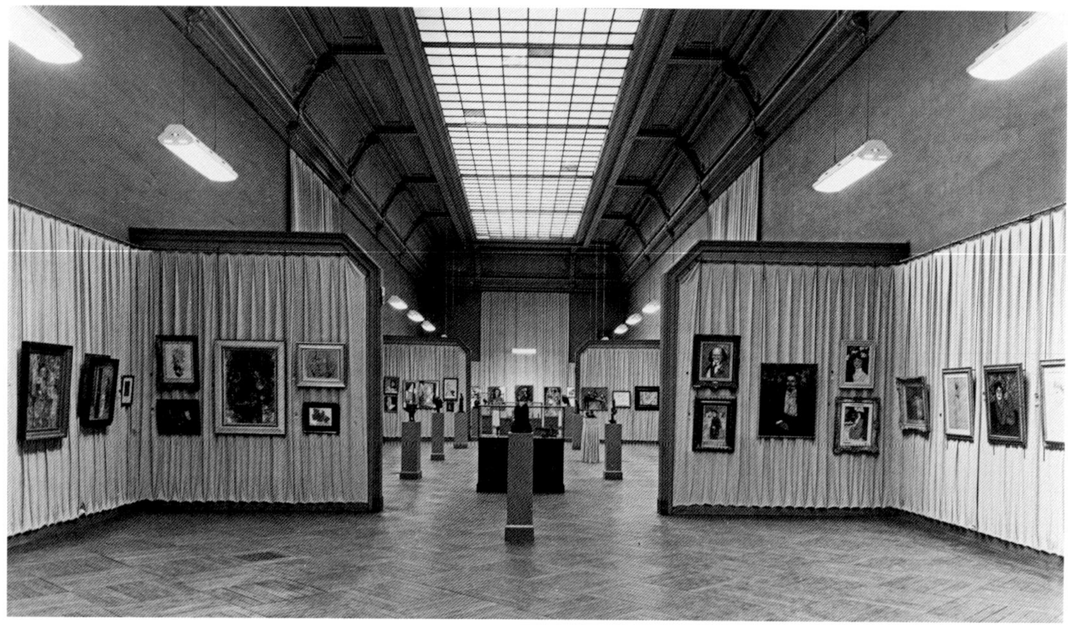

6. View of the exhibition *Picasso: Exposition organisée sous l'égide du Syndicat d'Initiative de Lyon* at the Musée de Lyon, 1953. Picasso Archives, Musée national Picasso–Paris

Lyon, Musée de Lyon. *Picasso: Exposition organisée sous l'égide du Syndicat d'Initiative de Lyon*. June–September. Catalogue (fig. 6)
On view: a bronze cast of *Head of a Woman (Fernande)* (1906; plate 4); one painted bronze from the Glass of Absinthe series (1914; plates 21–26); *Still Life* (1914; plate 15*); a bronze cast possibly of *Head of a Woman* (1931; SP 128-II); a bronze cast titled *Woman Sleeping* and dated 1932 in the catalogue; *Little Girl with a Ball* (1931; SP 112-II); *Woman Leaning on Her Elbow* (1933; SP 153-II); *The Reaper* (c. 1934; SP 234-II); *Cock* (1933; SP 155-II); *Death's Head* ([1941]; plate 82); a bronze cast titled *Head of a Woman* and dated 1943–44 in the catalogue; six unidentified bronze casts dated 1945 in the catalogue (probably a selection from SP 303-II to 316-II, 322-II to 331-II); *Goat Skull and Bottle* (1951–53; SP 410-IIa); a painted bronze of *Woman Reading* (1951–53; SP 462-IIa–c) and a painted bronze of *Crane* (1951–52; SP 461-IIa–d); and twelve ceramics

Milan, Palazzo Reale. *Pablo Picasso*. September 20–November 20. Catalogue
This exhibition included thirty-two sculptures, fourteen ill.; and forty-one ceramics, five ill.

New York, Curt Valentin Gallery. *Picasso, 1950–1953*. November 24–December 19. Catalogue
On view: bronze casts of *Cock* (1932; plate 58), ill., *Angry Owl* (1950; SP 404-II), ill., and *Owl* ([1950–51]; SP 403-II); *Woman Reading* (1951–53; plate 121*), ill., *Still Life: Pitcher and Figs* (1951–53; SP 460-IIb), ill., *Little Owl* (1951–53; SP 476-II), ill., and *Little Owl* (1951–52; plate 120); eleven painted terracotta sculptures, four ill.; and six ceramics, two ill.

New York, Curt Valentin Gallery. *Sculpture and Sculptors' Drawings*. December 22, 1953–January 24, 1954. Catalogue
On view: a bronze cast of *Head of a Woman (Fernande)* (1906; plate 4), ill.; and *Still Life: Pitcher and Figs* (1951–53; probably SP 460-IIb)

Amsterdam, Stedelijk Museum. *Picasso: Lithographieën, Aquatintes, Bronzen*
On view: bronze casts of *Standing Woman* (1945; SP 305-II), *Seated Woman* (1945; SP 325-II), and probably *Hand with Sleeve* (1947; SP 338-II); and seven unidentified sculptures listed in the catalogue

1954

London, Lefevre Gallery. *Picasso 1938–1953*. May. Catalogue
On view: Crane (1951–52; plate 122*); and bronze casts of *Baboon and Young* (October 1951; plate 116) and *Crouching Cat* (1943; SP 278-II); all ill.

Paris, Musée municipal d'art moderne. Xe Salon de Mai. May 7–30. Catalogue
On view: Pregnant Woman, first state (1950; likely SP 349-II)

New York, Curt Valentin Gallery. *In Memory of Curt Valentin, 1902–1954. An Exhibition of Modern Masters Lent by American Museums*. October 5–30. Catalogue
On view: a bronze cast of *Head of a Woman* (1909; plate 11), ill.

London, Institute of Contemporary Arts (ICA). *Collages and Objects*. October 13–November 20. Catalogue
On view: Still Life (1914; plate 15*)

1955

London, Marlborough Fine Art. *Picasso: 63 Drawings (1953–1954) and 10 Bronzes (1945–1953)*. May–June. Catalogue
On view: a bronze cast of *Pregnant Woman*, first state (1950; SP 349-II); a painted bronze of *Goat Skull and Bottle* (1951–53; SP 410-IIa or plate 123); bronze casts of *Flowers in a Vase* (1951–53; SP 413-II), ill., *Woman's Head* (1951; SP 411-II), ill., and *Baboon and Young* (October 1951; plate 116), ill.; and bronze casts of five unidentified figurines dated between 1945 and 1947 in the catalogue

New York, Curt Valentin Gallery. *Closing Exhibition: Sculpture, Paintings, and Drawings*. June 8–August. Catalogue
On view: a bronze cast of *Head of a Woman (Fernande)* (1906; plate 4); *Still Life: Pitcher and Figs* (1951–53; SP 460-IIb), ill.; bronze casts of two unidentified figurines dated 1947 in the catalogue; and three unidentified terracotta sculptures

New York, Fine Arts Associates (Otto M. Gerson). *Rodin to Lipchitz*. October 25–November 30. Catalogue
On view: Owl with Raised Wings (1950; SP 404-IIIa), ill.

Munich, Haus der Kunst. *Picasso 1900–1955*. October 25–December 18. Catalogue. The exhibition traveled to the Rheinisches Museum Köln-Deutz, Cologne, December 30–February 29, 1956; and the Kunstverein in Hamburg, Kunsthalle-Altbau, March 10–April 29, 1956
This exhibition included thirty-five sculptures, seven ill.; and thirteen ceramics, four ill.

1956

New York, Kootz Gallery. *Picasso*. March 12–April 7. Catalogue
On view: bronze casts of *Baboon and Young* (October 1951; plate 116) and *Cock* (1932; plate 58), both ill.

New York, Galerie Chalette. *Picasso: "The Woman." Paintings, Drawings, Bronzes, Lithographs*. April 16–May 19. Catalogue
On view: bronze casts of *Standing Woman* (1945; SP 303-II, 304-II, 305-II, 312-II, and 328-II), all ill.

New York, Fine Arts Associates (Otto M. Gerson). *Rodin to Lipchitz, Part II*. October 9–November 3. Catalogue
On view: Glass of Absinthe (1914; plate 25*), ill.; and an unidentified painted ceramic of *Owl* (1953; SP 403-III), ill.

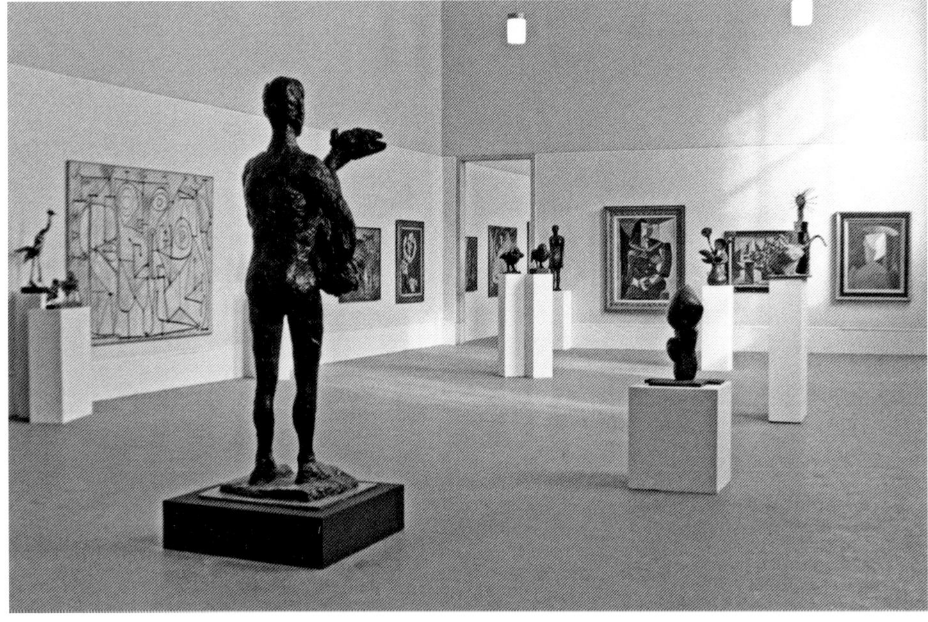

7. View of *Picasso: A Loan Exhibition of His Paintings, Drawings, Sculptures, Ceramics, Prints, and Illustrated Books* at the Philadelphia Museum of Art, 1958. Archives of the Philadelphia Museum of Art

Zurich, Kunsthaus Zürich. *Skulpturen von Malern von Daumier bis Picasso*. October 26–end of November. Catalogue
On view: bronze casts of *The Jester* (1905; plate 3), *Head of a Woman (Fernande)* (1906; plate 4), *Head of a Woman* (1909; plate 11), and *Bouquet of Flowers* (1951; SP 470-II), ill.; and seven unidentified bronze casts (probably a selection from SP 303-II to 316-II, 322-II to 331-II)

Oslo, Kunstnerns Hus. *Picasso, Malerier, Tegninger, Grafikk, Skulptur, Keramik*. November–December. Catalogue
On view: bronze casts of *The Jester* (1905; plate 3), ill., *Flowers in a Vase* (1951–53; SP 413-II), ill., and *Crouching Cat* (1943; SP 278-II); twelve unidentified bronze casts dated 1945 in the catalogue (probably a selection from SP 303-II to 316-II, 322-II to 331-II); bronze casts of *Head of a Woman* (1951; probably SP 411-II), *Bouquet of Flowers* (1951, possibly SP 470-II), *Still Life with Bouquet* (1951, SP-468-II), and *Vase of Three Heads* (May 13, 1955; SP 502-II); and six ceramics, one ill.

1957

New York, Fine Arts Associates (Otto M. Gerson). *Picasso, Sculpture (Part I)*. January 15–February 9. Catalogue
This exhibition included twenty-three bronzes and painted bronze casts, eighteen ill.; and three painted ceramics, one ill.

New York, The Museum of Modern Art. *Picasso: 75th Anniversary Exhibition*. May 22–September 8. Catalogue. The exhibition traveled to the Art Institute of Chicago, October 29–December 8; and Philadelphia (extended version; see Philadelphia 1958)
This exhibition included forty-five sculptures, thirty-six ill.

Rotterdam, Museum Boymans. *Picasso ceramiek*. July. Catalogue
This exhibition included seventy-four ceramics, thirty ill.

Milan, Palazzo dell'arte. *Undicesima triennale di Milano: Esposizione internazionale delle arti decorative e industriali moderne e dell'architettura moderna*. July 27–November 4. Catalogue
On view: a bronze cast of *The Bathers: Man with Folded Hands* (1956; SP 504-II); and a bronze cast titled *Bouquet* in the catalogue

1958

Philadelphia, Philadelphia Museum of Art. *Picasso: A Loan Exhibition of His Paintings, Drawings, Sculptures, Ceramics, Prints, and Illustrated Books*. January 8–February 23. Catalogue (fig. 7)
This exhibition included forty-six sculptures, thirteen ill.; and seventy-five ceramics, fifteen ill.

New York, Cooper Union Museum. *Ceramics by Picasso*. March 28–May 10. Catalogue
This exhibition included ninety-two ceramics, fourteen ill.

Brussels, Palais international des beaux-arts. Expo 58: Exposition Universelle et Internationale de Bruxelles. April 17–October 19. Catalogue
On view: a bronze cast of *She-Goat* (1950; plate 119)

Paris, Maison de la pensée française. *Cent cinquante céramiques originales*. March 8–June 30. Catalogue
This exhibition included 150 ceramics, twenty ill.

New York, Galerie Chalette. *Sculpture by Painters*. October 16–November 29. Catalogue
On view: a bronze cast of *Standing Figure* (1958; SP 540-II), ill., two bronze casts of *Standing Woman* (1945; probably a selection from SP 303-II to 316-II, 322-II to 331-II), and two additional bronze casts titled *Dove* and *Bull* in the catalogue

New York, Saidenberg Gallery. *A Selection of Works by Picasso in Ten Media*. November 18–December 27. Catalogue
On view: bronze casts of *Mask of a Woman* (1908; SP 22-II), *Head of a Horned Animal* (1950; SP 515-II), *Pigeon* (1953–54; SP 497-II), and *Woman with Necklace* (1957; SP 511-II); three ceramics, all ill.; and, according to a note in the catalogue, a selection of other works in both categories

1959

New York, Fine Arts Associates (Otto M. Gerson). *Picasso: The Bathers*. February 10–March 7. Catalogue. The exhibition traveled to the Museum of Fine Arts, Boston, March 15–April 15
On view: bronze casts of *The Bathers* (1956; SP 503–508-II), all ill.

London, Hanover Gallery. *Sculpture: Arp, Butler, César, Clatworthy, Effront, Giacometti, Kemeny, Maillol, Marini, Matisse, Picasso, Sager*. July 9–September 11. Catalogue
On view: bronze casts of *Head of a Woman (Fernande)* (1906; plate 4), *Kneeling Woman Combing Her Hair* (1906; plate 5), and *Standing Woman* (1945; SP 303-II, 305-II, and SP 323-II), all ill.

Kassel. II. Documenta: Kunst nach 1945, Internationale Ausstellung. July 11–October 11. Catalogue
On view: bronze casts of *The Bathers* (1956; SP 503–508-II), all ill.

Stockholm, Svensk-Franska Konstgalleriet. *Picasso*. September 26–October 18. Catalogue
On view: bronze casts of *Head of a Man* (1906; SP 9-II), *Head of a Woman (Fernande)* (1906; plate 4), *Head of a Woman* (1909; plate 11), *Hand with Sleeve* (1947; SP 338-II), *Standing Woman* (1945; SP 305-II, 311-II, SP 314-II, SP 322-II, SP 324-II, and SP 327-II), and *Seated Woman* (1945; SP 325-II), all ill.

1960
London, Marlborough Fine Art Limited. *XIX and XX Century Drawings, Watercolours and XX Century Sculpture*. February–March. Catalogue
On view: bronze casts of *The Jester* (1905; plate 3) and *Head of a Woman (Fernande)* (1906; plate 4), both ill.

New York, Sidney Janis Gallery. *Picasso, 1881– : His Blue Period (1900–1905), Collection of Pastels, Water-colours, and Drawings, also, the Complete Set of Small Bronzes of Female Figures, 1945–47*. April 25–May 21. Catalogue. The exhibition traveled to O'Hana Gallery, London, June 23–July 28; Stoneleigh Abbey, Warwickshire, July 30–August 14; and Galerie Motte, Geneva, August 23–September 10
On view: bronze casts of *Standing Woman* (1945; SP 303-II to 316-II, 322-II to 324-II, 326-II to 329-II), *Seated Woman* (1945; SP 325-II, 331-II), and *Hand with Sleeve* (1947; SP 338-II), all ill.

London, Tate Gallery. *Picasso*. July 6–September 18. Catalogue
On view: Still Life (1914; plate 15*), ill.

1961
Bremen, Kunsthalle Bremen. *Picasso. Druckgraphik, Gemälde, Handzeichnungen, Plastik*. June 23–August 6. Catalogue
On view: bronze casts of *Head of a Picador with a Broken Nose* (1903; plate 2), ill., *Standing Woman* (1945; SP 314-II), *Hand with Sleeve* (1947; SP 338-II), *Arm* (1959; SP 555-II), and two unidentified figures dated 1945 in the catalogue

Rome, Galleria dell'Obelisco. *Arp, Azuma, Braque, Butler, Calder, Callery, César, Ernst, Giacometti, Hoflenher, Lardera, Moore, Muller, Picasso*. December. Catalogue
On view: bronze casts of *Head of a Woman (Fernande)* (1906; plate 4) and *Kneeling Woman Combing Her Hair* (1906; plate 5), both ill.

New York, The Museum of Modern Art. *The Art of Assemblage*. October 2–November 12. Catalogue. The exhibition traveled to the Dallas Museum of Contemporary Arts, January 9–February 11, 1962; and the San Francisco Museum of Art, March 5–April 15, 1962
On view: Still Life (1914; plate 15*)

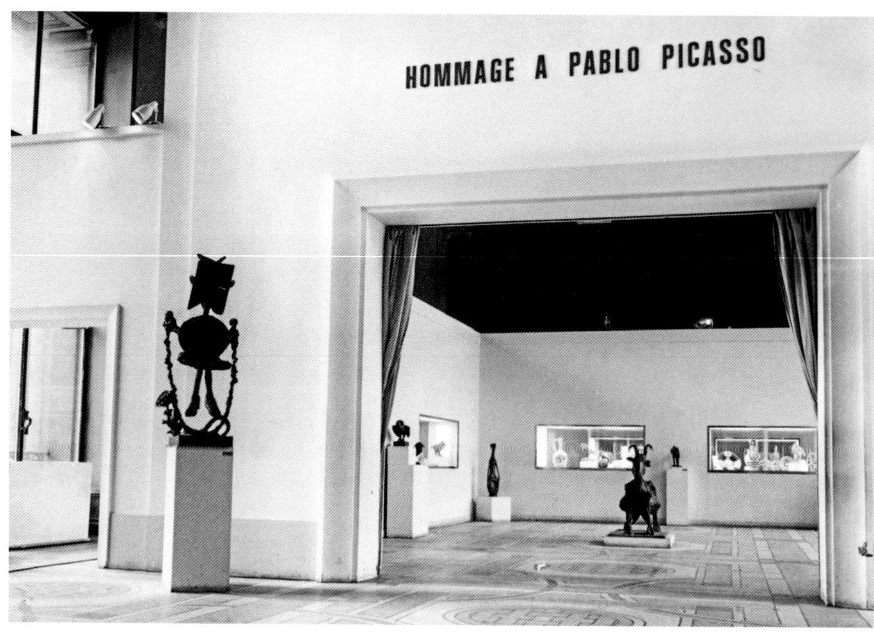

8. The entrance to the sculpture exhibition in the retrospective *Hommage à Pablo Picasso* held at the Petit Palais, Paris, 1966–67, with bronze casts of Picasso's *Little Girl Jumping Rope* (1950–[54]) at left and *She-Goat* (1950) center right. Archives Petit Palais. Musée des Beaux-Arts de la Ville de Paris

1962
New York, World House Galleries. *Sculpture: Daumier to Picasso*. February 20–March 17. Catalogue
On view: a bronze cast of *Standing Woman* (probably one of SP 303-II to 316-II, 322-II to 331-II)

New York, Otto Gerson Gallery. *Picasso: An American Tribute*. April 25–May 12. Catalogue
This exhibition included thirty-five sculptures, all ill.

New York, Otto Gerson Gallery. *Monumental Sculpture*. June–July 31. Catalogue
On view: a bronze cast of *The Bathers* (1956; SP 503–508-II); and *Woman with Outstretched Arms* (1961; plate 145*); both ill.

London, Hanover Gallery. *Sculpture: Arp, Butler, Cárdenas, César, Dodeigne, Ernst, Fullard, Giacometti, Ipoustéguy, Kalinowski, Metcalf, Picasso, Richier, Stuart, and Vail*. July 3–September 1. Catalogue
On view: bronze casts of *Head of a Woman (Fernande)* (1906; plate 4), *Kneeling Woman Combing Her Hair* (1906; plate 5), and *Arm* (1959; SP 555-II), all ill.

1963
Washington, D.C., Washington Gallery of Modern Art. *Sculptors of Our Time*. September 17–October 31. Catalogue
On view: Man with a Lamb (1943; plate 87*); and *Woman with Outstretched Arms* (1961; plate 145*); both ill.

Los Angeles, Felix Landau Gallery. *Pablo Picasso Sculpture*. November 18–December 7. Catalogue
On view: fourteen bronze casts of *Standing Woman* (1945; SP 303-II, 304-II, 306-II, 308-II to 310-II, 313-II to 316-II, 322-II to 324-II, 326-II); bronze casts of *Arm* (1959; SP 555-II) and *Winged Centaur with Owl* (1950; probably SP 382-II); and a painted bronze of *Bull* (1950; probably SP 392-II); all ill.

1964
Toronto, Art Gallery of Toronto. *Picasso and Man*. January 11–February 16. Catalogue. The exhibition traveled to the Montreal Museum of Fine Arts, February 28–March 31
On view: bronze casts of *Head of a Picador with a Broken Nose* (1903; plate 2), *The Jester* (1905; plate 3), *Head of a Woman (Fernande)* (1906; plate 4), *Head of an Old Man*, (1906; SP 9-II), *Mask of a Woman* (1908; SP 22-II), *Head of a Woman* (1909; plate 11), *Pregnant Woman* (1950; SP 349-II), *Head of a Woman* (1951; SP 411-II), and *Arm* (1959; SP 555-II), all ill.; and a bronze cast of *Seated Woman* (1902; plate 1) not included in the catalogue

Tokyo, National Museum of Modern Art. *Pablo Picasso Exhibition, Japan, 1964*. May 23–July 5. Catalogue. The exhibition traveled to the National Museum of Modern Art, Kyoto, July 10–August 2; and the Prefectural Museum of Art, Nagoya, August 7–18
On view: bronze casts of *Head of a Woman (Alice Derain)* (1905; SP 5-II), *Head of a Woman (Fernande)* (1906; plate 4*), *Standing Woman* (1945; SP 307-II and SP 308-II), and *The Bathers* (1956; SP 503–508-II); *Crane* (1951–52; SP 461-IIa); and a bronze cast of *Arm* (1959; SP 555-II); all ill.

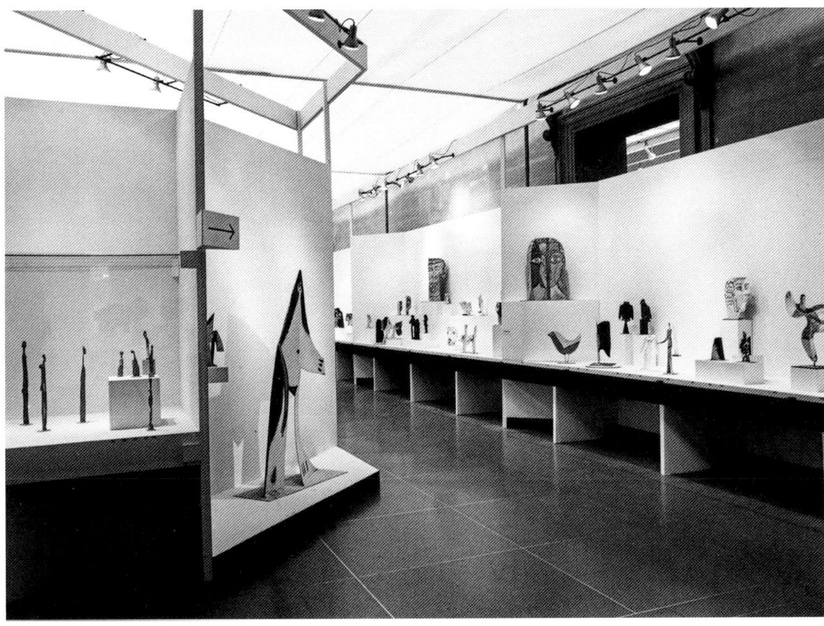

9. View of the exhibition *Picasso: Sculpture, Ceramics, Graphic Work* at the Tate Gallery, London, 1967. Picasso Archives, Musée national Picasso–Paris

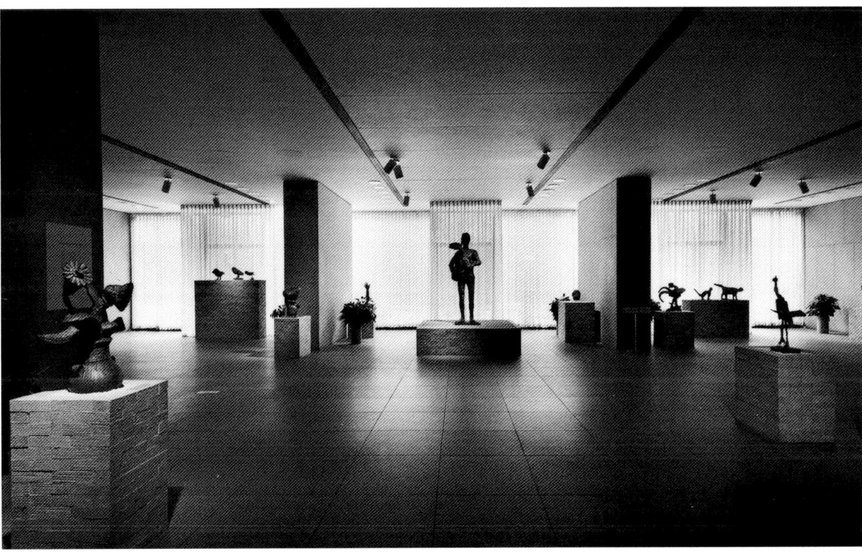

10. View of the exhibition *The Sculpture of Picasso*, The Museum of Modern Art, New York, 1967–68. Photograph by George Cserna. The Museum of Modern Art Archives, New York

1965

Stockholm, Nationalmuseum. *Picasso i Kiruna*. September. Catalogue
On view: bronze casts of *Head of a Man* (1906; SP 9-II), *Head of a Woman (Fernande)* (1906; plate 4), probably *Head of a Woman* (1906–07; SP 12-II), *Head of a Woman* (1909; plate 11), and probably *Hand with Sleeve* (1947; SP 338-II); and three unidentified bronze casts dated 1945 and 1948 in the catalogue

New York, Perls Galleries. *Pablo Picasso: Highlights in Retrospect*. October 12–November 20. Catalogue
On view: bronze casts of *Cock* (1932; plate 58) and *Arm* (1959; SP 555-II); and a painted ceramic *Owl* (1953; SP 403-III); all ill.

1966

Washington, D.C., Gallery of Modern Art. *Picasso since 1945*. June 30–September 4. Catalogue
On view: bronze casts of *Flowers in a Vase* (1951–53; SP 413-II), ill., *Bouquet of Flowers* (1951; SP 470-II), ill., *Head of a Woman* (1951; SP 411-II), ill., *Arm* (1959; SP 555-II), *Young Man* (1958; SP 509-II), ill., *Man with a Javelin* (1958; SP 543-II), ill., and *Bull* (1957; probably SP 528-II); nine unidentified bronze casts dated 1945–57 in the catalogue; and four ceramics, one ill.

Basel, Galerie Beyeler. *Picasso. Werke von 1900–1932*. November 26, 1966–January 31, 1967. Catalogue
On view: bronze casts of *The Jester* (1905; plate 3), *Head of a Woman (Fernande)* (1906; plate 4), and *Head of a Woman* (1909; plate 11), all ill.

Paris, Réunion des musées nationaux. *Hommage à Pablo Picasso. [Peintures, Grand Palais; dessins, sculptures, ceramiques, Petit Palais]*. November 18, 1966–February 12, 1967. Catalogue (fig. 8)
This exhibition included 187 sculptures and 116 ceramics, all ill.

1967

Basel, Galerie Beyeler. *Picasso. Werke von 1932–1965*. February–April. Catalogue
On view: a bronze cast of *Cock* (1932; plate 58), ill.; and two unidentified ceramics

Dallas, Museum of Fine Arts, and Fort Worth, Art Center Museum. *Picasso: Two Concurrent Retrospective Exhibitions*. February 8–March 26. Catalogue
On view: bronze casts of *The Jester* (1905; plate 3), *Head of a Man* (1906; SP 9-II), *Head of a Woman (Fernande)* (1906; plate 4), *Cock* (1932; plate 58), *Head of a Woman* (1951; probably SP 411-II), *Baboon and Young* (October 1951; plate 116), ill., *Arm* (1959; SP 555-II), and *Woman with Outstretched Arms* (1961; plate 145*)

London, Tate Gallery. *Picasso: Sculpture, Ceramics, Graphic Work*. June 9–August 13. Catalogue (fig. 9)
This exhibition included 203 sculptures and thirty-one ceramics, all ill.

New York, The Museum of Modern Art. *The Sculpture of Picasso*. October 11, 1967–January 1, 1968. Catalogue (fig. 10)
This exhibition included 204 sculptures and thirty-two ceramics, all ill.

REFERENCES

ADASKINA 2012 | Adaskina, Natalia. "Préface et notes." In Ivan Aksenov. *Picasso et alentours*, translated by Gérard Conio, pp. 7–33. Gollion, Switzerland: Éditions infolio, 2012.

AKSENOV 1917 | Aksenov, Ivan A. *Picasso i okrestnosti*. Moscow: Centrifuga, 1917.

ALEXANDRE 1900 | Alexandre, Arsène. *Exposition de 1900: L'Œuvre de Rodin*. Paris: Société d'Édition artistique, 1900.

ANTONIOU-NESJAR 2013 | Antoniou-Nesjar, Sylvia. "Pablo Picasso and Carl Nesjar." In Karin Hellandsjø, ed. *Picasso-Oslo: Art and Architecture in the Government Building Complex*, exh. cat., n.p. pamphlet. https://www.regjeringen.no/globalassets/upload/fad/vedlegg/bst/picasso-oslo.pdf. Oslo: Riksantikvaren–Directorate for Cultural Heritage, 2013.

ANTONIOU-NESJAR 2014 | ———. "Sylvette in Concrete." In Christoph Grunenberg and Astrid Becker, eds. *Sylvette, Sylvette, Sylvette: Picasso and the Model*, exh. cat., pp. 198–203. New York: Prestel, 2014.

APOLLINAIRE 1913 | Apollinaire, Guillaume. "Die moderne Malerei." *Der Sturm* 3, nos. 148–49 (February 1913): 272.

APOLLINAIRE 2000 | ———. *The Poet Assassinated*. Translated by Matthew Josephson. Cambridge, Mass.: Exact Change, 2000. Photographic reprint of a book originally published in New York by Broom, 1923.

APOLLINAIRE 2001 | ———. *Apollinaire on Art: Essays and Reviews 1902–1918*. Edited by Leroy C. Breunig. Translated by Susan Suleiman. Boston: Museum of Fine Arts, 2001.

ARAGON 1950 | Aragon, Louis. Preface. In *Picasso: Sculptures, dessins*, exh. cat., pp. 5–10. Paris: Maison de la pensée française, 1950.

ARAGON AND BRETON 1924 | Aragon, Louis, and André Breton. "Hommage à Picasso." *Paris-Journal*, June 20, 1924.

ASHTON 1972 | Ashton, Dore. *Picasso on Art: A Selection of Views*. New York: Viking, 1972.

BACH, ROWELL, AND TEMKIN 1995 | Bach, Friedrich Teja, Margit Rowell, and Ann Temkin. *Constantin Brancusi, 1876–1957*. Exh. cat. Philadelphia: Philadelphia Museum of Art; Cambridge, Mass.: MIT Press, 1995.

BALDASSARI 1997 | Baldassari, Anne. *Picasso and Photography: The Dark Mirror*. Translated by Deke Dusinberre. Exh. cat. Houston: Museum of Fine Arts, 1997.

BALDASSARI 2005 | ———. *The Surrealist Picasso*. Paris: Éditions Flammarion, 2005.

BALDASSARI ET AL. 2002 | Baldassari, Anne, et al. *Matisse Picasso*. Exh. cat. London: Tate, 2002.

BARR 1939 | Barr, Alfred H., Jr. *Picasso: Forty Years of His Art*. Exh. cat. New York: The Museum of Modern Art, 1939.

BARR 1946 | ———. *Picasso: Fifty Years of His Art*. New York: The Museum of Modern Art, 1946.

BARR 1957 | ———. *Picasso: 75th Anniversary Exhibition*. Exh. cat. New York: The Museum of Modern Art, 1957.

BEAUMELLE, MONOD-FONTAINE, AND SCHWEISGUTH 1991 | Beaumelle, Agnès de la, Isabelle Monod-Fontaine, and Claude Schweisguth, eds. *André Breton: La Beauté convulsive*. Exh. cat. Paris: Éditions du Centre Pompidou, 1991.

BERGAMIN 1937 | Bergamin, José. "Le Mystère tremble: Picasso furioso." *Cahiers d'Art* 12, nos. 4–5 (1937): 135–56.

BERGGRUEN 1998 | Berggruen, Heinz. *Highway and Byways*. Translated by Robin Benson. Yelvertoft Manor, Northamptonshire, UK: Pilkington, 1998.

BESNARD-BERNADAC, RICHET, AND SECKEL 1987 | Besnard-Bernadac, Marie-Laure, Michèle Richet, and Hélène Seckel. *Musée Picasso Catalogue sommaire des collections II: Dessins, aquarelles, gouaches, pastels*. Paris: Musée national Picasso, 1987.

BLANCHE 1932 | Blanche, Jacques-Émile. "Rétrospective Picasso." *L'Art vivant*, no. 162 (July 1932): 333–34.

BLANTON FREEDBERG 1986 | Blanton Freedberg, Catherine. *The Spanish Pavilion at the Paris World's Fair*. New York: Garland, 1986.

BOCCIONI 1913 | *1re exposition de sculpture futuriste du peintre et sculpteur futuriste Boccioni*. Exh. cat. Paris: Galerie La Boétie, 1913.

BOCCIONI 2009 | Boccioni, Umberto. "Futurist Sculpture." In Lawrence Rainey, Christine Poggi, and Laura Wittman, eds. *Futurism: An Anthology*, pp. 113–19. New Haven, Conn.: Yale University Press, 2009.

BOFARULL I SANS 1902 | Bofarull i Sans, Carles de. *Catálogo de la exposición de arte antiguo*. Exh. cat. Barcelona: Reproducciones artísticas Thomas, 1902.

BOIS 1998 | Bois, Yve-Alain. *Matisse and Picasso.* Exh. cat. Paris: Flammarion, 1998.

BOWLT 1988 | Bowlt, John E. "Between East and West: Russian Art of the Early Twentieth Century." In *Russian and Soviet Paintings 1900–1930*, rev. ed., exh. cat., pp. 29–41. Washington, D.C.: Hirshhorn Museum and Sculpture Garden, Smithsonian Institution, 1988.

BRASSAÏ 1999 | Brassaï. *Conversations with Picasso.* Translated by Jane Marie Todd. Chicago: University of Chicago Press, 1999. Published in French in 1964 as *Brassaï: Conversations avec Picasso.* Paris: Gallimard.

BRASSAÏ AND KAHNWEILER 1949 | Brassaï and Daniel-Henry Kahnweiler. *Les Sculptures de Picasso.* Paris: Les Éditions du Chêne, 1949. Published in English in 1949 as *The Sculptures of Picasso.* Translated by David B. Sylvester. London: Rodney Phillips.

BRETON 1925 | Breton, André. "Le Surréalisme et la peinture." *La Révolution surréaliste*, no. 4 (July 15, 1925): 26–30.

BRETON 1933 | ———. "Picasso dans son élément." *Minotaure*, no. 1 (June 1, 1933): 8–29.

BRETON 1961 | ———. "80 carats . . . mais une ombre (2 Novembre 1961)." In *Le Surréalisme et la peinture, 1928–1965*, rev ed., pp. 155–58. Paris: Éditions Gallimard, 1961.

BRETON 1999 | ———. *Break of Day.* Translated by Mark Polizzotti and Mary Ann Caws. Lincoln: University of Nebraska Press, 1999.

BURGESS 1910 | Burgess, Gelett. "The Wild Men of Paris." *Architectural Record* 27, no. 5 (1910): 400–414.

CABOT I ROVIRA 1901 | Cabot i Rovira, Joaquim. "August [*sic*] Rodin." *Pèl & Ploma*, no. 68 (January 15, 1901): 2–4.

CAHIERS D'ART 1948 | *Cahiers d'Art* 23, no. 1 (1948).

CAHN 2003 | Cahn, Isabelle. "Belated Recognition: Gauguin and France in the Twentieth Century, 1903–1949." In George T. M. Shackelford et al. *Gauguin Tahiti*, exh. cat., pp. 285–301. Boston: Museum of Fine Arts, 2003.

CAMERA WORK 1912 | *Camera Work* (August 1912), special issue.

CANADAY 1966 | Canaday, John. "Biggest One-Man Show on Earth." *New York Times*, November 18, 1966, p. 33.

CAPA 1974 | Capa, Robert. "Picasso." In *Robert Capa 1913–1954*, pp. 95–96. New York: Grossman, 1974.

CATONI 1990 | Catoni, Maria Luisa. "Parigi, 1904: Picasso 'iberico' e le 'Demoiselles d'Avignon.'" *Bolettino d'arte*, nos. 62–63 (July–October 1990): 117–30.

CHICAGO TRIBUNE 1967 | Artner, Alan G. "Chicago's Picasso Sculpture: The Unveiling of the Puzzling Sculpture Changes the Public Art Landscape." *Chicago Tribune*, August 15, 1967.

CLARIS 1901 | Claris, Edmond. "L'Impressionnisme en sculpture: Auguste Rodin et Medardo Rosso." *La Nouvelle Revue* (June 1, 1901): 321–36.

CLARIS 1902 | ———. "Renacimiento de la escultura." *La lectura* 2, no. 1 (1902): 86–99.

CLARK 2013 | Clark, T. J. *Picasso and Truth: From Cubism to Guernica.* Princeton, N.J.: Princeton University Press, 2013.

CLEEMAN 2012 | Cleeman, Jorgen G. "Kips Bay Towers." *Docomomo_US.org*, August 17, 2012. http://www.docomomo-us.org/register/fiche/kips_bay_towers_0.

CLIFFORD 1986 | Clifford, James. "Alberto Giacometti." *Sulfur*, no. 15 (1986): 38–41.

COCTEAU 1989 | Cocteau, Jean. *Journal 1942–1945.* Paris: Gallimard, 1989.

COEN 1988 | Coen, Esther. *Umberto Boccioni.* Exh. cat. New York: Harry N. Abrams, 1988.

CONQUÊTE 1942 | *Conquête du monde par l'image.* Edited by Noël Arnaud. Paris: Éditions de la Main à plume, 1942.

CONZEN 2005 | Conzen, Ina. *Picasso: Bathers.* Exh. cat. Ostfildern-Ruit, Germany: Hatje Cantz, 2005.

COUSINS 1989 | Cousins, Judith, with Pierre Daix. "Documentary Chronology." In William Rubin. *Picasso and Braque: Pioneering Cubism*, exh. cat., pp. 335–452. New York: The Museum of Modern Art, 1989.

COUSINS AND SECKEL 1988 | Cousins, Judith, and Hélène Seckel. "Éléments pour une chronologie de l'histoire des *Desmoiselles d'Avignon.*" *Les Demoiselles d'Avignon*, vol. 2, exh. cat., pp. 548–623. Paris: Éditions de la Réunion des musées nationaux, 1988.

COWLING 1985 | Cowling, Elizabeth. "'Proudly we claim him as one of us': Breton, Picasso, and the Surrealist Movement." *Art History* 8, no. 1 (March 1985): 82–104.

COWLING 1994 | ———. "Objects into Sculpture." In Cowling and John Golding. *Picasso: Sculptor/Painter*, exh. cat., pp. 229–40. London: Tate Gallery, 1994.

COWLING 2002 | ———. *Picasso: Style and Meaning.* London: Phaidon, 2002.

COWLING 2006 | ———. *Visiting Picasso: The Notebooks and Letters of Roland Penrose.* London: Thames and Hudson, 2006.

COWLING 2008 | ———. "The Sculptor's Studio: Picasso's *Bust of a Woman*, 1931." In *Picasso's Marie-Thérèse*, exh. cat., pp. 30–43. New York: Acquavella Galleries, 2008.

COWLING 2010 | ———. "The Rebirth of Venus: Women at Their Toilette." In Cowling and Richard Kendall. *Picasso Looks at Degas*, exh. cat., pp. 157–209. New Haven, Conn.: Yale University Press, 2010.

COWLING 2011 | ———. "The Image of Picasso-Sculptor in the 1930s." In John Richardson and Diana Widmaier Picasso. *Pablo Picasso and Marie-Thérèse: L'Amour fou*, exh. cat., pp. 257–91. New York: Gagosian Gallery, 2011.

COWLING 2014 | ———. "Picasso's *La femme à la clé* (1953–54): The Sculptor, His Model and His Assistant." In Christoph Grunenberg and Astrid Becker, eds. *Sylvette, Sylvette, Sylvette: Picasso and the Model*, exh. cat., pp. 210–17. New York: Prestel, 2014.

COWLING AND PULLEN 1994 | Unpublished viewing notes from Elizabeth Cowling's informal conversations with Derek Pullen, then head of sculpture conservation at Tate, on the occasion of the 1994 Tate exhibition *Picasso: Sculptor/Painter.*

COWLING, GOLDING, AND RUIZ-PICASSO 1994 | Cowling, Elizabeth, John Golding, and Claude Ruiz-Picasso. Catalogue. In Cowling and Golding. *Picasso: Sculptor/Painter*, exh. cat., pp. 255–87. London: Tate Gallery, 1994.

DAIX 1993 | Daix, Pierre. *Picasso: Life and Art.* New York: HarperCollins, 1993.

DAIX AND ROSSELET 1979 | Daix, Pierre, and Joan Rosselet. *Picasso: The Cubist Years 1907–1916.* Boston: New York Graphic Society, 1979.

DEROUET 2011 | Derouet, Christian. *Zervos et "Cahiers d'art."* Paris: Centre Pompidou, 2011.

DOÑATE 2001 | Doñate, Mercè. "Rodin y la escultura catalana." In Léal, Brigitte, and Maria Teresa Icaña, eds. *Paris Barcelona: 1888–1937*, exh. cat., pp. 242–57. Barcelona: Institut de Cultura de Barcelona; Paris: Réunion des musées nationaux, 2001.

DORONTCHENKOV 2009 | Dorontchenkov, Ilia. "Chronology." In *Russian and Soviet Views of Modern Western Art: 1890s to Mid-1930s*, pp. 311–22. Berkeley: University of California Press, 2009.

DRUICK 2006 | Druick, Douglas W. "Catalogue: 110. Paul Gauguin, *Mask of a Savage*." In Rebecca A. Rabinow, ed. *Cézanne to Picasso: Ambroise Vollard, Patron of the Avant-Garde*, exh. cat., pp. 372–73. New Haven, Conn.: Yale University Press, 2006.

DUBUFFET 1951 | Dubuffet, Jean. "Anticultural Positions." Lecture presented at the Arts Club of Chicago, 1951. Repr. in *Logos* 5, no. 2 (Spring/ Summer 2006). http://www.logosjournal.com/ issue_5.2/dubuffet.htm.

EXPOSITION INTERNATIONALE UNIVERSELLE 1900 | *Exposition internationale universelle de 1900: Catalogue général officiel: Œuvres d'art, Exposition centennale de l'art français (1800–1889)*. Paris: Lemercier, 1900.

FAIRWEATHER 1982 | Fairweather, Sally. *Picasso's Concrete Sculptures*. New York: Hudson Hills Press, 1982.

FEUILLES VOLANTES 1927 | "Les Expositions Paris et ailleurs." *feuilles volantes*, supplement to *Cahiers d'Art* 2, nos. 7–8 (1927): 3–4.

FITZGERALD 1987 | FitzGerald, Michael C. *Pablo Picasso's Monument to Guillaume Apollinaire: Surrealism and Monumental Sculpture in France 1918–1959*. PhD diss., Columbia University, 1987.

FLETCHER 2003 | Fletcher, Valerie J. "Process and Technique in Picasso's *Head of a Woman (Fernande)*." In Jeffrey Weiss, Fletcher, and Kathryn A. Tuma. *Picasso: The Cubist Portraits of Fernande Olivier*, exh. cat., pp. 166–91. Princeton, N.J.: Princeton University Press, 2003.

FOREST 1999 | Forest, Dominique. "Le *Guernica* de sa sculpture." In Jean Lacambre and Forest. *L'Homme au mouton Picasso*, pp. 21–27. Paris: Éditions de la Réunion des musées nationaux, 1999.

GALERIE CHARPENTIER 1954 | *Tableaux moderne; sculpture, bronzes*. Paris: Galerie Charpentier, March 30, 1954.

GALERIE FLECHTHEIM 1913 | *Beiträge zur Kunst des 19. Jahrhunderts und unserer Zeit. Eröffnungs-Katalog*. Exh. cat. Düsseldorf: Galerie Flechtheim, 1913.

GALERIE FLECHTHEIM 1919 | *Ostern 1919*. Exh. cat. Potsdam: G. Kiepenheuer, 1919.

GALERIE FLECHTHEIM 1929 | *Seit Cézanne in Paris*. Exh. cat. Berlin: Galerie Flechtheim, 1929.

GALERIES GEORGES PETIT 1932 | *Exposition Picasso*. Exh. cat. Paris: Galeries Georges Petit. 1932.

GEELHAAR 1993 | Geelhaar, Christian. *Picasso: Wegbereiter und Foerderer seines Aufstiegs 1899–1939*. Zurich: Palladion/ABC, 1993.

GEISER 1933 | Geiser, Bernard. *Picasso: Peintre-graveur*. Vol. 1. Bern: B. Geiser, 1933.

GERSH-NEŠIC 2005 | Gersh-Nešic, Beth S. *"La Jeune Sculpture française": André Salmon on French Modern Art*. Cambridge, UK: Cambridge University Press, 2005.

GERSON 2014A | Gerson, Scott. "*Guitar* [1912]: Conservation Notes." In Anne Umland and Blair Hartzell, eds. *Picasso: The Making of Cubism 1912–1914*, pp. 3.23–3.27. New York: The Museum of Modern Art, 2014.

GERSON 2014B | ———. "*Guitar* [1914]: Conservation Notes." In Anne Umland and Blair Hartzell, eds. *Picasso: The Making of Cubism 1912–1914*, pp. 15.10–15.11. New York: The Museum of Modern Art, 2014.

GILOT AND LAKE 1964 | Gilot, Françoise, and Carlton Lake. *Life with Picasso*. New York: McGraw-Hill, 1964.

GIMÉNEZ MARTÍN 2012 | Giménez Martín, Carmen. *Pablo Picasso's Woman with a Vase*. Madrid: Real Academia de Bellas Artes de San Fernando, 2012.

GINEX 2004 | Ginex, Giovanna. "Snapshots from the Studio of Umberto Boccioni." In Laura Mattioli Rossi, ed. *Boccioni's Materia: A Futurist Masterpiece and the Avant-garde in Milan and Paris*, exh. cat., pp. 63–81. New York: Solomon R. Guggenheim Museum, 2004.

GODEFROY AND MCCULLY 2010 | Godefroy, Cécile, and Marilyn McCully. *Pablo Picasso: 43 Works*. Exh. cat. Madrid: Fundación Almine y Bernard Ruiz-Picasso para el Arte, 2010.

GOEPPERT, GOEPPERT-FRANK, AND CRAMER 1983 | Goeppert, Sebastian, Herma Goeppert-Frank, and Patrick Cramer. *Pablo Picasso, The Illustrated Books: Catalogue Raisonné*. Geneva: Patrick Cramer, 1983.

GONZÁLEZ 1931-32 | González, Julio. "Picasso sculpteur et les cathédrales" (1931–32). In Josephine Withers. *Julio González: Sculpture in Iron*, pp. 132–45. New York: New York University Press, 1978.

GONZÁLEZ 1936 | ———. "Picasso sculpteur. Exposition de sculptures récentes de Picasso: Galerie 'Cahiers d'Art.'" *Cahiers d'Art* 11, nos. 6–7 (1936): 189–91.

GONZÁLEZ 2007 | ———. "Picasso Sculptor." In Jon Wood, David Hulks, and Alex Potts, eds. *Modern Sculpture Reader*, pp. 129–30. Leeds: Henry Moore Institute, 2007.

GOUGH 1999 | Gough, Maria. "*Faktura*: The Making of the Russian Avant-Garde." *RES: Anthropology and Aesthetics*, no. 36 (Fall 1999), special issue edited by Joseph Koerner: 32–59.

GREENBERG 1986 | Greenberg, Clement. "The New Sculpture" (1949). In John O'Brian, ed. *Clement Greenberg: The Collected Essays and Criticism*. Vol. 2, *Arrogant Purpose, 1945–1949*, pp. 313–19. Chicago: University of Chicago Press, 1986.

GRUNENBERG AND BECKER 2014 | Grunenberg, Christoph, and Astrid Becker, eds. *Sylvette, Sylvette, Sylvette: Picasso and the Model*, exh. cat. New York: Prestel, 2014.

HARTZELL 2011 | Hartzell, Blair. "Chronology." In Anne Umland. *Picasso Guitars 1912–1914*, exh. cat., pp. 97–99. New York: The Museum of Modern Art, 2011.

HARTZELL 2014A | ———. "*Guitar* [1912]" and "*Guitar* [1912]: Provenance." In Anne Umland and Hartzell, eds. *Picasso: The Making of Cubism 1912–1914*, pp. 3.2–3.22 and 3.28–3.31. New York: The Museum of Modern Art, 2014.

HARTZELL 2014B | ———. "*Guitar* [1914]" and "*Guitar* [1914]: Provenance." In Anne Umland and Hartzell, eds. *Picasso: The Making of Cubism 1912–1914*, pp. 15.2–15.9 and 15.12–15.15. New York: The Museum of Modern Art, 2014.

HEUMAN 2008 | Heuman, Jackie. "A Technical Study of Picasso's Construction 'Still Life' (1914)." *Burlington Magazine* 150 (November 2008): 749–54. Repr. in *Tate Papers*, no. 11 (April 1, 2009), http://www.tate.org.uk/download/file/fid/7282.

HODIN 1964 | Hodin, J. P. "Quand les artistes parlent du sacré." *XXe Siècle*, no. 24 (December 1964), special issue titled *Permanance du sacré*: 17–27.

HÔTEL DROUOT 1921 | *Catalogue des tableaux, gouaches & dessins*. Sale cat. Hôtel Drouot, Paris, June 13–14, 1921.

INTERNATIONAL EXHIBITION 1913 | *Catalogue of International Exhibition of Modern Art: Association of American Painters and Sculptors*. Exh. cat. New York: Vreeland Advertising, 1913.

JACOB 1927 | Jacob, Max. "Souvenirs sur Picasso contes par Max Jacob." *Cahiers d'Art* 2, no. 6: 199–203.

JOHNSON 1976 | Johnson, Ron. *The Early Sculpture of Picasso: 1901–1914*. New York and London: Garland, 1976.

JOHNSON 1977 | Johnson, Una E. *Ambroise Vollard, Editeur: Prints, Books, Bronzes*. Exh. cat. New York: The Museum of Modern Art, 1977.

JOZEFACKA AND MAHLER 2014 | Jozefacka, Anna, and Luise Mahler. Catalogue of the Collection. In Emily Braun and Rebecca Rabinow, eds. *Cubism: The Leonard A. Lauder Collection*, exh. cat., pp. 242–301. New York: The Metropolitan Museum of Art; New Haven, Conn.: Yale University Press, 2014.

KACHUR 1993 | Kachur, Lewis. "Picasso, Popular Music and Collage Cubism (1911–12)." *Burlington Magazine*, no. 135 (April 1993): 252–60.

KAHNWEILER 1952 | Kahnweiler, Daniel-Henry. "Huit entretiens avec Picasso." *Le Point* 7, no. 42 (October 1952): 22–30.

KARMEL 1993 | Karmel, Joseph Low [Pepe]. *Picasso's Laboratory: The Role of His Drawings in the Development of Cubism, 1910–1914*. PhD diss., New York University, 1993.

KENDALL 2010 | Kendall, Richard. "The Ballet: 'Work, Pleasure and Vice.'" In Elizabeth Cowling and Kendall, eds. *Picasso Looks at Degas*, exh. cat., pp. 105–55. New Haven, Conn.: Yale University Press, 2010.

KOMARDENKOV 1973 | Komardenkov, Vasilii. *Dni minuvshie*. Moscow: Sovetskii khudozhnik, 1973.

KRAMER 1967 | Kramer, Hilton. "Art: First Major Show of Picasso Sculpture Opens." *New York Times*, October 12, 1967, p. 55.

KRAMER 1971 | ———. "Picasso Gives Work to Museum Here." *New York Times*, February 11, 1971, pp. 1 and 34.

KUNSTHAUS ZÜRICH 1932 | *Picasso*. Exh. cat. Zurich: Kunsthaus Zürich, 1932.

KURCHANOVA 2013 | Kurchanova, Natasha. "Anna Begicheva: How I Remember Tatlin." *Res: Anthropology and Aesthetics*, nos. 63–64 (Spring/Autumn 2013): 299–313.

LÉAL 1996 | Léal, Brigitte. *Musée Picasso Carnets, Catalogue des dessins*. Vols. 1 and 2. Paris: Réunion des musées nationaux, 1996.

LEBON 2003 | Lebon, Elisabeth. *Dictionnaire des fondeurs de bronze d'art, 1890–1950*. Perth: Marjon éditions, 2003.

LEIRIS 1929 | Leiris, Michel. "Alberto Giacometti." *Documents*, no. 4 (September 1929): 209–14.

LEVEL 1928 | Level, André. *Picasso*. [Paris]: Éditions G. Crès et Cie, 1928.

LEYMARIE 1966 | Leymarie, Jean. Introduction. In *Hommage à Pablo Picasso*, exh. cat., n.p. Paris: Réunion des musées nationaux, 1996.

LEYMARIE 1971 | ———. *Picasso, Métamorphoses et unités*. Geneva: Skira, 1971.

LIFE 1944 | "New French Art: Picasso Fostered It Under Nazis." *Life* (November 13, 1944): 72–76.

LIFE 1957 | "Picasso the Sculptor: Colossus of Painting Reveals His Prowess in Another Art." *Life* 43, no. 16 (October 14, 1957): 77.

LONDON GALLERY 1947 | *The Cubist Spirit in Its Time*. Exh. cat. London: London Gallery, 1947.

LORD 1983 | Lord, James. "Giacometti and Picasso: Chronicle of a Friendship." *New Criterion* 1, no. 10 (June 1983): 16–24.

LORD 1985 | ———. *Giacometti: A Biography*. New York: Farrar, Straus and Giroux, 1985.

MALO 1941 | Malo, Pierre. "Picasseries et Picasso." *Comœdia: Hebdomadaire des spectacles, des lettres et des arts* (August 1941): 6.

MALRAUX 1976 | Malraux, André. *Picasso's Mask*. New York: Holt, Rinehart and Winston, 1976.

MATISSE 1941 | "Henri Matisse—First Encounter with African Art, 1906." Interview by Pierre Courthion, 1941. In Jack Flam with Miriam Deutch, eds. *Primitivism and Twentieth-Century Art: A Documentary History*, pp. 31–32. Berkeley: University of California Press, 2003.

MCCULLY 1982 | McCully, Marilyn, ed. *A Picasso Anthology: Documents, Criticism, Reminiscences*. Princeton, N.J.: Princeton University Press, 1982.

MCCULLY 1994 | ———. "Julio González and Pablo Picasso: A Documentary Chronology of a Working Relationship." In Elizabeth Cowling and John Golding. *Picasso: Sculptor/Painter*, exh. cat., pp. 211–21. London: Tate Gallery, 1994.

MCCULLY 1997 | ———. "Chronology." In McCully and Natasha Staller. *Picasso: The Early Years, 1892–1906*, exh. cat., pp. 21–51. New Haven, Conn.: Yale University Press, 1997.

MCCULLY 2007 | ———. *Picasso: Small Figure, The Collection in Context*. Exh. cat. Málaga: Museo Málaga, 2007.

MCCULLY 2011 | ———. *Picasso in Paris 1900–1907: Eating Fire*. Exh. cat. New York: Vendome, 2011.

MERLI 1942 | Merli, Juan. *Picasso: El artista y la obra de nuestro tiempo*. Buenos Aires: El Ateneo, 1942.

MERLI 1948 | ———. *Picasso: El artista y la obra de nuestro tiempo*. 2nd rev. ed. Buenos Aires: Editorial Poseidón, 1948.

MERLIN 1944 | Merlin, Arthur. "Le Salon d'automne devient cette année le Salon Picasso." *Libération* (October 7, 1944).

MONOD-FONTAINE 1982 | Monod-Fontaine, Isabelle. "Braque, le lenteur de la peinture." In *Georges Braque, les papiers collés*, exh. cat., pp. 37–42. Paris: Centre Georges Pompidou, 1982.

MONOD-FONTAINE 1984A | ———. "Chronologie et documents." In *Daniel-Henry Kahnweiler: Marchand, éditeur, écrivain*, exh. cat., pp. 93–167. Paris: Centre Georges Pompidou, 1984.

MONOD-FONTAINE 1984B | ———. "Georges Braque." In Monod-Fontaine et al. *Donation Louise et Michel Leiris: Collection Kahnweiler-Leiris*, exh. cat., pp. 24–35. Paris: Centre Georges Pompidou, 1984.

MONOD-FONTAINE AND CARMEAN 1982 | Monod-Fontaine, Isabelle, with E. A. Carmean. *Braque: The Papiers Collés*. Exh. cat. Washington, D.C.: National Gallery of Art, 1982.

MÜLLER 2002 | Müller, Markus, ed. *Pablo Picasso: The Time with Françoise Gilot*. Exh. cat. Bielefeld: Kerber, 2002.

NASH 1995 | Nash, Steven A. *Picasso: The Sculptor*. Exh. cat. San Francisco: California Palace of the Legion of Honor, 1995.

NYSON 1937 | Nyson, Benedict. "Modernism Is Now Verboten." *New York Times*, July 25, 1937, p. 4E.

O'BRIAN 1976 | O'Brian, Patrick. *Picasso: A Biography*. New York: Putnam, 1976.

OLIVIER 1965 | Olivier, Fernande. *Picasso and His Friends*. New York: Appleton-Century, 1965.

ORS 1930 | Ors, Eugenio d'. *Pablo Picasso*. Paris: Éditions des Chroniques du jour; London: A. Zwemmer, 1930.

PARIGORIS 1984 | Parigoris, Alexandra. "Picasso Plastiken. Düsseldorf." *Burlington Magazine* 126, no. 970 (January 1984): 59–60.

PENROSE 1967 | Penrose, Roland. *The Sculpture of Picasso*. New York: The Museum of Modern Art, 1967.

PENROSE 1981 | ———. *Picasso: His Life and Work*. Third ed. Berkeley: University of California Press, 1981.

PETIT PALAIS 1966 | *Hommage à Pablo Picasso: peintures, Grand Palais; dessins, sculptures, céramiques, Petit Palais.* Introduction by Jean Leymarie. Exh. cat. Paris: Ministère d'État Affaires Culturelles and Réunion des musées nationaux, 1966.

PICASSO 1937 | "Pablo Picasso—Discovery of African Art, 1906–1907." Interview by André Malraux, 1937. In Jack Flam, with Miriam Deutch, eds. *Primitivism and Twentieth-Century Art: A Documentary History*, pp. 33–34. Berkeley: University of California Press, 2003.

PIEYRE DE MANDIARGUES AND MONOD-FONTAINE 2007 | Pieyre de Mandiargues, Sibylle, and Isabelle Monod-Fontaine. "Biography." In Monod-Fontaine. *André Derain: An Outsider in French Art*, exh. cat., pp. 241–55. Copenhagen: Statens Museum for Kunst, 2007.

POGGI 2012 | Poggi, Christine. "Picasso's First Constructed Sculpture: A Tale of Two Guitars." *Art Bulletin* 94, no. 2 (June 2012): 274–98.

PREJGER 1961 | Prejger, Lionel. "Picasso découpe le fer." *L'Œil: Revue d'art mensuelle*, no. 82 (October 1961): 28–33.

PREJGER 1994 | Lionel Prejger interviewed by Elizabeth Cowling and Christine Piot. "Picasso's Sheet-Metal Sculptures: The Story of a Collaboration." In Cowling and John Golding. *Picasso: Sculptor/Painter*, exh. cat., pp. 241–53. London: Tate Gallery, 1994.

RAINEY, POGGI, AND WITTMAN 2009 | Rainey, Lawrence, Christine Poggi, and Laura Wittman, eds. *Futurism: An Anthology*. New Haven, Conn.: Yale University Press, 2009.

RAMIÉ 1976 | Ramié, Georges. *Picasso's Ceramics.* Translated by Kenneth Lyons. New York: Viking Press, 1976.

READ 1994 | Read, Peter. "From Sketchbook to Sculpture in the Work of Picasso, 1924–32." In Elizabeth Cowling and John Golding. *Picasso: Sculptor/Painter*, exh. cat., pp. 199–210. London: Tate Gallery, 1994.

READ 2008 | ———. *Picasso & Apollinaire: The Persistence of Memory*. Berkeley and Los Angeles: University of California Press, 2008.

RICHARDSON 1985 | Richardson, Brenda. "Annotated Chronology of Cone Acquisitions." In Richardson, with William C. Ameringer et al. *Dr. Claribel & Miss Etta: The Cone Collection of the Baltimore Museum of Art*, pp. 163–94. Baltimore: Baltimore Museum of Art, 1985.

RICHARDSON 1962 | Richardson, John, ed. *Picasso: An American Tribute*. Exh. cat. New York: The Public Education Association, 1962.

RICHARDSON 1991 | ———. With Marilyn McCully. *A Life of Picasso, 1881–1906*. New York: Random House, 1991.

RICHARDSON 1996 | ———. With Marilyn McCully. *A Life of Picasso: The Painter of Modern Life 1907–1917*. New York: Random House, 1996.

RICHARDSON 2007 | ———. *A Life of Picasso: The Triumphant Years, 1917–1932*. New York: Knopf, 2007.

RICHARDSON 2010 | ———. *Picasso: The Mediterranean Years, 1945–1962*. Exh. cat. London: Gagosian Gallery/Rizzoli, 2010.

RICHARDSON 2014 | ———. *Picasso & the Camera*. New York: Gagosian Gallery, 2014.

RIEDL 1962 | Riedl, Peter Anselm. "'Masque d'homme': Ein Frühwerk Pablo Picassos." In *Jahrbuch der Hamburger Kunstsammlungen*, vol. 7, pp. 83–92. Hamburg: Dr. Ernst Hauswedell, 1962.

RITCHIE 1952 | Ritchie, Andrew Carnduff. *Sculpture of the Twentieth Century*. New York: The Museum of Modern Art, 1952.

RMN 1979 | *Picasso: Œuvres reçues en paiement des droits de succession*. Exh. cat. Paris: Éditions de la Réunion des musées nationaux, 1979.

ROSSO 1902 | Rosso, Medardo. 1902. "De l'impressionnisme en sculpture." In *De l'impressionnisme en sculpture: Auguste Rodin et Medardo Rosso; lettres et opinions de Rodin, Rosso, [et al.]*, pp. 47–55. Paris: Éditions de "La Nouvelle Revue," 1902.

ROWELL 1973 | Rowell, Margit. "Jean Dubuffet: An Art on the Margins of Culture." In *Jean Dubuffet: A Retrospective*, exh. cat., pp. 15–34. New York: Solomon R. Guggenheim Museum, 1973.

RUBIN 1972 | Rubin, William. *Picasso in the Collection of The Museum of Modern Art*. Exh. cat. New York: The Museum of Modern Art, 1972.

RUBIN 1984 | ———. *"Primitivism" in 20th Century Art*. New York: The Museum of Modern Art, 1984.

RUBIN 1996 | ———, ed. *Picasso and Portraiture: Representation and Transformation*. New York: The Museum of Modern Art, 1996.

RUBIN 2012 | ———. *A Curator's Quest: Building the Museum of Modern Art's Painting and Sculpture Collection, 1967–1988*. New York: Overlook Duckworth, 2012.

RUIZ-PICASSO 1994 | Ruiz-Picasso, Claude. "The Valley of Gold: Picasso as Potter." In Elizabeth Cowling and John Golding, *Picasso: Painter/Sculptor*, exh. cat., pp. 223–27. London: Tate Gallery, 1994.

SABARTÉS 1948 | Sabartés, Jaime. *Picasso: An Intimate Portrait*. Translated by Angel Flores. New York: Prentice-Hall, 1948.

SADÍLKOVÁ AND HUBATOVÁ-VACKOVÁ 2002 | Sadílková, Pavla, and Lada Hubatová-Vacková. "Chronologie." In Jana Claverie, ed. *Vincenc Kramář: Un Théorician et collectionneur du cubisme à Prague*, exh. cat., pp. 191–310. Paris: Éditions de la Réunion des musées nationaux, 2002.

SALLES 1958 | Salles, Georges. "Les Baigneurs de Picasso." *Quadrum: Revue international d'art moderne* 5 (1958): 4–10. Trans. in *Picasso: The Bathers* (New York: Fine Arts Associates, 1959).

SALMON 1919 | Salmon, André. *La Jeune Sculpture française*. Paris: Messein, 1919.

SALON D'AUTOMNE 1904 | *Catalogue des ouvrages de peinture, sculpture, dessin, gravure, architecture et art décoratif exposés au Grand Palais des Champs-Elysées du 15 octobre au 15 novembre 1904*. Exh. cat. Evreux: Hérissey, 1904.

SALON D'AUTOMNE 1906 | *Catalogue des ouvrages de peinture, sculpture, dessin, gravure, architecture et art décoratif*. Exh. cat. Paris: Société du Salon d'Automne, 1906.

SALON D'AUTOMNE 1944 | *Catalogue des ouvrages de peinture, sculpture, dessin, gravure, architecture et art décoratif exposés au Grand Palais des Champs-Élysées*. Exh. cat. Paris: Société du Salon d'Automne, 1944.

SALTO 1917 | Salto, Axel. *Klingen* 1, no. 2 (November 1917).

SAWICKI 2015 | Sawicki, Nicholas. "Ripolin, Flags and Wood: Picasso's 'Violin, Wineglass, Pipe and Anchor' (1912) and Its Cubist Frame." *Burlington Magazine* 157 (January 2015): 18–26.

SAYAG AND LIONEL-MARIE 2000 | Sayag, Alain, and Annick Lionel-Marie, eds. *Brassaï: 'No Ordinary Eyes.'* London: Thames and Hudson, 2000.

SEITZ 1961 | Seitz, William C. *The Art of Assemblage*. New York: The Museum of Modern Art, 1961.

SKUPINA VÝTVARNÝCH UMĚLCŮ 1913 | *III. Výstava*. Exh. cat. Prague: Skupina Výtvarných Umělců, 1913.

SOIRÉES DE PARIS 1913 | *Les Soirées de Paris*, no. 18 (November 15, 1913), Guillaume Apollinaire and Jean Cérusse, eds., photographs by Émile Délétang.

SPIES 1971 | Spies, Werner. *Sculpture by Picasso*. New York: Harry N. Abrams, 1971

SPIES 1995 | ———. *Wege zur Skulptur, Die Carnets Paris und Dinard von 1928 aus der Sammlung Marina Picasso*. New York: Prestel, 1995.

SPIES AND PIOT 1983 REV | Spies, Werner, with Christine Piot. *Pablo Picasso. Das plastische Werk: Werkverzeichnis der Skulpturen in Zusammenarbeit mit Christine Piot*. 2nd ed. (revised and expanded). Exh. cat. Ostfildern and Stuttgart: Hatje Cantz, 1983.

SPIES AND PIOT 2000 | ———. *Picasso: The Sculptures*. Exh. cat. Ostfildern and Stuttgart: Hatje Cantz, 2000.

STALLER 1997 | Staller, Natasha. "Gods of Art: Picasso's Academic Education and Its Legacy." In Marilyn McCully. *Picasso: The Early Years, 1892–1906*, exh. cat., pp. 67–85. New Haven, Conn.: Yale University Press, 1997.

STEPAN 2006 | Stepan, Peter. *Picasso's Collection of African & Oceanic Art*. New York: Prestel, 2006.

STRIGALEV AND HARTEN 1993 | Strigalev, Anatolij, and Jürgen Harten. *Vladimir Tatlin Retrospektive*. Exh. cat. Cologne: DuMont, 1993.

TÉRIADE 1928 | Tériade, E. "Une Visite à Picasso." *L'Intransigeant* (November 27, 1928): 6.

TÉRIADE 1932 | ———. Interview with Picasso. *L'Intransigeant* (June 16, 1932). Repr. *Verve* 5, nos. 19–20 (1948).

TORRAS 2010 | Torras, Montse. "Reactions to the Work of Degas in Picasso's Circle (1881–1900)." In Elizabeth Cowling and Richard Kendall, eds. *Picasso Looks at Degas*, exh. cat., pp. 298–307. New Haven, Conn.: Clark Art Institute, 2010.

TUMA 2003 | Tuma, Kathryn A. "*Le Peau de chagrin*." In Jeffrey Weiss, Valerie J. Fletcher, and Tuma. *Picasso: The Cubist Portraits of Fernande Olivier*, exh. cat., pp. 128–63. Princeton, N.J.: Princeton University Press, 2003.

UMLAND 2011 | Umland, Anne. *Picasso Guitars 1912–1914*. New York: The Museum of Modern Art, 2011.

UTLEY 2000 | Utley, Gertje R. *Picasso: The Communist Years*. New Haven, Conn.: Yale University Press, 2000.

VENTURI 1953 | Venturi, Lionello. *Pablo Picasso: catalogo della mostra*. Exh. cat. Rome: De Luca, 1953.

VERDET 1952 | Verdet, André. *Le Chèvre (et la légende de Vallauris)*. Paris: Édition de Beaune, 1952.

WEISS 2003 | Weiss, Jeffrey. "Fleeting and Fixed: Picasso's Fernandes." In Weiss, Valerie J. Fletcher, and Kathryn A. Tuma. *Picasso: The Cubist Portraits of Fernande Olivier*, exh. cat, pp. 2–48. Princeton, N.J.: Princeton University Press, 2003.

WEISS 2008 | ———. "Picasso Raisonné." In Patricia G. Berman and Gertje Utley, eds. *A Fine Regard: Essays in Honor of Kirk Varnedoe*, pp. 119–33. Aldershot, UK, and Burlington, Vt.: Ashgate, 2008.

WIDMAIER PICASSO 2003 | Widmaier Picasso, Diana. "Between Form and Medium." In *The Sculptures of Picasso*, exh. cat. New York: Gagosian Gallery, 2003.

WIDMAIER PICASSO 2004 | ———. "Marie-Thérèse Walter and Pablo Picasso, New Insights into a Secret Love." In Markus Müller, ed. *Pablo Picasso and Marie-Thérèse Walter: Between Classicism and Surrealism*, exh. cat., pp. 27–35. Bielefeld: Kerber, 2004.

WIDMAIER PICASSO 2006 | ———. "Vollard and the Sculptures of Picasso." In Rebecca A. Rabinow, ed. *Cézanne to Picasso: Ambroise Vollard, Patron of the Avant-Garde*, exh. cat, pp. 182–88. New Haven, Conn.: Yale University Press, 2006.

WIDMAIER PICASSO 2014 | ———. "Pablo Picasso's Sheet-Metal Sculptures, Vallauris 1954–1965: Design, Materials and Experimentation." In Christoph Grunenberg and Astrid Becker, eds. *Sylvette, Sylvette, Sylvette: Picasso and the Model*, exh. cat., pp. 160–175. New York: Prestel, 2014.

WITHERS 1978 | Withers, Josephine. *Julio González: Sculpture in Iron*. New York: New York University Press, 1978.

ZERVOS 1927 | Zervos, Christian. "L'Art nègre." *Cahiers d'Art*, no. 7–8 (1927): 229–30.

ZERVOS 1928 | Zervos, Christian. "Les Sculptures des peintres d'aujourd'hui." *Cahiers d'Art* 3, no. 7 (1928): 277–89.

ZERVOS 1929A | Zervos, Christian. "Picasso à Dinard, été 1928." *Cahiers d'Art* 4, no. 1 (1929): 5–11.

ZERVOS 1929B | Zervos, Christian. "Projets de Picasso pour un monument." *Cahiers d'Art* 4, nos. 8–9 (1929): 342–53.

ZERVOS 1930 | Zervos, Christian. "Les Expositions à Paris et ailleurs, Sculptures de Matisse (Galerie Pierre)." *Cahiers d'Art*, no. 5 (1930): 275–77.

ZERVOS 1932A | Zervos, Christian. "Picasso." *Cahiers d'Art* 7, nos. 3–5 (1932), special issue on Picasso: 85–88.

ZERVOS 1932B | Zervos, Christian. "Quelques notes sur les sculptures de Giacometti." *Cahiers d'Art* 7, no. 7 (1932): 337–42.

ZERVOS 1932C | Zervos, Christian. "Picasso." *Cahiers d'Art* 7 (June 1932), special issue titled *Exposition d'œuvres de Picasso aux Galeries Georges Petit*: 2–3.

ZERVOS 1932–52 | Zervos, Christian. *Pablo Picasso*, vols. 1–5. Paris: Éditions "Cahiers d'Art," 1932–52.

ZERVOS 1945–46 | Zervos, Christian. "L'Homme à l'agneau de Picasso, juillet 1942–octobre 1943." *Cahiers d'Art* (1945–46): 84–112.

ZERVOS 1967 | Zervos, Christian. *Pablo Picasso*, vol. 18. Paris: Éditions "Cahiers d'Art," 1967.

PHOTOGRAPH CREDITS

Photo Maurice Aeschimann: p. 173; p. 200; p. 216, plate 90; p. 216, plate 91; p. 216, plate 92; p. 216, plate 93; p. 217, plate 94; p. 217, plate 95; p. 217, plate 96; p. 217, plate 97; p. 217, plate 98; p. 271.

Albright-Knox Art Gallery/Art Resource, NY: p. 267.

Courtesy Archivo Histórico de la Ciudad de Barcelona: p. 38.

© The Art Institute of Chicago: p. 41, fig. 16; p. 68; p. 69; p. 260, fig. 19; p. 284; p. 285.

Courtesy Bibliothèque nationale de France, Paris: p. 17.

© 2015 Artists Rights Society (ARS), New York/ADAGP, Paris [Georges Braque]: p. 72.

© Estate Brassaï-RMN: p. 12. Copy photo Jean-Gilles Berizzi: p. 185, fig. 4. Courtesy Skira Editore SpA: p. 19, fig. 10; p. 19, fig. 11; p. 21; p. 136, fig. 5.

© Estate Brassaï-RMN/© Centre Pompidou, MNAM-CCI/Photo Philippe Migeat: p. 136, fig. 6; p. 142; p. 144, fig. 21; p. 185, fig. 5.

© Estate Brassaï-RMN/© RMN-Grand Palais/Art Resource, NY: p. 295; p. 296 top left; p. 296 top center; p. 296 bottom center. Photo Daniel Arnaudet: p. 294 top left; p. 296 center; p. 296 middle right; p. 296 bottom right; p. 297 top right; p. 297 middle left; p. 297 center. Photo Michèle Bellot: p. 32. Photo Béatrice Hatala: p. 137, fig. 7. Photo Thierry Le Mage: p. 297 bottom left. Photo Hervé Lewandowski: p. 296 top right; p. 296 middle left; p. 296 bottom left. Photo Franck Raux: p. 102; p. 132; p. 180; p. 188, fig. 9; p. 188, fig. 10; p. 294 top right; p. 294 middle left; p. 294 middle right; p. 294 bottom left; p. 294 bottom right; p. 297 top left; p. 297 top center; p. 297 middle right; p. 297 bottom center; p. 297 bottom right.

Courtesy Bridgeman Images: p. 280.

© Photographie Bulloz/Petit Palais/Roger-Viollet: p. 76; p. 252, fig. 7; p. 310.

© Burgess, Frank Gelett (1866–1951)/© RMN-Grand Palais/Art Resource, NY/Photo Madeleine Coursaget: p. 57, fig. 13.

© International Center of Photography/Courtesy Magnum Photos [Robert Capa]: p. 190, fig. 16.

© Henri Cartier-Bresson/Magnum Photos: p. 20.

Photo Cathy Carver: p. 49; p. 238.

© Centre Pompidou, MNAM-CCI/Bibliothèque Kandinsky: p. 138, fig. 12.

© CNAC/MNAM/Dist. RMN-Grand Palais/Art Resource, NY: p. 239. Photo Georges Meguerditchian: p. 93.

© 2015 Artists Rights Society (ARS), New York/ADAGP, Paris [André Derain]/Courtesy Archives Taillade: p. 54, fig. 7.

Photo Bill Dewey: p. 198.

© Robert Doisneau/Rapho: p. 191, fig. 18; p. 214.

© 2015 Artists Rights Society (ARS), New York/ADAGP, Paris [Jean Dubuffet]: p. 24, fig. 16.

© Succession Marcel Duchamp/ADAGP, Paris/Artists Rights Society (ARS), New York 2015: p. 16, fig. 5.

© DWP Editions: p. 252, fig. 6.

Courtesy Éditions Cahiers d'Art: p. 53, fig. 5; p. 61, fig. 20; p. 80, fig. 13; p. 80, fig. 14; p. 107, fig. 7; p. 109, fig. 11; p. 109, fig. 12; p. 189, fig. 14; p. 206.

Courtesy Lynn G. Epsteen: p. 78, fig. 8.

Photo Gerald Friedli: p. 245.

© Fundación Almine y Bernard Ruiz-Picasso para el Arte/Photo Eric Baudouin: p. 92; p. 174; p. 175; p. 220; p. 221. Photo Marc Domage: p. 115; p. 170, plate 70; p. 171; p. 230; p. 274; p. 282.

Courtesy Fundación Almine y Bernard Ruiz-Picasso para el Arte. All rights reserved: p. 37, fig. 8; p. 70; p. 134; p. 135, fig. 3; p. 137, fig. 8; p. 137, fig. 9; p. 137, fig. 10; p. 138, fig. 11; p. 140, fig. 14; p. 251, fig. 4; p. 257, fig. 15.

Courtesy Gagosian Gallery: p. 272; p. 273.

Photo Claude Germain: p. 194; p. 244.

© J. Paul Getty Trust: p. 248.

Getty Research Institute, Los Angeles: p. 187.

© Alberto Giacometti Estate/Licensed by VAGA and Artists Rights Society (ARS), New York: p. 18, fig. 8. Courtesy Bibliothèque Kandinsky, Paris: p. 18, fig. 7.

Photo Patrick Goetelen: p. 89.

© Albert Harlingue/Roger-Viollet: p. 111, fig. 16.

Photo Béatrice Hatala: p. 34, fig. 1.

© Collection Hegewisch at Hamburger Kunsthalle/Photo Elke Walford: p. 42, fig. 19.

Courtesy Hiroshima Museum of Art: p. 36.

Photo © imageArt, Claude Germain: p. 152; p. 224; p. 225.

Courtesy Institute of Art History ASCR, Prague: p. 40, fig. 12.

© Jasper Johns/Licensed by VAGA, New York, NY: p. 26, fig. 19.

© Francois Kollar-RMN/© Ministère de la Culture/Médiathèque du Patrimoine, Dist. RMN Grand Palais/Art Resource, NY: p. 305, fig. 2.

© Krugier & Cie, Geneva/Photo Patrick Goetelen/Sparte: p. 170, plate 69; p. 218; p. 219, plate 100; p. 219, plate 101; p. 222, plate 104; p. 222, plate 105.

Courtesy Kunst- und Museumsbibliothek/Rheinisches Bildarchiv: p. 192; p. 193.

Courtesy Kunsthaus Zürich: p. 140, fig. 15; p. 305, fig. 1.

Courtesy Quentin Laurens Archives: p. 39.

© Artist Rights Society (ARS), New York [Dora Maar]/© RMN-Grand Palais/Art Resource, NY/Franck Raux: p. 145, fig. 23.

© Man Ray Trust/Artists Rights Society (ARS), New York/ADAGP, Paris 2015: p. 147, fig. 25. Courtesy Guy Ladrière, Paris: p. 78, fig. 9; p. 81, fig. 15.

© 2015 Succession H. Matisse/Artists Rights Society (ARS), New York: p. 18, fig. 9. Courtesy The Baltimore Museum of Art: p. 37, fig. 9.

Copy photo © The Metropolitan Museum of Art: p. 108.

© Lee Miller Archives, England 2015. All rights reserved: p. 24, fig. 17; p. 57, fig. 12; p. 78, fig. 10; p. 209, fig. 7; p. 262, fig. 22.

Photo Mitro Hood: p. 45.

© Musée d'art moderne de la Ville de Paris/Roger-Viollet/Courtesy Parisienne de Photographie: p. 46; p. 47; p. 48.

Musée du Quai Branly/Scala/Art Resource, NY: p. 55, fig. 9.

Courtesy Musée Rodin, Paris: p. 35, fig. 3.

Courtesy Museu Picasso, Barcelona: p. 35, fig. 4. Photo Gasull Fotografia: p. 13.

© Museo Picasso Málaga/Photo Marc Domage: p. 223, plate 107; p. 229. Photo Rafael Lobato: p. 223, plate 106.

© Museu Nacional d'Art de Catalunya, Barcelona 2015/Photo Calveras/Mérida/Sagristà: p. 52, fig. 3.

© 2015 Museum of Fine Arts, Boston: p. 41, fig. 17.

Digital image © The Museum of Modern Art, New York: p. 15; p. 16, fig. 5; p. 18, fig. 7; p. 18, fig. 8; p. 18, fig. 9; p. 19, fig. 10; p. 19, fig. 11; p. 20; p. 26, fig. 19; p. 27; p. 39; p. 40, fig. 13; p. 40, fig. 14; p. 42, fig. 18; p. 43, fig. 21; p. 53, fig. 5; p. 59, fig. 16; p. 59, fig. 17; p. 60, fig. 18; p. 61, fig. 21; p. 72; p. 75, fig. 3; p. 75, fig. 4; p. 79, fig. 11; p. 79, fig. 12; p. 80, fig. 14; p. 81, fig. 16; p. 104, fig. 2; p. 105, fig. 4; p. 107, fig. 7; p. 107, fig. 8; p. 109, fig. 11; p. 109, fig. 12; p. 135, fig. 2; p. 136, fig. 5; p. 141; p. 143, fig. 18; p. 143, fig. 19; p. 143, fig. 20; p. 145, fig. 24; p. 182; p. 189, fig. 14; p. 206; p. 207; p. 22; p. 250; p. 253, fig. 9. Photo George Cserna: p. 311, fig. 10. Photo Thomas Griesel: p. 262, fig. 23. Photo Jonathan Muzikar: p. 232; p. 233; p. 236; p. 237; p. 241; p. 268; p. 269. Photo Soichi Sunami: p. 253, fig. 8.

© 1971 The New York Times. All rights reserved. Used by permission and protected by the Copyright Laws of the United States. The printing, copying, redistribution, or retransmission of this content without express written permission is prohibited: p. 77, fig. 6.

Courtesy New York University Archives/Photo Dean Brown: p. 28.

© Roland Penrose (1900–1984)/© RMN-Grand Palais/Art Resource, NY: p. 311, fig. 9.

Courtesy Philadelphia Museum of Art: p. 309.

© RMN-Grand Palais/Art Resource, NY [Robert Picault]: p. 209, fig. 5; p. 209, fig. 6; p. 210, fig. 9; p. 212, fig. 11 p. 212, fig. 12; p. 213, fig. 13; p. 213, fig. 14.

Courtesy the author's family [Lionel Prejger]: p. 257, fig. 14.

Courtesy private collection: p. 14; p. 255, fig. 11.

© edwardquinn.com: p. 23; p. 202; p. 246; p. 249; p. 255, fig. 12; p. 256; p. 263, fig. 24; p. 263, fig. 25. Courtesy Edward Quinn Archives: Back cover.

© Robert Rauschenberg Foundation/Licensed by VAGA, New York: p. 26, fig. 20.

© RMN-Grand Palais: p. 54, fig. 8.

© RMN-Grand Palais/Art Resource, NY: p. 43, fig. 20; p. 50; p. 58; p. 73; p. 122; p. 137; p. 163, plate 62; p. 186; p. 210, fig. 8; p. 211; p. 215; p. 258, fig. 17; p. 259; p. 260, fig. 20; p. 307, fig. 5; p. 308. Courtesy Quentin Laurens Archives/Photo Mathieu Rabeau: p. 40, fig. 15. Courtesy Valencia/Julio González Archives, Paris/Photo Mathieu Rabeau: p. 113, fig. 17. Photo Daniel Arnaudet: p. 12; p. 35, fig. 5; p. 53, fig. 4. Photo Michèle Bellot: p. 110, fig. 13; p. 110, fig. 14; p. 258, fig. 16. Photo Gerard Blot: p. 228. Photo Madeleine Coursaget: p. 105, fig. 3. Photo Adrien Didiejean/Mathieu Rabeau: p. 44; p. 66; p. 67; p. 86; p. 87; p. 99; p. 114; p. 123; p. 128; p. 129; p. 156; p. 275; p. 283. Photo Béatrice Hatala: p. 52, fig. 2; p. 64; p. 65; p. 82; p. 88; p. 90; p. 91; p. 100; p. 101; p. 106, fig. 5; p. 107, fig. 9; p. 116; p. 117; p. 118; p. 119; p. 120; p. 121; p. 130; p. 131; p. 148; p. 149; p. 150; p. 151; p. 154; p. 155; p. 157; p. 162, plate 59; p. 164, plate 63; p. 164, plate 64; p. 172; p. 177; p. 178; p. 226; p. 227; p. 235; p. 242. Photo Thierry Le Mage: p. 53, fig. 6; p. 56; p. 104, fig. 1; p. 139; p. 162, plate 60; p. 163, plate 61; p. 165, plate 65; p. 165, plate 66; p. 184; p. 188, fig. 11. Photo Hervé Lewandowski: p. 52, fig. 1; p. 189, fig. 13. Photo René-Gabriel Ojéda: p. 37, fig. 7. Photo Mathieu Rabeau: p. 29; p. 55, fig. 10; p. 63; p. 111, fig. 15; p. 113, fig. 19; p. 124; p. 125; p. 126; p. 127; p. 147, fig. 26; p. 170, plate 71; p. 183; p. 189, fig. 12; p. 190, fig. 15; p. 191, fig. 17; p. 276; p. 277; p. 279. Photo Franck Raux: p. 2; p. 30; p. 132; p. 144, fig. 22; p. 180; p. 188; p. 196, plate 83; p. 196, plate 84; p. 197; p. 208, fig. 3; p. 208, fig. 4.

Courtesy The Russian State Archive of Literature and Art (RGALI): p. 16, fig. 4; p. 77, fig. 7.

Photo Peter Schibli, Basel: p. 281.

Courtesy Skira Editore: p. 143, fig. 20.

© SOM: p. 261.

Courtesy Stadt Köln/Photo Rheinisches Bildarchiv: p. 264–65.

Al Startzman/© Houston Chronicle. Used with permission: p. 254.

© 2015 Estate of Alfred Stieglitz/Artists Rights Society (ARS), New York: p. 59, fig. 17.

© Tate, London 2015: p. 59, fig. 15; p. 85; p. 161.

Courtesy Thomas Ammann Fine Arts AG, Zurich: p. 240.

Photo Kevin Todora: p. 243.

Courtesy Valencia/Julio González Archives, Paris: p. 113, fig. 18.

Photo Marc Vaux: p. 306.

© VG Bild-Kunst Bonn/© Städel Museum—ARTOTHEK: p. 60, fig. 19.

© Victoria and Albert Museum, London: p. 34, fig. 2.

TRUSTEES OF THE MUSEUM OF MODERN ART